THE STRUCTURED SELF IN HELLENISTIC AND ROMAN THOUGHT

The Structured Self in Hellenistic and Roman Thought

CHRISTOPHER GILL

OXFORD
UNIVERSITY PRESS

OXFORD
UNIVERSITY PRESS

Great Clarendon Street, Oxford OX2 6DP

Oxford University Press is a department of the University of Oxford.
It furthers the University's objective of excellence in research, scholarship,
and education by publishing worldwide in

Oxford New York

Auckland Cape Town Dar es Salaam Hong Kong Karachi
Kuala Lumpur Madrid Melbourne Mexico City Nairobi
New Delhi Shanghai Taipei Toronto

With offices in

Argentina Austria Brazil Chile Czech Republic France Greece
Guatemala Hungary Italy Japan Poland Portugal Singapore
South Korea Switzerland Thailand Turkey Ukraine Vietnam

Oxford is a registered trade mark of Oxford University Press
in the UK and in certain other countries

Published in the United States
by Oxford University Press Inc., New York

First published 2006

British Library Cataloguing in Publication Data
Data available

Library of Congress Cataloging in Publication Data
Data available

Typeset by SPI Publisher Services, Pondicherry, India.
Printed in Great Britain on acid-free paper by
Biddles Ltd., King's Lynn, Norfolk.

ISBN 978-0-19-815268-2

To Karen

Preface

This book has been my principal research project since the completion of *Personality in Greek Epic, Tragedy, and Philosophy: The Self in Dialogue* (Oxford University Press, 1996). There have been three main phases of activity. Between 1995 and 1998, I completed a first draft of about two-thirds of the book. The pace of completion slowed in 1998–2001 while I was Head of Department. Final writing and revision took place in 2001–4. At each stage, I have received generous help, which I am happy to acknowledge here.

I am grateful to the University of Exeter for research study-leave in the two academic years 1995–6 and 1997–8. A further stimulus has been the vibrant and supportive research ethos in the Department of Classics and Ancient History, centring on our weekly seminar. My colleagues Richard Seaford and Tim Whitmarsh also made valuable comments on a draft of Chapter 6 (and, in Tim's case) Chapter 7.

Other scholars have been exceptionally helpful in reading and commenting on parts of the book. In particular, Julia Annas, David Sedley, and Richard Sorabji commented on the whole first draft. Also, David Sedley and Tony Long read the first three chapters of the final version, and Tony also read parts of Chapter 6. Gail Fine commented on 6.6, which discusses her work. Other scholars, including Shadi Bartsch, Brad Inwood, and Gretchen Reydams-Schils, have read parts of the book at various stages. Their responses have often been detailed, incisive, and enormously helpful to me. Indeed, they have sometimes raised issues to which I am conscious of making only a partial response. I feel privileged to be working at a time and in an area in which constructive dialogue, transcending differences of approach and opinion, is such a central part of the study of antiquity. Of course, all remaining mistakes and faults are my responsibility.

The development of the book has also been taken forward by seminar-papers and visiting lectures throughout the whole period of research and composition. I am grateful for many helpful comments on these occasions, which have made a real difference to the overall form and detailed analysis of the book. The contexts of these papers include conferences on a range of topics: ancient and modern ethics (Bonn, Exeter), emotions in antiquity (Edinburgh, Heidelberg), the ancient philosophy of mind, and of self (Helsinki, on two occasions), body and mind (Munich), Plato (Athens and Delphi, Frankfurt, Granada, Jerusalem, Liechtenstein, Piacenza, Toronto, Würzburg—many of these organized by the International Plato Society),

Seneca (Chicago, Leeds). They also include seminar-papers or visiting lectures in these venues: Cambridge 'B' Club, Center for Hellenic Studies, Washington DC, Centre Gernet and École Normale Supérieure, Paris, Institute of Classical Studies, London, Southern Association for Ancient Philosophy, the Universities of Berlin (Humboldt), British Columbia (Vancouver), and Victoria (Lansdowne lectures). Published versions of these papers are included in the References in this book and cited in footnotes. Where the argument of this book is especially close to part of a published article, this is highlighted in the notes.

I am most grateful to Kerensa Pearson for her characteristically careful work in preparing the final version of the typescript. Many thanks too to Hilary O'Shea for her advice and support, and to all those involved at Oxford University Press for their meticulous and patient work in producing this book, especially Belinda Baker, the copy-editor.

I would also like to record two, more personal, debts. Like many classical scholars, I was first drawn to the study of antiquity by an inspirational school teacher. Iolo Davies, Classics teacher at Cowbridge Grammar School and a life-long friend, was, and has remained, an influential exemplar of independence of mind and personal engagement with the subject matter of the discipline. My wife Karen, as well as supporting my work in many other ways, has made a special contribution to this book. Her powerful response to a serious illness has helped to shape my understanding of the significance of central ideas in this book, especially 'the structured self' and the 'holistic' approach to personality. This book is dedicated to her with much love.

C.G.

Contents

PART II THE UNSTRUCTURED SELF: STOIC PASSIONS AND THE RECEPTION OF PLATO

PART III THEORETICAL ISSUES AND LITERARY RECEPTION

Note on Conventions

The abbreviations for ancient authors and works are normally those used by H. G. Liddell, R. Scott, and H. S. Jones, *A Greek–English Lexicon*, 9th edition (Oxford, 1940), and P. Glare (ed.), *Oxford Latin Dictionary* (Oxford, 1982). Authors and texts cited are given in full form in the Index of Ancient Passages. In Latin quotations, *u* is used rather than *v* except in personal names, as in the *Oxford Latin Dictionary*. All quotations in Greek, Latin, and other foreign languages are translated. Translations are mine unless otherwise attributed. Texts and translations are those of the most recent Oxford Classical Text (or, where none is available, Budé edition), except as indicated. Where quotations are attributed to A. A. Long and D. N. Sedley, *The Hellenistic Philosophers* (Cambridge, 1987) (LS), their translation is used, modified as indicated. References to Galen, *On the Doctrines of Hippocrates and Plato* (*PHP*) are to De Lacy's edition (1978–84), cited by book, chapter, paragraph, and in some cases page and line number. Translations from *PHP* are those of De Lacy except when otherwise indicated.

All secondary works cited by author and date are included in the References at the end of the book. Early modern thinkers such as Descartes, Kant, or Locke, are normally cited by reference both to the book, chapter, or paragraph divisions of the original works and to the pages of modern editions; the modern editions cited are included in the References. Internal references are made by section, or page, or take this form: 'see text to nn. 43–4 above', referring to the same chapter, unless other marked. 'He/she' and 'her/him' are used indifferently as indefinite personal pronouns, even when summarizing ancient authors who use only masculine pronouns for this purpose. When translating ancient authors, their practice of using masculine forms in this way is retained.

Commonly used abbreviations in this book, which do not appear in this form in Liddell, Scott, and Jones or the *Oxford Latin Dictionary*, are as follows:

Arist. *NE*	Aristotle, *Nicomachean Ethics*.
DK	H. Diels and W. Kranz (eds.), *Die Fragmente der Vorsokratiker*, 10th edn., 2 vols., Berlin: Weidmann, 1961.
Epicur. *K. D.*	Epicurus, *Kuriai Doxai* (*Key Doctrines*).
Gal. *PHP*	Galen, *de Placitis Hippocratis et Platonis* (*On the Doctrines of Hippocrates and Plato*).

Gal. *QAM*	Galen, *Quod Animi Mores Corporis Temperamenta Sequantur* (*The Soul's Dependence on the Body*).
LS	A. A. Long and D. N. Sedley, *The Hellenistic Philosophers*, 2 vols., Cambridge: Cambridge University Press, 1987.
SVF	H. von Arnim (ed.), *Stoicorum Veterum Fragmenta*, Leipzig: Teubner, 1903–5.

Introduction

At the heart of this book is a single, though complex, question. What is new and distinctive about the conceptions of self developed in Hellenistic philosophy and perpetuated in Roman thought? More precisely, what is new about the ideas of selfhood and personality evolved by Stoicism and Epicureanism, two major innovative Hellenistic philosophies?[1] And how do their ideas—or what is distinctive about them—relate to earlier Greek thought and to other theories of their period? The book is subdivided into three parts with a view to presenting my answer to this question and exploring the implications of this answer.

In the first and longest part ('The Structured Self in Stoic and Epicurean Philosophy'), I examine what seems to me to lie at the core of Stoic and Epicurean thinking on human personality. This is a striking combination of types of holism (psychophysical and psychological) and naturalism with certain key 'Socratic' claims or ideals. In this part of the book, I am equally concerned with Stoicism and Epicureanism. I set out to show how these two theories, which are in other ways strongly opposed, converge in holding this combination of ideas about human selfhood and personality. I discuss how their shared ideas relate to the background of earlier Greek thought and how they differ from other conceptions in the Hellenistic–Roman period, notably those of (what we call) Middle Platonism.

The second part ('The Unstructured Self: Stoic Passions and the Reception of Plato') is, in effect, a case study illustrating the overall thesis of the book. I examine in some depth a single theory, the Stoic analysis of passions or emotions, which exemplifies the salient characteristics of the idea of 'the structured self'. I also explore in this context questions about the history and reception of ideas in antiquity that are crucial for the book as a whole.

In the third part ('Theoretical Issues and Literary Reception'), I explore two types of implication of the claims made in the first two parts about Stoic and Epicurean thinking about selfhood and personality. One is that what is innovative and distinctive in Hellenistic–Roman thought about selfhood is

[1] For briefer discussion of Scepticism, the third major new theory of this period, in connection with the topic of subjectivity, see 6.6 below.

not, as is sometimes claimed, a shift towards a heightened interest in subjectivity. Stoic–Epicurean ideas, in particular, are no less objectivist in approach than earlier Platonic or Aristotelian ones but they differ because of their focus on (what I am calling) 'the structured self'. The second implication relates to the relationship between the philosophical ideas examined here and subsequent Greek and Roman literature. I suggest that the contrasting philosophical approaches examined here are reflected in differing literary representations of stability and disintegration of character, as exemplified in Plutarch's *Lives*, Senecan tragedy, and Virgil's *Aeneid*.

This summary of my aims raises several questions about the terms used here. I clarify these points before explaining more fully the main claims and project of the book. First, in what sense is this a book about 'the self'? Second, what does 'the structured self' signify? Third, what is meant by 'Hellenistic and Roman thought'?

The English terms, 'self', 'personality', also 'personhood' or 'personal identity' or 'character', are not precise, technical terms, but have a range of, partly overlapping, connotations.[2] These include those of individual distinctiveness or uniqueness.[3] They also include those of psychological (or psychophysical) structure,[4] or of what is essential or fundamental to our nature as human beings or persons.[5] My interest here is, very largely, in the second set of ideas, rather than the first. I am concerned with ancient thought about what is important about us as human beings or psychophysical wholes or as instantiations of psyche, rather than about what it is to be a (uniquely) particular person or to be *me*. Scholars working on ancient thought are sometimes concerned to distinguish ideas about self from those about personality or personhood and they may have a special interest in the distinctive connotations of 'self', including self-awareness or subjectivity. I do not share these concerns. My aim is to analyse ancient ideas about selfhood or personality, broadly understood, without drawing a sharp distinction between self and

[2] For parallel comments and references, see Gill (1996*b*), 1–2.

[3] See e.g. *Oxford English Dictionary* (1989) (= *OED*), 'personality', 2a: 'That quality or assemblage of qualities which makes a person what he is, as distinct from other persons: distinctive personal or individual character, esp. when of a marked or notable kind'; see also sense 3b, 5a, and *OED* 'self', senses 3, 4a.

[4] See e.g. *Chambers Dictionary* (1960), 'personality': 'the integrated organisation of all the psychological, intellectual, emotional, and physical characteristics of an individual, especially as they are presented to other people.' See also *OED* 'personality', sense 2c, and the combinations e.g. 'personality structure', listed in sense 7.

[5] See e.g. *OED*, 'self', 3: 'That which in a person is really and intrinsically *he* (in contradiction to what is adventitious); the ego (often identified with the soul or mind as opposed to the body); a permanent subject of successive and varying states of consciousness.' See also *OED*, 'personality', senses 1a, 1c, 3a. On this definition of 'self' and its conceptual basis, see 331–3 below.

personality.[6] Also, as I bring out in Chapter 6, I am sceptical about the relevance to Hellenistic–Roman, as well as Classical Greek, thought of some of the main modern connotations of 'self', namely subjectivity and self-consciousness, understood in terms of 'I'-centred subjectivity.

The term 'the structured self' in my book title has both specific and broader connotations. Mainly, and more specifically, I use this term to encapsulate the distinctive and innovative features of Stoic and Epicurean thinking about selfhood and personality. These centre on a combination of ideas, explained below, in both aspects of which the notion of structure has a special importance. Stoic–Epicurean thought, as I interpret this, sees human beings, like other animals, as structured wholes or units rather than as a combination of a psychic 'core' and a body or as a complex of distinct psychic parts. Also, the 'Socratic' claims crucial for Stoic–Epicurean thought give a special place to the achievement of a certain type of—ethical and psychological—structure, associated with 'wisdom', which constitutes the ideal norm for both theories. The idea of the '*un*structured self', which also figures sometimes in this book, refers to character-states which fall short of this type of ideal (ethical and psychological) structure. In another sense, *all* selves are seen as structured in Stoic–Epicurean thought because they constitute psychophysical wholes or units. These distinctive Stoic–Epicurean ideas about psychophysical and ethical structure are sometimes defined, in this book, by contrast with some earlier Platonic or Aristotelian or contemporary (for instance, Middle Platonic) ideas.[7] But, as I also bring out, a concern with structure in one of these senses, especially the second (ethical) sense, is partly shared with these other theories, though combined with a rather different view of human personality.[8] To this degree, concern with structure and its absence is a more pervasive feature of Hellenistic–Roman thought on selfhood and personality, and one that is prefigured especially in certain aspects of Platonic thought. This concern also underlies salient features of Greek and Latin literature in this period, as I show in Chapter 7.

What is meant here by 'Hellenistic and Roman' thought? The Hellenistic period is, typically, defined in political terms, as the epoch in which Alexander and his successors spread Greek culture over the Mediterranean prior to the unification of the whole region under the Roman Empire.[9] But, as some

[6] By contrast, Long and Sorabji in recent writings and work in progress, are more concerned with 'self', by contrast with 'personality'; Sorabji, in particular, is more concerned with individual selfhood. See e.g. Long (1992), (1997), discussed in 6.4 below, text to nn. 161–3, and (1996), ch. 12, discussed in 6.5, text to n. 175.

[7] See e.g. 1.2, 3.4, 4.3, and 6.3 below.

[8] See e.g. 4.3 and 7.2, on Plutarch.

[9] Conventionally, the period is defined as falling between the death of Alexander the Great in 323 BC and the battle of Actium in 31 BC.

scholars have recently underlined, political and intellectual eras do not necessarily coincide. There is a growing tendency to distinguish an earlier Hellenistic period from a later. The later period, sometimes called 'post-Hellenistic', is seen as running (roughly) from the start of the first century BC to the end of the second century AD. In the earlier Hellenistic period, philosophical activity centred on the evolution of new ideas, with little explicit commentary on previous theories even when their ideas were adopted. In the later Hellenistic period, in various schools, there was an increasing move towards explicit commentary. There was also a growing trend to appropriate previous thinkers such as Plato or Pythagoras as predecessors or authorities.[10] As this point indicates, it is particularly difficult to draw a sharp distinction between later Hellenistic and Roman philosophy. Roman thinkers such as Lucretius, Cicero, and Seneca are both indispensable sources for Hellenistic philosophy and also, in effect, independent later Hellenistic thinkers, adopting and to some degree modifying earlier Hellenistic ideas.

In this book, taken as a whole, I am concerned with both phases of Hellenistic philosophy, including the contribution of Roman thinkers. I also aim to correlate Hellenistic ideas with earlier ones, especially Plato's. In the first part of the book, which analyses the idea of the 'structured self' in Stoicism and Epicureanism, the focus is on the earlier and more innovative phase, though many of the sources are taken from the later period. In Part II, my interests range right across the whole Hellenistic–Roman period. I seek to reconstruct the history of the Stoic theory of the passions (especially the relationship between Chrysippus and Posidonius) and also the critical responses to which this theory gave rise in Plutarch and Galen in the first and second centuries AD. In Chapter 6, especially 6.6, my examination of the relevance of subjectivity to ancient conceptions of self embraces ideas ranging from the fourth century BC to the second century AD. In Chapter 7, the scope of the enquiry is extended to the reception of Hellenistic (and Classical) philosophical ideas on ethical psychology in Plutarch's biographies and Roman poetry of the first centuries BC and AD. Thus, 'Hellenistic and Roman thought' is understood rather broadly in this book, though the central concern is with Hellenistic philosophy in the narrow sense, particularly Stoic and Epicurean conceptions of selfhood and personality.

What is the combination of ideas on which, I suggest, Stoic and Epicurean approaches converge, and which constitutes the conception of the structured

[10] See further M. Frede (1999*a*), esp. 774–8, 783–4; Sedley (1997*b*), (2003), 20–4. On 'post-Hellenistic' philosophy, see Boys-Stones (2001), esp. ch. 6, and Sharples and Sorabji (forthcoming). See also 4.1 below, text to nn. 25–34. below.

self?[11] One aspect of this set of ideas is a holistic and naturalistic conception of human personality. Human beings, like other animals, are seen as psychophysical and psychological wholes or units. They are not seen as a combination of a psychic or mental core or essence and a body, or as a complex of distinct psychic parts, conceived as independent sources of motivation. This holism is combined with three types of naturalism. One type is a focus on the natural (birth-to-death) life of human beings as fundamentally embodied rational animals. A second type of naturalism is the belief that all human beings are constitutively capable of a form of natural development that shapes all aspects of the personality and is capable, in principle, of leading anyone to perfect wisdom. A third type (which I call 'rich naturalism') is the idea that the understanding of nature in the full sense involves combining and in some sense synthesizing the insights of ethics, physics, and logic, rather than reducing or subordinating ethics to—for instance—physics. These types of holism and naturalism are combined with certain 'Socratic' ethical claims or ideals. One of these is that the achievement of happiness is 'up to us' (implying that it is also 'open to us') through virtue and rational reflection in a way that is not constrained by our inborn nature, upbringing, or social situation. Another is that happiness involves a time-independent perfection of character, marked by freedom from passion or distress, and invulnerable to contingent circumstances. A third claim is that only the fully rational and virtuous (or wise) person is fully integrated or coherent while non-wise people are relatively incoherent and lead incoherent lives.

To what extent is this analysis of the distinctive character of Stoic and Epicurean thinking about selfhood a new one? Scholars have sometimes, in recent years, ascribed one or other type of holism or naturalism to Stoicism or Epicureanism.[12] Also A. A. Long, in particular, has stressed the seminal influence of Socrates on Hellenistic philosophy in general, especially Stoicism.[13] But this is the first work, I think, which presents the combination of these two types of idea, taken as constituting an integrated set of themes, as crucial for both Stoicism and Epicureanism, and as marking a key point of difference from some earlier, contemporary, and later theories. The combination of holism and naturalism with 'Socratic' ideals may seem surprising. Those ideals might seem better suited for combination with other types of

[11] The following outline is, of course, very broad and generalized, and is simply a foretaste of ideas explored especially in Chs. 1–2 below.

[12] For instance, there has been extensive discussion of physicalism in Epicureanism and of unified (holistic) psychology in Stoicism; see further 1.5 and 4.5 below.

[13] See Long (1988) (=1996: 1–34), (1999*b*); also (2002), ch. 3. See also Vander Waerdt (1994*b*), part 2; Alesse (2000). On the influence of the image of Socrates on the visual representation of intellectuals in the Hellenistic–Roman period, see Zanker (1995).

theory, notably the kind of core-centred thinking about human personality and the idealist or transcendental world-view we sometimes find in Plato's dialogues. Indeed, versions of these 'Socratic' ideals can be found in combination with a dualist world-view, for instance, in Plato's *Phaedo* and in some aspects of Plutarch's (Middle Platonic) thought.[14] But it seems to me that the combination of a holistic and naturalistic conception of human personality with certain, strikingly rigorous or paradoxical, 'Socratic' ethical ideas is central to the special character of Stoic and Epicurean thought. It is this combination that underlies certain parallel features in Stoic and Epicurean thinking about ethical psychology and about ideal norms of human character, as I bring out in Chapter 2. This combination also gives rise to a shared Stoic–Epicurean pattern of thinking about psychological and ethical development. This pattern can be defined by contrast with strands of Platonic and Aristotelian thought which contribute to the accounts of ethical development offered by Middle Platonic thinkers such as Antiochus or Plutarch.[15] It is also this combination of ideas that constitutes what is so distinctive in Chrysippus' theory of the passions. This in turn arouses the critical responses of Plutarch and Galen, which are based on their commitment to the part-based psychology they derive from Plato and Aristotle.[16] Thus, I suggest that exploring this combination of seemingly different types of idea is crucial both for defining the special quality of Stoic and Epicurean thought on selfhood and personality and for explaining the ancient debates and criticisms which it provokes.

What, exactly does 'Socratic' mean in this connection and why the inverted commas or 'scare-quotes'? As explained in Chapter 2, Stoic and Epicurean approaches diverge to some extent on this point. The Stoics, throughout their history, seem to have explicitly regarded Socratic ethical thought, especially (though not solely) as conveyed by Plato, as a prime source of inspiration. They also saw Socrates as an ethical exemplar and as one of the very few credible candidates for being a 'wise person' in the full sense.[17] The Epicureans tended to view Socrates, and Socratic-Platonic thought generally, in a negative light. However, at the same time, Epicurus and his followers adopted from Democritus and succeeding thinkers ethical ideas which have a good

[14] See 2.2 below, text to nn. 71–5, and 4.3 below, text to nn. 143–5.

[15] See esp. 3.2, 3.4 (on Antiochus and Arius Didymus), and 4.3, text to nn. 113–14, 7.2 below (on Plutarch). The main point of contrast is between the holistic (Stoic–Epicurean) and core-centred or part-based psychology (Antiochus, Plutarch) that is taken to underlie human development.

[16] On the combination of Socratic ideals and holism in Chrysippus' theory, see esp. 4.4 below, text to nn. 213, 245. On the part-based reactions of Plutarch and Galen, see 4.3–4.

[17] See further Sedley (1993); Vander Waerdt (1994*b*), part 2; esp. Striker (1994); Long (1996), 23–32; (2002), ch. 3; Annas (1994); Alesse (2000).

deal in common with the ideas adopted by Stoics from Socrates. Also, as noted earlier, Socrates stands as a looming presence over Hellenistic philosophy in general, in a way that is likely to have influenced even schools such as the Epicurean which did not acknowledge him as a model. Socrates became, from an early stage, a key symbol for the idea that philosophy is not just a medium for developing ideas and arguments. Philosophy was presented as a basis, and in some sense an authoritative one, for setting ethical norms by which people in general—and not just philosophers—should frame their lives. In other words, Socrates served as a symbol for the idea that philosophy was not just a 'second-order' activity, analysing ideas that already formed part of social discourse. Philosophy was a project that *made a difference* to what should count as norms of character and conduct. Both the Stoic and Epicurean schools adopted this conception of the status and role of philosophy, in partial contrast with the rather more 'academic' (in the modern sense) view of philosophy developed in the schools of Plato and Aristotle.[18] This Socratic conception of the role of philosophy underlies the ethical claims noted earlier, especially the first, that happiness is 'up to us' through virtue and rational reflection.[19] It is possible that Socratic influence also helped to shape the Epicurean as well as Stoic versions of all three ethical claims, even if this influence is not acknowledged. Also, the Epicurean versions of these ideas, like the Stoic ones, are 'Socratic' in the sense that they resemble themes closely associated with Socrates in our sources.[20]

The last point made, together with some earlier ones, brings out a further, more general, feature of this book. An important dimension of its argument centres on attempts to trace the reception of ancient ideas *within antiquity*. This partly reflects a more widespread tendency in scholarship on ancient philosophy.[21] Apart from the inherent interest of this topic, scholars are increasingly aware that our sources for ancient ideas—particularly for

[18] For some related comments, see Long (1999*b*), 618–23. An index of the difference from the approach of the Academy and Peripatos or Lyceum (the schools of Plato and Aristotle) is the Stoic–Epicurean idea that philosophy *as a whole* (and not just ethics, for instance) has a practical objective, an idea linked with their 'rich naturalism'. See further 3.3 below, text to nn. 172–9, and 3.5, text to nn. 264–78.

[19] The key point of connection is the thought that philosophy can help to lead *anyone* (in principle) to a type of happiness that is time-independent, invulnerable, and that constitutes a special type of cohesion of character.

[20] See further on the sense in which these ideas are 'Socratic', 2.2 below, text to nn. 37–40, 47–59, 76–87, and on the relationship between Socratic and Epicurean thought, 2.3 below.

[21] See e.g. (on the ancient reception of Plato's *Timaeus*), Reydams-Schils (1999) and (2003); also Sharples and Sheppard (2003). On the correlated topic of the modern reception of ancient ideas, see e.g. Miller and Inwood (2003), on early modern and Hellenistic philosophy, and White (2002), chs. 1–2, on the modern reception of Greek ethics.

Hellenistic philosophy but also for Socrates—[22] are often not just neutral reporters but are engaged participants in continuing and often intense debates. This feature is particularly important in Part II. As I stress there, the project of trying to reconstruct and interpret the Stoic theory of the passions is, to a large extent, a matter of critical engagement with our prime sources for the theory, Plutarch and Galen, who are also opponents and rivals of Stoic ethical psychology. This topic also bears on a more general dimension of the book's argument. The Stoic–Epicurean idea of the structured self is partly characterized here by contrast with certain features of Platonic and Aristotelian thought, notably their core-centred and part-based thinking about human personality, which was perpetuated by Middle Platonic thinkers such as Antiochus and Plutarch. On the other hand, for the Stoics especially, some aspects of Platonic thought also served as a positive influence, and one that shaped the holistic side of their thought as well as the 'Socratic' ethical claims.[23] But their appropriation of Plato, which was sometimes explicit, especially in later Hellenistic philosophy, was misinterpreted or disputed by subsequent thinkers, notably Plutarch or Galen, who themselves claimed to be the true inheritors of the Platonic conception of human personality.[24] The study of the reception of ancient ideas in antiquity is thus intimately bound up with the attempt to chart the history of ancient ideas of self.

I close this discussion by considering the relationship of this book to a previous study on a related theme: *Personality in Greek Epic, Tragedy, and Philosophy: The Self in Dialogue* (Gill 1996*b*). Both books represent attempts to encapsulate distinctive features of ancient thought about selfhood in successive periods of antiquity, though in rather different ways. The earlier book was divided equally between literature and philosophy, tracing analogous conceptions in both areas. The present book is more focused on philosophy;[25] the final chapter considers the possible influence of philosophical ideas on Roman literature especially. The argument of the previous book was centred on a contrast between 'objective-participant' and 'subjective-individualist' ideas of personality. The latter idea was presented as distinctively modern whereas the former was taken to be characteristic of Greek thought,

[22] On this aspect of the study of Socrates, see e.g. Kahn (1996), ch. 1, and Vander Waerdt (1994*b*), part 1.

[23] See e.g., on the influence of Plato's *Timaeus* on the Stoic holistic world-view, 1.3 below, text to nn. 41–8, and on Stoic thinking about the embodied psychological system, 5.1 below.

[24] See further 4.3 below (Plutarch), 4.4 (Galen), and 4.6 (Posidonius).

[25] The present book also engages more directly with current scholarly debates in relevant aspects of ancient philosophy. See e.g. 1.5 on the debate aroused by Sedley's ideas about 'emergent dualism' in Epicureanism, 3.3 on the issues raised by Annas's claims about nature in Stoic ethics, and 4.5–6 on controversies about the history of Stoic psychology.

though also available as a conceptual option in modern thought.[26] This contrast also reappears in the present book, in the discussion in Chapter 6 of the theoretical issues in selfhood raised by the preceding analysis of the salient features of Stoic–Epicurean, and some other Hellenistic–Roman, conceptions of personality. I maintain that Hellenistic–Roman thought on personality, like Classical Greek thinking, is best interpreted as 'objective-participant' in approach. My view runs counter to the claim sometimes made that the Hellenistic–Roman period sees a shift towards a more subjective and individualistic approach to self. The emphasis here is on the question of the relevance to Hellenistic–Roman thought of subjectivity, rather than of individuality. Indeed, the present book includes less discussion of social ethics, as this bears on ancient thinking about selfhood, than the previous book.[27]

A more general difference between the two studies is that the previous book centred on a contrast framed in what is sometimes called 'observer's language' (that is, *our* modern categories) whereas the present one is centred more on distinctions which belong rather to 'participant's language' (the categories of ancient thought).[28] Although the idea of the structured self (taken as a whole) is not an explicit theme of Hellenistic–Roman debate, the various component strands of this idea do form part of ancient discussions and controversies. In particular, the contrast between unified or holistic and core-centred or part-based conceptions of personality figures prominently in philosophical debate in this period. This issue is intertwined, in ways outlined earlier, with the contrast between Stoic or Epicurean and Platonic–Aristotelian (or Middle Platonic) thought.[29] The 'Socratic' ethical ideals are also linked with certain well-defined Hellenistic–Roman controversies, for instance, about whether the ideal character-state is that of 'freedom from passion' or 'moderation of passion' and how far happiness depends on external goods.[30] My discussion also underlines contrasting patterns in ancient thinking about ethical development,[31] and also divergent views about whether there can be stable, though

[26] See Gill (1996*b*), esp. Introduction and ch. 6.

[27] Contrast Gill (1996*b*), esp. chs. 2, 5. The reduced role of social ethics here simply reflects considerations of space and emphasis. I hope to explore elsewhere the significance of the idea of the (Stoic–Epicurean) 'structured self' for understanding Hellenistic–Roman social ethics. For some discussion of Stoic–Epicurean social ethics (the validation of objective' (not 'reactive') attitudes to other people), see 7.4 below, text to nn. 189–207.

[28] On this type of distinction, see 6.1, below, text to nn. 1–2.

[29] See further 4.1 below.

[30] On these debates (as they bear on this topic), see e.g. 3.4 below, text to nn. 206–7, 218–24, 4.3 below.

[31] See 3.2; also, on the implications of this contrast 6.5 below, text to n. 183, and 7.1, text to nn. 5–9.

defective, character-states.[32] On these latter topics, the conceptual differences between different ancient theories are evident, even though they do not seem to have given rise to explicit debate. In these ways, the present book is organized more than its predecessor around explicit ancient ideas and controversies. However, in broad terms, my two books form complementary parts of a—still continuing—project to chart the salient features of ancient thinking on human selfhood and personality in a way that is designed to promote and deepen our own engagement with these ancient ideas.[33]

[32] See e.g. 4.3 below, text to nn. 15–20 (Plutarch), 4.5 below, text to nn. 251–66, 5.2, text to nn. 133–7 below (Chrysippus, perhaps influenced by Plato). On the possible relevance of this point to literature, see Ch. 7, esp. 7.2 below, text to nn. 43–9, 7.3, text to nn. 94–104, 7.4, text to nn. 133–8.

[33] In a book in progress I examine the interplay between philosophical and medical conceptions of human personality in the 2nd c. AD, with special reference to Galen and Marcus Aurelius.

Part I

The Structured Self in Stoicism and Epicureanism

1

Psychophysical Holism in Stoicism and Epicureanism

1.1 PRELIMINARIES

What, then, is new and distinctive in Hellenistic conceptions of self? The answer offered here is that, at least in Stoicism and Epicureanism, it inheres in the features I am associating with the idea of the structured self. As explained in the Introduction, these features consist in a combination of holistic and naturalistic views of human nature or personality with a certain set of 'Socratic' ethical claims. In this chapter and the next two, I set out salient aspects of this shared, or converging, Stoic–Epicurean conception of self.

One key feature on which Stoic and Epicurean ideas converge is in conceiving human personality as a psychophysical and psychological unit or structured whole. There is a clear contrast with other ancient views (earlier, contemporary, or later), which identify what is distinctive or valuable in us as a determinate core or essence, typically mind or reason, and which see human beings as a combination of distinct parts, such as body and psyche or, within the psyche, reason and emotion or desire. In this chapter, I focus on Stoic and Epicurean thinking on psychophysical holism. I underline the parallels between their ideas on this topic, which are illustrated in each theory by their thinking on animal, including human, development (1.4–5). I begin by setting these Stoic and Epicurean ideas against the background of Platonic and Aristotelian thought, accentuating both the contrast with earlier core-centred and part-based thinking and also ways in which Platonic or Aristotelian thought anticipates Stoic–Epicurean holism (1.2). I also offer suggestions about the route by which Stoics and Epicureans converged in holding these ideas—in spite of other important differences—in part through their distinct but related responses to the late fourth-century intellectual context in which their theories were formed (1.3). The main type of naturalism explored here is a focus on the natural life of human beings as fundamentally embodied rational animals. The chapter concludes with a short discussion of Stoic and

Epicurean thinking about—what we call—personal identity, highlighting links with their conception of human beings as psychophysical units (1.6).

A further overall thesis of this chapter is that Epicureanism and Stoicism can be seen as sharing, or converging on, a philosophical position which we can call 'substantial holism', that is, holism as regards reality or substance. The salient mark of this position is that reality is viewed as a unified or integrated whole, rather than as a—perhaps uneasy—combination of radically different kinds of entity. Similarly, goodness or excellence and its opposite are conceived in terms of differing states or qualities or levels of complexity of this integrated whole, rather than as constituting one kind of entity as opposed to another. The obvious contrast is with what could be called 'substantial dualism', a position of which we can find versions in Plato's thought and also in Middle Platonism or Neoplatonism. A full examination of this idea would form the basis of another, and differently formulated, type of book; but it is useful, none the less, to view the points made here about psychophysical and psychological holism within this larger conceptual framework.

1.2 PLATONIC AND ARISTOTELIAN BACKGROUND

I begin by highlighting salient features in Platonic and Aristotelian thought which help to provide a historical context for the emergence of the distinctive set of Stoic–Epicurean ideas about personality (the structured self) outlined earlier (xvi–ii above). I seek to identify *both* features of Platonic and Aristotelian thought that are significantly different from the Hellenistic pattern *and* those which have some points of similarity to this pattern. The question of which Platonic and Aristotelian ideas may actually have helped to shape the emergence of the Stoic–Epicurean pattern—either by influence or by reaction—is taken up in the next section.

First, I offer illustrations from Plato and Aristotle of (what I am calling) 'core-centred' or 'essence-centred' thinking about the person, and also of 'part-based' thinking about human psychology. These are aspects of fourth-century thinking about personality which serve to define, by contrast, the Stoic–Epicurean mode, especially, the conception of human beings as cohesive psychophysical and psychological wholes. These features of Platonic and Aristotelian thought were also adopted in later Hellenistic thought, especially by Middle Platonic thinkers such as Antiochus and Plutarch. The influence of these Middle Platonic thinkers helps to explain their (partly) negative response to the Stoic version of the holistic model.[1] However, I also highlight dimensions of Platonic and Aristotelian thought which in some ways prefigure the Hellenistic holistic model. The Platonic and Aristotelian ideas outlined raise complex interpretative issues, but I do not engage with those issues here. My aim here is the strictly limited one of mapping key aspects of the intellectual background against which Stoic and Epicurean ideas about personality were formed.

What is meant by 'core-centred' or 'essence-centred' thought about personality? Plato's *Alcibiades 1*, examined in detail later (6.3), offers a clear example. Having raised the question 'what we ourselves are' (128e10–11), Socrates offers as an answer the soul or personality (psyche)[2] rather than the body (129c–130c), dismissing the idea that 'the combination of the two' (*sunamphoteron*, 130a9), body and psyche, could be so characterized (130b–c). This answer is refined in the suggestion that the psyche recognizes itself when it looks at the region of the psyche where virtue is present, specifically, wisdom and knowledge, which is presented as the god-like aspect, though one which also confers other virtues, such as self-control (132c–133c).[3] This passage exemplifies several features of the type of thinking I have in view. One part—or, better, aspect or dimension—[4] of the psyche is specified as our core or what we ourselves ('really') are. This aspect is defined partly by the possession of a certain capacity (here, for knowledge or wisdom) and partly by the expression of a certain nature, such as divine or god-like nature. Sometimes, a reflexive relationship is involved, for instance, self-knowledge. In the *Alcibiades*, as elsewhere in ancient thought, the reflexive relationship is taken to be explained by the nature of the core or essence and not vice versa.[5]

In two other famous Platonic passages, we find a similar set of ideas. Near the end of the *Republic*, after arguing for the immortality of the psyche, Socrates draws a distinction between the psyche as it is 'in truth' (*alētheia*) and as it is in its currently embodied condition. The claim is that, 'in truth', the psyche consists only of the rational, cognitive dimension, and that the present polymorphous (tripartite) condition of the psyche is a product of its embodiment.[6] The psyche in its present state is compared to a human statue

[1] See further 3.4 and 4.1–4 below.

[2] Generally, Greek and Latin terms are transliterated in this book, but I normally treat 'psyche' as a naturalized English term.

[3] See further 6.3 below, text to nn. 57–8.

[4] The idea of 'part' can be seen as problematic in this connection, because being a part might seem to signify secondary status, whereas the key point is that this entity is primary to our nature. See further 6.3 below, text to n. 108.

[5] On this point, see 6.3 below, text to nn. 94–100.

[6] A similar contrast is drawn more briefly, in connection with the idea of self-knowledge, in Pl. *Phdr.* 230a.

that has been sunk under the sea and become encrusted, making it seem 'more like a beast than its natural character' (*hoios... phusei*, 611d5–6). To discover this natural character we have to look at the psyche's love of wisdom, which shows 'that it has a natural kinship with what is divine and immortal and permanent'. If it were able to express this impulse towards the divine completely, it would realize its 'true (uniform) nature' (612a3) and would get rid of its current complexity.

In Plato's *Phaedo*, very similar claims about human nature are made, though as part of an argument for the immortality of the psyche, rather than as a specification of what is essential to us. The argument turns on a contrast between two categories of existing things: permanent, self-identical, non-material Forms and variable, non-uniform, material particulars. It is maintained that the psyche is cognate with the first category and the body is cognate with the second, and that, therefore, the psyche is more likely to survive death than the body. This is coupled with the claim that the psyche is best able to realize its natural kinship to the non-material Forms by separating itself from the body and the pleasures, pains, and desires generated by the body. The psyche is also more likely in this way to achieve immortality after death (78d–84b). Although this argument is not couched as one about 'what we ourselves are' or 'the true nature of the psyche', it is similar in drawing qualitative distinctions between aspects of our nature and in the criteria used to demarcate these aspects.

Two famous chapters in Aristotle's discussions of friendship, *Nicomachean Ethics* (*NE*) 9.4, 9.8, like Plato's *Alcibiades*, bring together the themes of reflexivity (here, self-love) and what is essential to us.[7] *NE* 9.4 begins with the claim that the marks of proper friendship are both derived from, and most fully expressed in, a person's relationship to himself (1166^{a}1–2). This is then modified by saying that this only applies to the good person's relationship to himself. The salient marks of friendship are said to be (1) wishing good things for the friend for the sake of the friend and (2) sharing the friend's life. The idea of 'what each one is' or 'seems to be' (*hoti hekastos esti* or *einai dokei*) is introduced in connection with the first mark of friendship. The good person, but not the bad, wishes good things to himself and does so for his own sake. Earlier in the argument, Aristotle defines the best form of friendship (that based on virtue) as friendship directed at what the person is 'in himself' (*kath' hauton*).[8] Here, this idea is reformulated as friendship directed at what 'each one seems to be' (1166^{a}17). This is taken to be our capacity for thought and reasoning (*to dianoētikon, to nooun*). Although the kind of thought is not

[7] On this point, see further 6.3 below, text to nn. 98–100.

[8] See *NE* 1156^{a}11–12, ^{b}10–11.

specified precisely, what seems to be meant is the kind of practical reasoning that is associated with ethical virtue, combined with the kind of contemplative reasoning expressed in pleasurable observation of one's own good actions.[9] The good but not the bad are said to be capable of directing this kind of well-wishing at themselves and of being at one with themselves, and in this sense they alone are capable of self-love.[10]

NE 9.8 contains a comparable, though not identical, line of thought.[11] The initial, and controversial, claim, is that one should be a self-lover (*philautos*), even though this term is conventionally used as criticism. Aristotle then describes conventional self-lovers as those who allocate themselves a larger share of material goods and bodily pleasures and who in this sense 'gratify their desires and in general their feelings (*pathē*) and the irrational part of their psyche' (1168^{b}16–17, 20–1). By contrast, Aristotle describes the good self-lover as someone who competes, and allocates himself a larger share, in practising virtue, even when this means giving up the goods desired by the conventional self-lover. This kind of person is more of a self-lover than the other type because he loves 'the most controlling part' (*to kuriōtaton*) of his personality, that is, his mind (*nous*), as expressed (by implication) in virtuous practical reasoning (1168^{a}28–31, 35). 'It is clear that this is what each one is, or mostly, and that this is what the good person loves most' (1169^{a}2–3). It is also claimed that the self-lover in this sense can combine the greatest degree of self-love with the best form of friendship towards someone else.

NE 10.7–8 also makes prominent use of the idea of 'what each one is' in the course of a famous and controversial discussion of the highest possible human happiness. The key relevant point is indicated in these two quotations:

> If happiness is activity in accordance with virtue, it is reasonable that it should be according to the highest [or 'most dominant', *kratistē*] virtue; and this would be the virtue of the best part of us (*ariston*). This part is mind (*nous*) or whatever seems to be our natural ruler and guide and seems to understand what is fine and divine, being itself either divine or the most divine element in us. Thus, the activity of this part in accordance with its proper virtue would be perfect (*teleia*) happiness. As has been said, this activity is contemplative (*theōrētikē*).[12]

> If the mind [*nous*, capable of contemplation, *theōria*] is divine by comparison with the human being [as a whole], the life of the mind (*kata touton*) must be divine by

[9] Practical reasoning (wishing and acting deliberately) is indicated in *NE* 1166^{a}14–15 and in 1166^{b}6–11 (the corresponding inferior state). 1166^{a}23–9, taken as continuing ^{a}13–23, suggests, rather, the kind of 'acts of contemplation' (*theōrēmata*, ^{a}26) involved in pleasurable observation of one's own good actions (on which see *NE* 9.9, esp. 1169^{b}33 and 1170^{a}2).

[10] *NE* 9.4, especially 1166^{a}10–29, ^{b}6–25.

[11] On some key differences, see Annas (1993*b*), 254–62.

[12] *NE* 1177^{a}12–18, sentence structure modified as in Irwin (1985), 284.

comparison with the [purely] human life... one should as far as possible make himself immortal (*athanatizein*) and do everything to live in accordance with the best thing (*kratiston*) in himself... This would seem to be what each one is, if it is the authoritative and better part. It would be odd for someone to choose another's life instead of his own. (1177^{b}30–1178^{a}4)

The obvious point of contrast with *NE* 9.4, 9.8 is that 'what each one is' is identified with the mind's capacity for theoretical contemplation rather than for practical reasoning linked with ethical virtue. The grounds for regarding the latter rather than the former as 'what each one is' (as expressing our distinctively human nature) are clearly articulated in 10.8. Aristotle describes practical reasoning as 'yoked together with' ethical virtue, and both of these as 'interlinked' with the emotions (*pathē*) and thus forming part of our life as a psychological (and psychophysical) 'compound' (*suntheton*) that makes up the human being (1178^{a}14–21). By contrast, contemplative mind is 'small in bulk', and in some sense 'separate' from the life of the human psychophysical compound. But a series of arguments are offered for concluding that contemplative mind is 'what each one is', in that it is 'dominant' (*to kurion*) and the highest part of us (*kratiston*) and also 'better' (*ameinon*) and greater in power and honour than practical reason.[13]

These examples, though not exhaustive,[14] may be taken as illustrating the general pattern of thought, in which we find a range of partly overlapping contrasts used to characterize what is essential to us. The broadest contrast is between body and psyche (*Alcibiades*, *Phaedo*); in *Phaedo* 80c–84b, this is reconceived as a contrast between the psyche freeing itself from the body or binding itself to it. Elsewhere, the contrast is between different aspects or dimensions of the psyche: between the emotional aspect and (practical) reason (Arist. *NE* 9.4, 9.8),[15] or between the psyche as a tripartite complex (including spirit and appetite) and as purely rational and cognitive (Pl. *R.* 10).[16] A further contrast, drawn most explicitly in Arist. *NE* 10.7–8 but implied elsewhere, is that between theoretical or contemplative reason or

[13] *NE* 1177^{b}34–1178^{a}3, 5–6, 22. The claim about self-immortalization is often linked by scholars with Aristotle's conception of god, as 'thought thinking itself' (*Metaph.* 12.7, 12.9), and with 'active mind' as a quasi-external, non-material presence within us (*de An.* 3.5, 3.7). For discussion, from different standpoint, see e.g. Lear (1988), 1–14, 135–51, 293–320; Nussbaum and Rorty (1992), chs. 17–19; Gerson (2004).

[14] Other suggestive Platonic parallels include the call to 'become like god' in *Theaetetus* 175e–177b, where the philosophical life is presented as combining 'wisdom and true virtue' (176c44–5). On this passage and its Middle Platonic influence, see Annas (1999), ch. 3; also Sedley (1999*b*), (2004), 74–86. On this strand in Plato's thinking, which was of intense interest to the Neoplatonists, see Gerson (2002).

[15] See 9.4, esp. 1166a13–23.

[16] See also Pl. *Phd.* 80c–84b, esp. 83c–84b, in which philosophy is seen as freeing the psyche from the pleasures and pains which are the result of involvement with the body; and *Phdr.* 230a.

mind (*nous*) and practical reason, the latter being seen as acting in conjunction with the body-based emotional part of the psyche.[17]

How should we conceive the 'parts' or aspects being contrasted and the overall picture of the human being that is implied? In one sense, the contrast is between different psychological capacities or functions. But the functions are also sometimes characterized by their goals and thus as sources of motivation; they are also identified by the objects or spheres of reality with which they are related. For instance in Plato, *Republic* 10 (611e), the 'true' psyche is described as naturally 'cognate' (*sungenēs*) to the 'divine' objects of wisdom and activated by an impulse (*hormē*) to gain contact with them.[18] In Arist. *NE* 9.4 and 9.8, the expression of (mostly practical) reason is seen as a goal and thus as a source of motivation.[19] The model of the human being implied in all these cases is that of the person as a—more or less unified—'combination' of body and psyche, or psychological functions, not a cohesive unit or whole.[20]

There is one further important feature of this type of thinking. It embraces two rather different ways of defining our 'core', 'essence', or 'what we ourselves are'. This can be defined as what is most characteristic and distinctive of human nature, or at least the human psyche, as a whole. Alternatively, it can be defined as the highest of the capacities we have, even if this is not representative of our nature as a whole human being or a whole psyche. This contrast is most clearly acknowledged—as that between 'human' and 'divine' lives—by Aristotle in *NE* 10.7–8. It is also implied in Plato's contrast between the 'complex' and the 'uniform' psyche in *Republic* 611e–612a and *Phaedrus* 230a. Of the other examples discussed here, Aristotle's specification of 'what each one is' in *NE* 9.4, 9.8 seems to belong to the first (human) group and the Platonic discussions in the *Phaedo* and *Alcibiades* to the latter (divine) group.[21] This divergence implies the existence of extensive debate on this topic in Greek philosophy of the period, which has been echoed in contemporary classical scholarship.[22] But, for my purposes here, the divergence

[17] This contrast is prefigured in Pl. *R.* 611c–612a, especially 611e.

[18] Similar ideas are implied in *Phaedo* 79d, 80e, 84a, and Arist. *NE* 10. 7

[19] See esp. *NE* 1166^{a}17–23, 1168^{b}28–34.

[20] See e.g. 'combination' (*suntheton*), Arist. *NE* 1178^{a}20; 'both together' (*sunamphoteron*), i.e. body and psyche, Pl. *Alc.* 130a9.

[21] This point is not explicit in *Alc.* 129c–130c, where the contrast is simply between psyche and body (the psyche being what 'the human being' is, 129e, 130c). But in 133a–c, our essence is specified as the 'divine' capacity for knowledge and thinking; if 133c8–17 is authentic, the link with 'god' is further explicated.

[22] For a lucid review of scholarly debate about Arist. *NE* 10.7–8, in particular on whether these chapters are consistent with *NE* (or Aristotelian theory) as a whole, see Kenny (1992), 4–42, 86–93. See also Gill (1996*b*), 370–83, referring to previous views, and White (2002), ch. 6.

between these variant ways of defining our essence is less important than the contrast between core-centred thinking about personality and the holistic pattern displayed in Stoicism and Epicurean theory.

What, in broad terms, is this difference? Partly, it is one of focus. Whereas one type of thinking focuses on identifying cores or essences, the other focuses on wholes. One pattern aims to define what human beings are essentially or in their core, the other on what we are as psychophysical and psychological wholes. For the second way of thinking, questions about the cohesion, integration, or unity of wholes, including human beings, are crucial in a way that they are not for the first way of thinking. A further difference lies in the understanding of more advanced or complex functions, such as gaining knowledge of truth. In the first view, these functions are, typically, allocated to the core or essence (for instance, 'mind' or 'reason') by contrast with the other parts (for instance, 'body' or the 'non-rational' part). In the second, holistic, view, gaining knowledge of truth is seen as a more advanced or complex function of the whole entity, for instance, the human being as a psychophysical and psychological whole. This in turn implies a view of the human being as able to develop layers of capacities or functions, superimposed on each other but coherently related to each other. There is also a difference as regards value. For the first way of thinking, what is seen as having value is the essence or core. In some cases, this is because the core provides access to another, more valuable, realm, for instance, that of divinity or truth. For the holistic approach, the whole is itself of value. If there is differentiation in value, greater value tends to be given to more complex or advanced functions, though these are still seen as functions of a cohesive whole.

There is one further, and related, feature of Platonic and Aristotelian thought that can be sharply differentiated from the Stoic–Epicurean holistic approach. Human motivation in Plato and Aristotle tends to be analysed by reference to certain 'parts' or aspects of the psyche, which are sometimes characterized as either rational or irrational (or non-rational).[23] A prominent, and influential, example appears in Book 4 of Plato's *Republic* (435c–439d), where motivation is subdivided into reason and appetite (*epithumia*) and appetite is presented as being in conflict with reason. The sense in which reason and appetite are separate parts is also relatively clear in this argument, namely as independent, and potentially conflicting, sources of motivation.[24]

On analogies between this strand of ancient thinking and modern thinking about the relationship between the concepts of person and human being, see Gill (1990*d*), introduction, 7–10.

[23] The question whether the contrasting part lacks reason or is in some sense rational but capable of conflicting with reason is one of the characteristic issues of this kind of thinking; see further Chs. 4–5 below.

[24] See further on this argument, and its possible influence on Stoic thought, 5.2 below.

This psychological model, while introduced with great emphasis in the *Republic*, is not uniformly maintained in that dialogue or elsewhere in Plato. Rather, it is one of a series of accounts of motivation, in the *Republic* and in other dialogues, centred on the idea of interplay, including conflict, between the rational part of the psyche and one or two other parts, such as appetite and 'spirit', *thumos*, which are described as relatively irrational (or non-rational).[25] Aristotle, while evolving his own psychological framework, also subdivides motivation into a rational factor and desire (*orexis*),[26] though these are normally seen as working together and as enabling, in adult humans, deliberate desire or choice (*prohairesis*).[27] In his ethical works, Aristotle characterizes degrees of ethical virtue in terms of the relationship between a rational and irrational (or non-rational) part. In 'akratic' (partially defective) people, Aristotle sees appetite as sometimes in conflict with practical reasoning.[28] In these respects, at least, Aristotle also adopts a part-based model of motivation and subdivides the psyche into rational and irrational parts. This part-based approach to human psychology goes naturally with the core-centred thinking illustrated earlier, and both features can be contrasted with the emphasis on psychological, as well as psychophysical, integration in Stoic and Epicurean thought.

However, there are aspects of Platonic and Aristotelian thinking which are closer to the holistic approach subsequently developed by the Hellenistic theories. I take, first, the question of the larger world-view and conception of reality, considered as a framework within which to view humans and other animals as physical and psychological entities. Although Plato, in some of his dialogues, offers clear statements of ontological dualism, the *Timaeus* can be read as providing a more 'one-world' picture. The physical world is presented as an expression of order and purpose; both at the cosmic and the human level, body and psyche are presented as fundamentally integrated.[29] This vein in Plato's thought exhibits some similarities to a central theme in Aristotle's thought, his 'hylomorphism', that is, the theory that primary substances (real objects) constitute the embodiment of form in matter. This Aristotelian theory is seen as applying to the psyche–body relationship as well as to other types of object or entity.[30] A further relevant feature is the development

25 For bipartite or tripartite pictures of the psyche, see e.g. *R.* 10, 602e–606d, *Phdr.* 246a–b, 253c–256e, *Ti.* 69–72, *Lg.* 644c–645b.

26 See e.g. Arist. *On the Movement of Animals* (*de Motu Animalium*)(*MA*), ch. 6, esp. 700b18–23. The 'rational' aspect is subdivided into 'appearance', 'sensation', and 'thought'; 'desire' is subdivided into 'wish', 'spirit', and 'appetite'.

27 *NE* 1112^{b}31–1113^{a}12, 1139^{b}4–5, *Eudemian Ethics* (*EE*) 1226^{b}21–5.

28 *NE* 1.13, esp. 1102^{b}13–1103^{a}3; and 7.3, especially 1147^{a}31–1147^{b}5.

29 See 1.3 below, text to nn. 41–8.

30 See 1.3 below, text to nn. 70–3.

of medical practice and thought from the fifth century onwards. Greek medicine adopts a body-based approach to human nature, and this results in medical theories in the third centuries which have striking parallels with Stoicism and Epicureanism.[31] In short, we can identify in the fourth century a number of strands that might have stimulated the holistic world-view and the picture of humans and other animals as psychophysical wholes that is characteristic of Stoicism and Epicureanism.

A similar point can be made about the Platonic and Aristotelian background to Stoic and Epicurean thinking about psychological cohesion. Broadly speaking, the two Hellenistic schools offer, in different ways, accounts of motivation and emotion that presuppose that humans and other animals operate as psychologically unified wholes. They assume that it is *not* the case that, in adult humans, reason and emotion or desire constitute radically separate and potentially conflicting sources of motivation.[32] They also present as the ideal outcome of ethical development character-states which are marked by an exceptional degree of psychological cohesion, even allowing for their general view that reason does not conflict with emotion or desire.[33]

There are several well-marked features of Platonic and Aristotelian thought that can be taken as prefiguring, in part at least, this aspect of Stoic–Epicurean thinking. The most obvious case is the account of motivation implied in certain early Platonic dialogues, notably the *Protagoras* and the *Gorgias*, which are generally taken as reflecting the thinking of the historical Socrates. The 'Socratic paradoxes' underlying Socrates' arguments (namely that virtue is one, that virtue is knowledge, and that no one does wrong willingly but only out of error), seem to presuppose a unified picture of human psychology, in which emotion and desire reflect beliefs and reasoning or the agent's degree of ethical understanding.[34] On the face of it, there is a sharp contrast between this view and the part-based psychology of other Platonic dialogues (notably the *Republic* and *Phaedrus*). But there are also dimensions in the thought of Plato's middle and later periods[35] that imply that psychological cohesion is

[31] See Gundert (2000) on Hippocratic thought on the psyche–body relationship and von Staden (2000), on parallels between Stoic and Epicurean thought and that of the 3rd-c. medical practitioners, Herophilus and Erasistratus.

[32] See 2.2 below, text to nn. 76–88, 2.3, text to nn. 210–30, 3.3, text to nn. 104–28.

[33] See 94–5, 122–6 below.

[34] See esp. Pl. *Prt.* 352b–361c, *Grg.* 466b–468e; see further Mackenzie (1981), chs. 9–10; Gosling (1990), chs. 1–2; Price (1995), 14–27; Penner (1991), (1997), (2005). Related features include the unified picture of desire presupposed in Diotima's theory of love in the *Symposium* (204d–212a, cf. Price 1995: 8–14) and, according to Penner and Rowe (2005), the theory of desire in the *Lysis*.

[35] On Platonic chronology, I follow Kahn (2002) in supposing that we can discern three broad groups of Platonic writings (with *Republic* and *Phaedrus* in the second group), but that we cannot identify the chronological order of dialogues within each group.

both an ideal and, to some extent, a fact of human existence. In the *Republic*, for instance, the presentation of ideal justice as a state of inner 'harmony' (443c–e) implies that cohesion can, in principle, be achieved even within a part-based psychological framework. In a different way, the account of the defective character-types in *Republic* 8–9 also implies that there is a close correlation between an agent's overall belief-set and the pattern of her emotions and desires, even in the case of imperfect people.[36]

There are clear analogues between the thinking of the *Republic* and Aristotle's ethical theory on this point. Aristotle, while presupposing a part-based model, presents the ideal character-state as one in which inclinations of desire and emotion are fully in line with beliefs and practical reasoning. This comes out clearly in his contrast between the complete virtue of temperance or moderation (*sōphrosunē*) and the partial virtue of self-restraint (*enkrateia*). In temperance, desire is wholly at one with reasoned judgement, and in self-restraint, reasoned judgement is effective in mastering desire.[37] Aristotle's analysis of courage (*andreia*) represents a striking instance of the idea of the co-functioning of practical reasoning and emotion in ethical virtue. The brave person is 'free from disturbance' (*anekplēktos*), as far as a human being can be, in moments of danger, and takes a virtuous pleasure in achieving his goal (of being virtuous) in spite of the pain involved.[38] More broadly, a mark of being fully virtuous is that the person acts and feels virtuously, and does so 'for its own sake' or 'for the sake of the fine', and does so 'firmly and unchangeably' (*ametakinētōs*).[39] These points relate to the presentation of the ideal character. There is more room for debate about Aristotle's view of the psychological cohesion of non-ideal people. But his presentation of 'akratic' people (whose desires are out of line with their ethical beliefs and reasoning) as relatively exceptional implies the view that, in general, both virtuous and non-virtuous *do* have desires and emotions in line with their reason.[40]

What are the implications for this enquiry of the presence of these different strands in Platonic and Aristotelian thought? In the first instance, my aim has been simply to characterize the Stoic–Epicurean holistic approach by contrast with (Platonic–Aristotelian) core-centred and part-based thinking and by partial comparison with the more holistic aspects of earlier theory. But

[36] See further Gill (1996*b*), 245–60; also 5.2 below, text to nn. 107–18.

[37] See Arist. *NE* 1.13, esp. $1102^{b}13$–28, 7.9, esp. $1151^{b}32$–$1152^{a}6$.

[38] See Arist. *NE* 3.6–9, esp. $1115^{b}11$, $1117^{a}35$–$^{b}3$.

[39] See Arist. *NE* 2.4, esp. $1105^{a}30$–3, also e.g. $1115^{b}11$–13.

[40] This seems to be implied by the contrast between (consistent) self-indulgence and (inconsistent) *akrasia* ('weakness of will') in *NE* 7.8. However, *NE* 9.4, especially $1166^{a}10$–29, $^{b}6$–25, outlined above (6–7) suggests a rather different view: that only the good are cohesive. On this point, see further Gill (1996*b*), 360.

what, if anything, can we infer about the process by which Epicurus and the early Stoics actually developed their versions of psychophysical and psychological holism? This is the question I turn to next.

1.3 CONVERGING HOLISTIC WORLD-VIEWS

> Despite their radically divergent versions of the world and of human beings, Epicureans, many Stoics, and the more significant early Hellenistic physicians share a constellation of convictions concerning soul and body... for example, that all *psychē* is *sōma* ['body'] but not all *sōma* is *psychē*; that only what is spatially extended, three-dimensional, and capable of acting and being acted on exists; that the soul meets these criteria of existence; that the corporeal *psychē*, like the rest of the rest of the body, is mortal and transient; that the *psychē* is generated with the body; that it neither exists before the body nor exists eternally after its separation from the body—that is, the soul does not exist independently of the body in which it exists.

In this striking claim, with which I am much in agreement, Heinrich von Staden (2000: 79) encapsulates certain shared features of the thought of Stoics and Epicureans, as well as that of medical thinkers and practitioners such as Herophilus and Erasistratus. He thus identifies key aspects of the types of psychophysical holism and naturalism in Stoic and Epicurean thought examined later in this chapter (1.4–5). In this section, I take up a question raised both by von Staden's statement and by the thesis I am maintaining. How did philosophical theories (Stoicism and Epicureanism) that are so strongly opposed on other central issues come to hold a fundamentally similar (holistic) view on the psyche–body relationship? How is their formulation of these ideas at the end of the fourth century BC and the start of the third related to the background of fifth- and fourth-century thought? My responses to these questions are framed in general terms, and are designed to outline a larger historical and conceptual context in which to locate the more detailed discussion of psychophysical and psychological holism in Stoicism and Epicureanism which follows.

I begin by highlighting some of the apparent obstacles to the thesis that the Stoics and Epicureans have a shared holistic outlook. On the face of it, their world-views are very different. The Stoics see the universe as a unified living organism, pervaded by divine rational providence. The Epicureans believe that atoms and void are the basic elements of reality and that the universe is the product of random conjunctions of atoms. In ethics, there is a comparably sharp contrast: the Stoics maintain that virtue is self-sufficient for happiness, whereas the Epicureans present pleasure as the basis of happiness and see virtue as only instrumental for gaining pleasure. There is an analogous contrast in the type of theories which form their main philosophical influences. The Stoics are strongly and explicitly influenced by Socrates and Plato, and perhaps also by Aristotle. The Epicureans, while presenting themselves as intellectually independent, seem to be most strongly influenced by rival philosophical approaches to the Platonic–Aristotelian tradition, particularly those of Democritus and post-Democritean thinkers. Given these differences, what makes it plausible to think that they might have converged in their philosophical outlook in the way suggested here?

One answer to this question has already been offered, in effect, in the preceding section. There are, certainly, aspects of Platonic and Aristotelian thought which these Hellenistic schools did *not* follow—and may have reacted against—namely the core-centred and part-based thinking illustrated in the previous section. But Plato and Aristotle, along with other earlier thinkers, also offered lines of thought which could have served to shape in a positive way the Hellenistic holistic approach. In particular, the combination of Plato's *Timaeus*, Aristotle's hylomorphism, and the development of Greek medicine could have exercised a powerful influence on the formation of a unified view of reality and of human beings as psychophysical wholes. Plato and Aristotle also offered ways of conceiving human beings as (actually or ideally) psychologically cohesive, though within a part-based and core-centred framework of thinking about human motivation.

These suggestions take us some way towards seeing how these schools *might have* formulated their holistic conception of the psyche–body relationship and about reality in general. But can we form a more precise view—even a conjectural one—about how they actually *did* reach these ideas? Some recent scholarship on the responses of Stoicism and Epicureanism to their formative influences offers suggestive pointers in this direction. While these studies are not focused precisely on the issue raised here—the emergence of the holistic conception of human personality—they still provide, at least, a speculative picture of how this conception may have been formed. In broad terms, they suggest that Stoic theory can be understood as a *naturalistic* version of (certain strands in) Socratic and Platonic thought. In particular, Stoicism offers a one-world version of (what can be read as) Plato's most one-world dialogue, the *Timaeus*. Epicureanism, on the other hand, can be seen as a *non-reductive* version of Democritean atomism, which also provides the basis for a unified account of the natural universe. In ethics, Stoicism offers a version of Socratic–Platonic ideals which renders them compatible with a naturalistic account of the world and human life. Epicureanism, analogously, offers a much more fully theorized and systematic account of hedonism than we can attribute to Democritus or the

Cyrenaics and one that is also consistent with their holistic and naturalistic world-view. Both Hellenistic theories also evolve conceptually sophisticated, non-reductive, accounts of the relationship between logic, ethics, and 'physics' (that is, the study of nature). In these ways, both theories qualify or counteract the stark philosophical opposition between their main influences—Platonism and Democriteanism. Thus, the two schools *converge* in the type of accounts they give on a series of major topics, even though they do not explicitly *agree* and collaborate in philosophical partnership. In particular, they converge in presenting psyche and body, and also human beings and other animals, as relatively complex material structures (or wholes) within a universe that is similarly conceived. This shared picture is part, at least, of what I am calling their 'psychophysical holism', with which we can couple their psychological holism, according to which human—and other animal—psychological functions form an integrated and coherent set. In so far as the two theories share, in this respect, a common world-view, we can also ascribe to them 'substantial holism', that is, holism about substance or the core principles of reality.

How far does recent scholarship support this picture of the formation of Stoic and Epicurean thought of this kind? One question that has been intensively examined is the possible role of Plato's *Timaeus* in helping to shape the Stoic world-view and the Stoic account of the core principles of reality.

Some of the main relevant points of contact are brought out in this comment by Sextus Empiricus, the second-century AD Sceptic:

> [Plato] offered an account whose meaning was the same as Zeno's. He too said that the universe (*to pan*) was the most beautiful of things, that it was a piece of handiwork achieved on natural principles, and that, according to the likely account, it was a living animal (*empsuchon zōon*), possessing mind and reason.[41]

In both the *Timaeus* and Stoicism, the universe is conceived as a living and rational animal, a combination of cosmic psyche and body.[42] An obvious difference is that the Platonic universe is the product of a transcendent 'craftsman-god', whereas the Stoic god is immanent in the normal operation of the universe. But the fundamental Stoic principles, the active and passive principles, can be seen as based on the relationship between the Platonic craftsman-god, combined with the world-soul, and the 'receptacle', the spatial vehicle of generation.[43] In both theories, the universe is seen as the best that

[41] S.E. *M.* 9.107; this passage is also cited as 1.110 in *Stoicorum Veterum Fragmenta* (*SVF*) = von Arnim (1903–5).

[42] Cf. Pl. *Ti.* 30b–c, esp. b7–8, 'the cosmos is a living animal, endowed with mind', also 31b–37c, with *SVF* 1.110, just cited, and Long and Sedley (1987) (= LS) 54, esp. A, F–G.

[43] On the craftsman-god (demiurge) and receptacle, see Pl. *Ti.* 28a–29a, 29e–30b, 49a–52c. On the Stoic principles and their relationship to Plato's *Timaeus*, see LS 44, 46, also LS i. 271–2, 277, 319; see also below.

can be conceived and as an expression of providential care and rationality.[44] This point bears on the presentation of the human body and the embodied human psyche. The human head is taken in both theories as a key instance of providential design, limited only by certain necessary material constraints.[45] One of the functions of the human head is that it enables human beings to see and recognize the structure, order, and rationality in the universe and to mould themselves on this pattern.[46] A clear corollary of these shared Platonic and Stoic themes is that what is bad in the universe is not conceived as what is bodily or material, by contrast with what is ideal or derives from psyche or mind. Rather, what is bad in both theories is the product of failure in natural development, a point which applies to Plato's thinking on (body-based) psychic illness and Stoic thinking on the psychophysical diseases that count as 'passions'.[47] In broad terms, then, Plato's *Timaeus*, sometimes seen in modern times too as Plato's most one-world dialogue,[48] may have played a key role in shaping the unified world-view of Stoicism.

In exploring these points further, I take up the question how far the early Stoics may have based their account of the core principles of reality on Platonic ideas, especially those of the *Timaeus*. There have been several important recent treatments of this question;[49] I focus here on a possible route of intellectual transmission, suggested by David Sedley, which is also adopted by John Dillon in his history of Plato's school in the fourth century.[50] Sedley gives special attention to a late fourth-century Academic (Platonic) way of reading the *Timaeus*, outlined by Theophrastus, the successor of Aristotle. This is confirmed by a similar account of fourth-century Academic principles provided by Cicero.[51] This evidence indicates how Xenocrates, the second head of Plato's school in the fourth century, may have interpreted the *Timaeus*, and how Polemo, his successor, may have transmitted those ideas to

[44] Cf. Pl. *Ti.* 29e–30c, 36e–37a, with LS 54 H–N.

[45] Cf. Pl. *Ti.* 73e–76d, esp. 75b–c, with *SVF* 2.1170 (= Gel 7.1.7); Cic. *N.D.* 2.142–6.

[46] Cf. Pl. *Ti.* 47b–d (on the cosmos as a harmonic or mathematical embodiment of order, 39b–c, taken with 35a–37c), 90a–d, with Cic. *N.D.* 2.37–9, 133, 140, 145, 153–5.

[47] Pl. *Ti.* 86b–89d. See further Gill (2000*b*), and 3.5 below, text to nn. 325–39; also on Stoic passions and Plato's thought more generally, see Ch. 5 below.

[48] See e.g. Brisson (1992), 41–3, 47–8; D. Frede (1996); Gill (2000*b*); Johansen (2004). See also, from this standpoint, Zedda (2003), on Plato's world-soul, and Burgess (2002), (2004) on Plato's account of the human body.

[49] See e.g. Hahm (1977), ch. 2, esp. 47–8; Reydams-Schils (1999), 42–59.

[50] Sedley (2002), the main points summarized in Sedley (1999*a*), 385; Dillon (2003*a*), 168–74; see also Dillon (2003*b*).

[51] Theophrastus fr. 230 (in Fortenbaugh *et al.* 1992) (= Simplicius, *in Phys.* 26.7–15), translated in Sedley (2002), 42; Cicero, *Academica* 1.24–9, translated by Sedley (2002), 53–4, excerpts translated by Dillon (2003*a*), 168–72.

Zeno, the founder of Stoicism.[52] The key feature of this Academic framework is that Plato's demiurge has been merged with the world-soul and correlated with the 'receptacle' to produce two principles. These are (1) an immanent moving causal principle identified with god and (2) matter. Matter, as such, is without qualities; it only acquires determinate properties through the operation of god, identified with perfect reason and the world-soul. A twofold framework of core principles of reality is a feature of fourth-century Academic thought, going back to the two principles (the One and the Indeterminate Dyad) in Plato's own reported oral teachings.[53]

The Stoic principles are the same as those ascribed to the fourth-century Academy, that is, god and matter or the active and passive cause. However, an important difference is that in Stoicism these are, explicitly, physical or 'bodies'. Having body is the standard mark of 'being' in Stoicism. 'Body' is defined by 'threefold extension along with resistance', and also by the capacity to act and be acted upon.[54] The latter criterion may have Platonic roots, but it is applied by Stoics in a more systematic way and treated as basic to the account of the core principles of reality.[55] These two principles are the only permanent elements; but they are only conceptually distinguishable from each other, since the universe as a whole represents the complete fusion of these principles. This point may be linked with a further difference between Platonic (or Academic) and Stoic thinking. In Platonic thought, value or goodness is, typically, attached to one side of the polarity of principles. For instance, accordingly to the conclusion of Plato's reported lecture 'On the Good', 'The Good is the One', rather than the Indeterminate Dyad.[56] In Stoic

[52] Zeno's teachers, as given in our ancient sources, include Polemo, along with Crates the Cynic (Sedley 2003: 9–11). Xenocrates was head of the Academy *c.*339–*c.*314, and Polemo was head *c.*314–*c.*266. Theophrastus succeeded Aristotle as head of the Peripatos (Lyceum) *c.*322–*c.*286. Zeno (who lived *c.*334–*c.*262) founded the Stoic school around 300.

[53] The other sets of twofold principles are One and Multiplicity (Speusippus), the Monad and the Dyad or Multiplicity (Xenocrates); see further Dillon (2003*a*), 40–2, 99–100. The status and philosophical implications of the evidence for Plato's unwritten teachings are immensely controversial among modern scholars. My own view is that Plato probably did discuss these ideas but that they did not form the doctrinal underpinning for the written dialogues; see Gill (1993).

[54] See LS 44, esp. B, and 45, esp. C, E–F (F cited in text). On the 'incorporeals', place, void, time, and the *lekton* (roughly, 'intelligible content'), which have secondary or derivative being, see Sedley (1999*a*), 395–402.

[55] See Pl. *Sph.* 247d–e: the capacity to act and be acted on as a mark of being, presented as a revision of the materialist claim that physical contact is the criterion (246a–b). The Stoics' move of arguing that only bodies (including the bodily principles) have being is seen by Sedley as combining *both* these criteria: Sedley (1999*a*), 383–5, following Brunschwig (1988), also LS i. 273–4.

[56] Aristoxenus, *Elementa Harmonica* 2.1, pp. 30.20–31.2 Meibom. A similar distinction in value is implied in subsequent Academic and Platonic polarities, and also in the Pythagorean ideas on which they seem to have drawn, e.g. the Table of Opposites (Arist. *Metaph.* 1.5, esp. 986a22–6). See further Kahn (2001), chs. 4–5, esp. 65–6; Dillon (2003*a*), esp. 40–2, 99–101, 153–4.

thought, goodness, which is closely linked with wholeness, order, and structure, is, typically, ascribed to the universe as a whole, which is an inseparable fusion of active rationality and matter, and to other structured entities within the universe, including virtuous human beings.[57] As just noted, Plato's *Timaeus* goes a long way in this direction, presenting the universe as a whole as good, ordered by divine providence, and exhibiting in-built structure.[58] But there are, none the less, certain ways in which Plato's dialogue highlights degrees of imperfection within the universe, including certain aspects of human nature; and, to that extent, the *Timaeus* offers a less uniformly positive view of the natural universe than Stoicism.[59]

Sedley's reconstruction of the Platonic basis for the Stoic principles, if accepted, provides a partial answer to the question of how the Stoic holistic world-view emerged. The Stoic world-view represents a more holistic version of the (relatively) unified view of the natural universe offered in Plato's *Timaeus* and mediated by the early Academy. How far should we also think that the *Timaeus* helped to shape Stoic ethical thinking and their conception of the relationship between humanity and the natural cosmos? Plato's thought, especially in the *Timaeus*, is sometimes seen as being a decisive influence on this subject. Gábor Betegh, for instance, highlights the linkage between the advocacy of the best human life at the end of the *Timaeus* and Diogenes Laertius' formulation of the standard Stoic characterization of the goal of life as 'following nature'. The common feature is the idea that we achieve happiness by ensuring that the rationality (or *daimōn*) within us is well ordered and matches the order and rationality in the universe.[60] This achievement depends in part, in both Plato's dialogue and Stoicism, on gaining an understanding of the ordered nature of the universe and using this as a pattern for our own character and life. The presence of this strand in Stoic thought is taken to explain why we find some evidence suggesting that physics provides a conceptual basis for ethics.[61]

[57] See LS 60, especially A, G–H; see also 3.3 below.

[58] See text to nn. 41–8 above. On this dimension of Pl. *Ti.* see e.g. Steel (2001) and Johansen (2004), esp. chs. 4–5.

[59] See e.g. the indications of a (comparatively) lower level of being, order and goodness, in the account of the creation of humanity and other animals (*Ti.* 41a–44c). The *Timaeus* is usually seen as marking the limits of divine order by the mind–necessity contrast in 47e–48a. But, for a challenge to that view (or, at least, an alternative reading that may have been adopted in the 4th-c. Academy), see Sedley (2002), 73–6, followed by Dillon (2003*a*), 173–4.

[60] Cf. esp. Pl. *Ti.* 90c4–6: 'because he always takes care of that which is divine, and has the *daimōn* that lives with him well-ordered ... he will be supremely happy', with D.L. 7.88: 'the virtue of the happy person and his good flow of life are just this: always doing everything on the basis of the concordance of each person's *daimōn* with the will of the administrator of the whole', trans. as in Betegh (2003), 279 and 286. For this comparison, see also Reydams-Schils (1999), 69–70.

[61] Betegh (2003), esp. 275–8, 289–93, 296–300. See also White (1979), 177–8.

In offering this view, Betegh assumes the validity of one interpretation of the core thesis of Stoic ethics, which one might call the 'cosmic' or 'providential' reading. This, certainly, forms one strand in the ancient evidence; but, as I argue later, it is not as pervasive as is sometimes claimed and coexists with other ways of formulating the key Stoic ethical principles.[62] Also, I think that the links traced by Betegh between Plato's *Timaeus* and Stoicism can be seen as constituting a rather different, and, in a sense, more holistic, line of thought. I share his view that, in both theories, goodness is conceived as manifested in order, structure, and harmony, and that both Plato's Timaeus and Stoicism recognize goodness both in the natural universe and (to some degree at least) in human nature.[63] But the salient thought is not so much that human beings achieve happiness by patterning themselves on the cosmos, as the (unique or primary) instantiation of goodness. Goodness is, rather, instantiated in *all* forms of ordered wholeness.[64] Similarly, in Stoicism at least, coming to know the good is not a matter of grounding ethics on physics. Rather, it is a matter of combining or synthesizing ethics, physics, *and logic*, and recognizing goodness, as ordered wholeness, in all three areas and in their interconnections.[65] The latter thought is also anticipated in the *Timaeus–Critias*, in the way that these dialogues link ethico-political themes and study of the natural universe.[66] Also, the *Timaeus* as a whole is explicitly structured as a logical or dialectical argument, whose early stages, especially, centre on the relationship between goodness and the universe.[67] So Plato's *Timaeus* may have been instrumental in suggesting the whole approach that I am calling 'rich naturalism', centred on the synthesis of ethics, physics, and logic, which is closely linked in Stoic thought with their holistic conception of reality.[68]

What about the influence of Aristotle on Stoicism? Aristotelian thought has often been seen as the main starting-point for understanding Stoic ethical or psychological theories.[69] His conception of substance or reality might seem particularly relevant to this topic. Primary substances, for Aristotle, are,

[62] Betegh (2003), esp. 273–8, 283–8. See further 3.3 below, centred on Cic. *Fin.* 3.20–1.

[63] Betegh (2003), esp. 290–1.

[64] See 3.3 below, text to nn. 104–28.

[65] See 3.3 below, text to nn. 145–79.

[66] See *Ti.* 17a–27b, linking the ideal state of Plato's *Republic*, the Atlantis story broached in the *Critias*, and Timaeus' account of the natural universe. See further Pradeau (1995); Johansen (2004), chs. 1–2.

[67] See esp. Pl. *Ti.* 29e–38b. On the dialectical form of Pl. *Ti–Criti.*, see Osborne (1996); Johansen (2004), 177–97.

[68] See further on relevant aspects of Platonic thought and its relationship to Stoicism, Gill (2000*b*), 70–7, (2004*c*), (2004*d*).

[69] See e.g. (on ethics) Annas (1993*b*); (on Stoic psychology) A. C. Lloyd (1978), Inwood (1985), ch. 1; (on Epicurean psychology), Furley (1967), 161–237.

standardly, concrete objects conceived as embodied form.[70] To put the point differently, his polarity of form and matter seems to prefigure the Stoic polarity of active and passive principles. This Aristotelian theory is sometimes characterized as 'hylomorphism', that is, the idea that substance (the primary kind of reality) consists in form or shape (*morphē*) embodied in matter (*hulē*).[71] An instance of this principle is that psyche is 'the substance, in the sense of form, of a natural body potentially having life' (*de An.* 2.1, 412a20).[72] Indeed, the Aristotelian principles of form and matter have sometimes been seen as underlying the Stoic ones, either on their own or in combination with the Platonic or Academic principles.[73]

It is quite possible that the Aristotelian ideas *did* play a significant role in shaping Stoic thought. However, there are certain reasons for caution about placing too much weight on the role of Aristotle in this respect. One reason is that it is unclear how much detailed knowledge there was of Aristotle's philosophy among thinkers outside his school. In particular, it is uncertain how far the school-treatises—that is to say, what *we* mean by Aristotle—were read and studied outside the school, at least in the early Hellenistic period. There is a well-known report by Strabo that the treatises were lost between the death of Theophrastus (*c.*286) and their publication by Andronicus at some point between 60 and 20 BC.[74] F. H. Sandbach was especially sceptical about the influence of Aristotle, pointing out that there were, in fact, surprisingly few direct references to Aristotle in our sources for early Stoicism or Epicureanism.[75] However, Jonathan Barnes (1997*b*) has subsequently made a thorough analysis of Strabo's report, casting doubt on many features of it. In particular, he argues strongly against the idea that Andronicus' publication of an 'edition' of Aristotle's works (whatever that means exactly) inaugurated a new era of detailed study of Aristotle's texts. Michael Frede (1999*a*: 772–5) also claims that there is evidence that the beginnings of detailed commentary on Aristotle went back beyond Andronicus' 'edition' to the early first century BC, and perhaps earlier. However, Barnes does not deny that Aristotle's

[70] See e.g. Arist. *Metaph.* 7; for lucid discussion of a complex subject, see also Lear (1988), 265–93.

[71] See e.g. (in connection with Aristotle's psychology) van der Eijk (2000), 63–9.

[72] See further Arist. *de An* 412a19–21, 27–8. Similarly, Aristotle's theory has been seen as anticipating modern functionalism, in which, in some versions at least, mental states are seen as 'functional states of the physical systems that realize them'. See Cohen (1992), 58 (cited), and Nussbaum and Putnam (1992). For a challenge to this interpretation of Aristotle's theory, Burnyeat (1992).

[73] See e.g. Hahm (1977), ch. 2, esp. 47–8, on Aristotelian influence, and Reydams-Schils (1999), 42–60, on the fusion of Platonic and Aristotelian influences, the latter mediated by Theophrastus.

[74] Strabo 13.1.54, cf. Plu. *Sulla* 26.

[75] Sandbach (1985). For a similar view, as regards Epicurus, see Bignone (1936).

school suffered a decline in activity and importance after the death of Theophrastus. It also remains uncertain exactly how much detailed knowledge there was of Aristotle's school-texts outside the school in the Hellenistic period, especially in the early part.[76] Of course, core Aristotelian ideas could also have been transmitted through Aristotle's own published works (now largely lost) and also, perhaps in modified form, by Theophrastus, a contemporary of Zeno and Epicurus.[77] But these considerations, taken together, suggest there may be a mismatch between the typical modern picture of the development of ancient philosophy in this period, in which Plato, Aristotle, and early Hellenistic philosophy form an unbroken sequence, and the way that the situation may have appeared to Zeno and Epicurus at the end of the fourth century.

Also, at the conceptual level, there are significant differences between Aristotelian and Stoic principles. One important difference, applying also to the relationship with Platonic ideas, is that the Stoic principles are understood as physical entities, 'bodies', in a way that is not true of Aristotle's causes.[78] Aristotle's view of the natural universe as embodying in-built purpose or teleology, according to which each species seeks to realize its natural goal, might seem close to the Stoic providential world-view. But the Stoic conception of providence has a divine, and cosmic, dimension that reflects Plato's *Timaeus*, rather than Aristotle. The Stoic picture is also linked, as Sedley points out, with a markedly un-Aristotelian conception of god.[79] So, although we cannot rule out the possibility of Aristotelian influence, it may be more fruitful to focus on Plato, with whom the links with Stoicism seem better supported by evidence.

So far, I have offered some justification for the idea that the Stoic, unified or holistic, world-view can be understood, in large measure, as a naturalistic version of Platonism. What about the suggestion that Epicureanism represents a more sophisticated and non-reductive version of Democritean atomism? How far does this view of Epicureanism serve to support the idea that this theory converges with Stoicism in offering a holistic picture of reality in which animals, including human beings, are conceived as structured psychophysical wholes or organisms?

[76] Barnes (1997*b*), 13, 44–5 (the latter passage contrasting general knowledge of Plato's works with that of Aristotle). For some evidence of knowledge of Aristotle's school-texts in the Hellenistic period, for instance, among Epicureans, see Barnes, 14–16.

[77] See further Long (1998), 375–9; Reydams-Schils (1999), 47–52.

[78] See LS 44 A, E, 45 A–B. See also Sedley (1999*a*), 385, and Reydams-Schils (1999), 56–60, who contrasts the Stoics with Plato in this respect.

[79] Sedley (1999*a*), 386, highlighting the links with Plato's idea of soul as a self-mover (e.g. *Phdr.* 245–6, *Lg.* 896–9), rather than Aristotle's idea of god as unmoved mover (*Metaph.* 12.7).

Although we have lost all but fragments of Democritus' writings and most of Epicurus' *On Nature*, it seems clear that Democritus (born *c*.460BC) provided the framework for Epicurus' world-view and contributed, at least, towards the formulation of Epicurus' hedonist ethics. On the face of it, the Democritean world-view, which Epicurus adopts, presents a strong contrast to the Stoic one. The universe is analysed as the random outcome of interaction between the basic physical elements of reality, atoms moving in void, with no scope for in-built natural purpose. However, the contrast is less extreme than it first appears. Both Democritean atomism and Stoicism maintain that reality is ultimately physical. Both theories also aim to show how the perceptible universe can be analysed in terms of a set of core principles or entities of great theoretical simplicity: active and passive principles, on the one hand, and body (specifically, atoms) and void, on the other. The Democritean theory also, like the Stoic one, represents a sophisticated response to current philosophical debate. Greek atomism is usually regarded, following Aristotle's account, as an attempt to reconcile the demand of Eleatic thinkers (Parmenides, Zeno) that 'being' should be conceived as permanent, unitary, and unchanging with the need to account for the diverse and mobile universe that we see around us. This reconciliation is achieved by explaining the phenomenal world as the product of the interaction of certain permanent, unchanging, indivisible elements of being, namely the atoms, whose movement is made possible by assuming non-being or space.[80] Epicurus, essentially, takes over this world-view and presents it in a more fully theorized and systematic form, which responds, by implication at least, to philosophical issues and developments since the work of Democritus.[81]

To what extent does Epicurus' world-view introduce substantive modifications to that of Democritus? In particular, in what respects is it, as suggested earlier, a non-reductive version? Given the deficiencies of our evidence, it is not easy to pinpoint key changes. Also, even when Epicurus signals differences, he may be reacting against interpretations and modifications of Democritus' theory by subsequent thinkers, rather than against Democritus himself. However, there are at least two respects in which Epicurus seems to offer a non-reductive version of Democriteanism. These are singled out in a study of the relationship of Epicurus to Democritus and his post-Democritean thought by James Warren.[82]

[80] See Arist. *GC* 1.8; for useful overviews, see Furley on 'Democritus' and Wardy on 'Atomism' in the *Oxford Classical Dictionary* (*OCD*).

[81] Sedley (1998*a*), ch. 4, and (1999*a*), 362–82, reconstructs the core principles of the Epicurean conception of nature from Epicur. *Ep. Hdt.* (especially 38–73) and Lucretius.

[82] Warren (2002). His main theme is ethics, but ethics interlocks with other issues. On what is presented by ancient sources as the post-Democritean intellectual tradition down to Epicurus, i.e. the thought of Metrodorus, Anaxarchus, Pyrrho, and Nausiphanes, see his ch. 1, esp. p. 11.

The main relevant subject is that of the properties of phenomenal objects.[83] The issues may seem rather technical, but they have potentially large implications. The starting-point is this well-known statement by Democritus: 'By convention (*nomos*) sweet, by convention bitter, by convention hot, by convention colour, but in truth (*etos*) atoms and void'.[84] The precise significance of this statement is not easy to define. Is the claim that our knowledge of truth extends only to atoms and void or also that nothing else really exists? Should we see this as a sceptical thesis, denying the possibility of knowledge of secondary qualities such as sweetness and heat, or as a reductivist or eliminative one, claiming that such qualities only have a real (ontological) basis at the atomic level? It seems that different thinkers between Democritus and Epicurus—including Pyrrho, the originator of Scepticism—interpreted the meaning rather differently and that the statement served as a stimulus to different types of sceptical or reductive theories. Epicurus seems to have understood the statement as expressing a strong reductionism about being, and one that he rejected.[85] Although Epicurus, like Democritus, sees atoms and void as the only things that have existence *in themselves*, he also insists that secondary properties exist and are knowable as the properties of real objects at the phenomenal (supra-atomic) level. In the *Letter to Herodotus* (*Ep. Hdt.*), 68–71, Epicurus defines with some care the ontological status of both permanent and transitory (accidental) properties. These exist and are in principle knowable either as the constituents of the nature of real, that is, bodily, objects or as properties which are in accordance with those objects as experienced. The existence and knowledge of these properties is asserted and defined at the supra-atomic level; Democritus' reductive or eliminative approach—as Epicurus understands this—is rejected.[86]

What are the larger implications for understanding the Epicurean worldview and thus for correlating its outlook with Stoicism? The main outcomes for my topic are these. Epicurus adopts a version of atomism that allows him to recognize the reality, intelligibility, and coherence of the macroscopic, supra-atomic world. It also enables him to analyse objects within that world, including human beings and other animals, as relatively complex but coherent wholes, with their own determinate existence and structure. The

[83] For the second subject, the relationship between ethics and physics, see discussion below.

[84] Democritus DK fr. B9 (= S.E. *M.* 7.135), trans. Warren (2002), 7, who also cites other ancient sources for this statement.

[85] See Warren (2002), 7–9, 24–6, 86–97, esp. 92–3, 125–8, 193–200. Brunschwig suggests that Epicurus overstated Democritus' reductionism or eliminativism, in relation to his own thought. See Brunschwig's preface to Morel (1996), 11–12, 22–9 (a reference I owe to Warren 2002: 193 n. 1).

[86] Sedley (1999*a*), 379–82. For ways of understanding the notions of 'reductive' and 'eliminative' materialism and the difference between these, see Irwin (1991*a*), 57; O'Keefe (2002), 158–60 (with reference to Epicurus).

nature of this existence and the maintenance of this structure properly constitute subjects of ethical as well as emotional importance for the relevant kinds of entity—for instance, human beings. Hence, Epicurus' ethics can, in certain respects at least, be related to his physics (though not reductively) in a way that is not possible for Democritus. In all these respects, the Epicurean world-view, despite its very different conceptual foundations, offers a complex but unified and naturalistic picture of the world that has much in common with that of Stoicism.

How, in broad terms, does Epicurus conceive these aspects of his world-view? For instance, how does he understand the causal or explanatory relationship between the two levels of reality, that is, atoms and supra-atomic objects? We find two main types of explanatory pattern. Some features of the phenomenal world, for instance, the special properties of psychic activity, are explained by positing distinctive types of atoms. However, it is also sometimes claimed that the distinctive features of the supra-atomic world are explicable by reference to interactions at the atomic level without one-for-one correlation between the two levels. The latter kind of explanation is sometimes characterized as the 'emergence' of supra-atomic features.[87] It has also, been claimed by Sedley that Epicurus conceives of 'radically *emergent* characteristics', notably, the developed psychic characteristics of human beings, which have *no* equivalent at the atomic level.[88] Sedley interprets in this way Epicurus' analysis of development in *On Nature* 25. However, Sedley's view is highly controversial, as I bring out later.[89] Like some other scholars, I assume that the Epicurean world-view is unified in the sense that all entities are seen as physical and, ultimately, atomic. But this is compatible with also recognizing supra-atomic entities as real and with forms of analysis and explanation that do not necessarily refer directly to the atomic level.[90]

There are certain other ways in which Epicurean atomism is rendered compatible with a picture of the world as one of (supra-atomic) real, stable, and coherent entities. For instance, despite arguing that the universe is the product of random interaction between atoms, Epicurus also sets out to account for the regularity and order in nature stressed by other theories, including those of Plato's *Timaeus* and Stoicism. This is achieved, in part, by presenting atomic composition as subject to law-like principles of causation

[87] See further Hankinson (1999), 501–3; Warren (2002), 67–71; the second type of explanation is sometimes seen as less conceptually sophisticated than the first. On psychic atoms, see 50–1 below.

[88] Sedley (1988), 321–2, his italics.

[89] See 1.5 below, esp. text to nn. 223–39.

[90] See esp. text to nn. 240–72 below.

such as, 'Nothing comes into being out of what is not' (*Ep. Hdt.* 38).[91] This principle is further specified by the idea that all things are generated from the appropriate 'seeds' under appropriate circumstances. In this way, Epicurus' theory of atomic combination incorporates a biological dimension.[92] It is an extension of this line of thought which enables Epicurus to treat animals and other natural kinds as cohesive physical and psychological units or organisms with a distinctive structure and set of capacities. Also relevant is his belief that those animal species which have survived over time and regenerated themselves have done so because of their inherent fitness.[93] Hence, despite his denial of in-built cosmic order or providence, Epicurus also shows in his own terms how the phenomenal, supra-atomic world displays regularity and intelligibility. This provides the basis, at least, for understanding how human beings and other animals have determinate natures or 'constitutions', and for seeing these constitutions as facts which have importance for ethical and emotional life as well as for the study of nature.[94]

The question of the relationship between ethics and physics is the second topic on which Warren sees a major distinction between Democritus, or some of his followers, and Epicurus. Democritus' emphatic distinction between 'conventional' qualities and 'true' (that is, atomic) facts (DK B9, see 24 above below) makes it difficult to see how one could ever connect ethics and the study of nature. Indeed, in most of the ethical fragments attributed to Democritus, there is no explicit linkage with Democritean physics. In fact, it is far from easy to see how his stress on ethical agency and the power of human reason is compatible with atomic determinism. There are, however, some fragments in which Democritus seems to suggest some kind of connection, though the interpretation of these fragments is much disputed.[95] Also, some post-Democritean thinkers appear to have used Democritus' distinction between 'conventional' and 'true' facts as the basis for an account of the relationship between branches of knowledge. For instance, this distinction seems to have contributed towards Pyrrho's scepticism about knowledge of the world, which also has ethical implications. Nausiphanes seems to have developed the idea

[91] On the line of argument, see Sedley (1999*a*), 363–6, and, on the explanatory status of such principles, see Hankinson (1999), 498–500.

[92] Epicur. *Ep. Hdt.* 39; Lucr. 1.159–73; S.E. *PH* 3.17–18. See also Sedley (1999*a*), 363–4, and (1998*b*), 193–8, clarifying differences between the use of the term 'seeds' by Epicurus and by Lucretius.

[93] Lucr. 5.837–77 (= LS 13 I); also Furley (1999), 432.

[94] On 'constitutions' in Epicureanism (as in Stoicism), see 1.4 below, text to nn. 129–36, 161–73, 1.5, text to nn. 204, 253–64, 2.3, text to nn. 172–4.

[95] See further Warren (2002), ch. 2, focusing on DK B191. On the ethical fragments ascribed to Democritus (or Democrates), which give a prominent role to rational agency, see 2.3 below, text to nn. 151–60.

which Democritus may have pioneered that ethics can be grounded on the study of nature (*phusiologia*).[96]

Epicurus, by contrast, evolves a more complex and subtle theory of the relationship between ethics and physics; and this fact underlies, it has been suggested, his negative comments about Democritus or post-Democritean figures such as Nausiphanes.[97] Although this too is a topic that has generated considerable scholarly debate, some points are generally now accepted. On the one hand, Epicurean ethics and physics seem to have been constructed as independent bodies of theory. There is no reason to think that key Epicurean distinctions, such as that between kinetic and katastematic pleasures, were grounded in an analysis of atomic-level facts.[98] On the other hand, Epicurus is wholly explicit that ethics and physics are both designed to serve an ultimately practical goal, that of achieving happiness. Also, logic (or canonic) plays an integral role in physics as well as ethics, and thus forms part of this practical project.[99] This integrated project is brought out very clearly in Lucretius' poem *On the Nature of the Universe*, in which the ethical implications of the study of nature are emphatically spelled out. For instance, in Book 3, Lucretius shows how a proper understanding of our human nature as temporary psychophysical (and ultimately atomic) units supports the conclusion that 'death is nothing to us' (3.830) and that fear of death should not prevent us from achieving peace of mind. Here, we can see how one of the outcomes of Epicurean physics, the recognition that human beings have a finite life-span as psychophysical units, is shown to have a direct bearing on ethics.[100] The same is also true of Epicurus' analysis of the ethical implications of his (atomically based) account of human development in *On Nature* 25.[101] Thus, we can see how Epicurus' critique of the Democritean or post-Democritean version of the relationship between ethics and physics results in a more complex and, again, non-reductive analysis of this relationship.

Obviously, much more could be said about the relationship of Stoicism to Plato and of Epicureanism to Democritus.[102] All I have wanted to offer here are plausible general accounts of the way that the two theories seem to have responded to their intellectual background by formulating the kind of holistic

[96] Warren (2002), chs. 4 and 7, esp. 86–97, 169–81, also 71–2.

[97] See Warren (2002), 189–200; on Epicurus' reaction against Democritean determinism, see 1.5 below, text to nn. 277–8.

[98] See e.g. Sedley (1998*b*), esp. 134 n. 8; on the kinetic–katastematic distinction, see 2.3 below, text to nn. 165–78.

[99] See further 3.5 below, text to nn. 266–78.

[100] See further 2.3 below, text to nn. 223–30.

[101] See 3.5 below, text to nn. 283–93.

[102] See further Chs. 4–5 below (on Plato and Stoicism), and 1.5 below, text to nn. 277–8, 2.3, text to nn. 151–60 (on Democritus and Epicurus).

picture of reality that I am attributing to them. I conclude this discussion by explaining more fully what I mean by a 'holistic' picture of reality, and how the contrast with Plato and Democritus can help us to define what this involves. On the face of it, what Epicureanism and Stoicism have in common is a form of monism, namely the shared assumption that reality is, ultimately, physical or 'body' (plus void, in Epicureanism).[103] This is an important shared feature and one with far-reaching consequences for their psychological and ethical ideas. But more significant, I think, is (what I am characterizing as) their 'holistic' world-view, by contrast with the ancient theories which are their most important influences. The holistic character of the theories derives, in part, from the fact that they offer an inclusive but integrated account of the world and of reality.[104] Within this integrated world-view, specific kinds of entity, for instance, human beings, are also conceived as relatively cohesive (psychophysical and psychological) wholes or as coherent but relatively complex structures within a universe that is also so understood.

The holistic character of the theories can be brought out by contrast with Platonic or Democritean thought. The contrast is obvious with the kinds of dualism to be found in Plato's *Phaedo*, namely between Forms and particulars, body and psyche, mind and emotions or desires. There is also a marked difference from the types of dualism found in fourth-century Academic thought, which constitute versions of Plato's reported distinction between the One and the Indeterminate Dyad. In the Platonic and Academic theories, we have a radical distinction between types and levels of being, or between full and partial 'being'. We also have a sharp differentiation in value, with goodness associated with one side of the polarity. There is a contrast of a different kind with the type of reductionism exemplified in Democritus fr. B9, discussed earlier. Democritean thought here exhibits in its own way a dualism between the atomic and phenomenal level. But, in this case, the phenomenal is reduced to the atomic (or eliminated altogether as a serious candidate for full existence). Put differently, the body, far from being presented as the lower level of reality (as in Plato's *Phaedo*) has become, instead, the sphere of 'being' and 'truth'.[105]

[103] See LS 5 and 45.

[104] The classic example of ancient monism is, rather, Parmenides' theory, which denies reality to anything other than unitary 'being'. One aspect of the holistic character of the Stoic and Epicurean theories is their view that complete wisdom consists of a combination and perhaps synthesis of logic, ethics, and physics, an idea I characterize as 'rich naturalism'. (See further 3.5 below.)

[105] On Plato's *Phaedo*, see 6 above; on Academic dualism, see n. 56 above; on Democritus fr. B9, see text to nn. 83–6 above.

The Stoic and Epicurean theories also treat as fundamental a certain type of polarity, namely that of the active and passive principles or of body (or atoms) and void.[106] But these principles, while influenced, it would seem, by Platonic and Democritean polarities, are differently conceived from those. The Stoic–Epicurean principles do not represent radically contrasted forms of being and value in the same way. Their function is to enable the construction of inclusive but cohesive (and in this sense, holistic) accounts of reality and the universe. These accounts, in turn, present the universe, and natural kinds such as human beings, holistically, that is, as inclusive but coherent wholes. Hence, elements which, in a dualistic framework, would appear as part of the polarity of being and value, or which could be subsumed under that polarity, figure as relatively structured entities or states. This, I shall suggest, is how psyche is conceived in both Stoicism and Epicureanism, along with the set of psychological—and also psychophysical—capacities which are characteristic of human beings and other animals. Even advanced capacities are so understood, though in a dualistic framework they might be assimilated to one side or other of a polarity (reason or emotion, for instance) or be reduced to merely bodily or atomic status. In contrasting these Hellenistic theories with Platonic-type dualism or Democritean reductionism, I am not overlooking the probable role of Plato and Democritus in shaping the distinctive form of the Stoic and Epicurean approach. As suggested earlier, Plato's *Timaeus*, which can be read in a non-dualistic way, along with Democritean atomism and perhaps Aristotelian hylomorphism, seems to have offered an important prototype for the kind of world-view I am characterizing as 'substantial holism'. But the Stoic and Epicurean theories go further in that direction, and they do so in a systematic way that seems to indicate a deliberate intellectual strategy.

1.4 PSYCHOPHYSICAL HOLISM: STOICISM

I now explore the idea that Stoic and Epicurean thought about psyche–body relations and advanced psychological functions is marked by a holistic approach. In discussing ancient thinking about the psyche–body relationship, like other scholars, I deploy a combination of methods to define the distinctive character of the relevant type of ancient thinking. One is to use modern categories which are standard in the theory of mind or ontology, such as substantial dualism or reductive materialism, to correlate ancient and modern

[106] See text to nn. 54–5 and 80–1 above.

concepts.[107] The other is to employ or coin terminology which is designed to encapsulate the characteristic standpoint of the ancient theory or theories, even if this diverges somewhat from modern categories. The latter method is the more important when, as here, the aim is to define patterns of thinking that are not confined to psychology but which bear on ethics and other areas relevant to the multi-faceted idea of self.[108] In modern terms, both Stoicism and Epicureanism exhibit, I think, a combination of non-reductive physicalism and non-dualistic interactionism in their thinking about the psyche–body relationship and about advanced psychological functions. They are physicalists in regarding the psyche as a form of body, though this does not involve reducing all psychological processes to (merely) physical or material ones or eliminating all analysis in non-physical terms. They are interactionists in that they conceive all psychological activities as involving the interaction of psyche and body. But interaction is not conceived in dualistic terms, that is, as the interaction of two entities which are of radically different kind and value, as in, for instance, the dualism of Plato's *Phaedo*.[109]

However, I focus, here at least, on trying to use or coin language which brings out shared or converging distinctive features of these two Hellenistic theories. The term 'psychophysical holism' is intended as a pointer towards these distinctive features. One of these features is the idea that human beings (and other animals) are to be understood as relatively complex but structured psychological-cum-physical units or wholes. This idea is elaborated in ways that are characteristic of each theory, for instance, in Epicureanism, by the idea that the psyche is a form of structured atomic matter and that organic entities such as human beings constitute integrated systems of atoms. In Stoicism, two related themes of this type are that human beings, as psychophysical wholes, fall within a spectrum of more or less complex structures, and that animal and human development can be understood, in part at least, in relation to this spectrum. In examining Stoicism, I first outline certain key relevant themes and then consider in more detail the implications of two specific accounts, the descriptions by Hierocles and Seneca of the early stages of animal development, taken in the larger context of the Stoic theory of development as 'appropriation'.

There is one respect in which psychophysical holism is a more integral element in the Stoic world-view than in the Epicurean one. This is that the universe as a whole and all determinate entities within it, and not only what

[107] On relevant modern terminology of this type, see Irwin (1991*b*), 57.

[108] On the conceptual scope of this study, see Introd. above, text to nn. 3–6.

[109] For analyses of Stoic or Epicurean psychology in modern terms which, though differently framed, are, I think, compatible with that outlined here, see e.g. Annas (1992), 2–6; Long (1996), 224–7.

are normally regarded as living things, are seen as combinations of an active, animating principle and body.[110] This follows from the set of universal twofold principles noted earlier, that of the active and passive principles or god and matter. It is the combination of these two principles that produces in each case determinate objects or 'qualified matter' (*SVF* 2.320). The active principle is identified with *pneuma*, 'breath', at least by Chrysippus, the most systematic and sophisticated Stoic theorist.[111] The relationship between *pneuma* and matter (*hulē*) is characterized as 'total blending'. This is a form of combination which falls between 'juxtaposition', in which the elements are combined but retain their character, and 'fusion', in which the elements wholly submerge their nature in each other. Total blending involves a thorough interpenetration of the two elements while allowing each to retain their nature and to be, in principle, recoverable.[112] The active principle, or active element, serves to 'sustain' or 'hold together' (*sunechein*) matter in a way that gives objects their coherent form and structure. It also does so by providing objects, both material or animate, with *tonos*, 'tenor, tension, or tensility'. 'Tension' here does not signify 'conflict', but, rather, the capacity of three-dimensional bodies to maintain their shape, stability, and overall character.[113] If we take these points together, it is clear that psychophysicalism of a strong type is a fundamental part of the Stoic world-view, both as regards the universe as a whole and individual (whole) entities within it.

However, to characterize this aspect of Stoic thought as 'psychophysicalism' is not quite accurate. This is because the psyche–body relationship is not unique but forms one of a series of relationships created by the interplay between active and passive principles. More precisely, 'unified bodies' (*henōmena*), which include 'grown together' or organic bodies (*sumphua*), can be placed on a spectrum according to the degree of tension that characterizes the movement of the active element which sustains the body. This spectrum of degrees of tension forms a natural hierarchy which Philo, for instance, presents in these terms:

Intelligence (*nous*) . . . has many powers, the tenor kind, the physical, the psychic, the rational, the calculative . . . Tenor (*hexis*) is also shared by lifeless things, stones and

[110] See 1.3 above, text to nn. 54–5. On the Platonic origin of the idea that 'the world at its most basic level of existence … is an intelligent organism' (Long 1999*a*: 561), see text to nn. 41–2 above and LS i. 319.

[111] Other Stoic accounts give this role to fire or air (or both), but not to earth or water, the remaining two elements. See LS 47, e.g. F, H, M and i. 286–9. Chrysippus was head of the School *c.*230–206 BC, after Zeno, the founder, and Cleanthes.

[112] LS 48; also Long (1996), 230–1; von Staden (2000), 99–100.

[113] See e.g. LS 47 G: 'air and fire because of their tensility (*eutonia*) can sustain (*sunechein*) themselves, and by blending with the other two [earth and water] provide them with tension (*tonos*) and also stability and substantiality'. See LS i. 288–9.

logs, and our bones, which resemble stones, also participate in it. Physique (*phusis*) also extends to plants, and in us there are things like plants—nails and hair. Physique is tenor in actual motion. Soul (psyche) is physique which has acquired impression and impulse. This is also shared by irrational animals. (LS 47 P)

This passage illustrates two features of the theory. One is that different sustaining causes, through differing degrees of tension, establish the character of more or less complex entities. The other is that these causes build or supervene on each other within a single entity. Hence, in human beings and other animals the structure of bones is the work of *hexis*, organic growth and nutrition derive from *phusis*, and functions such as impression, impulse, and movement belong to psyche. The spectrum continues with reason (*logos*), which supervenes on the other causes, and 'passes judgement on impressions, rejecting some of these and accepting others, in order that the [rational] animal may be guided accordingly' (LS 53 A(5)). But movement up the scale does not involve the loss or discarding of the lower types of tension or structure. In the developed human being, as Philo's quotation implies, successive degrees of tension are built into the organism: bones are shaped by *hexis*, growth by *phusis*, and impression by psyche. To this degree, the character of the functioning human adult is layered, as these different types of tension coexist within the same organism. Thus, the key notion is not so much *psychophysicalism*, though this remains a convenient label; the basic relationship is that of tension (structure) established between *pneuma*, as active, sustaining cause, and matter (*hulē*).[114]

Given this plurality of coexisting aspects—these degrees of tension—within a single complex organism, such as an adult human being, what constitutes its cohesion or wholeness? This question is raised, by implication at least, in this comment by von Staden (2000: 100):

the greater the tension, the more complex and adaptable the unified functioning of the relevant body, and hence the higher its place within the natural hierarchy... the more complex and diverse the capacities and behaviour of a living thing, the greater the degree of unification it requires to be a single, coherent functioning being.

This is a crucial question for the Stoics, given their emphasis both on the cohesion and on the structured complexity of entities at various levels, and it is a question which recurs in different forms both in ancient debate and in modern scholarship. There are at least three ways in which cohesion is secured. The simplest, already noticed, is that of *addition*; more complex is the fact that functions *supervene* on each other and are *transformed* in

[114] By analogy with Aristotelian 'hylomorphism', one might call this principle 'hylopneumatism'.

character in the process; the third is that of *systematic coordination*. Whereas the unity or structure of a stone is conferred solely by the relatively low tension of *hexis*, the human being contains an internally layered set of such tensions, from *hexis* to *logos*.[115] Second, and implied in the idea of 'layering', is that the higher state both presupposes or builds on the lower state and also modifies or transforms its operations. The second point is illustrated, for instance, in this passage:

Nature (*phusis*)... is no different in regard to plants and animals [when it directs both] without impulse and sensation, *and in us certain processes of a vegetative kind take place*. But... animals have the *additional* faculty of impulse, through the use of which they go in search of what is appropriate to them... And since reason, by way of a *more perfect management*, has been bestowed on rational beings, to live correctly in accordance with reason comes to be natural for them. *For reason supervenes (epiginetai) as the craftsman of impulse.*[116]

This passage brings out clearly the fact that 'nature' (*phusis*), operates in us, as in plants, as that which shapes nutrition and growth. But this process is also informed, in animals, by the functions associated with psyche (impulse and movement) which enable animals, for instance, to go in search of food appropriate to them to maintain their constitution. Reason (*logos*) too is both an additional structuring agency and one which transforms impulse, for instance by 'rejecting some of these and accepting others, in order that the [rational] animal may be guided accordingly' (LS 53 A(5), cited earlier). The notion of 'supervening' (or of one function, such as reason, being a 'craftsman' of another) seems to signify this combination of layering of functions and modifying or transforming them. A more striking instance of the latter theme is Hierocles' description of the birth of an embryo as involving the 'change' (*metabolē*) of *phusis* into psyche. What is involved in this process is that the animal being born acquires psyche *in addition to phusis*, although this may also bring about a transformation of the kind of functions exercised.[117]

The third way in which the Stoic account of animal psychology envisages cohesion is by assuming systematic coordination. Coordination is seen as brought about, especially, by a unitary 'control-centre' (*hēgemonikon*), an idea widely seen as a Stoic innovation.[118] The specific functions of the control-centre are impression, assent, impulse, and perception; another function is that of coordinating the other seven psychic functions, those of the five senses, utterance, and reproduction. The coordinating role of the *hēgemonikon* is

[115] See further Annas (1992), 52–4; Long (1996), 230–1.

[116] Diogenes Laertius (D.L.) 7.86 (LS 57 A (4–5)), with omissions and added italics.

[117] LS 53 B(2–3); also Long (1996), 236–9.

[118] See e.g. Annas (1992), 61–4; Long (1999*a*), 572.

expressed by a series of images: a tree-trunk and its branches, an octopus and its tentacles, a spider in the centre of its web.[119] Since the Stoic model is a psychophysical one, the control-centre is allocated a physical place, namely the heart, and the associated communication-system (though conceived as based on *pneuma*), is taken to operate through the veins and arteries. Chrysippus, in particular, is insistently criticized for this location by Galen, the second-century AD doctor and philosopher and an important source for this topic. A special ground of criticism is that Chrysippus failed to take account of the discovery (by vivisection in Ptolemaic Alexandria) of the directing role of the brain and the nerves by Herophilus and Erasistratus.[120] However, as several recent discussions have pointed out, Galen's criticisms are not wholly justified. Chrysippus, who does not claim to be basing his location of the control-centre on experimental research, is simply following one longstanding strand of ancient thinking about the site of the psychological centre,[121] and is, in any case, explicitly tentative in his location. His crucial concern is to identify a *single* control-centre, and the heart strikes him as the best candidate, given its accepted role as the seat of emotions and its links with voice-production (and thus the expression of thought) through the wind-pipe. Arguably, his model, though mistaken in its location of the psychological centre, captures better than Galen's three-location model the unified picture which he wants above all to convey.[122]

Stoic thinking about the psychophysical cohesion of animals, including humans, clearly, draws on a rich intellectual background. For instance, the idea of a *scala naturae*, a spectrum of psychological capacities, against which to locate human and animal functions, recalls Aristotle especially.[123] But the distinction between psyche and *phusis* is, markedly, un-Aristotelian; Aristotle thinks of 'psyche' as including all life-functions, including those of plants, and in this respect is closer to traditional Greek linguistic usage.[124] Von Staden suggests that Chrysippus' use of the distinction between *phusis* and psyche may be influenced by analogous contrasts drawn by Herophilus and

[119] LS 53 G(7), (Calcid. *in Timaeum* 220), also 53 H.

[120] Galen, *On the Doctrines of Hippocrates and Plato* (*de Placitis Hippocratis et Platonis*) (*PHP*), Books 2–3. On Herophilus and Erasistratus, see von Staden (2000), 87–96. Their respective dates are Herophilus (*c.*330–250), Erasistratus (*c.*320–240) and Chrysippus (*c.*280–*c.*206).

[121] The proponents of the heart included Empedocles, Aristotle, and Epicurus. Praxagoras (who flourished around 300 BC) may have been a particularly influential proponent (see Annas 1992: 21–2; Long 1999*a*: 568). On the heart–brain debate, see von Staden (2000), 87.

[122] See Mansfeld (1991); Annas (1992), 69–70; Long (1999*a*), 567–70; also the thorough examination of Gal. *PHP* 2–3 in Tieleman (1996). See further 4.4 below.

[123] See Inwood (1985), 9–41.

[124] See Everson (1991*b*), introd, 3–4; van der Eijk (2000), 59, 64; for earlier Greek usage, see Claus (1981); Bremmer (1983).

Erasistratus, in spite of the fact that Chrysippus does not follow them in the location of the psychological centre. These Alexandrian doctors seem also to have used their distinctions to limit 'psychic' functions to those related to movement and, in modern terms, cognitive functions.[125] More broadly, the attempt to correlate psychological functions with animal and human physiology, and to identify a control-centre and communication-system goes back at least to Plato's *Timaeus*, in addition to medical research on this subject.[126]

Despite these possible influences, the Stoic analysis emerges as a strikingly original and conceptually powerful analysis of psychophysical coherence. In combination with related aspects of their thinking, it carries important implications for their ethical theory and thus for their ideas about selfhood more generally. One is that the distinction between animate and non-animate creatures is not fundamental; nor is that between human beings and other animals or other natural kinds. The key categories, outlined earlier, are subdivisions of a scale of types of sustaining cause and 'tension'; and these distinctions, such as psyche and 'nature' (*phusis*), do not correspond with those between living and non-living entities or between different natural kinds. Since the Stoics have sometimes been taken to be, in a problematic way, anthropocentric in their approach to psychology and ethics,[127] it is worth underlining this contrasting aspect of their theory. This feature can be linked with other, more explicitly ethical, themes. One is that perfect wisdom is understood as the most complete type of psychophysical tension (*eutonia*, 'good tension'). This state is also characterized as *diathesis*, a technical term for the most completely 'tensed' and thus stable character (LS 47 S). This can be connected, in turn, with their view that humans who fall short of perfect wisdom lack 'good tension' and stability, and are marked by weak and fluctuating attitudes. A further related point is that the wise, who exhibit this psychophysical tension and stability, persist, as psychophysical wholes, after death. These ideas are explored more fully later.[128] Here, I simply point out that Stoic ideas about psychophysical cohesion or wholeness have broader implications, including ethical ones, for their thinking as a whole.

[125] Von Staden (2000), 98, also 90, on Herophilus' distinction between psychic and natural capacities (based on the discovery of the difference between perceptive and motor nerves) and 95–6, on Erasistratus' distinction between psychic and non-psychic natural functions. See also Long (1999*a*), 568.

[126] On the possible influence of the embodied (though tripartite) psychic model of *Ti.* 69–72, see Gill (1997*a*). On medical influences, see Annas (1992), 20–6. On Aristotle's thinking on the location of the psychological centre, see van der Eijk (2000), 68–9, and on later Aristotelian thinking, see Annas (1992), 26–33—neither are clearly influential on Stoic thinking.

[127] Texts often cited in this connection include LS 36 E, 54 N, 57 F(5). See further Sorabji (1993), 20–8, 123–4, 199.

[128] See 2.2 below, text to nn. 14–19.

So far, I have discussed these ideas in general terms. I now look more closely at two Stoic discussions of early animal development, by Hierocles and Seneca. I consider especially what they say about the role of self-perception or self-awareness in this process, which is presented as part of the process of appropriation to oneself or to one's 'constitution' (*sustasis* or *constitutio*). This feature of Stoic thinking, especially as presented by Cicero (*On Ends* 3.16), is interpreted by Troels Engberg-Pedersen as reflecting the idea that the emergence of 'I'-centred self-consciousness forms a crucial stage of human development. I examine his interpretation later (6.4), as part of a larger enquiry into the question whether Hellenistic thought, and especially Stoicism, exhibits a shift towards a subjective conception of selfhood. I am sceptical of the idea that Stoic texts (including Cicero's *On Ends* 3.16) provide evidence for such a shift. The discussions of animal development by Hierocles and Seneca examined here seem to me to be centred on the idea of animals as psychophysical and psychological wholes. Their conceptions of self-perception and self-awareness is, I think, fundamentally different from Descartes's conception of 'I'-centred self-consciousness (to which Engberg-Pedersen refers), which played a key role in the emergence of modern ideas about selfhood and subjectivity. I suggest that these Stoic ideas are better interpreted by reference to modern non-Cartesian ideas about psychology, including those of Dennett and Davidson, which express what I call an 'objective' approach to psychology.[129]

The relevant discussions by Hierocles and Seneca explore aspects of the Stoic theory of development as 'appropriation' (*oikeiōsis*). This theory is widely regarded as one of the most innovative and important features of Stoic thinking. The central idea is that animals, including humans, are naturally adapted to develop in a way that preserves themselves, or their constitution, and other members of their kind. The two aspects of this process, preserving oneself and preserving others, seem to be conceived as distinct, though related and equally natural. Self-love and self-perception figure as part of the first aspect of the process of personal development, centred on preserving oneself, in both animals and humans. A salient feature of the theory, considered later, is that in adult humans the preservation of oneself and of others is crucially informed by rationality.[130]

[129] On 'subjective' and 'objective' approaches to psychology and the role of Cartesian ideas of self-consciousness in the development of modern thinking about subjectivity and 'self' (understood in subjective terms), see 6.2 below. For Engberg-Pedersen's reference to Cartesian thinking about self-consciousness in connection with Stoicism, see 6.4 below, text to nn. 124–5.

[130] On the second, rational stage, see 3.2–3 below; on the social aspect of *oikeiōsis*, see LS 57 D–H. On *oikeiōsis* in general, see Pembroke (1971); Kerferd (1972); Inwood (1985), ch. 6; Engberg-Pedersen (1990*b*) (discussed in 6.4 below); Annas (1993*b*), ch. 5 and 262–76; Striker (1996), ch. 13; Inwood and Donini (1999), 677–82, 727–31.

The term *oikeiōsis*, as used by the Stoics, is usually translated as 'appropriation' or 'familiarization', and is seen as derived from *oikeios* ('one's own' or 'appropriate'). The core idea is that of making something or someone 'one's own'. The significance of this term is indicated in this passage by Diogenes Laertius:

[The Stoics] say that an animal has self-preservation as the object of its first impulse, since nature from the beginning appropriates it, as Chrysippus says in his *On Ends* book 1. The first thing appropriate (*prōton oikeion*) to every animal... is its own constitution (*sustasis*) and the consciousness (*suneidēsis*) of this. For nature was not likely either to alienate (*allotriōsai*) the animal itself, or to make it and then neither alienate it nor appropriate it (*oikeiōsai*). So it remains to say that in constituting (*sustēsamenēn*) the animal, nature appropriated it to [the animal] itself. This is why the animal rejects what is harmful and accepts what is appropriate.[131]

This passage can be seen as implying the kind of psychophysical holism outlined earlier in this section. Nature, taken collectively, is seen as one such whole, and this larger whole 'appropriates' the smaller one.[132] It does so by bringing it about that the smaller one, the animal, 'appropriates itself' and thus expresses its own potential wholeness (its constitution). This is achieved by ensuring that the 'first thing [that is] appropriate' to an animal is its own constitution and the consciousness of this. This appropriation of the animal to its constitution is expressed, in the first instance, in the fact that it accepts what is 'appropriate' to it and thus preserves its life.[133]

The role of self-awareness in this process can be illustrated, first, by a passage from Cicero's account:

[The Stoics] hold that as soon as an animal is born—for this must be the starting-point—it is appropriated to itself (*ipsum sibi conciliari*) and led to preserve itself and to love its own constitution (*suum statum*) and those things which preserve its constitution, and to be alienated from its death and from those things that seem to lead to death. They prove that this is so from the fact that, before either pleasure or pain has affected them, infants seek what preserves them and reject the opposite, something which would not happen unless they loved their constitution and feared death. But it cannot be the case that they desire anything unless they have a sense of themselves (*sensum sui*) and therefore love themselves. Hence it must be realized that the principle (*principium*) has been drawn from self-love.[134]

131 D.L. 7.85 (LS 57A(2)), trans. slightly modified.

132 'Nature' here, probably means both human and cosmic nature, as in D.L. 7.89. The Stoic theory of 'appropriation' involves both these conceptions of nature as well as deploying agent-centred, and also 'cosmic', perspectives, on nature. See further, on the interpretative issues raised by this aspect of their theory, 3.3 below.

133 'Appropriate' here translates *oikeion*; for a different, but related, Stoic concept, that of 'appropriate acts' (*kathēkonta*), see LS 59 (which LS translate as 'proper functions').

134 Cicero *On Ends* (*de Finibus* = *Fin.*) 3.16, trans. Brunschwig (1986), 128, slightly modified.

The main point of this, rather complex, passage seems to be this. The (alleged) fact that young animals seek what preserves them, rather than pleasure,[135] supports the Stoic view of natural development as appropriation. But this is so only if we recognize the existence of a set of interconnected motives, which are conceived as forms of relationship to oneself. Of these motives, the most basic is (1) having a sense or awareness (*sensus*) of oneself, which forms the basis for (2) love of oneself or one's constitution. Self-love, in turn, underlies (3) the desire to preserve oneself, which is manifested in (4) seeking what preserves one's constitution and avoiding the opposite. When interpreted in the light of this set of motives, animal behaviour, seen as directed at self-preservation rather than pleasure, is taken to provide empirical support for the Stoic principle (*principium*), that nature 'appropriates' or 'owns' each animal by appropriating it to itself or to its constitution.[136] This passage also implies that development is a matter of coming to recognize and instantiate your constitution as a psychophysical whole, an idea made explicit by Hierocles and Seneca.

These sources indicate the theoretical background for the most extended Stoic treatment that we have of animal self-awareness. Understood as 'self-perception', this forms the subject of the main surviving part of *Elements of Ethics* by Hierocles, a late but orthodox Stoic writing around 200 AD.[137] This extract illustrates his approach:

> We should realize that as soon as an animal is born it perceives itself... The first thing that animals perceive is their own parts... both that they have them and for what purpose they have them... Therefore the first proof of every animal's perceiving itself is its consciousness (*sunaisthēsis*) of its parts and the function for which they were given. The second proof is the fact that animals are not unaware (*anaisthētōs diakeitai*) of their equipment for self-defence. When bulls do battle with other bulls or animals of different species, they stick out their horns, as if these were their congenital weapons for the encounter. Every other creature has the same disposition relative to its appropriate (*oikeion*) and, so to speak, congenital (*sumphues*) weapon.[138]

135 This is directed at the competing Epicurean claim (Cic. *Fin.* 1.30) that the desire for pleasure is primary.

136 This interpretation draws on Brunschwig (1986), 128–33, and M. R. Wright (1991), 124–5. For the 'principle' of the final sentence, see also D.L. 7.85, cited above. Wright, however, takes *principium* to be the 'primary instinct' of self-preservation, which is cited in support of this principle. For a different (subjective) interpretation of the 'self-consciousness' involved in Cic. *Fin.* 3.16, see Engberg-Pedersen (1990*b*), 66–71, discussed in 6.4 below.

137 See Long (1996), 251–2, who points out that, despite its fragmentary state, this is our only surviving Stoic technical treatise on the foundations of ethics, as distinct from works of practical ethics and summaries of doctrines. The edition of Bastianini and Long (1992) contains a new text, together with translation and full commentary in Italian; the only earlier edition was that of von Arnim (1906). Apart from the extracts in LS (53 B, 57 C–D), there is no English translation known to me.

138 1.37–8, 51, 54–5, 2.1–9 (numbers refer to columns and lines of papyrus); LS 57 C, abbreviated, trans. slightly modified.

Like other Stoics, Hierocles holds that the fact that animals act instinctively to preserve themselves shows they have love or affection for themselves, and this in turn proves that they are from birth 'appropriated' to themselves and their constitutions.[139] The point on which he focuses, in the first part of his treatise, is that animals perceive themselves, and that this self-perception underlies the way they seek to preserve themselves. In framing his argument, Hierocles seems to be trying to meet two kinds of objection made by ancient critics of the Stoic theory. One is that animals do not perceive *themselves*, as distinct from perceiving external objects; the other is that animal self-perception, or self-awareness, does not start at birth.[140] The passage quoted earlier falls within Hierocles' arguments for the claim that animals perceive themselves at all. He refers especially to the instinctive awareness that animals have of their own specific means of self-defence, the 'congenital' or 'appropriate' weapon by which they express their self-appropriation. Some of his stronger arguments refer to natural means of self-defence of which the animal itself is instinctively aware but which are not evident to an outside observer, such as the deer's reliance on speed of running rather than its impressive but cumbersome horns.[141] The second set of arguments is designed to prove that animal self-perception is continuous and that it begins from birth. These arguments are more theoretical in character, though they include some (allegedly) empirical observations, such as that human behaviour shows self-awareness in sleep.[142]

The question that concerns me, in the first instance, is that of the conception of 'self-perception' and 'self' implied in Hierocles' arguments. A. A. Long highlights the contrast between this conception and modern post-Cartesian ideas of self-consciousness (1996: 256). For Descartes, 'we' (humans) are 'immediately conscious' of all psychological processes, including perception. This consciousness is thus, in effect, a type of *self*-consciousness: 'nothing can be in me, that is, in my mind, of which I am not conscious'.[143] The idea that all psychological processes are conscious is reinforced by Locke: it is 'impossible for any one to perceive without perceiving that he does perceive . . . consciousness always accompanies thinking [taken to include perception]'.[144] A related

[139] See points 5–6 (referring to Hierocles 6.24–7.50) in the summary of the extant parts of the treatise given in Long (1996), 262–3.

[140] For this interpretation, see Long (1996), 255; on the second type of objection, see Inwood (1984), 167–78. The two sets of arguments are those in 4(i) and 4(ii–iii) respectively in Long's summary (1996: 263).

[141] See Hierocles 2.46–3.2; also Inwood (1984), 160–1.

[142] Hierocles 5.1–30. Brunschwig (1986), 139–44, is critical of Hierocles' argumentation, especially because it draws on adult human behaviour to support claims about instinctive animal behaviour. For a more positive appraisal, see Inwood (1984), 158–67.

[143] See 6.2 below, n. 13. See also Wilkes (1988), 214–17.

[144] Locke, *Essay*, 2.27.9, cited from Nidditch (1975), p. 335.

idea is that we have immediate and certain (incorrigible) access to our psychological processes. So, for Hume, 'the perceptions of the mind are perfectly known'[145] and 'consciousness never deceives'.[146]

The contrast between this conception of self-consciousness and Hierocles' idea of self-perception is stark. This is not simply because of Descartes's mind–body dualism and his related view that non-human animals are incapable of consciousness and self-consciousness.[147] It is also because Hierocles discusses types of phenomena which fall outside what a Cartesian type of view would regard as conscious (or self-conscious) perceptions at all. These include behaviour during sleep, taken by Hierocles as evidence for self-perception. They also include, in the passage cited earlier, an animal's 'consciousness' (*sunaisthēsis*) of its bodily parts as a means of self-defence. Indeed, at one point, Hierocles characterizes animal self-perception as the kind of psychophysical event in which there is perception (or 'grasp', *antilēpsis*) of *all* parts of the body and psyche.[148]

The passage in which Hierocles characterizes self-perception in this way sheds light on the Stoic ideas about animals as psychophysical wholes outlined earlier.

> Since an animal is a composite (*suntheton*) of body and psyche, and both of these are tangible and impressible and of course subject to resistance, and also blended through and through, and one of them is a sensory faculty (*dunamis aisthētikē*) which undergoes movement... it is evident that an animal perceives itself continuously. For by stretching and relaxing, the psyche makes an impression on all the body's parts, since it is blended with them all, and in making an impression it receives an impression in response. For the body, just like the psyche, reacts to pressure; and the outcome is a state of their joint pressure upon, and resistance to, each other... it [this outcome] travels... to the control-centre, with the result that there is an awareness (*antilēpsis*) both of all the body's parts and of those of the psyche. This is equivalent to the animal's perceiving itself.[149]

This passage brings out vividly the features of Stoic thinking noted earlier, including the idea that psyche is integrated with body by 'complete blending', and that perception is a process of internal psychophysical communication. The capacity of an animal, of any sort, to perceive itself from birth is an

[145] Hume, *Treatise*, 2.2.6, cited from Norton and Norton (2001), p. 237.

[146] Hume, *Enquiry*, 7.1.13, cited from Beauchamp (1999), p. 138.

[147] See further Smith and Jones (1986), chs. 2–3.

[148] Hierocles 5.1–30, 2.1–9, cited above, and 3.19–52, respectively; see further Long (1996), 255–6, 259–61.

[149] Hierocles 4.38–53 = LS 53 B(5–9), trans. slightly modified. 'Control-centre' (LS 'commanding-faculty'): the Greek is *hēgemonian t[ou stē]thous*, 'rulership of the chest', apparently standing for *hēgemonikon* (see LS ii. 312).

indication that it functions from the start as a cohesive psychophysical organism.[150] The passage also brings out the role of the *hēgemonikon* ('control-centre'). Like other psychological functions, this is itself physical, since psyche is conceived in Stoicism as animating warm breath or *pneuma*; and its workings involve the total interpenetration of psychological and bodily processes. The *hēgemonikon* is understood as the centre of a comunication-system, running throughout the body, and it is repeatedly described in terms which underline its unifying role.[151] Thus, although its role is broadly comparable to the Platonic or Aristotelian 'mind' or 'reasoning part', it is more firmly and explicitly integrated with the body, and is, correspondingly, less likely to be contrasted with it in the way that mind or psyche sometimes is in Plato or Aristotle, and also, of course, Descartes.[152]

Are there modern non-Cartesian concepts that can be usefully compared with Hierocles' thinking about animal self-perception? Long cites the idea, coined by Charles Sherrington, of 'proprioception', as distinct from 'exteroception', that is, perception of external objects. Proprioception is 'that continuous but unconscious sensory flow from the movable parts of our bodies (muscles, tendons, joints) by which their position and tone and motion are continually monitored and adjusted'.[153] Long suggests that the Stoics, like modern neurologists, are 'interested in the principle that enables animals to function internally as well-organised wholes, coordinating their movements and ensuring that the deployment of their bodily parts is appropriate to their environment' (1996: 258–9). The comparison between self-perception and proprioception, as distinct from exteroception, seems to work best in that part of the treatise where Hierocles distinguishes self-perception from perception of external things. Here, Hierocles is arguing that external perception presupposes self-perception and that self-perception is prior to external perception.[154] Elsewhere in the treatise, he seems to use 'self-perception' more broadly, to signify the combination of internal and external perception that enables an animal to recognize what promotes or threatens

[150] See LS 47 N, 48 C(9–10), 53 G-H; also Long (1996), 240–2.

[151] The *hēgemonikon* is compared to a tree-trunk, octopus, or spider; see *SVF* 2.836, 2.879. See LS 53 F–H, K–N; also Annas (1992), 61–70; Long (1996), 233–5, 239–43. On *pneuma*, see LS 47, esp. G, M–Q. See also text to n. 111 above.

[152] The contrast between psyche (or mind) and body is marked in Pl. *Alc.* 129c–130c, *Phd.* (e.g. 78d–84b), Arist. *NE* 10.8, 1178^{a}14–22 (also *de An.* 3.5 and *Metaph.* 12.9). See further 1.2 above, and 6.3 below esp. text to nn. 57–8; also 2.2 below, text to nn. 93–113, 2.3, text to nn. 194–206, on quasi-dualism in Stoicism and Epicureanism.

[153] Long (1996), 258, citing Sacks (1987), 43, which refers to Sherrington (1906). Brunschwig (1986), 137, also links the idea of proprioception with Stoic thinking about self-awareness.

[154] See e.g. Hierocles 5.52–6.24; also Long (1996), 260–1.

its self-preservation.[155] In these cases, Hierocles' use of 'self-perception' is closer to the broad sense—recognition of what 'belongs' to one's constitution—attached by other Stoics to 'self-awareness'.[156]

Another way of characterizing the type of thinking involved in Hierocles' conception of self-perception is by reference to contemporary debate in the philosophy of mind about whether animals have beliefs. From a Cartesian standpoint, beliefs are conscious mental states of which animals are incapable. Some non-Cartesian thinkers, for instance, Donald Davidson, hold that we cannot ascribe beliefs to animals because they cannot use language, and language is a prerequisite for having beliefs. Daniel Dennett, on the other hand, argues that beliefs can be attributed appropriately to animals if there is 'an order which is there' in their behaviour which is effectively explained and predicted by attributing beliefs to them. Attributing beliefs to animals, or other entities, is, on this view, a means of explaining coherent, goal-directed behaviour, rather than of making claims about the existence of mental states, as in the Cartesian approach.[157] It is possible that we should see Hierocles' attribution of self-perception to animals (including, but not limited to, humans) as a move of the same general type. The attribution is designed to provide a mode of explanation for 'an order which is there' in the coherent, goal-directed behaviour of animals; it is not a claim about conscious mental states.

The parallel between Dennett's move and Hierocles' is not exact, in that perception, conceived as the capacity to respond to 'impressions', falls squarely within the capacities attributed to non-human animals by the Stoics,[158] whereas Dennett's attribution of beliefs to animals is controversial. What is innovative in Hierocles' argument, in the context of Stoic thought, is the attribution to animals of self-*perception* rather than self-awareness more generally. However, the point of the comparison between Hierocles' thinking

[155] See LS 57 C, cited in text to n. 138 above, in which self-perception is illustrated by the case of animals using their own natural bodily 'weapon' to counter the threat (recognized by external perception) posed by other animals. Here 'self-perception' is used broadly, to cover the ability of animals to correlate their natural capacities with those of other animals. See also 3.19–52; and Long (1996), 256.

[156] See Brunschwig (1986), 136–7, referring to the various kinds of internal and external awareness that are included in Seneca's account of animals' awareness of their constitution (*constitutionis suae sensus*) in Sen. *Ep.* 121.5–15.

[157] See further on this debate (and its relevance to ancient philosophy of mind), Gill (1991), esp. 170–3, referring to Dennett (1976), esp. 179, 181–7. The phrase 'an order which is there' is taken from Anscombe (1957), 79; see also Davidson (1985); and Jeffrey (1985), whose position on animal beliefs is similar to Dennett's.

[158] See e.g. LS 53 A(4–5). In Stoicism (and other ancient theories) controversy centred, significantly, on the question whether animals had rationality as well as perception, and not on whether they had self-consciousness; see Sorabji (1993), part 1, esp. ch. 1.

and Dennett's, as with proprioception, is to indicate the general type of psychological theory involved. The prominence in the theory of the idea of relationship to oneself does not indicate a theory centred on subjectivity of a Cartesian or post-Cartesian kind. Neither the criteria used to define 'self-perception' nor the methodology deployed require reference to the idea of the 'I' as a centre of self-consciousness or subjectivity. As in modern neurology or functionalism, what is being analysed, from a third-person standpoint, are animals viewed as coherent organic psychophysical systems. In terminology explained later (6.2 below), Hierocles analyses animal self-perception in 'objective' (not 'subjective') terms, and also employs an 'objectivist' methodology in his enquiry.

Seneca's letter (121) on the same subject confirms this way of understanding the psychological model implied, while also clarifying certain questions raised by this model.[159] Starting from the question whether all animals have a sense, or awareness, *sensus*,[160] of their constitution, Seneca, like Hierocles, argues that animals have an instinctive awareness from birth of their natural capacities.[161] A striking example, designed to counter the Epicurean view of instinctive behaviour (that it aims at pleasure), is that of the infant who, after falling down, and even while crying (*cum fletu*), struggles *painfully* (*per dolorem*) to exercise its natural capacity to stand up again (8). Seneca also confirms Hierocles' general account of this awareness in animals and human children, namely as an instinctive sense of the way that each species is naturally equipped, by bodily shape or capacities, to maintain its existence and characteristic form of life (21–4).

Seneca's letter confronts two objections to this theory. One is that it is incredible that animals and children should be able to understand what 'constitution' means, that is, in Stoic terms, 'the ruling part of the psyche [i.e. the "control-centre"] related in a certain way to the body' (10).[162] Seneca thinks this objection can be easily met. What is involved is not analytic understanding, that is, grasping the *definition* of 'constitution', but instinctive understanding expressed in action (11). Developing this point, Seneca draws a parallel between the (instinctive) understanding we humans have of our mind (*animus*) and that which animals have of their constitution (12).

[159] Though written earlier (1st c. AD), Seneca's account provides more analysis on certain points than Hierocles' longer, but incomplete, treatment, as is stressed by Brunschwig (1986), 135–44.

[160] For this term, broader in meaning than perception, see Cic. *Fin.* 3.16; see also 'consciousness' (*suneidēsis*) in D.L. 7.85, cited in text to n. 131 above.

[161] For this theme in Hierocles, see text to nn. 138–42 above. Chrysippus seems to have made the claim repeatedly that 'we have an appropriate disposition [*oikeiōsis*] relative to ourselves as soon as we are born and to our parts', LS 57 E(1).

[162] On the *hēgemonikon* and its relation to the body, see text to nn. 118–22 above.

However, we should not conclude from this that Seneca holds, like Descartes, that humans, but not animals, have minds and that humans also have direct, incorrigible access to the contents of those minds.[163] 'Mind' (*animus*) must here serve as shorthand for the distinctive character of adult human psychological functions, namely, their being rational. Also, the relevant way that 'we know' (*scimus*) the meaning of 'constitution' is by the instinctive use of these human functions, in a way that is parallel to the use by animals of their functions, including psychological ones, and not by Cartesian self-conscious introspection.[164]

The second objection is more searching. The idea that creatures are appropriated to their constitution from birth is not consistent, it is argued, with the sharp discontinuity claimed in Stoicism between children who are not yet rational and adults who are. 'How then can a child be appropriated (*conciliari*) to a rational constitution, when he is not yet rational?' (14). The child–adult relationship is the source of a number of substantive issues in Stoicism.[165] Seneca's response is to draw a distinction not found in other Stoic sources between appropriation to ourselves, as living a single, continuous life, and to our constitution at a given time (infancy, childhood, and so on, 16–17). 'Although each one has at different times a different constitution, the appropriation to one's own constitution is the same' (16). The question of the extent to which we have a continuous identity throughout our lives figures elsewhere in ancient thought, including Stoicism, as well as in modern thought.[166] The way that Seneca poses his view at one point might suggest a modern concern with the question whether 'I' (as a unique individual) persist through different phases of development: 'but I am the same, although I have been an infant, a child, and a youth' (16). But what is crucial here is that the continuity affirmed by Seneca is not that of *me*, as a locus of unique, personal identity, but that of *appropriation* to my constitution at any given time. The only form of this appropriation discussed in the continuation of Seneca's letter is the preservation of one's life, a form shared by animals and humans. But Seneca's point also holds good in the

[163] See text to n. 143 above.

[164] See also Brunschwig (1986), 137, who describes this 'self-awareness' as 'proprioceptive' (cf. 41 above). Animals have a *hēgemonikon*, though not a rational one; on this point, see Inwood (1985), 32, 72.

[165] See 4.6 below, text to nn. 374–88, for Posidonius' thinking on childhood development and the question of how to understand the growth of rationality. Posidonius is cited at the start of Seneca's letter (121.1), and is, presumably, one of the sources for the arguments.

[166] See e.g. (in ancient thought), Pl. *Smp.* 207d–208b, Plu. *Mor.* 473d. See (in modern thought) Williams (1981), 5–14; Parfit (1984), part 3, esp. chs. 10, 13. On the relationship between these ancient and modern debates, see Price (1989), 34–5, 50–3; Gill (1994), 4626–7, 4637–8. On related puzzles about identity in Stoicism (and Epicureanism), see 1.6 below.

case of the more advanced, rational development characteristic of adult humans at their best, which also counts as 'appropriation' to one's nature, as an adult.[167]

In other sources too we find variation between the idea of appropriation 'to oneself' and 'to one's constitution'; how significant, within Stoicism generally, is this variation? One ancient commentator tells us that some Stoics adopted the idea of appropriation to oneself, whereas others, who are described as giving a 'more subtle' and more 'fully articulated' account, introduced the idea of appropriation to one's constitution.[168] Some scholars think that Chrysippus refined the earlier idea (perhaps Zeno's) of appropriation to oneself to that of appropriation to one's constitution and its preservation.[169] However, if this is so, the innovation does not seem to have introduced a significant distinction between the two formulas; and, apart from Seneca's discussion in 121.14–17, just outlined, the two formulas seem to be used as equivalents.[170] The fact, as it seems to be, that there is no clear differentiation of meaning between the two expressions is highly suggestive as regards the psychological model involved. What this implies is that, in modern terms, the constitution *is* 'the self'.[171] Put more precisely, and in ancient terms, the relationship 'to oneself' could also be understood-perhaps better understood—as a relationship 'to one's constitution'. There is an interesting contrast with certain features of Platonic and Aristotelian thought, in which reflexive relations such as self-love are analysed in terms of a relationship to what is 'essential' or highest (that is, one's mind), and not to one's psychophysical constitution as a whole.[172] Indeed, the introduction of the idea of a relationship 'to one's constitution' might have been designed to mark the difference from these Platonic–Aristotelian themes.

But what is the precise significance of this idea? The principal point seems to be to underline the idea, central to Stoic theory, that human beings, like other animals, are integrated psychophysical organisms or living structures. Hence, 'self-perception' and 'self-love' are functions which express the instinctive desire of living organisms to maintain their structure. The Stoics, like Plato and Aristotle, attribute more advanced, rational functions to (adult)

[167] On this type of development, see 3.2–3 below.

[168] Alexander of Aphrodisias, a thinker in the Aristotelian tradition, *de Anima* 150.28–33 Bruns (= *SVF* 3.183).

[169] See Inwood (1983), 192 and references in 199–200 n. 6. See also Brunschwig (1986), 133, who suggests in n. 39 that the quotation of Chrysippus in D.L. 7.85 may have extended only to the first words, including the 'constitution' formula. For a different reading of the evidence, see Pembroke (1971), 145–6, n. 77.

[170] See e.g. Cic. *Fin.* 3.16, D.L. 7.85, cited in text to n. 131 above; also Hierocles 6.52–3, 7.48–9.

[171] On 'the self' as a distinctively modern expression, see 6.3 below, text to nn. 64–5.

[172] See 6.3 below, esp. text to nn. 94–100; also, in outline, 1.2 above, text to nn. 4–5.

humans than to other animals. But these are conceived as the more complex functions of an integrated organic structure and not as the functions of a higher or essential 'part' such as 'reason' or 'mind'. The definition of 'constitution' cited by Seneca (*Ep.* 121.10), 'the ruling part of the psyche [i.e. *hēgemonikon*] related in a certain way to the body', which applies both to human and non-human animals, illustrates this point. We (humans) are not combinations of two, or more, separate entities, psyche or mind and body. We (humans and other animals) are 'constitutions', in which the—psychophysical—ruling part is related in a certain specific way to the other psychophysical parts. Hence, the desire to maintain one's specific type of organic structure can be expressed, with equal appropriateness, as 'love of' (or 'appropriation to') 'oneself' or to 'one's constitution'.[173] Thus, this terminological innovation, like the larger theory of appropriation with which it is linked, as so far examined here, reflects the centrality for Stoicism of the idea that humans and other animals are psychophysical wholes.

1.5 PSYCHOPHYSICAL HOLISM: EPICUREANISM

In considering psychophysical holism in Epicureanism, I begin with the question of how to categorize the approach in modern terms. There has been much recent debate about this, a good deal of which centres on the correct way to interpret a recently deciphered set of fragmentary passages from Epicurus' *On Nature* which are now generally ascribed to Book 25.[174] However, I think it is possible to identify a credible overall account of Epicurus' position, which accommodates the relatively complex ideas of the passages in *On Nature* 25 without supposing that Epicurus gives up his physicalist assumptions. There is no doubt that Epicurus is a physicalist (and a materialist)[175] in maintaining that bodies (and void) are the only things that exist in themselves.[176] Epicurus is also explicit in maintaining that the psyche is a body, and so in this sense his psychology is materialist or physicalist.[177] But what sort of physicalist is he? 'Physicalism' is a broad and complex notion. Its typical ancient form, Annas suggests, is holding that

[173] See also Inwood (1983), 192–3, (1984), 163.

[174] On these passages, see text to nn. 223–72 below.

[175] What is the difference? For Everson (1999), 546–7, a materialist 'accepts that all individual substances are composed of matter', whereas physicalism 'must give some sort of priority to the physical over the mental'.

[176] See LS 5; also text to n. 80–1 above.

[177] Epicur. *Ep. Hdt.* 67 (= LS 14 A(7)), discussed below.

'everything that exists, including the psyche, falls under *phusikē*, enquiry into the constituents and structure of the universe'.[178] Can we be more precise about the form of physicalism that Epicurus maintained? Stephen Everson outlines two possibilities, 'ontological' and 'explanatory' physicalism:

> according to [ontological physicalism], mental events are a species of physical event and themselves satisfy physical descriptions. Explanatory physicalism, in contrast, does not require that mental events should be identical with physical events—merely that all events should be explicable by reference to physical events.[179]

Everson argues that, although a case could be made for placing Epicurus in either category, there are good grounds for attributing to him the stronger position of ontological physicalism. Epicurean arguments on a whole series of questions imply not simply that psychological phenomena can be explained in physical terms, but also that they are identical with physical events. They are physical events, in the first instance, because the psyche is a body as well as being a fully integrated part of a body, namely that of an animal. But these physical events can also be explained at a more fundamental level, that of atomic physics. Everson's examples of the latter point include Lucretius' analyses in atomic terms of the psychological characteristics of certain species, of the role of (physical) images in stimulating animal movement, and of the atomic basis of the onset of emotion.[180] Everson also explains in this way the passages in Epicurus' *On Nature* 25 and the theory of the swerve that have, by contrast, sometimes been explained in terms of 'emergent dualism', rather than physicalism.[181]

Everson's account might seem, at first sight, to ascribe to Epicurus the 'reductive' (or eliminative) position of Democritus that there is no reality or truth at the level of phenomenal objects but only at the atomic level.[182] But Everson is not denying that Epicurus thinks that phenomenal objects are real and that there can be true statements about them. The thesis ascribed to Epicurus is not that only atoms are real, or that atoms are more real than phenomenal bodies. Both phenomenal bodies (of which the bodily psyche is a part) and atoms are real, and there can be knowledge of them and true statements about them. But atomic physics offers a more profound or fundamental mode of analysis or explanation, and one in which it is supposed that events at the phenomenal level are identical with events at the atomic

[178] Annas (1992), 3, 'soul' revised to 'psyche'; see also her 2–9.

[179] Everson (1999), 558, cf. 546–50.

[180] Everson (1999), 550–3, referring to Lucr. 3.182–8, 4.877–91, 3.288–93.

[181] Everson (1999), 553–7; see further text to nn. 224–35 below; on the swerve, see 3.5 below, text to nn. 302–11.

[182] Democritus DK fr. B9, discussed in text to nn. 83–6 above.

level.[183] Everson also refers to a further salient feature, which contributes in another way to establishing the non-reductive character of Epicurus' theory. Epicurus rejects explanations which are framed in terms of natural teleology or of what Aristotle would call the 'form' or 'essence' of an object.[184] But this does not mean that, for Epicurus, analysis must be based on the nature of atomic *constituents*. Epicurus also holds that 'certain systems of atoms cannot be understood other than as *systems* of atoms', and that 'one cannot understand the behaviour of certain systems of atoms—i.e. humans—without describing it as the behaviour of a *system*—i.e. of the person—and so as having psychological causes'.[185] I think this is an important insight, and that it enables us to see how Epicurus may hold a physicalist view of human nature and psychology, and may, indeed, be an 'ontological physicialist', and yet still conceive human beings as cohesive and structured psychophysical wholes.

Assuming the validity of this kind of theoretical framework, I consider more closely certain core features of Epicurus' theory. I illustrate first, his physicalism about the psyche, then, his psychophysical holism, and the degree to which this holism involves ideas about psychophysical system or structure. In this respect, I think we can see points of convergence with the Stoic approach, in spite of substantive differences in the overall frameworks. The first point, the physical nature of the psyche, is a straightforward one, and is made emphatically in the relevant section of Epicurus' *Letter to Herodotus* (63–7), of which the closing words are these:

> The 'incorporeal', according to the prevailing usage of the word, is applied to that which can be thought of in itself. But it is impossible to think of the incorporeal in itself except as void. And void can neither act nor be acted upon, but merely provides bodies with motion through itself. Consequently, those who say that the psyche is incorporeal are talking nonsense.[186]

Here, Epicurus brusquely dismisses any form of psyche–body dualism, such as that in Plato's *Phaedo*. The only non-physical entity as such he recognizes is void; and void is simply space through which body moves.[187] Hence, if psyche is said to be non-physical, it must be void—which is certainly not what Plato's

[183] This is, at least, how I understand Everson's conception of ontological physicalism. The position, as so interpreted, can also be described as 'token identity physicalism' (Annas 1993*a*: 58–9, n. 30). For O'Keefe (2002), esp. 158–9, 167, the position outlined here *is* a form of reductionism, to be contrasted with the eliminative materialism of Democritus.

[184] Everson (1999), 549; the rejection of natural teleology is explicit (e.g. Lucr. 4.834–7), that of Aristotelian form is implicit.

[185] Everson (1999), 549 and 557. For a similar suggestion, see O'Keefe (2002), 159–60.

[186] LS 14 A(7), trans. modified (*per se* replaced by 'in itself', twice).

[187] See LS 5, and text to n. 80 above.

Socrates has in mind in the *Phaedo*.[188] It is worth noting that, as in Stoicism, the capacity to act and be acted on is taken as a criterion of independent being and used to support the claim of physicalism.[189]

As so far outlined, Epicurus' position might seem better characterized as monism—physicalism about everything including the psyche. But, here as elsewhere, I think the theory is better understood as holistic. Epicurus' central point is that animals (including humans) constitute psychophysical wholes.[190] The phrasing of the relevant passage (like much of Epicurus' extant writing) is awkward, overemphatic, and has been variously interpreted. However, the stress on psychophysical holism comes over strongly, particularly in von Staden's ultra-literal translation:[191]

> The psyche is a fine-textured body (*sōma*), which is spread along the whole of the aggregate (*athroisma*); [psyche is a body] most similar to breath (*pneuma*) which has a certain blending (*krasin*) of warmth, and [psyche is a body] in one way similar to the former [breath], in another way to the latter [warmth]. But [psyche] is the part (*meros*) [of the whole aggregate] which, by virtue of the fineness of its parts, has acquired a great difference, even from these things themselves [breath and warmth], yet it [the psyche] is liable to co-affection (*sumpathes*), more so with the former [breath], but also with the rest of the aggregate. The capacities of the psyche make all this evident, and so do its affections, mobilities, acts of thinking, and the things deprived of which we die. And we must hold on to [the fact] that the psyche bears the greatest responsibility for sense perception (*aisthēsis*): psyche would not have acquired perception if it were not somehow covered by the rest of the aggregate. The rest of the aggregate, having provided the psyche with this responsibility [for perception], itself in turn acquired from it [the psyche] a share in such an accidental property (*sumptōma*)—though not a share of all the attributes which the psyche has obtained and possesses. For this reason, when the psyche has been removed, it [the rest of the aggregate] does not have perception.

Certain claims emerge clearly, as is widely agreed, though other points are more debated. The first is that the psyche is 'body', *sōma* (material or physical). It follows that the conventional psyche–body contrast must be discarded; and this is duly replaced by a contrast between the psyche, which

[188] On Plato's *Phaedo*, see 1.2 above, text to nn. 6–7.

[189] See text to nn. 54–5 above. Perhaps we should suppose that Epicurus also draws this criterion from Plato, *Sph.* 247d–e, in spite of his generally anti-Platonic stance.

[190] Like the Stoics (but unlike Aristotle, text to n. 124 above), Epicurus does not attribute psyche to plants. By contrast with Stoicism, the claim about animal psychophysicalism is not part of a larger view of the universe as the product of an active and a passive cause.

[191] Epicur. *Ep. Hdt.* 63–4. See von Staden (2000), 81, 85; I have modified his layout, repunctuated, and made other minor changes and omissions, but have mainly used his translation and some of his explanatory glosses in square brackets. For an alternative translation, see LS 14 A(1–4).

is a 'part' (*meros*) of the overall whole and 'the rest of the aggregate' (*athroisma*), the latter being Epicurus' new term for the psychophysical whole. What is also evident is that psychic capacities and functions, such as perception and thinking, and, indeed, life itself, depend on the integration and co-working of the (physical) psyche and the rest of the aggregate.[192] This is conveyed, for instance, by Epicurus' repeated use of 'with-' or *sun*-compounds, such as 'liable to co-affection' (*sumpathes*, 63), 'born together at the same time' (*hama sungegenēmenon*, 64), 'contiguity and co-affection' (*sumpatheia*, 64).[193] It is also conveyed by the point, reiterated in the rest of section 64 of the letter, that functions such as perception are not essential properties of either psyche or the rest of the aggregate but are accidental properties. More precisely, they are *shared* accidental properties, and are shared if and only if the two partners are engaged in the various *shared* activities (indicated in the *sun*-compounds) that make-up psychophysical life.[194] It has often been supposed that the first part of paragraph 63 also refers to the specific kind of material body that constitutes psyche (a 'blend', *krama*, of certain kinds of fine and mobile atom). But von Staden argues, convincingly I think, that in the letter Epicurus' concern is just to assert the physicality of the psyche, and to clarify ways in which this physicality makes the psyche, in different ways, both like and unlike other physical entities.[195] Von Staden is also right, I think, not to see here any reference to 'parts of the psyche' of the kind identified in other sources.[196] The key claim here is simply that psyche and (in conventional terms) body constitute a psychophysical whole or unit, by contrast, for instance, with non-materialist views of psyche of the type dismissed in paragraph 67.

Two other aspects of Epicurean thinking can also be seen as exhibiting holism of a related kind, and as contributing in different ways to the picture of animals as psychophysical wholes. These are points which also involve the idea of a psychophysical system or structure, a feature which the theory has in common with Stoicism. The first point relates to the atomic basis of the distinctive character of the psyche, characterized in one source

[192] 'Without the body, the psyche no longer exists or functions as psyche, but is just scattered atoms; without the psyche, the body no longer exists or functions as a body, but is a mere corpse', Annas (1992), 149, 'soul' modified to 'psyche'.

[193] The first of these cases refers to the linkage between psyche and *pneuma*, but also to the linkage with 'the rest of the aggregate', as do the other two cases.

[194] See also von Staden (2000), 86–7; on 'essential' and 'accidental' properties, see Epicur. *Ep. Hdt.* 68–73, Lucr. 1.445–82.

[195] See von Staden (2000), 80–6; contrast Kerferd (1971), 84–92; Annas (1992), 137–8. The passage seems to allude to the claims made elsewhere about the composition of the psyche (similarity to warmth and breath, fineness); but this is not the point at issue here.

[196] See also Kerferd's view (1971: 92–6).

(Aëtius 4.3.11 = LS 14 C) as: 'a blend (*krama*) consisting of four things, of which one is fire-like, one air-like, one wind-like, while the fourth is something which lacks a name... The wind... produces movement in us, the air produces rest, the hot one produces the evident heat of the body, and the unnamed one produces sensation in us'. The move of positing a specific type of atomic basis for psychological functions has sometimes been seen as theoretically primitive. It has been compared unfavourably with the move, also found in Epicureanism, of explaining features of the phenomenal world by the combination or interaction of atoms which do not correspond in a direct way to the phenomena explained.[197] But the former move has other parallels in the theory, and this feature supports Everson's characterization of Epicureanism as 'ontological' and not just 'explanatory' physicalism.[198] Also, what is envisaged is not just one-for-one equivalence between atom-type and psychological feature, though this is also part of the theory.[199] There is also the idea that the psyche consists of a distinctive kind of blend or mixture (*krama*) of exceptionally mobile or warm atoms. The blend creates a special type of complex unity and, to some degree, a kind of system or structure; and it is this complex synthesis that enables complex psychophysical functions, such as sensation. Lucretius, in particular, clarifies this dimension of the theory:

> The primary particles of the elements so interpenetrate each other in their motions that no one element can be distinguished and no capacity spatially separated, but they exist as multiple powers of a single body (*unius corporis*)... heat, air and the unseen force of wind when mixed form a single nature (*unam naturam*), along with that mobile power [the unnamed fourth element] which transmits the beginning of motion from itself to them, the origin of sense-bearing motions through the flesh.[200]

It is the completeness of the blend of these specific atomic types that enables this relatively advanced capacity. The distinctive role of the—otherwise rather mysterious—fourth element is, indeed, to enable this cohesive unity. Lucretius compares the role of the psyche as a whole, though invisible, in permeating and animating the body and the role of the fourth element in permeating and unifying the psyche. The fourth element is, in this sense,

[197] See e.g. Sharples (1991–3), 189–90; Hankinson (1999), 501–2; Warren (2002), 69–71. Warren suggests Epicurus may have been influenced by Democritus' reported view that thought depends on a 'mixture' (*krasis*) in the body, 67–9, and that, in this respect, Epicurus did not emancipate himself sufficiently from Democritus' more reductive approach (on which, see 1.3 above, text to nn. 83–6).

[198] See text to n. 179 above.

[199] For one-to-one correlations between dominant atom-types in the psychophysical make-up and the character-types of animal species, see Lucr. 3. 288–306 (= LS 14 D(4)).

[200] Lucr. 3. 262–5, 268–72 (LS 14 D(1)), cf. 282–7 (LS 14 D(3)).

'the psyche of the psyche' (*anima animae*), although, as Lucretius twice reminds us, it is physical and operates on and through the body.[201]

The appeal to a nameless element based on no empirical evidence has sometimes been seen as a weakness in the theory. But Julia Annas (1992: 139–40) argues that it is consistent with Epicurus' physicalist approach to psychology to hypothesize a physical explanation for the distinctive qualities of sensation and other psychological processes. Also, as I have suggested, this feature fits in with the generally holistic approach of Epicurean (and Stoic) theory. Just as advanced and complex functions such as sensation and thought are explained by reference to the *integration* of psyche and body, creating what is, in effect, *one* synthesized whole, so a special role in enabling this process is allocated to an element within the psyche, whose function is that of *integrating* the psychic atom-types, and producing what Lucretius calls 'a single nature'.[202] The style of explanation, then, is to identify what gives a complex whole its wholeness and cohesion, and hence what enables sophisticated types of activity. There is a sharp contrast with the type of thinking found in Plato and Aristotle, for instance, in which advanced functions such as thought are attributed to some part, core, or essence of the person, which is also sometimes treated as virtually or actually separate from the person, and as 'divine' or 'external'.[203]

Epicurean thinking about the organization of psychological functions within the body also, I think, expresses a similar pattern of thought. At first sight, the Epicurean picture seems to be contrasted with the Stoic and to be closer to Platonic–Aristotelian thinking because we are told, in some sources, that Epicureans subdivide the psyche into 'rational' and 'irrational' parts (*logikon* and *alogon*). But Lucretius may reflect more accurately the main emphasis in this aspect of Epicurean theory. Although there are two psychological entities, *animus* and *anima*, 'mind' and 'spirit', Lucretius stresses, first, that they operate in a closely interconnected way and, second, that they are bodily entities and are fully integrated with (the rest of) the body:

the mind and spirit are firmly interlinked and constitute a single nature (*unam naturam*), but the deliberative part which we call the mind is, as it were, the chief, and holds sway throughout the body. It is firmly located in the central part of the

[201] Lucr. 3.273–81 (LS 14 D(2)), noting the repeated 'in the whole body', *corpore toto*, 276, 281.

[202] For this analogy, and the phrase cited, see the Lucretius passage cited in the preceding paragraph.

[203] See 1.2 above. The fact that the Middle Platonist Plutarch treats the fourth element as the source of reasoning and emotion (i.e. the functions of the *animus*) may reflect an inappropriately part-based reading of the Epicurean conception of psychic blend. See *Mor.* 1118 D (=Usener 314), also Kerferd (1971), 84–5, and, for similar (inappropriate) ways of reading Stoic or Epicurean theories, see 2.3 below, text to nn. 201–2, 3.4, text to nn. 191–2.

chest. For that is where fear and dread leap up, and where joys caress us; therefore it is where the mind is. The remaining part of the psyche [i.e. the spirit], which is distributed throughout the body, obeys the mind and moves at its beck and call.[204]

Although, as Lucretius goes on to explain, the *animus* sometimes has thoughts or emotions which do not affect the *anima* or the body, the main thrust of his account is on the interconnection of 'mind and spirit'—typically characterized as a linked pair—and body. Thus, for instance, when the *animus* experiences intense fear, the *anima* 'shares the feeling' (*consentire*), thus producing powerful psychophysical effects such as simultaneous pallor and sweating. Both actions initiated by the *animus* (which produce cooperative responses from the *anima* and body) and physical states such as being wounded (which have an impact on the *animus*) show the fundamental integration of the *animus–anima* complex with the body (that is, the *rest* of the body).[205] Lucretius' statement that the two psychic parts make up 'a single nature' (*unam naturam*) anticipates his later claim that the four types of psychic atom do the same,[206] and indicates that the same type of holistic thinking is operative in analogous ways as regards these two aspects of the theory.

I suggested earlier that these features of Epicurean thinking, as well as conveying the thought that living creatures are psychophysical wholes, also express the idea that these wholes constitute systems or structures. There are a series of ways—different in type but cumulative in effect—in which this idea manifests itself. One, noted already, is that the four types of psychic atom form a unified nexus or 'blend' (*krama*). Another is the point, just illustrated, that the *animus–anima* complex forms a psychological system which is integrated with physiology and physical functioning. Related themes, noted earlier, are that natural kinds are reproduced from their own (biological) 'seeds' and that the survival of specific kinds over time reflects the fitness and coherence of their bodily make-up.[207] A further related point is that natural kinds have certain stable kinds of temperament, reflecting the predominant

[204] Lucr. 3. 136–44 (=LS 14 B(1)), trans. slightly modified. I take it that, in the phrase translated as 'the remaining part of the psyche', Lucretius is using *anima* to mean the whole of the psyche (i.e. the equivalent of the Greek term, *psuchē*), a usage he explains in 3. 421–4 (=LS 14 F(1)); 'the remaining part' signifies *anima* in the narrow sense, i.e. 'spirit'.

[205] Lucr. 3. 145–76 (= LS 14 B(2–3)), esp. *consentire* (153), 'the spirit is interlinked (*coniunctam*) with the mind' (159), 'the nature of the mind and spirit [is] corporeal' (161–2), 'mind and spirit are constituted (*constare*) with a corporeal nature', 166–7, 'the mind is affected jointly with (*consentire*) the body, 169, also 175–6. Cf. the *con*-compounds with the *sun*-compounds (body and psyche) in Epicur. *Ep. Hdt.* 63–4.

[206] Lucr. 3. 270; cf. text to n. 200 above.

[207] See text to nn. 92–3 above. The idea that the fit species which survive are physiologically coherent is implied by the *incoherence* of the species which die out (Lucr. 5.837–48, = LS 13 I (1)).

atomic type (within the overall psychic blend) in each species.[208] Most suggestive of all—and what Everson has most in mind in talking of '*systems* of atoms'—is the thought that adult human beings constitute complex psychological (and also psychophysical) structures, in which advanced capacities such as that for taking responsibility for their actions represent 'developments' in their original atomic (psychophysical) 'constitution' (*sustasis*). The implications of the last—more complicated—idea I take up in considering Epicurean thinking in general about advanced psychological functions (which are also advanced forms of psychophysical wholeness).[209] But I want to signal here that the last motif represents one of a series of different ways in which the idea of animals as psychophysical wholes is combined with the idea of them as systems or structures (at a basic level, systems of atoms).

What do the Epicurean and Stoic theories, as so far examined here, have in common to justify the claim that they share, or converge on, psychophysical holism? Both theories are physicalist in the sense that they maintain that all independently real objects, including the psyche, are physical, and, indeed, are material objects or 'bodies'.[210] For the Stoics, the relevant form of physical existence is that which derives from the 'total blending' of *pneuma* (as active cause) and matter, a principle which applies to all organic and inorganic objects and not just animals. There is no exact equivalent for this general principle in Epicureanism, though there are some suggestive analogues regarding the specific question of the psyche–body relationship. On the face of it, the thought that the four types of psychic atom constitute a unified 'blend' might seem close to the Stoic idea of 'complete blending'. However, the Epicurean theme is more narrowly conceived; a closer parallel with the Stoic principle is the Epicurean thesis that psyche and body are thoroughly integrated in their workings.[211]

[208] Lucr. 3. 282–306 (= LS 14 D(3–4)).

[209] See text to nn. 240–6 below; also 2.3 below. esp. text to nn. 124–30.

[210] See text to nn. 54–5 and 80–6 above. The Stoics also explicitly recognize a category of 'incorporeals' (place, void, time, and *lekta*, i.e. 'the content of rational impressions' (D.L. 7.63) which are 'an ineliminable part of the world's structure' (Sedley 1999*a*: 402). Also, god considered in abstraction 'is an intelligent energizing power' (LS i. 278). These features of Stoic thought about the properties of real objects might be seen as comparable with the non-material 'emergent properties' of the (material) psyche posited by Sedley (1983, 1988). (I owe this suggestion to David Sedley). However, Sedley also recognizes that '[o]nly bodies have "being"' in Stoicism' (1999*a*: 395) and that the idea of abstracting god from matter is, in reality, 'an impossibility' (LS i. 278). In the following discussion, I assume that the Stoic–Epicurean physicalism is of a type that rules out emergent dualism (even of properties of psyche), but I acknowledge that a different and more inclusive view of Stoic–Epicurean physicalism (or psychophysicalism) could be maintained.

[211] On the points noted in this para., see 1.4 above, text to nn. 110–14, and text to nn. 197–203 above. Note also the use of 'with-compounds' (*sun-* or *con-*compounds) in text to nn. 190–6 above to convey the idea of psyche–body integration.

There are also striking parallels as regards the way the psychic functions are correlated with physiology and bodily operations. The Epicurean *animus*, like the Stoic *hēgemonikon*, is the seat both of emotions and reasoning,[212] and it is located in the heart, partly because of the longstanding linkage between that organ and emotion. Just as the Stoic *hēgemonikon* is conceived as the central locus of a nexus of functions (including sensation), operating like an octopus with tentacles, so the *animus* is the organizing agency, while the *anima* operates throughout the body, though normally in conjunction with the *animus*.[213] Indeed, in this respect, both the Stoic and the Epicurean models resemble the psycho-physiological system as presented by Alexandrian medicine, based on the combination of a central directive agency (the brain) and a communication-system running through the body (central nervous system).[214] Epicurean and Stoic thinking on this topic was, of course, in its main lines, formulated *before* these Alexandrian discoveries, although there is evidence that later members of the schools were aware of them.[215] But the idea of a unified, heart-centred psychophysical pattern correlated with physiology was already well articulated by Greek medicine, notably Praxagoras, by the end of the fourth century.[216] Indeed, the idea of a coordinated psychological and physiological system was a prominent feature of Plato's *Timaeus*, though linked with a part-based model of the psyche.[217] So the similarities between the Epicurean, Stoic, and Alexandrian models probably reflect the converging outcome of physicalist (more precisely, psychophysicalist) thinking about the body and psychic processes, rather than direct influences between these theories.

I have just highlighted a series of ways in which Epicurean thought, as well as expressing psychophysical holism, also conveys the thought that living creatures, especially human beings, constitute more or less complex psychophysical systems or structures. Some of those ideas have clear parallels in Stoicism, including, of course, the idea that the embodied psyche represents

212 Lucr. 3.140–2: *because* emotions are present here, it is *therefore* (*ergo*) to be understood as the seat of reasoning and mind (*mens animusque*) (= LS 14 B(1)), cited at text to n. 204 above.

213 See further (Stoic model), text to nn. 118–19, 204–6 above. One point of localized contrast is that the Stoic *hēgemonikon* is involved in sensation (though the five senses also constitute, in some sense, distinct parts of the psyche, LS 53 G–H), whereas sensation seems to be the work of the Epicurean *anima*, rather than the *animus*. See text to nn. 149–51 above, also Lucr. 3.350–69.

214 See von Staden (2000), 87–96.

215 On possible influence on Chrysippus, see von Staden (2000), 102–5, and on indications of later Epicurean awareness of these discoveries, Annas (1992), 145. On Lucretius' startling neglect of these innovations and of the debate they generated, see Lucr. 3.788–93 = 5.132–7, and Sedley (1998*a*), 68–72.

216 See Annas (1992), 20–6.

217 Pl. *Ti.* 69–72; also Gill (1997*a*), and 299–304 below.

an anatomically based system.[218] The Stoics also maintain in a much stronger form than the Epicureans (reflecting their conviction about natural teleology) the idea that natural kinds are coherent and functionally effective psychophysical structures.[219] Also, as illustrated later, the Stoics also believe that adult humans develop in a way that leads them to embody complex psychological (and also psychophysical) structures, through the development of advanced capacities, notably that of rational agency.[220] Indeed, the whole idea of 'structure' (as order or system) is much more explicit in Stoicism than Epicureanism at virtually every level of their thinking on this subject.[221] One manifestation of this tendency already noted is the idea that all entities consist of a structure produced by varying degrees of 'tension' in the operation of *pneuma* on matter, an idea which has no obvious analogue in Epicureanism.[222] However, the idea of animals as not only psychophysical wholes but also psychophysical systems or structures has a firm place in Epicurean as well as Stoic thought. More broadly, the pattern of thinking about human personality I am seeking to analyse here (in Epicurean and Stoic thought) can, in a number of ways, be conceived as 'structure-centred' (as well as holistic), by contrast with the core-centred or part-based thinking found in, for instance, Plato, Aristotle, and Middle Platonic thinking.

In illustrating Stoic thinking about psychophysical holism, I have considered certain discussions, by Hierocles and Seneca, of animal (including human) development. Similarly, I think that Epicurean thinking about psychophysical holism is illustrated by his view of animal and human development, notably in certain passages from Epicurus' *On Nature* 25. The situation is complicated by the fact that the relevant texts, while widely recognized as important evidence, are poorly preserved and difficult to interpret.[223] David Sedley, who contributed greatly to making these texts accessible for modern scholarly discussion,[224] saw them as expressing 'emergent dualism', as regards the properties of psyche. Subsequent scholars have tended to be sceptical of that view, and have seen the passages as expressing

218 See text to nn. 119–21 above.

219 See text to nn. 45–6 above (also LS 54, especially P), and nn. 92–3 above.

220 See 3.2–3 below.

221 See e.g. Cic. *Fin.* 3.74, on their philosophical system as an ordered structure, and White (1979), 156–7, on cosmic, social, and ethical order or structure in Stoicism.

222 See text to nn. 110–14 above. Epicurean *pneuma*, also, is 'breath' and not a universal 'active cause'.

223 For extracts, see LS 20 B–C (also 20 j in vol. ii); also Arrighetti (1973), sect. 34. The attribution to Book 25 was made in Laursen (1987).

224 On earlier study of the texts, see Sedley (1983), 16–18. Sedley (1983) gives a text, translation, and detailed analysis, a process taken further by Laursen (1987), (1988), (1995), (1998).

the kind of systematic physicalism that is taken to be characteristic of Epicureanism,[225] an interpretation I follow. The subject has been intensively debated, and there is no need to re-examine the issues in detail. But it is worthwhile outlining the debate and restating the basis for the physicalist reading, which I take to support the claim made here that Epicurus' thinking on development displays psychophysical holism.

Certain features of Epicurus' discussion are both clear and widely agreed. Epicurus asserts that human beings are properly held responsible for their actions because of the way they develop, in contrast to (wild) non-human animals. He argues, specifically, against those who maintain that human action is constrained by necessity in a way that undermines responsibility. A crucial part of the argument consists in showing that the opposing (determinist) position is self-contradictory, because arguing for a philosophical position amounts to making a stand for which one takes responsibility.[226] Sedley suggests, plausibly, that the main, though implicit, target of Epicurus is certain post-Democritean thinkers, who suppose that human actions are determined by physical (atomic) causes in a way that negates responsibility.[227] This (post-Democritean) view seems to be an inference from Democritus' reductionist thesis that 'in truth', by contrast with 'convention', there are only atoms and void.[228] However, much more controversial is Sedley's claim that Epicurus' anti-reductionism involves emergent dualism as regards psychic properties.

Some of the salient interpretative issues come out in these two passages:

From the very outset we always have seeds directing us towards these, some towards those, some towards these *and* those, actions and thoughts and characters, in greater and smaller numbers. Consequently, that which we develop—characteristics of this or that kind—is at first absolutely because of us; and the things which of necessity flow in through our passages from that which surrounds us at one point come to be because of us and because of the beliefs of ours which are from us ourselves.[229]

Many [developments] which have a nature which is capable of becoming productive of both this and that through themselves do not become productive, and it is not

[225] See e.g. Laursen (1988); Annas (1993*a*); Sharples (1991–3), 183–7; Hankinson (1998), 226–32; Purinton (1999), 285–94; Bobzien (2000); O'Keefe (2002). However, von Staden signals support for Sedley's view in (2000), 86 n. 11.

[226] See LS 20 C(3–12); on this 'self-refutation' strategy, see Sedley (1983), 25–7.

[227] See Sedley (1983), 29–36; see further on the post-Democritean tradition and Epicurean responses, Warren (2002), esp. 193–200.

[228] See DK fr. B 9, discussed in 24 above. See further Annas (1991), 86–8; Everson (1999), 556–7. O'Keefe (2002), 167–71, argues that the position rejected by Epicurus is eliminative rather than reductive.

[229] LS 20 C(1), *On Nature* 34.26 Arrighetti (1973). Trans. as in LS, but modified at various points in line with Bobzien (2000), 297.

because of the same cause in the atoms and in themselves. These in particular we combat and rebuke... in accordance with their nature which is disturbed from the beginning, as is true of all animals. For in their case the nature of the atoms has contributed nothing to some of their actions, and to the extent of their actions and dispositions, but the developments themselves contain all or most of the cause of some of these things. As a result of that nature some of the atoms' motions are moved in a disturbed way, not in every way through the atoms, but through what enters... from the environment into the natural... combating and advising many people together, which is opposed to the necessary cause of the same kind. Thus when something develops which has some distinctness among the atoms in a differential way, which is not like that from a different distance, it acquires a cause from itself, then transmits it at once to the primary natures and in some way makes all of it one.[230]

A marked feature of these and related passages is the claim that 'we ourselves' or the 'developments' (*apogegenēmena*) play a significant role as causes. A connected feature is a contrast between 'we' or 'developments', on the one hand, and 'atoms' (or 'the nature of the atoms') or 'nature' (or 'original constitution'), on the other.[231] What larger picture of human nature and reality is implied in this contrast? Sedley argues for what is sometimes called 'emergent dualism'. Given a certain level of material complexity, mental capacities 'emerge', which are distinct in kind from, and causally independent of, the material make-up of the entity concerned.[232] The contrasts noted earlier are taken to imply that 'self-determining animals (including humans)' develop 'selves which are *not* identical with their constituent atoms'. 'The self becomes responsible as soon as the animal develops a certain type of characteristic over and above his atomic make-up'; 'In Epicurus' view matter in certain complex states can take on non-physical qualities which in turn bring genuinely new behavioural laws into operation'.[233] The final sentence of the second passage cited earlier, rather differently translated, was taken by Sedley as especially significant. The development was taken to embody a radical (even 'transcendental') distinctness from the atomic basis.[234] But the development was also seen as having a decisive impact on the atomic make-up (the 'primary substances'), an impact some-

[230] LS 20 B(6–7), *On Nature* 34.21–2 Arrighetti (1973). Translation as in Annas (1993*a*), 56–7; for differences from the translation in LS, based partly on the readings of Laursen (1988), cf. (1998), see Annas's footnotes; on some important differences, see nn. 234, 240, 244–5, 253 below.

[231] See further Annas (1993*a*), 57–8.

[232] On different senses of 'emergence', see Asmis (1990), 290–1; also Warren (2002), 196–7, n. 13.

[233] Quotations from Sedley (1983), 38–9. Sedley (1988), 321–2, speaks of 'radically *emergent* properties' (his italics) and suggests that, according to Epicurus, 'matter can ... acquire entirely new, non-physical properties, not governed by the laws of physics'. See also LS i. 110.

[234] Sedley (1983: 37) translates: 'thus when a development occurs which takes on some distinctness from the atoms in a transcendent way [literally, 'separative' or 'discriminating',

times characterized as 'downwards causation', taken to mean that mental events have causal effectiveness at the atomic level.[235]

Sedley's view has been criticized on three, related grounds. It has been argued that the relevant passages are too uncertain in their textual readings and interpretation to support such a radical thesis.[236] It has been doubted that Epicurus could have introduced a major breach in his characteristic physicalism without this arousing ancient comment and criticism.[237] It is claimed that the theory can be more plausibly analysed in different terms. Annas, for instance, suggests that, of modern types of theory, 'token identity physicalism' is a more likely candidate: that is, the theory according to which every single mental event is identical with a single physical event.[238] It has also been maintained that the features of the passages taken by Sedley to show emergent dualism can be more plausibly interpreted in physicalist terms,[239] a line of interpretation adopted in the following analysis.

For instance, the contrasts noted earlier can be understood as identifying different aspects within the developing human (or animal), understood as a psychophysical whole, rather than between emergent mental states or properties and the atomic or physical make-up. The main point is to highlight the difference between the developing personality and the *original* or *earlier* nature or state. The original nature may be characterized as 'the atoms' (or 'nature of the atoms') or 'constitution', rather than 'developments' or what is 'from us',[240] even though those latter features are also instantiations of our

dialēptikon] ... he acquires responsibility which proceeds from himself; then he straightaway transmits it to his primary substances and makes the whole of it into a yardstick' (cf. LS 20 B(5)). Note also Sedley's translation of *heterotēta tōn atomōn*, 'distinctness from the atoms'; for an alternative, 'distinctness among the atoms', see n. 244 below. For a different reading or interpretation of the phrases translated by Sedley as 'primary substances' (i.e. atoms) and 'into a yardstick', see n. 245 below.

[235] On 'downwards causation', see Sedley (1988), 316–24. See further Warren (2002), 196, with references to previous discussions; also text to n. 246 below.

[236] See e.g. Everson (1999), 555.

[237] See e.g. Annas (1993*a*), 59 n. 30, point (2). However, Sedley (1983), 49–51, takes Cic. *de Fato* 23–5 as evidence that Carneades recognized that the Epicurean analysis of voluntariness involves autonomous (i.e. physically uncaused) movements. (Carneades' criticism is not directed at this analysis but at the Epicurean move, which he sees as unnecessary, of positing an atomic swerve.) On the swerve, which represents a breach in normal causation (though not in physicalism) see 3.5 below, text to nn. 302–11.

[238] Annas (1993*a*), 58–9 n. 30, point (1). On modern categories including token materialism, see Irwin (1991*b*), 57. See also the discussion of 'ontological physicalism', text to nn. 179–81 above.

[239] See references in n. 225 above. The following discussion draws especially on Annas (1993*a*) and Bobzien (2000).

[240] On this translation of *para hēmas*, see Annas (1991), 90, and Bobzien (2000), 293–8. The more common translation is 'up to us', but this might be taken to imply (what Bobzien) calls the 'independent-decision-faculty' model, on which see text to nn. 265–6 below.

atomic make-up or constitution. More precisely, the passages cited earlier, together with some others, can be taken as challenging the claim that human beings are appropriately exempted from responsibility for the moral quality of their actions and character because of the necessity imposed on them by their inborn nature or socially given upbringing. Hence, as it is put in another passage, 'we [appropriately] rebuke, oppose and reform each other as if the responsibility lay also in ourselves and not just in our congenital make-up [or constitution, *sustasis*] and in the accidental necessity of that which surrounds and penetrates us' (LS 20 C(2)). Similarly, in the first passage cited earlier (LS 20 C(1)), the main point is to stress that the way we develop is 'from us' (*para hēmas*), and that we respond to environmental factors ('the things that of necessity flow in through our passages from that which surrounds us') because of our existing belief-set at any one time ('the beliefs from us which are from us ourselves').

The second, longer passage cited earlier[241] can also be seen as centring on the importance of holding people responsible for the quality of their actions and character and not allowing them (or others) to negate this responsibility by attributing it to their congenital nature. This underlies the recurrent contrast between 'themselves' or 'the development', on the one hand, and 'the atoms' or 'the nature of the atoms' or 'that nature', on the other. The situation involved is one in which someone has a 'nature which is disturbed from the beginning', who will therefore find it more difficult to develop properly. None the less, in the case of such people, 'the nature of the atoms [that is, the congenital make-up] has contributed nothing to some of their actions ... but the developments themselves contain all or most of the cause of some of these things'.[242] In the following sentence, environmental factors *are* cited as a contributory factor promoting the disturbed behaviour.[243] But the decisive factor is again identified as being 'when something develops which has some distinctness among the atoms in a differential way'.[244] This development consists in the person choosing one or other action or way of life out of those made possible by the congenital or environmentally shaped character. The developing person 'acquires a cause from itself' which it transmits to the 'primary natures' (pre-existing natural traits) and makes all this into 'one', or

[241] LS 20 B(6–7), but cited in Annas's trans.; see n. 230 above.

[242] LS 20 B(3), trans. Annas (1993*a*), 56, cited above; the LS translation of this passage is similar. On this point, see also O'Keefe (2002), 180–2.

[243] See 'through what enters ... from the environment into the natural'; there is then a lacuna of about 20 words before the words 'combating and advising', which (I take it) refer to attempts by others to counteract the emerging pattern of 'disturbed' behaviour; cf. 'we combat and rebuke', earlier in the passage (LS 20 B(2)).

[244] For this way of understanding *heterōtēta tōn atomōn*, see Laursen (1988), 12–13; Annas (1993*a*), 56; Purinton (1999), 290–4; O'Keefe (2002), 173–6.

a cohesive character.[245] Hence, if the passage involves 'downwards causation', this is best understood as the process by which we (as psychophysical wholes) shape our pre-existing characters by thought and conscious effort, rather than as an exercise of purely mental causation on our physical make-up.[246]

In interpreting Epicurus' line of thought, a relevant fact, as Annas emphasizes (1993*a*: 65–70), is Epicurean thinking about the differences—and partial similarities—between humans and non-human animals. Often, in ancient philosophy, a sharp contrast is drawn between human and animal minds, with 'reason' used as the main point of demarcation.[247] Although this contrast can be found in at least one Epicurean source,[248] it is also sometimes made in a nuanced form, allowing some rational capacities to at least some non-human animals.[249] It is consistent with the latter, broader, view that the main distinction in Epicurus' *On Nature* 25, and also in Lucretius, seems to be between wild and tame animals, even though the prime example of tame animals is that of human beings or 'us'.[250] The Epicurean concern, we might say, is with agency, and, in so far as tame animals exhibit agency—notably, in Lucretius' use of a horse as his example of 'free will' (*libera uoluntas*) and the initiation of motion—[251] they can count as agents too.

Hence, wild animals are presented as predisposed by their congenital species-specific nature to certain types of emotional reaction such as anger or timidity.[252] In their case, 'we excuse wild animals, weaving together their developments similarly with the constitution into one thing, but not using either the way of advising or reforming'. In the case of tame animals (including, of course, human beings), even if we abuse them, we do so as a means of advice, particularly if their chosen course of action 'is similar to the original

245 There are two differences from Sedley's interpretation of this passage (n. 234 above). (1) *prōtōn phuseōn*, 'first natures', is taken to mean the original or pre-existing character, rather than the atoms; (2) Laursen's reading (1988: 9) *mian pōs hapasan* is adopted instead of Sedley's *kanona pasan*. The overall idea is that the agent, as part of character-development, integrates ('makes one') her pre-existing and developed characteristics. However, even if 'first natures' is taken to mean 'atoms', the process of character-shaping can still be conceived without positing dualism. See further Laursen (1988), 15–16; Bobzien (2000), 326–7; O'Keefe (2002), 176–9.

246 See further Sharples (1991–3), 183–7, and references in n. 245 above.

247 This is so in Stoic thought (at least, between adult humans and non-human animals). See Inwood (1985), 72–5, 79–80, 187–95; Gill (1991), 184–92; see further Sorabji (1993), part 1, esp. 7–16, 20–8.

248 See e.g. Hermarchus, cited by Porphyry, *On Abstinence* 1.10.1–12.7 (LS 22 N, esp. (10)).

249 Animals in some sense recognize (*sunoran*), but do not understand, concepts such as healthy and expedient; see Annas (1993*a*), 68–9, citing Polystratus, *On Irrational Contempt for Popular Opinions* 7.6–8

250 For the tame–wild contrast, see e.g. Lucr. 1.15, 163, 2.343, 921, 1081–3; also LS 20 j, discussed below.

251 Lucr. 2.251–93 (LS 20 F), esp. 256–7, 263–76.

252 Lucr. 3.288–322; see further Annas (1993*a*), 66; Bobzien (2000), 325.

constitution when this is bad'.[253] Both of the longer fragments from *On Nature* 25 (LS 20 B, C) underline the fact that 'they' or 'we' (mainly or wholly human beings) have an in-built capacity to develop in more than one possible way, a capacity that is, presumably, derived from our, relatively complex, atomic structure.[254] Epicurus does not explicate what this capacity consists in. But the reference to 'beliefs that come from ourselves' makes it natural to connect this capacity with that for belief-formation and to link this in turn with the (partial) contrast drawn elsewhere between humans and animals concerning the understanding of concepts.[255] Again, the possession by human beings of more advanced rational functions, enabling scope for variation from our inborn or environmentally shaped inclinations, can be conceived as a property of relatively complex physical or psychophysical units in a way that does not require the hypothesis of the emergence of non-physical properties.[256]

The evidence so far summarized might be taken as showing that these Epicurean passages *can* be interpreted in physicalist terms, rather than those of emergent dualism, but not, perhaps, that they *must* be so interpreted. Are there considerations which justify drawing that further inference? In general, as we have already seen, Epicurus' claim that the psyche is 'body' and, indeed, has an atomic basis is explicit and unequivocal.[257] Lucretius, in a poem whose close dependence on Epicurus' *On Nature* has been brought out by Sedley, devotes one entire book out of six to a sustained argument for psychophysical unity or holism.[258] Against that background, any qualification of physicalism would surely need to be explicated and justified more fully than is the case in the passages from *On Nature* cited by Sedley. In addition, certain other texts noted by Annas and Bobzien point more positively towards psychophysical unity. For instance, one passage presents memory as a causally effective factor (which 'brings about some things at once and increases others') on three kinds of 'primary constitution'. These are that of '(1) the atoms and at the same time of (2) what has been developed, and in another way to (3) [the

[253] LS 20 j (LS vol. ii only), trans. Annas (1993*a*), 61, following Laursen (1988), 17. Cf. LS 20 B(2), where the possession of a disturbed nature 'from the beginning' is ascribed to 'all animals' (presumably, all wild ones).

[254] See the first sentences of LS 20 B(1) and C(1), the two passages cited above from *On Nature* 25.

[255] For this (partial) contrast, see n. 249 above. This capacity for belief-formation underlies the ability of humans (but not wild animals) to counteract to a considerable degree their natural defective inclinations by reason (*ratio*), Lucr. 3. 307–22, esp. 307–9, 321.

[256] For this point, see O'Keefe (2002), 163–5.

[257] See especially LS 14 A, discussed in text to nn. 186–96 above. For a brief response to this point, see Sedley (1988), 325–6.

[258] See e.g. Lucr. 3. 136–76 (LS 14 B), 417–62 (LS 14 F). On the influence of *On Nature* on Lucretius' poem, see Sedley (1998*a*), esp. ch. 5.

constitution] when it has been increased, by which we do all our actions'. Although it is difficult to determine the precise significance of this threefold typology, the fact that memory (or 'a motion analogous to memory') is operative in all three types or stages of our constitution suggests that these are being treated as on the same level of being rather than as ontologically distinct (that is, physical or mental).[259]

A second passage on the kind of necessity involved in development points in the same direction. The passage is complex and hard to interpret; its gist is summarized by Susanne Bobzien in these terms:

> That an individual develops a soul and that that soul has a disposition and motion of a particular size are necessary. But the specific qualities of that soul and its specific developments *when it (or the person whose soul it is) advances in age* are not internally necessitated. Rather, *when the soul... advances in age*, it will be able to develop from itself, or from the cause from itself.[260]

The passage is similar in theme to those cited earlier from *On Nature* 25 (LS 20 B and C(1)). It centres on the idea that, whatever kinds of compulsion or necessity are operative in our development from our 'first constitution', they still allow scope for the developing person to act as a cause 'from itself'. The main contrast here is between the 'first constitution' and the developing 'soul'. But there is no suggestion here that the first constitution is atomic whereas the developing soul is an (emergent) non-atomic entity; the different factors are all treated as in the same category of being. This reinforces the claim that in the other passages too (LS 20B and C(1)), the contrast is between factors in development which are of the same ontological type, rather than being differentiated as atomic and (emergent) mental entities. It also supports the idea that the 'downwards causation' in LS 20 B(5) is that exercised by the developing self on her character as a whole, rather than that of mental on physical nature.[261]

[259] 34.20.6–14 Arrighetti (1973), trans. Annas (1993*a*), 60, numbers added; see also Laursen (1988), 10–11. Presumably, these three factors are either what is sometimes called 'person-stages' (memory or quasi-memory is operative over time) or three levels or aspects of the person at any one time. The latter reading might be supported by 34.11, Arrighetti (1973), cited by Annas (1993*a*), 59–60, and taken to illustrate the idea that we can talk about a person, at any one time, *qua* (*hē*(*i*)) atoms or *qua* mover or agent. As Annas underlines (1993*a*: 60–1), 34.20. 6–14 links the atomic and developing constitution more closely with each other than with that which is 'increased', thus counteracting the idea that the first two factors (atoms and agent) are substantially different in kind from each other.

[260] Bobzien (2000), 324, her italics, summarizing another passage from *On Nature* 25, 34.24 Arrighetti (1973), cited with text and translation. Her translation is based on that of Laursen (1998), 51–2; see also Annas (1993*a*), 60.

[261] See text to n. 246 above.

These passages, taken in the light of Epicurus' general position, give force to the claim that the implied conception of human nature is that of a psychophysical unit (on an assumption of ontological physicalism).[262] As so interpreted, these texts can help us to define more precisely the kind of unity or holism involved in the Epicurean conception of person or self. Annas notes the tendency for the terms 'us' and 'developments' to be used interchangeably and to be presented as the effective cause of our actions.[263] What underlies this usage is the thesis that it is *as a developing agent* that I (by contrast with a wild animal) am properly treated as responsible for my actions and character. What is also implied is a certain conception of what is, in a certain sense, 'personal identity'. As Annas puts it: 'I am the whole person, then, and have a development; but I can be said to *be* that development, just insofar as I am thought of as developing'. She explains in a similar way the analysis of human agents (or 'us') in terms of the combination of the atomic constitution, on the one hand, and the development, on the other: 'to explain what *I* am we need to refer not just to my having an atomic constitution but to the fact that my atomic constitution can develop—an agent, in fact'.[264] Both comments underline that Epicurus has in view a conception of the human being as a unified psychological—and psychophysical—agent or entity even though he is also identifying various factors by which to define the status of the human being as a cause and bearer of responsibility.

The implied idea of human identity or personality is further explicated by Bobzien through a distinction she draws between two conceptions of agency: the 'independent-decision-faculty model' and the 'whole-person' model. Characteristic of the first model is the idea that 'I', 'the one who decides [is] causally detached not only from external impacts, but also from my past experiences, from my present character and dispositions, from my desires and inclinations, perhaps even from my memories and factual beliefs'. She associates this model with the kind of 'indeterminism' according to which 'I can be held morally responsible for an action of mine only... if I was free to decide or choose otherwise'. In the alternative pattern, the agent is identified with 'the person's mind (or large parts thereof), including the person's system of beliefs, memories, character dispositions, desires and emotions'. In this model, 'moral responsibility for an action is typically *not* based on the causal undeterminedness of the agent's *decision*, but, on the contrary, on the fact that

262 For this category, see text to nn. 179–81 above.

263 In LS 20 C(1), 'developments' depend on 'us', whereas in 20 B, 'developments' are characterized as causal agents; hence, in 20 B(5), it is difficult to know whether the subject is 'he' (the person) or 'it' (the development).

264 Annas (1993*a*), 57, 63, her italics; no special (e.g. uniquely first-personal) weight is intended in her use of 'I'. On 'personal identity' in Epicureanism, see further 1.6 below.

the action is dependent on the present overall disposition of the person's mind'.[265] Bobzien's distinction has a special interest in this context because it overlaps, at least, with the distinction between 'core-centred' and 'holistic' conceptions of the person drawn earlier (1.2 above). A version of the first model of agency can be found, for instance, in Kant's idea of the 'transcendental' freedom we have as rational agents; it has also sometimes been ascribed to Plato.[266] As I bring out later (3.5 below), Bobzien's idea of 'whole-person' agency can help us see how Epicurean and Stoic ideas about responsibility converge, and also what picture of human personality they imply.

Here, my concern is only with the way this distinction bears on the interpretation of the passages from Epicurus *On Nature* 25, and on the implied conception of personality. Bobzien suggests that the independent-decision-faculty model and associated indeterminism are explicit or implied in certain readings of this theory, including Sedley's.[267] However, she argues, convincingly, that the relevant model is the 'whole-person' one. Among the reasons she offers is the fact that Epicurus is not concerned in these texts with the coercion 'of *one part* of the mind (the power of volition) by *other parts* of the mind, in particular by the person's *present* character dispositions', as he would be if he were assuming an independent-decision-faculty model.[268] Rather, Epicurus consistently focuses on the challenge posed by the idea that the person's agency (her overall mental disposition at any one time) is coerced by the weight of her past character, taken as a whole. Hence, Epicurus' recurrent linkage between development and responsibility and his insistence that the process of development is not (or should not be) constrained by 'our congenital make-up and... the accidental necessity of that which surrounds and penetrates us'.[269] That the threat is to the whole person, and not simply the quasi-separate decision-making faculty, is implied, she argues, by Epicurus' reference to the development of 'a soul with a disposition and movement of this particular size' or 'of this or that kind'.[270] She also interprets in this way LS 20 B(5) (in her translation): 'he receives the causal responsibility... and then he immediately imparts this to his first natures and somehow makes the whole of it into one'. This is taken to refer to the modification of our character as a unified and complex whole, involving,

[265] Bobzien (2000), 290–1, her italics, last phrase slightly modified for clarity.

[266] See 3.5 below, text to nn. 261–3.

[267] Bobzien (2000), 291, esp. n. 9, referring to Sedley (1983), 49, and Sharples (1991–3), 178, 187–8, among other discussions.

[268] Bobzien (2000), 316, her italics.

[269] LS 20 C(2), LS trans., cited by Bobzien (2000), 317–18.

[270] 34.27 Arrighetti (1973), cited by Bobzien (2000), 324.

for instance, the gradual revision of the belief-set that shapes our actions, rather than the exercise of a causally independent faculty of volition.[271]

The implications of Bobzien's contrast in models of agency and the nature of Epicurean thinking about psychological holism are discussed further later.[272] Here, I want simply to suggest that the inclusive and holistic model of personality presented by Annas and Bobzien as implied in these Epicurean texts fits coherently with the psychophysical holism that they also see as expressed there. In principle, perhaps, emergent dualism *could* be combined with Bobzien's 'whole-person' model of agency (if this was confined to the person as a psychological unit) and with Annas's picture of the Epicurean person as a developing whole agent. However, the combination of psychophysical and psychological holism is a more natural one; and Epicurus' texts in *On Nature* 25 are of special interest in this context because, as interpreted here, they illustrate this combination.

1.6 PUZZLES ABOUT IDENTITY

I close this chapter with a short discussion of two puzzles about identity raised in Stoicism and Epicureanism. Why are these puzzles relevant to this enquiry? They are—up to a point at least—puzzles about *personal* identity and to this extent germane to a study of Hellenistic conceptions of personality or selfhood. Also, the conception of personal identity assumed in the puzzles is a physicalist or material one, and this reflects the importance of the role played by physicalism in the two theories, as illustrated in this chapter. However, in neither case does the puzzle explore the full range of conceptual material considered in this chapter for understanding (what we should conceive as) 'personal identity'. In both cases, the puzzle centres on issues relating to uniqueness and individuation. But in neither case does the puzzle draw out what is, on the face of it, an implication of the two theories, as presented here, namely that each of us constitute unique psychophysical wholes. Why is this so? Should we conclude, against the evidence so far considered, that the two theories did *not* conceive human beings (and other animals) as psychophysical wholes? That, I think, would be an unwarranted inference. A more plausible view is that, although the two Hellenistic theories

[271] Bobzien (2000), 326. She also interprets in this way Lucretius' account of character-development in 3.307–22, stressing that this, ideally, involves the rational modification of our dispositional traits, taken as a whole and assumed to have an atomic basis.

[272] See further 2.3 below, text to nn. 184–93, and 3.5, text to nn. 245–63.

have the resources to conceive human beings (and other animals) both as unique and as psychophysical wholes, these two ideas were not combined—at least not in this type of debate. This, in turn, suggests that there are limits in the extent to which we can identify the modern philosophy of personal identity and Hellenistic philosophical debate.[273]

In each case, I outline the puzzle and summarize what seems to be a credible recent interpretation. Then taking the two puzzles together, I consider the extent to which we do, or do not, find an analogue here for modern debate about personal identity.

The key passage for the Stoic puzzle is this:

> Chrysippus ... in his work *On the Growing* [*Argument*], creates a freak of the following kind. Having first established that it is impossible for two peculiarly qualified individuals to occupy the same substance jointly, he says: 'For the sake of argument, let one individual be thought of as whole-limbed, the other as minus one foot. Let the whole-limbed one be called Dion, the defective one Theon. Then let one of Dion's feet be amputated.' The question arises which one of them has perished, and his [Chrysippus'] claim is that Theon is the stronger candidate. These are the words of a paradox-monger rather than of a speaker of truth. For how can it be that Theon, who has had no part chopped off, has been snatched away, while Dion, whose foot has been amputated, has not perished? 'Necessarily', says Chrysippus. 'For Dion, the one whose foot has been cut off, has collapsed into the defective substance of Theon. And two peculiarly qualified individuals cannot occupy the same substrate. Therefore it is necessary that Dion remains while Theon has perished.[274]

In providing a context for this puzzle, I draw on David Sedley's analysis, recently supplemented by John Bowin.[275]

The location of the extract, it seems clear, is a response by the third-century Stoic theorist Chrysippus to an argument ('the growing argument') mounted by Academic (Platonic) sceptics in criticism of Stoic thinking. The Academic argument challenges the idea that living entities can grow and retain their determinate identity; if they grow, they change their (physical) identity and so become new entities—or die.[276] Chrysippus' response consists in maintaining that determinate entities are not characterized solely by their material nature ('substrate'); they are also characterized, as individuals, by being 'peculiarly

[273] On this point, see text to nn. 298–307 below.

[274] Philo (of Alexandria), *On the Indestructibility of the World* 48 (LS 28 P). Philo here speaks as an advocate of the Academic approach, though in general his position is more complex.

[275] Sedley (1982), which forms the basis for the discussion in LS i. 174–6, and Bowin (2003). Other relevant discussions include Lewis (1995) and Irwin (1996).

[276] LS 28 A(1–2), B; earlier versions of this argument feature in a fragment of the 5th-c. comic dramatist Epicharmus, Plato, *Smp.* 207d, and *Tht.* 152d–e, as part of the 'Heraclitean' version of Protagoras' theory.

qualified'.[277] This response was dictated partly by the claim that we can have knowledge (in principle, infallible knowledge) of *particular* entities and can thus recognize or reidentify them. This claim forms part of their positive or constructive—and non-sceptical—conception of knowledge.[278] Chrysippus' response, then, in part, is that the identity of objects is not determined solely by their material nature or 'substrate' but also by the fact that this material nature is peculiarly qualified. The growing argument, then, fails to undermine the Stoic account because it only addresses the question of material change without showing that this also involves change in the way that the substrate is peculiarly qualified.[279] Academics poured scorn on this twofold characterization of identity (material substrate and being peculiarly qualified).[280] But it is not clear that they discovered any powerful fresh argument against the Stoic theory as so formulated.

The function of the thought experiment about Dion and Theon seems to be to undercut the Academic growing argument on a specific point. Although there is room for debate about how to interpret the details, the argument seems to require that, though presented as a distinct individual, Theon is actually *part* of the original Dion, namely Dion minus a foot. When Dion has his foot amputated, the question arises which of the two is left. They cannot both be left, because (at least on Stoic principles) 'two peculiarly qualified individuals cannot occupy the same substrate'.[281] Why does Dion survive? This is partly because it is Dion who has lost his foot, whereas Theon never had one to lose. Also, Theon was always only a part of Dion, though he was conceptually distinct, and now Dion has 'collapsed into the defective substance of Theon'. (LS 28 P(6)). How does this bizarre example support the Stoic account of identity? For Sedley, the example shows how a case in which material change (in this case, material diminution) is actually 'a *condition* of enduring identity', and not, as claimed by the Academic growing argument, a cause of loss of identity.[282] For Bowin, the argument shows that the 'supersession of successive individuals undergoing growth results in the *incorporation* of the superseded

[277] The being or substance (*ousia*) of an entity is constituted by the combination of its material basis ('substrate') and its qualities, both common and individual or peculiar. The theory resembles Aristotle's theory of substance, but the qualities (unlike Aristotle's 'form') are conceived as physical entities; see LS 28, taken with i. 172–4; also, on Stoic principles and their background, text to nn. 54–9 above.

[278] Sedley (1982), 260–6; for background, LS 40.

[279] Stob. 1.177.21–179.17 (LS 28 D).

[280] See Plu. *Mor.* 1083 A–1084 A (LS 28 A, esp. (3–4, 7)), which, in effect, accuses the Stoics of a type of incoherent dualism; also 28 C.

[281] LS 28 P(6), cf. (2). Bowin (2003), 246–51, stresses, in qualification of Sedley (1982), 270, that this is a Stoic principle the Academics would not accept, though the thought experiment still has force in terms that they would recognize.

[282] Sedley (1982), 270, his italics.

individuals instead of their destruction'.[283] On either interpretation, the example is designed to undermine the Academic growing argument and thus Academic objections to the Stoic way of defining the identity of a substance, namely as a combination of material substrate and being peculiarly qualified.

The second puzzle falls within the series of arguments offered by Lucretius in the latter half of Book 3. The overall theme is that 'death is nothing to us' (830) if we accept the Epicurean thesis that we 'are constituted by the conjunction of body and psyche' (845–6). The point is reinforced in this way:

supposing that after our death the passage of time will bring our matter back together, and the light of life will be restored to us, even that eventuality would be of no concern to us (*nec... pertineat... ad nos*), once our self-recollection (*repetentia nostri*) was interrupted. Nor do our selves which existed in the past (*ante | qui fuimus*) concern us now: we feel no anguish about them. For when you look back at the entire past span of measureless time, and then reflect how various are the motions of matter, you could easily believe that the same primary particles of which we now consist have often in the past been arranged in the same order as now. Yet our minds cannot remember it. For in between there has been an interruption of life, and all the motions have been at random, without sensation.[284]

The thought experiment here is that, given the physical basis for our nature, and the infinity of space and time, our specific atomic combination might be reconstituted in the future or might have been in the past.[285] Even so, Lucretius maintains, there is no reason for fear about this future or past self of a type that should disrupt our peace of mind. Why not? According to one account, that of Antonina Alberti, this is because our identity is different from that of the other self. Although the physical (atomic) basis of our nature may be (or may have been) present, the other self will not be 'us'. This is because the psychological criterion of identity, namely memory—our own memory of our life (*repetentia nostri*)—is missing. Since the other self will not be 'us', we should not be concerned by the possibility of any harm to this self.[286]

Warren, however, has offered a challenge to this reading, and an effective one. He argues that Lucretius accepts the idea that the past or future person *is* 'us', by the only criterion of identity offered here, namely, the specific combination of atoms—presumably, psychic as well as bodily atoms.[287] What

283 Bowin (2003), 46, his italics. Relevant here is the point that Theon was all along *part* of the substance of Dion.

284 Lucr. 3. 845–61 (LS 24 E(3–4)), trans. slightly modified in line 846.

285 Indeed, it is suggested by Warren (2001*c*), 501, that, given these factors, recurrence is not just a hypothetical but an inevitable outcome.

286 Alberti (1990*a*), esp. 197–8. Lines 847–9 are taken to introduce a hypothetical (material) basis for repeated identity, which is negated by the reference to memory in 851, 858–60.

287 Lucr. 3.845–6: 'we who are constituted by the conjunction of body *and psyche*' (*corporis atque animae*).

Lucretius is denying is not that this other self is 'us', but that the existence of this self is 'of any concern to us' (*pertineat*... *ad nos*). This explains the importance of memory (*repetentia nostri*, 851, cf. 858–60). Memory, as pointed out earlier (69 above), is a unifying factor within any one life, and is also a crucial basis for concern within that life. But there is no memory across lives or through death. Hence, our future selves, if such there are, will not remember and be disturbed by our present lives any more than we are disturbed by the lives of our previous selves. So the important question for Lucretius does not centre on the recurrence of identity but on the role of memory in giving unity to lives.[288]

What follows from these puzzles for the larger questions raised earlier and for this enquiry more generally? First, in so far as the discussions refer to identity, they reflect the physicalism that we have seen is fundamental to both theories. For Stoicism, physical nature (the substrate) is one key aspect of substance. Although, as the puzzle brings out, another key aspect is being peculiarly (uniquely) qualified, this aspect too is conceived in physical terms, for instance 'as the breath which runs through a body and informs it'.[289] Analogously, in the Epicurean discussion, the sole criterion of identity cited is the unique conjunction of atoms (both bodily and psychic) that makes up our physical nature.[290] The puzzles, that is, do not lend support to the idea that these Hellenistic theories hold any version of psyche–body dualism.[291] On the other hand, the puzzles do not, on the face of it, reflect the psychophysical *holism* that I have presented as characteristic of the theories. The Stoic–Academic debate does not seem to involve the idea that the peculiar qualities of a substance might be—in some cases at least—psychological ones.[292] The thought experiment offered by Lucretius, as interpreted here, does not deploy memory as a psychological criterion of personal identity, though it does give memory a crucial role in the argument. This negative point can be taken with another. The puzzles outlined here seem to take us tantalizingly close to the issues and conceptual terrain of the modern theory of personal identity. For instance, questions of uniqueness are central in both Hellenistic and modern debates. The shared Stoic–Epicurean emphasis on the *combination* of physical and psychological features that is fundamental to human (and animal) nature

[288] Warren (2001*c*), esp. 503–7. Warren finds a similar emphasis on continuity in *this life* in two passages which seem to deny the possibility of reconstituted identity, Epicur. *SV* 14 and Lucr. 3.670–6 (the latter passage denies that immortality of the psyche—even this were possible—would confer continuity of memory).

[289] LS i. 172; see also text to n. 114 above.

[290] See text to nn. 295–6 below.

[291] Plutarch's accusation of quasi-dualism in LS 28 A(3–4, 7) is simply polemical and not justified by the theory.

[292] See n. 296 below.

seems to offer the prospect of a particularly rich account of personhood and personal identity—more so than in many modern theories, which stress either physical or psychological criteria.[293] And yet, in certain respects, as Warren underlines in his discussion of the Lucretian puzzle, the key issue is not quite the same as that of the modern theory of personal identity.[294]

What underlies these two general points regarding the Hellenistic puzzles? I take first the question of psychological criteria for identity. There are specific features of these discussions which make it inappropriate to include psychological criteria of identity. The Stoic argument does not bear only on those entities which have psychological life, namely humans and animals.[295] Although the examples in Chrysippus' thought experiment (Dion and Theon) are, in some sense, human beings, the metaphysical theory embraces all entities with a determinate identity. The Stoics are committed, perhaps recklessly, to the claim that *all* substances, including ears of corn and hairs, are peculiarly qualified and are, in principle, reidentifiable. The Academic growing argument and the Stoic counterclaims apply to all determinate entities and not only to human and other animals; and even in the latter case it is not clear that the peculiar qualities are psychological ones.[296] In the Epicurean puzzle, by contrast, the psychological dimension is important to the argument, which is one about 'us' (human beings). Also, to a degree at least, our identity is defined by reference to a psychological characteristic, in so far as we are said to constitute a distinctive combination of bodily *and psychic* atoms.[297] On the other hand, as already stressed, Lucretius' argument does not turn on the role of memory, at least as a psychological criterion of identity, but rather on the role of memory as unifying our life and concerns. Hence, there are specific features of the two discussions that make it inappropriate for them to refer to psychological criteria of identity. But this fact does not by itself invalidate the idea that human beings, and other animals, are in general conceived by the theories as psychophysical wholes. On the contrary, this idea is assumed, at least in the Epicurean example.

What about the relationship of these puzzles to the modern theory of personal identity? The point just made about the Stoic argument helps to show why Chrysippus' thought experiment only partly overlaps with those in

[293] See further, on modern theory of this type, Perry (1975), esp. introd.; Rorty (1976), especially introd.; Cockburn (1991).

[294] Warren (2001*c*), 507–8, discussed further below.

[295] On the scope of those entities possessing psyche in Stoicism, see text to n. 124 above.

[296] See Sedley (1982), 260–6. However Lewis (1995), esp. 97–100 and Irwin (1996), esp. 471–3, do suggest that the peculiar qualities are psychological in nature, while acknowledging that it is not straightforward to establish this point from the available evidence.

[297] Lucr. 3.645–6, taken with the hypothetical cases of atomic recomposition in 847–62 (LS 24 E(3–4)).

the modern philosophy of personal identity. Although the boundary of the class of 'persons' is a disputed one in modern thought,[298] it would certainly not include all the substances relevant to the Stoic–Academic debate. Although Chrysippus' thought experiment could, perhaps, be adapted to fit the concerns of modern personal identity theory, the need for adaptation underlines the difference of conceptual focus.[299] In the Epicurean case, the difference is more nuanced; we can pinpoint it by referring again to the contrasting interpretations of Alberti and Warren. John Locke uses a thought experiment which is, in some ways, remarkably close to that of Lucretius, and which may have been inspired by Lucretius. Alberti sees Locke's use of this example as similar in general type, though not identical in content. In her view, Locke sees memory as both a necessary and sufficient condition of personal identity, whereas Lucretius also posits a physical criterion (a unique atomic constitution) alongside the psychological one.[300] Warren suggests that Locke's use of a parallel type of example may have led Alberti—inappropriately—to assimilate Lucretius' argument to the type we find in Locke.[301]

Can we locate these differences between Hellenistic and modern thinking in a wider framework? The issues are complex, and some are brought out elsewhere in this book.[302] But some general comments may be helpful here. The modern philosophy of personal identity can be seen as a combination of the following features. (1) An analysis of the metaphysical status of entities, including their identity (their sameness over time and at any one time). (2) A focus on the metaphysical status and the ethical consequences of the status of 'persons' (viewed as the most advanced or complex type of living entity), typically human beings, but not exclusively so and not necessarily defined in species-specific terms. (3) An interest in what makes each member of the favoured class (persons or human beings) unique, on the assumption that the uniqueness is a salient feature of humanity or personhood. (4) A focus on the question of the salient criterion or criteria of personhood or personal identity, whether conceived as physical or psychological qualities or a

[298] Should it include non-human animals and human foetuses? If human beings are central examples of persons, is this by virtue of being animals or of qualities that are non-species-specific? See further references in n. 293 above; also Gill (1990*d*), part 1.

[299] The main adaptation would be to focus on (the equivalent of) 'persons', arguably, rational animals. On rational animals in Stoicism and the conceptual relationship to modern 'persons', see Gill (1991), 184–93.

[300] Locke, *Essay*, 2.27.14–16, in Nidditch (1975), 338–41: hypothetical transmigration of souls does not constitute continuity of identity because of the absence of memory and hence of consciousness of being the same self. See Alberti (1990), 201–3.

[301] Warren (2001*c*), 507–8.

[302] See Ch. 6, esp. 6.2. On the relationship between ancient and modern thinking about the category of persons, or personal identity, see further Gill (1990*d*, 1991); also Price (1989), 23–5, 30–5, Warren (2001*a*), esp. 162–74, (2004), ch. 2, esp. 76–93.

combination of both. (5) The definition of those criteria in terms of being 'I' or 'me', or having a first-personal viewpoint (which may include first-personal memory), or being a self-conscious subject.[303] Set against this very broad framework, we can see that the Hellenistic puzzles discussed reflect some, but by no means all, of these features. The Stoic thought experiment fits squarely into (1) and shares with (3) a concern with uniqueness (peculiarly qualified material existence), but it does not share any of the other features. The Epicurean puzzle reflects aspects of the first three features, while not fitting firmly into any one of them.[304] But, as interpreted here, feature (4) is not relevant, nor is (5), which is a subdivision of (4).[305] However, Locke's discussion of selfhood, self-consciousness, and memory, including the passage which recalls Lucretius, contains all five features, even though it is one of the first discussions in the modern theory of personal identity.[306] The rather limited degree of overlap between this area of modern theory and the concerns of the Hellenistic puzzles is an indicator of larger conceptual and cultural differences, some of which are pursued elsewhere in this book.[307] Here, my aim has been the more limited one of showing that these cases are compatible with the framework explored elsewhere in this chapter, despite at first glance seeming to point towards the rather different thought-world of modern identity theory.

[303] See further 6.2 below, text to nn. 12–21.

[304] The Epicurean discussion refers to the identity of human beings ('us') defined in terms of specific criteria (psychophysical atomic-based composition) which confer uniqueness at least at any one time or place (though this is replicable in infinite time or space).

[305] For alternative criteria of personhood, not based on the idea of the self-conscious 'I', see 6.2 below, text to nn. 27–33.

[306] On Locke and self-consciousness as a criterion of personhood, see 6.2 below, text to nn. 14–15.; see further Perry (1975), ch. 2; C. Taylor (1989), 159–76.

[307] Notably, these puzzles show the difference between ancient thought and modern 'subjective' ('I'-centred) thinking; see 6.2, and 6.6 below.

2

Psychological Holism and Socratic Ideals

2.1 PRELIMINARIES

One aspect of the substantial holism that I see as characteristic of Stoicism and Epicureanism is the idea of human beings, and other animals, as psychophysical wholes. Another aspect is psychological holism, of which there are two dimensions. One is that psychological capacities are seen as closely integrated with each other, and as functions of a coherent whole, rather than as expressions of radically distinct parts and of what is or is not the core or essence of the person. Another is that psychological capacities are seen as functions of a unified psychophysical whole and not as being mental by contrast with physical. In other words, in these theories, psychological holism is combined with psychophysical holism. These types of holism are also linked with one of the three types of naturalism noted earlier, namely a focus on the natural (birth-to-death) life of human beings as embodied rational animals, rather than, for instance, as temporarily embodied non-material souls.

As outlined in the Introduction, these types of holism (and naturalism) are also combined in these theories with a series of radical 'Socratic' ethical claims. (These are, in brief, that it is 'up to us' to achieve happiness through rational reflection and virtue, that happiness involves time-independent perfection of character, and that only those who achieve this state are psychologically and ethically coherent.)[1] It is the synthesis of holism and naturalism with these Socratic claims that makes up the distinctive Stoic–Epicurean conception of human personality that I am characterizing as 'the structured self'. This synthesis is the more striking, and seemingly paradoxical, because these ethical claims are ones that might seem to be more easily integrated with dualistic (part-based or core-centred) theories such as those found in some Platonic dialogues, notably the *Phaedo*, or in aspects of Middle Platonism or Neoplatonism. In fact, these Socratic claims *are* sometimes combined with types of dualism, both in Plato and later in the Platonic tradition. But, within the Hellenistic and earlier Roman Imperial period, they are more closely

[1] On these 'Socratic' claims, and on the sense in which they are 'Socratic', see 2.2–3 below.

associated with Stoicism than with Middle Platonism. This reflects the fact that, on a number of issues, Stoics adopted a set of 'hard' positions, which reflect these Socratic ethical ideas, by contrast with the more moderate positions often adopted by Middle Platonists. (Briefly, these 'hard' positions are that virtue is self-sufficient for happiness and does not require external goods, and that the virtuous person is characterized by 'freedom from passion' or from distress and not by the 'moderation of passion'.)[2] Epicureanism, despite its differences in approach and background from Stoicism, also makes similar ethical claims and adopts versions of the 'hard' positions. Both theories do so in ways that are, I think, consistent with their characteristic holism and naturalism. It is true that we can sometimes find expressions of (what one might call) 'quasi-dualism' in both Stoic and Epicurean sources, especially in works of practical ethics. But these are best understood, I suggest, as rhetorical ways of conveying the 'hard' ethical stances rather than as reflecting deliberate and theorized breaches in the holistic approach.

In the following two sections, I set out key features of Stoic and Epicurean thinking about psychological holism, the linkage with psychophysical holism, and the way these types of holism are synthesized with 'Socratic' ethical claims. Several of the topics discussed in broad terms here are examined in more detail in the following chapters, in a way that is designed to bring out more fully the cross-currents of ancient debate and issues raised by modern scholarly interpretation.[3] My aim here is simply to illustrate the main respects in which Stoicism and Epicureanism, in spite of their different starting-points, converge in psychological and psychophysical holism. I also aim to bring out what seems to me to be the coherence of their thinking in this respect, which is rendered more complex, but not undermined, by the synthesis with the 'Socratic' ethical claims.

2.2 STOICISM

Psychological holism is reflected in what have been recognized since antiquity as certain central and characteristic features of Stoic thought. One is the idea that virtue and vice are equally functions of a single, unified psychological control-centre (*hēgemonikon*), and one which, in adults, is informed by

[2] See further discussion below; on the contrast with Middle Platonic ideas, see text to nn. 32, 41 below.

[3] See 3.4 below, on ancient debate about happiness, and Ch. 4, esp. 4.3, on the competing ancient ideals of freedom from passion and control of passion. On interpretative issues in modern scholarship, see Ch. 6 below.

rationality. Similarly, 'reason' (which can be used as a normative idea, meaning 'right reason') and 'emotion' or 'passion' (taken to be defective reactions) are equally functions of this unified rational control-centre. Hence, virtue and vice, and (normative) reason and passion differ not because they are expressions of different parts of the personality. They differ, in part, because they reflect different sets of beliefs; in more Stoic terms, they reflect the difference between the possession of knowledge or wisdom and of ignorance or folly. They also differ in so far as they express a coherent or incoherent set of beliefs and pattern of affective reactions and actions. This reflects the Stoic view that *only* the achievement of ideal wisdom confers complete consistency of beliefs, affective reactions, and actions and that *all* states of character falling short of this are more or less incoherent and fluctuating. However, this difference between good and bad states does not stem from the dominance of different parts or sources of motivation within the personality, for instance, that of mind or reason, emotion or desire. It stems from the overall state of the personality, taken as a whole and including the person's belief-set, pattern of reactions, and mode of behaviour.

Thus, for instance, we are told that, according to the Stoics, 'virtue is a consistent character' and that 'happiness consists in virtue, since virtue is a soul which has been fashioned to achieve consistency in the whole of life'. Conversely, 'viciousness is a tenor or character which is inconsistent in the whole of life and out of harmony with itself... it is the source of disturbances which... are disorderly and agitated movements of the mind'.[4] The fact that the contrasted states of virtue and vice, or (normative) reason and passion, are equally functions of a single (rational) control-centre is indicated in these comments.

> passion is no different from reason, and... there is no dissension and conflict between the two, but a turning of the single reason in both directions... 'First of all we should bear in mind that a rational animal follows reason naturally, and acts in accordance with reason as if that were its guide. Often, however, it moves towards and away from certain things in a different way, pushed to excess in disobedience of reason.'[5]

These Stoic ideas were formulated in an intellectual context in which the more familiar view was that virtue and vice should be defined by reference to a part-based psychological model of the kind we find in Plato and Aristotle. Our main sources for Stoic psychology, particularly for the theory of the passions, are later thinkers such as Plutarch and Galen, who adopt the Platonic–Aristotelian model (as they understand this) and present the Stoic alternative

[4] D.L. 7.89 (LS 61A); Cic. *Tusc.* 4.29 (LS 61 O(1–2)).

[5] Plu. *Mor.* 446 F (LS 65 G(1)); Gal. *PHP* 4.2.10, quoting Chrysippus (LS 65 J(1–2)).

theory as incoherent or psychologically implausible. It is a rather complex and delicate task to construct from such sources a more historically credible account of the Stoic theory, and to reconstruct its relationship to Platonic thought, as I try to do in Chapters 4–5. But, in outline, my view is that the Stoic account of the passions consistently reflects the unified or holistic Stoic conception of personality and also brings out the psychological credibility and subtlety of that conception.

A second relevant feature of Stoic thought is the idea of development as 'appropriation' (*oikeiōsis*). Personal *oikeiōsis* is subdivided into two stages, the more basic stage shared by all animals and the more advanced stage limited to adult humans (rational animals). There is a distinct, though related, process of social *oikeiōsis*. As already illustrated (1.4 above), the first stage of personal appropriation is closely linked with psychophysical and, to an extent, psychological holism. Animals are seen as instinctively disposed to respond to their environment in a way that enables them to maintain their own 'constitution', for instance, by using their own distinctive means of self-defence and survival. The idea that animals function in a highly unified way is conveyed especially in the correlated ideas of (instinctive) self-perception or self-awareness and a 'control-centre' (*hēgemonikon*) which coordinates all psychological processes. The second, adult human, stage of personal *oikeiōsis* is presented in one particularly important Ciceronian passage, which has been intensively analysed by scholars (*de Finibus* (*Fin*). 3.20–2). One key feature of the account is a move from instinctive attraction to things that maintain one's constitution to increasingly rational and consistent selection of these things. A second is the recognition that virtue, understood as 'regularity and ... harmony of conduct' is the good, and the only thing that has intrinsic value. This leads to a revaluation of the natural advantages pursued first instinctively and then by deliberate selection in the earlier stages of development.[6]

On the face of it, the second stage of personal development is not closely linked with psychological or any other type of holism. It seems to express the Stoic adherence to the 'hard' ethical claims that virtue is the only good, that it is sufficient for happiness, and that it does not require the addition of external goods.[7] However, I argue in Chapter 3 that this account, taken with other evidence, reflects the holistic approach in several ways. First, the linear pattern, in which the gradual development of understanding carries with it a progressive shift in motivation, expresses the Stoic view that human beings

[6] Cic. *Fin.* 3.20–2 (LS 59 D, phrase quoted from D(4)).

[7] See further 3.4 below: the Middle Platonist Antiochus sees it as reflecting both an implausibly 'hard' ethical position and an unrealistically narrow (reason-centred) view of human nature.

function as unified psychological wholes. We can see a contrast with a Platonic–Aristotelian pattern of thinking in which ethical development is subdivided into two stages, with the habituation of emotions and desires providing the basis for a subsequent rational reorientation of goals. Second, the description of virtue (recognized as the good) as 'regularity and ... harmony of conduct' reflects the general Stoic presentation of the ideal ('wise') character-state as marked by internal structure, cohesion, and consistency of a kind that pervades the whole personality. This ideal reflects in turn the Stoic holistic outlook in that virtue and goodness are conceived as complete or perfected wholes rather than as cores or essences.

This Ciceronian account has sometimes also been taken as implying that the recognition of the order and structure of the natural cosmos provides the crucial motivating force for the realization that virtue (conceived as order and structure) is the only inherent good. Like Julia Annas, I am sceptical of this way of reading the key Ciceronian passage and certain related sources. Recognition of the structure, order, and rationality shared by the natural universe, the virtuous character-state, and systems of reasoning and knowledge does, certainly, form a crucial part of the kind of understanding attributed by Stoics to the ideal wise person. But, I suggest, this is better seen in the context of the Stoic version of 'rich naturalism', combining the insights of physics, ethics, and logic, than as expressing the idea that the natural cosmos, taken on its own, provides the basis for recognizing the nature of goodness. 'Rich naturalism', applied to Cicero's account and others, does, I think, enable us to define another sense in which the Stoic account of the motivational shift that follows the recognition of the nature of the good reflects the larger holistic outlook.[8]

Taken together, then, the two stages of the Stoic model of personal development provide a powerful expression of holism, one that embraces ethical and psychological dimensions and has far-reaching implications for understanding the coherence and impact of Stoic philosophy. Stoic thinking about human psychology and about personal development, especially the final stages, has sometimes been taken, in ancient and modern times, as expressing an extreme or narrow conception of human nature, especially by those who approach the topics assuming the validity of a part-based psychological model.[9] However, I think that there are strong grounds for seeing the Stoic approach as, rather, systematically inclusive, in particular as correlating a

[8] See 3.2–3 below, also, on 'rich naturalism', 3.5 below.

[9] See e.g. Antiochus' criticisms on this ground, 3.4 below, esp. text to nn. 52–4. A modern critic of (what he sees as) the narrow cognitivism of Chrysippean psychology, who also approaches the issue from a—broadly—Aristotelian, part-based standpoint, is Sorabji (2000), esp. chs. 2, 10, 12–13.

unified picture of human (and other animal) psychology with psychophysical holism. This comes out both in their account of impulse (notably the kind of impulse that constitutes a passion or emotion) and in their characterization of virtue as a psychophysical state.

The Stoics analyse motivation in terms of a response (that of an 'impulse', *hormē*) to an 'impression' or 'appearance' (*phantasia*). In the case of adult humans, the response is mediated by 'assent' (*sunkatathesis*) to an impression and the impression is rational.[10] It is plausible to see this account of motivation as designed to be more unified than those of Plato or Aristotle, since it avoids the distinction—and potential conflict—between reason and appetite or desire. Passions or emotions (*pathē*) constitute a subdivision of impulses; and the Stoic account of emotions has sometimes been seen as unduly rationalistic because of the weight given to beliefs (in Stoic terms, 'rational impressions') in generating emotions.[11] However, I think the theory is better understood as designed to be inclusive and to give a place both to beliefs and to affective reactions. More precisely, it is designed to underline the linkage, in adult humans, *between* beliefs and affective reactions. The reactions involved, such as contraction, swelling, and shrinking are explicitly psychophysical in character, as are the reactions identified in Hierocles' descriptions of psychological processes (40–1 above). This comes out, for instance, in this report of Stoic definitions of emotions: 'Distress is an irrational contraction, or a fresh opinion that something bad is present, at which people think it right to be contracted . . . Pleasure is an irrational swelling, or a fresh opinion that something good is present, at which people think it right to be swollen.'[12] The emotion involves two kinds of judgement: that something is good or bad and that it is (therefore) right or appropriate to respond affectively in a certain way. Assent to these judgements triggers the affective response involved, that is, the 'irrational contraction' or 'irrational swelling' cited at the start of each definition. Hence, the analysis not only presupposes a unified or holistic conception of psychological processes (according to which emotions are a direct response to beliefs to which we 'assent') but also assumes that those processes are physical ones and expressions of the psychophysical cohesion of the rational animal.[13]

[10] On the sense in which adult human impressions are 'rational', see 139 below.

[11] There are two main versions of this criticism: (1) the Stoic theory gives undue weight to beliefs, i.e. the cognitive dimension of emotions, and understates other dimensions; (2) the Stoic theory assumes, wrongly, that affective reactions can *only* be generated by beliefs. My comments here respond to the first criticism. See further on issues raised by the Stoic theory of Passions Gill (2005*a*) and Ch. 4 below.

[12] Andronicus, *On Passions* 1 (LS 65 B(1, 4)).

[13] See further 4.5 below.

The Stoics also sometimes underline the point that virtue, as well as (defective) emotion, is a function of our psychophysical life. The virtuous character is sometimes contrasted with the non-virtuous one by reference to the idea of 'good tension' (*eutonia*) and 'lack of tension' (*atonia*). What is contrasted in this way is the 'sinewy' consistency and stability of the virtuous character, as distinct from the inconsistency and vacillation (and thus lack of 'sinew') of the defective one. This usage reflects the central role of tension (*tonos*) as a causal principle in Stoic thought; as noted earlier, 'reason' (*logos*) belongs to a spectrum of degrees of tension which includes 'nature' and psyche. Long puts the point in this form: 'Viewed macroscopically, tension is that property of the divine *pneuma* or *logos* which makes it, in its interaction with matter, the universal principle of causation and dynamic coherence. Viewed microscopically and ethically, tension is a property of the human soul, which is itself a fragment of the divine *pneuma*.'[14] Hence, the Stoic Cleanthes characterizes tension both as a 'stroke of fire' and as a kind of 'strength and might' in the psyche which constitutes virtue.[15] It is true that an analogy is sometimes drawn between physical and virtuous 'sinew', and that the quality identified is a property of the person's psychological character rather than her body.[16] But elsewhere it is stressed that, since psychological states are also physical, virtues are an integral part of our psychophysical life. A passage from Stobaeus develops this line of thought: 'in substance [the virtues] are identical with the psychic control-centre; accordingly, [they say] that every virtue is and is called a body; for the intellect (*dianoia*) and the psyche are bodies. They believe that the inborn *pneuma*, which is warm, is psyche'. For similar reasons, the psyche is 'an animal', and so is the control-centre, and so is virtue, which is a function of the control-centre.[17] The seemingly bizarre idea that virtues are 'animals' or 'living creatures' is confirmed elsewhere, and supported on the same ground, that virtues are dispositions of a psychophysical mind or control-centre.[18] The aim of such passages must be to highlight the point that virtue, understood as 'good tension', is not a property of a non-material mind or reason but of a rational animal which is also an integrated psychophysical organism.

One rather surprising extension of this line of thought is the idea, found in at least some sources, that the psyche of all human beings survives after death, and that those of the wise survive longest, until the next conflagration of the universe. This might seem to constitute an intrusion of Platonic dualism,

14 Long (1996), 213; see also 1.4 above, text to nn. 110–14.

15 LS 61 C(5), also the relevant note in LS ii. 376.

16 See e.g. Gal. *PHP* 4.6.5–6; also Engberg-Pedersen (1990*b*), 188–9.

17 Stob. 2.64.19–65.4, 5b7, trans. Inwood and Gerson (1998), 206, modified.

18 LS 61 E, also 29 B (virtue as 'the mind disposed in a certain way').

implying the existence of a non-material soul; but this is not so. What it represents is a logical consequence of the thought that *pneuma* has a physical existence and that there are varying degrees of pneumatic tension, which are more or less cohesive and enduring. Hence, the wise, whose stable and virtuous character (*diathesis*) constitutes the highest possible state of pneumatic tension, will survive longest beyond the dissolution of the rest of the body. As one source puts it: 'the weaker [type of] psyche consists of a feeble compound [or blend, *sunkrima*], namely that of the uneducated; the stronger type (that of the wise) lasts till the conflagration of everything'.[19] So, even the Stoics' version of the immortality of the soul—their belief in the relative durability of certain types of psyche—reflects their overall psychophysical holism.

In the Introduction, I have suggested that a striking and distinctive feature of Stoic—and, in a different way, of Epicurean thought—is the combination of psychological and psychophysical holism with certain 'Socratic' ethical claims. I explore this suggestion more fully here in connection with Stoicism and, subsequently, Epicureanism. The pervasive influence of Socrates on Hellenistic philosophy has been a special theme of recent scholarship, one explored especially by A. A. Long. Long has emphasized that Socrates influenced a whole series of groups and thinkers who were strongly divergent in approach from each other, and who probably had very different ideas about exactly what Socrates stood for.[20] Common strands, however, were the idea that it was open to all human beings to pursue happiness through reasoned reflection and that philosophy could make a substantive difference in shaping the ethical ideals that should inform human life.[21] In the case of Epicurus and his school, Socratic influence was rather generalized and was intertwined with that of other fifth- and fourth-century thinkers, notably Democritus and his successors. For the Stoics, by contrast, Socratic influence was strong and explicitly recognized from the origins of the school and persisted, in varying degrees, throughout its history, exercising an especially strong impact on Epictetus.[22]

[19] Aët. *Plac.* 4.7.3 (= *SVF* 2.810); also *SVF* 2.809, 811, 815; on pneumatic tension see LS 47 (including 47 S on *diathesis*); on conflagration, LS 46. See further Annas (1992), 67–8; also Bonhöffer (1890), 54–67.

[20] See further Giannantoni (1991), a four-volume collection of ancient sources for Socrates. Kahn (1996), ch. 1, reviews key extracts and stresses the diversity of the picture of Socrates offered (also the quasi-fictional status of the genre of 'Socratic dialogue').

[21] Long (1999*b*), esp. 618–23, also (1996), 1–16; Vander Waerdt (1994*b*).

[22] For instance, Philodemus, the 1st-c.BC Epicurean, tells us that the Stoics 'are willing to be called Socratics', *On the Stoics* (*de Stoicis*), 12.3. On Socrates and Epictetus, see Long (1996), 2, and (2002), ch. 3. For a comprehensive account of Socratic influence on Stoicism, see Alesse (2000).

Recent scholarship in this area has focused especially on the idea that Socratic ethical ideas may have helped to shape Stoic thinking on value. Special attention has been paid to the thesis maintained at one point in Plato's *Euthydemus*, that only wisdom is good, and only ignorance is bad, and that the value of all other so-called 'goods' depends on whether or not they are controlled by wisdom. It has been suggested that this helped the early Stoics to formulate their claim that only virtue (understood as wisdom) was good, as well as serving as the starting-point for Stoic debate about exactly what that claim involved. A subsequent argument in the *Euthydemus*, raising further questions about the idea of wisdom or knowledge as the good, is also thought to have contributed to a subsequent Stoic–Academic debate on that question.[23] More broadly, a number of claims made by Socrates in Plato's dialogues, including the core ethical thesis of Plato's *Republic*, that justice is happiness, seem to have informed the Stoic idea that only what is good (understood as virtue) constitutes what is really beneficial.[24] It is also widely supposed that Socrates' denial of weakness of will (more precisely, his argument that pleasure or pain cannot overcome knowledge of good) in Plato's *Protagoras* influenced the Stoic unitary model of human psychology.[25] This argument is closely linked with a series of 'hard' or 'paradoxical' claims made or implied in Platonic dialogues, especially the *Protagoras* and *Gorgias*, such as that virtue is one or unified, that it is knowledge, and that no one does wrong willingly but only through error. Those ideas are also thought to have had a decisive influence on Stoic ethical thinking and to have informed their picture of human motivation.[26]

Should we suppose that the Stoics saw themselves as adopting the ideas of Socrates, as distinct from Plato? This is what we might suppose, from the contrast which emerged from the first century BC onwards, between the Stoic position, strongly influenced by Socrates, and Middle Platonic thought, which drew, instead, on a combination of Platonic and Aristotelian (and sometimes also Stoic) ideas.[27] The idea that Stoicism embodied a critical, or even antagonistic, stance towards Plato's thought is promoted by some thinkers operating within a Middle Platonic framework, notably Plutarch and Galen; and, on some points, notably political ideals, there is evidence of

[23] Pl. *Euthd.* 281d2–e5, 291b–292d. See further Long (1996), ch. 1, esp. 22–32 (first published as Long 1988); Annas (1994); Striker (1996), 316–24; Gill (2000*a*); McCabe (2002).

[24] See Inwood and Donini (1999), 687–90, referring to e.g. Pl. *Ap.* 30a–b, *Meno* 77b–78b; also *R.* 357a–358d. On this idea in Stoicism, see text to nn. 33–4 below.

[25] See e.g. M. Frede (1986), 96, 98; Gosling (1990), 48–9; Sedley (1993), 313–14.

[26] See e.g. Pl. *Prt.* 352b–360e, *Grg.* 466b–468e. On these Socratic claims, see Penner (1971), (1991), (1997), (2005); Mackenzie (1981), chs. 9–10. On links with Stoicism, see Alesse (2000), 289–343; Long (2002), 70–4.

[27] See, on Middle Platonism in general, Dillon (1977); also 3.4 below.

an explicit Stoic critique of Plato.[28] However, we need to be very cautious about attributing to the Stoics, or any ancient thinker, an equivalent for the sharp 'Socrates–Plato' contrast sometimes drawn in modern scholarship.[29] As Sedley (1993: 314) points out, 'it would be misleading to imply that any ancient reader of Plato operated with an entirely clearcut distinction between historically Socratic texts on the one hand and Platonic texts on the other'. Aristotle is relatively unusual in drawing an explicit distinction between 'Socratic' and 'Platonic' ideas, for instance, about virtue as knowledge and the unity of the psyche. He also offers a history of the development of Platonic thinking about Forms, in which Socrates is presented as making a specific contribution.[30] But even Aristotle does not couple this view with a systematic division between 'Socratic' and 'Platonic' dialogues, arranged on chronological principles, as some modern scholars have done. As Sedley (1996: 80) also points out, the typical ancient way of reading Plato seems to be 'unitarian', rather than based on the modern distinction between early (Socratic) and middle or late (Platonic) dialogues. Recent study and reflection on the nature of our evidence and on responses to Plato throughout antiquity have led some scholars to re-examine the Socrates–Plato distinction and to be much more cautious about using it than has been common in modern discussions.[31]

But how should we characterize the nature of the Socratic influence on the Stoics, if it is not interpreted as constituting the adoption of Socratic, as distinct from Platonic, ideas? One possible hypothesis is this. We might suggest that, from Zeno onwards, the Stoics are attracted to a series of 'hard' (radical or extreme) ethical positions. These include the ideas that virtue is sufficient for happiness, that it is knowledge, that it is one (or strongly unified), that virtue and happiness are 'up to us', that only the wise person is fully coherent, and that the best character-state is that of freedom from passion. These are all positions which were seen as 'hard' or extreme in Hellenistic–Roman philosophical debate, and for which there are analogous, 'soft', positions, sometimes adopted by Middle Platonic thinkers.[32] These are

[28] On Plutarch and Galen, see Chs. 4–5 below; on the Stoic critique of the political ideal of Plato's *Republic*, see 5.2 below, n. 68.

[29] An extreme, though influential, example of a sharp 'Socrates–Plato' distinction (within the Platonic corpus) is Vlastos (1991), chs. 2–3.

[30] See e.g. Arist. *MM* 1182a15–26, *Metaph.* 13.4, esp. 1078^{b}22–32. For discussion, from different standpoints, see e.g. Guthrie (1969), 425–30; Vlastos (1991), 91–8; Kahn (1996), 79–87.

[31] See e.g. Kahn (1996), esp. chs. 2–3; Cooper (1997), introd.; Annas (1999), 1–7; more generally, Annas and Rowe (2002).

[32] See also n. 41 below. For instance, Antiochus holds that virtue is *not* sufficient for *complete* happiness (3.4 below, text to nn. 205–7); and Plutarch, typically at least, presents the normative state as 'control of passion' rather than 'freedom from passion' (4.3 below). I am not implying that Middle Platonic thinkers *invariably* adopt the 'soft' position, only that this is a recognizable trend. By contrast, Eudorus of Alexandria adopts the 'hard' position that virtue is sufficient for

positions which were associated with Socrates, in a variety of writings, and for which the presentation of Socrates as a character was an important source of inspiration. But, for support and elaboration of these ideas, it is highly likely that the early Stoics also looked to what are (in modern terms) 'Platonic' sources, such as the *Republic*. Hence, it seems that the Stoics' aim was to establish a relatively coherent set of hard ethical claims, rather than to adopt the ideas of the historical Socrates by contrast with those of Plato. They also aimed to combine these with the kinds of naturalism and holism already discussed, for which, as we have seen (17–20 above), the *Timaeus*, a classically 'Platonic' text (in modern terms) was an especially important source of inspiration.

Some of the evidence for the early Stoic school enables us to see how this combination of hard ethical positions and holism or naturalism might have arisen. We are told that Zeno had four main teachers: Crates the Cynic, Polemo (head of the Academy), the Megaric Stilpo, and Diodorus Cronus.[33] The Cynic approach, that of Crates, is presented in ancient sources as derived from Socrates by way of Antisthenes and Diogenes. Cynicism embodies an extreme version of Socratic ethics, based on the radical distinction between nature and convention. Stilpo is also said to have maintained another 'hard' position, namely that the wise are self-sufficient and that things that affect the body are neither good nor bad. We can see how these two teachers may have promoted the central Stoic idea that virtue or wisdom is the only real good, that it is self-sufficient for happiness, and that conventional 'goods', such as health and wealth, are, in comparison with this, only 'matters of indifference'. Polemo, by contrast, maintained that there are bodily and external goods, though these are less in value than psychological goods, that is, the virtues. This line was not adopted by Zeno; but more influential on him was Polemo's view that ethical development involved acting 'in accordance with nature'. As well as providing a standard formulation of the Stoic goal in life, this may also have led Zeno and his successors to see things such as health as 'primary natural things' which we are drawn towards, first instinctively and then rationally, in order to develop our 'constitution'.[34] Put more broadly, this

happiness, while Philo of Alexandria maintains that the normative character-state is that of 'absence of passions' (Dillon 1977: 123–4, 151–2). For Middle Platonic positions on the relevant issues, see Dillon (1977), index under 'goods', 'passions', 'virtue'.

[33] This combination of teachers enables us to see how Zeno developed his distinctive tripartite philosophy, combining logic, ethics, and physics. Diodorus provided a training in logic or dialectic, while Polemo seems to have been an important influence on Zeno's physics (1.3 above, text to nn. 50–3); Polemo, together with the other two teachers, helped to shape the ethics.

[34] For this type of reconstruction, see Sedley (2003), 9–13; on Polemo's ethics, see Dillon (1977), 43–5, (2003), 159–66; on the Cynics, including Crates, as heirs of Socrates, see Long (1999*b*), 623–32. For a detailed study of the Socratic influence on early Stoics, see Alesse (2000), esp. chs. 1–4.

combination of influences may have served to provide a more naturalistic framework for the hard ethical positions adopted from Crates and Stilpo (and, ultimately, Socrates), and one that was compatible with the broader naturalistic and holistic world-view that Polemo also helped Zeno to develop.

Of the Socratic ideas which seem to have influenced the Stoics I focus on three, outlined earlier (2.1 above).[35] Why focus on these three? This is partly because these bear in a particularly illuminating way on the nature of the Stoic ideal character and on its development. To put this point differently, these themes have a special relevance for the area of overlap between ethical and psychological questions that is an especially important one for this enquiry into concepts of self and personality.[36] They are also ones that display with special clarity the synthesis of radical ethical positions with holistic and naturalistic conceptions of human personality that is characteristic of Stoic thought. Also, they are closely interlocked with other, and more intensively discussed, aspects of Socratic thought which have been taken by scholars to influence Stoicism.

I take first the idea that the achievement of happiness is 'up to us' through the exercise of reasoned reflection and virtue in a way that is not constrained by inborn nature, upbringing, or social context. Why should we associate this idea especially with Socrates? First of all, this is implied by the consistent presentation of Socrates as engaging, in principle, *anyone* in dialogue and urging people to re-examine their lives through reflective discussion and redirect them towards the pursuit of happiness through virtue. This is a marked feature of the depiction of Socrates in Plato's early dialogues, notably the *Apology*, but also of Xenophon's *Memorabilia*, and of other Socratic dialogues, such as Aeschines'.[37] It is consistent with a whole set of characteristically Socratic ideas, explored especially in Plato's early dialogues, such as that virtue is one, that it is knowledge, that no one does wrong willingly, and that virtue is—or is the key basis for—happiness.[38] This set of ideas implies that the achievement of happiness depends solely on the development of rational understanding or knowledge.

There is a marked contrast not only with traditional or conventional Greek thinking, which links happiness (and indeed virtue) much more closely with external circumstances such as wealth and length of life or with family and communal context.[39] There is also a contrast, of a different kind, with ideas

[35] See also Introd., text to nn. 50–3.

[36] On the scope of this enquiry, see Introd., text to nn. 2–6.

[37] See e.g. Pl. *Ap.* 21a–23b, 29d–30b, 31a–b, *La.* 187e–188c. A striking feature is the inclusion of people from all social classes, including women, particularly in Xenophon's writings.

[38] See text to n. 26 above.

[39] See Dover (1974), 174–5. These conventional views are reflected in Arist. *NE* 1.8–11.

about ethical education, in Plato's *Republic* and *Laws*, and Aristotle's ethical works. Although these writings share the Socratic view that the core basis for happiness is virtue and that virtue is centred on rationality and knowledge, they also lay down additional preconditions for the development of virtue. Although there are some variations between these theories, a shared feature is the requirement of specific kinds of (inborn) nature, habituation, and intellectual activities. A recurrent theme is that inborn nature of a certain type can enable or prevent the development of virtue—or, at least, that of the highest kind of virtue. Similarly, habituation of attitudes, practices, emotions, or desires is presented as a crucial prerequisite of the more purely rational aspects of this process. Also, specialized forms of theoretical knowledge, including those of mathematics and advanced or technical types of dialectical analysis, are depicted as a necessary basis for virtue or happiness of the highest type. This contrasting set of themes fits in with certain other distinctive Platonic–Aristotelian ideas, including a part-based or core-centred conception of human personality.[40]

The Stoics adopted the first (Socratic) approach to the development of virtue whereas at least some Middle Platonists, such as Plutarch, adopted the second, Platonic–Aristotelian, approach, partly in reaction against the Stoics.[41] What reason do we have to think that the Stoics saw the first approach as 'Socratic'? First, as Long brings out, the Socratic view that happiness is 'up to us' was conveyed in the genre of 'Socratic dialogues' by a range of writers, and was influential in the broad spectrum of fourth-century groups that saw themselves as inspired by Socrates.[42] Second, along with the other two Socratic themes considered here, this claim is consistent with other ideas which the Stoics consciously adopted from Socrates. These are that virtue is the only good and is a form of wisdom or knowledge and (implied in the claim that virtue is knowledge) that human motivation operates in a highly unified way.[43] Further suggestive indications are provided by Stoic practical ethics. For instance, as Long (2002) brings out, Socratic ideas and allusions are deeply embedded in the thought-system and teaching methods presented by Arrian as characteristic of Epictetus. A number of these bear directly on the present point. No Stoic writings bring out more clearly

[40] See 3.2 below, text to nn. 21–37.

[41] See e.g. on Plutarch, 4.3 below, text to nn. 113–14; also, on the mixed patterns of Antiochus and Arius Didymus, 3.4 below, esp. text to nn. 195–6, 211–13.

[42] Long (1999*b*), 618–23, esp. 618–19: 'The strongest and most diffused element in this Socratic tradition is the notion that it is the task of philosophy to establish rational foundations for an individual's happiness'. See also 623: 'a Socratic lifestyle is one in which a person is . . . in control of his or her own life, and uses reason as the instrument of satisfying the conditions of happiness'.

[43] See text to nn. 23–6 above.

than Epictetus' *Discourses* the message that the achievement of happiness is 'up to us' (*eph' hēmin*), because it depends on rational reflection and virtue and not on 'externals'. The figure of Socrates, as elsewhere in Stoic writings, appears as a paradigm for this idea, and also for the related theme that happiness achieved in this way is 'invulnerable' to changes in external circumstances.[44] What is more unusual, but highly significant, is that this motif is coupled with the re-creation, in some of Epictetus' discourses, of Socrates' distinctive method of ethical education by directed, inferential questioning. Further, Epictetus is shown as emphasizing certain features of Stoic thought that fit in with this adoption of a quasi-Socratic teaching method. These include the idea that all human beings are capable of forming a true conception of certain fundamental notions, such as goodness, and also of responding to the motivational power of this conception. They also include the idea that we are all capable of examining our own beliefs (in Stoic terms, 'impressions') to establish their consistency with each other and with these basic notions. Thus, Epictetus at least, associates this theme very closely indeed with Socrates' ideas, character, and distinctive method of discussion; and, although he may well take this linkage further than other Stoics, it seems very likely that he is building on a longstanding set of Socratic associations.[45]

I have suggested that the Stoics both take over salient Socratic ideas and do so in a way that is consistent with their characteristic holism and naturalism. This applies clearly to their theory of personal development as 'appropriation', cited earlier as expressing, in its two main stages, psychophysical and psychological holism (77–9 above). One of the main points of this theory is to convey the thought that human beings are naturally adapted to develop an understanding of the good (and thus of happiness) *regardless* of other differences in innate character, upbringing, social context, or even intellectual gifts. Another is that what people come to understand is that virtue is the only intrinsic good and that it is sufficient for happiness. Also, the acquisition of this understanding is taken, *by itself*, to bring about a fundamental reshaping of motivation. Further, this reshaping of motivation is seen as affecting the *whole* personality, and not just a rational 'core'. Correspondingly, this process is not seen as requiring a preliminary stage of habituation of emotions or desire. These are all features which reflect salient differences from the Platonic–Aristotelian patterns of ethical education, also adopted by some Middle Platonic thinkers such as Plutarch, in which development is subdivided between a habituative stage, focused on emotions and desires, and an intellectual one, directed at

[44] See e.g. Epict. *Handbook* 51, *Diss.* 1.26.15–18, 1.29.15–19, 2.2.8–9; on Socrates and invulnerability, see text to nn. 52–9 below.

[45] See Long (2002), ch. 3, referring esp. to 2.26, 1.11.5–15, 1.22.1–2, 2.11.1–8, 3.12.15.

reason or knowledge. They are also features which express, in various ways, the Socratic idea that it is open to everyone to develop towards complete happiness through reasoned reflection and virtue, an idea linked with the—equally Socratic—unified conception of human psychology. The Stoic version expresses these ideas in the form of a systematic theory, whereas in the 'Socratic dialogues' (especially Plato's) they are presented indirectly through what are often puzzling or confrontational dialogues.[46] Stoicism also expresses these ideas in a way that reflects the types of holism and naturalism that we have found to be characteristic of their outlook.

The second Socratic theme adopted in this way by the Stoics is the idea that happiness involves a time-independent perfection of character, marked by freedom from passion and distress. What I have in view here is the Stoic version of the ideal of invulnerability of character, which was a pervasive norm in Hellenistic and Roman thought and culture.[47] In Stoic and Epicurean thought, in particular, this ideal is symbolized by three recurrent motifs. One is that the normative wise person remains undisturbed and happy even on the rack of torture, because her happiness and peace of mind depend on her virtuous character not on external circumstances.[48] A related idea is that greater length of life does not increase happiness any more than reduced length of life decreases it. Although happiness is a property of lives rather than characters, the happiness of the life is taken in these theories to depend on the character of the person. Once the state of perfect wisdom has been reached, the happiness which is consequential on wisdom is not increased by greater length of life. My use of the phrase 'time-independent' perfection of character is designed to underline this striking idea.[49] A third motif is that your happiness is not diminished by the harm or death of those dear to you. A recurrent symbol for this idea, one also adopted by other philosophical approaches, was Anaxagoras' reported saying, when his son's death was announced, that 'I knew I was the father of a mortal'.[50] In interpreting this third feature in both Stoicism and Epicureanism, it is vital to see that it is compatible with full-hearted commitment to benefiting other people,

[46] On the interpretative issues raised by Plato's 'Socratic' dialogues, see Gill (2001*b*), reviewing Beversluis (2000).

[47] See discussion below, also 2.3 below, text to nn. 207–9, 223–47, 4.3, text to nn. 144–5, 7.2, text to nn. 43–9.

[48] For Stoic versions of this idea, see e.g. Cic. *Fin.* 3.42, 5.84. The image of the just person on the rack of torture (whose happiness Socrates is asked to prove) in Pl. *R.* 361c–362a, esp. 361e4–362a2, may have been an influential prototype.

[49] See e.g. Cic. *Fin.* 3.46, 76.

[50] See e.g. Plu. *Mor.* 474 D, also 463 D; D.L. 2.13; Cic. *Tusc.* 3.30, 58. On the use of this dictum in Stoic (and other Hellenistic) writings, see Gill (1994), 4613.

including those dear to you, and does not reflect the idea that you secure your own happiness by insulating yourself from other people.[51]

How did Socrates come to be associated in Stoic thought with the ideal of invulnerability? One of the most prominent aspects of the presentation of the figure of Socrates in fourth-century Socratic literature is his self-control as regards emotions and desires and his imperviousness to physical hardship and dangers. Xenophon's comment is typical: 'Socrates was the most self-controlled (*sōphronestatos*) of all men over sex and bodily appetite, the most resilient in relation to winter and summer and all exertions, and so trained for needing moderate amounts that he was satisfied when he had only little'.[52] Different Socratic writers, as it seems from our surviving sources, conceive this feature in rather different ways. In Phaedo's *Zopyrus*, this trait is presented as the result of deliberate self-control exercised on an inborn nature prone to sensuality.[53] In Antisthenes, the ideal character-state, exemplified by Socrates, is that of 'toughness' (*karteria*) and 'self-mastery' (*enkrateia*), as regards emotions and desires. This is presented as the outcome of the deliberate and systematic pursuit of virtue, conceived as being 'self-sufficient' (*autarkēs*) for happiness.[54] Although Stoic writers draw on a variety of sources in their picture of Socrates' character, particularly Xenophon,[55] Plato's depictions have a special importance for Stoicism. Epictetus' practice may again be taken as exemplary, though it is confirmed by that of other Stoic writers, such as Seneca.[56] Epictetus repeatedly cites episodes from Plato's dialogues in which Socrates is shown as emotionally invulnerable to dangers or to pressures.[57] A favourite instance is Socrates' intransigent response to the threats to his life from his accusers or the jury as presented at his trial in Plato's *Apology*.[58] Other examples include Socrates' sexual indifference to Alcibiades'

[51] See further (in Stoicism) 6.5 below, text to nn. 216–23, and Long (2002), 244–50. On the compatibility of interpersonal or social engagement and the individual pursuit of happiness in Stoicism, see esp. Reydams-Schils (2002) and (2005), and, in Epicureanism, Warren (2004), ch. 5.

[52] Xen. *Mem.* 2.1.1, trans. Long (1999*b*), 622.

[53] See Kahn (1996), 11–12, with references.

[54] See Kahn (1996), 7–8, referring esp. to D.L. 6.11.

[55] See e.g. the examples listed in Long (1996), 2 n. 2.

[56] See e.g. Sen. *On Peace of Mind* (*de Tranquillitate Animi*) 5.2–4 (see Gill 1994: 4620–2), *On Consistency* (*de Constantia*) 7.3, 18.5. See further, esp. on Socrates' courage in the face of death, Griffin (1976), 369–74, 385, (1986). However, Sedley (1999*b*), 149–51, suggests that the use of examples such as Socrates was characteristic of later Stoic writings (i.e. from Panaetius onwards), rather than early Stoic thought.

[57] For a series of such examples, see Epict. *Diss.* 4.1.159–172, referring to e.g. Pl. *Crito* 45c–d (163), *Ap.* 32b (164).

[58] See e.g. Epict. *Diss.* 1.29.18, 2.2.15–18, 3.23.21, referring to Pl. *Ap.* 30c–d; 1.9.24, 3.24.99, referring to Pl. *Ap.* 28e; 1.26.18, 3.12.15, referring to Pl. *Ap.* 38a. See further Dobbin (1998), 229–30, commenting on Epict. *Diss.* 1.29.16–21.

physical attractiveness in Plato's *Symposium* and his calm attitude towards his imminent death in Plato's *Phaedo*.[59]

Can Epictetus' practice help us to see why Plato's presentation of Socrates may have been a special source of inspiration for Stoic thinking about invulnerability? Epictetus seems especially drawn to cases where Socrates' response is unqualified and single-minded, rather than ones which suggest that he controls emotions or desires by conscious effort (as he was presented in Phaedo's *Zopyrus*).[60] Also, Epictetus is especially attracted to cases where the theoretical basis for Socrates' response is made explicit. This comes out in the assertion by Plato's Socrates at his trial (frequently cited by Epictetus) that 'Anytus and Meletus can kill me but they cannot harm me' (*Ap.* 30c8–9).[61] Socrates' emphatic affirmation implies an unqualified lack of fear rather than the control or suppression of fear. Also, the line of argument preceding the comment suggests the theoretical basis for Socrates' lack of fear. This is the belief that one is only *harmed*, in a real sense, by becoming worse in ethical character, not by suffering the kind of external damage (condemnation and execution) that Socrates' accusers want to bring about.[62] This instance can be taken as exemplifying a more general feature of Stoic responses to Socrates, especially as presented by Plato, which surely contributed to the formulation of their version of the ideal of invulnerability. The presentation of Socrates was taken by them as exemplifying *apatheia*, the complete *absence* of emotions such as fear, rather than what came to be called *metriopatheia*, the control or moderation of an emotion by a deliberate act of reason.[63] Also, Plato's Socrates, especially, may have been used by them as a symbol for *apatheia* because some Platonic dialogues, at least, bring out with special clarity the theoretical grounds for not feeling fear in such situations. In addition to the *Apology*, another favourite text for Epictetus was the *Gorgias*. As Long (2002: 70–4) shows, Epictetus' citations of this argument add up to a summary of an ethical theory, according to which wrongdoing is the result of error in the attempt to realize the universal objective of doing what is good. To be harmed, then, goes along with *doing* injustice, and with having the kind of

[59] See Epict. *Diss.* 2.18.22, referring to Pl. *Smp.* 219b–e; 1.29.65–6, referring to Pl. *Phd.* 116d, 117d.

[60] See n. 53 above. A Platonic example of self-restraint (not cited by Epictetus) is Socrates' report of his control of lust aroused by the sight of Charmides' beautiful body in Pl. *Chrm.* 155d.

[61] See references in n. 58 above. Long (2002: 68) also highlights the probable influence on Stoic thought of Socrates' claim that no harm can come to a good person in life or death (Pl. *Ap.* 41d).

[62] Pl. *Ap.* 30b–d, taken in connection with Socrates' mission to urge the Athenians to 'take care of their psyche', i.e. improve their character, not their body (29d–30b) and his comments on the unreasonableness of fearing death in 29a–b.

[63] For this contrast, see Dillon (1983), and 3.4 below, text to nn. 207, 224, 4.3.

character expressed in wanting to do injustice, rather than with *suffering* it. Socrates' grasp of this point, implied in his comment in *Apology* 30c8–9, could be taken by the Stoics as showing why he feels no fear on this occasion, rather than feeling a fear that he needs to control or suppress.

How does Stoic thinking about the ideal of invulnerability reflect the combination of Socratic ethical claims and of psychophysical holism and naturalism? In answering this question, it is helpful to see Stoic thinking on this topic as one of two possible ways of thinking about invulnerability implied in Plato's writings. As already suggested, Stoic thinking represents a more holistic and naturalistic version of certain 'hard' ethical claims embodied especially in what modern scholars see as early Platonic dialogues, such as the *Gorgias* and *Protagoras*. These claims include the ideas that virtue is one, that it is knowledge, that no one does wrong willingly, that virtue is self-sufficient for happiness, and that doing wrong is worse than suffering it. Implied in the combination of these claims is a unified psychological model according to which human beings act and feel in a way that corresponds to their state of knowledge or ignorance of the good (which all people seek to obtain).[64] Plato's Socrates is both the main dialectical spokesman for these ideas and also their principal symbolic vehicle. He can be seen as already possessing the kind of knowledge that constitutes virtue or, at least, as understanding fully what these arguments imply, and acting and feeling accordingly.[65]

Broadly speaking, this seems to be how the Stoics read the early Platonic dialogues and the representation of the figure of Socrates there. They themselves formulated theories, such as that of the passions and of the correlated ideal of *apatheia* (absence of passion), which are based on the premise that people's affective lives and actions reflect their degree of ethical understanding or ignorance along the lines suggested in these Platonic dialogues. Where their theory differs is partly in its explicitness and systematic character. But it also differs in the introduction of an account of natural development (as 'appropriation'), in which human beings are seen as disposed to progress towards the kind of knowledge of the good that Socrates saw as the ideal outcome of human life. It also differs in analysing states of human knowledge and ignorance holistically, as functions of the whole psychophysical personality of the adult human being (or rational animal). This point has been made earlier in connection with the theory of the passions (79 above). Analogously,

[64] See text to nn. 23–6 above.

[65] The question whether Socrates can *both* consistently deny knowledge about the subjects into which he enquires *and* have the virtues that depend on (or are identical with) this knowledge has been much discussed in recent scholarship; see e.g. Benson (2000), 238–49.

wisdom is seen not just as a state of ethical knowledge but also one that informs the (psychophysical) personality of the wise person at virtually every level. Stoic images of invulnerability such as that of the wise person happy on the rack or of Socrates unmoved at his trial and death imply not just a certain kind of psychological character. They also suggest a certain kind of physical state, that of 'sinewy' cohesion or tension (*eutonia*), reflecting the kind of bodily or 'animal' state that is constituted by virtue.[66] The Stoics might have seen that last thought prefigured in representations of Socrates, including those of Plato. His body itself is presented as 'invulnerable' to sexual desire, physical pain, fear, and alcohol.[67] Indeed, the depiction in Plato's *Phaedo* of the response of Socrates' body to the impact of hemlock poisoning expresses a similarly calm, measured, and (relatively) impervious type of response, and one that is strikingly different at least from most ancient accounts of the effects of hemlock.[68] The Stoics might have read this scene as implying that Socrates' virtue had become so much part of his character that it determined the way that his body reacted to hemlock-poisoning.[69] The Stoics could also have located that kind of image of invulnerability in a comprehensive theory of natural development and correlated psychophysical states, outlined earlier (77–80 above).

The distinctive character of Stoic thinking on invulnerability and their use of Socrates as a symbol of this ideal can be defined by contrast with another ancient approach. This is the dualist conception of invulnerability that we can see as expressed in the ideas of Plato's *Phaedo*, which is symbolized by the presentation of Socrates there. The argument of this Platonic dialogue centres on radical metaphysical contrasts between body and psyche (or mind) and particulars and Forms.[70] These contrasts also inform some of the points made by Socrates about virtue. Emotions and desires are presented as a product of the linkage of the psyche with the body; and conventional types of virtue, such as self-control and bravery, are characterized negatively as the 'exchange' (*amoibē*) of one set of body-based pleasures and pains for another. By

[66] See text to nn. 14–18 above.

[67] See e.g. Pl. *Smp.* 219b–220c, 221a–b, 223c–d; also references in nn. 57–9 above.

[68] Pl. *Phd.* 117e–118a (following the description of Socrates' unemotional response to the prospect of death in 116b–117e). See Gill (1973), which stresses the contrast from other ancient and modern accounts of the symptoms of hemlock-poisoning. However, Bloch (2002), drawing on a wider range of evidence (especially modern medical accounts), argues that Plato's account is historically accurate in its presentation of Socrates' death.

[69] Cf. the Stoic idea that the cohesive and structured character of the wise person (his 'good tension', *eutonia*) might enable his psyche to persist after death, 80 above. I am not aware of any evidence that the Stoics *actually did* interpret the scene in this way, though Socrates' courage at the prospect of death, certainly, was sometimes regarded by them as a paradigm for passionless virtue; see n. 59 above.

[70] See further 1.2 above, text to nn. 6–7.

contrast, *true* or *real* (*alēthēs*) virtue is said to depend on the purging or purification of the psyche (or mind) from the body, a process carried out by philosophy and by the search for (non-empirical) knowledge that this expresses.[71] Features of the characterization of the figure of Socrates can be seen as symbolizing the possession of this type of virtue—or at least the understanding of what it involves.[72] Socrates' exceptionally brave and unemotional response to the prospect of death at the end of the dialogue might be taken, from this standpoint, as illustrating the kind of mind that has 'purified' itself from the body by philosophy and thus from the emotions and desires that are the outcome of linkage with the body.[73] Against the background of this line of thought, the exceptionally calm and measured character of Socrates' death by hemlock-poisoning may be taken as symbolizing the response of a mind that is wholly ready to purify itself from the body. This can plausibly be taken as a Platonic way of reading the significance of the scene, by contrast with the 'Stoic' interpretation of his bodily reactions suggested earlier.[74] A dualist conception of invulnerability and *apatheia*, of this type, figures in Plutarch's Middle Platonic pattern of thinking, alongside the ideal of 'moderation of passions' (*metriopatheia*), as brought out later (4.3 below). Also, in *Tusculans* 1, Cicero adopts this way of thinking about invulnerability, and uses Socrates' courage at his death, together with other key motifs from the *Phaedo*, as an exemplar for this ideal.[75] This point illustrates vividly how the Platonic Socrates, particularly at the moment of death, could be used in Hellenistic–Roman thought as a symbol for invulnerability on the basis of rival conceptions of human nature and personality.

The third theme involving a merger of Socratic claims and Stoic holism is less well marked than the other two; but it is, none the less, an important and suggestive one. This is the idea that only the rational and fully virtuous person

[71] Pl. *Phd.* 68c–69c, esp. 66b–d, 68d–69c, also 83a–84a.

[72] For the final qualification, see n. 65 above.

[73] Socrates' readiness for death expresses the attitude of one who has 'practised' for death in the way suggested in *Phd.* 67e–68b.

[74] Contrast the response of those reluctant to leave the body—they become ghosts because the psyche is still partly embodied, weighed down by its 'earthy' or 'heavy' character (81a–e). For this reading of the scene, see Gill (1973) and for the contrasting 'Stoic' reading, which is not explicit in any extant Stoic work, see text to n. 69 above.

[75] See Cic. *Tusc.* 1.71–5, esp. 71: 'when [Socrates] was holding the cup in his hands, he spoke as one who was not being forced to his death but was ascending to the skies (*in caelum... escendere*)'. Other themes based on the *Phaedo* include the idea of philosophers 'practising death' (*Tusc.* 1.74, cf. Pl. *Phd.* 67e–68b). On Cicero's philosophical position in *Tusc.*, see Lévy (1992), 445–94, (2003); and on his philosophical affiliation in general, a version of Academic Scepticism, see Glucker (1988). In the *Tusculans*, Cicero combines a strongly Platonic approach in Book 1 with a positive treatment of Stoic therapy in *Tusc.* 3–4 (on which see Graver (2002*a*); Tieleman (2003), ch. 6). On Cicero and unitary or part-based conceptions of the psyche, see 4.1 below, text to nn. 35–9.

is psychologically cohesive whereas anyone who falls short of this normative state is incoherent in character and way of life.[76] This idea is implied by the fact that the desired outcome of personal development (understood as 'appropriation') is complete consistency in patterns of rational selection and response.[77] It is also an explicit and emphatic part of the theory of the passions. Those subject to the passions—which means everyone apart from the normative wise person—display reactions which are 'fluttering' or 'feverish' and lacking in coherence. This is so even though we also find evidence for the belief that different people are dispositionally inclined to experience certain kinds of passion.[78] This idea also fits with other well-marked themes in Stoicism according to which failure to achieve complete wisdom necessarily entails complete lack of wisdom.[79] Why should one see this Stoic idea as Socratic in origin or inspiration? It is not an explicit thesis in the early Platonic dialogues or Socratic dialogues by other authors. In fact, the clearest anticipation of this theme comes in what modern readers see as a 'Platonic' (not 'Socratic') dialogue, the *Republic.* The depiction of the series of defective psychological types in Books 8 and 9 suggests that the further removed they are from the ideally just character-type the more internally conflicted and incoherent they are in motivation and way of life.[80]

However, this is another idea that the Stoics may well have derived from the set of 'hard' ethical claims associated with Socrates, such as that virtue is one, that it is knowledge, and that no one does wrong willingly.[81] What these claims imply is that virtue constitutes a unified or structured state of character, consisting in, or grounded on, knowledge. Possession of this structured character entails *complete* consistency in one's belief-set (or knowledge-set). Since wrongdoing results from error not conscious choice, it will also imply consistency in motivation, action, and affective responses. Ideas of this kind were held by the Stoics about the normative wise person;[82] and it is plausible to see them as inspired by the Socratic claims that were taken as fundamental to their ethical thinking. Portrayals of Socrates could, again, have been taken as emblematic of this motif. For instance, the representation of the Socrates–Alcibiades relationship in Plato's *Symposium* and, it seems, Aeschines' *Alcibiades*, underlines the contrast between Socrates' consistency in ideas and

[76] For this idea, see further 4.5, 5.2, 7.3–4 below.

[77] See e.g. Cic. *Fin.* 3.20–1 (also 146–7 below), *Off.* 1.100, 111; D.L. 7.89.

[78] See LS 65 A(2), G(3), R–S. See further 4.5 below, text to nn. 245–66.

[79] LS 61 I(1), S–T.

[80] See 5.2 below, text to nn. 115–35.

[81] See text to nn. 23–6 above.

[82] See references in nn. 48–51 above; also LS 65 W, Cic. *Fin.* 75–6.

attitude and Alcibiades' fluctuating objectives in life and violent mood-swings.[83] In Plato's *Phaedo*, the close of the dialogue especially highlights the contrast between the fact that Socrates' actions and emotions (even his style of death) consistently reflect the implications of the argument, whereas the reactions of others, despite having accepted his conclusions, show an emotional intensity not consistent with those conclusions.[84] More broadly, Plato's dialogues in particular do not only underline the contrast between the *logical* inconsistencies (the incoherent belief-sets) of Socrates' interlocutors and Socrates' consistency—at least, his consistent search for consistency of belief.[85] They also emphasize the fluctuating *emotional* responses of the interlocutors to Socratic probing of their belief-sets and imply, at least, that there is a linkage between these two kinds of incoherence.[86] A similar pattern is sometimes evident in Epictetus' version of Socratic arguments, in particular the set-piece *Discourse* 1.11, whose explicit subject is the interlocutor's incoherent (and misguided) pattern of responses to his daughter's illness.[87] This seems to be another case where a distinctive Stoic theme derives from reflection on hard Socratic ethical claims, combined with reflection on Socrates as a symbolic figure. Again, as brought out later, this idea is developed in a way that reflects Stoic psychological and psychophysical holism, in the Stoic theory of the emotions or passions.[88]

A contrasting view is, again, implied in certain strands of Platonic–Aristotelian thought and made explicit in Plutarch's fusion of these strands in his essay, *On Ethical Virtue*. Plutarch appeals to Aristotle's distinctions between the full virtue of temperance (*sōphrosunē*), the partial virtue of self-restraint (*enkrateia*), the partial vice of incontinence (*akrasia*), and the full vice of intemperance (*akolasia*).[89] Plutarch presents these as distinct and relatively stable states. More specifically, he emphasizes the difference between the internally conflicted and incoherent character of the akratic person and the stable, though defective, character of the intemperate person, who consistently has excessive sensual desires (*Mor.* 445 B–446 C). More broadly, he presents this as a credible set of ethical and psychological distinctions which

[83] See Pl. *Smp.* 215b–222b, esp. 216a–c and 219b–e; *Alcib. 1*, esp. 134c–135e. On Aeschines' portrayal, see Kahn (1996), 19–23. This feature informs Plutarch's presentation of Alcibiades as 'chameleonic' (7.2 below, text to nn. 32–7).

[84] See Pl. *Phd.* 115a–116a, 117b–e. See also text to nn. 67–9 above.

[85] On this process see (from various standpoints), Vlastos (1994), ch. 1; Benson (2000). part 1; Beversluis (2000); Gill (2001*b*).

[86] Much of the interpersonal drama of the early Platonic dialogues derives from this source, e.g. in *Gorgias* (on which see Kahn 1983) or *Protagoras* (on which see Beversluis 2000: 257–90).

[87] See Long (2002), ch. 2, esp. 77–9; also (1996), 277–80.

[88] See 4.5 below, text to nn. 180–91, 267–78, 4.6, text to nn. 333–5, 5.2.

[89] For these distinctions, see e.g. Arist. *NE* 1.13, $1102^{b}13$–28, 7.1, $1145^{b}8$–20.

is made possible by the part-based model adopted by Plato and Aristotle, in which types of ethical character are defined by the extent to which the rational part shapes and controls the non-rational desires and appetites.[90] By contrast, Plutarch complains, the Stoic unified model effaces this important set of distinctions by identifying reason with emotion or desire (*Mor.* 447A–C). An implication of Plutarch's view is that the Stoics conflate intemperance with incontinence, assimilating the relatively stable vice to the internally conflicted one. Plutarch's view represents a plausible way of interpreting a set of ideas in Aristotle, which have partial parallels in Plato,[91] although there are, in fact, ideas in both thinkers that prefigure the Stoic view.[92] Here again, Plutarch's (Middle Platonic) approach serves to highlight by contrast the Stoic pattern of thought in which a theme with Socratic roots is elaborated in terms of psychological and psychophysical holism.

So far I have been assuming that Stoic thought consistently reflects psychological and psychophysical holism even when it is expressing its own version of 'hard' Socratic ethical claims. But is this really the case? This is a question that needs to be tackled because there are certain passages, particularly in works of Stoic practical ethics, that seem to express, instead, psyche–body dualism or at least, core-centred thinking of the kind I have presented as characteristic of Plato and Aristotle or Middle Platonism. How can we explain this if, as I have suggested, the holistic approach is a deliberate and systematic feature of Stoic (and Epicurean) thought?

Epictetus' *Discourses*, for instance, contain several striking examples, including these passages from 1.3:

> since in our birth we have these two elements mingled within us, a body in common with the animals, and reason and intelligence in common with the gods, many of us incline towards the former relationship, miserable as it is and wholly mortal, and only some few to the divine and blessed one . . . 'For what am I? A poor miserable man' they say, and 'This poor wretched flesh of mine'.[93]

This comment is on similar lines: 'Wherever "I" and "mine" are placed, to there the creature inevitably inclines: if they are in the flesh, the authority must be there, if in one's volition (or 'choice', *prohairesis*), there, if in external things, there'.[94] A similar contrast is couched in the form of the question: 'what is the

[90] *Mor.* 446 D–E , taken with 441 F–442 E , 443 C–D ; also 4.3 below.

[91] A further Platonic idea that could be cited in this connection is that of the determinate, but defective, character-types in *R.* 8–9, which constitutes different patterns of relationship between the three parts of the psyche; but see also following note.

[92] See e.g. Arist. *NE* 9.4, $1166^{b}3$–29, *EE* $1240^{b}24$–7, arguing that only the good are internally unified and are therefore capable of self-love; see also Gill (1996*b*), 358–60. For the series of character-types in *R.* 8–9 as implying a similar view, see 5.2 below, text to nn. 115–35.

[93] Epict. *Diss.* 1.3.3, 5, trans. Hard in Gill (1995), slightly modified.

[94] Epict. *Diss.* 2.22.19, trans. Long (2002), 222.

principal part (*proēgoumenon*) in us, and what is our substantial and what our essential nature (*hupostatikon kai ousiōdes*)?' Epictetus also poses this imagined question (to Epicurus): 'What is there within you which deliberates, which examines everything, and which, with regard to the flesh itself, determines that this is the principal part?'[95] In another passage, Epictetus uses the contrast 'mine' and 'not mine' to express his reiterated distinction between what is and is not 'up to us', that is, within or outside the scope of our choice or *prohairesis*. He develops the contrast in an imagined dialogue, in which someone insists on maintaining his chosen course of action in spite of intimidation: '"Betray the secret". I will not betray it, for this is up to me (*ep' emoi*). "Then I will fetter you". What are you saying, man? Fetter me? You will fetter my leg; but not even Zeus himself can get the better of my choice'.[96]

Similar contrasts are drawn in Marcus Aurelius' *Meditations*; two striking passages are worth noting.

> Ensure that the governing and pre-eminent (*hēgemonikon kai kurieuon*) part of your psyche remains indifferent to every movement, smooth or violent in your flesh, and let it not combine with them, but circumscribe itself, and restrict these affections to the members of the body.
>
> This thing, whatever it is that I am, is mere flesh (*sarkia*), and some breath (*pneumation*), and the governing faculty (*hēgemonikon*). Despise the flesh—mere blood and bones, and a mesh of interwoven nerves and veins and arteries. Consider too what kind of thing your breath is: a stream of air, and not even forever the same, but expelled at each moment and then drawn in anew. So that leaves our third part, the governing faculty.[97]

Broadly similar, seemingly dualist, statements can be found sometimes in Seneca, two of which are worth noting here. In the preface to the *Natural Questions* (13), Seneca identifies as the difference between god and us that god is entirely reason whereas we have reason as our 'better part'. In *Letter* 65.18, he characterizes the wise person as one who, 'though he is stuck in his body, yet is absent from it in the best part of himself and directs his thoughts to the realm above'.[98]

How are we to explain expressions of this kind, which seem to run counter to the kind of holistic thinking I have presented as central to Stoicism? One factor—though not a decisive one—is that this type of expression tends to

[95] Epict. *Diss.* 1.20.17–18, trans. Hard in Gill (1995), slightly modified.

[96] Epict. *Diss.* 1.1.23, trans. Hard in Gill (1995), slightly modified.

[97] M.A., extracts from 5.26 and 2.2, trans., Hard in Gill (1997*b*), punctuation slightly modified.

[98] Both examples cited by Long (2002), 177, whose translation of *Ep.* 65.18 is used. The phrase 'the realm above' is paralleled in *Natural Questions*, Preface, 13, where the study of nature is said to draw the mind 'upwards' towards the divinity embodied in the universe.

appear in works of practical ethics rather than in more technical contexts. Although, in general, writings of this type strongly reflect mainstream Stoic ideas, the formulation tends to be studiously non-technical and sometimes reflects a distinctive personal idiom. It is thus less surprising that we should find examples of core-centred thinking in such works, in spite of the fact that the main lines of Stoic thinking, which are also reflected in these writings, point towards a holistic conception of human nature.[99] But the crucial point, I think, is one made by Long in connection with Epictetus. Epictetus is not, in passages such as those cited, making a metaphysical claim about the mind–body relationship or about (what we would call) 'personal identity'. He is using seemingly dualist or core-centred language to make an essentially moral or ethical point. The point is that we should (in a non-technical sense) 'identify' ourselves with our *prohairesis*, our capacity for rational agency, volition, and choice. This is one of the formulations by which Epictetus expresses his recurrent contrast between what is and is not 'up to us' (within or outside our *prohairesis*).[100] Part of the point of this contrast is to convey the central Stoic theme, which has, as I have just stressed, Socratic roots, that the achievement of happiness through reasoned reflection and virtue is 'up to us' in a way that is not constrained by external factors such as our inborn nature, upbringing, or situation. We all have the capacity to exercise our rational agency by taking virtue as our goal, rather than (in more technical language) 'indifferents' such as sensual pleasure, here identified as our body or flesh.[101] The idea that this capacity is unconstrained is expressed by saying that, for instance, someone can fetter one's leg but not one's *prohairesis* (or 'me', in an ethical sense). Epictetus assumes that 'invulnerability', in a strong sense, belongs only to the normative wise person, not to those taking this state as their ultimate goal.[102] But even those who only aspire to this state can recognize the invulnerable or unconstrained character of their rational agency *provided that* they undertake in a systematic way the developmental programme of which we are all constitutively capable as rational animals.[103]

But how can we be sure that Epictetus or Marcus is *not* using this type of language to make a substantively philosophical point, even if a non-standard one?[104] In the case of Epictetus, a well-known Stoic teacher, this would be very

[99] See further 6.5 below, esp. text to nn. 197–207.

[100] Long (2002), 158–62, 199, 207–10, 222–9.

[101] Epictetus presupposes the idea of 'indifferents' (see e.g. *Diss.* 1.20. 6–7, 12) although he typically avoids this type of technical vocabulary in the *Discourses*.

[102] For passages in Epictetus that suggest this idea, see 6.5 below, esp. text to nn. 201–7, 228–9.

[103] See e.g. Epict. *Diss.* 1.1, esp. 10–12, 21–5, 1.2.12–19, 1.4, 1–4, 18–27; see further 6.5 below, text to nn. 208–10, 224–35.

[104] One of the passages cited earlier (*Diss.* 1.20.17–18) *is* making a philosophically substantive point: Epictetus is using core-centred language to challenge Epicurus' claim that pleasure

surprising. But, in any case, as Long points out, Epictetus indicates elsewhere that he shares the normal Stoic—non-dualist—view that the mind's substance is *pneuma* ('breath').[105] As regards psychological holism, Epictetus' distinctive three-point programme for ethical development, like the standard Stoic theory of development on which it is based, presupposes a unified psychological model in which motivation is shaped by beliefs and by progress in understanding.[106] So we have good reasons for preferring an interpretation of Epictetus' language which is consistent with psychophysical and psychological holism. Marcus Aurelius is not, of course, a Stoic teacher, and, on some points at least, there is room for raising questions about his doctrinal orthodoxy.[107] But Marcus too, in a number of ways, makes clear his acceptance of the Stoic view that human minds are physical entities. In his case too, the contrast drawn in the passages cited seems to be, essentially, an ethical one, a way of framing the (self-delivered) injunction towards a virtuous rather than sensual response. This is virtually explicit in the continuation of the two passages cited earlier. In 5.26, referring to the movements in the flesh, he continues:

> when they communicate themselves to the mind by virtue of that other sympathy, *as must occur in a unified organism* (*sōma hēnōmenon*), you should not attempt to resist the sensation, which is only natural, but ensure that the governing faculty (*hēgemonikon*) does not add to it from itself by judging it to be good or bad.[108]

Marcus recognizes that we constitute a psychophysical whole (a 'unified organism' or 'body') and that certain sensations are natural and will make an impact on the control-centre by the internal 'sympathy' in our bodies (which Hierocles links with 'self-perception').[109] His point is that one should not judge this sensation to be good or bad, but only (by implication) at most a preferred indifferent. This is the process he has in mind in advising himself not to 'combine' with the movements of the flesh and to 'restrict' them to the

(including physical pleasure) is the overall good. The language used is not particularly appropriate for either Epicureanism or Stoicism (see also Antiochus' use of inappropriate part-based language in criticism of Stoic ethics, 3.4 below, text to nn. 189–95). However, there is no indication that Epictetus is introducing a new type of Stoic metaphysical doctrine.

105 Long (2002), 158, referring to Epict. *Diss.* 2.32.3, 3.3.22. On *pneuma*, see LS 47 and 1.4 above, text to nn. 110–14. On the combination of metaphysical monism and ethical quasi-dualism in Stoic thought more generally, see Long (1999*a*), 560–2.

106 For this programme, see esp. 3.2 below, text to nn. 19–20, 42–6, 73–5 (LS 56 C); see further 6.5 below, text to nn. 194–207.

107 Especially on the question repeatedly raised by Marcus whether the universe is based on 'atoms or providence'. See e.g. M.A. *Med.* 4.3, 6.10, 7.32, 8.17, 9.28, 9.39, 10.6, 11.18, 12.24. For recent discussions of this point, see Annas (2004); Cooper (2004*a*).

108 Trans. Hard in Gill (1997*b*), with added italics.

109 See 1.4 above, text to nn. 137–52.

members of the body. Similarly in 2.2, the other passage cited, he urges himself not 'to be drawn this way and that, like a puppet, by every uncooperative impulse (*hormē akoinōtaton*)'. The comment, though partly couched in Platonic language, that of the psyche as a 'puppet',[110] assumes the standard Stoic view that human beings act and feel according to a belief-based impulse (*hormē*). In saying that we should 'despise the flesh' and identify ourselves with our control-centre, Marcus means that we should not respond to passions (characterized in standard mode as fluctuating, drawing us 'this way and that')[111] but work towards a more 'cooperative', reasonable, and virtuous mode of response. Similar points could be made about Seneca's use of apparently dualist expressions.[112]

The preceding discussion may have helped to show why Stoic writers might be drawn towards using quasi-dualist language with Platonic connotations to express this kind of ethical message, without intending this language to suggest metaphysical innovation. I have pointed to a series of ways in which the Stoics seem to be strongly influenced by 'hard' ethical claims closely associated with Socrates, especially as his ideas and character are presented in Plato's dialogues. These are combined with a nexus of ideas about emotions and human development implying psychological and psychophysical holism. Given this background, it is less surprising that Stoic writers should occasionally use language which evokes Platonic dualism or core-centred thinking to make ethical points which themselves evoke the core claims of Plato's Socrates.[113] This makes it easier to see why they might not expect these ethical points to be taken to imply a commitment to Platonic dualism or a core-centred conception of personality. Thus interpreted, passages of this kind confirm the view I have presented here of the Stoic holistic outlook rather than undermining it.

2.3 EPICUREANISM

In the case of Epicureanism too, my view is that the conception of human personality expresses a combination of psychological and psychophysical holism and Socratic ethical ideas of the same general type. The first part of this

[110] Pl. *Lg.* 644d–645b: the human psyche compared to a puppet pulled by strings, i.e. (mostly) the emotions; but one of the strings is reason and we should cooperate with this.

[111] See e.g. LS 65 A(2), G(3), R.

[112] For these expressions, see n. 98 above. On Seneca's thinking on psychology, see 215 below.

[113] There may, of course, be additional reasons why specific Stoic thinkers use Platonic language. On Posidonius and Plato, see 4.6 below, text to nn. 346–92; in the case of Marcus, there may also be influence from Middle Platonism.

suggestion is not especially controversial. Recent accounts of Epicurean psychology have stressed, for instance, that, as in Stoicism, the conception of emotions and desire is markedly belief-based or cognitive and, to this extent, reflects a unified picture of human psychology.[114] As regards the synthesis of psychological with psychophysical holism, the Epicurean analysis of the initiation of action envisages a role both for 'mind' as a source of action and for 'images' (*eidōla, simulacra*), understood as physical entities which activate the animal as an integrated psychophysical whole.[115] At the level of ideals, the Epicurean account of happiness or the good life is defined, emphatically, in terms of a combination of physical and psychological pleasure.[116] To put the same general point in different terms, the salient distinctions, regarding human nature and motivation, are framed in terms which cut across the mind–body or reason–desire contrasts which are characteristic of Platonic–Aristotelian part-based psychology and core-centred thinking (1.2 above).[117] This applies, for instance, to Epicurean distinctions such as that between 'natural' and 'empty' desires (or emotions) or between 'kinetic' and 'katastematic' pleasures.[118]

More controversial is the idea that the Epicurean version of psychological and psychophysical holism is combined with *Socratic* ethical ideas. Unlike the Stoics, the Epicureans did not present themselves as inspired by Socrates; and Epicurus' immediate followers at least were strongly critical of Socrates. He was characterized by them as (in Long's terms) 'the complete anti-Epicurean—a sophist, a rhetorician, a sceptic, and someone whose ethical enquiries turn human life into chaos'.[119] However, the strength of their attacks does not indicate that Socrates was without significance for them—rather the reverse. As Long also suggests (1996: 10–11), 'Epicurean criticism of Socrates can be seen . . . as a means of undercutting the most obvious alternative models of the philosophical life—Socrates as interpreted by Stoics and Academics'. To put the point more broadly, the attacks by Epicurus' followers reflect Socrates' towering presence in the fourth and third centuries BC as a symbol for the power of philosophy to change human lives and as a paradigm for the philosophical life and character.[120] Epicurus' followers, in effect, aimed to

[114] That is, the theory does not imply a strong contrast between reason and desire/emotion of the type implied in Pl. *R.* 435–441 (on which see 5.2 below, text to nn. 75–101). See further Annas (1992), 191–9; also Mitsis (1988), 40–51.

[115] See e.g. Lucr. 4.877–906, taken with Annas (1992), 175–80; on the role of 'mind' (*mens* or *animus*) in activating animal movement understood as a psychophysical process, see also Bobzien (2000), 309–16.

[116] See e.g. LS 21 A(6), B(1).

[117] On apparent exceptions to this generalization, see 114–17 below.

[118] See e.g. LS 21 I–J, Q–R, discussed below.

[119] Long (1996), 9; see also Riley (1980); Kleve (1983).

[120] See also Long (1999*b*), 620: Socrates 'was a precursor of Epicurus himself in his devoted band of followers and the paradigm he afforded of someone perfected in his own practices'.

replace Socrates as a symbolic figure by Epicurus;[121] but this objective points to a strong awareness of the key ethical claims associated with Socrates, rather than lack of interest in these claims.

Epicurus was, it seems, more positively influenced by Democritus in ethics as well as in his atomic physics.[122] But, in certain important ways, Democritus' ethical thought can be seen as reinforcing the 'Socratic' ethical ideas on which I am focusing. Also, it may well be Socrates, together with some of the figures from the post-Socratic (or post-Democritean) tradition, rather than Democritus himself, who contributed most towards two distinctive features of Epicurean ethics. These consist in a strikingly austere or rigorous attitude, surprising in a hedonist philosophy, and a fondness for emphatic paradox. These features are evident in one of the fundamental principles of Epicurean ethics: the—much-debated—formulation of the goal of life, pleasure, in negative terms, as the *absence* of physical pain and mental distress (*aponia* and *ataraxia*). They are also visible in the Epicurean forms of the three aspects of the ideal of invulnerability shared with Stoicism. Two of these represent Epicurean versions of the thought that the wise person is happy on the rack of torture and that length of life has no bearing on one's happiness. The third expression of invulnerability is the claim that 'death is nothing to us'. Our happiness, it would seem, is threatened neither by the loss of others dear to us nor even by the loss of ourselves. As in the case of Stoicism, these motifs evoke Socrates' paradoxical mode of argument and his ultra-rigorous personal style, displayed especially in Plato's dialogues. As in the case of Stoicism, the Epicurean version of these strong ethical claims is conceived in a form that is fully—if perhaps surprisingly—consistent with the conception of human beings as psychologically cohesive, embodied rational animals with a finite life-span. Although there were, probably, various influences on these expressions of invulnerability, that of Socrates seems likely to have been a crucial one. Hence, the combination of Socratic ideals with psychological and psychophysical holism is not just a point on which Epicureanism, as it was put earlier, *converges* with Stoicism. It is also a feature that offers the prospect of taking us to the heart of the Epicurean conception of human personality and selfhood.[123]

[121] On aspects of the process of establishing Epicurus as a symbol figure see e.g. Caizzi (1993), 323–9; Warren (2004), 9–10; also, on the role of sculpture, Frischer (1982); Zanker (1995), 113–29. Epicurus' death-bed letter became a key element in this process, competing with Plato's presentation of Socrates' fortitude in death; see text to nn. 234–47 below, also 2.2 above, text to nn. 68–75.

[122] Epicurus' hedonism, for instance, develops Democritus' presentation of *euthumia* ('cheerfulness') as the proper human objective; see e.g. DK fr. B 191. See further text to nn. 151–6 below.

[123] On the points outlined in the preceding paragraph, see text to nn. 161–87, 207–50 below.

I move now to the Epicurean version of the three relevant Socratic ethical ideas; the question of the compatibility of these themes with their holistic outlook will be considered in each case. The most straightforward theme is the Epicurean version of the idea that complete happiness is open to all human beings as such and is attainable through virtue[124] and rational reflection in a way that is not constrained by one's inborn nature, upbringing, or social situation. Several salient points come out in these two passages from Epicurus and Lucretius respectively:

Let no one either delay philosophizing when young, or weary of philosophizing when old. For no one is under-age or over-age for psychic health. To say either that the time is not ripe for philosophizing, or that the time for philosophizing is gone by, is like saying that the time for happiness either has not arrived or is no more. So both young and old must philosophize—the latter so that although old he may stay young in good things owing to gratitude for what has occurred, the former so that although young he may be like an old man owing to his lack of fear of what is yet to come. Therefore we must practise the things which produce happiness, seeing that when happiness is present we have everything, while when it is absent the one aim of our actions is to have it.[125]

Likewise the human race. Even though education (*doctrina*) may produce individuals equally well turned out—it still leaves those original traces of each mind's nature (*naturae cuiusque animi*). And we must not suppose that faults can be completely eradicated, so that one man will not plunge hastily into bitter anger, another may be assailed too readily by fear, or the third type not be over-indulgent in tolerating certain things. There are many other respects in which various natures and consequently the behaviours of human beings must differ, but I cannot now set out their hidden causes, nor can I find enough names for all the shapes of primary particles from which this variety springs. But there is one thing on which I see I can state this matter: so slight are the traces of our natures which reason (*ratio*) cannot expel from us, that nothing stands in the way of our leading a life worthy of the gods.[126]

The main relevant features of the background for the second passage have been discussed earlier (1.5 above). Human beings are psychophysical entities, with inborn temperamental tendencies. The variations, presumably, like those of different animal species, reflect the predominance of the components of psychic atoms, such as those which are fire-like or air-like, which promote a tendency to anger or fear.[127] Where human beings differ from (wild) animals

[124] On Epicurean thinking on virtue, see text to nn. 210–16 below.

[125] Epicur. *Ep. Men.* 122. The translation is mostly based on LS 25 A, but adopts that of Inwood and Gerson (1997), p. 28, in the fourth sentence (LS 25 A(2)), in which LS interpret the significance of *men*... *de* differently.

[126] Lucr. 3.307–22, trans. LS 14 D(5), slightly modified in line 315 following Bobzien (2000), 325.

[127] See Lucr. 3. 262–306 (LS 14 D (1–4)), also 1.5 above, text to nn. 197–201, 208.

is in their capacity to modify their behaviour, in part through responding to praise and criticism by others. It is their capacity to bring about 'developments' which are distinct from the original constitution which makes human beings—and tame animals—active causal agents who are responsible for the quality of their character.[128] On the interpretation offered earlier, this capacity does not require us to postulate the existence of 'emergent' mental (non-physical) causes. This capacity for development is envisaged as a psychological-*cum*-physical state. The passage just cited suggests that this capacity derives from a greater degree of complexity, and thus scope for variation, in the human atomic constitution.[129] The 'downwards causation' suggested in *On Nature* 25 by Epicurus seems to be that exercised on our unified (psychophysical) nature by the process of development rather than that of purely mental characteristics on our atomic constitution.[130] The claim made by Lucretius, in line with the passages from *On Nature*, is that, whatever our inborn nature, we can all achieve complete happiness ('a life worthy of the gods'), even if 'traces' (*uestigia*) of our natural defects remain (Lucr. 3.319–22).

The distinctive features of the Epicurean view, as presented by both Epicurus and Lucretius, come out clearly if we juxtapose this view to a well-known Aristotelian discussion along similar lines. In *NE* 3.5, Aristotle also argues that we acquire responsibility for our actions by the role we play in our own development. A key part of Aristotle's argument is that, because of this role, we are at least 'co-responsible' (*sunaitioi*) for the character we acquire, regardless of the inborn tendencies we have to choose in certain ways.[131] This degree of similarity led David Furley to suggest that the Epicurean account was based directly on Aristotle's discussion.[132] However, leaving aside the question whether Epicurus had access to the relevant Aristotelian school-texts,[133] there are important differences between the two approaches. Aristotle's main concern, which he himself compares with that of law-courts, is with the retrospective question whether someone is properly held responsible

[128] See 1.5 above, text to nn. 247–56.

[129] 'There are many other respects...' (Lucr. 3.315–17), cited above; see also the first sentences of LS 20 B and C, which can be taken as implying that human beings have a more complex atomic psychic structure than (at least) wild animals and that their greater capacity for development reflects this structure.

[130] See 1.5 above, text to nn. 235, 246, 261.

[131] Arist. *NE* 1114^{a}31–^{b}25.

[132] Furley (1967), 184–95, 233–7, based mainly on the evidence of Lucretius (Furley's study predates recent work on the passages from Epicurus' *On Nature* 25).

[133] This question, raised especially by Bignone (1936) and Sandbach (1985) (see also 1.3 above, text to nn. 74–7), is addressed briefly by Furley (1967: 164–6). Barnes (1997*b*), 14–15, identifies some of Aristotle's school-texts that Epicurus seems to have known (not including the ethical works); on the problems surrounding the transmission of the ethical treatises, see Barnes, 57–9.

for the actions they have committed in the past and for the formation of the character that has led to those acts.[134] The Epicurean concern, implicitly in *On Nature* 25, and explicitly in the two passages cited here, is either prospective or neutral as regards temporal sequence. The central claim is that *at any time* in our lives we are capable of taking forward our development, and of doing so until we secure happiness or 'a life worthy of the gods'.[135] This marks the second main difference from Aristotle's discussion. Aristotle maintains that, even though our character may become unchangeable at a certain point in our lives, we are still properly held responsible for the way it has developed.[136] From the Epicurean perspective, no such point exists. That is why, as stressed in the first passage cited (*Ep. Men.* 122), young and old alike should actively engage in philosophy with a view to securing happiness.

Aristotle's approach reflects his general belief, noted earlier, that the full development of virtue and happiness depends on a combination of the right kind of inborn nature, upbringing (conceived as habituation), and rational reflection, of the kind promoted by his ethical teaching.[137] The Epicurean discussions contain no comparable emphasis on the role of habituation; in Lucretius' discussion, for instance, the only two factors mentioned are inborn nature and education or reason (*doctrina, ratio*). In the relevant passages from *On Nature* 25, praise and blame is not presented as a vehicle of social habituation but as a means of promoting a process of rational development of which human beings are constitutively capable.[138] Habituation is not necessarily conceived as a wholly non-rational process in Aristotle.[139] But Aristotle himself links the importance of habituation in ethical development with the fact that ethical character (by contrast with intellectual virtue) involves the non-rational aspect of our personality.[140] It is plausible too to link this idea with his claim that, at a certain point in our lives, our characters may no longer be open to change by conscious choice.[141] In the Epicurean framework, by contrast, there is no equivalent for the Platonic–Aristotelian distinction between rational and non-rational parts of

[134] Arist. *NE* 1113^{b}21–1114^{a}3. On the links with Athenian law-court practice, see Irwin (1980), 119–20.

[135] See esp. Epicur. *Ep. Men.* 122 (LS 25 A); Lucr. 3.319–22 (LS 14 D(4)), also LS 20 B, C(1–3).

[136] Arist. *NE* 1114^{a}3–21.

[137] See further 3.2 below, text to nn. 30–7.

[138] LS 20 B(2), C (2–4); the latter passage is concerned to meet the objection that praise and blame necessitate; but neither Epicurus nor his imagined opponent present praise and blame as methods of habituation.

[139] See further on this point Sherman (1989), ch. 5, (1997), ch. 2, esp. 78–83, ch. 6, esp. 241–3.

[140] See e.g. *NE* 2.1, esp. 1103^{b}13–25; 2.2, esp. 1103^{b}33–1104^{b}3; 2.3, esp. 1104^{b}3–13; and, more generally 1.13, 10.9.

[141] Arist. *NE* 3.5, 1114^{a}3–21, esp. 9–10.

the psyche.[142] Correspondingly, the process of ethical education, designed to lead us from 'empty' desires and emotions to 'natural' ones, is one that can continue throughout our lives. These salient differences between the Aristotelian discussion and the Epicurean approach bring out the connection in Epicureanism between the unified or holistic psychological model and their thinking about our life-long capacity for developing complete happiness, a connection also found in Stoicism.[143]

The first passage cited earlier (the preface to Epicurus' *Letter to Menoeceus*) illustrates the Epicurean view, while also suggesting themes linked with the Epicurean version of the ideal of invulnerability. The passage emphatically presents philosophy as the vehicle for securing happiness throughout an entire life, not just in youth or early adult life. Although, here and elsewhere, Epicurus speaks of 'practising' or 'rehearsing' (*meletan*) the philosophical doctrines that make for happiness, this should not be taken as denoting a process that is habituative in a non-rational sense.[144] As the rest of the letter makes plain, what is envisaged is the construction of a well-grounded set of priorities, involving the active exercise of rational reflection.[145] At the same time, the passage seeks to erase an idea which in other ethical theories (Platonic–Aristotelian ones, for instance) underlies such long-term planning. This is that a human life has a natural shape or narrative, centred on the evolving stages of youth, maturity, and old age.[146] The Epicurean life, as pictured here and elsewhere, is a continuum, in which the same medium (philosophy) is equally appropriate at any time as the vehicle of happiness.[147] The conventional idea that life forms a temporal sequence of stages is replaced by the theme that we should aim to create a *unified* life, consisting in a continuous state of freedom from distress (*ataraxia*). In this passage, this is achieved by combining 'gratitude for what has occurred' in the past and 'lack of fear of what is yet to come'.[148] The fact that this unified life negates the

[142] The distinction between *logikon* and *alogon* ('rational' and 'non-rational') parts sometimes found in our sources corresponds to Lucretius' distinction between *animus* and *anima*, and not to Plato's distinction between reason and appetite/spirit (*R.* 435–41) or Aristotle's rational and non-rational parts in *NE* 1.13 (i.e. distinct sources of motivation). See further Annas (1992), 144–7, and 1.5 above, text to nn. 204–6.

[143] See 2.2 above, text to nn. 6–9, 36–46.

[144] On Epicurus' teaching methods, including the role of apparently habituative elements such as memorization, see Nussbaum (1994), ch. 4, esp. 129–33.

[145] See Epicur. *Ep. Men.* 127–32 (LS 21 B).

[146] On such stages in Platonic–Aristotelian accounts of ethical development, see 3.2 below, text to nn. 21–37 (by contrast with Stoic thinking).

[147] See also Warren (2004), 133–4, referring to evidence including Epicur. *Vatican Sayings* 17; and 146–52, esp. 146–7, referring to extracts from Philodemus' *On Death*, e.g. 12.26–13.17 Kuiper (1925).

[148] Epicur. *Ep. Men.* 122 (LS 25 A(2), cited above, with LS trans. modified). See also LS 24 D and text to nn. 239–40 below.

standard picture of time-based maturation is underlined in the unexpected fusion of the characteristics of youth and age.[149] By the same token, the comments also signal the theme that length of life is irrelevant to happiness, a feature linked, paradoxically, with the idea that we can secure a life 'worthy of the [immortal] gods'.[150]

What reason do we have for thinking that this 'Socratic' theme reflects the direct influence of Socrates on Epicurean thought? Democritus might seem a more plausible source, since he was explicitly regarded by Epicurus as a major influence, though not one to be followed uncritically.[151] Among the ethical fragments ascribed to Democritus, we can find several which suggest that human beings are capable of achieving happiness by effective management of actions and attitudes. Charles Kahn (1985: 26) identifies as a recurrent motif 'the role of reason in human life' through which 'thoughtful judgement and careful reflection can protect us against the uncertainties of fortune on the one hand and self-inflicted grief on the other.' Fragments which indicate this view include DK B 171: 'Happiness (*eudaimoniē*) does not dwell in flocks or gold; the psyche is the home of the daimon ("spirit" or "fortune")'. In similar vein, B 191, one of the most substantial Democritean fragments, presents 'mind' (*gnōmē*) as the principal determinant of our success or failure in producing 'cheerfulness' (*euthumiē*), particularly by the attitudes we adopt towards the (external) success and failure of other people.[152] One can see how, if this kind of approach were developed systematically—rather more so than is evident in the surviving fragments—we would have a clear prototype for the Epicurean emphasis on the life-long capacity to secure happiness by rational reflection.

It would be much more certain that Democritus was a significant precursor of Epicurus on this point if it was clear that (1) he had successfully reconciled his atomic physics with his ethical guidance, and (2) he had done so in a way that provided a theoretical basis for a conception of free will and responsibility. However, it is not at all clear that this is the case, as James Warren brings out in a careful study of the relevant evidence. He concludes that, despite some suggestive phrases in the ethical fragments, we simply cannot tell whether or not Democritus systematically linked his atomic physics with his ethics.[153] Epicurus' critique of Democritus in *On Nature* 25 seems to be based

149 This feature generates the difficulty in knowing quite how to translate this sentence, as indicated in n. 125 above. See also Warren (2001*a*), 163–6.

150 See further Warren (2000), (2004), ch. 4, esp. 110–35, and discussion below, esp. text to nn. 223–30.

151 For evidence on this point, see Warren (2002), 25–6.

152 See further Kahn (1985), 12–15.

153 Warren (2002), 71–2, after an examination centring on the claim that 'Souls moved out of large intervals (*diastēmatōn*) are neither well settled nor cheerful (*euthumoi*)' (B 191), discussed

on the view that Democritus fails to recognize that his physics, notably his reductive physicalism with its deterministic implications, runs counter to the idea that we can take effective charge of our own lives.[154] Of the previous followers of Democritus, Epicurus is especially critical of Nausiphanes; and his negative attitude may be a response to Nausiphanes' attempt to ground ethics on *phusiologia*, the study of nature.[155] Warren's conclusion, then, is that Epicurus is innovative in his project of reconciling atomic physics with the idea that we are responsible for the direction of our lives.[156]

If we focus on Democritus' ethical ideas, setting aside the question of the integration of ethics and physics, is it clear that Epicurean thinking on our life-long capacity for securing happiness was decisively influenced by Democritus, as distinct from Socrates? It was noted already in antiquity that Democritus' idea that the roots of happiness lie in our own capacity for reasoned reflection has clear parallels, notably in Plato.[157] As Kahn points out (1985: 26–8), the idea also strongly evokes the representation of Socrates and Socratic ideas in a variety of sources. It is Socrates who is repeatedly shown as addressing *anyone*, at any stage in their life, and urging them to take charge of their search for happiness, for instance, by the 'care of the psyche' advocated in Plato's *Apology* (29e–30b).[158] Also, it is Socrates' distinctive line of argument which prefigures the Epicurean (and Stoic) unified psychological model, in which desires and emotions are seen as dependent on beliefs, or rather on the degree of knowledge or ignorance.[159] This theme, though sometimes implied in Democritus' fragments, is also coupled there with comments that suggest a stronger opposition between reason and emotion or desire.[160] The argumentative style of Epicurus' exploration of the idea of our capacity for securing our

in Warren, 58–71. Vlastos (1945–6) was more confident about the linkage, based especially on *metarusmousa* ('reshaping' minds) in B 33.

[154] See Warren (2002), 193–200, also 7–9 on Democritus' reductive physicalism in B 9 (discussed in 1.3 above, text to nn. 83–6), and 69–71, on the determinist implications of this physicalism. See also LS 20 B (13–14), taken with LS i. 108.

[155] Warren (2002), 169–81; for Epicurus' criticism of Nausiphanes, see Cic. *ND* 1.73.

[156] The precise character of that reconciliation has been variously interpreted, as illustrated earlier (1.5 above, text to nn. 226–71).

[157] See Stob. 2.52.13–53.20 (based on Arius Didymus), which links Democritus B 171, cited above, with Pl. *Ti.* 90a and *Lg.* 636e; I owe this reference to Julia Annas (2002). Hence, the Democritean version of this idea could be combined with that of other Hellenistic–Roman theories; see e.g. Plu. *Mor.* 467 A, taken with Gill (1994), 4624.

[158] See text to n. 37 above.

[159] See text to nn. 25–6 above. There is a natural connection between this unified psychological model and the idea that the development of understanding and character can continue throughout life; see text to nn. 125–36 above.

[160] See, on the one hand, DK B 191, which suggests that 'mind' can produce 'cheerfulness' (*euthumiē*), and, on the other, the contrast between reason (or oneself) and emotion/desire in B 214, 234, 236, and between psyche or mind and body in B 159, 223.

happiness also recalls that of Socrates, particularly as presented by Plato, rather than the remaining fragments of Democritus. Ideas such as the erasure of the distinction between youth and age and the replacement of conventional views about the shape of a human life with the ideal of a life unified by one's state of mind (*Ep. Men.* 122) evoke the paradoxical mode of the Platonic Socrates rather than the blander tone of Democritean ethical advice.

The other two Socratic themes, time-independent perfection of character and the unity of the wise person, can be taken together. I begin by locating them against certain central features of Epicurean ethics, and then bring out how those features imply psychological and psychophysical holism. I also underline the striking combination of holism (and naturalism) with Socratic ethical ideas, and consider how far those ideas seem to derive directly from Socrates.

The core Epicurean ethical thesis, which distinguishes this approach from most other ancient theories, is that the overall goal of happiness is constituted by pleasure. The claim that this thesis is self-evidently true is supported by their version of the 'cradle argument':

> as soon as every animal is born, it seeks after pleasure and rejoices in it as the greatest good, while it rejects pain as the greatest bad and, as far as possible, avoids it; and does this when it is not yet corrupted, on the innocent and sound judgement of nature itself. Hence [Epicurus] says there is no need to prove or discuss why pleasure should be pursued or pain avoided. He thinks these matters are sensed just like the heat of fire, the whiteness of snow and the sweetness of honey, none of which needs confirmation by elaborate arguments; it is enough to point them out.[161]

However, this appeal to the self-evident and 'natural' character of the good is coupled with a highly revisionist account of pleasure—a combination which is typical of the theory—[162] namely as the *absence* of pain in the body (*aponia*) and of distress in the psyche (*ataraxia*). As Cicero puts it: 'when we are freed from pain, we rejoice in the actual freedom and absence of all distress; but everything in which we rejoice is pleasure, just as everything that distresses us is pain; therefore the complete removal of pain has rightly been called pleasure'.[163] This thesis was strongly criticized in antiquity for its counterintuitive and negative character. But there is a more positive, and revealing, way of characterizing the claim.[164] This is that just *being alive*, or fulfilling one's nature or 'constitution' as

161 Cic. *Fin.* 1.30 (LS 21 A(2)). On the precise status of this claim see Brunschwig (1986), 115–22; Sedley (1998*b*), 136–9. For the Stoic version of this argument, which may have been designed to respond to the Epicurean version, see 37–9 above.

162 On this point, see Annas (1993*b*), 188–200, esp. 200.

163 Cic. *Fin.* 1.37 (LS 21 A(6)); see also LS 21 B(1). This theory involves the denial of any state intermediate between pleasure and pain of the type suggested by Plato in *R.* 583c–584a.

164 Cicero criticizes the theory as contrary to normal conceptions of pleasure: *Fin.* 2.5–19, Plutarch criticizes it, in part, for its negative character: *Mor.* 1091 A–1092 A. See further on these criticisms Stokes (1995); Boulogne (2003), 150–82, esp. 170.

a psychophysical entity, is inherently pleasurable—provided we do not wreck this state by mismanaging our lives and by adopting false beliefs. Support for this way of understanding the Epicurean thesis can be found in their innovative conception of katastematic pleasure and in the distinction between necessary and natural desires and their opposites.

The distinction between kinetic and katastematic pleasure, though clearly important, is not fully explicated in our sources. It resembles one drawn in earlier Greek philosophy, between the pleasure of satisfying a need and so restoring our natural state and that of normal functioning without any previous need or lack. Cicero, for instance, illustrates the distinction in this way: 'Quenched thirst involves katastematic pleasure, but the pleasure of the actual quenching is kinetic'.[165] However, Epicurus' one surviving comment on the subject points in a different direction: 'Freedom from disturbance (*ataraxia*) and absence of pain (*aponia*) are katastematic pleasures; but joy and delight (*chara* and *euphrosunē*) are kinetic pleasures'.[166] Apart from the fact that this refers to psychological, rather than physical, pleasures, this suggests a distinction between lasting states and episodes, with no reference to a preceding lack. The core thought underlying the distinction may be this. Simply being alive, if one is free from physical and psychological pain, is fundamentally pleasurable; and this state can also be described as 'katastematic' pleasure. Other pleasures are merely *variations* of this;[167] and this goes for episodes of pleasure (including the psychological experiences of joy and delight) as well as the transient process of restoring our physical and psychological condition to its painless state.[168]

What does the term 'katastematic' connote? There is no explanation of this in Epicurean sources; but our evidence suggests two main associations. One connotation is that of our *natural* state. The phrase 'natural state' (*phusikon katastēma*) figures in one source deriving from Epicurus.[169] This comment can be taken together with the repeated idea that the pursuit of pleasure (meaning, primarily, katastematic pleasure) is 'natural' or 'cognate' or

165 Cic. *Fin.* 2.9 (LS 21 Q(2)), trans. modified. For earlier distinctions of this type, see e.g. Pl. *Phlb.* 46b–52b; Arist. *NE* 10.3, 1173^{b}7–20, *MM* 2.7, 1204^{b}37–1205^{a}6.

166 D.L. 10.137 (LS 21R(1)), trans. modified.

167 For kinetic pleasure as that which 'varies' (but does not increase) katastematic pleasure, see Cic. *Fin.* 2.10 (LS 21 Q(3)), also LS 18 E(1)).

168 For an interpretation of the type outlined here, see Striker (1996), 205–8; Sedley (1998*b*), 129–30, 142–4; Erler and Schofield (1999), 654–7; see also Gosling and Taylor (1982), 374–88. A stronger version of this thesis, in which kinetic pleasure consists *only* in variation of katastematic pleasure (and not in its restoration) is maintained by Diano (1935), (1974), 28–128; also Rist (1972), 106–8, 170–2. On scholarly debate on this point, see LS, vol. ii, notes on 21 Q and S.

169 Fr. 73 Arrighetti (1973), lines 16–17, a fragmentary letter to Metrodorus; also fr. 416 Usener, a late source.

'appropriate' to us.[170] A connection might be seen with Aristotle's conception of pleasure as the 'unimpeded' exercise of our natural state, or as that which completes and perfects (or 'supervenes on') the exercise of a natural function.[171] The term *katastēma*, like *sustasis*, can thus be seen as denoting a (psychophysical) 'constitution', which we are instinctively disposed to express, and whose expression or realization is inherently pleasurable. We may also see a linkage with the Epicurean theory of natural development. According to this theory, human beings are constitutively capable of developing beyond their inborn 'constitution'.[172] But their advanced or developed state can also be characterized as a 'constitution' (*sustasis*).[173] 'Katastematic' pleasures, understood as those of the 'natural state' (*phusikon katastēma*) or 'constitution', can be seen as those most characteristic of the fully developed human being, or complex rational animal, when realizing this constitution properly. If this connection holds good, there is a parallel with the Stoic theory of development as involving the appropriation of our (developing) constitution, in spite of other differences between the two theories.[174]

A second, and related, connotation of the term *katastēma* is with stability, rather than motion or process; hence, Long and Sedley (1987) translate *katastēmatikos* as 'static'. The term *katastēma* can be linked with other Greek terms (*katastasis*, *kathistasthai*) signifying lasting 'state' or 'settling' into a state.[175] As with the connotations of 'nature', this term also evokes earlier Greek thinking about pleasure, notably the debate about whether pleasure should be understood as the maximization of episodes of satisfaction or as the expression of a stable and ordered state. These contrasting ideas were vividly illustrated in Plato's *Gorgias* by Socrates' contrast between leaky, sieve-like, jars and solid ones, an image taken up by Lucretius.[176] In giving priority

170 See e.g. Epicur. *Ep. Men.* 129 (*sungenikon*, 'cognate', *oikeian*, 'appropriate'); Stob. 2.46.21–2 ('being appropriately (*oikeiōs*) disposed'); D.L. 10.34, pleasure is 'appropriate' (*oikeion*), pain is 'alien' (*allotrion*); Usener 398, 509. See further Annas (1993*b*), 188–9; also Sedley (1998*b*), 138–9, answering Cicero's criticism that the 'cradle argument' demonstrates the primacy of kinetic, rather than katastematic, pleasure.

171 See Arist. *NE* 7.12, esp. 1153^{a}12–15, 10.4, esp. 1174^{b}31–3. The term *kathestēkuia* (cognate to 'katastematic'), figures in these arguments, signifying our 'settled' state, as distinct from that needing replenishment (e.g. *NE* 1153^{a}2–6).

172 For *sustasis* in this sense, see LS 20 C(2), j (LS vol. ii only).

173 See 34.20.6–14 Arrighetti (1973), discussed by Annas (1993*a*), 60–1 (see 1.5 above, text to n. 259).

174 On the Stoic theory of *oikeiōsis* and our developing *sustasis*/*constitutio*, see 1.4 above, text to nn. 131–6, 161–73.

175 See LSJ, *katastasis*, sense II.2, *kathistēmi*, senses B.5–6. See Diog. Oen. fr. 28, col. VI Chilton, esp. lines 4–7 (= fr. 29, col. I William). This combines the idea of 'states' (by contrast with 'actions') with the idea that the removal of disturbance and 'unnatural' desires (lines 5–7) results in pleasure 'of states', i.e. katastematic pleasure.

176 See Pl. *Grg.* 493a–494b; also Lucr. 3.931–9, 1003–10, 6.9–25; for related ideas in Epicurus, see *K. D.* 10 (LS 21 D(3)), *Ep. Men.* 128. See also Warren (2004), 137. Erler and Schofield (1999),

to 'static', rather than kinetic, pleasure, Epicurus adopted a sharply divergent version of hedonism from the Cyrenaics, for whom pleasure consisted in the maximization of episodic processes of satisfaction.[177] These two connotations of *katastēma*, those of our 'natural state' and of 'stable condition', are connected by the Epicurean conviction that our natural state is one of stability and calm, rather than of process and agitation. Both these associations are summed up in this Epicurean dictum: 'the stable condition (*eustathes... katastēma*) of the flesh, and the confident expectation of this contain the most secure joy for those who are capable of reasoning.'[178] As explained shortly, this passage is also suggestive for Epicurean thinking about psychological integration and about the ideal character-state.

First, however, we need to take note of a further important distinction, between types of desire. Some are natural and necessary, others are natural but not necessary, others again are neither natural or necessary, but are said to be 'empty', or the product of 'empty opinion' (*kenodoxian*).[179] This typology can be linked with that between kinetic and katastematic pleasure, though this link is not made explicitly.[180] Natural and necessary desires can be seen as those for objects which produce katastematic pleasure. The stress in our sources is on the physical aspect: for instance, the desire for food when hungry is a natural and necessary desire for the katastematic pleasure of *aponia* (absence of physical pain).[181] But I take it that 'natural and necessary' desires would include the desire for *ataraxia* (freedom from psychological disturbance), which, for Epicurus, depends on a proper understanding of nature.[182] Desires that are natural but not necessary are for objects that 'vary' katastematic pleasure; examples given in our sources are sex and expensive food. These can be taken to be desires for kinetic pleasures, at least for those which are natural. The examples given of desires which are neither natural or necessary but which derive from 'empty opinion' include 'garlands or the

656 n. 41, compare Aristotle's idea that certain pleasures (e.g. sight) are those of our 'settled' nature (*phuseōs kathestēkuias*) (*NE* 1153^{a}2–6, *MM* 1205^{b}20–8). But they also point out, appositely, that 'Epicurus' innovation is to make the settled state of our nature *itself* a pleasure' (their italics).

177 See D.L. 2.86–9, 10.136. See further Annas (1993*b*), 230–2; Erler and Schofield (1999), 654–6; also (with a new view of the Epicurean–Cyrenaic relationship), Warren (2001*a*), 161–78.

178 Plu. *Mor.* 1089 D (LS 21 N), trans. modified and repunctuated; for further references to this dictum, see Usener 68.

179 See e.g. Epicur. *Ep. Men.* 127 (= LS 21 B(1)), LS I, Usener 456.

180 This linkage is made by Fowler (1997), 25–6; also, by implication, Sedley (1998*b*), 130.

181 See e.g. LS 21 I, and (in Usener 456) the scholion on Arist. *NE* 3.13, and Plu. *Mor.* 989 B; also LS G(1).

182 Epicur. *Ep. Men.* 127 (LS 21 B(1)) links necessary desires with the production of happiness, specified in 128 as *ataraxia* as well as bodily health. On the understanding of nature as crucial for producing *ataraxia*, see e.g. *K.D.* 10–12.

erection of statues' (that is, prizes or symbols of social status) and the desire for food or sex or clothing 'of a certain kind', as distinct from the desire for food or sex as such.[183]

Further exploration of this distinction can help to bring out the extent to which Epicureanism, like Stoicism, holds a unified or holistic conception of human psychology. The contrast between 'natural' and 'empty' is applied to emotions as well as desires; and the basis of the contrast lies in the type of belief or quality of understanding underlying the emotion or desire. Two types of false belief, in particular, are singled out as promoting 'empty' desires or emotions. One is the mistaken belief that the objects arousing desire yield katastematic pleasure, when they do not, and when they do not even yield kinetic pleasure.[184] An analogous error is the 'intense enthusiasm' aroused by 'desires which do not lead to pain if they are unfulfilled', which have their origin in 'empty opinion'.[185] Similarly 'empty' is the kind of emotion—anger, for instance—that regards punishment or correction (*kolasis*) as an inherent source of pleasure.[186] Another important type of empty belief relates to 'the infinite' (*to aoriston*). The mistake lies in thinking that pleasures such as eating, that are 'natural', can be increased infinitely, by elaborate food; or that such pleasures can be prolonged infinitely, in spite of the finite nature of human lives.[187]

In Stoicism, all emotions or passions, apart from the 'good emotions' (*eupatheiai*) experienced by the wise person, are presented as a product of error and something that should be extirpated. The Epicurean position is not quite so absolute; for instance, Epicureans recognized a type of 'natural anger' which the wise person might experience, though with certain very special preconditions.[188] However, Epicureanism does involve a very radical critique of emotions, including those that are normally taken to be a fundamental part of human life, such as fear of death, grief, and desire for possessions. This critique derives from the idea that such emotions depend on empty or misguided beliefs and will be removed by the correction of such beliefs.[189]

183 See a scholion on *K. D.* 29 (= LS 21 I); and a scholion on Arist. 3.13, in Usener 456. See further, on the latter point, Annas (1989), 149–52, and (1993*b*), 192–3.

184 See e.g. Epicur. *K. D.* 7: people pursue fame and position (cf. the garlands and statues of the scholion on *K. D.* 29), thinking falsely that this will yield the 'natural good' of a self-sufficient life. See further Procopé (1998), 179.

185 *K.D.* 30 (LS 21 E(3)); see further Annas (1993*b*), 192–3.

186 See e.g. Phld. *Ira* 42.22–34, cited by Annas (1989), 154–5.

187 See Annas (1992), 191. Relevant sources include *K.D.* 15, 18–21, 30, *V.S.* 59, 69, Usener 202–3, 465, 485.

188 See further 7.4 below, text to nn. 197–207.

189 See e.g. the first four *Key Doctrines* and Philodemus' *Tetrapharmakon* ('Four-fold Remedy'): 'Nothing to fear in god, nothing to feel in death, good can be attained, bad can be endured', trans. Gaskin (1995), 77, slightly modified; see also LS 25 J. Also Lucr. 3.978–1023; Cic. *Fin.* 1.59–61; and Diano (1974), 266–8.

The assumption that emotions and desires depend directly on beliefs might seem to be contradicted by Lucretius' suggestion that an underlying fear of death generates a whole series of secondary emotions and desires, including 'greed and the blind craving for honours'.[190] Similarly, Lucretius claims that people 'hate themselves' and feel disgust for life because they do not recognize the cause of their own unhappiness (3.1053–79). These ideas might seem to run counter to the view that emotions depend directly on beliefs. They may seem to indicate a divided model of the personality, involving unconscious beliefs and unrecognized motivation, that anticipates Freud.[191] However, the central thought assumed in such passages is that people have empty beliefs about the way in which (in Epicurean terms, katastematic) pleasure, including freedom from disturbance, can be obtained.[192] Both the secondary emotions, such as acquisitiveness, and the underlying one (fear of death) are taken to depend on such erroneous beliefs. Although the connection between these two beliefs, and the role of this connection in producing these emotions, is presented as unrecognized by those concerned, the connection can, in principle, be fully recognized, and Lucretius' aim in this context is to promote this recognition.[193]

In presenting emotions and desires (both 'natural' and 'empty') as grounded on beliefs, Epicureanism adopts a holistic view of human psychology. Also, as argued earlier, psychophysical holism is fundamental to Epicurus' conception of the psyche (as expressed in *Ep. Hdt.* 63–7, for instance) and the picture of development given in *On Nature* 25. Against this background, it may seem surprising that Epicurean sources, including Epicurus himself, regularly contrast the 'mind' (*dianoia*) and the 'flesh' (*sarx*), or psyche and body, in discussions of pleasure.[194] This might lead us to infer the intrusion of psyche–body dualism or core-centred thinking of the kind found in Plato and Aristotle (1.2. above). But that inference would not be justified. For one thing, this contrast is drawn, typically, in passages, such as the *Key Doctrines*, where Epicurus is summarizing ethical themes for a wide audience, or in later sources based on this type of material. Epicurus here couches his ideas in ordinary language, with relatively few technical terms or explicit revision of concepts. There is a marked difference in style from, for instance, *Ep. Hdt.* 63–7, where Epicurus is explicitly revising the conventional

[190] Lucr. 3.59–86, line 59 quoted. The paradoxical idea that fear of death can generate desires which lead someone to commit suicide (79–82) is criticized by Sen. *Ep.* 24.22.

[191] See e.g. Segal (1990), 23–5; Nussbaum (1994), 196–201.

[192] For this theme, see Lucr. 2.14–61 (LS 21 W(3–7)).

[193] For this view, see also Warren (2004), 21, n. 3; see further Diano (1974), 269–71.

[194] See e.g. Epicur. *K.D.* 18 (LS 21 E(1)), *K.D.* 20 (24 C(2)); D.L. 10.137 (LS 21 R(2)); Cic. *Tusc.* 5.95, Diog. Oen. 38.1.8–3.14 (LS 21 V).

psyche–body distinction (48–50 above). There is a difference also from Epicurus' *On Nature* 25 or Lucretius' Book 3, where, in more or less technical language, the authors analyse the nature or workings of the psyche in explicitly physical terms.[195] Although our sources do not offer a 'translation' of the mind–flesh distinction into physicalist or psychophysicalist terms, it would, presumably, be possible for them to do so, along the lines of the revision of the psyche–body distinction provided in *Ep. Hdt.* 63–7. Other Epicurean distinctions, such as those between katastematic and kinetic pleasures or between *animus* ('mind') and *anima* ('spirit'), might be deployed for this purpose. The main point would be that both types of pleasure ('mind-based' and 'flesh-based') form part of an interconnected set of functions belonging to the psyche–body 'aggregate' (*athroisma*), as indicated in *K.D.* 9, discussed below.

It is also important to take note of the overall point of the passages in which the mind–flesh or psyche–body distinction is drawn. The aim is not to suggest that the mind or flesh are different kinds of ontological entity or that their aims and activities are fundamentally distinct. A crucial function of the mind is to reason so as to maximize bodily pleasure, as indicated in this passage, often cited in antiquity: 'The stable state (*eustathes* . . . *katastēma*) of the flesh and the confident expectation of this contain the highest and most secure joy for those who are *capable of reasoning* (*epilogizesthai*).'[196] There is a close link between the mind–flesh distinction and the contrast between the capacity for short-term and for long-term responses.[197] It would not be quite right to say that the mind–flesh distinction is simply identical with this contrast between types of capacity; sometimes the pleasures are envisaged as different in other ways. But it is clear that *the* (not simply, *a*) key role of the mind is to engage in long-term planning and reflection in order to maximize katastematic and kinetic pleasure for the body—as well as for the mind. Hence, for instance, 'The body rejoices just as long as it perceives a present pleasure; but the mind perceives both the present pleasure, along with the body, and foresees the one that is coming without allowing the past one to flow away' (Cic. *Tusc.* 5.95 (LS 21 T)). At the same time, it is stressed that the ultimate aim of what might otherwise seem to be *purely* mental or intellectual activities, above all, understanding the nature of the universe, is to produce the katastematic pleasure of absence of distress.[198] The two aims are brought together, for instance, in *K.D.* 20 (LS 24 C(2)): 'but the intellect (or mind, *dianoia*), by making a rational calculation of the end and limit which govern the flesh, and by dispelling the

[195] See e.g. LS 14 B–D, 20 B, C(1–2), discussed in 1.5 above.

[196] See text to nn. 199–202 below. Plu. *Mor.* 1089 D (LS 21 N), italics added and repunctuated; for other ancient citations, see Usener 68. On *epilogizesthai*, see text to nn. 200–3 below.

[197] See e.g. LS 21 R (2), T, 24 C(2).

[198] LS 25 A(3), B–C, K.

fears about eternity, brings about the complete life'. Generally, we are not explicitly reminded that the intellect (*dianoia*) denotes one of the functions of the heart-based *animus*, which forms part of a coherent psychophysical whole (or 'aggregate'). But the role envisaged for the intellect, and more broadly, for the coordinated functions of psyche and body—namely achieving the linked goals of a 'complete life' free from physical pain and psychological disturbance—is wholly consistent with this implied picture.

Epicurus also underlines in various ways the distinctively holistic character of his thinking about the mind–body relationship and pleasure. One is through significant use of the word *epilogizesthai* (or *epilogismos*), that figures, for instance, in the passage just cited (*K.D.* 20). The precise significance of the Epicurean term remains a matter of debate. But two well-marked connotations which bear on the present topic are those of reasoning which is empirically grounded (based on the facts of experience) and reasoning which is directed 'towards' (*epi*) the practical achievement of the Epicurean goals.[199] The term thus reflects the general Epicurean stress on the idea that, in forming objectives, the mind should work for the sake of the body or the good of the whole, embodied person. There is a clear contrast with the recurrent Platonic–Aristotelian idea that reason (*logos*), or 'mind' (*nous*, *dianoia*) has desires or objectives *of its own*.[200] The kind of challenge posed by such ideas to a Platonic–Aristotelian approach is illustrated by Plutarch in one of his critiques of Epicureanism. He rejects the ideas that physical pleasure can provide a secure basis for an account of happiness and that intellectual activities should be seen as having an ulterior objective.[201] Writing from an explicitly part-based psychological standpoint, he thus reasserts the 'core-centred' thinking that forms a significant strand in the Platonic and Aristotelian thought on which he draws.[202]

A similar Epicurean point is emphasized in different ways. For instance, several passages stress the fundamental character of physical needs and pleasures in a way that seems especially designed to provoke dualist sensibilities of a Platonic type.[203] Related ideas are conveyed more subtly in two striking

[199] See further Sedley (1973), 27–34; Schofield (1996), 230–6, esp. n. 12. Another important usage is in LS 20 C(6), translated there as 'reasoning it empirically'.

[200] For this as a shared idea of Socrates, Plato, Aristotle, and the Stoics—but not the Epicureans—see M. Frede (1996), 17–18. For some relevant passages, outlined in 1.2. above, see Pl. *R.* 612a, *Phd.* 78d–84b, Arist. *NE* 10.7. Pl. *R.* 586e–587a might *seem* similar to Epicurean thought on the role of reason, but actually gives reason a more independent role (see further Gill 1996*b*: 296–7).

[201] *Mor.* 1091 A–D , 1092 A–1094 D. See further Boulogne (2003), 167–82, suggesting that the criticisms reflect Plutarch's polemical objectives rather than his interpretative grasp of Epicureanism.

[202] Plu. *Mor.* 1096 D–E; on Plutarch's psychological standpoint, see 4.3 below.

[203] See e.g. LS 21 G(1), L–M. For an explicit rejection of *Phaedo*-type dualism, see *Ep. Hdt.* 67.

passages, both of which centre on 'counterfactual' (unreal but imaginable) situations.

> If the causes of the pleasures of the dissipated released mental fears concerning celestial phenomena and death and distress, and in addition taught the limit of desires, we should never have any reason to reproach them [i.e. the dissipated] since they would be satisfying themselves with pleasures from all directions and would never have pain or distress, which constitutes the bad. (*K.D.* 10 (LS 21 D(3))

This comment might aggravate people who have Platonic–Aristotelian assumptions in a number of ways. Most obviously provocative is the claim that the pleasures of the dissipated are not bad in themselves (that is, as vices) but because they are ineffective in producing pleasure and avoiding pain or distress 'which constitutes the bad'.[204] But the passage also presents, though in this counterfactual form, the Epicurean ideal of coordinating mental and physical activities in a way that produces 'pleasures from all directions', that is (psychophysical) katastematic pleasures.

The second passage is yet more suggestive: 'If every pleasure were condensed in ⟨location⟩ and duration and distributed over the whole of the aggregate (*athroisma*) or the dominant parts of our nature, pleasures would never differ from each other'.[205] The text and interpretation of this passage has been much debated.[206] But, leaving other difficulties aside, the passage does convey some points relevant here. The salient thought seems to be that, if the difference between katastematic and kinetic pleasures and also between psychological and physical pleasures were modified by 'condensation' and 'distribution', these pleasures would be the same in nature and, presumably, value. In other words, there is no *fundamental* (for instance, ontological) distinction between them, but only a difference in location and duration. The passage seems to assume that at present pleasures are not distributed *equally* over our bodily aggregate; mental pleasures, presumably, are concentrated in the heart-based 'mind' (*animus*). However, to say this is to imply the idea, already entailed by Epicurean psychology, that 'mental' pleasures *are* located within the 'aggregate' and are functions of our bodily make-up. Thus, the situation envisaged, though hypothetical, represents a holistic ideal, both in the sense that it presupposes psychophysical holism and—though hypothetically—an embodied (holistic) fusion of all types of pleasure.

[204] Contrast, for instance, the relative evaluations of pleasure and virtue in Pl. *R.* 583a–588a or Arist. *NE* 10.5.

[205] Epicur. *K.D.* 9 (LS 21 D(2)), trans. modified.

[206] See further LS vol. ii, note to 21 D(2), with references to other discussions, including Gosling and Taylor (1982), 378–82.

Against the background of Epicurean thinking about psychological and psychophysical holism, I return to the two Socratic claims outlined earlier and the question of how far the Epicurean version of these claims is derived directly from Socrates. The first claim is that complete happiness involves a time-independent perfection of character, marked by freedom from passion or distress and in this sense by 'invulnerability'. The Epicurean version of this claim was associated with motifs also found in Stoicism. This similarity was noted in antiquity, though critics of Epicureanism tended not to accept that the Epicurean versions were justified by the theory. Among the similarities noted by Cicero is the idea that, once wisdom has been attained (as understood in each theory), length of life makes no further addition to the happiness which is the result.[207] A further and yet more striking similarity lies in the idea that the wise person will be happy on the rack of torture, despite the fact that, in both theories, the person is conceived not as a divine mind or essence, but as a fundamentally embodied human being. The classic formulation of this in Epicureanism seems to have been that the wise person, even in the bull of Phalaris, an instrument of extreme torture, will say, 'how sweet this is, and how unimportant this is to me'.[208] The fact that, in one source, he also 'cries and groans' underlines the point that, as in Stoicism, the wise person who manifests this total consistency of character is also conceived as embodied.[209]

The second Socratic claim is that only the fully rational and virtuous person is fully cohesive in her character and way of life whereas non-wise people are psychologically as well as ethically incoherent and lead incoherent lives. The question of virtue is one on which Stoics and Epicureans markedly diverge. The Stoics present virtue as the only good and virtue as therefore sufficient for happiness. The Stoic ideal person is conceived as someone whose virtue shapes her belief-system and character, producing a consistency and stability which rule out the possibility of erroneous belief-based passions and so produces freedom from passion.[210] The Epicureans regard pleasure (understood as absence of pain and distress) as the good and see virtue as instrumental in gaining pleasure, though also as 'inseparable' from the achievement of pleasure.[211] Despite this substantive difference between the

[207] Cic. *Fin.* 1.63, 2.87–8, 3.46–7. In 2.88, Cicero underlines the similarity between Stoic and Epicurean thinking on this point, though he also thinks that this claim is only credible on the basis of the Stoic (virtue-centred) position, and not the Epicurean (pleasure-centred) one; see further Warren (2004), 131–2.

[208] See the passages assembled in Usener 601, including Cic. *Tusc.* 2.17–18, 5.31; also Plu. *Mor.* 1088 B and 1090 A (Usener 600). In Stoicism, cf. Cic. *Fin.* 3.42, an idea challenged by Antiochus in *Fin.* 5.84.

[209] D.L. 10.118; on this point in Stoicism, see 2.2 above, text to nn. 66–9.

[210] See e.g. Cic. *Tusc.* 5.81–2 (LS 63 M), *Fin.* 3.75–6, LS 41 G; see further 3.2–3 below.

[211] See LS 21 B(1–2, 6), O–P, contrast the Stoic view in LS 63.

two theories,[212] Epicureans and Stoics converge in the strong contrast drawn between the cohesion of the wise person's character and the incoherence of the non-wise.[213] Cicero's account brings out this feature of Epicurean thought and the parallel with Stoicism. The lives and state of mind of the non-wise are internally conflicted by misguided (or 'empty') desires and emotions—above all the fear of death—which compete with each and have no underlying structure.[214] Lucretius develops this theme and also brings out the rationale for the incoherence of the lives and character of the imperfect. It is the *unacknowledged*, as well as ungrounded, fear of death that generates a series of secondary, but also 'empty' emotions and desires, which produce internal disturbance and incoherence in people's lives. The restless energy and fitful intensity of such lives is a reflection of the failure to recognize, and to counteract, the underlying fear of death.[215] Lucretius also underlines the contrast with the consistency and continuity of pleasure of the fully achieved Epicurean life, made possible by Epicurus, who is himself presented as the paradigm for this character and way of life.[216]

The Epicurean characterization of the cohesion of the wise person includes one motif which is not paralleled in Stoic thought. This is that the wise person's life is unified by the right attitude to past, present, and future, thus ensuring that there is a continuum of pleasure, regardless of other contingent variations or phases in her life. As Cicero puts it: '[The wise person] remembers the past with pleasure, grasps the present with a recognition of how pleasant it is, and does not rely on the future; he looks forward to it, but enjoys the present' (*Fin.* 1.62). The motif is a recurrent one: we are told that the wise person 'will always have a supply of tightly knit pleasures (*perpetuas et contextas uoluptates*), since the anticipation of pleasures hoped for is united (*iungeretur*) with the recollection of those already experienced' (Cic. *Tusc.* 5.96). This theme figures in the preface to *Ep. Men.* (122), discussed earlier; and this example brings out that the idea of a continuum of pleasure, like that of the 'complete life', *replaces* normal ways of thinking about the passage of

212 The gap is somewhat narrowed by the fact that Epicurus also sees virtue as 'inseparable' from 'living pleasurably' (*Ep. Men.* 132, LS 21 B(6)). On the question of the compatibility of this claim with the idea of virtue as instrumental, see further Gill (1996*b*), 395–7; also Mitsis (1988), ch. 2; Annas (1993*b*), 342–50.

213 On the partial contrast with Platonic–Aristotelian (and some Middle Platonic) thought, see text to nn. 89–92 above and 4.3 below, text to nn. 115–20.

214 Cic. *Fin.* 1.57–62. Cicero's spokesman for Epicureanism claims (*Fin.* 1.161) that his account of the happiness of the wise person is better than the Stoic account, a claim disputed by Cicero in 2.88–9.

215 Lucr. 3.41–93, 1053–94.

216 Lucr. 2.1–61, 6.1–28 (LS 21 W–X). On Epicurus as a paradigm of the virtues in Lucretius, see further n. 245 below; also nn. 120–1 above.

time, and helps to explain the sense in which the Epicurean ideal is 'time-independent'.[217]

What underlies the Epicurean conviction that the wise person is able to view past, present, and future with uniform pleasure? In particular, what defence has Epicurus against the criticism made by Cicero that a philosophy which places the chief good in pleasure rather than virtue is not entitled to be confident that this will be secured in a way that makes the wise person's happiness invulnerable and independent of the passage of time or of contingent circumstances (*Fin.* 2.86–9). There are two, interdependent, dimensions in Epicurean thinking on this subject. One relates to the management of desires and actions, the other to the understanding of the nature of human life and to the implications of this for our emotions and desires.

On the first point, the core strategy, outlined in the *Letter to Menoeceus*, is the restriction of desires to those which are natural and necessary—necessary, that is, for the natural goal of securing freedom from physical pain and psychological disturbance.[218] Time is relevant to this strategy in various ways. On the one hand, as stressed by Annas, this is a programme for one's life, considered as a whole, and not just a matter of accumulating temporary or moment-by-moment pleasures, as advocated by the Cyrenaics.[219] The strategy also presupposes, as Warren emphasizes, a reasonable degree of confidence about the future: it is not just 'the stable state of the flesh' but also '*the confident expectation of this*' that contains 'the highest and most secure joy for those who are capable of reasoning'.[220] This confidence constitutes a different way of understanding the distinction between the Epicureans and Cyreanaics; given their more inclusive conception of what counts as 'pleasure', the Cyrenaics have less reason for confidence that the future will, in fact, yield pleasure. To this degree, Epicureans are justified in looking forward, as well as backwards (and at the present) and in identifying a continuum of pleasure that can survive the passage of time and the contingencies this brings.[221] At the same time, the Epicureans are all too well aware

[217] See text to n. 125 above, esp. the idea that 'although old he may stay young in good things owing to gratitude for what has occurred . . . although young he may be like an old man due to his lack of fear of what it yet to come.' On the 'complete life', see below.

[218] Epicur. *Ep. Men.* 127–32 (LS 21 B); see also text to nn. 179–83 above.

[219] Annas (1993*b*), 37–9. Irwin (1991*a*) sees this difference as reflecting a distinctive Cyrenaic conception of (temporary) personal identity.

[220] Plu. *Mor.* 1089 D (LS 21N), trans. modified with added italics.

[221] Warren (2001*a*), esp. 135–6, 161–2, 174–9. Warren contests the idea (n. 219 above) that this difference between Epicureans and Cyrenaics centres on a difference in thinking about personal identity (2001*a*: 162–74). He argues that *Ep. Men.* 127–32 constitutes a 'hedonic calculus', but one centred on setting overall priorities, rather than on a Benthamite project of maximizing pleasures. See 2001*a*: 137–48, 157; for a partly contrasting view, Annas (1993*b*), 189–90.

of, at least, one contingent fact that will ensure that the future will not bring pleasure—namely the inevitability of our death. But, as they also stress, this will not be *our* future, and so this is only an apparent exception to their general programme.[222]

The last point needs to be taken with the second relevant theme in Epicurean thinking, one explored by several recent treatments.[223] This is the thought that human beings attain the god-like state of happiness to which they properly aspire by understanding and accepting their un-god-like temporality. It is the knowledge of the nature of the universe and thus of human existence as that of a fundamentally temporary psychophysical (atomic) compound that is crucial for this purpose—and which itself constitutes a god-like kind of knowledge.[224] It is this knowledge that can remove the *pleonexia* ('acquisitiveness') that makes people desire infinite life. It can also remove the 'empty' fear of death—and what follows death—that poisons experience by generating a plurality of secondary (empty) emotions and desires. This, in turn, is crucial for achieving the continuum of *ataraxia* (absence of disturbance) and—as far as possible—*aponia* (absence of pain) that is seen as characteristic of the gods, once the nature of the gods is properly grasped.[225] An implication of this line of thought is that the Epicureans—like Socrates in Plato's *Phaedo*—advocate 'rehearsing for death'. But they do so in explicit denial of the belief in human immortality (at least, that of the disembodied psyche or mind) that is coupled with this advice in the *Phaedo*.[226] This second strand of Epicurean thought contributes a further dimension to their confidence about the pleasures of the future, in spite of the contingencies that the passage of time can produce. A striking way of formulating this view of death is by reference to the idea of the 'complete life'. Thus, 'a correct understanding that death is nothing to us makes the mortality of life enjoyable, not by adding infinite time, but by ridding us of the desire for immortality'. Similarly, whereas 'the flesh places the limits of pleasure at infinity', the mind (*dianoia*), 'by dispelling the fears about infinity, brings about the complete life, so that we no longer need the infinite time'.[227]

What, exactly, is implied in the idea of the 'complete life' (*pantelēs bios*)? In trying to grasp this, it is useful to consider an objection posed by Gisela Striker to Epicurus' claim that his theory takes away the fear of death.

[222] They also deny that our death brings pain or disturbance: LS 24.

[223] Warren (2000) (2004), esp. ch. 4; also Rosenbaum (1990); Nussbaum (1994), 192–238.

[224] Warren (2000), 251–3, referring, for instance, to Lucr. 1.72–9.

[225] Warren (2000), 236–44, referring, for example, to Epicur. *Ep. Men.* 124.

[226] Phld. *Mort.* 38.14–19 Kuiper (1925), cited by Warren (2000), 241–2, (2004), 151–2. The comparison with Pl. *Phd.* 67e–68b is my suggestion.

[227] Epicur. *Ep. Men.* 124 (LS 24 A(2)), *K.D.* 20 (LS 24 C(2)), trans. modified.

Perhaps, Striker argues, Epicurus counters the position of those who fear death because they desire immortality (or 'infinite time'). But Epicurus does nothing for those who fear death because they do not want to see their lives cut short before they have had the chance to live out a life of normal length. The argument does not address those who think, like Aristotle, that human happiness requires a 'complete life' in the sense of a normal life-span.[228] However, Epicurus might reply that what matters is not whether or not our life matches some external standard of length. A life just *is* the period from birth to death (whatever its length). We make our life complete not by completing a certain length of time but by bringing it about that our life is completed, and unified, by a continuous line of katastematic pleasure. If we can bring this about, the *whole* life will be complete. The fact that the life might have lasted longer has no bearing on *our* life, since that ceases at death.[229] Also, Epicurus might argue, adopting the right attitude to time, and recognizing its irrelevance to happiness, is a key component in making the life, at any one time, complete (that is, full of katastematic pleasure and free from disturbing hope and fear), even for those who only want *more time* and not infinite life. It is only adopting this attitude that makes the present truly pleasurable, by negating the desire for *more time* than you presently have. It is in this sense, perhaps, that 'infinite time and finite time contain equal pleasure, if one measures the limits of pleasure by reasoning'.[230]

The fact that Epicureans hold that what matters is not length of life but achieving the ideal character-state (regardless of the length of time) can be understood in another way, which marks a further point of convergence with Stoicism.[231] The ideal character can be conceived as a certain type of structure; and it seems that just to instantiate this structure constitutes, in itself, the highest form of human happiness. The question of how long one does so, or what actions and outcomes follow from instantiating this structure, seems to be secondary, or even irrelevant. A related idea, which figures in both theories, is that wisdom, the ideal character-state, constitutes a kind of finishing-line for human attainment. Once the line is crossed, no further degree of improvement is possible.[232] It is true that the same point could be made about the core-centred theories reviewed earlier. For Plato in the

[228] See Arist. *NE* 1098a18–20, also 1.10. Striker (1989); also Annas (1993*b*), 346–7.

[229] For passages relevant to this line of thought, see Epicur. *Ep. Men.* 125–6 (LS 24 A(5–6)), Lucr. 3.830–42, 900–4 (LS 24 E(1–2,7)).

[230] Epicur. *K.D.* 19 (LS 24 C(1)). For a similar line of argument, see Warren (2004), ch. 4, esp. 115–35, 153–9, including a distinction between more or less radical (Epicurean) versions of the idea that additional time does not increase happiness (130).

[231] For this shared idea, see references in n. 207 above.

[232] See e.g. LS 61 S-T, 63 I (Stoicism); also 3.3 below, text to nn. 122–8. In Epicureanism, katastematic pleasure, once achieved, cannot be increased, only varied, LS 21 C(1), E(1). On the

Phaedo, or for Aristotle in *NE* 10.7–8, achieving the divine state of philosophical contemplation of truth represents the ceiling of human achievement and the realization of the essential core of the personality. To that degree, by implication at least, length of life and external actions and achievements are, at most, secondary criteria of human happiness.[233] What is striking, even paradoxical, about the adoption of this idea by Stoicism and Epicureanism is that they combine it with a one-world view in which human beings are seen as fundamentally embodied psychophysical organisms. One might expect such a world-view to lay greater stress on considerations such as length of psychophysical life and external actions rather than the achievement of an ideal character-state. However, the stress on the importance of realizing an ideal character-state is retained in these theories, but with a different (structure-centred) conception of what constitutes this ideal. The paradoxical character of the Epicurean ideal—but also its coherence—is brought out in Epicurus' famous death-bed letter.

> I wrote this to you on that blessed day of my life which was also my last. Strangury and dysentery had set in, with all the extreme intensity of which they are capable. But the joy (*echaron*) in my mind (*psuchēn*) at the memory of our past conversations was enough to counterbalance this. I ask you, as matches your life-long companionship with me and with philosophy: take care of the children of Metrodorus.[234]

Critics of Epicureanism, such as Cicero and Plutarch, even if admiring the courageous, and generous, attitude, doubt that the philosophy can justify the attitude. They question, in particular, whether a theory which places such value on the absence of physical pain, can justify attaching so little importance to this pain.[235] But these doubts may not be justified. The theory, as noted earlier, allows for a contrast between states of the mind and body, even though the mind is, of course, also conceived as physical.[236] The recognition that 'pain . . . when acute is there for a short time', and that 'death is nothing to us', can be seen as underlying Epicurus' ability to counteract his physical pain.[237] Above all, the passage illustrates the idea that the wise person 'will always have

'internalized' conception of happiness presupposed in both theories, see Annas (1993*b*), 347–50, 405–11, 428–30.

233 See 1.2 above, esp. text to nn. 6–7, 12–13.

234 D.L. 10.22 (= LS 24 D, trans. modified); see other references in Usener 138. The past tenses are designed to suit the time of reading the letter, and not, obviously, of writing it.

235 See Cic. *Fin.* 2.98–9; Plu. *Mor.* 1089 F–1090 A, 1099 D–E.

236 See text to nn. 194–8 above; also n. 208 above for the recurrent idea that the wise person will feel pleasure in the bull of Phalaris. Hence, the suggestion of Cicero (*Fin.* 2.98) and Epictetus (*Diss.* 2.23.21–2) that the mind–body contrast drawn in the letter is inconsistent with Epicurean theory is not justified.

237 LS 21 C(2) and 24 A(1).

a supply of tightly-knit pleasures', focused here on 'the recollection of those already experienced', that is, 'the memory of our past discussions', and perhaps also his addressee's 'lifelong companionship with me and with philosophy'.[238] The underlying point, then, is not just that mental pleasure counterbalances physical pain. It is also that the unity and stability of Epicurus' character-state (which is also a psychophysical state) is sufficient to counteract the occurrent, though intense, physical pain, the transience of which Epicurus recognizes. As so understood, Epicurus' response has a natural place in his holistic conception of personality, even though an analogous response could also have been conceived in part-based and core-centred terms, as in Plato's famous characterization of Socrates' unmoved response to his imminent death in *Phaedo* 115a–118a.[239]

In these ways, we can see how Epicureanism combines psychological and psychophysical holism, and the kind of naturalism that is focused on our finite, birth-to-death life, with Socratic ethical ideals of time-independent perfection and invulnerability. How far, in the case of these themes, is it reasonable to see this line of thought as derived directly from Socrates? As in the case of the previous Socratic theme discussed (103–9 above), the acknowledged influence of Democritus may have gone some way in suggesting this approach. As Kahn points out, '*autarkeia*, "independence, self-sufficiency," is as conspicuous in the fragments as is *euthumiē*', reflecting the role of 'thoughtful judgement and careful reflection' in protecting us against external contingency and internal disturbance.[240] The important fragment B 191 combines the advocacy of a strategy for shaping your desires with advice about adjusting your attitudes to life in such a way as to secure 'cheerfulness'.[241] Another potentially important influence is brought out in Warren's study of the post-Democritean ethical tradition (2002). This is the characterization of the goal of life in negative terms, prefiguring the negative formulations of Epicurean invulnerability (*a̲ponia*, absence of pain, and *a̲taraxia*, absence of disturbance). Thus, we are told that Nausiphanes, Epicurus' former teacher, took as his ideal *a̲kataplēxia* ('unshakeability'), which anticipated Epicurean *a̲taraxia*.[242] We are also told that Epicurus, as well as Nausiphanes, was especially

[238] Cf. LS 21 T, cited above, with LS 24 D. Given Epicurus' understanding of death (as the end), pleasure in the past cannot, of course, be united here with 'anticipation of pleasure hoped for', though he might (I think, consistently) anticipate *others'* pleasure. See further (also on the consistency of his appeal to Idomeneus for help to Metrodorus' children), Warren (2001*b*), (2004), ch. 5.

[239] See further 2.2 above, text to nn. 67–75.

[240] Kahn (1985), 26, referring to frs. B. 176, 210.

[241] Cf. B 68; thus Democritus partly anticipates the twofold Epicurean strategy outlined in text to nn. 218–27 above.

[242] Warren (2002), 39, 164–6. The technical term for such *a*- formulations is 'alpha-privative'.

impressed by the character (*diathesis*) and life-style of Pyrrho (D.L. 9.64), the founder of one strand of ancient scepticism, a feature linked with his (sceptical) assertion that 'all things... are equally indifferent (*adiaphora*), indeterminate (*astathmēta*), and unjudged (*anekrita*)'.[243] Although, as Warren also stresses, Epicurus did not follow the ethical approaches of either of these figures,[244] it is still possible that they contributed towards the striking formulation of his ideal in negative terms and in a way that combines hedonism with the ideal of invulnerability and exceptional consistency of character.

However, in appraising the influence of these figures on Epicurus, it is unrealistic to ignore the pervasive role of Socrates. As noted earlier, Socrates served as a paradigm in this period for the idea that philosophy has the power to set norms for character and behaviour which are substantively different from those of conventional life. In particular, he was presented in a variety of sources both as advocating an exceptional type or degree of self-control (*sōphrosunē*) and instantiating this in his own personality and life. As Long has brought out (1999*b*: 618–23), Socrates thus acted as paradigm for widely differing philosophical groups, and also inspired the symbolic or exemplary role played by intellectuals such as Pyrrho or, in the Cynic movement, Diogenes. Hence, in taking up ideals such as invulnerability to external contingencies or internal emotions and preternatural consistency of attitude and character, Epicurus was participating in a widespread adoption of Socratic themes and characteristics. The critical stance towards Socrates of Epicurus' followers, rather than Epicurus himself, noted earlier (101–2 above) may reflect a deliberate move to replace Socrates by Epicurus as a personal as well as philosophical paradigm. For Lucretius, Epicurus becomes the archetype for a series of (innovatively conceived) virtues.[245] The often-cited deathbed letter of Epicurus seems to have emerged as a rival to Plato's picture of the death of Socrates as an illustration of invulnerable consistency of attitude.[246] It also seems likely that Socrates' philosophical style, especially as depicted by Plato, helped to shape Epicurus' inclination to produce innovative and paradoxical formulations, such as the idea that 'death is nothing to us' or that of the 'complete life' (unimpaired by the prospect of termination by death).[247] In these respects, at least, Socrates, as presented in the formative

243 Warren (2002), 87–8, 100, 160–4, 176.

244 Warren (2002), 196–200, linking Epicurus' attitude with the rejection of reductive materialism or scepticism (taken by these earlier thinkers to be derived from Democritus).

245 Lucr. 1.69–79 (courage), 5.13–54 (heroic benefaction), 5.1194–1203 (piety); on the innovative quality, see Gill (1996*b*), 395–7.

246 Citations of the letter include D.L. 10.22; Cic. 2.96; Sen. *Ep.* 22.5; see Usener 138 and n. 234 above.

247 See LS 24 A(1), E(1), C(2–3).

period of Epicureanism, seems to have exerted a direct influence on the Epicurean adoption of these ethical ideals.

How far Socrates' thinking, as presented in any of the Socratic writings, also shaped the detailed content of Epicurus' philosophy, including its version of psychological holism, is more open to question. The strategy of management of desires and pleasures outlined in Epicurus' *Letter to Menoeceus*, which includes an attempt to counteract the impact of current impressions, by contrast with future ones, has been seen as influenced by the hedonic calculus offered by Socrates in Plato's *Protagoras*.[248] A more localized, though suggestive, point is the adoption by Lucretius of the imagery used by Socrates in Plato's *Gorgias* to contrast the stable pleasure offered by Epicureanism with the 'leaky' life-style advocated by other forms of hedonism.[249] It is conceivable that the psychological monism implied in Plato's *Protagoras* and *Gorgias*, in which emotions and desires are seen as dependent on beliefs—or rather degrees of knowledge and ignorance—could have been influential on Epicurus as well as on the Stoics.[250] However, I think the more plausible view is that Epicurus and his followers aimed to synthesize Socratic ideals, such as those discussed earlier, with forms of holism and naturalism that have distinct origins.

[248] Epicur. *Ep. Men.* 127–32 (LS 21 B); Pl. *Prt.* 356a–357b; Warren (2001*a*), 148–54.

[249] See n. 176 above.

[250] On Socratic psychological monism, see text to nn. 25–6 above; also 3.2 below, text to nn. 71–2.

3

Development and the Structured Self

3.1 PRELIMINARIES

The third chapter in the first part of this book focuses on Hellenistic–Roman thought about the development of ethical character. Stoic and Epicurean thinking on development, particularly in its early stages, has already figured prominently in a previous chapter (1.4–5), in connection with the idea of psychophysical holism. Here, I examine questions raised by the more advanced stages of human development, especially as conceived in Stoicism. The Stoic pattern is defined in part by contrast with Platonic–Aristotelian thinking, continued in Middle Platonism, as presented by Antiochus and Arius Didymus. I also discuss certain shared features of Stoic and Epicurean thinking about ethical development, which bring out further salient features of the combination of Socratic ideals and types of holism and naturalism that I characterize as the idea of 'the structured self'.

In Stoicism, my concern is mainly with one particularly important source for advanced personal development, the implications of which have been a subject of intense debate in recent scholarship: Cicero, *On Ends* (*de Finibus* (*Fin.*)) 3.20–1 (LS 59 D). First (3.2), I highlight the contrast between the Stoic pattern and a Platonic–Aristotelian one, which is sometimes adopted in Middle Platonism. I suggest that this contrast reflects, in part, the difference between the Stoic holistic view of personality and the part-based psychological model found in these other theories. Second (3.3), I consider the relevance for my enquiry of a continuing debate about the significance of Cicero's account. A crucial dimension of this debate is the question of how to understand the motivational shift that is central to Cicero's presentation, from attraction to primary natural things to the recognition that 'the good' (or virtue), understood as order and harmony, is the only inherently desirable thing. Scholarly argument has centred on the question whether this shift is motivated by the idea of realizing one's human (rational) nature through virtue or by modelling oneself on the cosmos, as the paradigm of order. I argue for a version of the former view. In doing so, I stress the extent to which virtue and the good are conceived in Stoicism in a 'holistic' way, in terms of a linkage between wholeness, structure, and benefit. Hence, the motivational shift towards valuing the good described by Cicero can be seen as being—in part at least—attraction to what gives wholeness and structure to one's human nature. However, I do not deny that the concept of good in Stoicism in general, and by implication in Cicero's account, is broader than simply human good, and is, indeed, a trans-categorical idea. But I suggest that this aspect of the concept of good is better understood by reference to the synthesis of ethics, physics, and logic, than by the idea of patterning oneself on the universe. In other words, this aspect of Stoicism reflects what I am calling the 'rich naturalism' which is a further shared distinctive feature of Stoic–Epicurean thought, and one that bears directly on their conception of human personality. This discussion thus shows how exploration of aspects of the idea of the structured self can take us to the heart of key ethical as well as psychological questions in Stoicism.

The account of development offered by Antiochus, the first-century BC Middle Platonist, is often contrasted to the Stoic theory by reference to the fact that Antiochus presents an analysis of ethical motivation which is based—or more explicitly based—on the idea of realizing one's human nature.[1] I recognize the force of this contrast, to some degree at least. However, my concern here (in 3.4) is with a rather different distinction. Both in Antiochus and in Arius Didymus, we find versions of the idea of development as 'appropriation' (*oikeiōsis*) which reflect a Platonic–Aristotelian, part-based approach to psychology, rather than a holistic one. Antiochus also, misleadingly, characterizes the Stoic theory in terms of his own approach.

Finally (3.5), I consider certain general shared features of Stoic and Epicurean thinking about development, which coexist with their contrasting theories about determinism and free will. I discuss the implications of the 'whole-person' model of causation which is taken by Susanne Bobzien to apply to both theories in spite of other differences. In this connection I explore the idea that 'rich naturalism', involving a synthesis of ethics, physics, and logic, is a feature of both theories. This idea is deployed in Stoic and Epicurean theories of causation and underlies their thinking on the way that human development involves agency and responsibility. I suggest that the idea of 'rich naturalism' helps us to define the type of objectivism that is characteristic of their philosophical outlook. More broadly, this idea helps us to specify the version of the 'objective-participant' approach to human personality which is associated with the conception of the structured self in Hellenistic philosophy, a theme explored further in Chapter 6.

[1] See e.g. White (1979). Of course, the extent to which this constitutes a point of contrast to Stoicism depends on whether Stoic ethical theory is interpreted in cosmic or self-realizationist terms; see 3.3 below.

3.2 STOIC DEVELOPMENT AND PSYCHOLOGICAL HOLISM

In illustrating Stoic thinking about the advanced stages of human personal development, I focus on the implications of a single, very important, passage (Cicero, *On Ends* (*Fin.*) 3.20–1), which forms part of their theory of development as 'appropriation' (*oikeiōsis*). In exploring these implications, I underline the connections between Cicero's account and Stoic thinking in general about the motivation of action and the nature and development of rationality. Subsequently (3.3), I relate the passage to Stoic ideas on the formation of knowledge of the good and the way that this knowledge shapes motivation. In both cases, I aim to bring out the characteristic Stoic linkage between a holistic and naturalistic conception of human personality and salient Socratic ideas. The main Socratic theme relevant to this section is that all human beings are constitutively capable of developing towards full virtue and happiness, in a way that is not constrained by their inborn nature, upbringing, or social context. The relevance of this theme is brought out especially by contrast with a Platonic–Aristotelian pattern of thinking in which those factors *are* seen as determining the scope of possible development. A further Socratic idea which is especially relevant to this section is a unified—rather than part-based—model of human psychology.[2]

I first cite the passage from Cicero, which falls within his account of key features of Stoic ethics:

(3) ... the first 'proper function' (*officium*) (this is my term for *kathēkon*) is to preserve oneself in one's natural constitution; the second is to seize hold of the things that accord with nature and to banish their opposites. Once this procedure of selection and rejection has been discovered, the next consequence is selection exercised with proper functioning; then, such selection performed continuously; finally, selection which is absolutely consistent and in full accordance with nature. (4) At this point, for the first time, that which can be truly called good begins to be present and understood. For a human being's first affiliation is towards those things that are in accordance with nature. But as soon as he has acquired understanding, or rather the conception which the Stoics call *ennoia*, and has seen the regularity and, so to speak, the harmony of conduct (*rerum agendarum ordinem et... concordiam*), he comes to value this far higher than all the objects of his initial affection; and he draws the conclusion that this constitutes the highest human good which is worthy of praise and desirable for its own sake. (5) Since that good is situated in what the Stoics call *homologia* ('agreement' (*conuenientia*) will be our term for this, if you don't mind)—since it is in this, then, that that good consists to which everything is the means, that good which is the

[2] On these links with Socrates, see 2.2 above, text to nn. 25–6, 36–46, 2.3, text to nn. 124–43, 184–93, and discussion below.

standard of all things, right action and the right itself (*honeste facta ipsumque honestum*), which is reckoned the only good, though later in origin, is the only thing desirable through its intrinsic nature and value, whereas none of the first objects of nature is desirable for its own sake.[3]

Virtually every aspect of this account raises substantive interpretative questions. But, initially, I note certain relatively straightforward features,[4] before proceeding to more complex issues. What the account presents is an ideal pattern of development, culminating in perfect virtue or wisdom. It is not completed by all human beings, though all human beings, on becoming adult, thereby move from the instinctive to the rational phase. Also, the whole process is one which all adult humans are, in principle, capable of completing.

To make sense of the account, we need to see that rational development is located against three different levels of value, which are well marked in Stoic ethical theory. The first is that of 'the things that accord with nature' (*ea quae secundum naturam*), sometimes called 'primary natural things'. These are the states or conditions towards which living creatures are instinctively attracted in the first stage of development (1.4 above). These conditions preserve and maintain our 'constitution' as psychophysical organisms; for humans, they include health, prosperity, social well-being and status.[5] The second level is that of *kathēkonta* (translated as *officia* by Cicero), rendered by Long and Sedley as 'proper functions', and, more commonly, as 'appropriate acts'. This is a broad category in Stoicism, defined as 'something which . . . has a reasonable justification' and 'an activity appropriate to constitutions that are in accordance with nature'.[6] As a category, it includes at least two types of value which are relevant here, those of primary natural things and acts of perfect virtue (*katorthōmata*). For all animals, it is, in the first instance, 'appropriate' to pursue the primary natural goods that maintain their constitution, the point made at the start of the passage just cited (LS 59 D(3)). However, as human beings become adult, it is also appropriate to pursue these rationally, that is, to select them and reject their opposites in a considered or deliberate way. This is suggested by the comment that 'the next consequence is selection exercised with proper functioning' (*cum officio*).[7] The third level of value, broadly speaking, is that of complete virtue ('right actions and the right itself', LS 59 D(5)).

In this process of development, the three levels are related to each other in two different ways. On the one hand, the three levels are integrally connected

[3] Cic. *Fin.* 3.20–1 (LS 59 D(3–5)), including LS subdivisions, trans. slightly modified.
[4] See also the brief analysis in LS i. 368.
[5] For examples of these primary natural things, see LS 58 A(4), C(2).
[6] Stob. 2.85.14–15 (LS 59 B(1)); D.L. 7.107 (LS 59 C), trans. slightly modified.
[7] Cic. *Fin.* 3.20 (LS 59 D(3)); also LS ii. 357, and M. R. Wright (1991), 130–1.

in that each level provides the material for advancing to the next. Pursuing the primary natural things is itself an appropriate act (or 'proper function'), and pursuing them in a way that expresses human rationality is appropriate for the human constitution. However, simply performing proper functions or appropriate acts does not constitute complete virtue. Precisely what constitutes complete virtue, for Stoicism, is a matter of considerable debate (3.3 below); but it includes the idea that appropriate acts are done in a way that expresses the state of mind, character, and understanding of a perfectly virtuous or wise person. In this respect, selecting the primary natural things through the performance of proper functions constitutes the 'material of virtue' (*hulē tēs aretēs*), provided that such selection is made virtuously, or at least in a way that promotes the development of virtue.[8] On the other hand, the Stoics see a radical disjunction between the type of value represented by the primary natural things and by virtue. As Cicero puts it here, 'that good which is the standard of all things, right action and the right itself... is the only thing desirable through its intrinsic nature and value, whereas none of the first objects of nature is desirable for its own sake' (*Fin.* 3.21 = LS 59 D(5)). Although the primary natural things are still properly classed as 'preferable' to their opposites, they are 'matters of indifference' (*adiaphora*), by comparison with virtue, the only unqualified good. It is this combination of ideas, seeing qualified value in the primary natural things but seeing virtue as the only good, that was absolutely characteristic of Stoicism and which aroused fierce criticism from ancient opponents such as Antiochus.[9]

The conception of value implied in this account, and, above all, the 'hard' ethical thesis that virtue is the only good, are likely to have been based on Socratic thinking, particularly as presented in Plato's *Euthydemus*.[10] Another Socratic theme is strongly implied in Cicero's account, and one which is central to the complex of ideas I am characterizing as 'the structured self'. This is the idea that all human beings are constitutively capable of developing to the point of gaining complete happiness, through virtue and rational reflection, regardless of the specific character of their inborn nature, upbringing, and social context. In Stoicism, this is expressed, for instance, in such claims as that, 'All human beings have the starting-points of virtue by nature', and that, 'Virtue is teachable... as is evident from the fact that inferior people

[8] See LS 59 A, B, F(4), G, I. See also Inwood and Donini (1999), 727–31, esp. 729.

[9] See LS 59 D(6) (Cic. *Fin.* 3.21); LS 58, 64. Kidd (1971*b*) remains a very good discussion of these levels of value. Antiochus' criticisms are directed at the idea that only virtue, and none of the primary natural things, is properly characterized as 'good'; see 3.4 below. Zeno's pupil Aristo denied that primary natural things had *any* value, but this line was not adopted by mainstream Stoicism (LS 58 F–G).

[10] See 2.2 above, text to nn. 23–6.

become good'.[11] Cicero's account of the final stage of personal development stresses this point. Coming to recognize that only the good is desirable for its own sake is 'in accordance with nature, and stimulates us to desire it far more strongly than we are stimulated by all the earlier objects [the primary natural things]'.[12] This claim is the more striking since it presents as natural an outcome—seeing virtue alone as the good—that some ancient critics of Stoicism, including Antiochus, regarded as highly *un*natural.[13] The thesis might seem the more surprising since the Stoics also acknowledge that there are certain factors, namely 'the persuasiveness of impressions and the conversation of the majority of people', which—in some sense, 'naturally'—militate against this recognition.[14] It is this view about the naturalness of the progress and result of the developmental process that partly explains the contrast explored shortly with the Platonic–Aristotelian pattern, based on the combination of inborn nature, habituation, and rational reflection.

What underlies the Stoic claim that this developmental process is a natural one? Part of what is involved is a belief—shared with the Epicureans—that all human beings have the natural capacity to form conceptions of ideas, including god and good, which are seen as fundamental for living a human life. These conceptions are described by both theories as *prolēpseis* ('preconceptions' or 'anticipations'), a name which highlights their *prior* or fundamental character. Although the characterization of these conceptions, in both theories, might seem to indicate that they are innate, what is innate, and universal, is, rather, the *capacity* to form such ideas. The complete understanding of the meaning of these conceptions requires both relatively advanced forms of rationality and extensive empirical experience. But both Stoics and Epicureans maintain that the acquisition of such knowledge is a universal human capacity.[15]

This set of ideas explains what might otherwise seem a rather puzzling combination of emphases in Stoic thinking about knowledge of the good. On the one hand, there is stress on the *naturalness* of forming an understanding of good. We are told, for instance, that 'the idea of something just and good is acquired naturally (*phusikōs*)'. We also hear that 'the theory of good and bad things . . . is most in harmony with life and connects best with the innate preconceptions (*emphutai prolēpseis*)'.[16] On the other hand, accounts of the

[11] See Stob. 2.65.8 and D.L. 7.91 (LS 61 L and K), trans. modified in each case.
[12] Cic. *Fin.* 3.21 (LS 59 D(6)); also *Fin.* 3.23.
[13] See 3.4 below.
[14] See Galen, *PHP* 5.5.14, D.L. 7.89; also 4.5 below, text to nn. 233–7.
[15] See 180–1 below.
[16] D.L. 7.53 (LS 60 C), and Plu. *Mor.* 1041 E (LS 60 B).

formation of understanding of the good stress the complex cognitive process that is involved. Cicero, for instance, provides this outline:

> Since the conceptions of things arise in minds if something has become known, either by experience or combination or similarity or analogy, it is by the fourth and last of these that a conception of the good has arisen. For when the mind by means of analogy has climbed up from those things which are in accordance with nature [i.e. the primary natural things], it then arrives at the conception of the good.

As well as stressing the advanced nature of the cognitive process, Cicero also underlines the special and exceptional character of the understanding thus acquired.[17] As some recent accounts have suggested, this combination of emphases can be explained, in part at least, by exploring the implications of the linkage in Stoic theory between the acquisition of knowledge of the good and the advanced stages of ethical development, as presented in texts such as Cic. *Fin.* 3.20–1. What seems to be implied by this linkage is that, on the one hand, human beings have, universally, a natural capacity to develop to the point where they reach complete understanding of the good, and thus recognize its unique and inherent value. On the other hand, this is a very demanding and, in a sense, exceptional achievement since its completion is identical with *becoming* wholly good and with developing complete wisdom.[18] What it means to become good or perfectly wise, according to Stoic theory, are questions considered later (3.3. below). But what this linkage helps us to see is why the Stoics stress both the universality of the natural capacity to understand the good and the complex and demanding nature of the process by which complete understanding of the good is acquired.

Cicero's account of rational development thus displays very clearly one of the two Socratic themes noted earlier.[19] What reason is there for thinking that these themes are combined with a holistic conception of personality, in which human beings are viewed as psychological (indeed, psychophysical) wholes? On the face of it, the process described seems purely cognitive or rationalistic, thus confirming a view that has been sometimes been held about Stoic ethical psychology in ancient and modern times.[20] However, I think that this interpretation of the significance of this passage and the larger view of Stoic

[17] Cic. *Fin.* 3.33–4 (LS 60 D(1–2), cited). Cicero also emphasizes that the good is known 'from its own specific power' and that the 'specific value of virtue' has a significance which is different in kind from that of other values (LS 60 D(3–5). See also Sen. *Ep.* 120. 3–5, 8–11 (LS 60 E). On concept-formation in Stoic theory, see further LS 39 D-F; also M. Frede (1999*c*: 319–21); Hankinson (2003: 62–4).

[18] See Jackson-McCabe (2004), and Inwood (2005), ch. 10; also M. Frede (1999*b*).

[19] See text to n. 2 above.

[20] See e.g. Antiochus' view (3.4 below). For a sophisticated modern version of this view, focused on a detailed reading of Chrysippus' theory, see Sorabji (2000), esp. chs. 1–2, 11–13.

psychology are both mistaken, and that the Stoic picture of advanced development, like that of the early stages (1.4 above), implies a holistic theory of considerable conceptual power and credibility. To bring this out, I contrast the Stoic account with another well-marked ancient pattern of ethical development, which presupposes a part-based psychological model. I also show that the Stoic picture implies a theory of the motivation of action, and of what 'rationality' means, that is consistently holistic in conception.

The alternative ancient pattern is one of which we can find versions in, for instance, Plato's *Republic* and *Laws*, and Aristotle's ethical writings; later examples, explicitly based on the Platonic and Aristotelian versions, can be found in Plutarch and Galen, combined with criticism of the Stoic approach. A key feature of this pattern is that development is subdivided into two stages, a habituative phase, often closely tied to involvement with family or communal values, and a rational, and specifically theoretical, phase, centred on dialectical analysis of ideas of value. This twofold phasing is explicitly linked with the division of the psyche into rational and irrational (or non-rational) parts. Plato's *Republic* represents a particularly clear example. Ethical education is subdivided into two stages, one centred on the combination of musical and literary culture (*mousikē*) and athletics (*gumnastikē*), the other on mathematics and dialectic. The first stage is directed at the entire class of guardians in the ideal state, most of whom will only become 'auxiliaries'; the second stage is designed for the élite subgroup of guardians being prepared for the role of philosopher-ruler.[21] It is also indicated that the first stage, while not wholly lacking in a rational or cognitive dimension, is directed primarily at the non-rational parts of the psyche, 'spirit' (*thumos*) and appetite (*epithumia*). This stage is intended to habituate the developing child and young adult, and, more specifically, her 'spirit' and appetite, in behaviour, attitudes, and normative ideals which express the ethical belief-system of the community, centred on an interconnected set of virtues. The process is presented as 'harmonizing' the two non-rational parts of the psyche to the rule of reason.[22] The second stage is focused on the rational part of the psyche, and is designed to enable it to realize its capacity for abstract thought (through mathematics) and theoretical analysis (through dialectic). The educational programme culminates in understanding the nature of the virtues and, especially, the good, taken as constituting the key aspect of knowledge in the full sense.[23] There are indications that the second stage is designed to produce a kind of

[21] Pl.*R.* Books 2–3, esp. 414b, 416a–b, Book 7, esp. 518d–519b, 525b–c, 535a–537c, 539d–540c.

[22] See esp. Pl. *R.* 441e–442a, also 401d–402a, 411e–412a, 429e–430a, 522a.

[23] See Pl. *R.* 521d–534c, esp. 531c–d, 533b–534c.

internal 'harmony' and 'integration' between the psychic parts or motives of a type that is still more complete than that produced by the first stage of the programme.[24]

Plato's *Republic* presents the two-stage pattern in its most schematic form; but the core features recur in other ancient versions. In Plato's *Laws*, there are salient differences from the *Republic*, bearing on the political structure, the forms of discourse within the community, and the degree of emphasis on mathematics and dialectic.[25] But we find here also an essentially two-stage pattern. Both the educational programme and the communal life of the adult citizen-body are presented as vehicles for habituation in, and engagement with, a shared set of beliefs about values, centred on the virtues. This is explicitly focused on the non-rational part of the psyche, and on the shaping of emotions and desires,[26] though it also involves the promotion of rational or cognitive responses to the belief-system of the community, communicated especially through the preludes to the legal code.[27] An intellectually and ethically élite group, the 'nocturnal council', is presented as enabled to proceed, following training in abstract thought, to dialectical analysis of the virtues that underpin the life of the community.[28] Book 10 of the *Laws* also offers a specimen of how philosophical analysis of the nature of the universe could be used to support the ethical and religious belief-set of the community.[29]

In Aristotle's ethical writings, the development of virtue is presented as arising from a combination of inborn nature (*phusis*), habituation (*ethos*), and rational reflection (*logos*). If someone is not ethically disabled by defective inborn nature, and is properly habituated in appropriate actions, attitudes, and beliefs, through the familial and communal context, he will have the basis for developing complete virtue including ethical understanding.[30] He will have what Aristotle calls 'the that' or 'the facts' (*to hoti*) of ethical life. But ethical development is only completed by the combination of 'the that' with 'the why' (*to dioti*), that is, by shared reflection, analysis, and debate about core

[24] See Pl. *R.* 485d–486b, 500b–d, 586e–587a. See further Gill (1985), (1996*b*), 266–71, 292–7, (1998*b*), 196–214, (2004*d*); also, on the role of mathematics, Burnyeat (2000), discussed by Gill (2004*c*).

[25] See further on the distinctive features of Plato's *Laws*, Gill (2003*a*); on the political ideal (the unified community), Pradeau (2002*b*), ch. 5.

[26] See e.g. *Lg.* 653a–c, 654c–d, 655d–656b, 658e–660a; also 643e–645c, 649a–650b.

[27] See e.g. *Lg.* 716a–719a (imagined address to colonists), 719e–723d (preludes to laws).

[28] Pl. *Lg.* Book 12, esp. 961d–968a.

[29] Pl. *Lg.* Book 10, esp. 885b–890c, Book 12, 966d–968a; also Gill (1985), 11–12. See further, on ethical psychology and the promotion of a belief-structure in the community, Bobonich (1996) and (2002).

[30] As is stressed by Sherman (1989), 176–84, (1997), ch. 2, esp. 78–83, ch. 6, esp. 241–3, 'habituation' in Aristotle need not be taken as a process of mindless conditioning.

ethical ideas, of the type offered in Aristotle's classes on ethics in the Lyceum and expressed in his school-texts.[31] Reflective discussion, focused on questions such as the nature of the virtues, and the relationship of virtue to happiness, provides a cognitive understanding, which can both inform ethical action and lead to a revision of ethical priorities.[32] Aristotle, like Plato, adopts a part-based model of the psyche, and the two main phases of ethical development seem to be correlated with this division, though less explicitly than in Plato.[33] As in Plato, 'virtue' is taken to be marked by a high degree of 'harmonization' or integration of motivation, though within a part-based framework,[34] and theoretical reflection can enhance this unity (though it can also introduce new tensions).[35] Plutarch, in his essay, *On Ethical Virtue*, examined later, adopts what he sees as a shared Platonic and Aristotelian pattern of thinking about ethical education and contrasts it sharply with the Stoic pattern which he rejects as psychologically implausible. He spells out the linkage between phases or types of ethical development and the capacities of different parts of the psyche with explicit reference to Platonic and Aristotelian ideas.[36] In Galen's essays on ethical development, there are some additional elements, derived from his attempt, in part at least, to integrate medical considerations alongside the framework transmitted especially from Plato and Aristotle. But in his approach too, we find the idea that ethical development depends on a combination of habituation and rational (especially dialectical) reflection, correlated with the part-based psychological model that he adopts in explicit rejection of the unified Stoic model.[37]

How far should we suppose that the Stoics themselves were deliberately offering an account of ethical development that was distinctively different from that of Plato and Aristotle—in so far as they had detailed knowledge of Aristotle's school-texts?[38] This raises a general question, which arises especially in connection with the Stoic reception of Plato, and one I discuss in full in connection with the Stoic theory of passions (Chapters 4–5 below). By the time of Plutarch and Galen, the first and second centuries AD, the battle-lines

[31] See Arist. *NE* 1.3–4, esp. 1095^{b}3–8, also 1098^{a}33–b4, and 10.9; see further Burnyeat (1980), 71–3, Sherman (1989), 196–7; Gill (1996*b*), 272–5.

[32] See Annas (1993*b*), esp. chs. 1, 18.

[33] At least, this is implied by his distinction between ethical and intellectual virtue, correlated with distinct parts of the psyche: Arist. *NE* 1.13, 2.1, *EE* 2.1, esp. 1219^{b}26–1220^{a}12. Presumably, intellectual virtues such as practical wisdom and excellence in deliberation (*NE* 6.5, 9) can include making effective use of ethical reflection.

[34] See *NE* 1.13, esp. 1102^{b}26–8, 3.12, esp. 1119^{b}15–18; also 1.2 above, text to nn. 27–8, 34–40.

[35] *NE* 10.7–8 seems to introduce new tensions by advocating the superior preferability of the theoretical to the ethical life. See further Gill (1996*b*), 370–83; White (2002), 244–64.

[36] Plu. *Mor.* 443 C – 444 D; see further 4.3 below.

[37] See Hankinson (1993).

[38] On the last point, see 1.3 above, text to nn. 74–7.

are clearly drawn: the psychological models are sharply opposed and the Platonic–Aristotelian pattern of development is explicitly linked with the part-based model. But how far back can we push this awareness? Galen encourages us to see Chrysippus in particular as deliberately rejecting the Platonic–Aristotelian part-based psychological model and his successor Posidonius (*c.*135–*c.*50 BC) as consciously readopting this model. But, as I argue later (4.1), it is far from clear that this is the right way to reconstruct the history of Stoic thought on this question, though Posidonius certainly does show a keen interest in the picture of ethical development offered in Plato's *Republic* and *Laws.*[39] A more plausible view, I think, is that, from Zeno onwards, Stoics took a non-doctrinaire view of earlier theory, especially Plato's (or that of the Academy), adopting or modifying what they found useful for the construction of their own line of approach, and ignoring or merely noting what they found less congenial. Thus, as suggested earlier, in formulating their overall world-view and their account of reality, they offered a naturalistic (and holistic) version of Plato's *Timaeus*, which they probably read as a 'one-world' vision.[40] As regards psychology too, Stoics, including Chrysippus, may have adopted a good deal of Platonic thought, even in the *Republic*, while not, however, adopting the part-based psyche.[41] So we cannot be sure that the Stoics actually saw themselves as rejecting the Platonic–Aristotelian pattern of ethical development, although their own analysis, as embodied in the theory of 'appropriation', is sharply different from this pattern.

But just how different is the Stoic picture? The Stoic account might seem basically similar, in so far as it assumes two stages, a non-rational one (for children and non-human animals) and a rational one, for adults.[42] But this apparent similarity is rather misleading. There are several important differences, which come out if we focus on the point that the Platonic–Aristotelian pattern presents ethical development as depending on a combination of inborn nature, habituation, and (dialectical) reason. First, the Stoics believe that all humans beings as such are constitutively capable of carrying out the full developmental process towards complete wisdom and virtue—even if, in fact, hardly anyone does so.[43] Hence, they do not accept that a person's inborn nature (or natural type, as presented in Plato's *Republic*)[44] plays a crucial role in determining how far someone gets in the developmental process. Nor is

[39] See 4.6 below, text to nn. 351–3, 366–80.

[40] See 1.3 above, text to nn. 41–59.

[41] See further 5.2 below.

[42] For the two phases, see D.L. 7.86 (= LS 57 A(4–5)), and Cic. *Fin.* 17, 20–1 (= LS 59 (D), esp. (3)), cited above.

[43] See further text to nn. 11–14 above.

[44] See Pl. *R.* 414b–415c; on the influence of inborn nature, see Arist. *NE* 10.9, esp. 1179^{b}4–31.

there an emphasis on habituation, either in the pre-rational or the rational stage of the Stoic picture. This difference does not derive from a belief that there are no lasting psychological dispositions, although this belief has sometimes been attributed to the Stoics.[45] The point is, rather, that the Stoics do not explore, as Plato and Aristotle do, the linkage between habituation and the training of the non-rational part of the psyche since they do not accept the existence of a separate non-rational part. Thirdly, the rational stage of development is not conceived as a distinct, reflective or dialectical one, superimposed on the basis of a habituated set of attitudes and beliefs. Rationality is expressed in the form of 'selection', a practical activity, directed at obtaining the primary natural goods, and, increasingly, at doing so in the right (virtuous) way. Even at the final stage, the relevant action is 'choice' or 'taking' (*hairesis*) the right thing for the right reason.[46] This does not mean that there is not an extensive role for rational reflection about ethics in Stoic theory. But the theory does not present the 'rational' stage as a distinct, advanced stage of development, but as a characteristic of all adult behaviour, though one that is, typically, only realized imperfectly. Underlying all these differences is the fact that the Stoics envisage motivation in animals, human children, or adults, as involving the psyche (or the psychophysical entity) as a unified whole. Hence, there is no stage in the part-based Platonic–Aristotelian pattern which corresponds exactly with either phase in Stoic development.

To form a more precise view of the way in which the Stoic view of adult development is unified or holistic, we need to take into account their theory of motivation and of the growth of rationality. The Stoic theory of motivation has been much examined in recent years, and there is broad agreement at least about the main lines of the theory.[47] The theory applies, in general terms, to both human and non-human animals. 'Ensouled things [animals] are moved "by" themselves when an impression (or appearance, *phantasia*) occurs within them which calls forth an impulse (*hormē*).'[48] A specific feature of the world 'appears' or 'impresses itself on' the animal in a certain way.[49] Certain impressions motivate action, namely those which impel 'an appro-

[45] See Inwood (1985), 34–41, arguing against Pohlenz's suggestion that there were no lasting dispositional states in Stoic psychology. This does not mean the Stoics recognized 'parts' (sources of motivation) in the Platonic–Aristotelian sense (see further Chs. 4–5, esp. 5.2).

[46] For the distinction between 'selection' (*eklogē, selectio*) of indifferents and 'choice' (literally, 'taking') (*hairesis, sumere*) of the good, see Inwood (1985), 201–15. The distinction is implied in Cic. *Fin.* 3.20–1 (= LS 59 D(3–4)).

[47] See Inwood (1985); also Price (1995), ch. 4; Brennan (1998), (2003).

[48] LS 53 A(4); movement 'by' is contrasted with movement 'out of' which occurs also in inanimate things.

[49] 'Impressions' are of very wide scope in Stoic thought, including what are, in other theories, 'perceptions', 'memories', and 'thoughts'; see Long (1996), 266–72.

priate act' or 'proper' function (*kathēkon* or *officium*). As noted earlier, 'an appropriate act' is a broad category in Stoicism, embracing an instinctive response to what answers to a natural need (hunger, for instance), on the one hand, and the considered judgement that this is the right thing to do, on the other.[50] The key point is that the impulse to act in a given way is an appropriate response to the specific impression that has been formed.[51]

The overall pattern of motivation applies both to rational animals (adult humans) and non-rational ones, that is, human children and non-human animals. But there are certain distinctive features of motivation in adult humans: 'A rational animal, however, in addition to its impressionistic nature, has reason which passes judgement on impressions, rejecting some of these and accepting others, in order that the animal may be guided accordingly' (LS 53 A(5)). What is involved in this additional process of rejection or acceptance? There are two main aspects. One is that the rational animal needs to give 'assent' (*sunkatathesis*) to an impression before the impulse to action occurs.[52] The other is that the impressions of rational animals have linguistic content, as is indicated in these two passages:

> a rational impression is one in which the content can be exhibited in language.
>
> all impulses are acts of assent and the practical impulses also contain motive power. But acts of assent actually differ in their objects: propositions (*axiōmata*) are the objects of acts of assent; but impulses are directed towards predicates (*katēgorēmata*), which are contained in a sense in the propositions.[53]

The response of the rational animal differs in two ways. (1) The impression has linguistic, and specifically propositional, content, such as 'this food looks good'. (2) She must assent to this proposition before the impulse to eat is activated. She assents or fails to assent to the proposition as a whole, but the impulse is directed specifically at the predicate (for instance, 'looks good'). It is the fact that the predicate highlights something that makes a response 'appropriate' that explains why assent to the impression stimulates an impulse to act in a given way.[54]

[50] See text to nn. 6–7 above.

[51] See Stob. 2.86.17–18 (LS 53 Q(1)): 'What activates impulse ... is precisely an impression capable of directly impelling a proper function'. The linkage comes out more clearly in the translation in Inwood (1985), 224: 'What stimulates impulse is nothing but a hormetic presentation (*phantasia hormētikē*) of what is obviously [or immediately, *autothen*] appropriate'; see further Brennan (2003), 268–9.

[52] The 'assent' may precede the impulse or be a condition of its (simultaneous) occurrence; hence, we are told that 'all impulses *are* acts of assent' (LS 33 I(1)), my italics, cited more fully below.

[53] LS 33 C and I, both abbreviated.

[54] 'Propositions' are statements or assertions, and 'predicates' are what is asserted about a given subject. The content of an impression corresponds to a non-material 'sayable' (*lekton*),

What conception of 'rationality' underlies the Stoic distinction between adult humans—and gods—on the one hand,[55] and non-human animals and human children, on the other? The distinction between human adults and children seems especially arbitrary. Why should becoming an adult make such a difference?[56] A salient consideration is that the Stoics understand 'reason' not as a single function or motive, but as—at least—an interconnected set or system of capacities.[57] Hence, although human children and non-human animals are recognized as displaying some aspects of these capacities, they are also seen as incapable, or (in the case of human children) not yet capable, of mastering the structured set of capacities that constitutes reason.[58] For instance, in *On Duties* (*de Officiis* (*Off.*)) 1.11–14, Cicero, drawing on Stoic sources, presents human adults as characterized by a linked set of capacities. These are for logical reasoning, language, sociability in family and communal life, the desire for truth, and the ability to recognize order and rationality in nature. The interdependence of these capacities can be illustrated by, for instance, language and logical reasoning. Language as a system implies the ability to draw inferences, enabling the speaker to decode signs and to recognize that a given word or proposition signifies a certain meaningful content. Language also provides a means by which the speaker can specify connections between objects or events in the world and draw inferences from those connections.[59] Similarly, the formation of conceptions and preconceptions, including those of goodness, is derived by a combination of empirical observation and reasoning, which itself depends on the use of language.[60] The formation and application of concepts is, in turn, a prerequisite for rational selection and choice, which are key elements in (adult) human ethical development. It is by building up and applying a systematic understanding of conceptions of value that we become able to 'select [and

but an impression is a material event, a certain configuration of *pneuma*. See further Price (1995), 146–7; Brennan (2003), 261 n. 8; for the formulation in this paragraph, see Gill (1991), 185–6.

[55] For this, perhaps unexpected, linkage, see e.g. LS 60 H, 63 F(3), also 67 K–L.

[56] Also, when does adulthood begin? Seven is marked as the age by which preconceptions are formed (LS 39 E(4)), 14 the age by which there is a grasp of language as a system of significance (D.L. 7.55). See further Inwood (1985), 72.

[57] See further on the meaning of 'reason' in Stoicism 3.3 below, text to nn. 94–8, 4.5, text to nn. 197–212.

[58] See Inwood (1985), 72–80. This is one of the reasons that leads Davidson (1985: 475) to deny animals rationality, understood as 'a pattern of beliefs that logically cohere'; for a comparison between Davidson and the Stoics on this point, see Gill (1991), 184–92. On Stoic thinking on animal capacities, see also Sorabji (1993), 20–8, esp. 28, questioning my comparison between the Stoics and Davidson.

[59] See LS 53 T–U, 33 C–D; also Gill (1991), 186–8.

[60] For instance, reasoning by 'similarity or analogy', Cic. *Fin.* 3.33 (LS 60 D(1)).

reject] on the basis of preferential reason'.[61] In short, rational capacities are conceived as an integrated set and as informing all aspects of adult human functioning, including emotions and desire, and not only those conventionally regarded as 'rational'.

Should we suppose that the transition from childhood to adulthood in human beings is a gradual and piecemeal one or a sharp and radical one? Psychological plausibility, together with the complexity of the notion of 'reason' in Stoicism, seems to point towards a gradual transition. But, as Tad Brennan comments (1998: 58 n. 5), much of the evidence indicates belief in a sharp and radical distinction, at age 14, and this goes with some other important, 'all or nothing', distinctions in Stoicism, such as that between virtue and vice or between wisdom and folly. Brad Inwood suggests that the Stoics (like modern legislators) were concerned to identify a definite age at which to locate the start of moral responsibility.[62] But I think another factor may be decisive, in this distinction and in others, and one that relates to the holistic approach that is characteristic of the Stoics, as explained shortly (144 below).

These points about Stoic thinking on motivation and rationality give us the basis, at least, for defining the way in which their thinking on advanced stages of rational development, as exemplified in Cicero *Fin.* 3.17, 20–1, expresses a holistic conception of personality. There are three main aspects. One is that the actual process of motivation is conceived in a highly *unified* way, in contrast to Platonic–Aristotelian part-based accounts of motivation. Another is that motivation is envisaged as reflecting the *whole* state or character of the developing agent at any one time. Thirdly, the motivational response is located, for both non-rational and rational animals, in the larger context of the *holistic* view of reality, a fact which raises complex interpretative issues explored in the next section.[63]

Of these three aspects, the first is the most straightforward.[64] The account is psychologically holistic both in not assuming a plurality of 'parts', or distinct sources of motivation, and in presenting motivation as a focused response to some feature of a situation. This unified character of the analysis comes out most clearly by contrast with the part-based account of Plato's *Republic* 4, in which motivation is presented in terms of the interplay between three potentially conflicting sources of motivation, namely, reason, spirit, and appetite.[65]

[61] LS 58 E(3); also 59 D(3).

[62] Inwood (1985), 74–5, see also 72–4, 79–80.

[63] See also the discussion of 'rich naturalism' in 3.5 below, esp. text to nn. 312–23.

[64] See also the discussion of the Platonic–Aristotelian background in 1.2 above, esp. text to nn. 2–28.

[65] Pl. *R.* 435c–441c; see further 5.2 below.

The Stoic picture has sometimes been seen as much closer to the Aristotelian pattern. This is especially so in the case of Aristotle's account of animal motivation, including that of humans, which is conceived as the activation of desire (*orexis*) by perception, 'appearance' (*phantasia*), and thought, and in which motivation is analysed in terms of propositional statements and inferences ('practical syllogisms').[66] However, the difference from the Aristotelian pattern comes out most clearly if we compare the two accounts of adult human motivation. For Aristotle, adult 'actions', in the fullest sense, are based on choice (*prohairesis*), and choice is a combination of reasoning and desire, following deliberation between alternatives.[67] Although it is possible to draw an analogy between the stages and categories of the two models,[68] the Stoic pattern is more unified. In Aristotle, choice involves the integration of two distinct agencies—which are capable of coming apart in the case of 'akratic' ('weak-willed') people.[69] In the Stoic picture, the acts of 'impression', 'assent', and 'impulse' are neither subdivided between reason and desire nor seen as the outcome of their coordination. These acts are equally rational functions of a unitary control-centre (*hēgemonikon*), which is, in adult humans, wholly rational in its operation. Although it is seen as possible—indeed, desirable—to reflect before assenting to an impression that invites action, this is conceived more as a process of verification than of weighing up the merits and demerits of alternative courses of action, as in Aristotelian deliberation.[70] The Stoic account is often, and plausibly, seen as closer still to the model implied in Socrates' arguments in Platonic dialogues such as the *Protagoras* (352b–360e) and *Gorgias* (466b–468e). Here, what are conventionally seen as conflicts between doing what is good or right and following pleasure are re-analysed as the failure to recognize what one really wants or as imperfect calculation of benefits. The underlying assumption is that recognition of what is beneficial (right, good, or pleasurable) will produce the motivation to obtain this benefit. On this point, as on much else, Stoic thought seems to emerge as a response to Socratic ideas, as expressed especially, though not exclusively, in Plato's early dialogues.[71] But whereas the Socratic model, as

[66] See e.g. Inwood (1985), 9–17, referring esp. to Arist. *MA* 700^b18–23, 701^a31–6. See further (on relevant similarities), Gill (1991), 171–92.

[67] Arist. *NE* 3.3, esp. 1112^b31–1113^a12, 6.2, esp. 1139^b4–5: 'choice' is either 'desiderative mind' (*orektikos nous*) or 'mind-based desire' (*dianoētikē orexis*)', *EE* 2.10, esp. 1226^b10–20, choice is 'deliberative desire' (*bouleutikē orexis*), 17.

[68] See, in particular, A. C. Lloyd (1978), who thinks the Stoic account presents as a simultaneous process what is, for Aristotle, a phased one. See also Gill (1996*b*), 50–2.

[69] *NE* 1.13, esp. 1102^b13–1103^a3, and 7.3, esp. 1147^a31–1147^b5, in which appetite (*epithumia*) becomes unhinged from the agent's (normal or better) process of practical reasoning. On Stoic thinking about psychic conflict, see 4.5, below, esp. text to nn. 192–244.

[70] See further Brennan (2003), 262–3.

[71] See further 2.2 above, esp. text to nn. 23–6.

presented by Plato, is embedded in intense, paradoxical arguments with interlocutors who have radically opposed assumptions, the Stoic account is fully and systematically articulated and forms part of a developed psychology and world-view. Thus, the following quotation from Epictetus might hold good, broadly speaking, both for Socrates and for the Stoics; but it is the Stoics who provide a systematic theory in which to locate the idea:

> for all human beings there is one and the same origin [of action] ... for impulse toward something the origin is the feeling that it is beneficial (*sumpheron*) to me. It is impossible to judge that one thing is beneficial but to desire something else, or to judge that one thing is appropriate (*kathēkon*), but have an impulse toward something else.[72]

The unified character of Stoic thinking on psychology is also conveyed in this characterization of 'impulse' by Brennan (2003: 267): 'It is a mental event that synthesizes a description of a particular, determinate state of affairs with an evaluative attitude toward that state of affairs and leads to immediate action. It is the causally sufficient, immediately antecedent, psychological motivation of an intentional action.'

This is one aspect of the holism of the Stoic conception of advanced human motivation. A related aspect is that the motivation constitutes a unified response that reflects the state of the agent (or animal) at any one time, conceived as a unified whole. More precisely, the response is to an impression that some aspect of the situation is 'appropriate' (advantageous or beneficial) for the agent, conceived as a unified whole, at any one time. This dimension of the Stoic theory has already been illustrated in Hierocles' picture of the animal as a unified psychophysical organism responding to the environment with a combination of self-perception and impulse and of Seneca's account of the developing animal as 'appropriated' to her constitution at any one time (1.4 above). It is also implied in the Ciceronian passage cited earlier (*Fin.* 3.17, 20–2 = LS 59D). At each stage of the developmental process, the human being responds, as a unified entity, to the recognition that such-and-such an act represents what is 'appropriate' at that stage. In human children, as in non-human animals, this is an instinctive response towards some 'primary natural thing' that will help the child to maintain her constitution, for instance, by eating food when hungry.[73] In the subsequent stages, the unified motivation is

[72] Epict. Diss. 1.18.1, translated by Brennan (2003), 268. See also the comment in Brennan (2003), 267: 'One cannot have an impulse without acting on it—the very having of it [i.e. the assent to the impulsive impression] is the initiation of the action envisaged in the impression'.

[73] Thus 'the first "proper function"... is to preserve oneself in one's natural constitution; the second is to seize hold of the things that accord with nature and to banish their opposites' (LS 59 D(3)); see also text to nn. 3–5 above.

also directed to the developing recognition of what is appropriate. The fact that, in subsequent stages, the response is characterized in rational terms ('selection', 'understanding', 'draws the rational conclusion')[74] should not be taken as implying that the process involves only one psychological 'part' or source of motivation. As outlined earlier, the development of rationality informs *the whole of* the person's psychological life. This aspect of the holistic view, combined with the idea of determinate developmental stages, may be the key factor shaping the Stoic idea, noted earlier, that there is a sharp, radical break between childhood and adulthood. The thought seems to be that an animal is *either* rational (as are gods and adult humans) *or* non-rational (as are non-humans and human children). The animal's responses and motivation are considered as a whole, and regarded as equally directed at what is 'appropriate', but within an explanatory framework based on the contrast between rationality and non-rationality. In the same way, and perhaps for analogous reasons, a sharp and radical break is posited between those who are or are not perfectly wise, that is, between those who do or do not progress to the final stage in the developmental schema Cicero describes.[75]

I noted earlier the contrast between the Stoic conception of development and the Platonic–Aristotelian pattern adopted by Plutarch and Galen. Superficially, the two patterns seem similar because both envisage, in human beings, a phased progression from a non-rational state (in children) to a rational one (in adults), with scope for degrees of progress within the rational phase. But the transition between the two stages is differently conceived, and is also less radical in the case of the Platonic–Aristotelian picture. The non-rational, or less rational, parts represent continuing dimensions in the psychological life of adult humans; hence, they need to be shaped (or 'harmonized') by habituation in the first phase, to provide a foundation for the development of the distinct part, reason, in the second phase. The process of harmonizing non-rational parts continues in this phase, in a perhaps altered form.[76] In the Stoic pattern, reason is not a 'part' in this sense, but—at least—a set of structured capacities which shape *the whole of* the adult's psychological life, that is, her impressions, assents, and impulses.[77] This does not mean, of course, that the Stoic theory leaves no scope for emotion and desire. The Stoics have a fully elaborated account of emotions to be examined in depth later (Chapter 4 below). But emotions, whether good or bad, are fundamentally rational responses (impulses) and not functions of a

[74] *selectio, intellegentiam, cognitione et ratione collegit*: LS 59 D(3–4).

[75] LS 59 D(4–5); also LS 61 S–U. See further on this aspect of Stoic thought, Inwood and Donini (1999), 724–7.

[76] See text to nn. 22–4, 34 above.

[77] See text to nn. 55–61 above.

distinct or quasi-distinct part of the psyche. They are also conceived holistically, in so far as they are seen as expressing the totality of a person's belief-set at the relevant time. The status of bad emotions or 'passions' can be defined in relation to Cicero's developmental schema, though they do not figure in his picture of ideal human development. Those who experience passions are those who fail to progress to the final stage within adult rationality, and who, correspondingly, regard 'preferable indifferents' as though they were good. In normative terms, such experiences are 'irrational', though, as just stressed, they reflect the rationality of the adult human agent, for instance, her (mistaken) beliefs, and, more broadly, her overall belief-set at any one time. In this respect also, then, the Stoic conception of adult development implies a unified, holistic conception of personality.

3.3 STOIC DEVELOPMENT AND ETHICAL HOLISM

In this section, I focus on the ethical implications of Cicero's account of the advanced stages of personal development. In particular, I consider this question: what is it that motivates the shift from selecting primary natural things, as ends in themselves, to seeing virtue alone as the good? This question has been much debated in recent scholarship, and some of the issues raised are relevant for my enquiry. The developmental process culminates in the recognition that 'regularity and . . . harmony of conduct' constitutes the only thing that is good in itself (LS 59 D(4)). I consider how this idea fits into the larger framework of Stoic thinking about virtue and the good, and I suggest that this framework reflects a holistic ethical outlook as well as psychological holism. It expresses the idea that goodness belongs to entities, including human beings, conceived as structured wholes rather than as containers of 'cores' or 'essences' which are the primary bearer of value. I also bring out the way that this type of holism is combined with key Socratic ethical ideas, including those which I am associating with 'the structured self'. As well as the thought that human beings are naturally constituted to develop towards virtue and happiness, illustrated in the previous section, Stoic thinking on this subject includes versions of the ideas that wisdom constitutes a time-independent, invulnerable perfection of character, and that only the wise person is wholly consistent and coherent. I also suggest that the Stoic holistic understanding of the concept of good involves a combination and, to some extent, synthesis of logic, ethics, and physics, an idea which I associate with that of 'rich naturalism'.

A striking feature of Cicero's account is a certain type of linkage between stages two and three of the account of ethical development cited earlier.[78]

> Once this procedure of selection and rejection has been discovered, the next consequence is selection exercised with proper functioning (*cum officio*); then, such selection performed continuously; finally, selection which is absolutely consistent and in full accordance with nature... But as soon as he has acquired understanding, or rather the conception which the Stoics call *ennoia*, and has seen the regularity and, so to speak, the harmony of conduct (*rerum agendarum ordinem et... concordiam*), he comes to value this far higher than all the objects of his initial affection; and he draws the conclusion that this constitutes the highest human good which is worthy of praise and desirable for its own sake. (Cic. *Fin.* 3.20–1 = LS 59 D (3–4)).

In the first part of the passage, Cicero describes the process by which selection becomes increasingly focused on what is appropriate (*cum officio*), that is, on what is most 'natural' for humans to select. By implication, at least, this is behaviour which displays what the second part of the passage calls 'regularity... and harmony of conduct', in that it constitutes an increasingly structured and rationally grounded pattern. The implied linkage between these two features is underlined by the intermediate words: 'At this point, for the first time, that which can be truly called good begins to be present and understood (*inesse incipit et intellegi*)'. These words suggest that, when selection becomes 'absolutely consistent and in full accordance with nature' (*constans consentaneaque naturae*), this means that the person has now come to know the good. They also imply that the increasingly ordered character of the person's selection, even prior to complete knowledge of the good, is a significant pointer to the nature of the good, as presented here, namely 'regularity... and harmony of conduct'. This linkage implies that an intensification in consistency, order, and structure forms an integral part of ethical development.

But what model of ethical development should we use to make the best sense of this account, taken in the larger context of Stoic ethical theory? How, in particular, should we explain the motivational shift that leads one to see the primary natural things as merely 'matters of indifference' in relation to virtue, which is seen as the only good and inherently desirable thing? Two general types of model have been employed in recent discussions. One model, which we may call 'self-realizationist', explains the shift in motivation by reference to the idea of realizing, through virtue and knowledge of the good, one's human nature as a rational creature. The other, which we may call 'cosmic', stresses, rather, the importance of patterning oneself on the order embodied in the

[78] For full citation and an analysis of the three stages, see 129–31 above.

natural universe and of seeing virtue as a way of expressing this order in one's own life and character.

Versions of the first model have been offered by Max Pohlenz, Troels Engberg-Pedersen, and Julia Annas.[79] I focus on Annas's version, which raises a number of important conceptual questions relevant for this enquiry. First, however, I consider the 'cosmic' approach, which is more widely held by current scholars. Gisela Striker's incisive statement (1996: 225–31) can be taken as exemplifying this approach. According to Striker, Cicero's account suggests that an understanding of cosmic nature as ordered, structured, and rational provides the basis of the motivational shift to regarding virtue as the only inherent good. But what can support this claim, since cosmic nature makes no explicit appearance in Cic. *Fin.* 3.20–1, though it has a prominent normative role elsewhere in Stoic thought? Striker observes that 'the good' is presented, initially, not as 'virtue' but as 'the regularity and... harmony of conduct' (Cic. *Fin.* 3.21, LS 59 D(4)). She also notes the feature of Cicero's account just highlighted here. The stage immediately preceding the realization that 'regularity and harmony' is the good is marked by a move towards regularity and harmony, as selection is based on increasingly rational and consistent principles (LS 59 D(3)). This has led some scholars, including Engberg-Pedersen, to suggest that the motivational shift is based on the desire for self-realization: as one recognizes one's essential rationality, one seeks to realize this and comes to see this (rational self-realization) as the good.[80] Striker is critical of this move; as she sees it, Cicero 'seems rather to suggest that self-preservation is *replaced* as a primary goal by the desire for order and harmony' (her italics).[81] Striker reconstructs the shift in this way:

> First one discovers the order and harmony of one's own natural conduct. Then one realizes that this must be a result of rational planning by nature, since real goodness can be found only where there is rationality... As a rational being one then comes to think that the best or only way to bring order and harmony to one's own life consists in following nature. But the final good is the best human life—therefore it must be a life 'in agreement with nature'.[82]

[79] (The following three paragraphs are based on Gill (2004*f*), 103–6.) These three versions differ significantly from each other. See Pohlenz (1940), 1–47, and Annas (1993*b*), ch. 5, discussed further below. On Engberg-Pedersen (1986) and (1990*b*), 64–100, see 6.4 below.

[80] See Engberg-Pedersen (1986), 156–62, (1990*b*), 84–7.

[81] Striker's criticisms (1996: 226–7) are especially directed at Pohlenz (including his 1959: 117); for similar criticisms of Pohlenz, see White (1979), 144–7. White argues that the self-realization approach is more characteristic of Antiochus' version of *oikeiōsis*, as presented in Cic. *Fin.* 4–5 (see further 3.4 below).

[82] Striker (1996: 230). 'Living in agreement with nature' is one of the standard Stoic formulations of the goal of life or happiness in Stoicism; see LS 63 A–C.

Recognizing one's own rationality and order does not generate the desire for self-realization; rather, it enables an understanding of rationality and order as being, in itself, good. Striker maintains that cosmic nature is, typically, seen in Stoicism as the supreme paradigm of order, structure, and rationality (1996: 228–30). The developing agent, Striker suggests, will come to see her emerging rationality and order as a product of nature's providence. Therefore, she will seek to live a life 'in agreement with nature', characterized by rationality and order. This move is taken to provide the motivation that explains the shift from seeking advantages to choosing the good, as the only proper object of desire (1996: 225–31). On this interpretation, Cicero's account is seen as consistent with other evidence suggesting that, as Striker puts it, 'the foundations of Stoic ethics are to be sought... in cosmology or theology'.[83]

This type of interpretation is adopted by several other recent treatments.[84] However, it raises certain problems, especially as a reading of the Ciceronian text, which are underlined especially by Julia Annas (1993*b*). Annas stresses both that there is no explicit mention of cosmic nature as a paradigm of rational order in Cic. *Fin.* 3.20–1 and that Cicero identifies as the good 'right actions and the right itself', that is, virtue, characterized in human terms. She argues that Cicero's account reflects, in a quite straightforward way, what was recognized in Hellenistic debate as the core Stoic ethical claim: namely that virtue is the only good and that it is self-sufficient for happiness.[85] However, there then arises, for her as for Striker, the question of how to explain the motivational shift from seeking 'preferable things' to choosing virtue. To a degree, Annas takes it as significant that the passage does *not* explicitly offer an explanation. The main point of the passage is, simply, to present in narrative form the claim that it is natural for human beings to develop towards this recognition of the absolute primacy of virtue. But, in so far as the passage does imply an explanation, Annas sees it as centring on a growing recognition of what rational consistency involves.[86] The Stoic thesis, explained by comparison with Kant, is taken to be that the natural course of human development will lead us to see that we have overriding *reasons* to

[83] Striker (1996), 231, cf. 228. See e.g. Plu. *Mor.* 1035 A–C, including (LS 60 A): 'There is no other or more appropriate way of approaching the theory of good or bad things or the virtues or happiness than from universal nature and from the administration of the world'; also LS 60 B, Cic. *Fin.* 3.73.

[84] See e.g. M. Frede (1999*b*); White (1985), (2002), 312–17; Betegh (2003), esp. 283–5. See also, less focused on Cic. *Fin* 3.20–1, Inwood and Donini (1999), 675–6, 682–4; Schofield (2003), 242–6.

[85] Annas (1993*b*), 166–8; the presentation in Cic. *Fin.* 3–5 of the Stoic and Antiochean positions takes this feature of the Stoic theory as central.

[86] Annas, like Striker, takes note of the indications of developing rationality in Cic. *Fin.* 3.20–1 (LS 59 D(3–4)).

give priority to virtue and that to do so is consistent with our nature as rational agents. It is this kind of rational consistency that Cicero has in view when he speaks of *homologia*, that is, 'agreement' with our rational nature.[87] The introduction of the idea of agreement with cosmic nature is, Annas suggests, 'far-fetched', as a reading of the passage (1993*b*: 170 n. 46). More generally, Annas stresses that the theory of *oikeiōsis* belongs within Stoic *ethics*, and that it involves only the kind of claims (notably, about the self-sufficiency of virtue for happiness) which are central to Stoic ethical theory. She does not deny the importance of the evidence, stressed by Striker, that the Stoic conception of cosmic nature, based on physics, was seen as supporting their ethical theses. But she denies that, in orthodox Stoicism at least, the cosmic perspective adds any substantive new content to ethics. Study of the Stoic world-view contributes, rather, a wider context in which to place the idea that *it is natural* for human beings to recognize that virtue is self-sufficient for happiness. It is this, rather limited, role that the idea of 'nature' has in the Stoic theory of *oikeiōsis*, rather than the more substantive role in explaining the development of ethical motivation that Striker attributes to this idea (Annas, 1993*b*: 159–66).

Annas's interpretation of the role of nature in the Stoic theory has proved very controversial, and Striker's approach is more characteristic of current scholarship.[88] But, as Annas highlights, cosmic nature does not figure explicitly in Cicero's account. And this fact does, indeed, raise difficulties for the idea that cosmic nature serves as a paradigm for goodness in this passage and provides the key basis for the motivational shift. There is also force in Annas's claim that different Stoic sources offer significantly different perspectives on this topic, and that some sources give a much bigger role than others to the role of cosmic nature.[89] Indeed, this point is now being more fully acknowledged by other scholars.[90] Also, her questioning of the idea that cosmic nature serves as an external 'foundation' for Stoic ethics, or that this kind of

[87] Annas (1993*b*), 168–72: see esp. 170: 'The idea is that we can appreciate rational consistency, which is not just the consistency of reasons for getting what we happen to want, but the consistency of reasons... that a rational person would have and act on. We come to see that rational consensus makes a claim on us which has nothing to do with, and indeed can override, our own desires and wants'.

[88] For critical responses to Annas's view see Cooper (1995) (with a response in Annas 1995), also Cooper (1996); Inwood (1995), esp. 653–61; Betegh (2003), 273–8. For parallels to Striker's view see n. 84 above.

[89] The cosmic theme is not prominent in Stobaeus' summary of Stoic ethics, based on Arius Didymus (Inwood and Gerson 1997: pp. 203–32), or in Cic. *Fin.* (except for *Fin.* 3.73), though it is prominent in D.L. 7.85–9. See further Annas (1995); also Engberg-Pedersen (1990*b*), 24–5, 32–5.

[90] See esp. Schofield (2003), 236–46; also, though with more qualifications, Inwood (1995), 653–5; Long (1996), 152–5, (2002), 204–5.

foundationalism forms part of ancient—as distinct from modern—ethical thought, merits serious consideration.[91]

I think that Annas's criticisms of the 'cosmic' reading of the Ciceronian account, and, more generally, the 'self-realizationist' view of the theory, can be strengthened by reference to other evidence on Stoic beliefs about virtue and the good. This evidence bears on my enquiry here in several ways. First, it shows that Stoic thinking on ethics, as well as psychology, displays the kind of holistic approach I am presenting as characteristic of the theory. Second, it illustrates in another way how holism in Stoic theory is combined with 'hard' ethical positions based on Socrates, including the ideal of invulnerable perfection of character and the thesis that only the wise person is consistent and coherent. Third, it helps us to form a clearer picture of the ideal character in Stoicism and thus of their version of the structured self (in its highest manifestation).

There are quite full discussions of virtue and the good in the two main ancient doxographical (or 'text-book') accounts of Stoic ethics, in Diogenes Laertius and Stobaeus, which can be supplemented from other sources.[92] One way of encapsulating the salient motifs is this. Virtue and the good can be seen as two correlated and interdependent notions. Both notions centre on two linked themes, those of benefiting, on the one hand, and of wholeness, structure, and cohesion, on the other. Goodness is defined by the conferring of benefit or the beneficial. It is also manifested in the wholeness, structure, cohesion, and in this sense the 'perfection', of a whole series of types of entities. The link between these two strands is, by inference at least, that goodness benefits by the very fact that it provides or constitutes the cohesion or structure of entities as unified wholes. Similar points could be made about virtue. Virtue is that element or factor that *consistently and invariably* benefits, as distinct from providing localized or intermittent benefits. The virtues, in themselves, constitute a structured and unified whole or set. They also confer structure and unity on the entities in which they are present, and thus enable the perfection of them as wholes. The benefit or goodness which virtue confers—or, in another sense, which it consists in—derives from its character of being a structured whole and from its role of conferring structure on entities considered as wholes.

I illustrate this general account of goodness and virtue before focusing on two ideas which are of special interest for this enquiry, that of the unity or

[91] See also Annas (1999), ch. 5, esp. 110–12. See further Gill (2004*f*, 2005*b*). On the relationship between 'external' and 'internal' foundations for ethics, see also Gill (1990*a*), (1996*b*), 430–43. See also Gill (2004*e*) on the background of scholarly debate about the relationship between ancient and modern ethics.

[92] D.L. 7.90–104, trans. Inwood and Gerson (1997), pp. 192–5; Stob. 2.58.5–75.6, sections 5b–o, trans. Inwood and Gerson (1997), pp. 203–11; also LS 60–1.

inter-entailment of the virtues and the cohesion of the virtuous character. 'Good' is, standardly, defined as 'benefit or not other than benefit'.[93] 'Good' is also defined as 'that which is perfectly in accord with nature for a rational being, qua rational', a category of which virtue is given as an example.[94] The point is not, I think, that 'rationality', in itself, constitutes the good. Rather, the thought is that the perfection of a structured whole is good, and the more complex the whole the better, provided it is still unified and structured. This may be what informs the subsequent point in the same account: 'the perfect good is honourable (or 'fine', *kalon*), because it has all the features sought by nature or because it is perfectly symmetrical'.[95] This line of thought also underlies Seneca's discussion of the nature of good, which contains this comment: 'that is finally perfect which is perfect in accordance with universal nature, and universal nature is rational'.[96] Rational entities constitute more complex entities than non-rational ones; their perfection therefore represents a higher expression of goodness (structured and cohesive wholeness) than that of simpler, non-rational entities. An extension of this line of thought also underlies, I think, the idea that the universe as a whole, conceived as a rational animal, is the paradigm of goodness or perfection, and also of benefit. This is not, I think, because special status is being attached to the cosmos qua cosmos. Rather, it is because the cosmos is the most inclusive, structured whole that can be conceived, and so its perfection represents the most complete type of goodness.[97] We should also bear in mind that rationality, in Stoicism, is not just a specific type of entity or capacity but is the highest form of 'tension' produced by the active cause or *pneuma*. That is to say, rational entities form the most complex type of structured and stable entities.[98] So, overall, 'goodness' connotes both benefit and structured, unified wholeness, the two ideas being taken to be mutually informing.

The meaning of virtue, outlined earlier, is closely correlated with that of good. A key underlying thought, going back to Plato's Socrates, is that virtue is the only thing that benefits consistently and universally, whereas other things confer partial and intermittent benefit.[99] Similarly, virtue is that which confers benefit on the larger whole in which it is present. 'Virtue... is

[93] S.E. *M.* 11.22 (LS 60 G(1)). See also the fuller definitions in D.L. 7.94 and Stob. 2.69.11–70.7, sect. 5d, trans. Inwood and Gerson (1997), pp. 208–9.

[94] D.L. 7.94, trans. Inwood and Gerson (1997), p. 193.

[95] D.L. 7.100, trans. Inwood and Gerson (1997), p. 194.

[96] Sen. *Ep.* 124.14 (LS 60 H(4)).

[97] See e.g. LS 54, esp. A, B, E–H.

[98] See 1.4 above, text to nn. 110–14.

[99] On the link with Socratic thought, see Inwood and Donini (1999), 687–90; also, on the influence on Stoic ethics of Pl. *Euthd.* 278e–281e, Long (1996), 23–32; McCabe (2002); also 2.2 above, text to n. 23.

generally a sort of completion [or perfection, *teleiōsis*] of each thing'; that is, it brings about the perfection of wholes which makes them good.[100] A discussion by Sextus Empiricus, in particular, works out the whole–part relationship in Stoic thought in some detail. Starting from the formula that 'good is benefit or not other than benefit', he explains that virtue constitutes 'benefit', whereas the virtuous person and friend are 'not other than benefit'. Good things are wholes of which virtue is a part, and virtue makes the whole good by informing it with benefit.[101] Stobaeus reports a set of typologies bearing on the relationship of virtues to other goods. The point of the categories is partly to convey the superior permanence of virtue, but also to bring out the way in which virtue informs other qualities or capacities of the good person and confers on them their beneficial and stable character.[102] One of the ideas reported is that 'all the virtues are both instrumental and final goods. For they both generate happiness and they complete it, since they are its parts'.[103] Here again, virtue functions as the part which confers benefit on the whole and so makes it good. Thus, both the ideas of virtue and good, in related ways, combine the notions of 'benefit' with that of perfected wholeness and structure.

I now consider three, more specific, ways in which the ideas of goodness and virtue are closely linked in Stoic thought with those of wholeness and structure. The first idea is that the virtues form a unified or structured set. Again, the basic thought goes back to Plato's Socrates, whose arguments imply the unity of virtue, a view adopted by Aristo, an early and ultra-Socratic Stoic.[104] Zeno, however, seems to have argued that the four cardinal virtues, while distinct, were all correlated forms of knowledge or prudence (*phronēsis*), and that, taken together, they mapped out the main fields of virtue.[105]

[100] D.L. 7.90, trans. Inwood and Gerson (1997), p. 192.

[101] S.E. *M.* 11.22–6 (= LS 60 G): see esp. (4) 'Since then, virtue is a part of the virtuous man and his friend, and parts are neither the same as wholes or other than wholes, the good man and his friend have been called "not other than benefit" by contrast with virtue, a part which constitutes "benefit directly"' (2). Some of the points made are attributed to 'sons of the Stoics' (LS 60 G(3)), rather than the Stoics as such; but the line of thought fits in with longstanding Stoic themes.

[102] See e.g. Stob. 2.73.7–10 (= LS 60 J(3)), based on the distinction between goods 'in process', 'in state', and 'in tenor': '"In tenor" (*hexis*) are not only the virtues but also the other expertises in the virtuous man which are modified by his virtue and become unchangeable, since they become like virtues.' Sometimes, *diathesis*, 'character' is used as a technical term to signify the special permanence of virtue (LS 60 L, cf. 47 S). See further LS i. 376.

[103] Stob. 2.72.3–6 (= LS 60 M, in part).

[104] See e.g. for Socratic thinking on the unity of virtue, Pl. *Prt.* 329b–333b, 359a–360e; see further Penner (1973); Vlastos (1973), 221–65; Cooper (1998*b*), 235–47. On Aristo, see LS 61 B(2–3), also LS i. 358–9; on Aristo as ultra-Socratic, Schofield (1984). On the influence of Socrates on this vein of Stoic thought, see Alesse (2000), 293–309.

[105] LS 61 B(5), C(1–3); also Cooper (1998*b*), 261–4.

I focus on Chrysippus', rather more elaborated, version of this theory. In this version, the virtues are inseparable in that 'he who has one has them all, and he who acts with one virtue acts with all'. Although the virtues differ in their 'main topics' (*kephalaia*), their primary area of expertise and operation, the virtues also involve, in a secondary way, the topics of the other virtues. For instance, the topic of prudence (*phronēsis*) is, 'in the first instance, considering and doing what is to be done, and in the second instance, considering what one should distribute (and what one should choose and what one should endure) for the sake of doing what is to be done without error'.[106] The primary topics of the other virtues are, for moderation, making the impulses stable, for courage, considering what one should endure, and, for justice, looking to what is due to each person. But, despite being distinct in this way, 'all the virtues consider the topics of all (the virtues) and those which are subordinate to each other' in a primary or secondary way.[107]

What, precisely, does this theory of primary and secondary reference consist in? In one interpretation, what is involved is, first, that each virtue is exercised in a specific area of conduct, for instance, justice in matters involving distribution. The reference to secondary topics, in this view, means only that the practice of each virtue is not inconsistent with the exercise of the other virtues.[108] A stronger interpretation is offered by John Cooper, who suggests that the topics are ones that bear on the doing of any action, whatever area of conduct it falls within, such as that of distribution and endurance. As he puts it, 'the thought is that in *each* action, there is room for some due distribution of something to someone... and room for something to be endured', and so on. 'Thus, if one is to make one's impulses precisely correct, one must know what action it is that has to be done and why, and what it is that has to be endured in doing it and why—all of that must be taken into account in the particular way that one shapes and constitutes the impulse of selection and choice that is to lead to the action itself'.[109] On either view, and especially that of Cooper, the theory represents a striking illustration of the idea that the virtues constitute an interlinked set or system in themselves and that they also produce cohesion, harmony, and structure in the character and

106 Stob. 2.63.8–10, 11–15, sect. 5b5, trans. Inwood and Gerson (1997), p. 205. The phrases in brackets have been supplied by the editors of the text, Wachsmuth and Hense (1884–1912). The term *kephalaia* is translated as 'perspectives' in LS 61 D.

107 Stob. 2.63.24–5, section 5b5, trans. Inwood and Gerson (1997), p. 205.

108 See LS i. 384; also, framed more positively, Long (1996), 217–19.

109 Cooper (1998*b*), 253–61; quotations from 258. Note esp. D.L. 7.126, trans. Cooper (1998*b*), 259: 'the things to be done are also to be chosen, to be endured, to be held to, and to be distributed'.

life of the person who possesses the virtues.[110] The theory also shows how the Stoics could take an idea which had been linked with the part-based conception of personality (as was Plato's famous analysis of the four cardinal virtues in the *Republic*)[111] and rework it in terms of a unified psychology. Although, for instance, 'enduring' is the main function of courage and 'making the impulses stable' is that of moderation or temperance, these should not be regarded as 'emotional' functions, by contrast with 'rational' ones, since they fall within the scope of a psychological framework that is unified and is, in adult humans, informed by rationality.[112]

Another relevant theme, and one which also reflects the combination of Socratic ethical ideas and a holistic outlook, is that the character of the virtuous person is marked by consistency, unity, structure, and harmony. Here is a typical formulation: 'Virtue is a consistent character (*diathesis*), choiceworthy for its own sake and not from fear or hope or anything external. Happiness consists in virtue since virtue is a psyche which has been fashioned to achieve consistency (*homologia*) in the whole of life'.[113] What ideas underlie this kind of characterization? One, just noted, is the idea that the virtues themselves constitute an internally consistent structure. The virtues, clearly, stand at the centre of Stoic thinking about character or ethical personality. However, the Stoics are also interested in the way that virtue can inform other aspects of the personality and the whole life of the virtuous person. Hence, another relevant idea, already noted, is that the interlinked exercise of the virtues gives rise to further capacities, qualities, or states, which 'supervene' (*epiginesthai*) on this exercise.[114] Stobaeus speaks of 'capacities (*dunameis*) which 'come as a result of practice, for example, health of the psyche, and its soundness and strength and beauty'. We are also told that 'the health of the psyche is a good blend (*eukrasia*) of the beliefs in the psyche'. Also, 'just as beauty of the psyche is symmetry of its limbs constituted with respect to each other and the whole, so too the beauty of the psyche is a symmetry of reason and its parts with respect to the whole of it and to each other'.[115] These further qualities 'supervene' on the virtues; put differently, the virtues 'perfect' or 'complete' the character and life of the person involved.[116] The idea of a

[110] See also Stob. 2.73.23–74.1, sect. 5l, trans. Inwood and Gerson (1997), p. 210: 'a complex system of craftsmanlike knowledge, which provides its own stability, which is what the virtues are like'.

[111] Pl. *R.* 441c–443e; on the Stoics and Plato's *Republic*, see further 5.2 below.

[112] See 2.2 above, text to nn. 10–13, and 3.2 above, text to nn. 47–62.

[113] D.L. 7.89 (= LS 61 A), trans. slightly modified.

[114] Stob. 2.62.15–20, sect. 5b4, trans. Inwood and Gerson (1997), p. 205.

[115] Stob. 2.62.18–24, and 2.63.1–5, sect. 5b5, trans. Inwood and Gerson (1997), p. 205, slightly modified.

[116] See D.L. 7.90–1; also LS J–M, discussed in text to nn. 102–3 above.

supervenient beauty, deriving from the coordinated exercise of the virtues, was stressed especially by Panaetius, and associated by him with the idea of 'seemliness' (*to prepon* or *decorum*). The central Stoic ideal of consistency is extended by Panaetius in the thought that we must work for consistency, and thus, seemliness in the way that we exercise the interconnected set of virtues.[117]

Other features too are said to supervene on the virtues or are presented as consequential on the possession of the virtues. For instance, happiness (*eudaimonia*) is said to supervene, when appropriate acts (*kathēkonta*) 'acquire the additional properties of firmness and tenor and their own particular fixity' (LS 59 I, ascribed to Chrysippus). What seems to be envisaged here is, partly, the way in which an appropriate act becomes a 'perfectly right act' (*katorthōma*), when it derives from the character of someone with complete wisdom, which is marked by firmness and fixity as well as by harmonious consistency.[118] But the idea of supervenience may also express the relationship of happiness to virtue in Stoicism. Although happiness is derived from, and inseparable from virtue, it is conceptually distinct. It is distinguished as a form of life from virtue, which is a quality of character. But the distinctive marks of happiness, such as 'good flow of life' (*eurhoia biou*) or 'peacefulness and tranquillity', derive from the cohesive interconnection of the virtues and form an extension of the qualities, such as beauty and harmony, which supervene on that interconnection.[119] This set of connected ideas is indicated by Seneca, in a passage which shows how we can infer the nature of happiness from concrete expressions of virtue: 'That man's orderliness (*ordo*) revealed it [happiness] to us, his seemliness (*decor*), consistency (*constantia*), the mutual harmony of all his actions, and his great capacity to surmount everything. From this (*hinc*), we perceived that happiness which flows on smoothly, complete in its own self-mastery.'[120] A further feature, to be examined later is the experience of 'good emotions' (*eupatheiai*), which are the affective corollary of the possession of the virtues as a matched set.[121]

Common to all these themes is the idea that the virtues, once developed, inform the personality as a whole. The structure created by the interconnected virtues also produces, by supervenience, a whole series of capacities, affective states, and a mode of life (happiness). This larger, and more inclusive, whole

[117] See Cic. *Off.* 1.93–6, 98, 100, 111; Panaetius was head of the Stoic school in the late 2nd c. BC.

[118] See LS 59 J–K; also LS i. 361; and Long (1996), 210–12.

[119] On these marks of happiness, see LS 63 A(2), B(4), F(1). LS 63 A, B, F also illustrate this view of the relationship between virtue and happiness, on which see LS i. 398–400.

[120] Sen. *Ep.* 120.11 (LS 60 E(8)), cited more fully in text to n. 166 below.

[121] See e.g. D.L. 7.116–17, and 4.2 below, text to nn. 83–8.

is also characterized by an exceptional kind of unity, cohesion, and structure, conveyed through a series of themes, such as harmony, beauty, and good flow. Although this enables the Stoic ideal to have greater psychological richness and complexity than would the bare idea of possessing the virtues, none of these further ideas involves any breach in the unified or holistic psychology that is characteristic of Stoicism.

Also associated with these three versions of the linkage between goodness and wholeness is a set of 'all or nothing' ideas. These ideas, like some other Stoic themes, can be seen as expressions of the Socratic claims that happiness involves invulnerable (time-independent) perfection of character and that only the wise person is fully coherent in character and mode of life.[122] The relevant Stoic ideas are, seemingly, paradoxical and were endlessly criticized or ridiculed in antiquity; but they convey a revealing message in this context. One such idea is that the wise or perfectly virtuous person possesses *every kind of* skill, whereas even partial deficiency deprives someone of expertise in *any* skill. A correlated idea is that there is an absolute gulf between wisdom and non-wisdom, regardless of how much progress someone has made towards wisdom.[123] Analogously, we find the idea, just noted, that the virtuous person is characterized by complete consistency, internal order, and stability. The non-wise, by contrast, exhibit radical inconsistency and fluctuation.[124] The underlying point here is that it is the systematic and interconnected structure of virtue or goodness that is crucial and that this needs to be present *as a whole* before *any* of the associated benefits can result. Without this informing structure, the building-blocks—perhaps better, the pieces of the jigsaw—lack the framework that enables *any* of the elements to make sense.[125]

How does this holistic way of thinking about virtue and good relate to the other kinds of holism attributed to them so far in this study? Stoic thinking about psychological holism, discussed in the previous section, and about ethical holism, considered here, reflect what I have called their 'substantial holism' (1.3 above), that is, the holistic view of reality and the world. The Stoic view on this point can be defined by contrast with the Platonic and Academic ideas that seem to have been crucial influences on their thought. In

[122] For other such ideas in Stoicism, and on the sense in which they can be seen as 'Socratic', see 2.2 above, text to nn. 47–92.

[123] LS 61 G, S–U; Stob. 2.65.7–68.23, sections 5b8–13, trans. Inwood and Gerson (1997), pp. 206–8. See also Inwood and Donini (1999), 724–7.

[124] See text to nn. 113–17 above, see further 4.5, esp. text to nn. 212–66 and 5.2 below, esp. text to nn. 125–35.

[125] For an analogous suggestion about Stoic thinking on rationality, see 3.2 above, text to nn. 55–61.

what one might call 'substantial dualism', reality and value, in the strongest sense, is attached to one side of a duality rather than the other: for instance, to Forms, rather than particulars, One rather than Indeterminate Dyad, psyche rather than body, mind or reason rather than emotions or desire.[126] Stoicism seems to react, systematically, against this outlook, both in psychology and ethics. Human beings and other animals are conceived as psychophysical and psychological wholes; value is attached to them as wholes, and special value to more complex and structured wholes.[127] A similar pattern of thinking seems to underlie the Stoic ideas about virtue and goodness, which are closely linked with those of wholeness and unity. Virtue is conceived, first, as a type of structured whole (the inter-entailing set of virtues), and, second, as that which informs and unifies individual character and life.[128] Goodness is closely linked with wholeness and structure: special value is attached to more complex—but still unified and structured—entities. Although reason has a crucial role in giving structure to complex entities, including the psychological processes of adult human beings, value attaches to the complex but unified structure, not to reason as a 'core' or 'essence' or privileged 'part'.

Against the background of this general view of virtue and the good in Stoicism, I return to the question of how to make the best sense of Cicero's description of the final stage of ethical development in *Fin.* 3.20–1. As noted earlier (147–8 above), one prevalent approach to this question, exemplified by Striker, stresses the importance of cosmic nature, especially in its providential role, as a paradigm of rational order, in serving to bring about the final motivational shift. A key argument for this view is that it is only by reference to the cosmic perspective that we can explain why someone should go from valuing 'preferable things' such as health and continued life, as goals of selection, to regarding virtue in itself as the only good. The outcome of the developmental process is one in which we come to accept all events, including 'dispreferable things', such as one's death or that of family-members, as part of an ordered, rational, cosmic pattern which embodies goodness.[129] However, other interpreters, such as Annas and Engberg-Pedersen, question the relevance of this idea to Cicero's account or to the Stoic conception of ethical development. They point out that there is no explicit reference to cosmic order or to the thought that recognizing the goodness of cosmic order brings

[126] See 1.3 above, text to no. 104–5 (also 1.2, text to no. 14–23).

[127] See 1.3 above, text to nn. 104, 106.

[128] A similar pattern can be found in Stoic thinking about social relations. For some relevant evidence, see LS 67 A, L, 57 F(2–3); also White (1979), 156, who accentuates the importance in this context of terms such as *kosmos* ('order'), *sustēma* ('organization').

[129] For versions of this line of argument, see Striker (1996), 229–30; Cooper (1995), 595; Schofield (2003), 244–6; White (1985), (2002), 313–14.

about the motivational shift described.[130] These scholars suggest that the change in motivation described by Cicero can be interpreted purely by reference to the agent's developing self-understanding. Both emphasize, in different ways, the idea that the movational shift is linked with understanding oneself *as rational* and with coming to see rationality (in a normative, moral sense) as having an overriding or objective force.[131]

I think that the line of thought pursued here lends support to these scholars, at least in their scepticism about the need to see an allusion to cosmic nature and providentiality to make sense of Cicero's account of ethical development.[132] It is clear from the evidence about Stoic ethical thought outlined earlier that terms such as 'consistency' and 'regularity and... harmony of conduct' (LS 59 D(4–5)) can convey the idea of virtue and the good without any need for invoking the idea of cosmic order and providentiality. Also, the material considered here indicates a credible model of ethical development, which could explain the motivational shift described by Cicero without invoking the idea of cosmic order. First, we have the idea that human beings are constitutively capable of forming an understanding of the good, in part by observation of their own developing patterns of selection and of the (partial) good qualities of other people.[133] Second, we have the idea that virtue and goodness constitute the perfection of our existence as complex but unified and structured wholes.[134] These ideas, taken together, are sufficient to account for the thought, stressed by Cicero and some other sources, that the good, once understood, exercises an inherently motivating force.[135] The underlying idea is that we recognize in the good an expression of the complex structure and wholeness that is fundamental to our nature and which we ourselves express at the climactic stage of ethical development.[136] This, in turn, explains why we come to see the realization of virtue and the good as qualitatively different from securing the primary natural things that are the objects of selection in the previous stage. Thus, we can make sense of the

[130] See Annas (1993*b*), 170 n. 46; Engberg-Pedersen (1990*b*), 65–6, 94–7.

[131] See Annas (1993*b*), 168–72, esp. 170; Engberg-Pedersen (1986), 156–62, (1990*b*), 84–7.

[132] I am less convinced about the relevance of the idea of rationality, in a normative sense, as having overriding force. This interpretation seems to me to bring Stoicism too close to the Kantian pattern. On the question of the relevance of the Kantian pattern to ancient thought, see Gill (1996*b*) 246–7, 260–6, 326–33, 336–40.

[133] See text to nn. 15–18 above and nn. 62–71 below.

[134] See text to nn. 99–103 above.

[135] LS 59 D (4, 6); cf. LS 60 F.

[136] To this degree, this pattern is centred on the idea of self-realization, but conceived in more holistic terms than by Pohlenz (1959: 117), whose view is criticized by Striker (1996: 225), or by Antiochus (3.4 below). This pattern is also different from the type of self-realization envisaged by Engberg-Pedersen, centred on the subjective-objective contrast; see further 6.4 below.

sequence presented by Cicero without invoking an idea of cosmic order and providentiality that is, at most, only implicit in his account in 3.20–1.

Support for the claim that this is a well-marked approach to ethical development in Stoicism can be found in at least two works of practical ethics. In *On Duties* (*Off.*) 1, Cicero draws on a framework for promoting ethical progress derived from Panaetius, the last head of the Stoic school. A central motif is that we should aim at 'consistency' and at achieving the 'appropriate' or 'seemly' (*to prepon* or *decorum*) by correlating four roles (*personae*). One of these is our universal nature as rational agents who are capable of developing the virtues, conceived as an integrated set. The other three roles are subdivisions of our particular nature: our talents and inclinations, social background, and chosen way of life.[137] Here, as elsewhere, the ideal outcome is characterized in terms of order, structure, harmony, and consistency.[138] There is, however, no reference to cosmic order or providentiality. The approach advocated by Cicero is what is sometimes described by modern scholars as 'self-realizationist', that is, based on the development of our human, or rational, nature rather than on an appeal to cosmic order.[139] However, as Cicero spells out very clearly in *On Duties* 3, the ideal outcome of the developmental process is that obtaining preferable indifferents such as health and wealth is seen as radically different in value from selecting virtuously and achieving a virtuous character and way of life.[140] So it is not uniformly supposed in Stoic thought that reference to cosmic providence is the *only* way to understand the required motivational shift.

A similar point can be made about the three-stage developmental strategy that forms a recurrent theme in Epictetus' *Discourses*. Epictetus advocates, first, that we recognize that our happiness depends on what is 'up to us', through our exercise of rational reflection, and not on securing external goods. Second, we should use this recognition to inform our selection of, and impulses towards, what is 'appropriate' in, for instance, interpersonal and social behaviour. Third, we should aim at complete 'consistency' in the impressions that inform our selections and impulses.[141] This three-stage programme, like some other patterns in Stoic practical ethics, is, clearly, related to the kind of developmental process outlined in Cicero, *Fin.* 3.20–1, while not being identical in formulation.[142] The main relevant point here is

137 Cic. *Off.* 1.107–20, also 93–6, 98; see Gill (1988), 169–77.

138 See e.g. *Off.* 1.98: 'with order and consistency', *ordine et constantia*; 1.111, 'evenness in the whole of life', *aequabilitas uniuersae uitae.*

139 See e.g. White (1979), 146, 161–2, 176.

140 See e.g. Cic. *Off.* 3.7–19.

141 See esp. Epict. *Diss.* 3.2.1–5 (LS 56 C).

142 Similarities include the idea that the development towards complete human virtue and happiness is open to all human beings (is 'up to us'), that appropriate selection is a key part of

that this method, while directed at the same motivational outcome as *Fin.* 3.20–1 (and *On Duties*), is not presented as dependent on reference to cosmic order and providence.[143] This is the more striking because Epictetus sometimes does refer to the ethical implications of cosmic order and providence, as does Cicero, though less emphatically, in *On Ends*.[144]

What larger conclusions should we form about Stoic thinking in general about the basis of ethical understanding and motivation? This question, apart from being important for making sense of Stoicism, has a particular relevance for my enquiry. Earlier, I suggested that Plato's providential world-view in the *Timaeus*, perhaps mediated by Polemo, may have been a crucial influence on the formation of the Stoic holistic outlook. The Stoic ideals of (embodied) structure and harmony are also prefigured in the providential world-view of the *Timaeus*, where they are associated, for instance, with the world-soul and the ideal human character.[145] It might therefore seem to follow that I should also see the providential role of nature as a key theme, and perhaps *the* key theme, within the Stoic holistic outlook, with powerful implications for ethics. It is, certainly, the case that cosmic order and providentiality *does* sometimes figure in Stoic accounts of ethics. This idea plays a key role in Diogenes Laertius' account, where it is presented as underlying the theory of ethical development as 'appropriation' (*oikeiōsis*).[146] It is also deployed by teachers of practical ethics, including, sometimes, Epictetus, as one of the means by which they seek to promote ethical development.[147] However, I think it is less crucial and pervasive in Stoic thought than is often supposed. I also believe that it figures, typically, as part of a different, and more complex, pattern, which has at least partial analogues in Epicureanism. This is the idea that complete wisdom consists in a combination, and in some sense fusion, of the three branches of philosophy, logic, ethics, and physics. I associate this idea with the notion of 'rich naturalism', according to which the three branches of philoso-

development, that 'external' goods are valued substantially below virtue, and that 'consistency' is the goal. On this method, see further 6.5 below. However, see Long (2002), ch. 7, esp. 182–9, who suggests that Epictetus de-emphasizes the Stoic theory of appropriation, preferring to appeal to 'god' as a basis for the idea that all human beings are fundamentally capable of ethical responses.

[143] It is sometimes argued that Epictetus' three-stage method corresponds to the division: physics–ethics–logic; but this claim (of which I am sceptical) does not amount to invoking cosmic providentiality; see 6.5 below, text to nn. 229–35.

[144] See e.g. Epict. *Diss.* 1.14, 16; see further Long (2002), ch. 6. See also Cic. *Fin.* 3.73.

[145] See 1.3 above, text to nn. 41–59.

[146] D.L. 7.85–9; Cooper (1995), in his critique of Annas (1993), ch. 5, sees this line of thought as the basis of Cicero's account of development in *Fin.* 3.17, 20–1. See also Schofield (2003), 239–46, who sees Diogenes' version as representing one of two main ways of interpreting Stoic ethics.

[147] See n. 144 above.

phy are mutually supporting and reciprocally related. This is not the kind of naturalism in which, for instance, ethics is reduced to physics or is presented as conceptually dependent on foundations supplied by physics.[148]

To provide a context for this suggestion, I refer again to recent scholarly debate, especially the contribution of Annas. Annas is sometimes taken as simply discounting the relevance of cosmic nature, or physics, to Stoic ethics; but her position, which has been progressively refined, is more complex, and credible, than this. In *The Morality of Happiness* (1993*b*), 173–7, Annas does present the emphasis on cosmic nature in Cleanthes (second head of the Stoic school) and in, for instance, Marcus Aurelius, as a minor strand in Stoic thought and as a less philosophically sophisticated version of the theory. However, she has subsequently qualified this claim, accepting that this constitutes *one*—but not the only—line of thought about the basis of Stoic ethics.[149] A second claim, which she has not withdrawn, is that study of Stoic philosophy involves a two-stage process: one in which each part (for instance, ethics) is studied independently and a second stage in which each part is studied in a 'holistic' way, that is, in the light of all three parts. She sees the second stage as providing a larger conceptual framework but not as adding any substantively new content.[150] She finds support for this view in evidence that Chrysippus favoured the order logic–ethics–physics for the Stoic curriculum.[151] She also points to evidence that Chrysippus gave a significant role to dialectical debate, including the 'articulation' of ethical concepts, which she takes as supporting the idea that ethics was studied first in the curriculum and debated in its own terms.[152] However, critics of her position have pointed out that we also find alternative orders for the Stoic curriculum, including that of logic–physics–ethics, ascribed to Chrysippus among others.[153] Also, the evidence cited by Annas in support of the presence of purely ethical dialectic also refers to 'demonstration' of ethical principles, which could include demonstration from the principles of physics.[154] So the evidence for this question from our sources on the Stoic curriculum seems to support both types of interpretation.

148 There are, certainly, Stoic sources which suggest the latter idea, notably Plu. *Mor.* 1035 C–D (LS 60 A) (see also n. 83 above). But these passages constitute only a subdivision of the larger body of evidence bearing on this, philosophically complex, question.

149 Annas (1995), 604–5 n. 13, responding to Cooper (1995).

150 Annas (1993*b*), 163–5, (1995), 603–4.

151 Plu. *Mor.* 1035 A (LS 26 C), also D.L. 7.70 (LS 26 B(3)).

152 Annas (1993*b*), 163–5, referring to the discussion of book-titles of ethical treatises by Chrysippus in Brunschwig (1991).

153 D.L. 7.40–1 (LS 26 B(4)).

154 Cooper (1995), 597–8; Inwood (1995), 659–60; Betegh (2003), 275–8. The main book-title discussed is, 'That the ancients admitted dialectic along with demonstrations'; see Brunschwig (1991), esp. 95.

However, Annas has, subsequently, highlighted a further feature of the ancient evidence and offered another possible way of understanding the relationship between branches of knowledge in Stoicism. Although some sources suggest that there was a definite order in which the three parts were studied, we are also told that, according to some Stoics, 'no part is given preference over another, but they are mixed together.'[155] Annas finds here support for the idea that the conceptual model is 'non-hierarchical' and reciprocal.[156] It follows that, despite some evidence pointing the other way,[157] physics is no more foundational for ethics than is ethics—and logic—for physics. The importance of the idea that philosophy should work to combine, and in some sense synthesize, the findings of logic, ethics, and physics, has also been emphasized by Pierre Hadot.[158] The possible linkage between logic and ethics has been much less examined than that between ethics and physics; but Long has gone some way in this direction.[159] This seems to me the most promising starting-point for understanding the Stoic view of the relationship between the branches of philosophy. I explore this suggestion later in this chapter, taking up especially the—difficult—question whether the goal is the *combination* of all three branches or some more complete *synthesis*, including the analysis of ideas in a 'trans-categorical' way.[160] This feature of Stoic thinking also provides a basis for making sense of their version of the idea of 'rich naturalism'.

I close the present discussion by outlining ways in which the combination of ethics, physics, and logic can be seen as contributing to our understanding of 'good'. This point can be taken with another, well-marked theme in Stoic thought. This is that theory needs to be thoroughly integrated with practice if it is to make any real contribution (as it can) to ethical development.[161] Hence, what is required is to see how practical life and theory can reinforce each other in giving us the complete understanding of goodness that will bring about the motivational shift described by Cicero in *Fin.* 3.20–1. I begin by considering one element in this process that has been rather under-examined in recent scholarship, namely the role of social interaction in the

[155] D.L. 7.40 (LS 26 B(4)).

[156] Annas (1999), 111–12; her main topic here is the attempt by later Platonists to find this (Stoic) model in Plato.

[157] See e.g. LS 60 A–B, stressed by Striker (1996), 228.

[158] See e.g. P. Hadot (1979), 208–11, 215–18.

[159] See esp. Long (1996), ch. 8, and LS 31 B(1), C(1). However, Long himself favours a version of the 'cosmic' approach to the nature and basis of Stoic ethics; see Long (1996), ch. 6, in particular the postscript, added in 1995 (152–5).

[160] See 3.5 below, esp. text to nn. 312–23.

[161] This theme is stressed especially by Epictetus; see 6.5 below, text to nn. 213–36, esp. nn. 235–6.

practical side of this process, a subject illustrated in Seneca's letter 120.[162] Seneca here tackles an issue which arises directly out of Cicero's account in *Fin.* 3.20–1, or at least out of the theory that it reflects. This is the question how we can use our natural capacity for knowing the good in spite of the fact that we live in societies in which examples of perfect virtue (wise people or 'sages') cannot be observed directly. Seneca, like Cicero in *Fin.* 3.33, stresses the role of our natural cognitive capacities, notably for analogy.[163] More specifically, Seneca outlines a series of strategies by which we can extrapolate from imperfect, real-life or traditional examples to a conception of a more unqualified type of virtue.[164] For instance, Roman exemplary stories of specific acts of exceptional virtue, attached to figures such as Fabricius or Horatius Cocles, can offer an important, if only one-dimensional, insight into virtue (5–7). We can also learn, partly as counterexamples, from people whose behaviour appears good in one context but not in another.[165] But we can learn most, by contrast, from someone who displays complete consistency.

> We saw someone who was kindly to his friends, forbearing to his enemies, dutiful and pious in his public and private behaviour . . . Moreover he was always the same and consistent with himself in every action, good not through policy but under the direction of a character such that he could not only act rightly but could not act without acting rightly. We perceived that in him virtue was perfected . . . We grasped moderation, courage, prudence, justice and gave to each its due. From whom did we perceive virtue? That man's orderliness (*ordo*) revealed it to us, his seemliness, consistency (*constantia*), the mutual harmony (*concordia*) of all his actions, and his great capacity to surmount everything. From this we perceived that happy life which flows on smoothly, complete in its own self-mastery.[166]

By contrast, most of us are riddled by inconsistency in behaviour and attitudes. 'No one can play one role except the wise person; the rest of us are polymorphous (*multiformes*)' (120.22).

Seneca's discussion here is suggestive, rather than expository or analytic.[167] But it illustrates several points bearing on the contribution of practical life to coming to know the good. It brings out—what can, of course, be shown from

[162] For helpful discussion of this letter, see Inwood (2005), ch. 10.

[163] Sen. *Ep.* 120.4–5, presented as a way in which we can develop the 'seeds' of knowledge of the good that we have by nature (cf. text to nn. 11–18 above).

[164] These strategies include 'admiring' actions 'as if (*tamquam*) they were perfect' and 'pretending not to notice' (*dissimulauimus*) failings, 5.

[165] 120.8–9; this feature may be linked with concept-formation 'by opposition', D.L. 7.53 (LS 39 D(6)); see Pohlenz (1940), 87.

[166] 120.10–11 (LS 60 E(7–8)).

[167] Among the questions raised by Seneca's letter are his reasons for casting the account of coming to know the good in the past tense, as though it were a familiar part of everyone's (past) experience (which it is not); and the identity of the ideal figure outlined in 120.11–12 (Socrates

other sources—that ethical development in Stoicism necessarily involves interpersonal and social interaction, even though this does not play the habituative role allocated to it in the Platonic–Aristotelian pattern.[168] The fact that Cic. *Fin.* 3.20–1 does not explicitly refer to the role of social engagement and observation of others, as Seneca does, does not mean that any special weight is being given to *individual self*-observation, as Engberg-Pedersen suggests.[169] It is notable that Seneca's characterization of the type of person that enables us to understand the good highlights the same features that figure in Cicero's description of the good, namely 'regularity and... harmony of conduct' (*ordinem et... concordiam*), as well as in the preceding account of increasingly consistent (*constans*) selection.[170] Seneca's description also alludes to other central Stoic themes considered here, including the unity or inter-entailment of the virtues, the cohesion of the wise person's character (and the incoherence of the non-wise), and the invulnerability of the wise person's happiness.[171] In so doing, Seneca highlights the way in which social observation and interaction can provide reasons for seeing goodness or virtue as characterized by unity, harmony, and order, as well as for regarding this state as inherently attractive.

What about the contribution of theory, especially the combination of logic, physics, and ethics, to helping us understand the good? As regards physics, scholars such as Striker have stressed the idea that the natural universe, conceived as a rational whole, instantiates certain standard Stoic definitions of 'good', including 'what is perfect according to nature' and 'perfection of rational nature'.[172] Striker herself takes this evidence as showing that cosmic nature serves as *the* paradigm of goodness in Stoicism; but we can take it, instead, as showing that nature represents *one* of a number of such exemplars. In considering the role of logic or dialectic, we need to be aware of the breadth of this branch of knowledge in Stoicism, which embraces the analysis of language, discourse, and concepts, as well as formal logic. 'Logic', in this sense, partly plays an enabling role. In the theoretical sphere, it enables the analysis (in ethical theory) of the concept of good and of other notions of

and Cato are his standard paradigms). On these questions and possible responses, see Inwood (2005), ch. 10. For the suggestion that the use of specific exemplars for ideal wisdom is characteristic of later, rather than early, Stoicism, see Sedley (1999*c*), 150–1.

[168] See further 6.5 below, esp. text to nn. 214–23; for the contrasting Platonic–Aristotelian pattern, see 3.2 above, text to nn. 21–37.

[169] See Engberg-Pedersen (1986), 156–62, (1990*b*), 84–7. In other words, the Stoic pattern can be interpreted in objective-participant rather than subjective-individualist or objective-individualist terms (see further Gill 1996*b*: 364–70, and 6.4 below).

[170] Cf. Cic *Fin.* 3.20–1, and Sen. *Ep.* 120.11–12.

[171] See also text to nn. 104–25 above.

[172] Striker (1996), 229–30, referring to, for instance, Cic. *Fin.* 3.33 and D.L. 7.94.

value. In the practical sphere, logic functions as the means by which we give coherence and structure to our belief-system in the process of forming knowledge. At the same time, logic, like physics, and like the combination of the three branches of knowledge, itself serves as an expression of structure, order, and coherence, a point brought out with special force by Cicero (*Fin.* 3.72–4). Ideas of this type are implied in the—seemingly paradoxical—Stoic claims that dialectic not only enables virtue but *is* a virtue, and that 'the wise person is always a dialectician'.[173]

Taking all these points together, we might offer the following general picture of coming to know the good. This is a matter of applying our natural human intelligence and our capacity for recognition of fundamental concepts, and of doing so across the whole range of our practical and theoretical life.[174] In forming a picture of this process, we need to remember that analogy plays a key role in enabling us to form a conception of the good, by enabling us to identify similarities through comparison of different things, and, significantly, different *kinds* of things (LS 60 D(2), E(3)). The salient marks of goodness are order, structure, and rationality, marks which, we have seen, are also naturally linked with the ideas of wholeness and benefit.[175] Recognizing these features in one's own development towards virtue through increasingly well-grounded selection plays a crucial part of this process.[176] But so too does the recognition, by analogy, of comparable features in other people's actions and character, and also in social and political structures and organizations.[177] At the level of theory, it is a matter of forming a coherent understanding of logic, ethics, and physics, and of coming to see that the underlying structure, interconnections, and core concepts of these branches of philosophy also display the salient marks of goodness.[178] A further, and vital, dimension is that of correlating the marks of goodness in practical life and in theory.[179] Naturally, this is a hugely complex and demanding process and one that explains why 'wisdom' (including the full actualization of coming to know the good) is a seemingly unattainable ideal in Stoicism. But the immediate

[173] D.L. 7.46 (LS 31 B(1)), and 7.83 (LS 31 C(1)); see further LS 31 D, J, R–T, taken with Long (1996), ch. 8.

[174] On gaining knowledge of the good, see 171 above, text to nn. 16–18. This paragraph is based on Gill (2004*f*), 113–14.

[175] LS 60 G–I. The underlying thought seems to be that order, structure, and rationality are fundamental to what makes things whole and that those features necessarily benefit both the whole and its component parts, whereas their opposites necessarily harm them. See further text to nn. 93–103 above.

[176] Cic. *Fin.* 3.20–1 (LS 59 D(3–5)), discussed in 3.2 above, text to nn. 4–9.

[177] LS 60 E, 67, esp. K, L, P, M–S, taken as implying that conventional states manifest goodness (incompletely) in the degree to which they exhibit structure, order, and rationality.

[178] See e.g. Cic. *Fin.* 3.72–4.

[179] See further on this point, Gill (2004*f*), 119–24.

relevant point—if this account is correct—is that the idea of good is, essentially, trans-categorical, and is not derived primarily from any one branch of philosophy, such as physics, or from any one area of experience.

3.4 A CONTRASTING PATTERN: ANTIOCHUS AND ARIUS DIDYMUS

The distinctive character of Stoic thinking about development can be clarified by contrast with two other theories from the later Hellenistic period, those of Antiochus and Arius Didymus. Although both theories adopt the Stoic move of giving a central role to ethical development, and of using this as a way of presenting a certain conception of the good, they combine this with Platonic and Aristotelian ideas, including a largely Aristotelian account of happiness. A related feature is that the whole process of development is presented as 'self-realization', in the sense of fulfilling one's human nature. In the Stoic pattern, by contrast, only the first stage is explicitly presented in that way, as the realization of one's constitution, whereas the second stage culminates in the recognition of the absolute value of good rather than one's own nature.[180] (In neither case, should we suppose that 'self-realization' has the subjective or individualist connotations that it sometimes has in modern thought.)[181] However, the feature of these other Hellenistic theories that is of most interest here is their adoption of a core-centred and part-based view of human nature. Human beings are seen as combinations of distinct parts (body and psyche or rational and irrational parts of the psyche), and those parts are graded as more or less valuable, sometimes by using 'human' and 'divine' as normative categories. Antiochus also characterizes Stoic thinking, from a critical standpoint, in these terms, and seems not to recognize what is substantively different in Stoic conceptual language. These theories thus highlight, by contrast, the distinctive psychological and ethical holism of the Stoic pattern. The same is true, as we see later, of Plutarch and Galen, except that in those cases, the divergent approaches to psychology are explicitly recognized and constitute a major grounds of criticism.[182] A further point of interest is that

[180] For these two stages, see e.g. Cic. *Fin.* 3, 17, 20–1 (LS 59 D), and 1.4, 3.2–3 above. As illustrated in 3.3 above, the second stage can be interpreted in terms of self-realization or of modelling oneself on the cosmos, but the explicit subject is the recognition of the inherent and unique value of good. On this contrast between the Stoic and Antiochean (or Arian) patterns, see further White (1979), 147–59; Annas (1993*b*), 183–7, 282–3; Striker (1996), 269.

[181] On the subjective connotations of 'self' and related terms in modern thought, see 6.2 below, esp. text to nn. 8–21.

[182] See Ch. 4 below, esp. 4.3–4.

the discussions of Antiochus and Arius bring out the lines of connection between major controversies in Hellenistic ethics, notably about the nature of happiness, and competing (part-based or holistic) ways of understanding human nature and personality.

The nature of our evidence for these two thinkers, and also their status as thinkers, differs. Antiochus (*c.*130 – *c.*68 BC) developed a synthesis of Platonism, Aristotelianism, and Stoicism, based on the claim that in epistemology and ethics these theories shared certain fundamental (and true) principles. Although the evidence for Antiochus' philosophical position is rather complex, his status as an independent thinker and as a dissident member of the Academic (Platonic) school is well documented. His philosophy is, however, preserved only indirectly, especially by Cicero: the texts relevant here are the critique of Stoic ethics in Cicero *Fin.* 4 and the account of development in *Fin.* 5, both explicitly based on his approach.[183] Arius Didymus (*c.*70 – *c.*9 BC) was also a known historical figure, Augustus' court philosopher, and is usually regarded as a Stoic. He is generally identified with the 'Arius' whose *Epitome* of Peripatetic (Aristotelian), Platonic, and Stoic ethics is included in Stobaeus' collection of ancient philosophical ideas.[184] The text that concerns me here is his, heavily Stoicized, summary of Peripatetic ethics, which, following Annas, I see as reflecting a deliberate philosophical policy. Rather like Antiochus but independently, as far as we know, his aim seems to have been to combat scepticism by showing how these non-sceptical philosophies brought out the same essential truths from differing standpoints.[185]

Antiochus' central claim in ethics concerned the nature of happiness. This reflected the fact that the question whether or not virtue was sufficient for happiness had become a central one in Hellenistic ethics. Typically, the Stoic and Aristotelian positions on this were sharply contrasted. Whereas the Stoics maintained rigorously that virtue was sufficient for happiness, Aristotle and his followers, while regarding virtue as the key constituent of happiness, allowed that other factors had an effect in promoting or reducing happiness.[186] Antiochus, following a head of the Academic school in an earlier period, Polemo, argued that Platonic, Aristotelian, and Stoic thinking centred

[183] On Cic. *Fin.* 4–5, see Annas (1993*b*), 180–8, 277–9, 419–23. On Antiochus in general, see Glucker (1978); H. Tarrant (1985); Barnes (1989).

[184] See further Sedley (2003), 32; the identification of Arius Didymus with 'Arius' is challenged by Göransson (1995).

[185] On the summary of Aristotelian ethics, see Annas (1993*b*), 279–87, 317–20, 415–18. Arius' summary of Stoic ethics (in English translation) is available in Inwood and Gerson (1997), pp. 203–32; see also Long (1996), ch. 5. See further Fortenbaugh (1983); Hahm (1983).

[186] On this Hellenistic debate, see Irwin (1986); Annas (1993*b*), chs. 18–21. For Aristotle's position, see *NE* 1.7–11.

on the same fundamental thesis, namely that virtue was both necessary and sufficient for happiness. However, Antiochus also retained the idea, which was regularly associated with Aristotle in this period, that there were three kinds of good, those of the psyche, body, and external goods. He also rejected the Stoic move of presenting 'primary natural things' as 'matters of indifference' in comparison with virtue. He combined these seemingly different emphases by maintaining that, although virtue was sufficient for the happy life (*uita beata*), the happiest or completely happy life (*uita beatissima*) also required bodily and external goods such as friends and material possessions.[187]

This claim about happiness provides the context within which to place the question that is relevant here, that of Antiochus' conception of human nature and personality. In the critique of the Stoic position presented by Cicero, through the figure of Piso,[188] Antiochus characterizes the Stoic position on virtue as being, in effect, a claim about human nature. In denying that the primary natural things, which include health and other bodily advantages, are goods, the Stoics are said to present the human being as a psyche without a body. According to Antiochus, although Chrysippus claims only that the psyche (or 'mind' or 'reason') is the most important element in human beings, his ethical theory, in effect, treats the human being as *nothing but* the mind.[189] Referring to the Stoic idea that every animal is motivated by self-love and self-preservation, Antiochus argues that the Stoic view is really that humans should only love the best part of themselves—if we can describe mind as the *best* part when it is the *only* part that is valued.[190] He rejects the idea that the highest and most developed human function (which he associates with mind or reason) requires the devaluation of the more elementary functions and motives. Rather, he argues that the proper role of reason is to guide and enhance those other functions. He illustrates this point by imagining the art of viticulture embodied in the vine itself. Human beings are like a self-cultivating vine, in which reason 'crafts' impulse from within the body; and reason, like viticulture, should be seen as perfecting, rather than

[187] See Cic. *Fin.* 2.34, Books 4–5, esp. 4.2, 14–15, 19–23, 5.67–75, 77–95; also Cic. *Ac. Post.* 22–3. See further Annas (1993*b*), 419–23; also (on Polemo and Antiochus), Dillon (1977), 39–41, 56–8, 70–5 (on Polemo), Dillon (2003*a*), 159–66.

[188] The views expressed by 'Piso' in Cic. *Fin.* 4–5 are linked firmly with Antiochus in *Fin.* 5.6–8, 14, 75, 81, and the criticisms of the Stoics in Book 4 are wholly consistent with those views and are reasonably attributed to Antiochus.

[189] See Cic. *Fin.* 4.26–39, esp. 26–8; cf. Aug. *C.D.* 19.3, citing Varro, *de Philosophia* (see Dillon 1977: 71–2). Cicero's terminology for 'mind' varies between *animus* (4.26–8, 36), *mens* (28), *ratio* (35, 37–8). These seem to correspond, broadly, to *psuchē*, *nous*, and *logos*; but it is not clear that Cicero's usage is systematic.

[190] Cic. *Fin.* 4.35; for Stoic thinking on self-love, see Cic. *Fin.* 3.16–17, and 1.4 above, text to nn. 130–6.

superseding, the more elementary processes that form an integral part of human development.[191]

Antiochus' criticism of the Stoics on this point represents a striking mismatch between the theory criticized and the conceptual language used. Antiochus is, of course, right in saying that the Stoics believe that full ethical development brings with it a radical devaluation of the primary natural things in comparison with virtue (Cic. *Fin.* 3.20–2). Antiochus' distortion lies in the fact that he describes Stoicism as if it employed the kind of core-centred and part-based conceptual language sometimes found in Plato and Aristotle (1.2 above). The model ascribed to Stoicism is that in which the human personality consists of distinct parts (body and psyche or mind or reason), one of which is the essential or genuinely valuable part. By contrast, as stressed earlier, reason in Stoicism is precisely *not* a distinct part, but a function or capacity which, in adult humans, has the power to inform *all* the functions of the human being as a psychophysical unit. Full ethical development (that is, living the life according to nature and virtue) affects not just the rational functions in the conventional sense, such as thinking and knowing, but reshapes the whole personality of the person as a psychophysical organism. So the Stoics could have adopted Antiochus' image of the vine with an embodied reason to convey their view of how reason 'supervenes as the craftsman of impulse' in adult humans.[192]

Although the conceptual language of Antiochus' criticisms does not, I think, reflect that of Stoicism, it does reflect that of Antiochus' own theory. Antiochus sets out to recast salient features of Stoic thinking into an idiom derived from Plato and Aristotle, with a view to providing what he sees as a more convincing account of those features. Antiochus adopts the Stoic way of defining the goal of life, through a programme of ethical development from birth onwards; like them he sees this developmental programme as partly shared with other animals.[193] He also adopts the Stoic definition of the overall goal as 'the life according to nature';[194] and sets out to explain how virtue

[191] Cic. *Fin.* 4.38–9. There seems to be an allusion to the Stoic idea that, in adult humans, 'reason supervenes as the craftsman of impulse' (D.L. 7.86 = LS 57 A(5)). For the Stoic idea being criticized (that 'perfected reason', i.e. virtue, though a later development, replaces the impulse to pursue the primary natural things), see *Fin.* 3.23. For a rather different use of the vine-image, see *Fin.* 5.39–40.

[192] See n. 191 above. On reason as shaping the whole personality, see 3.2 above, text to nn. 72–7.

[193] See e.g. Cic. *Fin.* 4.16, 25, 28, 32, 34; 5.24–6, 38–40, 42–3; cf. *Fin.* 3.16, 62–3; also 1.4 above. This type of theory is sometimes called a 'cradle-argument'; see Cic. *Fin.* 5.55, and Brunschwig (1986), esp. 113–14.

[194] More precisely, he adopts a goal ('life according to nature') shared, though differently conceived, by Stoics and Academics such as Polemo and Carneades. See 4.14–15, 5.16–22, 24–6; also Annas (1993*b*), 182; Striker (1996), 262, 269–70.

comes to be valued for its own sake. However, the idiom in which this project is couched reflects two aspects of the Platonic–Aristotelian thinking illustrated earlier. It expresses the concept of the human being as a combination of psyche and body, seen as distinct entities, and to some extent the idea that there is a rational (or divine) core in the human personality. It also reflects the idea that the achievement of the goal consists in 'self-realization', notably in the (Aristotelian) form of the idea of realizing one's generically human nature.[195]

Central to Antiochus' theory—as also to Stoicism—is an ideal programme of development, in which humans go from elementary self-preservation to recognizing that virtue is inherently desirable and living accordingly. However, there are salient differences from the Stoic pattern and some of these derive from the difference between core-centred and holistic conceptions of human personality. Whereas, for the Stoics, reflexive ideas (such as self-love) tend to be associated only with the elementary stages of development, Antiochus presents the whole process as an expression of self-love and self-realization.[196] (The type of self that is realized is not that of the unique individual but that of one's generic nature as a human being.) In Stoic development, the idea of self-love is conceived as that of appropriation to one's constitution, that is, of one's nature as a unified living structure or psychophysical organism (1.4 above). In Antiochus' theory, human nature is presented as a combination of body and psyche, and the capacities of body and psyche are considered separately (*Fin.* 5.34–6). Those of the psyche are presented as more valuable than those of the body; and within psychic capacities most value is attached to those of 'reason, understanding, knowledge, and all the virtues' (*rationis et cognitionis et scientiae uirtutumque omnium*, 5.34). A further subdivision is drawn between 'natural' and 'voluntary' virtues, that is, between natural talents and ethical virtues such as practical wisdom and courage (5.36). The latter virtues are said to be superior to natural talents because they depend on the active expression of reason (*ratio*), which is the most 'divine' part of the human being; virtue is also defined as the 'perfection of reason' (*absolutio uirtutis*).[197] In this connection, the vine-image of 4.38–9 is re-used to make the rather different point that, if a vine could be equipped, like a

[195] See Arist. *NE* 1.7, esp. 1097^{b}22–1098^{a}18. In a broader sense, this way of conceiving the goal of life (as the realization of one's psychic or generic nature) goes back to Diotima's speech in Pl. *Smp.*, esp. 206c–209e or Pl. *R* 443c–444e, 588c–591e (happiness defined as the fulfilment of the nature of the human psyche).

[196] On Stoic thinking about self-love, see n. 190 above. On self-love as fundamental to each natural kind throughout its life, see *Fin.* 4.32 ('self-loving', *diligens sui*), also 5.24 ('every animal loves itself', *omne animal se ipsum diligit*), an idea explored systematically in 5.25–33.

[197] *Fin.* 5.38; note esp. 'reason... than which nothing is more divine in a human being'. See also 5.43, on following reason 'as if a divine guide' (*quasi deum ducem*).

human being, with a mind and reason, it too would value these as the highest expression of its—now extended—nature (5.40–1).

On the face of it, this programme resembles the Stoic two-stage pattern of human ethical development. But there are substantive differences. One is that the whole programme, and not simply its initial stage, is conceived as the expression of self-love; the emergence of reason, which marks a new stage in Stoic theory, is simply the continuation of this process. Thus, for Antiochus, development is, essentially, a one-stage programme.[198] Another is that Antiochus conceives reason in terms of the core-centred and part-based thinking found in Plato and Aristotle: reason is the most valuable ('divine') 'part', and not (as in Stoicism) a capacity which can in principle reshape every aspect of human psychophysical personality. Several other differences go along with these, some bearing on the early stages of development. In Stoicism, self-awareness is ascribed to human beings (and other animals) from birth; the relevant kind of self-awareness is an instinctive sense of what preserves one's psychophysical constitution. Antiochus, apparently criticizing this Stoic view, maintains that the acquisition of self-knowledge is a gradual one, and that it is only present completely when humans achieve the perfection of reason (5.41–3). Stoics coming after Antiochus (Hierocles and Seneca) attempt to meet this objection by analysing more precisely the nature of elementary self-awareness—namely as self-perception—or by arguing that appropriation to one's constitution is a feature of each phase of development, even though the relevant type of constitution (rational or non-rational) may vary.[199]

Antiochus does allow that human children have the 'seeds' (*semina*) and 'sparks' (*scintillas*) of the virtues from birth.[200] At first sight, this resembles the Stoic idea that 'all human beings have the starting-points (*aphormas*) of virtue by nature'.[201] But, in fact, the two ideas reflect a different way of thinking about development. For Antiochus, the point is that children have in an inchoate form the rationality whose perfection is virtue. The idea thus fits into his essentially single-stage picture of ethical development. For the Stoics, by contrast, children are pre-rational; and so is their self-awareness and

[198] This is linked with Antiochus' rejection of the Stoic claim that virtue has a fundamentally different type of value from that of the primary natural things taken as the goal of the first phase (that of self-love); see text to n. 187 above. A further difference is that the social aspect of development, treated as separate in Stoicism, is presented as an integral part of a single process. See *Fin.* 5.65–70, and contrast *Fin.* 3.62–8; also Annas (1993*b*), 275–9.

[199] See 3.2 above, text to nn. 11–18, 56–62; also Inwood (1984), 168–77, and 1.4 above, text to nn. 139–42, 162–7.

[200] Cic. *Fin.* 5.43, also 59–60. The image of 'sparks and seeds' also appears at 5.18 (on which see Annas (1993*b*), 183, n. 12).The image of seeds occurs in analogous contexts in Aristotle (*HA* 588^a33, *NE* 1179^b23–6), Epicurus (LS 20 C(1)), and Stob. 2.116.22, though they are linked with different conceptions of development.

[201] Stob. 2.65.8 (LS 61 L), my trans.

self-perception. Human children have 'the starting-points of virtue' in the sense that they can begin to form preconceptions, including those of the good. But these preconceptions cannot make sense, and thus help to provide the basis for virtue, until they are fitted into the structure of concepts and reasoning that begins with the emergence of adult rationality.[202]

A more complex respect in which Antiochus differs from Stoicism concerns the subsequent development of rationality and virtue. Antiochus presents two kinds of argument for the claim that the development of virtue is a natural one; the difference between these arguments is marked by a break at 5.46. Before 5.46, the main theme is that virtue develops in human beings through the recognition, whether nascent or explicit, that virtue represents the 'perfection' of our nature as rational creatures (5.38, 43). After 5.46, the stress falls, rather, on the idea that we can come to recognize virtue as desirable for its own sake, just as we recognize bodily and external goods as desirable in themselves.[203] There is a potential tension between these two ideas. One way of resolving this tension is offered by Nicholas White: 'being thus attracted to and motivated by justice for its own sake is itself a part of one's nature, and it is for this reason that being thus motivated by justice is claimed to be a part of our good'.[204] On this interpretation, development can be understood both as self-realization (of one's human, and specifically rational, nature) and as a process which culminates in recognizing virtue as desirable in itself.

On this interpretation, a point on which Antiochus' theory and Stoicism come very close—in seeing development as leading to the recognition of the inherent desirability of virtue—is still differentiated by the overall self-realizationist character of Antiochus' approach.[205] A related, and more obvious, point of difference is this. Although Antiochus presents virtue as both necessary and sufficient for happiness, he acknowledges that loss of other kinds of good diminishes *complete* happiness.[206] Similarly, he acknowledges that conflict can arise between the desire to act virtuously and the desire to pursue another kind of good, for instance, to save one's life. He also acknowledges that even the ideal wise person will be affected by the fear of death, as a

[202] See 140–1 above. These two stages within childhood development (forming preconceptions, starting to put them into a system) may help to explain why different ages (7 and 14) are given in Stoic sources for the beginnings of adult rationality; see LS 39 E(4) and D.L. 7.55.

[203] See 5.58–61, esp. 61: *honesta* (right acts) are desirable by their own nature and for their own sake and not only because of our self-love. The idea of virtue as desirable for its own sake is fundamental to Stoicism (*Fin.* 3.21); it figures also in earlier Greek philosophy, e.g. Pl. *R.* 358b–d; Arist. *NE* 1105^{a}32.

[204] White (1979), 152, referring to the emphasis on the naturalness of virtue in *Fin.* 5.58–60, 65–6 (after the significant break at 5.46). See also Annas (1993*b*), 184.

[205] For a comparable feature in Arius' theory, see text to nn. 220–2 below.

[206] See refs. in n. 187 above.

consequence of our natural desire for self-preservation.[207] These are all respects in which Antiochus' conception of ethical development differs from the Stoic one, in which ideal wisdom brings with it a complete reshaping of motives and emotions that eliminates this kind of conflict and emotional response. So Antiochus' theory, despite its general resemblance to Stoic thinking, differs both in its conceptual language and in the picture of human personality or selfhood conveyed through such language.

Although the precise relationship between Antiochus and Arius Didymus is unclear, many of the same points can be made about Arius' outline of Peripatetic ethics.[208] Here too we find the goal of life (or happiness) presented as the outcome of a programme of ethical development (conceived as 'appropriation', *oikeiōsis*).[209] As in Antiochus, this Stoic pattern is located in a framework that is fundamentally Aristotelian. Arius too conceives the development of virtue as the realization of our human nature and analyses human nature as a combination of more or less valuable 'parts'. In his account also, the idea of virtue as self-realization is combined with that of virtue as 'choiceworthy for its own sake'. As in Antiochus' theory, the personal and social sides of ethical development are seen as aspects of a single, essentially one-stage programme. Despite the relative shortness of the relevant discussion (eight pages of Greek text), there is more room for debate in Arius' case about the coherence and authorship of the theory. But I share Annas's view that the text can be seen as a considered response, of an Aristotelian type, to the Stoic theory of development.[210] Taken together, the theories of Antiochus and Arius show how Platonic–Aristotelian responses to the Stoic theory in this period are associated with a certain version of core-centred (and part-based) thinking about selfhood.

207 See *Fin.* 5.28–32 (esp. 32). Thus, although Antiochus apparently said that 'the wise person is never moved by desire nor excited by pleasure' (Cic. *Ac. Pr.* 135), and to this extent adopted the norm of *apatheia* ('absence of emotion'), he seems to have interpreted this in a sense that brought it close to the rival ideal of *metriopatheia* ('moderation of emotion'). See Dillon (1977), 77–8; and on these competing ideals, Dillon (1983), and 4.3 below.

208 For Greek text, see Stobaeus 2.116–52, of which 116–24 present the theory of development; for English translation of 2.116–24, see Görgemanns (1983), 168–73. For analysis, see Görgemanns (1983), 173–81; Inwood (1983), 190–201; Annas (1993*b*), 279–87, 415–18.

209 The use of the idea of *oikeiōsis* by thinkers working in an Aristotelian tradition such as Arius and Antiochus gave rise to the suggestion that this idea was derived from an Aristotelian source (probably Theophrastus) and only then adopted by the Stoics. But it is now generally accepted that the idea of *oikeiōsis* originated in Stoicism and was subsequently adopted in modified form by later Aristotelian thinkers. See Görgemanns (1983), 166–8; Annas (1993*b*), 280.

210 Görgemanns and Inwood (n. 208 above) see more disunity in argument and (perhaps) authorship. For the idea that the theory is specifically inspired by Aristotle's claims (*NE* 9.4, 8) about the compatibility of self-love and love of others, see Annas (1993*b*), 285–7.

Arius' account begins by outlining a broadly Aristotelian picture of human nature and ethical development. A bipartite model of the psyche, consisting of rational and irrational parts, is linked with a view of ethical development as depending on a combination of nature, habit, and reason.[211] This picture is very similar to that of Plutarch's *On Ethical Virtue*, though in Plutarch we find explicit opposition to the Stoic pattern, rather than assimilation of its categories.[212] Human nature is located as intermediate between divine and animal nature, linked to the first by the rational part and to the second by the irrational (Stob. 2.118.6–11). The emergence of virtue is associated firmly with self-realization (that is, realization of our human nature, conceived in part-based terms): 'the human being strives to exist, and is naturally appropriated to himself' (2.118.12–13). As in the Stoic theory of *oikeiōsis*, the initial impulses are directed towards 'the things according to nature' (though here these include pleasure, 2.118.15–16). Those impulses are given a self-realizationist twist by presenting them as responses to our parts and their functions, all of which are 'dear' (*philon*) to us (2.118.20–119.2). Virtue is presented, in the first instance, as emerging in the form of 'firm knowledge' that enables us to select the things according to nature and to reject their opposites. The terminology here is strongly Stoic, and so too is the idea that virtue emerges out of, and is appropriately expressed in, selection among primary natural things. The notable omission here, as in Antiochus' theory of development, is the characteristically sharp Stoic break from selecting between primary natural things to choosing virtue for its own sake.[213]

However, the idea that virtue is worth choosing for its own sake does figure prominently in the account. There are also indications that the recognition of the inherent value of virtue represents a distinct stage in ethical development. But this stage is still understood, as by Antiochus, as a linear continuation of our response to other kinds of goods, and not as marking a radical change in conceptions of value. This further stage is also located in a self-realizationist framework. So Arius' view, like Antiochus', can reasonably be interpreted as being that it is a function of our human nature that we can come to recognize the inherent desirability of virtue, though not in a way that involves the Stoic devaluation of other goods.

[211] The rational parts are further subdivided into scientific (*epistēmonikon*) and deliberative (*bouleutikon*); the irrational into appetititive (*epithumētikon*) and spirited (*thumikon*); the irrational part is also called (in Stoic terminology) 'impulsive' (*hormētikon*). See Stob. 2.117.11–18. Cf. Arist. *NE* 1.13, 2.1, 6.1; also (on the spirited part), Pl. *R.* 439e–441c; see further Annas (1993*b*), 281.

[212] See 4.3 below, which also discusses the relationship between the bipartite or tripartite psychology and the idea that development involves three distinct factors (inborn nature, habit, and reason).

[213] Stob. 2.119.4–19; contrast Cic. *Fin.* 3.20–2, discussed in 3.2–3 above.

The idea of something being 'choiceworthy for its own sake' is introduced first in connection with social relations. This is initially surprising, and the relevant section has been seen as an interpolation; but the linkage with the self-realizationist framework outlined earlier is indicated within the section and explicated subsequently.[214] Friendship (*philia*) and friendly acts towards family and friends are presented as responses to what is 'choiceworthy for its own sake' (*di' hauth' haireton*). Such friendship, which may be extended to human beings as such, derives 'from nature' since 'the human being is an associative and communal animal'.[215] What is 'choiceworthy for its own sake', the other people or the friendly responses to them? Both are, as is indicated within this section.[216] The continuation of the account brings out the analytic framework (2.122.7–10). Friends count as external goods which are 'choiceworthy for their own sake'; and still more so are bodily and psychic goods. So the virtues of the psyche, including social virtues, are more choiceworthy for their own sake than the people who are the recipients of (virtuous) friendship. However, it is made clear subsequently that this valuation does not mean that virtue is 'selfish' or 'self-loving' (*philautos*), but 'associative and political', in that it includes a social dimension. Also, social virtues are explicitly included in the 'whole divine chorus of virtues' that constitutes the key constituent of happiness.[217]

A similar set of valuations and line of argument is also found in Antiochus' theory.[218] In both theories this point fits into a similar self-realizationist and core-centred pattern. It is argued that, if the human being is 'choiceworthy for his own sake', so too must be his parts (body and psyche), their activities and their excellences (bodily beauty or health and psychic virtue). Arius then

214 The section is 2.119.22–122.7. This is preceded by the comment that 'the whole outline [of the ethical system] of this school is developed from this starting-point' (trans. Görgemanns 1983: 169). This can be interpreted as meaning that the (self-realizationist) framework outlined in 2.116.21–119.19 serves as a basis for what follows. For a different view, underlining the incoherence of the text, see Görgemanns (1983), 175–6; Inwood (1983), 191–2.

215 2.120.14 (*philallēlon... kai koinōnikon zōon*); cf. Aristotle's famous claim that the human being is a naturally political animal (*NE* 1097^{b}7–8). Arius uses in this connection terms (*oikeious, oikeiotētas*, 'relatives', 'connections') which are cognate with *oikeiōsis* (120.11, 13). But the underlying idea here seems to be that we are *naturally* adapted to recognize the *inherently choiceworthy* character of friendship (cf. 121.16–18); contrast the key role given to *oikeiōsis* in 2.118.11–14, 123.21–7.

216 Other people: 2.120.9, 121.25; the friendly response: 120.16–18, 121.16–17; 121.24–5; either (or both): 121.2–3. The linkage is explicit in 121.25: 'if the friend is choiceworthy for his own sake, so is friendship'.

217 2.125.21–2 and 127.3–9 (also 126.18–20).

218 See esp. Cic. *Fin.* 5.67–9: psychic virtues are more valuable (more integral to the highest good, i.e. happiness) than the external goods including friendships. However, those virtues are properly expressed in (among other ways) maintaining the friendships that constitute these external goods.

proceeds to define a set of analogies between aspects of the three types of good, while also maintaining a hierarchy of value (psychic, bodily, external).[219] This ordering of types of good is mostly asserted without much argument, perhaps because it is a well-marked feature of the Aristotelian tradition. However, one feature of ethical development is cited in support of this ordering.

> Virtue makes its entrance, as we have demonstrated, from bodily and external goods, but it turns towards itself and contemplates the fact that it is much more in accordance with nature than the bodily virtues, and is appropriated to itself as to something choiceworthy for itself, and is even more appropriated to itself than to the bodily virtues. So the psychic virtues are far more valuable.[220]

The backward reference ('as we have demonstrated') is to the idea noted earlier, that virtue arises out of the need for knowledge to guide selection between (in Stoic terms) primary natural things, understood here as bodily and external goods. This passage, unlike the previous one, identifies psychic virtue as an object of motivation in its own right ('choiceworthy for itself'). The natural capacity of human beings to develop in this way is signalled by the use of the verb cognate with *oikeiōsis*, used earlier in connection with appropriation to bodily and external things.[221] The presentation of 'virtue' (rather than the developing person) as 'appropriated' to itself is rather curious. It may indicate that this stage presupposes a degree of rational self-awareness of one's own virtue ('Virtue . . . turns towards itself and contemplates . . .') However, the main point is, probably, to underline the naturalness of the process involved. The achievement of (psychic) virtue carries with it a natural recognition of its own inherent desirability, as a standard part of the 'appropriation' of our own human nature. The contrast between attraction to bodily and external goods and to virtue, together with the implied reference to developing rationality, recalls the Stoic pattern. But the contrast here is less sharp; the appropriation to psychic rather than bodily and external goods is only a matter of degree. The overall idea is, rather, as in Antiochus, that our human nature is realized in recognizing the inherent attraction of virtue, even though we are not attracted to virtue *because* it constitutes a form of self-realization.[222]

[219] 2.122.11–13; for the argument as a whole, see 122.11–125.13. For comparable features in Antiochus' theory (except for the analogies between different types of good), see Cic. *Fin.* 5.34–8, 46–8.

[220] 2.123.21–7, trans. Annas (1993*b*), 284, modified.

[221] See 2.118.11–14 (also text to n. 213 above).

[222] See Cic. *Fin.* 5.58–61, esp. 61 (right acts intrinsically desirable and not just because of self-love); also text to nn. 202–4 above.

The contrast with the Stoic position is underlined in the definition of happiness which closes this account of development. Although the core idea is that of 'activity in accordance with virtue', this is coupled with the qualification '[in enjoyment of] bodily and external goods', which are seen as making an independent contribution to happiness.[223] The conclusion also indicates that the emotional ideal—as one would expect from the opening psychological model—is that of rational control of emotions and not the complete reshaping of emotions and character which is the Stoic ideal.[224] These points specify (in an Aristotelian, non-Stoic way) the conception of human nature that serves as the basis for this self-realizationist ethic.

3.5 STOIC–EPICUREAN DEVELOPMENT: DISTINCTIVE FEATURES

I now return to Stoic and Epicurean thought about development. My aim is to summarize a set of shared, or converging, distinctive features, and to consider how these contribute to the overall conception of human personality that I have described as 'the structured self'. Some of these features have been considered earlier in this study, in connection with one or other of the two theories; my focus here is on defining areas of common ground and salient differences from other approaches. These features include the fact that both theories maintain what Bobzien calls the 'whole-person' model of causation, despite holding radically different views about determinism. A further feature is the 'rich naturalism' which derives from their shared belief that wisdom, in the full sense, involves a combination, and perhaps synthesis, of ethics, physics, and logic. This belief forms a further strand in their holistic philosophical outlook and also has a bearing on their understanding of what 'whole-person' causation involves. Their thinking about rich naturalism contributes, in turn, to the kind of objectivism we find in these theories, and, in particular, to the sense in which they hold an objectivist conception of selfhood or personality, a question pursued further in Chapter 6, with special reference to Stoicism.

[223] 2.126.17–22. See further Annas (1993*b*), 285, 414–18. There is a partial contrast with Antiochus, for whom virtue is sufficient for the happy life (though not the completely happy one); see text to n. 187 above.

[224] See 2.127.20–1: (avoiding) 'overstep[ping] proper measures in their impulses', cf. 124.4–5: 'temperance... rids us of the excess of emotions' (trans. Görgemanns 1983, modified). The ideal is *metriopatheia* not *apatheia* ('moderation of emotion', not 'absence of emotion'); see n. 207 above.

I begin, however, by summarizing an aspect of their thinking which has already figured, at various points, in this study. This is the combination, in both theories, of a holistic and naturalistic conception of human personality with the Socratic ethical claim that all human beings are constitutively capable of achieving full happiness through rational reflection and virtue. What I want to accentuate here are certain striking similarities between the thinking of the two schools on this subject, and also the coherence of this line of thought in spite of some apparent tensions. Both theories maintain this claim despite also holding that human development is influenced by inborn or environmental, body-based characteristics and—often negatively—by beliefs transmitted through upbringing and social discourse. What renders their thinking on this subject coherent are two further ideas, which have been partly underlined already. One is their belief that human beings are constitutively equipped to form a true understanding of certain fundamental notions, such as 'good' or 'god', which bear directly on shaping our lives towards achieving happiness. The other is the unified or holistic psychological model, according to which changes and belief and the development of understanding affect motivation, character, and objectives in a way that is not disrupted by non-rational parts of the personality.

I take first their thinking on inborn temperamental characteristics. I noted earlier a well-known passage in Lucretius, which presents human beings, like animal species, as differentiated by innate (atomically based) inclinations, which reflect the predominance of heat or cold in their make-up. Hence, 'one man will . . . plunge hastily into bitter anger, another may be assailed too readily by fear, or the third type . . . be over-indulgent in tolerating certain things'.[225] What is less familiar is a similar idea in Stoicism. For instance, we hear from Galen that variations in the mixture (*krasis*) of air and fire that makes up psychic *pneuma* ('breath') produce differentiations in natural intelligence. Thus, 'Chrysippus has been made intelligent because of the well-tempered blend (*eukratos mixis*) of these two [elements], while the sons of Hippocrates . . . [have been made] swinish because of the boundless heat'.[226] There is also some evidence suggesting that emotional inclinations may also be influenced by innate make-up: 'there are variations in people's natures such that . . . some are lustful, others irascible, or cruel or arrogant'. These inclinations may contribute, at least, to the dispositional tendencies to

[225] Lucr. 3.311–13 (LS 14 D(4)), with omissions. Presumably, the variations reflect differing proportions of psychic atoms, e.g. fire-like or wind-like; see also 1.5 above, text to nn. 197–9, 208.

[226] Gal. *QAM*, ch. 4, 2.45.24–46.1 Marquardt *et al.* (1967), part of *SVF* 2.787, trans. Tieleman (2003), 150.

one or other emotion recognized by Stoicism.[227] A related Stoic belief, with close parallels in other strands of thought of the period, is that variations in natural intelligence are affected by the physical environment. Hence, 'at Athens the atmosphere is rarefied, resulting in the Athenians' reputedly sharp wits; while at Thebes it is heavy so that the Thebans are stout and tough' and, presumably, less mentally acute.[228] A further, more unusual, idea is that the attempt by midwives to counteract the transition from a warm, moist womb to cold, dry air by giving new-born babies a hot bath implants a life-long tendency to seek pleasure and to regard it as good.[229]

Epicureans and Stoics also have closely analogous ideas about the influence of social discourse, in the family and the larger community, in shaping beliefs about central notions bearing on our happiness. The focus, in both theories, tends to fall on the negative influence of this factor. For instance, the inscription of Diogenes of Oenoanda, an Epicurean of the second century AD, announces that: 'the great majority are all in common, as in a time of plague, sick with false opinions about things—and their numbers are growing ever bigger (for through copying each other one catches the sickness from another like sheep)'.[230] Typical subjects on which people infect each other with false beliefs in a way that disables them from acquiring peace of mind include the gods, death, and the nature of pleasure. Analogously, the Stoics identify as one of the two main factors that undermine ethical development 'the influence (or conversation, *katēchēsis*) of associates (or those around one, *tōn sunontōn*)'.[231] A typical subject on which error is socially propagated is the belief that 'preferable indifferents' such as health and wealth should be regarded as inherently good things. It is for this reason, in part, that the Stoics and Epicureans, along with other philosophers of the period, present their philosophy as providing a means of therapy or cure to counteract the errors promoted by conventional social discourse.[232] However, it is not the case, for

[227] Cic. *On Fate* (*Fat.*) 8. On dispositional tendencies to one or other passion or emotion, see e.g. Gal. *PHP* 4.5.21–2; Cic. *Tusc.* 4.24–9. On their status as—only relatively stable—dispositions, see 4.5 below, text to nn. 251–66. See also, on psychic health and illness as based on the proportion of air and fire in the psyche, Gal. *PHP* 5.3.7–10, cited by Tieleman (2003), 152.

[228] Cic. *Fat.* 7, trans. Sedley (1993), 314, slightly modified. For parallels, see e.g. the Hippocratic treatise *Airs, Waters, Places* 12, 24, Pl. *Ti.* 24c–d (see further Sedley 1993: 319 n. 20).

[229] Calcidius, commentary on the *Timaeus*, ch. 165 (*SVF* 3.229); see further Tieleman (2003), 160–2; also Long (1986). Contrast the Epicurean belief that the desire for pleasure is innate and evident from birth, Cic. *Fin.* 1.30 (LS 21 A(2)). See further on Stoic thinking on inborn and environmental factors, Bobzien (1998*a*), 290–4; Tieleman (2003), 146–66, 186–96.

[230] Fr. 2 Chilton, trans. Chilton (1971), 4.

[231] D.L. 7.89; in *PHP* 5.5.14, the influence is given as that of 'the many' or 'majority'.

[232] Epictetus' dialogues exemplify this method; see 6.5 below, text to nn. 219–27. On the idea of Hellenistic–Roman philosophy as therapy, see Nussbaum (1994), esp. chs. 4, 8, 9. On therapy

either school, that social discourse is wholly negative in its effect. For the Stoics, for instance, conventional ethical beliefs, practices, and roles, provide much of the framework from which we learn how to select 'appropriate things' (*kathēkonta*).[233] Also, as highlighted earlier, social engagement and observation can help to provide models of partial virtue from which we can construct an understanding of the good.[234] Even for the Epicureans, conventional beliefs about the gods, for instance, contain a core of recognition of their true nature, though one heavily overlaid with socially transmitted error.[235]

On the face of it, this nexus of Stoic and Epicurean beliefs might seem directly comparable with the Platonic–Aristotelian ideas reviewed earlier, 134–6 above, namely that ethical development depends on a combination of inborn nature, social habituation, and reason, and that the absence of any one factor can prevent this development. These beliefs might also seem to undermine the Stoic–Epicurean conviction that all human beings as such (as rational animals) are constitutively capable of achieving complete happiness. However, the consistency of their thinking on this point is secured by at least two other distinctive themes. One is the belief that all human beings have the natural capacity to form notions—in principle, true or correct ones—on important subjects, such as god or good. In both theories, these notions are sometimes presented in terms which might suggest that they are in some sense innate or inborn.[236] However, this runs counter to the fact that both theories present knowledge as empirically based. The notions involved ('preconceptions' or 'anticipations', *prolēpseis*) are ones which we are naturally disposed to form on the basis of perception, and which, once formed, help us to organize and structure our perceptions. What is 'inborn' or 'innate' is only the capacity to form such concepts, and not the concepts themselves. Within this shared line of thought, there are some variations of emphasis between the theories. For instance, it can be said that 'Epicurean preconceptions are naturally implanted from outside', through 'repeated sensory presentations',

as part of a system of practical ethics, see e.g. Stob. 2.39.20–41.25 (Philo of Larisa); also Brittain (2001), ch. 6; on genres of practical ethics; Gill (2003*d*), 40–4.

233 See LS 59, including the comments in LS i. 368 on 'roles' in Cicero and Epictetus; also Gill (1988).

234 Sen. *Ep.* 120 (excerpts in LS 60 E), taken with 3.3 above, text to nn. 161–171.

235 See LS 23 B, E. See further, on Stoic and Epicurean thinking on the degree of truth in conventional discourse, Scott (1995), 169–86. On the positive role of social discourse in ethical development in Epicureanism, see text to nn. 284–91 below.

236 See e.g. 'inborn' (*innata*), Cic. *N.D.* 1.44, 'implanted' (*insita*), Cic. *Fin.* 1.31 (Epicurean); 'formed in a connatural way' (*sumphuton*), Plu. *Mor.* 1070 C–D, 'acquired naturally' (*phusikōs*), D.L. 7.53 (LS 39 D(8)), cf. LS 39 E(3), 'implanted preconceptions' (*emphutōn prolēpseōn*), Plu. *Mor.* 1041E.

as distinct from socially transmitted beliefs. Stoic preconceptions, on the other hand, are 'rooted in human nature',[237] in the sense that we have an innate disposition to form such concepts.[238] Also, as recently argued, for Stoics, 'implanted' (*emphutos*) preconceptions, such as the concept of good, are ones that we develop through the natural developmental process of appropriation (*oikeiōsis*).[239]

For both theories, these notions are 'common' in the sense that all human beings are constitutively capable of forming them, regardless of other differences in natural capacities and social context. Although simply acquiring such notions does not, in itself, amount to knowledge, which involves a wider framework of understanding, this type of concept-formation plays a substantive role in the development of knowledge.[240] It does so, in particular, on subjects which are crucial for the achievement of happiness, as conceived in the two theories, such as the nature of god, pleasure, or good. For both schools, a key part of the role of philosophy—as exercised, for instance, through practical ethics—lies in helping people to recover or build on these preconceptions and to remove the obscuring layers of socially communicated errors. This conception of the role of philosophy is partly inspired by the project of Socratic dialectic, as the teachings of Epictetus especially bring out.[241] In another way, as Dominic Scott suggests, both Epicurean and Stoic ideas on preconceptions can be interpreted as naturalistic and empirical versions of the Platonic theme that knowledge of key concepts—or truths—is in some sense 'innate' and can be 'recollected' through philosophy.[242]

Stoic and Epicurean thinking on preconceptions thus constitutes a central part of the basis of the idea that all human beings are constitutively capable of achieving complete happiness, in spite of variations in natural intelligence or temperament and in familial and social context. A second relevant strand of thought, already examined separately in both theories, is the unified or holistic psychological model, which underlies Stoic thinking on the nature of rationality and the emotions and Epicurean ideas about 'natural' and 'empty' emotions and desires. Both theories see emotions and desires as belief-based in a way that enables development in understanding and the

[237] For this formulation of the contrast, see Asmis (1999), 279 (word-order rearranged), also 276–83 (on Epicurean thought).

[238] See also the contrast between the natural formation of preconceptions by empirical observation (Epicurean) and dispositional innatism, i.e. the innate disposition to form preconceptions (empirically) (Stoic), in Scott (1995), 190–210, esp. 190, 204.

[239] Jackson-McCabe (2004); see also 3.2 above, text to nn. 15–18.

[240] On 'common notions', see Scott (1995), 180–2; on preconceptions (or 'anticipations') in Stoic epistemology, see M. Frede (1999*c*), 318–21.

[241] Epict. 1.22.1–3, 9–10 (LS 40 S), 3.3.2–4 (LS 60 F); also Long (2002), 79–86.

[242] Scott (1995), 218–20 (also chs. 1–2 on Plato's theory).

removal of error to have a direct effect on motivation.[243] A further strand in their thinking is the idea that the possession of rationality brings with it the capacity to participate actively in the development of one's character and overall objectives, an idea already illustrated in Epicureanism, and brought out shortly in Stoicism.[244] It is this combination of ideas that renders the Stoic–Epicurean version of this 'Socratic' theme consistent with their overall holistic and naturalistic framework of thought.

The second shared feature of Stoic and Epicurean thought on development to be considered here is their use of what Bobzien calls the 'whole-person' model of agency, by contrast with the 'independent-decision-faculty' model. As I bring out below, the idea of 'whole-person' agency is related to, though not identical with, my use of the notion of psychological holism. This is one of a number of categories and contrasts which Bobzien has introduced with the aim of clarifying the ancient version of debate about free will and determinism. A further such contrast is between the idea that moral responsibility is grounded in the autonomy of the agent, on the one hand,[245] and the idea that it requires the ability to act in alternative ways in a given situation, on the other. A related distinction is between 'two-sided' and 'one-sided' versions of agency or 'potestation'. For the 'two-sided' version, to be an agent is to be capable of doing a specific action *or its opposite*. For the one-sided version, the agent is only capable (given her character, objectives, and so on) of performing the action she does perform in any given situation. But she is none the less responsible for the action if she acts as an autonomous, unconstrained agent.[246] The distinction between the 'whole-person' and 'independent-decision-faculty' models of agency is to be taken along with these other distinctions.

Bobzien uses these concepts to construct a picture of the ancient debate which is in some ways surprising, not least in the similarities she highlights between Epicurean and Stoic thought, but is still highly convincing.[247] Epicurean and Stoic views are normally sharply contrasted as representing the assertion of free will and indeterminism, on the one hand, and that of determinism on the other. Bobzien does not deny the validity of this broad

[243] See 2.2 above, text to nn. 9–13, 2.3, text to nn. 179–93, 3.2, text to nn. 64–77.

[244] See 1.5 above, text to nn. 229–71, and text to nn. 255–6 below.

[245] 'Autonomy' is taken by Bobzien to mean simply that 'it was the agent *and not something else* that was causally responsible for whether the action occurred'. For the contrast between agent autonomy and the capacity for alternative actions, see Bobzien (1998*b*), 135, cited, her italics, and (1998*a*), 278. 'Autonomy', as so understood, does not have the special (and sometimes subjectivist or individualist) sense (e.g. self-legislation, acting as a source of ethical value) that it has sometimes acquired in modern times: see further Gill (1996*b*), index s.v. 'autonomy'.

[246] Bobzien (1998*b*), 139–42, (1998*a*), 279–84.

[247] For a full appraisal of Bobzien (1998*a*), see Brennan (2001).

contrast; but she uses her distinctions to provide a more accurate analysis of the cross-currents of this debate. In her terms, both Epicurean and Stoic theories affirm agent autonomy (rather than the ability to perform an act and its opposite); that is they presuppose one-sided potestation. They also share the whole-person model of agency, rather than the independent-decision-faculty model.[248] Bobzien also argues that the first fully developed version of indeterminism which involves two-sided potestation is that of Alexander of Aphrodisias, the second-century AD Aristotelian commentator, whose theory emerges in part out of debate with Stoic determinism.[249] However, Alexander does not make the further move of introducing an independent-decision-faculty model of agency, to go with his theory of two-sided potestation.[250] This innovation emerges, along with conceptions of the 'will' as, in some sense, distinct from the personality as a whole, in accounts of 'free will' by later thinkers including Augustine, Kant, and Sartre.[251]

What, more precisely, do the Epicurean and Stoic accounts of agency have in common, on this view, and how does this bear on their picture of human development? In Epicureanism, in the account offered earlier (1.5 above), human beings, and to some extent tame animals, are conceived as capable of developing in an autonomous way that is not dictated by the constraints of their original constitution. The ability to develop in this way entitles us to be treated as the source of actions which come 'from us' (*par' hēmas*).[252] In Stoicism, adult human beings differ from other creatures (non-human animals and human children) because our actions involve 'assent' to 'rational impressions'. For this reason, actions are 'up to us' (*eph' hēmin*) or 'in our power' (*in nostra potestate*) in a way that is not true of other living creatures.[253] In both theories, being human—that is, being a relatively complex psychophysical unit—involves being capable of alternative courses of action.[254] But, on Bobzien's view, which I accept, what is crucial is not the

[248] See (on Stoicism), Bobzien (1998*a*), 276–90; (on Epicureanism), Bobzien (2000), 290–8.

[249] Bobzien (1998*b*), esp. 164–75; see also 143–6, discussing Aristotle's more limited (and not indeterminist) use of the idea of two-sided potestation. See also (1998*a*), 396–412.

[250] Bobzien (1998*b*), 171–2.

[251] See Dihle (1982), ch. 6, esp. 123–32, 143–4, on Augustine, and Gill (1996*b*), 445–6, on Kant and Sartre, stressing the difference from ancient theories in the conception of free will. By contrast, Bobzien (1998*b*), 170, sees Alexander's theory as similar to much contemporary thought (e.g. that of Dennett 1984) in *not* positing freedom of a 'will' in this sense.

[252] Bobzien (2000), 293–8, favours this, relatively neutral, translation of *par' hēmas* (a more common one is 'up to us') because it avoids the potentially 'two-sided' connotations of other translations.

[253] Cic. *Fat.* 39–43 (LS 62 C, esp. 4, 6, 9); again, the phrases used should not be taken to imply that the two-sided capacity is crucial.

[254] For this feature in Epicureanism, see LS 20 C(1), also 1.5 above, text to nn. 240–6; in Stoicism, adult humans can give or withhold assent (see Bobzien 1998*a*: 289).

(two-sided) capacity for alternative actions, but, rather, the ability to act in the complex but unified way—on the basis of beliefs, or with assent—that makes one an independent agent.

What picture of development is implied by the two theories and how does this involve a whole-person model? What it does *not* require is a process in which one part of us (will, reason, or mind) somehow stands apart from the rest of the personality and produces a new or revised character. Rather, what is envisaged is a process—typically, a gradual or piecemeal one—in which rational agency operates *within* this whole personality. Bobzien reconstructs this process, in each theory, in the following way, beginning with the Epicurean pattern:

A person may encounter beliefs, including value beliefs, which differ from those they have adopted and developed in line with their original constitution. These different beliefs are then transmitted to the original 'disposition of the soul' (the 'first natures') and made part of it, and as a result the overall disposition is—slightly—changed . . . At this point the disposition is no longer (fully) the result of internal and external necessity, but in part the result of conscious, rational, influencing.[255]

She reconstructs the Stoic pattern in a similar way:

Chrysippus would not claim that one's actions are determined by one's 'inborn' character traits. Rather, usually some actions will be in accordance with these traits, others will not. For what is decisive for how someone responds to the externally induced impressions is not this 'inborn' nature but the nature of the person's mind . . . The inborn character traits . . . are some of its many aspects, which together result in a specific pattern of tension of the mind's pneuma. Whether a person assents and acts depends on this state of tension of the entire individual nature of the person's mind at the time.[256]

The salient features of Bobzien's reconstructed pattern are that the personality functions as a whole and that causal agency, exercised in the formation of beliefs or in assent, reflects the character of this whole at the relevant time. Her accounts indicate how both theories can give a role to inborn or environmental influences on character, and to the influence of social discourse, and still see (adult) human beings as causal agents in their development, in a way that is coherent and that consistently reflects a 'whole-person' model of agency.

[255] Bobzien (2000), 326–7, based on passages in *On Nature* 25 (Arrighetti 1973: 34.24 and 34.22, Laursen 1998: 51–2, 22), taken with Lucr. 3.307–22, cited in Bobzien (2000), 323–6. On 'first natures', and on the developmental process involved, see 60–1 above.

[256] Bobzien (1998*a*), 297, drawing on evidence for Stoic thinking about developmental factors reviewed in 290–4 and analysed in the light of the model of agency of Cic. *Fat.* 39–43 (LS 62 C).

Can we identify ancient examples of the independent-decision-faculty model of agency with which to contrast the Stoic–Epicurean whole-person model? There are some possible cases, though not, I think, a fully developed alternative ancient theory of this type. For instance, Bobzien suggests that Cicero's criticisms in *On Fate* 9–11 (which are directed at Chrysippus' reference to inborn and environmental factors) imply assumptions of this sort. In drawing a contrast between our 'will' (*uoluntas*) or what is 'in our power' and our (given) nature (*natura*), a contrast that—he complains—Chrysippus fails to draw, Cicero seems to be using such an alternative model. His objections are not theoretically developed, and here as elsewhere, when he uses part-based psychological language, it is difficult to gauge how conscious he is of the conceptual implications of doing so.[257] But, on the face of it, this seems to be a case where a theory couched in the 'whole-person' mode is criticized in terms which are part-based and which perhaps imply the idea of an independent-decision-faculty.[258]

It might seem plausible that the kind of core-centred thinking in Plato and Aristotle reviewed earlier (1.2 above) should have given rise to the independent-decision-faculty model or, at least, to some embryonic version of this model. Brennan, reviewing Bobzien's book on Stoic determinism (1998*a*) makes this suggestion about the conception of mind in Plato's *Phaedo*. There, the real or essential person is the 'mind' (*nous*), as distinct from the emotions and body; and Brennan takes this as prefiguring 'the demand that a truly responsible agent be causally insulated even from their own character'.[259] Bobzien herself also highlights the contribution made by the later reception of Platos' ideas to two notable features of thought in the second century AD: a stress on the idea that what is 'up to us' is how we *choose* rather than how we *act* and an emerging focus on two-sided causal agency. Middle Platonists in this period interpret in the light of such ideas two aspects of the Myth of Er which closes Plato's *Republic*: the 'choice of life' made by the disembodied psyche and the assertion that 'responsibility lies with the chooser: god is not responsible'. However, as Bobzien also points out, this is very much a *re*interpretation of Plato. Plato's pre-natal choice of life is translated into the choice of actions within a life. In Plato's *Republic*, taken in its own terms, she suggests, the affirmation of the responsibility of the chooser seems designed to convey agent autonomy rather than the independent-decision-faculty model.[260]

257 See further 4.1 below, text to nn. 35–8.

258 Bobzien (1998*a*), 296–8. However, as she points out, Cicero's comments do not amount to invoking the idea of 'a causally undetermined deciding self' (298). There is a partial analogue in Antiochus' criticisms of the Stoic holistic psychological model from a part-based standpoint (168–9 above).

259 Brennan (2001), 283, referring to Pl. *Phd.* 66b–d; see also 1.2 above, text to nn. 6–7.

260 Bobzien (1998*b*), 156–64, esp. 161–2, referring to readings of Pl. *R.* 617e by Alcinous and Nemesius. See also Bobzien (1998*a*), 403–4.

Analogously, in modern times, Plato's *Republic* has sometimes been interpreted as prefiguring Kant's idea that, as rational creatures, we have 'transcendental' freedom of the will. Bernard Williams, for instance, characterizes as 'Platonic' the idea that 'I cannot be a fully free, rational, and responsible agent' unless 'the criticising self can be separated from everything that the person contingently is',[261] that is, in effect, a strong version of Bobzien's independent-decision-faculty model. However, as I have suggested elsewhere, Williams's view represents a retrojection of Kantian ideas on to Plato. The thinking of the *Republic*, at least, seems better understood in the light of the idea that ethical development depends on a combination of inborn nature, habituation, and dialectical education.[262] Thus, although some aspects of Platonic thought can be seen as containing the basis for an independent-decision-faculty model, we do not find in Plato a fully developed version of this alternative view of agency.[263]

As just indicated, there are close links between the contrast drawn in this study, between core-centred or part-based and holistic conceptions of self, and Bobzien's contrast between whole-person and independent-decision-faculty models of agency. The two categories are not identical; for instance, Bobzien's contrast is more narrowly focused on the question of causal agency. But the two contrasts are mutually informing; and my discussion of psychophysical and psychological holism in Stoicism and Epicureanism helps to explain why we find the whole-person model (rather than the alternative one) adopted in those theories. However, there is another factor that underlies the adoption of this model by these Hellenistic theories; this factor also brings out in a different way the holistic outlook that I see as characteristic of the theories. This is what I am calling 'rich naturalism', that is, the combination and, in some sense, synthesis of logic, ethics, and physics that is a further striking innovation of the theories. In general, it is plausible to suppose that this innovation was itself a key factor in making the free-will–determinism issue an explicit subject of theoretical debate in a way that it had not been in previous periods. Put very broadly, the issue arises out of the attempt to bring together, and reconcile, 'scientific' conceptions of human agency and personality and moral ones, as these notions were conceived at this time. As suggested later, this attempt, like other leading features of Stoic–Epicurean thought, was anticipated in a striking passage of Plato's *Timaeus*.[264] In

[261] Williams (1985), 110, taken with his more specific comments on Pl. *R.* in 28–9, 31. See also Nussbaum (1986), 138, 154–8, 160–3. For Kant's idea of 'transcendental' freedom, see Kant (1948), pp. 107–15 (Prussian Academy edition: iv. 446–55 of the *Groundwork*).

[262] Gill (1996*b*), 445–55; see also 3.2 above, text to nn. 21–4.

[263] See also text to nn. 324–38 below on a Platonic passage (in the *Timaeus*), which prefigures, rather, the whole-person model.

[264] See text to nn. 324–38 below.

Aristotle, by contrast, the various components of this debate—ethical, logical, causal—are treated in separate treatises and are not explicitly connected. (We can see the connections being made in second-century AD Middle Platonic philosophy, culminating in Alexander's version of an Aristotelian theory, designed to challenge the Stoic account.)[265] Stoicism and Epicureanism, on the other hand, set out specifically to provide an integrated philosophical curriculum and unified account of knowledge. One of the most important consequences of this integrated approach is the emergence of—what we call—the free-will–determinism debate. As I aim to bring out, this attempt to integrate the findings of logic, ethics, and physics—which is a further dimension of their holistic conceptual outlook—informs the kind of whole-person picture of human agency offered by each theory. This, in turn, bears on the sense in which each theory offers an objectivist view of the personality or self, a theme broached here and explored more fully in Chapter 6.

I begin with Epicureanism. Like Stoicism, this theory operates with a tripartite division of knowledge,[266] but not conceived in quite the same way. Rather than treating logic or dialectic as a separate branch of knowledge, Epicureans characterize this as 'canonic' and see it as a preliminary or subordinate part of physics. 'Canonic', literally, a 'measuring-stick' or standard (*kanōn*), is concerned with the methodology of enquiry designed to yield knowledge of truth. The central principle is that such enquiry should proceed, in a logical and systematic way, from what is 'evident', rather than 'non-evident'. The 'evident' is understood, typically, in empirical terms: the primary sources of empirical knowledge are taken to be perception, preconceptions, and feelings, though this does not rule out the use of other kinds of 'evident' principles, such as that 'nothing comes from nothing'.[267] In effect, then, Epicurus operates with a fusion of logic (canonic) and physics, a fusion which is displayed with particular clarity in Lucretius' highly systematic approach to the study of nature, which seems to be (mostly) based closely on the methodology of Epicurus' *On Nature*.[268] Epicurus may also have thought that ethics should have a similar methodological form and should consist in systematic inferences from what is 'evident' in this sphere, based on

[265] See further Bobzien (1998*b*), esp. 146–7, also (1998*a*), 396–412. The aspects combined include Aristotle's discussion of decision and what is 'up to us' in ethics (e.g. *NE* 3.5), his logical analysis of possibility and necessity (e.g. *On Interpretation* 9, 12–13), combined with his analysis of causes such as 'nature', 'chance', and 'purpose' in *Physics* and *Metaphysics*. For a modern synthesis of these Aristotelian elements, see Sorabji (1980).

[266] On the prevalence of this tripartite distinction in Hellenistic philosophy, see Algra *et al.* (1999), xiii–xvi.

[267] See further LS 17–18; Asmis (1999), 260–4.

[268] On this (generally) close dependence and on the forms of argument involved, see Sedley (1998*a*), chs. 3, 5, 7.

a combination of perceptions, feelings, and preconceptions, as well as on (allegedly) self-evident principles. Sedley has offered a reconstruction of the principles of Epicurean ethics along these lines, drawing primarily on Cicero's account in *On Ends* 1, seen as parallel in methodology, but not in content, to Epicurean physics.[269] If this is correct, then Epicurean logic is—or can be—fused with ethics as well as physics.[270] It is consistent with this view, that in the structure of Lucretius 3, ethical conclusions (above all, that 'death is nothing to us', 3. 830) are presented as following logically—according to Epicurean methodology—from the preceding analysis of the psyche–body relationship, an analysis which forms part of Epicurean 'physics'.[271]

The relation between ethics and physics is an important one for Epicurus, as in Stoicism, but is also open to various interpretations. A particularly revealing pair of comments comes in Epicurus' *Letter to Pythocles* (85–6:)

> First, we should not think that any other end is served by knowledge of celestial events... than freedom from disturbance and firm confidence, just as in the other areas of discourse... physics should not be studied by means of empty judgements and arbitrary fiat, but in the way that things evident require.[272]

On the one hand, Epicurus is quite explicit that physics is not studied as an end in its itself but that the objective, ultimately, is a practical one, to bring about peace of mind, especially by removing false ideas about death and the gods. But, on the other, it is also stressed that physics can only achieve this aim if it is conducted according to proper scientific methodology (beginning from 'things evident', *ta phainomena*, for instance) and thus, in principle, yielding knowledge of truth. This, relatively complex, position has given rise to various interpretative responses. Martha Nussbaum, for instance, has suggested that the practical (or 'therapeutic') objectives of Epicurean physics mean that its scientific methodology is—or could be—qualified or 'angled'.[273] However, the evidence can be read differently. Elizabeth Asmis suggests that Epicurus' epistemological theory offers a robust and coherent form of empiricism. Epicurean thinking on alternative or multiple explanations in physics

[269] Sedley (1998*b*). For a partly similar analysis of Cic. *Fin.* 1, see Striker (1996), ch. 10, especially 198.

[270] The logical or methodological structure is less clear in more informal or public writings, such as *Ep. Men.* or the collections of short sayings (e.g. *Key Doctrines*).

[271] Lucr. 3.94–416 offers thirty-three arguments for the inseparability of psyche and body, providing the basis for the conclusion that 'death is nothing to us' (830) and the ethical implications drawn in 831–1094. Warren (2004) provides a full analysis of the ethical implications, though this does not focus on the linkage between the two aspects (physical and ethical) of Lucretius' argument.

[272] D.L. 10.85, 86 (LS 18 C(1, 3). See also LS 25, especially B, D–E.

[273] Nussbaum (1994), ch. 4, esp. 124.

(which might seem to support Nussbaum's view) is compatible with this empiricist methodology. To put the point simply, the science needed to support ethics has to be *real science*, and not some watered-down version.[274]

Sedley raises a distinct but related issue about the relationship between ethics and physics in Epicureanism. His reading of the project of Epicurean ethics (1998*b*), just outlined, implies that the two areas are constructed on parallel principles but are independently grounded. Therefore, we should not suppose that Epicurean ethics is seen as reducible to, or conceptually dependent on, physics.[275] Warren has supported this position by examining evidence for Epicurean criticism of this type of reductionism in post-Democritean thought, especially Nausiphanes' apparent move to ground ethics on *phusiologia* (the study of nature).[276] Taking these various points together, a plausible overall view is that Epicurean thinking on the relationship between ethics and physics is broadly similar to that in Stoicism, as described earlier.[277] The two branches of knowledge are seen as conceptually independent and not reducible to, or subordinate to, each other.[278] But they are also mutually reinforcing; and complete knowledge requires them to be combined with each other and with logic (canonic) and, to some degree, synthesized. As in the case of Stoicism, determining the point at which combination passes into synthesis or fusion is difficult; but the issue of free-will–determinism provides a good context for trying to do so. It also offers material for determining how far these different branches of knowledge converge in presenting a single or unified picture of human personality.

As regards branches of knowledge, the general forms of Epicurean and Stoic theorizing about free-will–determinism seems to be broadly similar. In both theories, the relevant arguments seem to have been put forward in works falling within logic and physics (or physics informed by canonic, in Epicureanism). This topic does not seem to have formed a distinct section of ethical theory in either case.[279] On the other hand, it is wholly explicit for both schools that the relevant discussions have a bearing on an ethical question,

[274] Asmis (1999), including 288–90 on multiple explanations (see also Hankinson 1999: 505–7).

[275] (1998*b*), especially 134, n. 8.

[276] Warren (2002), esp. 169–81, 189–92, 198–200.

[277] See 3.3 above, text to nn. 148–79 developing the position outlined in Annas (1999), 111–12.

[278] The first sentence cited earlier (text to n. 272 above) might seem to imply the subordination of physics to the goals of ethics. But the point is, rather, I think, that *both areas* have the overall aim of securing human happiness (as analysed by ethical theory); note especially the final words of the sentence, 'just as in the other areas of discourse'.

[279] Hence, LS 62 ('Moral Responsibility' in Stoicism) is interposed by LS into a sequence which is otherwise closely based on the categories of Stoic ethical theory: see LS 56 A and LS i. 346. LS 20 ('Free Will' in Epicureanism) is mainly based on evidence taken from physics.

namely what justifies us in holding someone responsible for her actions or character and correspondingly liable to praise and blame (or exhortation, therapy, and advice).[280] Thus, overall, we can say that analysis of this topic falls *within* logic and physics (or physics-plus-canonic), but that it is designed to *support and reinforce* ethics. How far it is also conceived as modifying the character or content of ethical discourse or theory is something that needs to be considered with some care. This forms part of the larger question how far this type of theory involves not just a combination of branches of knowledge but also their synthesis or fusion.

In logic, or canonic, the main relevant theme in Epicurean thought is the denial of the principle of bivalence. This is the principle that all propositions are, determinately, *either* true *or* false, including propositions relating to future time. For Chrysippus, this followed from his belief in universal causal determinism. All events, past, present, and future, form a seamless web of causes; so statements about the future are, determinately, either true or false, regardless of whether their truth or falsity is known by anyone now. Epicurus, of course, was not aware of how Chrysippus would subsequently employ this principle. But Epicurus is presented by Cicero as denying bivalence as part of his general rejection of determinism (or Fate).[281] The other key relevant idea attributed to Epicurus falls within physics. This is the claim that the movement of atoms is not only the result of weight and impact. Atoms also sometimes 'swerve' (to a small or minimal extent) without prior cause. The idea of the swerve is presented as being introduced for two reasons. One is to explain the composition of the universe; otherwise, it might be supposed that atoms would have travelled for ever on perpendicular lines and never collided to form the universe as we know this. The other reason, more relevant here, is to explain free will and the initiation of action.[282] The other main relevant aspect of Epicurean theory, which also falls within physics, is the account of human development, coupled with arguments against determinism, in *On Nature* 25.

I begin by considering the implications of the passages in *On Nature* 25, whose picture of human development—as that of psychophysical wholes—has already been discussed here (56–66 above). First of all, what do these passages imply about the relationship between ethics and physics? In broad terms, the answer is quite clear: the passages present, from the standpoint of

[280] See e.g. LS 20 A–B, C, esp. (2), 62 D(1–3). On the significance of the final phrase in brackets, see text to nn. 336–9 below.

[281] See Cic. *Fat.* 21, 37 (LS 20 E(2), (H)). On bivalence in Stoic logic, see Bobzien (1998*a*), 61–74.

[282] See Cic. *Fat.* 22–3 (LS 20 E(2–3)); Lucr. 2.251–93 (LS 20 F); Diog. Oen. 32.1.14–3.14 (LS 20 G).

physics (and, presumably, as part of a methodologically structured argument)[283] an account of human development which justifies our treating people as responsible agents. That is, physics reinforces a concept that standardly forms part of everyday ethical discourse or practice and which is also presupposed in ethical theory. However, more specific points emerge from the two main passages regarding this relationship. Epicurus twice links the (alleged) fact of our responsibility with the social practice (which forms part of ethical life) of mutual criticism and correction.[284] This kind of linkage is rather common in Epicurean texts and is an index of the general claim that the Epicurean account of nature (physics) validates our standard ethical notions of responsibility, expressed in praise and blame.[285] But in these passages in *On Nature* 25 a further point emerges. The fact that we praise and blame each other in this way is taken to be a relevant piece of evidence on which this investigation, which forms part of physics, can draw. More precisely, it is taken to be relevant evidence that praise and blame are allocated 'as if the responsibility lay also in ourselves, and not just in our congenital make-up and in the accidental necessity of that which surrounds us' (LS 20 C(2)). This move might seem to betray logical circularity or to beg the question under debate. It seems unsatisfactory that an argument in physics designed to support the idea that we are right to treat people as ethically responsible should appeal to the fact that we praise and blame people as if they were ethically responsible. But this point needs to be taken with another, yet more striking one, if we are to take the full measure of Epicurus' approach here.

The passage just cited (LS 20 C(2)) forms the start of a notable, and much-discussed, feature of Epicurus' argument against determinism, that is, his 'self-refutation' strategy.[286] Epicurus maintains that anyone who argues for determinism in a way that involves denying the validity of the concept of responsibility (and the distinction between being responsible and being necessitated) 'refutes himself', that is, shows up his own self-contradiction. He does so partly

[283] Given the fragmentary state of the texts, the larger structure of argument and its methodology are not easy to define. For some comments, based on fragments from the later parts of Book 25, see Annas (1993*a*), 64–71; for an edition of all surviving fragments in Book 25, Laursen (1995), (1998).

[284] 'And with these we especially do battle, and rebuke them, hating them for a disposition which follows their disordered congenital nature' (LS 20 B(2)). 'And we can invoke... the fact that we rebuke, oppose and reform each other as if the responsibility lay in ourselves' (LS 20 C(3)).

[285] See Epicur. *Ep. Hdt.* 133–4 (LS 20 A(1)): 'while that which depends on us, with which culpability and its opposite are naturally associated'; Diog. Oen. 32.1.4–3.14 Chilton (LS 20 G), esp. 'if fate is believed in, that is the end of all censure and admonition, and even the wicked will not be open to blame'. See also e.g. Arist. *NE* 3.5, esp. 1113^{b}21–1114^{a}3.

[286] On this strategy, see e.g. Sedley (1983), 25–31; Bobzien (2000), 298–306; also n. 300 below.

because his argument (that we are not responsible agents) is in contradiction with his, and everyone else's, real-life practice in praising and blaming people as if they were responsible (20 C(4)). Also—and this is the most compelling point—his argument is inconsistent *with his action right now*, in engaging in argument at all. For to engage in argument, it is maintained, is to act on the assumption that you are responsible for the position you assert and to hold your interlocutor responsible for his position (20 C(3, 5, 6)). Arguments of this type are self-undermining unless they match the particicipant's actual behaviour, both in debate and in other contexts. They fail to show rationality of the type that Epicurean methodology regards as valid, that is, *epilogismos*, which seems to mean argument that is grounded on the facts of experience and which in turn feeds back into real-life practice and action.[287] A genuinely valid argument for determinism—if there could be one—would have to show that our preconceptions about responsibility and necessity are mistaken and so is the behaviour governed by these preconceptions.[288]

What bearing does Epicurus' self-refutation strategy have on the question of the relationship between ethics and physics? What seems to be implied by this point and the one noted earlier is that we conduct arguments in physics *as engaged ethical agents* and that we bring to bear, where relevant at least, the concepts, practices, and understanding developed in ethical experience. There is no requirement that, in an argument in physics, including one that has ethical implications, we should *set aside* our everyday ethical attitudes; on the contrary, consistency between the two areas is a requirement of properly conducted argument. Indeed, the point can be broadened further. As noted earlier, correct reasoning in physics depends on applying the principles of canonic, including argument correctly based on what is evident, for instance, preconceptions. This argument requires the participants to apply appropriately in physics what is evident in ethical practice, notably the preconceptions of responsibility and necessity. In other words, the validity of argument in physics depends, in this type of subject, on correct logical methodology in applying concepts that form part of normal ethical experience and which could also be analysed in ethical theory. To this extent, this argument depends on a combination, and perhaps fusion, of physics, ethics, *and logic* (or canonic) to make its point.

But what about the objection noted earlier that the argument seems to be circular or to beg its own conclusion? In assessing this objection, we need to

[287] On *epilogismos*, see Sedley (1983), 25–6; Schofield (1996), esp. 235–6. See also O'Keefe (2002), 165–6, underlining the linkage between the form of argument and the implied conception of humans as rational animals.

[288] LS 20 C(4, 8–12); on preconceptions, see text to nn. 236–42 above.

be clear about what we think the argument is designed to achieve. The objection will have force if we suppose that the argument aims to establish the validity of the ethical principle of responsibility *from scratch*, or, put differently, from inferences established purely *within physics*. In modern terms, we would be assuming that the argument would be trying to establish an ethical claim on purely scientific grounds.[289] But that is not a necessary, or even reasonable, expectation about this Epicurean argument or others. A much more reasonable expectation is that arguments in physics and in ethics, if both are conducted on sound methodological principles, should be mutually reinforcing or supporting. In this case, what the argument seems designed to provide is a (physics-based) picture of human development which is consistent with our preconceptions about responsibility and is equipped to meet objections which lack this consistency.[290] Thus, although, as we have seen, ethical theory and physics are normally conducted independently, this does not derive from strong assumptions about the radical distinction between (say) facts and values or between the world known to science and that experienced by ethical agents.[291] On the contrary, proper argument requires the merging of such forms of enquiry where this is appropriate, as well as the assumption that these forms of enquiry should be mutually supporting.

On this reading, then, Epicurus' account of human development in *On Nature* 25 constitutes a clear instance of what I am calling 'rich naturalism', that is, a non-reductive combination of ethics, physics, and logic. This account also implies further points regarding the unity of the person and the objectivist (more precisely, objectivist-participant) theoretical approach.[292] On the first point, the argument implies that there is and should be consistency between the conception of human personality presented in physics and that presupposed in ethical discourse and practice, and, presumably, also ethical theory. What the argument in physics aims to establish is the validity of the conception of the human being as a responsible agent; and this idea is also presupposed by normal ethical discourse. As the argument insists, especially in the self-refutation section, the person who engages in physical

289 In other words, if we suppose that the argument is intended as 'Archimedean', in the sense identified by Williams (1985), 28–9. On the problems raised by treating arguments in ancient philosophy (inappropriately) as 'Archimedean', see Gill (1996*b*), 358–60, 364–5, 428–9, 447–8.

290 Thus, Epicurus claims that the picture of development offered by his imagined necessitarian objector involves inconsistency with our preconceptions of responsibility and necessity: LS 20 C(2–12).

291 Famous modern distinctions of this kind include Hume's 'is–ought' distinction (*Treatise* 3.1.1, esp. para. 27, Norton and Norton 2001: 307); and Kant's distinction between the phenomenal and noumenal standpoints; see Kant (1948), pp. 111–19 (*Groundwork*, Prussian Academy edn., iv. 450–8).

292 On this terminology, see 6.2 below, also discussion below.

investigation and the person who engages in ethical discourse and practice are *the same person*, and this person is expected to apply the same preconceptions and modes of inference in each case.[293] So the argument presupposes another form of holism of outlook, not so much holism as regards the relationship between psyche and body but rather between the human being as conceived in ethics and in physics. As suggested shortly, a similar kind of holism is implied in Stoicism. In other ancient theories, for instance that of Aristotle, questions relating to moral responsibility are discussed separately (that is, in ethical works) from those relating to types of causation (which are treated as part of physics); and the aspiration to a unified view of the person, based on a convergence of ethics, physics, and logic, is much less evident. If there is a precursor to Epicureanism and Stoicism in this respect, it inheres, rather, in a striking passage from Plato's *Timaeus* discussed below.[294]

The same features just noted in *On Nature* 25 can also be used to clarify the sense in which this aspect of Epicurean theory displays objectivism and implies an objective-participant conception of personality. The significance attached to these terms is explained more fully in Chapter 6 (especially 6.2); but some relevant points can be made here. Both in Epicureanism and Stoicism, the objectivism derives, in part at least, from the 'rich naturalism' implied in their theory. The key underlying thought is not that ethical claims are grounded in facts established by physics and are thus shown to have an objective foundation of a type they would not otherwise have. It is, rather, that branches of knowledge which are independently grounded can also be used to reinforce each other by their findings. It is also that the combination—and, to some degree, fusion—of these independently grounded branches of enquiry provides the kind of coherent but inclusive knowledge that constitutes (objective) wisdom in the full sense.

The objective-*participant* character of the approach comes out clearly in features of the passages in *On Nature* highlighted earlier. Despite the fact that Epicurus presumes that human beings have the constitutional capacity to develop as responsible agents, the argument also assumes that these capacities are developed—in part at least—as a response to interactive discourse, that of praise and blame, encouragement and discouragement.[295] Although, in both Epicureanism and Stoicism, strong claims are made about our natural ability to form preconceptions on key ethical ideas, the theories still allocate a

[293] See text to nn. 286–8 above.

[294] See text to n. 265 above, and 324–34 below. Of course, Aristotle *can* be interpreted as aiming at this type of theoretical unity (see e.g. Irwin 1988); but the aspiration is much less explicit than in the Hellenistic theories.

[295] See esp. LS 20 B(1–2), C(1–3), 20 j. On the developmental process, see further text to nn. 284–5 above. On this feature of the argument, see also O'Keefe (2002), 180–1.

determinate role to social discourse in developing understanding, though not the same (habituative) function identified in the Platonic–Aristotelian pattern.[296] This role is indicated in Epicurus' references to interactive praise and blame, even though the main point of such references is to highlight the underlying assumptions of such discourse, rather than to define its role in development. A related point emerges from the self-refutation section of LS 20 C(3–12). This is not only that, as in Plato, for instance, the standard context for intellectual enquiry and for the attempt to achieve knowledge of objective truth is dialectical discussion between properly equipped and fully committed participants in dialectic.[297] It is also that—again as in Plato—participants in dialectic are presumed and expected to bring to bear their real-life character and attitudes in discussion and to display consistency between 'words and deeds'.[298] (In Plato's dialogues, a crucial part of the symbolic role of Socrates is the outstanding consistency between 'words and deeds' that he displays.)[299] In Epicurus' argument, such consistency is taken to prove or disprove the (objective) truth of the position maintained by the participant. In the self-refutation section, there is the further twist that dialectic itself is taken to provide a real-life context in which (real-life) beliefs and character can be identified, in a way that can be used to invalidate the argument—against responsibility—being mounted.[300] This is a further respect in which the discussion, to some extent, like that of Plato's *Alcibiades 1*, expresses an objective-participant conception of personality, in the linkage implied between proper forms of interactive and intellectual participation and the attainment of knowledge of objective truth.[301]

Some at least of these points, though not those relating to the objective-participant character of the approach, apply to the other main relevant theme in Epicurean physics, the idea of atomic 'swerve'. Attempts to define the proper role of the swerve in Epicurean thought face a number of acute difficulties, not least the fact that no discussion of this topic survives from Epicurus himself.[302] A further difficulty, underlined since antiquity, is that of

[296] See 3.2 above, text to nn. 21–37.

[297] See further, on this theme in Plato, Gill (1996*a*), 285–96, in the *Republic*, Gill (1996*b*), 279–83.

[298] For this theme, see e.g. Pl. *La.* 187e–189b. One aspect of this is Socrates' demand, 'say what you believe', on which see e.g. Vlastos (1991), 111–13 (challenged in Beversluis 2000: 37–58).

[299] See e.g. Pl. *Ap.* 29d–e, *Smp.* 218c–219e, *Phd.* 114d–e, 117c–118a.

[300] See LS 20 C(3–12), esp. (4, 6, 7). The analogous use of the self-refutation argument in Lucr. 4.469–521 (LS 16A), on which see Burnyeat (1978), does not carry the same 'objective-participant' connotations (though it is also objectivist in approach); but this does not mean that those connotations are not relevant in LS 20 C.

[301] On this point and Pl. *Alc.*, see 354–9 below.

[302] For the main ancient sources, see n. 282 above. On possible reasons why we have no surviving discussion of the swerve by Epicurus, see Purinton (1999), 294–5.

seeing how the idea of the swerve is compatible with the Epicurean assertion of human responsibility for actions.[303] This difficulty may seem especially acute for an interpretation such as Bobzien's, which stresses the importance of agent autonomy (and thus of consistency between character and action) rather than of indeterminism in the sense that agents can act in more than one possible way in a given situation. The existence of—random, uncaused—swerves at the atomic level, but also affecting human action, might seem easier to combine with the indeterminist interpretation of Epicurean theory than with Bobzien's (agent-centred) one.

Bobzien's response is to associate the swerve with the process by which a human being (or animal) forms her character, rather than supposing that a swerve is required for each voluntary action.[304] In the case of human beings at least, and perhaps tame animals, the swerve thus plays an analogous role in Epicurus' theory to that played in *On Nature* 25 by the idea that our development involves choosing between various possible courses of action and not automatically following our inborn nature.[305] However, as Bobzien argues, we do not need to assume that subsequent swerves precede every action; hence, humans are properly treated as responsible for the actions which—predictably—reflect their character or constitution, once developed.[306] Bobzien finds support for this view in the fact that, in the one surviving ancient description of the operation of the swerve, what is presented is a standard Epicurean account of animal action and movement. The animal operates as a psychophysical unit, in which the desire of the 'mind' (*animus* or *mens*) to move activates the body through the mediation of the 'spirit' (*anima*). The point on which Lucretius focuses is the contrast between voluntary motion of this kind and enforced behaviour, and it is in this connection that he refers to the swerve.[307] The role of the swerve, Bobzien argues, is to explain how animals, including humans, have volitions: this is because animals have relatively complex psychophysical constitutions.[308] On this view, the hypothesis of the swerve provides a—supplementary—explan-

[303] See e.g. Carneades' criticisms, reported in Cic. *Fat.* 23–5 (LS 20 E(4–7)); on those criticisms see Sharples (1991–3), esp. 179–82; Purinton (1999), 296–9. For a survey of modern interpretations designed to respond to this criticism, see Purinton (1999), 256–7.

[304] For this view, see also Furley (1967), 232.

[305] LS 20 B(1), C(1); see further 1.5 above, text to nn. 240–56. On the linkage between Epicurean thinking on development and on the swerve, see Bobzien (2000), 317–27.

[306] Bobzien (2000), 327–36.

[307] This contrast is taken by Bobzien to explain the slight pause before voluntary movement (Lucr. 2. 261–83, LS 20 F(2–3)), a pause sometimes explained by a preliminary atomic swerve. On the psychophysical model assumed, see 1.5 above, text to nn. 203–6. On animals (and not only humans) as agents in Epicureanism, see 1.5 above, text to nn. 247–56.

[308] Lucretius 2.251–93 (LS 20 F); Bobzien (2000), 307–20.

ation for the emergence of agent autonomy.[309] It thus also fulfils its other designated function of explaining why all events do not form part of an endless causal chain, which would (as Epicurus supposes) rule out the possibility of agent autonomy.[310]

Bobzien's interpretation of the role of the swerve, like those of other scholars, is conjectural and open to counterarguments. But, on any view, unless we conclude that the swerve is a conceptual failure, it has to be rendered consistent with agent responsibility, however this is understood.[311] Thus, Epicurus' thinking on the swerve also displays the themes outlined earlier. These are that ethics and physics are mutually reinforcing, that Epicurean objectivism rests, in part, on an assumed consistency between the findings of these branches of knowledge, and that the ethical agent and the object of scientific investigation are one and the same.

I deal with the Stoic theory of determinism more briefly, since some relevant points have already been made. As argued earlier (**162–6** above), I think that the relationship between the three branches of knowledge is better understood as reciprocal and mutually supporting, rather than as one in which ethics (or logic) is conceptually dependent on physics. As in Epicureanism, the main discussions fall within logic or dialectic and physics, rather than ethical theory, although the ethical implications of the enquiry are never lost sight of.[312] The logical side of the debate was intensively elaborated, particularly by Chrysippus. The central thesis, explored fully both in logic and physics, is that of universal causal determinism: all events are determined by a seamless web of interlinked causes and no event occurs randomly or without connection to the causal web.[313] In principle, if not in practice, the whole causal nexus is rationally predictable and is in this sense predetermined. Chrysippus' defence of human (adult) responsibility falls squarely within this picture. This is presented by Cicero as an awkward compromise between libertarian and necessity-based accounts of human nature.[314] However, the theory can be seen as fitting coherently within the Stoic theory of universal causal determinism. It is our Fate, as humans, to be neither (indeterminately) 'free' nor 'bound by necessity', but, rather, to respond to external

[309] It is supplementary to the explanation offered in Epicur. *On Nature* 25.

[310] For this function, see Lucr. 2.251–60; also Bobzien (2000), 308–9. The Stoics do not see determinism as incompatible with agency, as explained below.

[311] For other approaches, see Purinton (1999), 255–6. Purinton's own view revives the 'bottom-up' interpretation of Giusanni and Bailey, and assumes that each volition involves one or more swerves: for Purinton's reading of Lucr. 2. 251–93, see his (1999), 265–74.

[312] See n. 279 above.

[313] See further D. Frede (2003); Bobzien (1998*a*). This outline of Stoic determinism is based on Gill (2000*c*), reviewing Bobzien (1998*a*).

[314] Cic. *Fat.* 39 (LS 62 C(2)); see further Bobzien (1998*a*), 315–24.

stimuli as rational agents in line with our character as this has developed at any one time. Crucial for this analysis is the distinction between internal and external causes of action and the idea that adult humans must 'assent' to (rational) impressions as a prerequisite for action. In so far as human adults act only on the basis of assent and are in this sense the 'internal' cause of their actions, they are properly held responsible for those actions. Human action, understood as a rational response to external stimuli, also forms an intelligible part of the seamless causal web of Fate.[315]

It is a characteristic feature of the Stoic theory of determinism that discussion in each branch of knowledge, while independently argued, reinforces the relevant claims in other areas. For instance, Chrysippus' response, within logic, to the 'lazy' argument that there is no point in purposive action if everything is fated reinforces both his ethical and causal (physical) frameworks. His response depends on a distinction between simple and conjoined future statements (an example of the latter type is that *X* will happen if *Y* happens), combined with the idea of 'co-fatedness' of events.[316] The ethical implications of the causal framework are drawn out by Chrysippus himself, as reported by Aulus Gellius:

> 'Although it is true', he says, 'that all things are enforced and linked through fate by a certain necessary and primary rationale, nevertheless our minds' own degree of regulation by fate depends on their peculiar quality.' For if our minds' initial natural make-up is a healthy and beneficial one, all that external force exerted upon them as a result of fate slides over them fairly smoothly and without obstruction. But if they are coarse, ignorant, inept, and unsupported by education, then even if they are under little or no pressure from fated disadvantages, they still, through their own ineptitude and voluntary impulse, plunge themselves into continual wrongdoings . . . the very fact that it turns out this way is the product of the natural and necessary sequence of things called 'fate'. For it is in itself a virtually fated and sequential rule that bad minds should not be without wrongs.[317]

I assume that these comments are consistent with the view outlined earlier, according to which, although people have divergent inborn natures and are subject to different environmental and social influences, all human beings are constitutively capable of developing towards complete happiness through rational reflection and virtue. The central point here is that there is consistency between their developed character at any one time and the ethical quality of the actions they perform. This consistency reflects 'the natural and neces-

[315] Cic. *Fat.* 40–3 (LS 62 C(4–9)); Gellius 7.2.6, 11–13 (LS 62 D(4–6)). See further Bobzien (1998*a*), ch. 6, esp. 250–314; also, with a new, and persuasive, explanation of Cicero's distinction between 'complete and primary' and 'auxiliary and proximate causes' (*Fin.* 41), Bobzien (1999).

[316] See Bobzien (1998*a*), ch. 5.

[317] Gellius 7.2.6–10 (LS 62 D(1–3)), punctuation based on LS no. p. ii.

sary sequence of things called "fate" '.[318] This passage illustrates larger features of the theory, which parallel those already highlighted in Epicureanism. The analysis of human beings as agents within physics is in line with the conception of responsibility presupposed by ordinary ethical discourse and by theory. Relevant discussion both within logic and within physics assumes that the human beings there analysed are, in effect, *the same type of people* as are characterized in ethical discussion and theory. The objectivism of the theory depends, in part at least, on the way in which three areas of analysis reinforce each other and provide a mutually supporting and, in this sense, holistic framework of understanding and, in principle at least, knowledge.

I take it that these conclusions are relatively straightforward. What is more open to debate is whether we should see the intended outcome of this process simply as one in which the three branches of knowledge are combined or whether they are also in some sense synthesized or fused. The kind of fusion that might be involved here is not quite of the type considered earlier in Epicurus' *On Nature* 25, that is, in which real-life ethical assumptions are brought into debate about causal analysis within physics.[319] Rather, it is whether the effect of combining the three areas is, to some degree, to *modify and transform* ethical understanding. As noted earlier, in connection with debate about the significance of Cic. *Fin.* 3.20–1, it is sometimes claimed that the outcome of combining physics and ethics is to bring about this kind of transformation. In particular, it is maintained that it is *only* a recognition of the natural cosmos—or of the universe as a coherent nexus of fated events—as inherently ordered, structured, and in that sense 'good' that can bring about the crucial motivational shift required by the Stoic picture of ethical development. This can lead us not only to accept 'dispreferable' events but also to embrace them as part of the goodness (order, structure, coherence) of fate.[320] If scholars are right to claim the centrality of this theme, then the desired outcome of 'rich naturalism' in Stoicism is not only the mutual reinforcement of the three types of knowledge but also—in this respect at least—modification by fusion.

I think it is undeniable that the line of thought described forms *a* strand in Stoic thinking. It is expressed in some well-attested sources for Stoic theory as well as underlying some passages in Stoic practical ethics.[321] But I think it is

[318] See further on Gellius' evidence Bobzien (1998*a*), 293–301. Her reading does not stress the universal capacity for happiness, though I do not think she intends to deny this feature of the theory.

[319] See text to nn. 286–8 above.

[320] See text to n. 129 above.

[321] See e.g. Epict. 2.6.9 (LS 58 J), ascribed to Chrysippus. This theme is pervasive in Marcus Aurelius; see e.g. *Med.* 2.3, 3.16, 4.1; see further Rutherford (1989), 155–67; Annas (1993*b*), 175–6.

less prominent than is often claimed; also some passages taken to reflect this idea may be better interpreted as expressing a different but related one. This is, rather, the idea outlined earlier: that a proper understanding of the universal nexus of causes and of the logical relations governing possibility and necessity is wholly compatible with a picture of (adult) human beings as rational and responsible agents. Both in the passage of Gellius cited earlier and in a related passage from Cicero's *On Fate*,[322] the emphasis falls on the thought that agency confers responsibility rather than on the importance of 'fatalistic' resignation to the 'dispreferable' consequences of the cosmic order.[323] This suggests, in turn, that the dominant pattern in Stoic thought on determinism is the combination of the different branches of knowledge and their mutual reinforcement, rather than their fusion and mutual transformation—though the latter forms a further, if less prominent, strand.

I conclude this section by noting one earlier passage in Greek philosophy which, to some degree at least, prefigures Stoic–Epicurean thought in offering a unified (ethical-*cum*-physical) conception of the human being and in drawing out the implications of this unified account for the understanding of responsibility. The passage falls in Plato's *Timaeus* (86b–90d), a dialogue that, in a number of ways, anticipates, and may have helped to shape, the holistic outlook on humanity and the universe found in Stoic and Epicurean thought.[324] Plato's passage contains several arresting claims. One is that diseases of the psyche are the product of (largely congenital) defects of the body. Although the significance of the key sentence has been debated, I think the claim is the strong one that *all* psychic diseases, including what are normally regarded as moral defects such as sexual self-indulgence, are a product of the bodily constitution, sometimes coupled with a corrupting education.[325] This point is combined with the equally striking assertion that we should not hold such people responsible (*aitiateon*) or offer criticism (*oneidos*) of them. This is because 'no one does wrong willingly', and such defects occur 'against their will'. Rather than reacting with praise and blame, we should focus on therapy and the promotion of health.[326] This idea is also explored in a strongly

[322] Gellius 7.2.6–13 (LS 62 D), and Cic. *Fat.* 40–3 (LS 62 C(4–10)).

[323] For a similar view, see D. Frede (2003), 203–5; also Bobzien (1998*a*), 346–57, arguing that certain texts which advocate a related form of 'fatalistic' resignation are marginal to mainstream Stoic theory.

[324] See further 1.3 above, text to nn. 41–68, and 5.1 below. In Stoicism this influence is likely to have been direct and acknowledged. For Epicurus, followed by Lucretius, the providential world-view of the *Timaeus* was, rather, a target for criticism (Lucr. 5.156–234, taken with Sedley 1998*a*: 75–8), though it may, none the less, have exercised a more generalized influence on the substantial holism shared by Stoicism and Epicureanism (1.3 above, esp. 28–9).

[325] Pl. *Ti.* 86b1–2, taken with 86c–87b; also Gill (2000*b*), 59–65.

[326] Pl. *Ti.* 86d5–e3, 87b4–8.

physicalist way. First, it is emphasized that, since we constitute a 'combination' (*sunamphoteron*) of body and psyche, we should aim to create harmony and 'proportion' within both parts and in the relationship between them.[327] Also, the development of both bodily and psychic health and excellence are presented in physical terms, as the outcome of shaping oneself on the model of the ordered and structured cosmos. As regards the body, the recommendation is for a pattern of stable movement and exercise, avoiding the use of drugs which disrupt the body's natural processes.[328] Intellectual activity or philosophy, while presented as the realization of our divine aspect, is also characterized in physical terms, as the realization in us of the cyclic motions of the most divine element in the cosmos, the heavenly bodies.[329]

This arresting passage contains a number of themes which anticipate distinctive strands in Hellenistic or later ancient thought. The surprising claim that all psychic failings are to be seen as (largely) body-based defects or illnesses was taken up by Galen in a work centred on this theme.[330] Also, as Teun Tieleman has underlined, several motifs in this passage anticipate Stoic thinking about the sources of corruption, including the role allocated to inborn (body-based) defects and bad education. The passage also prefigures the pervasive Stoic presentation of moral vices as forms of psychic (and also psychophysical) illness or 'madness'.[331] The analysis of psychic and bodily health and excellence in terms of 'proportion', 'harmony', and 'structure' also strongly anticipates Stoic thinking.[332] The idea that ethical faults, as psychic illnesses, should be treated by therapeutic methods is a prevalent one in Hellenistic thought, including Stoic and Epicurean thought.[333] More broadly, these features of Plato's dialogue reflect the larger project of the *Timaeus*, which represents, in later terms, an attempt to combine physics and ethics, in a way that is also underpinned by a strong logical or dialectical argument. In modern terms, what is notable in the passage, and in the dialogue as a whole, is the attempt to combine, or indeed fuse, scientific and ethical perspectives on human nature, seen in the context of the universe.[334]

327 Pl. *Ti.* 87c–89a, especially 87d2–3, e5–6.

328 Pl. *Ti.* 88c–89d.

329 Pl. *Ti.* 90a–d. See further Sedley (1997*a*); Johansen (2000), 102–4, (2004), 150–2.

330 Gal. *QAM*, chs. 6 and 10; Kühn pp. 789–91, 812–13. See further Gill (2000*b*), 65–70; also Singer (1997*b*), locating *QAM* within Galen's thinking about psyche–body relations and types of explanation.

331 Tieleman (2003), 157–62, 186–90; for the relevant features of Stoic thought, see 262–6 below.

332 Pl. *Ti.* 87c–88b, taken with 32b–33a, 44c1–2, and 82a–b; see further Gill (2000*b*), 70–4, esp. 71 and 5.1 below, text to nn. 10–17.

333 See n. 232 above and discussion below.

334 For the dialectical argument, centring on the ethical implications of the analysis of the cosmos being offered, see esp. *Ti.* 29e–38b; also Osborne (1996); Johansen (2004), 177–97. On

Where, however, Plato's passage differs sharply from Stoic and Epicurean thought, at least as so far considered, is in the inference that this line of thought means that we should not blame people or hold them responsible, even for what are normally considered ethical failings such as lack of sexual self-control.[335] By contrast, as we have seen, Stoic and Epicurean theory combines a unified (ethico-scientific) picture of human beings as psychophysical wholes with an analysis of them as autonomous and responsible agents. In fact, this point of difference is only partial. As I bring out later, both Stoic and Epicurean thought do contain analogues for the idea that wrongdoing is a product of error and that the appropriate response is therapy or teaching, rather than blame or criticism. This is linked with the critique, in both theories, of reactive attitudes such as anger and blame, and the advocacy of a therapeutic or admonitory response to defective attitudes and actions.[336] This Stoic–Epicurean idea, like other of their distinctive and unconventional ethical claims, can, plausibly, be traced back to Socrates. Socrates is regularly presented, especially in Plato's dialogues, as arguing that 'no one does wrong willingly', but only in error, a theme sometimes coupled with Socrates' adoption of a therapeutic stance towards his interlocutor.[337] In this passage in the *Timaeus*, Plato, exceptionally, couples this Socratic thesis with a body-based analysis of defectiveness of character. This is linked, in turn, with an exceptionally sweeping exemption of people from responsibility for their faults and a recommendation of body-based therapy and education.[338] In Stoicism and Epicureanism, by contrast, a body-based—more precisely holistic—approach to human nature is the standard one. Also, both theories combine the view of people as psychophysical and psychological wholes with an analysis of them as responsible agents. They also see human beings as constitutively capable of responding to therapy and education—in principle, throughout their lives—and regard this as a further aspect of their capacity for agency and responsibility.[339] Thus, both Stoic and Epicurean theories adopt some of the striking themes in

the fusion of ethics and physics, see also Gill (2004*b*). On later ancient responses to Plato as a thinker who prefigures the Hellenistic–Roman project of unifying the branches of knowledge, see Annas (1999), 108–12.

335 See n. 326 above.

336 See 7.4 below, text to nn. 189–207; also Gill (2003*c*), 208–16.

337 See e.g. Pl. *Prt.* 352b–360e, *Grg.* 466b–468e; for Socrates as adopting the therapeutic approach, see e.g. *Grg.* 475d, 505c, also *Sph.* 230c–d; see also text to n. 241 above. On Socrates as prefiguring the idea of philosophy as therapy, see e.g. Nussbaum (1994), 53; Sellars (2003), 33–54.

338 See further Gill (2000*b*), 61–5, also Mackenzie (1981: 178) on Plato's 'odd experiment . . . with the idea that vice may be explained in terms of [body-based] psychic disease'.

339 See text to nn. 252–6 above and 6.5 below, text to nn. 183–93.

this Platonic passage, but produce a rather different, and more fully systematized, set of ideas. None the less, this passage in the *Timaeus* offers an arresting anticipation both of the Stoic–Epicurean synthesis of branches of knowledge and also of the motifs, regarding human nature and personality, that arise out of this synthesis.

PART II

The Unstructured Self: Stoic Passions and the Reception of Plato

4

Competing Readings of Stoic Passions

4.1 ANCIENT DEBATE ABOUT THE STOIC THEORY

In Part I of this book, I have explored, in relatively broad terms, salient features of the shared or converging set of ideas about human personality in Stoicism and Epicureanism that I associate with the notion of the structured self. Part II focuses, in a more concentrated and detailed way, on two related themes: the Stoic theory of the passions and the relationship of the Stoic theory to Platonic psychology. This Part constitutes, in effect, a case study for the larger claims of the book about the distinctive features of Stoic–Epicurean thought about personality and about the relationship of these features to early, contemporary, and later ancient thought.

This Part differs in another way from Part I. So far, the emphasis has been on positive aspects of the Stoic–Epicurean theories, in particular, their thinking about ideals of character and the process of development by which these ideals are realized. In this Part, I examine Stoic thinking about what is, in one sense at least, 'the *un*structured self'; that is, about the type of personality that *fails* to develop towards the ideal condition of cohesive structure.[1] This is the Stoic account of the passions or—bad—emotions (*pathē*).[2] This account is one of the most famous and influential, though also complex and problematic, features of Hellenistic and Roman thought about ethical psychology; and this is partly why it occupies a prominent place in this study. It is a theory which played a powerful role, along with other, competing, ancient ideas about emotions, in shaping the presentation of unstructured selves in Plu-

[1] In one sense, *all* selves are 'structured' in Stoic and Epicurean thought, in that they are conceived as (psychophysical and psychological) unified wholes and not as combinations of distinct or independent 'parts'. In another sense, however, the great majority of selves are 'unstructured', in failing to achieve the *ideal* structure. See further Introd., xv above.

[2] The relevant term *pathos* (plural, *pathē*) is broad in meaning, signifying emotions or passions or, more generally, anything that is suffered or undergone. I generally adopt the traditional English term for the Stoic theory, as being one way of conveying the central point that these responses are (in a sense to be defined) 'irrational' and misguided. Other terms used for the phenomena analysed by Stoicism are 'emotions' (Brennan 1998: 34), 'affections' (M. Frede 1986; Tieleman 2003: 15–16).

tarchean biography and Roman poetry.[3] The Stoic theory of the passions, taken together with the complex relationship of the Stoic theory to Platonic psychology, also illustrates larger features of Hellenistic–Roman thinking that are central to this book.

First, the Stoic analysis of the passions brings out in another way the psychophysical and psychological holism that I see as central to their outlook. It also shows how this is combined with Socratic ethical claims, in particular, that only the wise person is psychologically cohesive and that all non-wise people are more or less incoherent. The latter point is implied in what seems to me one of the most psychologically penetrating aspects of their thinking. This is the depiction of states of passion, including intense and violent emotion, as shot through with internal contradictions. This dimension of their thought, perhaps surprisingly, reflects in a consistent way their psychological holism.[4] Second, the Stoic theory of the passions, taken with the responses of other thinkers to their theory, helps us to map more effectively the history and cross-currents of Hellenistic–Roman debate about human personality. This debate displays in another way the contrast and opposition between core-centred or part-based and holistic approaches to the self that is a central theme of this book.

These two topics are intimately connected. Two of the most important sources for the Stoic theory of passions derive from highly engaged participants in this debate. These are Plutarch's essay *On Ethical Virtue*, and Books 4 and 5 of Galen's *On the Doctrines of Hippocrates and Plato* (*PHP*). Both these thinkers adopt versions of the part-based approach to psychology which they see as characteristic of Platonic–Aristotelian thought. As I aim to bring out, these assumptions colour their accounts of the Stoic theory, which they see as expressing a narrowly rationalistic and psychologically implausible view of human nature. Hence, recovering (what I see as) a more credible understanding of the Stoic theory depends, in part, on counteracting the negative picture offered in these sources and on reinterpreting the evidence they provide. The conceptual standpoints of Plutarch and Galen also influence their portrayal of the relationship of the Stoic theory to Platonic thinking, which is the second main theme of this Part. Plutarch and Galen, in different ways, offer themselves as the intellectual heirs of Plato and Aristotle in psychology, and present the Stoics, especially their main theorist, Chrysippus, as rejecting earlier thinking, particularly that of Plato. I will suggest that the ancient evidence, including that provided by Plutarch and Galen, permits a different, and much more complex,

[3] See Ch. 7 below, including discussion of Epicurean thinking on emotions (7.4, text to nn. 197–207, 158–60).

[4] See 4.5 below, text to nn. 192–244.

account of the relationship between Plato's thinking and the Stoics—and also between Plato's thought and later versions of Platonism. As already suggested (1.2 above), there are certain features of Platonic and Aristotelian thought, namely core-centred and part-based psychology, which are in sharp contrast with the Stoic holistic and naturalistic approach and which the Stoics did not adopt. But there are other aspects of Plato's ideas which prefigured—and might have influenced—the distinctive features of Stoic thinking on passions and on ethical psychology more generally, a theme explored especially in Chapter 5.

I begin with the second of these topics. In the remainder of this section, I attempt to reconstruct the history of ancient debate on this topic, in a way that is designed to challenge the influential picture given by Galen, in particular. This provides a framework within which to locate the more detailed examination of the evidence of Plutarch and Galen which follows in the rest of this chapter. Plutarch and Galen both present the Stoic theory as rejecting what they see as a Platonic–Aristotelian consensus—and one with intuitive appeal and widespread support—that the psyche consists of rational and irrational parts, and that passions or emotions constitute a function of the irrational part. They do not see the Stoic theory as based on what I am calling a 'holistic' or integrated account of the human personality. Rather, like Antiochus, they maintain that the Stoics identify the person or self with one 'part', namely the rational aspect of the psyche, and see emotions as stemming from that 'part'. In other words, they interpret the Stoic theory in terms of their own, part-based, psychological model, rather than recognizing that it offers a substantively different, unified and inclusive, conception.[5] Galen makes further, and more detailed, claims. He presents Chrysippus, rather than Zeno, as formulating the Stoic view of emotion in its most extreme, intellectualist form.[6] He also presents Chrysippus as rejecting the Platonic tripartite picture of the psyche, which Galen himself adopts as being both intuitively plausible and in line with empirical study of human physiology.[7] Galen also asserts that Posidonius, a leading Stoic thinker in the early first century BC, made fundamental criticisms of the mainstream (Chrysippean) Stoic psychological model, and, instead, adopted Plato's part-based model.[8]

How credible is the picture offered by Plutarch and Galen? Galen's comments are especially full and have provided the core of modern collections of evidence for the Stoic theory of passions, for instance, in von Arnim's

[5] See 4.2 and 4.5 below; on Antiochus, see 3.4 above, text to nn. 187–91. Both Plutarch and (to some extent) Galen adopt the Middle Platonic approach of which Antiochus is the pioneer. See Dillon (1977), chs. 2, 4, and pp. 339–40.

[6] See 246–9 below.

[7] See further n. 22 below and (on Galen's own views), 4.4 below.

[8] See 4.6 below.

standard volume on Stoic doctrines (1903–5 = *SVF*), Long and Sedley (1987), and the Edelstein-Kidd volume on Posidonius.[9] Modern scholarly accounts of the Stoic theory of passions have, for the most part, regarded Galen's view of Chrysippus as unduly negative and have presented Chrysippus' theory as internally consistent and, indeed, as one of the most powerful and coherent ancient accounts of emotions.[10] However, Richard Sorabji, in an important recent study (2000), follows Galen closely both in his history of the development of Stoic thought and in seeing Chrysippus' theory as over-intellectualist and lacking psychological credibility.[11] For the most part, most scholars (including those critical of Galen's negative treatment of Chrysippus) have tended to accept Galen's picture of Posidonius as, in effect, rejecting Chrysippus' unified psychology and adopting Plato's tripartite model.[12] However, in recent years, there have been strong challenges to Galen's picture of Posidonius. Janine Fillion-Lahille (1984) and John Cooper (1998*a*) have thrown doubt on the idea that Posidonius' criticism and replacement of Chrysippus' theory was as radical and thoroughgoing as Galen asserts. In supporting this view, I have also suggested that, in their theory of the passions, as well as in other aspects of their psychology, the early Stoics may have been much closer to Platonic thinking than Galen admits.[13] This suggestion is supported by other recent work highlighting the influence of Socrates and Plato on the evolution of Stoic thought more generally.[14] Recently, Teun Tieleman has undertaken a systematic reconstruction of Chrysippus' theory of the passions, which involves a root-and-branch critique of Galen's picture. Tieleman argues both that Galen's account of Chrysippus' theory seriously misrepresents its philosophical content and that, in all essentials, Posidonius also maintained this theory, while at the same time exploring its relationship to Platonic thought.[15] It is this critical approach to

[9] See *SVF* 1.205–15, 3.456–90; LS 65; Edelstein and Kidd (1972/1989); Kidd (1988). Other important sources include the 'doxographical' (text-book) accounts of D.L. 7.110–17; Stob. 2.88.8–93.13 (= sections 10–10e in Arius' summary of Stoic ethics, trans. Inwood and Gerson 1997, pp. 217–19); and Cic. *Tusc.* 3–4. On the sources, and the difficulties they present, see Tieleman (2003), 1–11.

[10] See e.g. Gould (1970), 181–96, esp. 192–6; Inwood (1985), 127–81, esp. 140, 143–5; Price (1995), 145–75.

[11] Sorabji (2000), part 1, sees Seneca, as well as Posidonius, as aiming to repair these deficiencies in Chrysippus' theory. On Sorabji (2000) see Graver (2002*b*) and Gill (2005*a*).

[12] See e.g. Inwood (1985), 131–2; Price (1995), 175–8; also Kidd (1971*a*), (1988).

[13] See Gill (1998*a*); also (1997*a*) and (2000*b*). A critical view of Galen's account of the Stoic theory of passions is also implied in Gill (1983*a*).

[14] See 1.3 above, text to nn. 41–68, 2.2, text to nn. 23–34.

[15] See Tieleman (2003), which includes a careful examination of Galen's methods, in ch. 1, based partly on Tieleman (1996), which discusses Galen's account of Chrysippus' *On the Psyche* in *PHP* 2–3.

Galen's evidence that I adopt here; apart from other advantages, I think this opens up the basis for a more credible picture of the relationship of Stoic thought to Plato on the emotions and on ethical psychology more generally.

I focus initially on a question which has received surprisingly little scholarly discussion but which is potentially very important. It is very clear in Plutarch, and still more, Galen, that the issue of whether one should hold a part-based or unified conception of the psyche had become a well-recognized issue of—often intense and polemical—debate. From what date and in what context did the debate take this form?[16] Of course, to some degree at least, this contrast can be traced back to ideas found in Plato and Aristotle. Also, the adoption by the Stoics and Epicureans of a distinctively unified (holistic) psychological model might seem to imply an awareness of this issue. Further, at some stage in Hellenistic–Roman thought, this contrast figured within the set of questions used as the basis for doxographical (handbook) summaries of previous philosophical positions.[17] But these points do not quite address the question I have in view. My question is: when does the issue emerge *in the form in which it is presented by Plutarch and Galen*? They characterize the debate as a straightforward, two-sided contest between a part-based model shared by Plato and Aristotle and a unified (or, as they see it, intellectualist) model adopted by the Stoics or, according to Galen, Chrysippus alone. Galen, at least, implies that the issues were defined in this way from an early stage. Certainly, he presents Chrysippus as, in effect at least, deliberately rejecting the Platonic–Aristotelian, part-based model, and Posidonius as deliberately readopting it.[18] But how far back does this view of the debate really reach? My working hypothesis is that this way of characterizing the debate belongs, essentially, to the period of Plutarch and Galen (the first and second centuries AD), and that in earlier ancient thought the issues were not conceived in terms of this stark opposition. Also, it is far from clear that thinkers prior to Plutarch saw Plato or Aristotle as holding a consistently part-based theory, which was radically different in kind from the unified picture adopted by the Stoics. I outline this view of the evolution of ancient thought in general terms, in preparation for the more detailed examination offered later of Plutarch's and Galen's treatments of this subject (4.2–6) and my own alternative account of the relationship between Stoic and Platonic psychology (5.1–2).

In both Plato and Aristotle, we find various psychological models offered in different contexts without a clear attempt to define an 'official' position. For instance, although the tripartite psyche is introduced with great fanfare in

16 The remainder of this section is a revised version of Gill (2005*a*), 460–7.

17 See further text to nn. 48–58 below.

18 See e.g. Gal. *PHP* 6.2.5, for a typically schematic contrast. See further 4.5–6 below.

Plato's *Republic*, subsequently in that dialogue Plato's Socrates deploys a bipartite version and also sketches a further one, in which the disembodied rational mind constitutes our sole true or essential nature.[19] Aristotle, in the *Nicomachean Ethics*, though he presents formally at one point a bipartite version, sometimes deploys ideas which suggest either a tripartite model or the idea of the mind as our real self.[20] In broader terms, we can find in Plato and Aristotle the expression of *both* (what I am calling) core-centred as well as part-based psychology *and* features that prefigure psychological and psycho-physical holism (1.2 above). This rather diverse and undoctrinaire approach to the topic, in both thinkers, helps to explain why later ancient thinkers with very different approaches found inspiration in Platonic and Aristotelian ideas. A further dimension, especially in Aristotle, is analysis of the nature of the psyche and of psychological questions, conducted in a way that (perhaps as mediated by Theophrastus), seems to have influenced the doxographical tradition and thus to shape later debate.[21]

Plato's non-doctrinaire approach, in particular, may also help to explain a relevant but puzzling feature of early Stoic thought which Galen underlines. Galen notes several times that, although Chrysippus commented on Plato's tripartite theory in the *Republic* and *Timaeus*, he failed to argue explicitly against it.[22] For Galen, this is a mark of Chrysippus' defectiveness as a theorist. While rejecting, by implication at least, the Platonic tripartite model (which Galen endorses), Chrysippus fails to offer the kind of refutation of Plato's model that Galen himself offers in the case of the Stoic theory.[23] In fact, Tieleman maintains, Galen may well exaggerate this point; Chrysippus' argument, in so far as we can reconstruct it, seems to have been designed to answer Plato, at least implicitly.[24] Even so, Galen's claim may, indeed, answer to a real feature of Chrysippus' practice, and one which marks a difference from Posidonius, and still more so Plutarch and Galen.

Although the nature of our evidence makes certainty impossible, it does not look as though the early Stoics, typically, saw themselves as *commentators*

[19] Pl. *R.* 436a–441c; 602c–603b, 604b–605c; 611b–612a. See also 5.2.

[20] *NE* 1.13, esp. 1102^b13–1103^a3 (bipartite model); 3.2 (anger–appetite contrast as regards motivation), 7.6 (anger–appetite contrast as regards incontinence); 10.7, esp. 1177^b30–1178^a3 (mind as real self).

[21] Arist. *de An.* 1.1, 402^a7–8, $^a23$–$^b3$. See further Tieleman (2003), 23–9 on this passage and its possible influence on the doxographical tradition and thus Galen. See also nn. 48–58 below.

[22] *PHP* 3.1.19–21, 4.1.6, 4.1.15, 4.3.6, 5.7.43, 5.7.52.

[23] In *PHP* 3.1.10–15, Galen reports Chrysippus as noting Plato's idea of the embodied tripartite psyche (*Ti.* 69–72), as part of a review of ideas about the location of the ruling part of the psyche, and, by implication, rejecting it. See further 5.1 below, text to nn. 35–8, on this passage.

[24] See Tieleman (1996), 140–6, referring to Chrysippus' *On the Psyche*; see further 5.1 below, text to nn. 39–41.

on Platonic texts or on the ideas they contain.[25] The themes of some Platonic dialogues were explicitly rejected (notably the class-based political ideal of the *Republic*);[26] but, in general, the early Stoics seem to have adopted some Platonic ideas and ignored others, whether based on the dialogues or on indirect sources, without necessarily feeling the need to render this process explicit. Their primary concern, it seems, lay in constructing their own theory, using a variety of earlier ideas and materials as sources of inspiration, rather than in specifying what was or was not different from previous theories. This seems to be the process involved, for instance, in Zeno's adoption of Polemo's version of the providential world-view of the *Timaeus*, discussed earlier. A similar process seems to have been at work in the adoption of Socratic ethical ideas (often based on Platonic sources) in combination with a largely innovative holistic and naturalistic approach to psychology and ethics.[27] I suggest later that the same pattern may also have been embodied in Chrysippus' response to Plato's presentation of the theory of the tripartite psyche in the *Timaeus* and *Republic*. Chrysippus, I think, adopted and developed salient features of Platonic thinking, including the idea of human psychology as a body-based system and the claim that imperfect psychological states are fundamentally incoherent. But he did not, of course, adopt the part-based approach as such, which is displayed with special force in *Republic* 4, and which helps us see what is at stake, philosophically, in the question whether or not the psyche has 'parts'.[28] If this is taken in combination with the internal diversity and the absence of a single 'official' doctrine on this subject in Plato's dialogues (or Aristotle's school-texts), we can more easily understand, I think, the failure on Chrysippus' part, on which Galen comments, to mount a full-scale, explicit critique of Plato's tripartite model.[29]

The position seems to be significantly different in the case of some later Stoics, notably Panaetius and Posidonius. They lived at a period of culture in which the transmission of, and commentary on, texts from an earlier period, including those of Plato and Aristotle, was becoming a more important part of philosophical activity.[30] Their later reputation as 'lovers of Plato and

[25] On the contrast with the later Hellenistic period, see text to nn. 30–4 below.

[26] See 5.2, n. 68 below.

[27] See references in n. 14 above, and 2.2 above.

[28] See 5.2 below, esp. text to nn. 75–80, on the latter question.

[29] See text to nn. 22–3 above.

[30] For this contrast between the different phases of Stoicism, and Hellenistic philosophy generally, see M. Frede (1999*a*), esp. 774–8, 783–4; also Sedley (2003), 20–4. Both scholars link this development with an emerging tendency in late Hellenistic (or post-Hellenistic) thought to trace ideas back to earlier 'authorities', especially Pythagoras and Plato; on this tendency, see Boys-Stones (2001), esp. ch. 6. See also Sedley (1997*b*) on the emergence of a commentary tradition on Plato's dialogues in the late Hellenistic period.

Aristotle' may reflect, in part at least, their participation in this process.[31] In the case of Posidonius' thinking on emotions, it is clear (in a way that is not clear in the case of Chrysippus) that, in offering his own ideas, he referred explicitly to certain Platonic texts, especially the account of the formation of character in early childhood and education in Book Four of the *Laws*.[32] Galen presents this process as one in which Posidonius rejected the Stoic, or at least Chrysippean, account of the emotions and adopted the Platonic tripartite model in its place, though no other ancient source presents Posidonius as radically abandoning orthodox Stoic thought in this way.[33] But a quite different interpretation is possible, as I suggest later. This is that Posidonius, unlike Chrysippus, discussed explicitly the relationship between Stoic theory and the Platonic texts. More precisely, what Posidonius may have been doing was *translating Platonic ideas into Stoic form*—the exact reverse of the way that Galen presents the position. This is a more plausible project for the leading Stoic of his day to have engaged in than the wholesale rejection of previous Stoic theory ascribed to him by Galen; it is also a project that is compatible with several of the passages that Galen himself cites in this connection.[34]

Is this the point at which the contrast between part-based and monistic conceptions of the psyche became defined as an explicit issue of debate? It is more likely, I think, that Posidonius, like Chrysippus before him, highlighted salient similarities between Platonic and Stoic thought without dwelling on the underlying conceptual differences. The difference between Posidonius and Chrysippus, in this respect, was probably only that Posidonius examined more explicitly the relationship between specific Platonic and Stoic ideas. Cicero provides evidence for thinking that the debate between part-based and unified approaches had not yet emerged as a well-established issue in the late first century BC. When discussing Stoic theory, Cicero sometimes uses language which seems more appropriate to a part-based psychological model such as Plato's.[35] Why does Cicero not see the inconsistency? Various reasons have been suggested for Cicero's usage.[36] But one plausible explanation is that Cicero conflates the two kinds of model because the contrast between them had not yet been clearly defined as an explicit issue of debate. In the relevant passages, it seems likely that Cicero is drawing on Panaetius and Posidonius,

[31] See e.g. Panaetius frs. 1, lxi van Straaten (1962).

[32] Gal. *PHP* 5.5.30–2; also 4.7.23, 5.6.19–22.

[33] Cooper stresses this point (1998*a*: 72), and references in his n. 5.

[34] See 4. 6 below, esp. text to nn. 351–92.

[35] Cic. *Off.* 1.101, 132, 2.8, *Tusc.* 4.10–11.

[36] 1. He was influenced by Posidonius' model (taken to be part-based): Inwood (1985), 140–1; Sorabji (2000), 103. 2. He is deliberately employing the language of Platonic dualism, which reflects his Academic (Platonic) intellectual affiliation: Lévy (1992), 472–80. 3. His concerns are moral rather than psychological: Tieleman (2003), 248–9.

so his failure to highlight the difference indicates that they too had not marked this as an issue.[37] Indeed, Cicero may be following texts which adopt the policy I ascribe to Posidonius (4.6 below), of reading Platonic ideas and texts in terms of Stoic psychology. The contrast between Cicero's vagueness on this point and his acute awareness of the key issues in his report of Antiochus' debate with the Stoics on ethical questions is very marked. There, the difference between the Platonic–Aristotelian and the Stoic positions, is explicit and forms the basis of sustained polemical debate.[38] Cicero's failure to isolate the psychological issue is also very striking, in view of the fact that he makes much of the question whether emotions should be moderated (the Platonic–Aristotelian view) or extirpated (the Stoic one).[39] It seems extraordinary that Cicero does not pick up the correlated issue of the contrast between part-based and unified (or holistic) conceptions of personality; yet this seems to be the case.

In Seneca's *On Anger*, we also find that the contrast between the moderation and the extirpation of emotions is a major issue of debate, but not one that is explicitly linked with the related contrast between models of personality.[40] In *On Anger* 1.7.2–3, for instance, Seneca makes comments which are compatible with either a unitary or a bipartite model.[41] In Letter 92, which argues at length for the central Stoic ethical claim that virtue is sufficient for happiness (including peace of mind), Seneca offers without comment at different points a bipartite and tripartite model of mind (92.1, 8). This issue might be seen as implied in the three-stage analysis of emotion in *On Anger* 2.2–4, but only if we take it that reference to pre-emotions implies an allusion to a non-rational part of the psyche, an inference that we do not have to draw from the passage.[42]

The first text in which the issue is made explicit, as far as I am aware, is Plutarch's essay, *On Ethical Virtue*. Here, the contrast between the Platonic–Aristotelian (part-based) and Stoic (monistic) psychological models is wholly explicit and polemically debated, from an anti-Stoic standpoint. It is also

[37] This may also be the explanation for Arius' use of dualistic language in his (otherwise largely orthodox) account of the Stoic theory of emotion, discussed in Inwood (1985), 142–3. For scepticism about the idea that Cicero's usage reflects that of Panaetius, see Tieleman (2003), 246–50.

[38] Cic. *Fin.* 4–5, esp. 4.2, 14–15, 19–23, 5.67–75, 77–95; see further Annas (1993*b*), 180–7, 419–23; also 3.4 above

[39] See e.g. Cic. *Tusc.* 4.41–2, 39, 57, noted in Sorabji (2000), 208–9.

[40] Sen. *On Anger* 1.7, 9–10, 3.6.1–2.

[41] We are told that reason (*ratio*) remains in control (*potens*) only if it is kept separate from emotions (*adfectus*), and that, when 'mingled' with them, it becomes their slave.

[42] Sen. *On Anger* 2.3.5, 2.4.1–2. Sorabji (2000), 72, sees allusions in the whole passage (2.2–4) to Posidonius' theory, though to his claims about animals, music and tears, rather than to Posidonius' (alleged) part-based psychology. See further on Sen. *On Anger* 2.2–4, in 279–81 below.

linked with a series of correlated contrasts, including that between the moderation and extirpation of emotions. This contrast is taken up subsequently by Galen (*PHP* 4–5) who argues in similar terms, though focusing on the contrast between a tripartite (rather than bipartite) and monistic model and combining it with his distinctive synthesis of Platonic–Aristotelian and medical ideas.[43]

Why does this conflict become explicit for the first time only in Plutarch?[44] The answer lies partly in features peculiar to Plutarch and Galen and to the way they define their positions as explicitly non- or anti-Stoic.[45] But there are also two other more general factors, relevant in differing degrees to both thinkers. One of these is the emergence of the broad movement we call 'Middle Platonism', which falls between the post-Platonic Academy and Neoplatonism. The latter two Platonic movements focus on the creative evolution of new ideas, in this respect like Stoicism. Middle Platonism, though not uncreative in its own way, has a more explicitly doctrinal, even doctrinaire, approach. There is a prevalent concern to distinguish and defend distinctively Platonic ideas from those of other schools, especially the influential Stoic school. (This concern coexists with a very broad and diverse conception of what should count as distinctively 'Platonic'.)[46] This approach is apparent from Antiochus onwards; but Antiochus' interests, as we have seen (3.4 above) centre on categories of value and ethical development. Plutarch is the first thinker, as far as I know, who extends this concern to ethical psychology, and who argues strongly, in *On Ethical Virtue*, for the Platonic–Aristotelian part-based model against the Stoic unitary view.[47] Galen also endorses what he sees as a shared Platonic–Aristotelian psychological model, though one that he also believes is supported by earlier medical thought and empirical evidence.[48]

[43] Plutarch lived in *c.* AD 45–125, and Galen AD 129–*c.*210/215. See further 4.2–4 below. As noted earlier, neither thinker recognizes that the Stoic theory constitutes a new, *holistic*, model.

[44] Inwood (1985), 139–43, cites certain other passages in this connection; but those passages do not, I think, identify this subject as an issue of explicit debate as Plutarch and Galen do.

[45] See further 4.2 and 4.4 below.

[46] On this movement, see Dillon (1977), and, on questions of doctrine and eclecticism in this period, see Dillon and Long (1988). On Middle Platonism and the emergence of the commentary tradition in late or post-Hellenistic thought, see M. Frede (1999*a*), esp. 776, 786–9; and Boys-Stones (2001), esp. ch. 7.

[47] Antiochus, as reported by Cicero, *Fin.* 4.26–39, esp. 26–8, criticizes the Stoics for an excessively rationalistic or intellectualist conception of human nature (for treating the mind as if it were the whole person), see 3.4 above, text to nn. 189–95. But he does not make it explicit, as Plutarch does, that two quite different models of personality are involved.

[48] See further 4.4 below. On Galen in the context of Middle Platonism, see Dillon (1977), 339–40.

A second important underlying factor has been highlighted by Tieleman, drawing on some recent work, especially by Dutch scholars. This is the effect of doxography, especially in the *Placita*-tradition, in shaping the ancient understanding of philosophical issues and of the history of ideas. 'Doxography', in this connection, signifies the attribution to earlier thinkers of determinate positions on a series of issues, which are often formulated in a highly schematic form. A key move in charting this process was played by Hermann Diels, who identified an otherwise unknown writer, Aëtius, as the source of two extant works of doxography (or collections of 'opinions', *placita*) deriving from the second and fourth centuries AD.[49] In the reconstructed Aëtian source, there are four main topics under which philosophical views are organized: the nature or substance of the psyche, its parts, the location of the ruling part, and the functions of the psyche.[50] We can see the origins of this kind of schema already in Aristotle's *On the Psyche*; and this set of questions seems also to be presupposed in a passage from Book 1 of Chrysippus' *On the Psyche*, cited by Galen.[51] But in the later works in this tradition, the schematization has become more elaborate and more rigidly applied.

Tieleman highlights ways in which the doxographical tradition seems to have shaped the approaches of Plutarch and Galen to psychological questions. For instance, the doxographical tendency to harmonize different schemes seems to underlie the readiness of both thinkers to treat Platonic tripartition and Aristotelian bipartition as variants of the same pattern.[52] We also find in both Plutarch and Galen the doxographical tendency to regiment under certain doctrinal headings the ideas of thinkers such as Pythagoras or Hippocrates whose work antedated the emergence of the relevant categories.[53] It also seems likely that the development of the doxographical approach helped to make the contrast between unified and part-based models of psyche an explicit subject of debate. For one thing, the doxographical approach would have heightened awareness of contrasting views and provided a schematic framework for identifying them. For another, the tendency, evident in the

[49] Diels (1879). These are the *Placita* of pseudo-Plutarch (2nd c. AD) and the *Eclogae* of Stobaeus (4th c. AD); Aëtius himself is supposed to have lived sometime between the 1st c. BC and AD. See further Tieleman (2003), 61; more generally Mansfeld (1990); Mansfeld and Runia (1997).

[50] Tieleman (2003), 23.

[51] See Arist. *de An.* 1.1, 402ᵃ23–ᵇ3, and Chrysippus cited in Gal. *PHP* 3.1.10–16. Theophrastus appears to be an important medium for the transmission of Peripatetic and other earlier ideas on this subject. See further Tieleman (2003), 21–3, esp. n. 23; also Mansfeld (1989) and (1990), esp. 3167–77, 3212–3216. See further 5.1 below, text to nn. 35–41.

[52] Tieleman (2003), 71, 82–4, 76–7; this assimilation was made easier because of variations in the usage of both Plato and Aristotle outlined earlier (nn. 19–20 above).

[53] Tieleman (2003), 62, 77–8.

pattern cited earlier, to *assume* that the psyche has parts might have made the Stoic theory seem non-standard and misguided, as it seems to Galen.[54] It is not easy to pinpoint the date at which the doxographical method began to exercise a marked influence in this respect. As noted earlier, one can see some indications of the method already in Chrysippus, or indeed Aristotle, though these are probably best understood as anticipations of what became a more formalized schema.[55] As also noted, Cicero and Seneca show little awareness of the debate between monistic and part-based approaches, although the influence of the doxographical tradition has been identified in their work.[56] It seems to be in the later first and second century AD that the combination of the doxographical tradition and the evolution of Middle Platonism,[57] among other factors,[58] leads to the emergence of the contrast between part-based and unified psychological models as an issue for explicit and intense debate.

As highlighted earlier, the discussions of Plutarch and Galen which present most starkly the contrast between part-based and monistic psychological models, particularly Galen, *PHP* Books 4–5, are the richest and most important sources for the Stoic theory of passions. But, if the view I have just been maintaining is correct, these thinkers are not simply, as is explicit, intellectual opponents and critical reporters of the theory but also import a more subtle form of misrepresentation. This is that they—particularly Galen—depict the conflict between part-based and monistic psychological models, which they are the first to make into an explicit and polemical issue, as already a well-recognized subject of debate from the early Stoics onwards. In this way, they offer an anachronistic picture of the evolution of the Stoic theory, for instance, as regards Chrysippus' response and Posidonius' relationship to

[54] See text to n. 50 above. In fact, the Stoics themselves (e.g. Chrysippus in Gal. *PHP* 3.1.11), as well as other ancient sources do sometimes identify psychic 'parts'; but these 'parts' are better understood as (psychophysical) 'functions' than as 'parts' in any stronger sense. See Tieleman (2003), 66, 70; and on the nature of psychic 'parts' in ancient thought, see 5.2 below, esp. text to nn. 75–80.

[55] See text to n. 51 above. Diels (1879) posited a work he called *Vetusta Placita*, located in the 1st c. BC, as a bridge between Theophrastus (seen as a crucial predecessor for this approach) and 'Aëtius' (Tieleman 2003: 61). Mansfeld posits the existence of a yet earlier work, the *Vetustissima Placita*, which could have helped to shape the approach and categories of thinkers in the 3rd c. BC such as Chrysippus: see Mansfeld (1989), 313, 334–42, (1990), 3167–77.

[56] See Mansfeld (1990), 3122–40.

[57] Plutarch's tendency to merge Platonic and Aristotelian thinking about psychic parts has roots both in earlier Middle Platonic thought (e.g. Antiochus) (see Dillon 1977: 193–8, also 72–8) and doxography (Tieleman 2003: 76–8).

[58] For Galen, a key factor is Chrysippus' error, as he sees it, regarding the location of the control-centre, by contrast with Plato's correct view. This gives a special importance to the contrast between unified and part-based psychological (and psychophysical) models; see 4.4 below, text to nn. 161–4.

Chrysippus or use of Platonic ideas. I am not saying that this distortion was necessarily deliberate. Plutarch and Galen may simply have projected backwards an awareness of a conflict which they themselves played a crucial role in defining. If this is so, their picture of ancient debate about emotions introduces a subtly misleading emphasis; and considerable work is needed to counteract this emphasis and to uncover a view of the ancient debate which is not coloured by this distortion. The remainder of this chapter, along with some other recent scholarship,[59] can be seen as a contribution to this larger project. At the same time, my aim is to bring out how Stoic thinking about emotions reflects their version of the combination of holism and Socratic ideals which I associate with the idea of the structured self, and how this line of thought interacts with contrasting (part-based) models in the Hellenistic and Roman periods.

4.2 PLUTARCH ON STOIC PSYCHOLOGY

I begin by considering Plutarch's essay *On Ethical Virtue*.[60] The principal interest of this work here is that it presents, in a relatively clear and straightforward way, the contrast between the Stoic theory of the passions, with its associated psychological model and ideal character-type, and an alternative approach to emotions and psychology, presented as based on Plato and Aristotle. The argument of *On Ethical Virtue* takes this general form. In the first half of the work (up to 447 A), Plutarch identifies certain central Stoic ideas and offers a competing (Platonic–Aristotelian) account of these ideas. In the second half, he engages in a closer, more dialectical, critique of the Stoic position from the same standpoint. In this section, I discuss the Stoic themes that Plutarch reports and his response to those themes. In the next section, I examine the approach that Plutarch offers as an alternative to the Stoic one, considering especially how far it differs from the Platonic and Aristotelian ideas that are presented as the basis of his view. Taken together, the two sections bring out how a Middle Platonist in the early Roman Empire sees the main competing current positions as regards models of human personality.

I focus on four passages in which Plutarch reports the Stoic position, and on the counterarguments he offers, as a way of displaying the two sides in this

[59] See esp. Cooper (1998*a*) and Tieleman (2003).

[60] That is, *Moral Essays* (*Moralia* [*Mor.*]), 440 D–452 D. For text and translation, see Helmbold (1970), and Dumortier and Defradas (1975). For editions with commentary, see Babut (1969*a*) and Becchi (1990*b*).

debate.[61] Plutarch does little to elucidate the Stoic ideas he cites; but I seek to explain them in the light of other ancient evidence and modern discussions. The first passage summarizes the core of the Stoic psychological model:

[Stoics all agree] that virtue is a certain character-state (*diathesis*) of the control-centre (*hēgemonikon*) of the psyche and a capacity produced by reason, or rather, reason itself when this is consistent (*homologoumenon*), firm and unchangeable. They also think that the emotional and irrational aspect of the psyche is not distinguished from the rational by some difference of nature,[62] but it is the same part of the psyche, which, indeed, they call mind and control-centre . . . it contains nothing irrational in itself, but is called irrational, whenever an excessive impulse becomes forceful and takes control and carries it away towards some outrageous act which is against the decision of reason. Indeed, they say that emotion [or 'passion', *pathos*] is reason of a wicked and unrestrained kind which derives from a bad and mistaken judgement and which has acquired force and vigour.[63]

One salient feature of the Stoic model is conveyed here: in virtuous and non-virtuous people alike, the psyche functions as a whole and not as a combination of rational and irrational parts. But what underlies, and makes sense of, this claim? The passage implies a number of key Stoic themes, some of which have already been considered here. One is that human beings, like other animals, constitute integrated psychological, as well as psychophysical, organisms, whose operation is guided by a single 'control-centre' (*hēgemonikon*).[64] The passage also reflects the distinctive Stoic view that, on becoming adult, all humans become rational in a way that informs their psychological life as a whole, and not just the functions, such as deliberating or gaining knowledge, conventionally classed as 'rational'.[65] These are features that I have presented as characteristic of Stoic psychological holism. The passage also implies an idea which I characterized as 'ethical holism'. This is that virtue is a state of character marked by a high degree of internal stability, harmony, and cohesion. This consists in the presence of a unified or interentailing set of virtues, which informs all other aspects of the personality.[66] As explained earlier, this state of character is the outcome of a process of ethical development that culminates in the recognition that virtue is the only good and the

[61] The four passages are *Mor.* 441 C–D, 446 F–447 A, 449 A–B, 450 C–D. Their content is widely recognized as authentically Stoic; they are cited by von Arnim as *SVF* 1.202 (also LS 61 B(8–11)), 3.459 (also LS 65 G), 3.439, and 3.390 respectively.

[62] Literally, 'by some difference and nature'.

[63] *Mor.* 441 C–D; in the last sentence I read *proslabonta* with most manuscripts. The translation is mine; for an alternative one, see LS 61 B(9–11).

[64] See 1.4 above.

[65] See 3.2 above, esp. text to nn. 47–75.

[66] See 3.3 above, esp. text to nn. 92–125.

only proper object of choice. This is linked with the recognition that the other objects to which we are naturally drawn, such as health and wealth, are 'matters of indifference', compared with virtue, and are, at best, merely, 'preferable'.[67] It is the completion of this process, and only its completion, that produces a character that is fully 'consistent' (*homologoumenon*) and stable. Plutarch's phrasing in this passage refers to this ideal, using the term *diathesis*, which is reserved in Stoic thought for the wholly stable character of the virtuous or wise.[68] Thus, in addition to the kinds of holism outlined, the passage also suggests the idea (which I have characterized as 'Socratic') that only the wise person is *fully* unified, coherent, and stable, and that all non-wise people are relatively incoherent and unstable.[69] Thus, while all human beings as such are in some sense 'rational' and unified by their rationality, only the wise person is *completely* unified and rational (in a normative sense). This complex, but intelligible, set of ideas underlies Plutarch's account of virtue in this passage.

A related set of ideas underlies Plutarch's comments on the Stoic conception of *pathos*, 'passion' or (bad) 'emotion'; these ideas have also been outlined earlier, but are explained more fully here and subsequently.[70] The passage implies two salient features of a passion in Stoic thought, namely that it is both an expression of reason and, at the same time, one that is mistaken, excessive, and forceful or violent. Like other impulses, passions depend on 'assent' to rational 'impressions' and are thus acts of reason.[71] But, unlike other impulses, they involve intense, even violent, psychophysical reactions. So the passion of distress (*lupē*) can be characterized equally as 'a fresh belief that evil is present' and as 'a shrinking before what is thought to be a thing to avoid'. The first formulation expresses the content of the impression (the relevant belief), the second the resulting impulse (involving an intense reaction).[72] The beliefs underlying the passion are mistaken or 'false' in the specific sense that 'preferable indifferents', such as health or wealth are taken to be 'good' (a status reserved for virtue). The description of a passion as an 'excessive' (*pleonazousa*) impulse partly reflects this point. The person

[67] See Cic. *Fin.* 3.16, 20–1; also LS 58–9, esp. 59 D. See also 3.2 above, esp. text to nn. 2–9.

[68] On ideal 'consistency' see Cic. *Fin.* 3.21; also LS 61 A, 63 A–C. On *diathesis*, see LS 60 J, L (and LS i. 376–7).

[69] On this idea, and the sense in which it is 'Socratic', see 2.2 above, text to nn. 76–92.

[70] See 2.2 above, esp. text to nn. 10–13, and 4.5 below.

[71] See 3.2 above, text to nn. 51–4.

[72] See Gal. *PHP* 4.2.1, p. 238, 27–8; 4.2.5, p. 240, 3–4. Thus, the fullest definition of distress is 'an irrational contraction, or a fresh opinion that something bad is present, at which people think it right to be contracted [i.e. depressed]', Andronicus, *On Passions* 1 (LS 65 B(1)); see also LS 65 C–D. See further Engberg-Pedersen (1990*b*), 179–81; Brennan (1998), 30–3; also 4.5 below, text to nn. 184–7.

concerned attributes 'excessive' value to a merely 'preferable' indifferent.[73] The passion is also 'excessive' in the sense, underlined by Plutarch, that it can become 'forceful' and powerful. Indeed, despite stemming from the belief of the person concerned, it can 'carry someone away' and lead her to act 'against the decisions of reason' (*Mor.* 441 C). This combination of 'rationality' and 'irrationality', which is perhaps the most paradoxical of the ideas associated with the Stoic theory of passion, is underlined by Galen, and is discussed fully in connection with his evidence.[74] But the crucial point is that the 'freshness' and intensity of the false belief and the force of the consequent impulse (the 'contraction' or 'swelling') have the power to prevent the person from forming a reasonable judgement or even to counteract a reasonable judgement that she does form.[75]

The last point allows the Stoics to explain the phenomenon normally understood as psychological division in a way that is consistent with their unified or holistic model of the psyche. This is the subject of two passages in *On Ethical Virtue*, each of which brings out different aspects of the Stoic analysis of psychological division.[76] The first passage is this:

> [The Stoics] say that passion is no different from reason, and that there is no dissension and conflict between the two, but a turning of the single reason in both directions, which we do not notice owing to the sharpness and speed of the change. We do not perceive that the natural instrument of appetite and regret, or anger and fear, is the same part of the psyche, which is moved by pleasure towards wrong, and while moving recovers itself. For appetite and anger and fear and all such things are corrupt opinions and judgements, which do not arise around just one part of the psyche but are the inclinations, yieldings, assents and impulses of the whole control-centre, and are, quite generally, activities which change rapidly, just like children's fights, whose fury and intensity are volatile owing to their weakness.[77]

The main theme here is that what is conventionally taken to be psychological division actually expresses the operation, in adult humans, of a unified, rational psyche, and, in particular, of its control-centre. Since passions are 'corrupt' expressions of the rational control-centre and reasonable impulses are also expressions of reason, both sides in the conflict derive from the same source. The fact that we, mistakenly, suppose that two 'parts' are involved is

[73] For a *pathos* as an 'excessive impulse' see LS 65 A(1) and Plu. *Mor.* 441 C. On passion as bound up with giving 'excessive' value to things, see Gal. *PHP* 4.5.21–2. See further Inwood (1985), 158–61; Engberg-Pedersen (1990*b*), 184–6, 193–7; for some qualifications, Brennan (1998), 39–44.

[74] See 4.5 below, esp. text to nn. 192–244.

[75] See Gal. *PHP* 4.2.14–18, 27, 4.6.35; also Plu. *Mor.* 450 C–D.

[76] *Mor.* 446 E–447A and 450 C–D.

[77] *Mor.* 446 F–447 A (= LS 65 G), trans. slightly modified.

explained by 'the sharpness and speed of the change'. The point is not that the people concerned are unaware that they are experiencing what they regard as psychological division or conflict. It is that they do not perceive *that it is the same* part of the psyche that is operative in each of the two or more states of mind.[78]

If Plutarch's passage is an accurate report of Stoic thinking, what kind of psychic division do the Stoics envisage? Plutarch, in his critique of this view, assumes that what is intended is conflict, or alternation, between 'reason' and 'passion', as these are understood in part-based terms. He claims that we can only understand why passion continues, after the intervention of reason, by assuming that two distinct psychic parts are involved (*Mor.* 447 B–C). His claim might seem to be supported by the fact that his report identifies two factors, 'appetite and regret (*metanoein*)' and states that the psyche 'is moved by pleasure towards wrong, and while moving recovers itself again (*epilambanesthai*)'. The second pair of phrases imply a relatively rational form of reaction against the passion which precedes it. But Plutarch also refers to the alternation between two different passions ('anger and fear'); and the explanation of psychological conflict offered in the last sentence of the passage takes the form of a general statement about passions as such ('appetite and anger and fear and all such things'). What underlies this comment is the Stoic claim, indicated also in the earlier passage discussed (*Mor.* 441 C–D), that only the character-state of the perfectly wise person is completely stable and 'consistent' (*homologoumenon*). Although Stoics recognize that other, non-wise people may have quasi-dispositional inclinations towards one or other passion, the general state of the non-wise is one of 'feverish' instability.[79] This explains Plutarch's description of passions in general as 'activities which change rapidly, just like children's fights, whose fury and intensity are volatile and transient'. Plutarch's description reflects the fact that the variation and conflict that the Stoics have mainly in mind is that which occurs between the fluctuating passions of a non-wise person; these are also conceived as expressions of reason, but 'corrupt' ones.

However, Stoic thinking does accommodate the idea that the passions of the non-wise alternate with more reasonable responses; indeed, this idea is fundamental to their conception of a passion. This comes out in the second passage on this subject in Plutarch's *On Ethical Virtue*, cited from Chrysippus' *On Inconsistency*.

[78] See esp.: 'We do not perceive that the natural instrument of appetite and regret ... is the same part of the psyche'. For Stoic recognition that people are aware of their own psychological division, see the Medea example, discussed in 4.5 below.

[79] See 4.5 below, esp. text to nn. 251–66.

Anger is a blind thing: often it prevents us from seeing the obvious, and often it stands in the way of what has been understood . . . When passions occur, they thrust out reasonings and divergent views and push on forcibly to actions contrary to reason . . . It is the nature of a rational animal[80] to apply reason to all his actions and to be guided by this; but often we reject it, when subject to a more violent movement. (*Mor.* 450 C–D)

This passage brings out two points which are illustrated more fully in Galen's evidence. One is that those who experience passions—that is, all non-wise human adults—are also capable, at other times, of forming views or impressions that are 'divergent' (*ta hōs heterōs phainomena*) from the misguided and unreasonable beliefs underlying the passions. The other is that, in subjecting ourselves to the opposed (passionate) belief and the subsequent impulse ('a more violent movement'), we are 'rejecting' reason or 'turning away from' it (*apostrephesthai*), a rejection which may be conscious.[81] Both these features of Stoic thought explain why Stoics think that psychological conflict can involve fluctuation between reasonable and unreasonable impulses as well as between different passions (as in *Mor.* 446 F–447 A). [82]

The contrasting affective state of the wise is the subject of the remaining report of Stoic doctrine in Plutarch's essay.

[The Stoics] call shame 'modesty', pleasure 'joy', and fear 'caution'. . . in place of distress and fear, they speak of 'gnawing' and 'perplexity' and gloss over desire with the term 'eagerness'. . . they call that joy, wish, and caution good emotions (*eupatheiai*) and not absences of emotion (*apatheiai*). (*Mor.* 449 A–B)

Plutarch presents this aspect of Stoic thinking as a concession forced on them by the psychological fact that reason and emotion arise from different sources and that virtue consists in emotion shaped by reason (449 A–C). In fact, the idea of 'good emotions', which occurs in most (though not all) ancient summaries of Stoic doctrine, has a coherent and intelligible place in their thinking.[83] The Stoics demarcate the four primary passions as appetite and fear, pleasure and distress, directed at what seems good or bad in the future and the present respectively. They identify three primary 'good emotions', corresponding to the first three primary passions: these are wish, caution, and joy. There is no equivalent for the passion of distress, because 'the wise person

80 That is, adult humans or gods; see further 3.2 above, n. 55.

81 As in the Medea example, see 4.5 below, text to nn. 218–44.

82 On the links between psychological conflict and failure in development, see 4.5 below (also 3.2–3 above).

83 The category of *eupatheiai* is not included in the account of passions in Stob. 2.86–93 (though it may be referred to in 2.69.1–4); but see D.L. 7.116 (= LS 65 F), taken with LS ii. 107; also Cic. *Tusc.* 4.12–14.

is not affected by the presence of what is bad (*praesentis mali*)'.[84] The terms 'gnawing', 'perplexity', and 'eagerness', misleadingly presented by Plutarch as 'good emotions', seem, rather, to be examples of the preliminary reactions (*propatheiai*), falling short of belief-based emotions, which even the wise person may experience.[85]

The basic structure of a 'good feeling' seems to be the same as that of a passion. Assent to an impression that something is good or bad, and that it is therefore appropriate to react accordingly, stimulates an impulse to feel in a certain way.[86] But there are two substantive differences. A bad emotion or passion (*pathos*) depends on placing an inappropriate value on 'preferable' indifferents such as health or wealth and taking them as good and inherently desirable. In the case of a 'good emotion' (*eupatheia*), there is no such mistaken valuation of preferable things. Indeed, it seems that good feelings are conceived, essentially, as reactions to the only things that are genuinely good or bad, namely virtue or vice, and not as responses to 'preferable' things at all. 'Joy' (*chara* or *gaudium*), for instance, is an appropriate response by a wise person to the presence of virtue in herself or in another wise person.[87] Second, although a good feeling is, in some sense, an affective reaction (an 'expansion', *elatio*, in the case of joy), it is marked by the calmness and consistency that is characteristic of the wise person, by contrast with the intensity and fluctuation associated with passion (Cic. *Tusc.* 4.12–13). Good emotions, then, form one of the types of psychological state which are informed by virtue and which make up the consistent and structured 'wholeness' of the character of the wise person.[88]

I have now considered Plutarch's reports of Stoic doctrines on ethical psychology in this essay and I have supplemented his, rather meagre, explanation of these points. How far, and how effectively, does he argue against the Stoic approach and for his own? In the first part of the essay, Plutarch offers little explicit argument against the Stoic theory he reports, proceeding, instead, to outline his contrasting, part-based, model, considered shortly (4.3 below). However, this procedure implies a response, which is made explicit in the latter

84 See LS 65 A(3–4), B, E–F. The wise person is not affected by 'the presence of what is bad' (Cic. *Tusc.* 4.14), because she is free from vice (the only thing that is bad) and is not adversely affected (i.e. made bad in character) by the vice of others.

85 See Graver (1999), 316–17. On 'pre-emotions', see further 279–81 below.

86 For the parallelism of structure, cf. LS 65 B, D with F; see also Brennan (1998), 30–6.

87 They are described as 'off-shoots' (*epigennēmata*) of virtue in D.L. 7.94; see also Sen. *Ep.* 59.2, 'expansion of the psyche relying on goods that are its own and are true' (*animi elatio suis bonis fidentis*). On 'good emotions' as correlated with good, rather than preferable indifferents, which are appropriate objects of 'selection', see Brennan (1998), 54–7, clarifying Inwood (1985), 174–5, and arguing against Nussbaum (1994), 399.

88 See further 3.3 above, esp. text to nn. 114–21.

half of the essay. This is, in the first instance, that the part-based model answers better to conventional intuitions and received opinions about our psychological experience.[89] But he also argues that the ideal and defective states recognized by Stoicism are more plausibly explained by the part-based model than the unified one. Plutarch's four reports focus on the contrast between the consistent and stable state of the virtuous or wise person and the fluctuation and incoherence typical of the non-wise. Plutarch's contrasting claim is that the stability and coherence that he also recognizes as a mark of ethical virtue is better understood as a form of harmony or moderation, achieved through the 'persuasion' of the non-rational part by practical reason.[90] Similarly, he suggests that the psychological incoherence that the Stoics (despite their unitary model) ascribe to the non-wise is better interpreted as the failure to create harmony between two, fundamentally different, parts.[91]

In the second half of the essay (from 447 B), Plutarch argues more directly against the Stoic theory. Like Galen, Plutarch focuses especially on the claim that the Stoics cannot explain psychological incoherence (such as 'weakness of will'), while he also seeks to undermine the Stoic idea of 'good emotions'.[92] However, as John Dillon suggests, Plutarch's critique of Stoic psychology is not very penetrating. In analysing the Stoic theory (in order to criticize it), Plutarch presupposes the validity of the part-based psychology for which he is arguing. He simply does not take seriously the idea that emotion could be understood as an expression of reason, even though he records at least one coherent Stoic statement of this idea (441 C–D), cited earlier.[93] In his comments on (one version of the) Stoic analysis of psychological conflict, Plutarch interprets this as being a conflict between reason and emotion, without giving serious consideration to the idea which he himself reports, that this constitutes fluctuation between (reason-based) emotions.[94] He assumes that the Stoics have no way of explaining the phenomenon of people acting against their better judgement, despite quoting a passage from Chrysippus on the 'rejection' of reason, an idea which seems to have played a key role in the Stoic explanation of this phenomenon.[95] The only Stoic counterargument with

[89] See e.g. *Mor.* 445 F–446 C (citation of poetic expressions of *akrasia*, presented as supporting Plutarch's view), a method also adopted by the Stoic Chrysippus; see also 447B, 448F.

[90] See *Mor.* 441 C–D, 442 C–443 C, 444 B–D, 445 B, 448 D–F.

[91] See *Mor.* 446 C–448 C, 450 B–E.

[92] See *Mor.* 447 B–448 C and 449 A–C, respectively; on Galen's analogous criticism, see 4.6 below, text to nn. 193–6.

[93] See also Dillon (1983), 512–15, who reconstructs the Stoic side of the debate that is not articulated by Plutarch.

[94] *Mor.* 447 A–C; also text to n. 77 above.

[95] See *Mor.* 446 E–448 C, also 450 C–D (on 'rejection of reason', see 4.5 below, text to nn. 194–201).

which he engages is the relatively minor claim that human reason, though essentially unified, can be divided in reasoning, as well as, by implication, in emotion. In fact, this claim is more defensible than Plutarch suggests; but Galen's evidence shows that the Stoics have much more to offer on the subject of psychological conflict than is indicated in this claim.[96] Similarly, the Stoic category of 'good emotions' is simply treated as a covert acknowledgment that virtue has to be analysed in terms of the moderation of emotion by reason.[97] Galen's discussion of Stoic psychological conflict is more illuminating, in spite of its more aggressive style, in part because it tries to expose self-contradictions within Stoic thinking and, by doing so, takes us deeper into the Stoic theory. This method of attacking Stoic ideas (that is, by exposing contradictions) is practised by Plutarch himself extensively elsewhere; but in this, rather non-technical essay, he confines himself to less searching forms of examination.[98]

Indeed, the general form of argument in Plutarch's *On Ethical Virtue* leaves it rather unclear what is at issue in this debate. If, as Plutarch suggests, both the Stoics and their opponents have broadly similar conceptions of ethical virtue and its opposite—namely as psychological coherence and incoherence—it may not seem to matter very much whether this is characterized in unified or part-based terms. It may, therefore, be unclear why the opposition between part-based and unitary psychological models is treated as so important by Plutarch, as well as by Galen. One question that Plutarch fails completely to ask is that concerning the grounds on which we characterize parts of the psyche as different or the same. Galen has more fully articulated views on that subject.[99] But, as I suggest later, we need to go back to Plato *Republic* 4, the first formal ancient argument that the psyche has parts, to form a clearer view of the philosophical issues raised by this question (5.2 below). As I have already argued (140–5 above), the Stoic aim is not to expand the scope of 'reason' in relation to other parts of the psyche but to define a new, holistic, conception of personality in which all psychological functions are, in human adults, informed by reason. Plutarch's readiness to assimilate the Stoic conception of reason to the Platonic–Aristotelian one (as he interprets this) quite obscures this innovation.

However, there are certain ways in which Plutarch's essay, despite its limitations, is a revealing document for understanding Hellenistic–Roman

[96] *Mor.* 447 c –448 c; the claim is defensible if we accept that reason is involved in emotional as well as deliberative conflict. On Stoic analysis of psychological conflict, see further 4.5 below.

[97] *Mor.* 449 a–c; also text to nn. 83–5 above.

[98] Contrast Plutarch's *On Stoic Contradictions* and *On Common Conceptions against the Stoics*; the method is derived from that of the sceptical Academy, especially Carneades.

[99] See e.g. Tieleman (2003), 34–9, referring to Gal. *PHP* 6.2.5.

debate on this question. This is partly because, as brought out more fully in the next section, the essay displays the connections seen in this period between a whole set of issues, and also between the positions typically adopted on those issues. It illustrates, for instance, how the unitary psychological model is often linked with the ideal of 'freedom from passion' (*apatheia*) and the part-based model with that of 'moderation of passion' (*metriopatheia*)—though it also shows how the part-based model can be linked with a version of *apatheia* (237–8 below). Less explicitly, it illustrates two conceptions of 'character', in the sense of a stable psychological structure. In one conception, exemplified here by Stoicism, stability and consistency of character is reserved only for the perfectly virtuous or wise. In the other (Platonic–Aristotelian) conception, 'character' (*ēthos*) is ascribed to a wide range of types of person, both virtuous and defective, even if the virtuous are seen as more completely stable and coherent (232–3 below). Plutarch's essay also implies a certain view about the historical evolution of Greek thought on these issues. His merging of Platonic and Aristotelian categories implies that Aristotle's ethical psychology developed a line of approach already mapped out in, for instance, Plato's *Republic* and *Phaedrus*.[100] However, the history of the Hellenistic reception of earlier ideas can be interpreted quite differently. In particular, as suggested later (Chapter 5 below), Stoic thought can also be seen as strongly shaped by Plato, though it does not adopt the part-based Platonic–Aristotelian psychological model favoured by Plutarch and some other Middle Platonic thinkers.

However, there is another, and more striking, respect in which Plutarch's essay takes us to the heart of certain key issues in this debate. This comes out early in *On Ethical Virtue*. After reporting the central Stoic claim of psychological monism (441 C–D), Plutarch responds in an apparently oblique way, by referring to—what Plutarch presents as—a strongly dualistic conception of the psyche at the cosmic as well as the human level in Plato's *Timaeus* (441 F–442 A). As Jan Opsomer underlines (1994: 36–41), Plutarch indicates his awareness, which is not otherwise apparent in the essay, that Stoic psychological monism is linked with the claim that the universe constitutes an integrated structure and one which is also pervaded by a unifying rationality. As I have suggested earlier (1.3 above), Stoic thinking about psychological integration and the role of reason forms part of a larger holistic philosophical outlook that bears on their thinking about the natural order and ethics. Their innovative conception of the self as a unified whole, one partly shared with the Epicureans, derives from this larger outlook. In challenging this monism, as a

[100] See esp. *Mor.* 441 F–442 C, also 443 C–D, 444 D–445 C, 452 B–D (cf. 443 C–D). See further text to nn. 110–12 below.

cosmic as well as psychological idea, Plutarch indicates that he recognizes that Stoic psychology forms part of a larger philosophical vision, even though the more narrowly focused argumentation in this essay tends to minimize this fact.

4.3 PLUTARCH'S PSYCHOLOGY

In considering Plutarch's competing view, I focus initially on the question of his intellectual position, and, especially, the way that he fuses Platonic and Aristotelian ideas. I then bring out several ways in which his treatment of these ideas reflects certain well-marked features of Hellenistic–Roman debate about emotions and psychology more generally. Finally, I consider certain more distinctive features of his thinking in this essay, including his ideas about psychological harmony and about the relationship between the norms of 'freedom from passion' and 'moderation of passion'.

Plutarch's philosophical position has been much discussed recently, and it is worth trying to state this in general terms, before considering *On Ethical Virtue* more specifically. In earlier scholarship, it was common to characterize thinkers such as Plutarch as 'eclectic', meaning that they simply selected different aspects of earlier theories without much regard to philosophical consistency. More recently, it has been stressed that most ancient thinkers regarded themselves as having a reasonably firm allegiance to one or other philosophical position or tradition. But what it meant to have a 'Platonic' or 'Peripatetic' position was a matter of continuing debate in antiquity; and this debate included the recognition of areas of common ground between different schools.[101] Plutarch regarded himself as a Platonist from an early stage in his life. But 'Platonism' is understood by Plutarch as sharing common ground with the Aristotelian position on, for instance, ethical psychology. Unlike some Platonists in his era,[102] Plutarch did not see Platonism as compatible with Stoic ideas, and is a largely consistent opponent of Stoicism.[103] One factor that

[101] A key study of this question is Dillon and Long (1988), especially Donini (1988) and Dillon (1988) on Plutarch. A striking example of (coherent) philosophical synthesis is that of Antiochus (see 3.4 above). In speaking of 'thinkers' here, I have in mind primarily those who were, in some sense, philosophers. How far this generalization extends beyond philosophical circles is more open to question; see further 7.4 below, esp. text to nn. 128–32.

[102] On Eudorus and Philo (both of Alexandria), two rather earlier thinkers who synthesize Platonic with Stoic (by contrast with Aristotelian) themes, see Dillon (1977), 123–5, 146–8, 151–2. Their views are of special relevance, since Plutarch's teacher Ammonius was also a Platonist from Alexandria (Dillon, 1977: 184–5, 189–92). On what 'Platonism' meant in this period, for thinkers such as Plutarch, see Boys-Stones (2001), ch. 6.

[103] But, for exceptions, see n. 129 below.

determines this stance is a pervasive dualism, in metaphysics as well as psychology, that puts Plutarch at odds with the unified world-view of Stoicism.[104]

The psychological model put forward in this essay by Plutarch, to counter the Stoic pattern, is presented as derived from Plato and Aristotle; and some features of Plutarch's essay are wholly recognizable from the Platonic dialogues and the surviving Aristotelian treatises.[105] From at least the late Hellenistic period (first century BC), and, certainly, in Plutarch's lifetime (*c.* AD 45–125), apparently by contrast with the early Hellenistic period, the school-texts of Aristotle were generally available and were, like the dialogues of Plato, becoming the objects of detailed commentary.[106] However, other aspects of Plutarch's essay, notably those relating to the ideas of the 'mean' and 'moderation of passion', while broadly Aristotelian, reflect a rather different way of thinking from that found in Aristotle's school-texts. There has been much recent debate about the intellectual influences on these latter aspects of the work. One factor is the reshaping of Aristotelian ideas to serve as a counterweight to the Stoic theory of the passions. Charting the history of this reshaping is not easy, given the complexity of the question and the inadequacy of our evidence; and there have been divergent interpretations of Plutarch's position. For instance, Pierluigi Donini sees Plutarch's approach as reflecting a well-established pattern of assimilation of Aristotelian ideas by Middle Platonism in the first and second centuries AD.[107] Francesco Becchi, on the other hand, argues that Plutarch draws on a more authentically Aristotelian tradition, though a tradition reshaped by the desire to oppose Stoic ethical psychology.[108] However, other scholars, especially Daniel Babut and Jan Opsomer, see in Plutarch's adaptation of the idea of the mean a more independent application of Platonic thinking to an originally Aristotelian concept. Babut and Opsomer also stress the importance of Plutarch's dualistic world-view, as a factor bearing on the significance attached to the mean, as well as on his larger response in this work to the Stoic theory of the passions.[109]

[104] See Babut (1969*b*), 298–301, 316–17; Dillon (1977), 199–208.

[105] Parallels to Plato and Aristotle are cited in the editions of Plutarch's essay by Helmbold (1970); Dumortier and Defradas (1975).

[106] See further M. Frede (1999*a*), 772–6, 784–5; Sedley (1997*b*); also n. 30 above and 213–14 above.

[107] Donini (1974), esp. 64–5, 80–1, (1986), esp. 214. Donini highlights the parallels with Alcinous' *Handbook* (trans. with commentary by Dillon 1993), ch. 24.

[108] For Becchi, the representatives of the more authentic Aristotelian tradition include Aspasius and (later) Alexander of Aphrodisias. Becchi sees in the Middle Platonic works (e.g. by Alcinous) cited by Donini a popularized and simplified Aristotelianism. See Becchi (1975), 180, (1978), 266, 275, (1981), 279–80. For a lucid summary of this debate, see Opsomer (1994), 33–6.

[109] See Babut (1969*b*), 298–301, 316–17, 321–33; Opsomer (1994); also, more briefly, Dillon (1977), 193–8. I am grateful to Alexei Zadorojnyi for guidance in charting Plutarchean scholarship.

In examining the significance of Plutarch's model for my enquiry, I focus first on the way the essay illustrates certain well-marked features of part-based thinking and then on certain more original features. In its general form, the ethical psychology offered by Plutarch as a counterweight to Stoicism is recognizable as a synthesis of Platonic and Aristotelian ideas. Like other Platonists in this period, Plutarch treats as unimportant the difference between Plato's (typically) tripartite model of the psyche and Aristotle's (typically) bipartite model.[110] The key point, for him, is that both these earlier thinkers treat as fundamental the contrast between distinct rational and non-rational (emotional or desiring) parts or functions of the psyche. Virtue, or more precisely ethical virtue, is defined in terms of the control of practical reason over the emotional part, a control which is exercised especially through the development, by habituation, of dispositions (*hexeis*) of 'character' (*ēthos*).[111] Virtue is also defined, in apparently Aristotelian language, as a 'mean' or 'moderate degree' in emotional response (*Mor.* 444 B–445 A). This bipartite model is alleged to explain the existence of degrees of virtuous cohesion or incoherence, such as 'self-control' or 'weakness of will' (*akrasia*), in ways that the Stoic monistic model cannot.[112]

Plutarch's discussion illustrates two well-marked points of contrast between Platonic–Aristotelian patterns of thinking and Stoic ones, although these are not central to his concerns in the essay. His account of 'character' (*ēthos*) presupposes the Platonic–Aristotelian pattern outlined earlier, according to which the development of virtue depends on the combination of nature (*phusis*), habit (*ethos*), and reason (*logos*). This pattern is set out in another essay of Plutarch's, *The Education of Children*, and it underlies Plutarch's thinking about the development of character in his biographies or *Lives*.[113] In *On Ethical Virtue*, Plutarch explicitly links the idea of ethical virtue (and its development) with that of the part-based psychological model. Ethical development depends on shaping the capacity (*dunamis*) for emotion through habituation (*ethos*) to the point where we acquire a stable disposition (*hexis*) which can be exercised in

[110] *Mor.* 442A–C, referring esp. to Pl. *Ti.* 69c–71d, *R.* 435b–442e, Arist. *NE* 1.13. On the Middle-Platonic tendency to conflate bipartite and tripartite psychology, see Vander Waerdt (1985), esp. 379–80; Dillon (1977), 194–5; on the possible influence of the doxographical tradition on this point, see Tieleman (2003), 76–8. As noted earlier, text to nn. 19–20 above, the bipartite–tripartite distinction is by no means a rigid one in Plato and Aristotle.

[111] Plu. *Mor.* 443 C–D, 443 E–444 D. See also Arist. *NE* 1.13, 2.1, 3, 5, 6, 3.3, 6.5; Pl. *R.* 395c–d, 401d–402a, *Lg.* 653a–c. See further on links between Plato and Aristotle on this subject, Gill (1996*b*), 247–60, 268–75.

[112] *Mor.* 445 B–E, 446 C–E; see also Arist. *NE* 1.13, 7.8–9; Pl. *Phdr.* 253c–e, 256a. On the latter point, see discussion below.

[113] *Mor.* 2A–B; see further 7.2 below, text to nn. 19–23.

combination with practical reason (*phronēsis*).[114] There is a clear contrast with the Stoic (and Epicurean) pattern according to which all human beings as such have the life-long capacity for developing complete virtue, although this contrast is not spelled out by Plutarch in this essay.

A second feature of the Platonic–Aristotelian pattern implied in Plutarch's essay relates to stability and coherence of character. The key point, already implied in Aristotle's theory, is that there can be stable, though defective, states of character as regards emotion and desire. Aristotle draws a distinction between these states (for instance, that of intemperance, *akolasia*) and the condition of internal conflict and inconsistency he calls *akrasia* (usually translated as 'weakness of will').[115] Plato's dialogues sometimes seem to imply a similar view; for instance, *Republic* Books 8–9 describe the development of what seem to be relatively stable and determinate—though also defective—character-types.[116] However, in Stoicism (as also Epicureanism), stress is laid on the idea that only the normative wise person is coherent and stable, and that the character and lives of non-wise people are marked by inconsistency and inner conflict.[117] Similarly, as I bring out later, in Stoicism, *all* states of passion are conceived as being, in effect, 'akratic' ones, a point linked with the belief that all human beings are constitutively capable of achieving full wisdom.[118] Plutarch's essay strongly endorses the Aristotelian framework, in particular the distinction between intemperance and *akrasia* ('weakness of will') which Stoicism implicitly rejects (*Mor.* 445 E , 446 C–D). Plutarch's reason for maintaining this distinction is not explicitly linked with the question of stability of character. His claim is that the Aristotelian distinctions, whose validity he assumes, are only intelligible if we explain them as different manifestations of the relationship between the rational and the irrational part of the psyche.[119] But it is clear from Plutarch's larger framework of thinking, in the *Lives* as well as the *Moral Essays*, that he does

[114] *Mor.* 443 C–D ; the pattern is strongly Aristotelian (see Aristotle references in n. 111 above). On the larger Platonic–Aristotelian pattern of development, see 3.2 above, text to nn. 21–37.

[115] See e.g. Arist. *NE* 7.8 (the contrast between self-indulgence and *akrasia*), also 1.13, 1102^{b}13–1103^{a}10, linking distinctions of this type with the part-based psychological model.

[116] See e.g. *R.* 550a4–b6, 553a–e, 559d–561e, 572c–573b.

[117] See 2.2 above, text to nn. 76–92, 2.3, text to nn. 209–39, 4.6 below, text to nn. 244–66. As explained in 5.2 below, text to nn. 121–35, this view is prefigured in Pl. *R.* 8–9, despite the initial impression given by this account. We also sometimes find a similar view in Aristotle: see e.g. *NE* 9.4, esp. 1166^{b}6–26, also *EE* 7.6, esp. 1240^{b}24–7 (see further Gill 1996*b*: 358–60).

[118] See 256–8 below.

[119] *Mor.* 445 B–E , 446 C–E . Plutarch goes on to consider a passage illustrating Stoic thinking about inner conflict (*Mor.* 446 E–447 C); but again his point centres on the explanatory power of the part-based model and not the contrast between Platonic–Aristotelian and Stoic ideas about stability of character.

think that there can be (at least relatively) stable but defective characters.[120] So his defence in *On Ethical Virtue* of an Aristotelian theme linked with this idea is an indication of a further important difference between the view he represents and the Stoic (and Epicurean) approach.

The third illustration of a well-known Aristotelian theme is more fully developed by Plutarch, and here the contrast with Stoic thought is more fully brought out. This is also a point on which we can see Plutarch reshaping and modifying earlier ideas in the light of current debate. This is Plutarch's presentation of the idea of the 'mean' (*meson*) and the related idea of 'moderation of passion' (*metriopatheia*). In Aristotle's ethical treatises, the idea of the mean is applied to actions as well as emotions. Essentially, the 'mean' signifies what is (objectively) appropriate or correct, given the ethical claims of the specific situation and the persons involved. As Aristotle points out, the requirement of appropriateness to specific persons and situations rules out an interpretation of the mean in purely arithmetic or quantitative terms.[121] In Plutarch, we find several, interconnected changes of emphases, which can be paralleled elsewhere in Hellenistic or Roman debate. The focus is almost entirely on emotion, rather than action; and the idea of appropriateness to specific circumstances is replaced by that of setting a limit to emotion as a source of motivational energy.[122] A dominant image is that of emotion as an impelling movement which, if not moderated, can become excessive, disordered, and can carry one away. Both the image and the terminology used are strongly evocative of Stoic thinking on passion. It seems clear that Aristotle's idea of the mean has been reconceived to provide an alternative to the Stoic analysis.[123] A related emphasis, which also marks a difference from Aristotle, lies in the idea that moderating, rather than 'extirpating', emotions is the right ethical strategy. We are told that 'reason does not wish to take away (*exairein*) emotion completely (that is neither possible nor an improvement)'; and that the aim is not 'freedom from emotions (*apatheias*), but proportion and moderation (or mean amounts) of emotions

[120] See 7.2 below, text to nn. 13–23, 43–9.

[121] Arist. *NE* 2.6, especially 1106^{a}26–^{b}7; also *EE* 2.3. See further Hursthouse (1980–1); Sherman (1989), 34–6, 123, 166–7; Gill (1996*b*), 71–3.

[122] Although *Mor.* 444 B is strongly reminiscent of Arist. *NE* 2.6, esp. 1106^{b}28–34 (including reference to 'everything that we *do*' and one, correct way of 'hitting the mark'), 444 B–D as a whole is centred on the idea of limiting emotion as a force. See also Annas (1993*b*), 61.

[123] See esp. *Mor.* 444 B: 'impulse (*hormē*) is produced through emotion (*pathos*) from character (*ēthos*), but it needs to be limited by reason (*logos*)'; 444 C: 'by limiting emotional movement (*pathētikē kinēsis*), reason implants ethical virtues in the emotional part'. For 'movement' as a key Stoic image for emotion, see LS 65 J(3, 7), P, and 268–9, 278 below; 'impulse' (*hormē*) is the standard Stoic term for motivation (e.g. LS 33 I).

(*summetrias pathōn kai mesotētas*)'.[124] A related theme is that emotion is a positive and necessary source of motivation towards virtue, especially important in ethical education, rather than being something that must be eradicated if virtue is to emerge.[125]

Several of the themes in Plutarch's discussion can be paralleled in other discussions of emotion in the period, for instance, Cicero's *Tusculans* and Seneca's *On Anger*, though both these authors support the Stoic side of the argument. We are told in these works that Aristotle advocates moderation of emotion, rather than that he advocates 'hitting the mean' in emotions as well as actions, as Aristotle's treatises suggest. Again, moderating emotions, rather than extirpating them, is presented by Cicero and Seneca as Aristotle's approach to the 'therapy' of emotions ('therapy' is not, in fact, an important idea in Aristotle's ethical treatises).[126] We are told that Aristotle regards anger as a necessary emotional stimulus for virtue, as distinct from the claim of the school-texts that 'good temper' is a virtue.[127] As in Plutarch, it seems clear that these writers, or the sources on which they draw, have reconceived Aristotelian ideas in a way that is designed to counter the influential Stoic approach to emotions, which has much in common with the Epicurean one.[128]

However, as is stressed by Babut and Opsomer, Plutarch's conception of the mean, and his conceptual framework in this essay, cannot be explained simply as the modification of Aristotelian ideas for an anti-Stoic programme.[129] His treatment, together with his anti-Stoic project, needs to be understood in the light of a dualist world-view, which builds on the kind of dualism sometimes found in Plato. After presenting the mean as the outcome of the moderation of emotion by reason (444 B–D), Plutarch analyses the sense of 'mean' that is involved. He rules out a number of possible senses: that of virtue as a

[124] *Mor.* 443 C and 451 C. On the advocacy of *metriopatheia*, not *apatheia*, see further Dillon (1983), esp. 512–15.

[125] *Mor.* 449 F, 451 D–452 A, esp. 451 D–E. The emotions are useful 'in standing by reasoning and intensifying (*sunteinonta*) the virtues: moderate anger (or spirit, *thumos*) does so for courage, hatred of bad does so for justice'. Here and in 449 F ('sinews', 'intensifying'), Plutarch seems again to be using Stoic terms for an anti-Stoic message; on 'sinews' and 'tension' as Stoic notions, see e.g. Gal. *PHP* 4.6.2–3, taken with Long (1996), 212–13.

[126] On the ideas of medicine and health in Aristotle's ethical treatises (which are different from Hellenistic–Roman ideas about therapy), see Nussbaum (1994), chs. 2–3.

[127] See e.g. Cic. *Tusc.* 3.22, 74; 4.39–46, esp. 43; Sen. *On Anger (Ira)* 1.7, 8.4–5, 9, 10.4, 11.1, 12.1–3, 14.1, 17.1. Contrast Arist. *NE* 2.6, 4.5. See further Graver (2002*b*), pp. xvii–xix.

[128] On Epicurean thinking on emotions, see 2.3 above, text to nn. 179–93 and 7.4 below, text to nn. 197–207.

[129] See references in n. 109 above. Plutarch's use of Aristotelian ideas is not always anti-Stoic; e.g. in *On Avoidance of Anger*, his use of such ideas brings him closer to Stoicism (see Kidd 1992: 171–3; Becchi 1990*a*).

compound of vices (as grey is a compound of white and black); or as an intermediate on the same scale as the vices (as eight is intermediate between four and twelve); or as being wholly separate from the emotional impulses that form the extremes.

But [virtue] is a mean ... in a sense like that which applies to musical sounds and harmonies. There the mean (*mesē*), a properly pitched note like the *nētē* or the *hupatē*,[130] avoids the sharpness of the one and the excessive heaviness of the other. Virtue is a movement (*kinēsis*) and capacity (*dunamis*) concerned with the irrational, which removes over-relaxed or over-strained impulse, and in general the excessive and the deficient, and puts each of the emotions into a moderate and faultless state. (*Mor.* 444 E–445 A)

Plutarch's analysis of the mean here diverges decisively from Aristotle.[131] In seeking to explain this account, it can be taken with another passage in which Plutarch uses Aristotelian vocabulary in a non-Aristotelian way. This comes at the very start of the essay, where Plutarch says of ethical virtue that 'it has emotion as its matter (*hulē*) and reason as its form (*eidos*)'. He couples this with the question whether the emotional part of the psyche has its own reason or is guided by that of another part (the latter is Plutarch's preferred answer).[132] In his definition of the mean in 444 E–445 A, Plutarch's point seems to be that, although the 'matter' of ethical virtue is emotion, virtue cannot be defined wholly in terms of emotion. Virtue as a mean is not to be understood as a compound of non-virtuous emotions, nor as intermediate between them, nor is virtue wholly distinct from emotion. Rather, it must be understood as the outcome of the process by which reason gives emotion its proper form, by implanting (as he puts it in 444 C–D) 'proportion and mean amounts of emotions'. Reason, then, 'informs' emotion by *harmonizing* it. In terms of the image of 444 E–445 A, it produces a kind of emotion (compared to a musical string or note) which is perfectly harmonized, avoiding the defects of strings which are too tightly or slackly strung. In a distinct but related discussion in *Platonic Questions* 9, Plutarch envisages reason as the mean (*mesē*) note harmonizing the other two notes: 'it slackens and tightens and generally makes [the other two notes] harmonious and concordant by

130 These three notes formed the basis of the Greek musical seven-note scale (heptachord); the *nētē* was the lowest in scale but highest in pitch, the *hupatē* was the highest in scale but lowest in pitch, the *mesē* intermediate (fourth out of seven); see further *OCD*, under 'Music' (A. D. Barker).

131 Aristotle defines virtue as a state (*hexis*), *NE* 1106^{b}36, and rules out the idea that it is a capacity (*dunamis*) or something in respect of which we are moved or affected (*kineisthai*), 1106^{a}4–9.

132 *Mor.* 440 D ; the former answer is that of the Stoics, Plutarch's target. On the Aristotelian form–matter distinction, see Arist. *Physics* 2.7.

removing the excess from either... for the moderate and commensurate are defined by a mean—or rather this is the purpose of the capacity of reason, to produce "means" in the emotions'.[133] In *On Ethical Virtue*, the characterization of virtue as a harmonic mean serves Plutarch's anti-Stoic objectives, because it presents virtue as, in essence, the outcome of a relationship between reason and emotion and not as a mode of reason. The stress on the idea of virtue as harmony and as a form of correct 'tension' takes on added point in this connection because those ideas were central ones for the Stoics too.[134] This definition can be taken together with a recurrent theme in the essay: that (ethical) virtue derives from the 'persuasion' of emotion by reason, a persuasion that can, at its best, produce 'harmony' between them.[135] A related theme is that both successful persuasion and failure presuppose that there are two distinct entities involved.[136]

From what source does Plutarch derive the idea of virtue as harmony, and what larger framework of thought does it reflect? Early in the essay, Plutarch links the idea of the harmonization of the irrational by reason with Pythagoras (441 D–E).[137] But he then proceeds to illustrate the part-based psychological model, with which the idea of virtue as harmony is linked, by reference to Plato's *Timaeus*.[138] The idea of virtue as a type of harmony and as dependent on reason's rule of the non-rational parts is prominent in Plato and is absolutely central to the *Republic*. A passage of special importance comes in *Republic* 4: the virtue of justice is described as an inner state in which the three parts of the psyche, like the three main notes on the scale (the *nētē*, *mesē*, and *hupatē*), are harmonized to each other.[139] The precise way to understand the musical image in *Republic* 4 is a problem taken up in Plutarch's *Platonic Questions* 9, noted earlier. After arguing for the correlation of the highest (*hupatē*) note with reason, the *mesē* with 'spirit', and the lowest (*nētē*) with appetite, Plutarch concludes by presenting reason as the *mesē*

133 *Mor.* 1009 A, trans. Cherniss (1976), slightly modified.

134 On virtue as harmony in Stoicism, see Long (1996), ch. 9, esp. 212–13 on tension; see *Mor.* 443 A and 1.4 above, text to nn. 110–14.

135 *Mor.* 441 E, 442 C, E–F (linked with the idea of harmony in 443 A), 445 B–E (including the idea of virtue as harmony in 445 C), 446 D–E.

136 See e.g. *Mor.* 445 B, 446 E.

137 Pythagoreanism was revived in the Hellenistic–Roman period and was taken up especially by the earlier Platonist, Eudorus; see Dillon (1977), 117–21, 126–9, and ch. 7. Pythagoras was sometimes treated as a kind of pre-founder of Platonism; see further Boys-Stones (2001), 118, 120.

138 *Mor.* 441 F –442 A, on the significance of this passage, see Opsomer (1994), and 228 above.

139 Pl. *R.* 443d–e; another prominent use of this image, and of the related one of 'tension', is in 410d–412a (*Mor.* 449 F refers to the idea of 'tension' in *R.* 411b). On 'harmony' in *R.*, see Gill (1985), 12–15, 21–4.

which harmonizes the other two notes (*Mor.* 1009 A, cited earlier). It seems reasonable to think that Plato's image of virtue as inner harmony, which is linked integrally with the Platonic part-based psychological model, is the key influence on Plutarch's specification of the mean as a harmonized middle string or note. As suggested earlier, a further factor may be the desire to reclaim an image (virtue as harmony or good tension) which had also been adopted by the Stoics. These two points are further linked in that the Stoics may well have been influenced by Plato in their adoption of this image, although they then interpreted it in the light of their monistic psychological model.[140] This may have motivated Plutarch to reclaim the image for the part-based psychological model he adopted, above all, from Plato.

Plutarch's use of the idea of virtue as a harmonic mean is, clearly, used to convey a dualistic model of the psyche, and, more generally, a dualistic world-view. There are, in fact, as sometimes in Plato (and Aristotle) two kinds of dualism involved. One is that between the rational and the non-rational parts of the psyche; the other is that between reason in its theoretical role, conceived as uniform, 'pure', and non-material, and reason as practical, conjoined with emotion in embodied human life.[141] The combination of dualism of this type and the idea of virtue as psychic harmony might seem paradoxical. The ideal of harmony might seem better associated with a more integrated psychological model, as it is in Stoicism, for instance.[142] The same point could be made about the combination of dualism and the ideal of *metriopatheia*, by contrast with *apatheia*. In Plato's *Phaedo*, for instance, dualism between psyche and body is linked with an ideal which is close to that of *apatheia*. The philosopher's liberation of the psyche from the body is seen as bringing with it a liberation from the emotions and desires which are derivative from the body.[143] It might seem that Plutarch's dualism should lead him in the same direction, though not towards the Stoic conception of *apatheia* as linked with psychological monism.

In fact, as shown especially by Babut, Plutarch displays, here and elsewhere a coherent combination of the ideals of *apatheia* and *metriopatheia*, and one that makes sense in terms of the kinds of dualism just noted. The combination comes out in this passage:

We must not say that every virtue involves a mean. Wisdom, which has no need of the irrational, is associated with the mind (*nous*) in a pure and emotionless (*apathē*) state,

[140] For this suggestion, see Long (1996), 214–15.

[141] On this contrast between practical and theoretical roles of reason, see, in Plutarch's essay, *Mor.* 443 E–444 D; in Pl. *R.* 518c–521b; Arist. *NE* 6.5, 7, 10.7–8.

[142] See text to n. 134 above.

[143] Pl. *Phd.* 66b–69c, 82e–84a. See also 1.2 above, text to nn. 6–7, and 2.2, text to nn. 67–75.

and is a self-sufficient extreme [or 'perfection', *akrotēs*] and capacity of reason . . . On the other hand, that virtue which is necessary because of the body and which needs . . . the service of the emotions as a kind of instrument for its practical aims, consists not in a destruction or negation of the irrational part of the psyche, but in an ordering and regulation [described earlier as the imposition 'not of freedom from emotions but proportion and mean amounts of emotions'].[144]

In other words, there are two ideals: *apatheia* for the mind as the vehicle of abstract thought and knowledge and *metriopatheia* for the body-based emotions as regulated by practical reason.[145] The combination is not incoherent; it reflects the combination of core-centred and part-based thinking outlined earlier in Plato and Aristotle (1.2 above). But it is substantively different from the Stoic idea of *apatheia* (or *eupatheia*), based on different assumptions about psychological (and psychophysical) unity.

Plutarch's essay, taken as a whole, represents a suggestive statement of the contrast between unitary and part-based conceptions of psychology, made from a strongly part-based, and sometimes core-centred, standpoint. It illustrates connections typical of that standpoint, for instance, between the ideal of 'moderation of passion' and the Aristotelian conception of 'character', understood in part-based terms. It also shows Plutarch developing some more distinctive themes within that approach, notably in the ideas of virtue as psychic harmony and *apatheia* ('freedom from passion') as a supplementary ideal. But Plutarch's rather generalized essay takes us only a certain distance in getting to grips with the Stoic theory of the passions and the issues that this raises for psychological debate in the first and second centuries AD. To make further progress with this topic, we need to examine our second ancient witness, Galen, who is both a more tenacious critic of the Stoic theory and an invaluable source for many of its most arresting ideas about human personality.

4.4 GALEN ON STOIC PSYCHOLOGY

The second ancient discussion of the Stoic theory of the passions examined here is that in Books 4 and 5 of Galen's *On the Doctrines of Hippocrates and Plato* (*PHP*). Like Plutarch, Galen contrasts Stoic monistic theory unfavour-

144 *Mor.* 444 C–D, also 443 C–D.

145 See also *Mor.* 440 D–E, 450 E–451 B; on *metriopatheia*, see text to nn. 124–5 above. See Babut (1969*b*), 321–33, esp. 330–3. Other passages on *apatheia* discussed by Babut in 322–3 include *Mor.* 165 C and 382 F.

ably with the part-based psychology of earlier Greek thinkers, especially Plato. Galen finds support for his view in—what he presents as—Posidonius' rejection of monistic psychology and his adoption of the Platonic tripartite model. Although Galen is a strong and polemical opponent of the Stoic account of the passions, his discussion is an indispensable source for this theory. In trying to bring out alleged self-contradictions in Stoic monism, and in examining (what he presents as) a major dispute between two leading Stoic theorists, Chrysippus and Posidonius, Galen provides a wealth of evidence not otherwise available. Like Plutarch's essay, Galen's discussion brings out how competing readings of Platonic philosophy became intertwined with debate about substantive issues in ethical psychology in later Greco-Roman thought.[146]

Several—though not all—recent scholarly accounts suggest that Galen's attack on the consistency and credibility of the orthodox (Chrysippean) Stoic theory is unjustified and that his evidence allows us to construct a more coherent picture.[147] I share this view. It is more normal to accept, in substance, Galen's claim that Posidonius rejected psychological monism and adopted Platonic tripartition. However, I follow the line taken by some recent treatments, that Galen's own evidence fails to bear out his analysis. I think that Posidonius' modification of orthodox Stoic monism was much less radical than Galen suggests, and that he used Platonic material—at most—to supplement Chrysippean psychology, rather than to undermine it.[148] This reassessment of the evidence of Galen provides the basis for the topic taken up in the next chapter, an attempt to reconstruct the significance of Platonic psychology for the early Stoics, notably Chrysippus. I think we can see how the Stoics may have seen the psychology of the *Timaeus* and *Republic* as, in certain key respects, prefiguring or supporting their conception of human psychology and the passions, rather than contradicting it, as Galen maintains.[149]

The underlying aim of my reconstruction of Stoic thinking and its relationship to Plato is to bring out in another way the salient characteristics of their theory, as I interpret these, especially the combination of psychophysical and psychological holism with Socratic ethical ideals. Thus, for instance, I will criticize Galen's assertion that there is a significant divergence between Zeno

[146] Galen (AD 129–*c*.210) wrote *PHP* 1–6 in AD 162–6; Chrysippus was head of the Stoic school in 232–*c*.206 BC; Posidonius lived in *c*.135–*c*.50 BC.

[147] See e.g. Gould (1970), 192–6; Inwood (1985), 140, 155–65, 172; Engberg-Pedersen (1990*b*), 182–93; Price (1995), 145–75; see esp. Tieleman (2003), chs. 3–4, 6. For a contrasting view, accepting in essence Galen's picture, Sorabji (2000), part 1.

[148] See Fillion-Lahille (1984); Cooper (1998*a*); Tieleman (2003), ch. 5.

[149] See Ch. 5 below.

and Chrysippus in their understanding of the kind of psychophysical state involved in passion; both thinkers, I suggest, conceive passion in similar (holistic, psychophysical) terms. I will also argue that the Stoic view of a passion as a state of internal conflict is consistent with their belief that people function as psychological wholes, in spite of Galen's claim that their thinking is incoherent on this point. Relevant to both features of Stoic thought is the combination of psychophysical and psychological holism with Socratic ethical ideas, notably the idea that only the wise person is *fully* coherent. This belief informs the Stoic idea that the inclinations of non-wise people towards one or other passion are only *relatively* stable and are more comparable to 'fevers' than consistent patterns of illness.[150]

As regards Posidonius, I am highly sceptical of Galen's claim that he abandoned (what I am calling) a 'holistic' view of human psychology in favour of a part-based account based on Plato. Although the evidence preserved by Galen suggests some modification of the Chrysippean theory, centring on the idea of passionate (or emotional) movements (*pathētikai kinēseis*), it is far from clear that this involves any significant breach with psychophysical or psychological holism. Posidonius' well-attested interest in certain aspects of Platonic thought, for instance about the early stages of human development, can be seen as reflecting the belief that, on certain points, Platonic thought prefigures (or can be assimilated to) Stoic thought.[151] Indeed, as already stressed in this study, Platonic—as well as Socratic—ideas seem to have contributed to the formulation of the Stoic holistic philosophical outlook from Zeno onwards.[152] So Posidonius' interest in Platonic thinking on development and psychology is less surprising than it might seem, though it is expressed in the form of detailed commentary on Plato's dialogues in a way that seems to be untypical of earlier Stoic thought.[153]

Why, on my view, is Galen such a misleading—though also crucial—source for the Stoic passions and for their psychology in general? More generally, why did Rome's most famous doctor in the mid-second century AD devote so much effort to challenging a theory formulated by Chrysippus in the third century BC, in part by reasserting the validity of the yet older Platonic account? A full answer to this question would be a large undertaking; indeed, modern scholarship is only now getting to grips with these and other interpretative and conceptual issues raised by the vast legacy

[150] See further 4.5 below, text to nn. 251–66.

[151] See 4.6 below, esp. text to nn. 366–88.

[152] See 1.1 above, text to nn. 41–68, 2.2, text to nn. 20–35.

[153] On the last point, see text to nn. 30–4 above.

of Galen's writings.[154] However, an outline reply can be offered, drawing on some important recent studies.[155] One relevant factor is Galen's extraordinary ambition not only to combine the roles of doctor and philosopher but also to synthesize the findings of medical research and experiment with key doctrines in the preceding Greek philosophical tradition, going back at least to Plato. Galen's *PHP* is a striking expression of this ambition. Books 1–3 are centred on the question of the location of the mind or governing-part (*hēgemonikon*), a question that had become central to psychological debate, and which is pursued further in Book 6. Books 4–5, marked as a digression, focus on the relationship between rational and non-rational parts. In both parts of the enquiry, Galen's attempted synthesis of medical and philosophical (especially Platonic) ideas is coupled with a sustained attack on the Stoic psychophysical and psychological model.[156]

Why does this project lead Galen into conflict with Stoicism? On some grounds, one might have expected Galen to form a positive view of their psychophysical and psychological holism. Heinrich von Staden suggests that, in many respects, Galen's thinking falls squarely within the same (broadly) naturalistic and physicalist approach to psychology that is shared by Epicureans, Stoics, and Hellenistic medical thinkers such as Herophilus and Erasistratus. As von Staden puts it:

> Fundamental to Galen's view of the body–soul relation are his views on humours, blendings or temperaments, capacities, bodily instruments, forms or parts of the soul, and the localization of various parts or forms or capacities of soul. The body is 'proximately composed' of the four humours (blood, black bile, yellow bile, and phlegm) whose proper blend is different in different parts of the body, so that the brain, the heart, and the liver, for example, each has its own proper blend.[157]

Also, despite his allegiance to Plato, Galen repeatedly refrains from passing judgement on general questions of psychology that are not amenable to his (broadly) empirical approach, such as the question whether any part of the psyche is non-material or immortal.[158] Indeed, in some contexts—though not *PHP*—Galen acknowledges points of similarity between his views and Stoic

[154] I plan to contribute to this process by a study centred on the relationship between Galenic and Stoic conceptions of human personality.

[155] For a helpful overall survey, including English translation of key texts, see Singer (1997*a*), esp. pp. viii–xviii; on Galen's method in general, see G. E. R. Lloyd (1996); Singer (1997*b*). On *PHP*, in particular, see Tieleman (1996), (2003). De Lacy's annotated translation of *PHP* (1978–84) is invaluable.

[156] See De Lacy (1978–84), i. 46–50; Tieleman (1996), pp. xxii–xxviii, (2003), 19–30. *PHP* 7–9, written later, deal with other areas of alleged agreement between Plato and Hippocrates. On Galen's psychology, see Hankinson (1991, 1993).

[157] See von Staden (2000), 106, transliterations in brackets omitted.

[158] See further von Staden (2000), 106.

ones. In an essay arguing for *The Soul's Dependence on the Body* (*QAM*), Galen cites the Stoics along with other thinkers in support of the idea that the psyche consists in a mixture or temperament (*krasis*) of the body.[159] Teun Tieleman points out that Galen at one point acknowledges his debt to Stoic thinking about physiology, regarding the idea that 'the four qualities [hot, cold, dry, wet] are specified in terms of the four humours, which are affected . . . by regimen.'[160] As von Staden underlines, we find in Galen (as well as in Stoicism and earlier medical writers) the contrast between 'natural' (purely organic) and 'psychic' functions, the latter subdivided into perceptive, motor, and 'hegemonic' activities, implying, arguably, that psychic functions constitute the more complex activities of a psychophysical whole.[161] Features such as this might have led Galen routinely to align himself with the Stoics (and Epicureans) as holding a unified, physicalist conception of human, or animal, psychology.

However, this is very much *not* what Galen actually does. Galen has two main grounds for his emphatic rejection of Stoic ideas, both of which derive in different ways from his objective of uniting medical science with Platonic thought, as he understands this. One reason, which is central to *PHP* 1–3, is the Stoics' failure to adopt the brain-centred picture of animal psychology which Galen took to have been established by medical research. The brain-centred nervous system had been discovered through human vivisection by two Alexandrian doctors, Herophilus and Erasistratus, in the third century BC. The Stoics adopted the idea, presupposed also by Herophilus and Erasistratus, that the body functions as a unified psychophysical system, and one in which *pneuma* (warm air or breath) is the main animating vehicle. But the Stoics failed to take up the idea that the brain is central to this system. Instead, they gave this role to the heart, in line with much earlier thought, particularly that of Praxagoras.[162] Galen is intensely critical of the Stoic heart-centred model. Galen maintained that his own experiments (on living animals and humans), as well as those of earlier doctors, had established beyond doubt the role of the brain as the focus of the nervous system and the seat of the *hēgemonikon*. He also argued that this brain-centred model was compatible with the Platonic tripar-

[159] Gal. *QAM* ch. 4, pp. 45.5–46.1 Marquardt *et al.* (1967) (= *SVF* 2.787), cited by Tieleman (2003), 149–50.

[160] *SVF* 1.132, 2.771, cited by Tieleman (2003), 153.

[161] See von Staden (2000), 107–11, who also notes that Galen sometimes combines this terminology with Platonic–Aristotelian psychic categories. On this distinction in Stoic thought, and its possible significance, see 1.4 above, text to nn. 113–17.

[162] See Annas (1992), 20–6, stressing the importance of the Stoics' adoption (by partial contrast with Aristotle, 17–20) of the idea of animal physiology as a centralized and unified system, with *pneuma* as the vehicle of communication. On the parallels (as well as differences) between the Stoic and medical models, see von Staden (2000), 87–105. The lifetimes of Herophilus, Erasistratus, and Chrysippus overlapped; von Staden (102–5) sees signs of possible influence on Stoicism from the medical writers, though not (obviously) on the location of the control-centre.

tite psyche, especially as presented in the *Timaeus*, in which the three functions (reasoning, spirit, and appetite) are located in three different parts of the body, the brain, heart, and liver. Galen further claimed that this view was anticipated in the Hippocratic Corpus, the earliest collection of Greek medical writings. On this basis, Galen argued that the Stoic unified, heart-centred psychophysical model was in conflict both with earlier medical and philosophical thought and with the results of experimental research.[163] In *PHP* 4–5, Galen confronted the related Stoic idea of psychological monism, arguing for the contrasting Platonic tripartite model, as he interpreted this. His grounds for criticism are examined later (4.5); but, in essence, Galen, like Plutarch, finds it simply incredible that (adult) human beings should be conceived as psychological wholes, whose functions, including emotions, are informed by rationality. He argues that the Stoic analysis of emotion, and psychic health and sickness, is riddled with self-contradiction, produced by the unavoidable acknowledgement of irrational parts in the psyche. Galen supposes that his part-based psychological picture is substantiated by medical or scientific research and that the Stoic unified psychological picture is vulnerable on this ground also, a theme developed in *PHP* Book 6.[164]

Problematic features of Galen's critique of Stoic psychological monism are drawn out in subsequent sections. I conclude these introductory comments on Galen's thinking by outlining certain related difficulties which have been identified in his arguments for the validity of his body-based tripartite psychological theory. These difficulties derive, in different ways, from Galen's assertion that three distinct locations in the body (brain, heart, and liver) operate as bases for separate sources of motivation. Tieleman questions whether this claim can, in fact, be supported, as Galen maintains, by reference to Platonic and Hippocratic sources. In Plato's *Timaeus*, Galen's main source, it is far from clear that heart and liver act as *independent* sources of motivation, as distinct from secondary or derivative agencies.[165] Tieleman also argues that, although Galen specifies some Hippocratic evidence for his claims that heart and liver were seen as origins for psychophysical activity, he fails to cite Hippocratic evidence supporting the location of the control-centre in the brain. Also, Galen does not succeed in showing that the Hippocratic texts reflect a *systematic* allocation of functions to parts in the way claimed.[166]

[163] See Hankinson (1991); Mansfeld (1991), 124–38; Tielemann (1996), pp. xxii–xxxvii.

[164] See Tieleman (2003), 19–39, including an outline of *PHP* Books 4–5 on 30–3. On the influence of doxography on Galen's thinking, see Tieleman (2003), ch. 2, esp. 61–5, 80–8. On Plutarch's analogous criticism of Stoic thinking, see 4.2 above, text to nn. 92–8.

[165] Tieleman (1996), pp. xxix–xxxi, referring to Pl. *Ti.* 70a–b, d–e (also 71a–d).

[166] Tieleman (1996), pp. xxii–xxxv, also noting that the *Placita*-tradition links Hippocrates with Plato as placing the control-centre in the brain. Tieleman acknowledges that G. E. R. Lloyd (1991), 398–416, takes a more positive view of the evidential base for Galen's claims about Hippocrates.

Jaap Mansfeld brings out a related, and still more damaging, problem in Galen's case. He argues that the logical outcome of Galen's experimentally based picture would be a highly unified psychological model, in which the motivation of action derives solely from the brain acting through the nervous system. The role which Galen allocates to the heart and liver, as seats of independent sources of motivation, cannot be squared, he claims, with Galen's own physiological picture.

> Because there are no motor nerves issuing from either the heart (the seat of anger, according to Galen) or the liver (the seat of desire, according to Galen), the two non-rational parts are in fact precluded from moving any muscle . . . it is reason, and reason alone, which makes the muscles move by means of the connecting nerves.[167]

Hence, the idea stressed by Galen that desire and anger can be 'stronger' than reason would need, for consistency with Galen's physiology, to be translated into the claim that reason supports desire and anger and so gives them the requisite strength of motivation. This is a view which, in fact, is much closer to the Stoic conception of psychic conflict, though this is not, of course, seen by them as conflict between psychic parts.[168] Galen argues that the (alleged) strength of anger and desire, acting in conflict with reason, runs counter to the Stoic unified psychophysical model. However, as Mansfeld points out, the Stoic unified model can be seen as a more logical outcome of previous medical research, including Galen's own experiments, than Galen's own tripartite model—apart from, of course, the Stoic positioning of the control-centre in the heart instead of the brain.[169] Although this issue is not pursued further here, these comments indicate that the physiological side of Galen's picture may give rise to analogous problems to those that emerge from study of his critique of the Stoic psychology of emotions.

4.5 GALEN ON CHRYSIPPUS

I now turn specifically to Chrysippus' theory of the passions; my aim is to use Galen's evidence to try to provide a more credible analysis of the theory than Galen himself offers. Tieleman (2003) makes the first systematic attempt to reconstruct Chrysippus' theory, in particular, his treatise *On the Passions* (*peri*

[167] Mansfeld (1991), 141.

[168] For the Stoic conception of psychic conflict, see 4.5 below, text to nn. 214–44.

[169] Mansfeld (1991), 138–45. On the interesting question how far *modern* scientific research might support a unified or part-based model, see Sorabji (2000), ch. 10, an issue I plan to pursue elsewhere.

pathōn), largely on the basis of a critical examination of Galen's evidence.[170] I summarize his main findings before focusing on three topics which are of special relevance to my larger theme. These topics consist in the question whether Zeno's thinking on passions differed significantly from that of Chrysippus, Chrysippus' ideas about passion and self-division, and his thinking about passionate quasi-dispositional states.[171] All three topics illustrate in different ways the combination of psychological and psychophysical holism with Socratic ideals that I am taking as characteristic of the idea of the structured self.

Chrysippus' (lost) treatise consisted of four books, of which the first three were, apparently, theoretical in character while the fourth ('therapeutic') book was more practical in orientation, though still firmly grounded in Stoic theory.[172] In Tieleman's reconstruction, the first book was centred on Chrysippus' elaboration of Zeno's analysis of passion (*pathos*), and the definition of the four basic passions (pleasure, appetite or desire, distress or grief, and fear) and subdivisions of these. Although the idea that passions are judgements was fundamental to both Zeno's and Chrysippus' versions of the theory, in Tieleman's view, both thinkers also stressed that passions constituted psychophysical reactions, such as contractions or expansions, correlated with judgements.[173] Book 2 seems to have consisted in discussion of 'problems' (*aporiai*), including the question of how to explain cases in which the two types of judgement associated with passion seem to come apart. A related topic was that of the source of the corruption of human judgements that leads to the generation of passions. We have no evidence for the contents of Book 3. The fourth ('therapeutic') book seems to have dealt with a range of topics, including the analogy between psychic and bodily health or sickness, weakness of character and the rejection of reason, passion as madness, and practical techniques of therapy of the passions.[174]

Books 4–5 of Galen's *PHP*, while not following the structure of Chrysippus' treatise on the passions, was explicitly designed as a sustained attack on its main theses. Book 4 focuses on the alleged inconsistencies and inadequacies

[170] Another important source, discussed in Tieleman (2003), ch. 6, is Cic. *Tusc.* 3–4, on which see also Graver (2002*a*).

[171] The discussion of the first topic is based on Gill (2005*a*), 453–4, and the second on Gill (1998*a*), 115–21.

[172] On the fourth book, see Tieleman (2003), ch. 4; on Stoic 'therapy', in general, see 3.5 above, text to nn. 336–9, 6.5 below, esp. text to nn. 245–66.

[173] On the issue of whether (as Galen claimed) these Stoic thinkers diverged significantly on this subject, see text to nn. 181–91 below.

[174] For an outline of topics, see Tieleman (2003), 325–6, based on the detailed analysis of chs. 3–4, and 6. The relevant sources are to be included in a new edition of the early Stoic fragments in progress at Utrecht University (revising *SVF*).

of Chrysippus' theory. The primary claim is that Chrysippus' unified or intellectualist psychology fails to provide a coherent explanation of the phenomena of passions and psychic weakness which Chrysippus himself presents as being in some sense irrational. Galen argues that there can be no convincing explanation of these phenomena by Chrysippus because he refuses to admit the presence of non-rational parts in the psyche, whereas (according to Galen) Posidonius did admit this. Book 5 develops this theme, focusing on purported incoherences and gaps in Chrysippus' use of the analogy between psychic and bodily health and beauty or proportion. Galen draws extensively on Posidonius' treatise on passions, maintaining that the later Stoic's treatment of themes such as childhood development and the question of the cause of passion constituted a radical critique of Chrysippus' analysis. Book 5 concludes by endorsing Plato's argument for distinct and independent psychic parts in *Republic* Book 4, a theme developed in Galen's comments on Plato's account of the embodied tripartite psyche in *PHP* Book 6.[175]

On the basis of his examination of the evidence for Chrysippus' treatise (and that of Posidonius), Tieleman offers an account which differs very markedly from Galen's.[176] In the first instance, he casts doubt on the claim that there were substantial differences in doctrine between Chrysippus, on the one hand, and Zeno or Posidonius, on the other. He also highlights at least two important features of Chrysippus' theory which Galen's treatment obscures. One is that Chrysippus' theory draws on the same causal analysis as his theory of determinism, namely that based on a combination of an antecedent (external) and a 'sustaining' cause (internal to the character of the agent). The judgement—more precisely, the two types of judgement—involved in passion represent a response based on the combination of how something 'appears' at the relevant time and the underlying character of the agent.[177] Chrysippus' definition of the nature of a passion and his therapeutic method reflect his view that both types of factors need to be borne in mind. The same point applies to his diagnosis of the problems recognized in Book 2 of the treatise—together with the analysis or solution of these problems, which Galen largely ignores.[178] A second and related factor is the physicalism (in my terms,

[175] For an outline analysis of Gal. *PHP* 4–5, see Tieleman (2003), 30–3, and on Galen's methods of interpretation, see Tieleman,19–60.

[176] See Tieleman (2003), 321–4, setting out his main conclusions.

[177] See Tieleman (2003), 108–13; on this causal analysis in connection with determinism, see 197–8 above. The two types of judgement (an innovation of Chrysippus) are 1. that something good or bad is present and 2. that it is appropriate to react in a certain way; see Tieleman (2003), 124–5; Sorabji (2000), 29–34. The use of the idea of 'character' in this connection needs to be qualified by Chrysippus' stress on the unstable quality of non-wise dispositions (Tieleman, 104–7, and 261–4 below).

[178] See Tieleman (2003), 122–32.

psychophysical holism) which Chrysippus, like other Stoics, applies to this subject. This physicalism underlies the understanding of passion as an occurrent or transient phenomenon and also of the longer term character-state. It also informs the analogy between psychic and physical health, which is, therefore, not to be seen as merely metaphorical.[179] Hence, Tieleman maintains, Galen's charge that Chrysippus' theory is narrowly rationalistic, and incapable of explaining the powerful and complex phenomena of emotional experience, is shown up as deeply misleading.

Tieleman's claims are radical and far-reaching, and are likely to generate continuing debate. But they are based on the most detailed and systematic examination of Galen's evidence and methods so far attempted, and they seem to me, in general, highly convincing. I concentrate on three specific questions raised by Galen's account of Chrysippus' theory. When these features of Chrysippus' theory are reclaimed from Galen's critical treatment (in the way suggested by Tieleman and some other scholars),[180] they can be seen as reflecting the characteristically Stoic combination of psychophysical and psychological holism with Socratic ideals. The first is the question whether there was a substantive difference between the definitions of emotions or passions offered by Zeno and Chrysippus. Galen repeatedly claims that there was such a difference: 'Chrysippus thought that the emotions *actually were* the judgements... whereas Zeno and many other Stoics thought the emotions occurred on the occasion of (*epi*) judgements, but (in the case of distress and pleasure at least) *actually were* the contractions and expansions'. Richard Sorabji, whose report of Galen's claims I have just cited, accepts that the difference was real and important;[181] but is he right to follow Galen on this point? Sorabji himself refers also to evidence that Zeno presented the reactions as based on judgements and that Chrysippus thought that emotional judgements were normally followed by reactions.[182] Can we be sure that the Stoics themselves saw the issue as being whether emotions were *either* judgements *or* (resulting) psychophysical reactions, as Galen maintains?[183]

179 See Tieleman (2003), 109–12, 146–66, 186–97.

180 See references in n. 147 above.

181 Sorabji (2000), 34–6, esp. 34, cited, with added italics, referring to Gal. *PHP* 4.2.5–6, 4.3.1–2, 5.1.4, pp. 240, 246, 248, 292. On conventions for referring to Gal. *PHP*, see xi above.

182 Sorabji (2000), 34–5, referring to Cic. *Tusc.* 3.75, Gal *PHP* 4.7.2–3; Sorabji, 36, referring to Gal. *PHP* 4.7.13–14.

183 Sorabji (2000), 35, argues that, unless we accept that Chrysippus redefined emotions as judgements, we cannot explain what is distinctive about the innovation (e.g. in Sen. *Ira* 2.2–4) of *pre*-emotions ('first movements'), since these will be indistinguishable from Zeno's reactive emotions. But to say this is to accept a misleading dichotomy: *either* judgements *or* reactions. If both Zeno and Chrysippus see emotions as judgement-based reactions (see discussion below), 'first movements' prior to judgements are still different from emotions. On pre-emotions, see 4.6 below, text to nn. 336–40.

In a recent study of this question, A. W. Price stresses, as I have done here, the integrated or holistic thinking underlying the Stoic account of emotion.[184] Although the Stoic analysis of emotion refers to the four key elements in their theory of human action (rational impression, assent, impulse, action), the salient point is that emotion is the outcome of the *combination* of these elements. This comes out in a wide range of ancient evidence for the theory, including the definitions of pseudo-Andronicus, in which emotions are characterized equally as the reaction (for instance, the contraction) or the judgement.[185] These two aspects are further linked in that the relevant judgement is that it is appropriate to react in the way that is actually occurring at the time. As Price puts it, 'distress and pleasure contain an internal cross-reference: distress is opinion-cum-contraction, pleasure opinion-cum-swelling, with the opinion prescribing the very movement that realizes it'. Price also suggests that there was only 'a fine point of divergence' between the two Stoic thinkers.: 'Zeno might have identified emotions with causal complexes wherein contractions and the like follow upon opinions, whereas Chrysippus might have thought that opinion of a kind constitutes emotion even before it causes (even if it always *does* cause) contraction or the like'.[186] The difference is, at most, one of emphasis rather than doctrine. For both Stoic thinkers, the emotion is also understood in physical terms: 'they invite us to analyse emotion as a psychophysical union of intentionality and physiology, while emphasizing that it is psychic assent that forms the locus of the subject's responsibility for his own emotions'.[187] On this view, which I share, the account of emotion demonstrates, strikingly, the combination of psychophysical and psychological holism I am presenting as characteristic of Stoic theory, in a way that differs only marginally between the two Stoic thinkers.

But, if this view is correct, why does Galen underline the contrast between Zeno and Chrysippus as he does, and should we not take this seriously, given that Galen had access to evidence now lost? Galen's claim forms part of his

[184] Price (2005); the remainder of this paragraph is based on Gill (2005*a*), 453–4.

[185] Andronicus, *On Passions* 1 (SVF 3.391 = LS 65B), e.g. 'Distress is an irrational contraction, or a fresh opinion that something bad is present, at which people think it right to be contracted'. Price stresses that the 'or' should not be seen as disjunctive; belief and contraction are interdependent and inseparable aspects of the same phenomenon of emotion. See also Gal. *PHP* 4.2.1–7, taken with Tieleman (2003), 119–22.

[186] Price (2005), 475, 473–4. Price also notes that we are told that Chrysippus thinks that the impulse is 'towards' (*epi* plus accusative) the contraction, while Zeno holds that emotions 'follow' or 'supervene on' (*epi* plus dative) judgements, Gal. *PHP* 4.7.14, 4.1.17. Thus, both thinkers, in slightly different ways, stress the integral linkage between belief and reaction.

[187] Price (2005), 475. On the psychophysical monism underlying the theory, see also Graver (2002*b*), 229. See also, denying a fundamental difference between Zeno and Chrysippus, Inwood (1985), 130–1; Inwood and Donini (1999), 699.

general project of driving a wedge between Chrysippus' psychological monism and the ideas of 'the ancients', which Galen endorses. 'The ancients' (*hoi palaioi*), for Galen, typically signify Hippocrates, Plato, and Aristotle (interpreted as sharing core ideas); but Galen sometimes recruits the earlier Stoic thinkers, Zeno or Cleanthes, in an effort to show that Chrysippean psychological monism is isolated and extreme.[188] So the motivation for Galen's assertion of this difference is not hard to see. But is the evidential support for the distinction well grounded? As Tieleman brings out, there is reason to doubt this. In one, rather full, passage where Galen, drawing on Posidonius' *On Passions*, examines Chrysippus' response to Zeno's definition of distress, the only significant change is the addition of the word 'fresh' to Zeno's definition as 'an opinion (or "judgement", *doxa*) that one is in the presence of something bad'.[189] In another passage, Galen, startlingly, presents it as an open question which view, exactly, Zeno holds on this subject, though elsewhere he makes quite definite statements about this.[190] He excuses himself from examining the point further by saying that he has decided to concentrate in *PHP* on the treatises of Chrysippus and Posidonius on passions. Given Galen's usual practice in commentary, as far as we can establish this, it seems quite possible that Galen has not actually consulted Zeno's book on passions at all, but is relying on inferences from statements about Zeno's view made by Chrysippus and Posidonius, inferences that are not clearly justified by any passage he cites.[191] It seems, then, that Galen's claim about the divergences between Zeno and Chrysippus derives from his polemical standpoint and his assumptions about the validity of part-based psychology, rather than from a securely based account of the differences between the two Stoic thinkers.

Second,[192] I focus on two, related, criticisms by Galen of Chrysippean thinking. One is that Chrysippus fails to give a clear or consistent account of the kind of irrationality involved in a passion. The other is that Chrysippus' analysis of passion involves reference to a type of self-division which his unified psychological model cannot accommodate. In the case of both criticisms, I think that Galen's own evidence, taken with other evidence for Stoic

[188] See Tieleman (2003), 40, 285, 295; see e.g. Gal. *PHP* 4.2.1, 4.3.1–2, 5.6.40–3. On the tendency in philosophy of this period to cite the authority of ancient wisdom in support of current positions, see text to n. 30 above.

[189] Gal. *PHP* 4.7.1–5, esp. 3 (cited in my translation); see Tieleman (2003), 115–18.

[190] Gal. *PHP* 5.40–6; more precisely, he says that, whichever view Zeno held (Chrysippean, Platonic, or intermediate), it does not require separate refutation. Contrast his comments in passages listed in n. 188 above.

[191] See Tieleman (2003), 85–6; and, on Galen's highly selective method of commentary, Tieleman, 48–9. We learn from Epict. *Diss.* 1.20.15, 4.9.6 that Zeno's treatises were still available for consultation in the 2nd c. AD.

[192] Discussion of this second topic is based on Gill (1998*a*), 115–21.

theory, allows us to recognize that the Stoic theory is both coherent and intelligible. I discuss this question at some length, because Galen's criticisms are potentially damaging. However, when more fully explained, I think this topic shows how Stoic holism could provide a psychologically powerful form of explanation for complex and seemingly paradoxical types of emotional state. Also, I think Chrysippus' treatment, especially his use of the example of Medea, may well have had an important reception in subsequent Roman poetry as well as in Epictetus' *Discourses*.[193]

Galen claims that Chrysippus' use of the notion of 'irrationality' is incoherent. This criticism is directed at passages such as the following, which Galen quotes from Chrysippus:

> Therefore some people say not inappropriately that a passion [*pathos*] of the psyche is a movement contrary to nature, as in fear and desire and the like. For all such movements and states are disobedient to reason and reject it; accordingly we say that such persons are moved irrationally [*alogōs*], not in the sense of reasoning poorly, as one might speak of someone who reasons the opposite of well, but in the sense of rejecting reason [*tou logou apostrophēn*].[194]

Galen suggests that in such passages Chrysippus is drawing a distinction between a passion and other kinds of ethical error or mistake (*hamartēma*).[195] But he argues that Chrysippus is unable to provide a proper account of this distinction. Galen claims that there are two—and only two—possible senses of 'irrational' (*alogon*) in Greek. These senses involve: (1) the defective use (*kakōsis*) of rationality or (2) the complete absence (*sterēsis*) of rationality. He applies this distinction to Chrysippus' (alleged) contrast between a passion and a mistake. He argues that, if an ethical mistake constitutes defective reason, the only sense available for 'passion' is that of the complete absence of reason. However, as he points out, this sense is ruled out by Chrysippus' central claim that passions (which occur only in adult humans) are judgements (*kriseis*), and that they do not arise in an irrational (*alogon*) part of the psyche because there is no such part. He criticizes on similar grounds Chrysippus' statement that people in passionate states are moved irrationally, that is, 'without reason and judgement' (*aneu logou kai kriseōs*). He concludes that Chrysippus neither provides a secure distinction between ethical mistake

[193] On Epictetus, see text to nn. 202–5 below; on the poetic reception, see Ch. 7 below, esp. 7.3.

[194] Gal. *PHP* 4.4.16–17, p. 254, 13–19, De Lacy trans. slightly modified.

[195] Is this distinction Galen's (see Hankinson 1993: 189–90, 192–7) but used to analyse Chrysippean theory, or is it also drawn by Chrysippus? It seems likely that Galen is analysing in these terms a contrast drawn more informally by Chrysippus: see *PHP* 4.2.12, p. 240, 26–7 (discussed by Galen in 4.2.24–7), 4.4.17, p. 254, 17–19 (discussed by Galen in 4.4.23).

and passion nor a consistent statement of the kind of irrationality involved in a passion.[196]

Can we make better sense of Chrysippus' characterization of a passion? One way of doing so, which I have deployed elsewhere, is to draw a distinction between 'functional' and 'normative' senses of rationality.[197] In this way, we can restate Chrysippus' claim as being that a passion is rational in a functional but not a normative sense. We can see this claim, and the implied distinction, implied in another Chrysippean passage cited by Galen: 'the rational animal is by nature such as to follow reason and to act with reason as his guide. But often he moves in another way towards some things and away from some things in disobedience to reason when he is pushed too much'.[198] Like other functions of adult human psychology, passions involve rationality. Specifically, as *hormai* (impulses or conations), they depend on assent (*sunkatathesis*) to impressions (*phantasiai*), which are rational in the sense that their content can be expressed verbally by the adult herself. A key point in Chrysippus' theory is that the impulse is triggered by assent to the content of the impression, more specifically, to the recognition that something is or is not beneficial.[199] Hence, in passages cited by Galen, Chrysippus can describe the passion of distress (*lupē*) equally as 'a fresh belief that evil is present' and as 'a shrinking before what is thought to be a thing to avoid'. The first formulation expresses the content of the impression, and the second the resulting impulse, which, in the case of a passion, brings with it intense psychophysical reactions.[200] The fact that a passion is a function of a distinctively rational animal (an adult human) is conveyed, as Galen recognizes, by the idea that it constitutes a 'rejection of reason', a formulation considered more fully shortly.[201]

For Chrysippus, a passion is 'irrational', or 'unreasonable', in a normative sense in at least two ways. First, the beliefs which underlie the passion are not

[196] See *PHP* 4.4.9–23, p. 252, 20–p. 256, 6; also 4.2.19–27, p. 242, 12–p. 244, 9; 4.3.5–6, p. 250, 27–252, 5; 4.5.16–17, p. 262, 15–23.

[197] For the application of this distinction to the Stoic theory of passions, see Gill (1998*a*), 114, 116–17; also, more generally, Gill (1996*b*), 180, 228, 248–52, 296–7. See further discussion of this distinction below.

[198] *PHP* 4.2.10–11, p. 240, 19–21. Stob. 2.88.8–90.6 (= LS 65 A) seems also to be trying to define this combination of functional rationality and normative irrationality (see esp. 2.89.4–5, 16–18, LS 65 A(6–7)); see further Inwood (1985), 143.

[199] See 2.2 above, text to nn. 10–13, and 3.2, text to nn. 47–75.

[200] *PHP* 4.2.1, p. 238, 27–8; 4.2.5, p. 240, 3–4. Thus, the most comprehensive form of definition of distress seems to be 'an irrational contraction, or a fresh opinion that something bad is present, at which people think it right to be contracted [i.e. depressed]' (LS 65 B(1)). See further text to nn. 185–6 above.

[201] See e.g. *PHP* 4.2.11–12, p. 240, 21, 23; 4.4.17, p. 254, 16–17; also Galen's discussion in 4.2.21–3, 4.4.6.

those which a perfectly reasonable or wise person would hold. As is clear from the passages cited by Galen to illustrate the alleged distinction between 'passion' and 'mistake', the problem is not that the person engages in defective reasoning. Epictetus underlines this point, referring to one of Chrysippus' favourite examples of passion, Euripides' Medea (especially *Medea* 1078–81). Medea's anger derives from the fact that she regards 'taking vengeance on her husband... as more advantageous [*sumphorōteron*] than saving the lives of her children'. She assents, consistently, to her impression (that it is right to take revenge on my husband, even if this involves the death of my children). The irrationality inheres in the defectiveness, or falsity, of the beliefs that underlie this impression (which Epictetus calls 'preconceptions', *prolēpseis*).[202] The crucial type of falsity underlying a *pathos* is that of mistaking preferable indifferents such as health, wealth, or social position for goods.[203] In this case, we have the further mistake of taking retaliation to be preferable, or rather, as Medea thinks, good and choiceworthy even at the cost of the life of her children. It is the 'fresh' (that is, still vivid and powerful) application, in a specific case, of a false belief of this kind that constitutes one part of the irrationality in a passion.[204] The other part is that, even if the person concerned recognizes the (normatively) irrational character of her passion, she is unable to correct this. Like running legs (an image repeatedly used by Chrysippus), the passionate impulse, though generated through logically sound assent to an impression which is based on the agent's underlying beliefs, is now outside the person's control.[205]

So, by applying the distinction between functional and normative senses of reason, it is possible to show that Chrysippus' conception of passion is coherent in ways not recognized by Galen. It is a further, and more difficult, matter to determine whether Galen is trying to make sense of a theory he does not really understand or is trying to subvert a theory which he grasps but with which he is in profound disagreement.[206] However, the use of this distinction in connection with Greco–Roman thought may seem problematic in ways that have been underlined by Michael Frede. Frede maintains that, while the

[202] Epict. *Diss.* 1.28, esp. 7–10, 28; see further Long (1996), 277–80, (2002), 76–7. On Chrysippus' references to Euripides *Medea*, see further below. This account of the irrationality of a passion reflects the fact, pointed out by Brennan (1998), 47–51, that, although a passion is sometimes described in Stoic sources as a false belief, this is not made part of the formal definition. It is the underlying or dispositional belief that is false, not the ocurrent belief contained in the impression.

[203] See further Brennan (1998), 30–3; Engberg-Pedersen (1990*b*), 184–6.

[204] On the significance of 'fresh', i.e. not just recent but still effective in producing an impulse (more precisely, the belief 'that it is appropriate to have an impulse'), see Inwood (1985), 146–55.

[205] See e.g. *PHP* 4.2.14–18, 27; 4.6.35; also text to nn. 55–61 below.

[206] The argument often has an aggressive, point-scoring tone, which suggests the latter attitude. See e.g. 4.4.1–6. See further Hankinson (1991), 209–18; Cooper (1998*a*), 103 n. 20; the analyses of Tieleman (1996, 2003) suggest the second alternative.

Stoics, together with Socrates, Plato, and Aristotle, use 'reason' in—what moderns see as—different senses, it is an essential part of their thinking that reason constitutes a single, though complex, entity. Although reason is used to signify a set of functions or capacities, a form of knowledge, a mode of desire, and a normative state, these are not normally marked as different senses by these Greek thinkers. Indeed, their arguments often depend on taking reason in at least two of these senses at any one time and on giving reason a weight which derives from this assumption. As Frede puts it:

> [These Greek thinkers assume that] reason has the function to guide us in our lives, a function which it can exercise because it is a cognitive capacity which provides us with the necessary knowledge about the world, but also the ability to recognize what is good and to move us towards it. [Two key aspects of this notion are] the assumption that [reason confers] a basic knowledge about the world, and the assumption that reason has its own desires.[207]

Frede's point, restated, is that, in these ancient thinkers, reason never has a *purely* functional sense, because it is always conceived as having normative weight. This normative weight is not something that is given arbitrarily to the notion of reason, but which derives from its objective character as a complex but integrated entity. Thus there is, on the face of it, a problem in using the contrast between functional and normative senses of reason in connection with ancient thought, at least if this contrast is intended to correspond to distinctions drawn within ancient thinking itself.[208]

In the case of Stoic thought, there is the further point that reason is not a single function but a connected set of capacities, which informs all the psychological functions of an adult human, including those normally classed as emotions and desires.[209] To put the thought more broadly, the significance of reason in Stoicism, like that of virtue and good, needs to be located within the holistic outlook that is characteristic of this theory. Reason is not, as it often is in Plato or Aristotle, a distinct part or independent source of motivation, albeit one that, as Frede points out, is also taken to have normative status.[210] Reason, is, on the one hand, the highest manifestation of tension, which constitutes objects, including animals, as stable and structured

[207] M. Frede (1996), 17; also 5–19; on contrasting, post-Classical, especially Christian, conceptions of 'reason', see Frede, 25–8. Another obvious contrast is with Hume's belief that 'Reason is, and ought only to be the slave of the passions', *Treatise* 2.3.3, para. 4, Norton and Norton (2001), p. 266. That is, reason is purely an instrumental function and not a source of motivation or bearer of normative status in its own right.

[208] This contrast can, none the less, be a useful way *for us* to unpack senses that we recognize are integrated in ancient thought; this is, broadly, how the contrast is used in Gill (1996*b*), 248–52.

[209] See 3.2 above, text to nn. 55–61.

[210] On 'core-centred' thinking in Plato and Aristotle, see 1.2 above.

entities. In another sense, reason, along with structure, order, and wholeness, is a salient mark of goodness, in the areas of reality grasped by the interlocking branches of knowledge—logic, ethics, and physics.[211] These features of Stoicism render even more complex the understanding of what reason means in the theory. But these features also suggest a way of restating the point made earlier. Instead of saying that non-wise adults have reason in a functional but not normative sense, we can say that they have reason (in all its senses) but in an inchoate and incomplete way. In particular, reason in non-wise people does not have the cohesion, structure, and wholeness that it has in a perfect, wise person. In non-wise people, as indicated earlier, passions involve reason in that they depend on beliefs and reasoning. Also, the formation of a set of beliefs and the drawing of inferences from these beliefs constitutes part of the process of building up the kind of system or structure that the Stoics conceive as reason. But non-wise people do not have the *kind of* beliefs that are characteristic of wise people, nor do their sets of beliefs and their other rational capacities have the *kind of* consistency and coherence that is characteristic of wise people.[212] In other words, the fact that such people are not to be considered as having reason in a normative sense is a product of the fact that their rational functions operate in a relatively undeveloped and unstructured way.

A corollary of this line of thought is the belief that only wise people have a fully stable and coherent character, whereas non-wise people are marked by fluctuations of attitude and mood and by internal incoherence. This is one of the 'Socratic' ideas that, I have argued, are typically combined with psychological holism in both Stoicism and Epicureanism.[213] Chrysippus' comments on this theme are a second major target of Galen's criticisms; and, again, close scrutiny of Galen's criticisms can help us to see the rationale of Stoic thinking. Galen highlights the apparent paradox that, in spite of his psychological monism, Chrysippus presents passions as involving certain kinds of inner pressure and conflict. He does so partly by repeatedly describing people in passions as 'pushed' (*ōtheisthai*) and 'moved' (*pheresthai*); as 'not in control of themselves' (*akrateis*); and as 'not in their right minds' (literally 'in themselves', *en hautois*).[214] Also, perhaps surprisingly, Chrysippus seems to have given special attention to cases which, apparently, involve conflict between beliefs and emotions, such as involuntary crying and the fading of grief over

[211] See further 1.4 above, text to nn. 111–14, 3.3, text to nn. 93–103, 172–9.

[212] On the development of reason, see 3.2 above, text to nn. 55–62 and on the coherence of the state of mind and character of the wise, 3.3 above, text to nn. 113–25.

[213] See 2.2 above, text to nn. 76–92, 2.3, text to nn. 210–22.

[214] See e.g. *PHP* 4.2.11–12, p. 240, 20–1, 25; 4.4.24, p. 256, 7–9; 4.6.24–6.

time, although the belief in the sadness of bereavement remains.[215] Even more striking is his interest in two other, related types of situation. One is that of people who acknowledge the 'irrational' character of their feelings but who, perversely, persist in them.[216] The other is that of people who are so 'carried away' by their passion that they cannot stop their 'running legs', even though they now recognize the unreasonable nature of their state. Euripides' Medea seems to have been Chrysippus' prime example of this state, and Galen gives this summary of Chrysippus' view of her state of mind:

> Medea, on the other hand, was not persuaded by any reasoning to kill her children; quite the contrary, so far as reasoning goes, she says that she understands how bad the acts are that she is about to perform, but her anger is stronger than her deliberations; that is, her passion [*pathos*] has not been made to submit and does not follow reason as it would a master, but throws off the reins and disobeys the command.[217]

Medea seems to have been of special interest to Chrysippus because she served as a striking illustration of the idea of passion as the 'disobedience' or 'rejection' of reason. Although it is clear that Chrysippus did not think that all types of passion exhibited this degree of conscious disobedience, it is significant that this case was a key example for his theory.[218]

Galen argues that the kinds of inner conflict that Chrysippus recognizes are only intelligible on the assumption that there is at least one non-rational part in the psyche; and that the relationship between these—fundamentally distinct—parts is, typically, that of a struggle for power.[219] This comes out in Galen's competing analysis of Medea's inner struggle in the monologue of Euripides' *Medea* (1021–80):

> She knew what an unholy and terrible thing she was doing, when she set out to kill her children, and therefore she hesitated... Then anger dragged her again to the children by force, like some disobedient horse that has overpowered the charioteer; then reason in turn drew her back and led her away, then anger again exerted an opposite pull, and then again reason. Consequently, being repeatedly driven up and down by the two of them, when she has yielded to anger [she says]:

[215] *PHP* 4 7.12–19; see further 4.6 below, text to no. 320–6. Tieleman (2003), 122–32, sees these as among the 'problems' (*aporiai*) Chrysippus tackled, and aimed to resolve, in Book 2 of *On Passions.*

[216] Thus, we hear 'lovers and ... angry persons [say] that they want to gratify their anger and to let them be, whether it is better [*ameinon*] or not', *PHP* 4.6.27, p. 274, 35–7, also 4.6.38–42.

[217] *PHP* 4.2.27, De Lacy trans. slightly modified; also 4.6.19–22, referring to Eur. *Med.* 1078–80. On the term translated 'throws off the reins' (*aphēniazein*), see 4.6 below, text to nn. 383–4 See further Gill (1983*a*), and (1996*b*), 227–32.

[218] For (partly contrasting) cases of 'blind' anger or inarticulate love, see *PHP* 4.6.43–6, 4.6.9, 19; for the idea of 'rejection' of reason see e.g. 4.2.10–12, 17, 27.

[219] See e.g. *PHP* 4.2.28–44, 4.4.35–7, 4.5.3–18; also Galen's summary of Platonic psychology, 5.7.12–25, 5.7.74–82. See further Mansfeld (1991), 133–5.

'I understand the evils I am going to do,
but anger prevails over my counsels' [*Med.* 1078–9].[220]

Galen contrasts the process described with an inner dialogue presented in Homer, *Odyssey* 20 (18–21), which Plato notes in connection with psychic division: 'she says that her anger overpowers her reason, and therefore she is forcibly led by anger to do the deed, quite the opposite of Odysseus, who checked his anger with reason.'[221] Galen's view is that we can only make sense of such cases of inner conflict by adopting Plato's tripartite model of the psyche (reason, spirit, and appetite), as he interprets this, namely as involving power-relationships between fundamentally distinct parts.[222] Galen claims that Posidonius held the same view, and that he rejected Chrysippus' theory on these grounds, a claim challenged shortly (4.6 below). None the less, it may seem that, in this respect, Galen identifies an important issue raised by Chrysippus' theory: is Chrysippus' account of psychic conflict consistent with his monistic psychology? One might argue that, on this point, Chrysippus' theory overreaches its powers of explanation;[223] and that the subsequent modifications of the theory by Posidonius and Seneca need to be understood on this assumption.[224]

However, this is not the only conclusion we can draw. I think that the inner conflict described by Chrysippus is fully intelligible in the light of his theory. Chrysippus' discussion of inner conflict is sometimes considered as a contribution to debate about the nature of *akrasia* (acting and feeling against one's own better judgement), a debate whose agenda is defined, above all, by Aristotle.[225] This is, to a degree at least, a reasonable way to locate the theory;[226] but we need also to underline the paradox that, for Chrysippus, in sharp contrast to Aristotle, *all* cases of *pathos* involve a certain type of

[220] *PHP* 3.3.14–16, p. 188, 18–25. The translation of *Med.* 1078–80 (De Lacy's) reflects Galen's understanding of their meaning; for a different version, see n. 240 below.

[221] *PHP* 3.3.17, p. 188, 30–2; see also Pl. *R.* 390d, 441b, *Phd.* 94d–e. Galen's analysis differs from these Platonic passages (and also from *Phdr.* 253–6) in being framed not just in terms of interplay between psychic parts but also of a 'she' (*autē*) who is dragged alternately by reason and anger. The latter formulation is, however, found in Pl. *Lg.* 644d–645a and (in psychic development) *R.* 550a–b, 553b–d; see also Gill (1983*a*), 145–6, n. 6.

[222] For Galen's psychological assumptions, see 4.4 above.

[223] This charge is made with special force in *PHP* 4.7.12–22.

[224] For this view, see Sorabji (1998), (2000), part 1.

[225] See e.g. Gosling (1990), ch. 5, esp. 57–60; Nussbaum (1994), ch. 10, esp. 383–6; Price (1995), ch. 4, esp. 152–67; these discussions all focus on Plu. *Mor.* 446 F–447 A (LS 65 G), a text considered in 4.2 above, text to nn. 76–9.

[226] One qualification regarding this view is the uncertainty about Hellenistic knowledge of Aristotle, and the fact that Plato, rather than Aristotle, seems to have been the thinker who principally set the agenda of ethical debate; see 1.3 above, esp. text to nn. 69–77.

akrasia.[227] What lies behind this view? As Troels Engberg-Pedersen emphasizes, it is crucial to correlate Chrysippus' thinking on passion as inner conflict with the fundamental Stoic idea that ethical development (understood as *oikeiōsis*, 'appropriation' or 'familiarization') is natural to human beings.[228] We need to bring together several key aspects of the theory of *oikeiōsis* explored in the preceding chapter. One is the belief that all human beings have, constitutively, the 'seeds' or starting-points of virtue.[229] This means not simply that, as Aristotle supposes, some human beings have the seeds of virtue but that these will develop into actual virtue only if nourished by the appropriate social and intellectual environment.[230] I think the Stoics maintain the stronger thesis that the capacity for virtue remains latent in all of us, in spite of the corrupting effect of our social environment.[231] The second relevant feature of their thinking is widely recognized as the crucial stage in the ethical development of adult human beings. This is the transition from being naturally drawn to pursue the primary natural goods (such as self-preservation, health, wealth) to seeing these, though preferable and worthy of selection, as matters of indifference in comparison with virtue. The rationality and 'consistency' (*homologia*) that is previously expressed in consistent selection of preferables comes to be understood as only fully expressed in the pursuit of virtue, which is the sole good and proper object of choice.[232]

These two features, taken together, give us the starting-point for explaining Chrysippus' view of passion as inner conflict. The point is not simply that passions centre on taking preferables, mistakenly, for goods. It is also that human beings, at some more or less conscious level, *recognize* that, in doing so, they are failing to exercise the natural human capacity to see virtue, not the preferables, as the only good. Relevant here is Chrysippus' account of the causes of the corruption (*diastrophē*) of the ethical development that is natural to human beings, apparently discussed in Book 2 of Chrysippus' *On Passions*.[233] One cause is the 'persuasiveness of impressions'; this manifests itself especially in the tendency, which is to some degree inherent in human

[227] On this feature of Chrysippus' thought, see also Inwood (1985), 162–5; Engberg-Pedersen (1990*b*), 182–9; Price (1995), 163–7. On the contrasting Aristotelian view, adopted by Plutarch, see 4.3 above, text to nn. 115–20.

[228] See Engberg-Pedersen (1990*b*), ch. 8, esp. 182–93; also Inwood (1985), ch. 5, esp. 155–65.

[229] See e.g. LS 61 L, taken with 65 J esp. (1); also D.L. 7.89; Cic. *Tusc.* 3.2.

[230] See Arist. *NE* 10.9, esp. $1179^{b}20$–$1180^{a}14$, taken with Burnyeat (1980), esp. 74–7. In Aristotle's view, only some human beings have the requisite natural starting-points, *NE* $1179^{b}7$–31.

[231] See 3.2 above, including contrast with Platonic–Aristotelian patterns of thought on development.

[232] See Cic. *Fin.* 3.20–1 (LS 59 D(3–5)); also 3.2–3 above.

[233] See further Tieleman (2003), 132–9.

nature, to form the impression that preferables are goods, and so to attach to them 'excessive' value. The 'fresh' application to specific cases of this false belief activates the combination of an 'excessive' and 'unnatural' impulse and intense, overwhelming psychophysical reactions that constitutes a passion.[234] The second cause is the 'conversation' (*katēchēsis*) of the majority of people.[235] Implied in this cause are two features of Stoic thinking about the role of society in ethical development. On the one hand, ethical and emotional engagement with the roles and practices of one's society is seen as playing a crucial part in enabling humans to understand what it means to treat virtue as the only good.[236] On the other hand, the discourse of one's society tends to promote the mistaken identification of preferables with goods (and, as the case of Medea indicates, mistakes about what properly constitute preferables).[237] Thus, social upbringing and participation contribute to both sides of the psychological conflict that Chrysippus identifies, providing both the action-guiding beliefs that generate passions and the competing recognition of the priority of virtue that generates freedom from the passions.

As so understood, the kind of inner conflict that Chrysippus associates with passion is compatible with his psychological holism. The conflict is not—as Galen presumes—between reason and anger or lust, conceived as fundamentally distinct psychological parts or sources of motivation, but between competing sets of beliefs, reasoning, and emotion.[238] Put in more Stoic terms, the conflict is between a set of false beliefs that generate passion and the inchoate ethical knowledge (understanding that virtue is the only good) that promotes the absence of passion (*apatheia*) or 'good emotions' (*eupatheiai*). Chrysippus seems also to assume that people in a state of passion are, at some more or less conscious level, aware of their failure to achieve a degree of rationality and virtue of which they are, fundamentally, capable. To this extent, Chrysippus' description of passion as the 'disobedience' or 'rejection' of reason signifies a process that is actually or potentially conceived under this description by the person concerned, and not just a metaphor which an observer might use to analyse the process.

[234] See *PHP* 5.5.14, 19; also 4.2.8, 14–18, 4.5.21–2. See further Inwood (1985), 158–61; Engberg-Pedersen (1990*b*), 184–6, 193–7; Brennan (1998), 39–44.

[235] *PHP* 5.5.14, given in D.L. 7.89 as 'the conversation of those around one [*tōn sunontōn*)'.

[236] See e.g. LS 59, esp. D(3–4), E(2), Q; also Kidd (1971*b*), (1978).

[237] For Epictetus' exploration of a similar set of ideas, partly in connection with Medea, see Long (2002), 74–86, and text to nn. 202–5 above.

[238] Cf. Chrysippus' analysis of Medea's state of mind, as that of a whole person alternating between two belief-sets, not conflict between psychological 'parts' of herself, as suggested in Gill (1983*a*), 138, 141.

This point must lie at the heart of Chrysippus' well-attested interest in the lines concluding the great monologue of Euripides' *Medea* (1078–9):[239] 'I know that what I intend to do is bad (*kaka*), but spirit (or anger, *thumos*) is master of my plans'.[240] Medea's decision to kill her children, like all adult human impulses, is based on beliefs and reasoning, such as that 'taking vengeance on my husband is more beneficial than saving the lives of my children'.[241] Medea herself, in Chrysippus' interpretation, sees the impulse involved as excessive and unnatural. Despite seeing this and thus expressing her latent rationality as a human being, she is unable to counteract the impulse (the 'running legs' of passion) which is based on the belief that retaliation is good. In this respect, she disobeys or rejects (under this self-induced pressure) a type of rationality whose validity she herself acknowledges.[242] A similar idea is suggested by the examples of the perverse rejection of good advice that Chrysippus seems to have cited in this connection, such as that of angry people saying 'that they want to gratify their anger and to let them be, *whether it is better or not*'.[243] In other cases, where there is no explicit comment on the irrationality of the act or feeling involved, the same point is implied by a contrast between states of mind before and after the passionate impulse. Thus, even in cases of inarticulate or 'blind' passion, the contrast with the preceding (partly) rational state suggests that a latent, and latently conscious, rationality underlies the passion.[244] All this is consistent with the

239 See esp. *PHP* 4.2.24–7, 4.6.19–22; Galen's repeated attention to these lines (e.g. in *PHP* 3.3.13–16, 3.7.14–16) seems to be designed to counteract Chrysippus' interpretation of them. Chrysippus' interest in E. *Med.* as a whole is indicated by D.L. 7.180. Tieleman (2003), 172, argues that Chrysippus' discussion formed part of the fourth ('therapeutic') book on passions, though there is a conceptual link with Chrysippus' definition of passion in Book 1. See Gal. *PHP* 4.2.1–27; Gill (1983*a*), 139–40; Tieleman (2003), 172, n. 115; and text to nn. 172–4 above.

240 This translation of 1079 is designed to be neutral between the traditional one, 'spirit is stronger than my reasonings/deliberations' (which fits better with Galen's picture of a struggle between two psychic parts, reason and anger), and an alternative one, 'spirit is master of [i.e. in control of] my [revenge-] plans'. The latter fits better with Chrysippus' picture as well as the required sense of Euripides' lines, but may not have occurred to Chrysippus. The traditional translation is assumed by Galen in *PHP* 3.3.16, and may have been assumed by Chrysippus, as paraphrased in *PHP* 4.2.27 (see text to nn. 217–18 above). See further Gill (1983*a*), 138, (1996*b*), 223–5, 227–32, esp. 232 n. 215; also Tieleman (2003), 171 n. 113, supporting the traditional translation.

241 See Epict. *Diss.* 1.28.7, and text to n. 202 above; Chrysippus, presumably, assumed that Medea's passion rested on some such reasoning.

242 See text to nn. 217–18 above; for a passion as 'excessive', 'unnatural', and like 'running legs', see *PHP* 4.2.15–18. See also Stob. 2.89.4–90.6 (= LS 65 A(5–8)). The parallel between Chrysippus' analysis of the Medea case (*PHP* 4.2.27), as interpreted here, and Stob. 2.90.2–6 (= LS 65 A(8)), suggests that the latter passage is also Chrysippean in thought, in spite of the reservations of Inwood (1985), 143; see also Price (1995), 150.

243 *PHP* 4.6.24–41, esp. p. 275, 30–1.

244 *PHP* 4.5.7–11 (Menelaus abandoning his previous decision to kill the guilty Helen when affected by her sexual appeal); 4.6.44–6 (contrast between people in states of 'blind' anger and

view offered earlier, that such inner conflict reflects a (partial) failure in ethical development and a consequential conflict between an impulse based on false ethical belief and the half-developed awareness of the falsity of the belief and the wrongness of the impulse.

Thus, Galen's evidence enables us to recognize the framework of thinking underlying Chrysippus' conception of psychic division, even though Galen himself presents this framework as incoherent or implausible. His evidence also helps us to define further a larger contrast in Hellenistic and Roman thought between different ways of thinking about lasting or stable structures of character, and one which bears on Chrysippus' conception of psychic division. This is the third topic to be considered here in Galen's reading of Chrysippus' theory. Stoic thinking on this subject also expresses the combination of psychological—and psychophysical—holism and the 'Socratic' motif that only the wise person is psychologically stable and coherent. In examining this subject, I concentrate on drawing out the implications of Galen's evidence for a striking feature of Stoic theory, rather than on counteracting Galen's polemical presentation.[245]

In Plutarch, as noted earlier, stable structures of character, of virtue and vice, are defined by reference to the control of reason over the irrational part, especially through the development of dispositions (*hexeis*) through habituation. In general, such thinking represents a fusion of Plato's focus, especially in the *Republic*, on the interrelations between the parts of the psyche and Aristotle's mapping of types of virtuous and defective dispositions, which succeed or fail in hitting the correct 'mean' in action and feeling.[246] A crucial assumption, made explicit by Aristotle, is that there can be stable but defective character-states as regards desire and emotion, and that there is a distinction between such character-states and *akrasia*, conflict or inconsistency as regards desire and emotion.[247]

Galen's emphasis in *PHP* is on occurrent (transient) psychological states and on the underlying structure of the psyche, rather than on lasting character-states. But it is clear that, like Plutarch, he sees such states as developed through the relationship between rational and non-rational

when they had 'earlier engaged in philosophical conversations'). On the Stoic use of these and other poetic examples, see Tieleman (2003), 170–87, supporting (in 171–6) the interpretation of the Medea case offered here also Gill (2005*c*).

[245] However, Galen's polemical presentation is evident here too to some extent; see text to nn. 267–71 below.

[246] See Plu. *Mor.* 443 C–446 E, taken with 4.3 above, esp. text to nn. 110–12 above; also e.g. Pl. *R.* 435b–444e; Arist. *NE* 2.5–7. On a contrasting strand in Platonic thought, see 5.2 below, text to nn. 121–35.

[247] See 4.3 above, text to nn. 115–19.

parts, and especially through the imposition of determinate patterns on the non-rational parts.[248] In his essay on *The Passions and Errors of the Psyche*, Galen, like Plutarch, focuses on ways in which emotions and desires can be informed by rational training, and, in this sense, 'persuaded' by reason.[249] Although his essay *On Characters* (*peri ēthōn*) has been lost, except for an Arabic summary, it seems to have stressed, like *PHP*, the Platonic idea that the 'spirited' (*thumoeides*) part can be used as the ally of reason to secure the obedience of the 'appetitive' (*epithumētikon*) part and so build up virtuous patterns of character.[250]

The Stoic view is starkly different. The difference lies not only in the monistic psychological model but also in the idea that the only stable character-state is that of the perfectly wise and that all other states are inherently unstable, fluctuating, and in conflict with each other and with the person's latent or partial rationality. This view has already been noted in Plutarch's essay and underlies Galen's account of Chrysippus' thinking about self-division.[251] But it is illuminated further in Galen's extensive critique in *PHP* 5.2–3 of Chrysippus' use of the analogy between physical and psychological health and sickness. Earlier in *PHP*, Galen comments on Chrysippus' idea that some non-wise people have quasi-dispositional states (regarded as types of sickness), such as being 'mad on women' or 'mad on birds' (*PHP* 4.5.20–2). Other sources confirm this idea; Cicero, in particular, underlines the point that these are, in some sense, dispositional patterns. Different people are 'more inclined' (*procliuiores*) to different 'sicknesses'; they show, for instance, 'irascibility' (*iracundia*) rather than just (occurrent) 'anger' (*ira*).[252] Some of the key categories are spelled out in this account in Stobaeus:

> A predisposition (*euemptōsia*) is a tendency towards [having a] passion . . . for example . . . proneness to irascibility (*orgilētēs*) . . . A disease (*nosēma*) is an opinion connected to a desire which has settled and hardened into a condition, in virtue of which people think that things not worth choosing are extremely worth choosing, for example, love of women, wine, or money. There are also certain states opposites to these diseases which turn up as antipathies (*kata proskopēn*), such as hatred of women,

[248] This is implied in Galen's critique of Chrysippus' use of the analogy between psychic states and physical health or disease (*PHP* 5.2.1–3.31, discussed below), and in his account of Posidonius' account of character-development (e.g. *PHP* 4.7.6–46, esp. 39–44), considered in 4.6 below.

[249] For translations of this essay (*Aff. Dig.*), see Harkins and Riese (1963), with interpretation, and Singer (1997*a*), 100–49. See Hankinson (1993), 198–204, noting in 203–4 the difficulty in determining whether the emotional goal for Galen is extirpation or moderation of passions. On a comparable complexity in Plutarch's thought, see 4.3 above, text to nn. 144–5.

[250] See *Aff. Dig.* 27; Hankinson (1993), 203; also *PHP* 5.7.44–82, discussing Pl. *R.* 439e–441b, 441e–442d.

[251] See Plu. *Mor.* 441 C–D, 447 A, and 4.2 above, text to nn. 78–9; also text to nn. 213–18 above.

[252] Cic. *Tusc.* 4.27.

wine, or money. Those diseases which occur in conjunction with weakness are called ailments (*arrōstēmata*).[253]

Recurrent features of these accounts include the idea of dispositions towards, and away from, certain passions,[254] and a class of diseases 'with weakness' (*met' astheneias*).[255] However, one should not infer from such typologies that these dispositions are conceived as highly determinate and stable states. This is not because Stoicism cannot conceive the idea of stable dispositions.[256] The point is that it is only the state of the perfect wise person that is seen as stable and consistent, thus meriting the term 'character' (*diathesis*), in the full sense.[257] These contrasting dispositions are marked by instability and incoherence, as well as by mutual conflict. Take, for instance, the class of ailments 'with weakness' (*arrōstēmata* or *aegrotationes*). This category is often explained by reference to Chrysippus' comments, recorded by Galen, about psychic 'weakness' or 'lack of tension' or 'sinew', *atonia*. Chrysippus has in view cases where people fall away from their good intentions, and from the rationality of which all adult humans are capable, through the persuasive impact of something taken (wrongly) to be good.[258] For these cases to reflect dispositions, the people concerned must be recurrently disposed to fall away from their good intentions.

George Kerferd has offered a more precise analysis of what is meant by 'ailments', which draws together several of the features in our evidence for the Stoic conception of psychic illness. He suggests that ailments are the outcome of a 'collision' (*proskopē*, *offensio*) between competing pro- and anti-passions, such as love and hatred of women. These ailments are 'weak' because the force of the original passion (say, love of women) has been weakened by the competing force of the passion 'colliding' with it (hatred of women).[259]

[253] Stob. 2.93.1–13 (= 10e), trans. Inwood and Gerson (1997), p. 219, slightly modified. See also D.L. 7.115; Cic. *Tusc.* 23–30; Gal. *PHP* 5.2, taken with Tieleman (2003), 186–7.

[254] See e.g. Stob. 2.93.4–6, 9–11; Cic. *Tusc.* 4.23–7, where the two types are presented as subdivisions of two of the primary passions, namely appetite and fear (LS 65 A(3–4)).

[255] i.e. *arrōstēmata*, Stob. 2.93.12–13; D.L. 7.115; (= *aegrotationes*, Cic. *Tusc.* 4.23).

[256] Modern scholars, following some ancient critics of Stoicism, have sometimes supposed that Stoic psychological monism meant that they only conceived of ocurrent states of the whole psyche. For critical analysis of this view, see Inwood (1985), 34–41; also Price (1995), 167–8.

[257] On Stoic terminology, and the contrast between *diathesis* ('character') and 'state' (*schesis*) or 'tenor' (*hexis*), see LS 47 S, 60 J(3), L (also LS i. 376), LS 61, esp. A.

[258] See Gal. *PHP.* 4.6.1–19. Chrysippus' example is Menelaus, whose 'weakness' leads him to abandon his intention to kill Helen because of the impact of her beauty. Medea is treated as a comparable example of persuasion by anger, 5.6.19–23. On the linkage between ailments and weakness or lack of tension, see Bonhöffer (1890), 275–6; Price (1995), 169; on weakness, see also Kidd (1983); Inwood (1985), 163–5; Engberg-Pedersen (1990*b*), 187–92.

[259] Kerferd (1983), 88–93, referring to *proskopē* (sometimes read as *prokopē*) in D.L. 7.113 and Stob. 2.93.10, and *offensiones* in Cic. *Tusc.* 4.23; on pro- and anti-passions, see n. 254 above. For a similar suggestion, stated in more general terms, see Price (1995), 169–70.

This is an intriguing suggestion, although I do not find it quite articulated in our—rather inadequate—texts on this subject.[260] However, whether or not 'ailments' were defined in precisely this way, this general line of explanation for dispositions to passions holds good. As Cicero puts it, 'the disturbing effect of corrupt beliefs warring against one another robs the psyche of health and introduces the disorder of disease'. As he explains, 'this feverish excitement of the psyche', when it 'becomes chronic and settled' creates 'disease and ailment' (Cic. *Tusc.* 4.23–4). The main point is that, even though such diseases are, in some sense, lasting or recurrent dispositions, they are also inherently unstable, because they are in conflict with tendencies to other passions or with latent, partly developed, rationality. This seems to be the point of Chrysippus' comment that the psychic state of inferior people is 'analogous to a body which is apt to fall into fever or diarrhoea or something else of that kind from a small or chance cause'.[261] On similar grounds, Chrysippus characterizes a passion, considered as an occurrent phenomenon, as 'a flutter' (*ptoia*) and as 'moving at random' (*pheromenon eikē*(*i*)).[262] The point of comparing such psychic states to fevers is to underline that, even if they are in some sense passionate dispositions, they are fundamentally unstable. This is made quite explicit in this comment of Chrysippus, cited by Galen: 'We must suppose that the disease of the psyche is most similar to a feverish physical state in which fevers and chills do not occur at regular intervals but irregularly and at random from the character (of the person) and at the incidence of small causes'.[263]

What is the nature of these dispositional or quasi-dispositional states? As Stobaeus puts it: 'A disease is an opinion connected to a desire which has settled and hardened into a condition (*hexis*), in virtue of which people think that things not worth choosing are extremely worth choosing'.[264] Presumably, the process of 'hardening' depends not simply on the duration or reiteration of such beliefs, but on the development of clusters of more or less consistent

[260] In Stob. 2.93.9–13, the class of anti-passions arising through collision or 'as antipathies' (*kata proskopēn*) seems to be distinct from the *arrōstēmata* ('ailments') listed in the next sentence, although Kerferd seems to identify them (1983: 90). Also, in Cic. *Tusc.* 4.23–4, *offensiones* seems to signify 'aversions' (anti-passions), opposed to the 'ailments' (*aegrotationes*), rather than the 'collisions' causing the ailments, as Kerferd suggests (1983: 92).

[261] Gal. *PHP* 5.2.3, p. 294, 34–6.

[262] Gal. *PHP* 4.5.6; also Stob. 2.88.11–12 (=LS 65 A(2)). See also Plu. *Mor.* 447 A: passions are 'activities which change rapidly like children's fights, whose fury and intensity are volatile owing to their weakness' (4.2 above, text to nn. 76–7).

[263] Gal. *PHP* 5.2.14, p. 298, 3–7, trans. De Lacy, slightly modified. 'Character', perhaps surprisingly (see n. 257 above), is *diathesis*. On the response of Posidonius to this view, see n. 334 below.

[264] Stob. 2.93.6–8, 10e, trans. Inwood and Gerson (1997), p. 219; cf. D.L. 7.115; also Inwood (1985), 163.

beliefs, which sustain each other. Can we provide a larger explanatory framework in which to place Stoic thinking about the inherently unstable quality of defective dispositional states? In broad terms, as already indicated, it reflects their theory of ideal—but also natural—development. Human beings are constitutively capable of developing both towards the recognition that virtue is the only good and towards the complete consistency of beliefs and character that constitutes perfect wisdom. Chrysippus describes this state as psychic 'proportion' (*summetria*), 'health', 'strength', and 'good tension' (*eutonia*), by contrast with the disproportion, weakness, and lack of tension that is characteristic of—even relatively stable forms of—psychic sickness.[265] The unstable and feverish character of non-wise dispositions, like the internally conflicted quality of occurrent passionate states, such as that of Medea, serves as an index of the failure of the human constitution to realize the health and cohesion that it potentially possesses. The implication is that, however people subjectively evaluate their situation, its defectiveness is objectively displayed by their internal incoherence and instability.[266]

Tieleman suggests that this feature of Chrysippus' thought, together with the larger contrast between psychic health and disease, should be seen as reflecting a systematic psychophysical holism (in my terms) which Galen's presentation partly obscures. As he points out, Galen criticizes Chrysippus' claim that psychic health is a 'proportion' and 'good blend' (*eukrasia*), fastening especially on Chrysippus' comment that what is involved is a proportion or blend of certain 'parts' or 'divisions' (*merē, merismoi*) of the psyche.[267] Galen assumes that the only sense that could, plausibly, be attached to such terms is the Platonic idea of psychic health as the harmonization of parts which are also distinct and independent sources of motivation.[268] He points out that the only psychic parts recognized by Chrysippus, such as the functions of sensation, voice, and sexuality, do not meet this criterion.[269] Galen also suggests another possible answer, drawing on a different Chrysippean idea, that reason is 'a collection of notions and concepts'.[270] Galen suggests that the 'proportion' and 'good blend' involved is that between sets of beliefs—or, rather, aspects of knowledge—a suggestion with some basis in

[265] Gal. *PHP* 5.2.26, 31–3; also Cic. *Tusc.* 4.30–2. See also Engberg-Pedersen (1990*b*), 187–92. On the developmental framework presumed, see 3.2–3 above, esp. text to nn. 114–21 on the character-states of ideal 'health', 'beauty', and 'proportion'.

[266] See further, on issues of subjectivity and objectivity, Ch. 6 below, and on a striking poetic illustration of this point (in Seneca's *Medea*), 7.3 below, text to nn. 103–16.

[267] Gal. *PHP* 5.2.31–5, 47–9, esp. p. 304, 11, 18, 21. See Tieleman (2003), 147–51.

[268] *PHP* 5.2.36–8, 5.3.19–30; and (on Platonic psychology), 5.7, esp. 5.7.34–73; see also 5.2, esp. 309 below.

[269] *PHP* 5.3.7; on these as the functions of a unified psyche, see LS 53 H.

[270] *PHP* 5.3.1 (= *SVF* 2.841), drawn from Chrysippus, *On Reason*.

Stoic thinking.[271] But Galen rejects the idea that psychic health can be defined in those terms, rather than those of the part-based psychology which he maintains.

However, despite what seems to be Galen's studied failure to engage with Chrysippus' theory, Galen does at one point cite (what Tieleman regards as) Chrysippus' key idea. This is that psychic health and beauty are based on a correct blending of the elements of hot and cold or, in the case of *pneuma*, air and fire.[272] In essence, the suggestion is that, for Chrysippus, psychic health and illness and the quasi-dispositional inclinations to different passions are seen as having a physical dimension and basis, in a way that reflects the psychophysical holism of the theory. Tieleman highlights a number of Stoic themes which support this view. For instance, he suggests that Chrysippus' presentation of psychic disease as consisting in a state in which 'fevers and chills do not occur at regular intervals but irregularly and at random' indicates an underlying failure of proportion between hot (fevers) and cold (chills) in the psychophysical state of the person concerned.[273] A formative influence on this failure to develop proportion is taken to be the practice of midwives in seeking to counteract the impact of cold on the newly born body by a warm bath. This both weakens the body's capacity to find a balance between warm and cold and encourages the erroneous belief that 'everything pleasant and agreeable is good and that everything that by contrast brings sorrow is bad'.[274] Tieleman also underlines the significance of evidence showing Stoic interest in physical regimen (diet and exercise), in particular the impact of wine even on the wise, which was generally seen as heating and 'moistening' cold or dry temperaments.[275]

[271] *PHP* 5.2.49: 'They [presumably, notions and concepts] are the parts of the psyche through which its reason and the disposition (*diathesis*) of its reason are constituted. A psyche is beautiful or ugly [that is, well or badly proportioned] by virtue of its control-centre being in this or that state with respect to its own proper divisions'; cf. 5.2.47. See also Cic. *Tusc.* 4.30: in psychic health, judgements and beliefs are in harmony, and 4.31.

[272] Tieleman (2003), 152, referring to *PHP* 5.3.7–10. Galen's recognition of this point is the more significant because he acknowledges elsewhere that he was influenced by this Stoic idea (see nn. 159–60 above).

[273] *PHP* 5.2.14 (= *SVF* 3.465), coupled with the idea that the psyche expands (with heat) in lust and desire and contracts (with cold) in fear and grief (*PHP* 4.3.2; Cic. *Tusc.* 4.15). On anger as a kind of inner inflamation, see *PHP* 3.1.25. The lack of proportion thus helps to explain the 'fluttering', fluctuating, character of passionate states (*PHP* 4.5.7; Plu. *Mor.* 446 F). See Tieleman (2003), 155–9.

[274] Calcidius, commentary on Pl. *Ti.*, ch. 165, last sentence cited; this passage is usually seen as expressing Stoic thinking on the causes of human corruption. See Tieleman (2003), 161–2, also 133–5 (as part of his reconstruction of Book 2 of Chrysippus' *On Passions*).

[275] Tieleman (2003), 162–6; on cognate Stoic thinking on the effect of environment on character, see Cic. *On Fate* 7–9 (also Tieleman 2003: 194).

Tieleman (2003: 323) is surely right to stress a side of Stoic thinking which, as he underlines, was de-emphasized, for different reasons, by both the main relevant sources, Cicero and Galen, and is often neglected by modern scholars, who stress, rather, the cognitive or rationalistic dimension of Chrysippus' theory. However, Galen has some basis for claiming that, for Chrysippus, a physical explanation by itself will not be sufficient.[276] Nor, of course, should we think in terms of the shaping of an irrational part by physical means in a way that influences the (independently conceived) rational part. Therefore, especially revealing are passages such as some of those cited earlier which indicate a combination or synthesis of physical and rational or cognitive processes.[277] Suggestive also is Tieleman's citation of the passage from Plato's *Timaeus*, which, like Stoic thinking on the sources of corruption, links physical and social (cognitive) factors in producing psychic illness.[278] In fact, I think more work may be needed to reconstruct fully the linkage between physical and rational factors in explaining, as far as our evidence allows, the psychophysical holism underlying Stoic thinking about psychic illness and quasi-dispositional inclinations to one or other passion. But I think Tieleman has helped to show the general form that such an explanation needs to take. Critically interpreted, Galenic and other evidence for Chrysippean thinking on these topics can enable us to see how this strand of Stoic thinking on—what one might call—the *un*-structured self matches the psychophysical as well as psychological holism that is characteristic of the overall theory.

4.6 GALEN ON POSIDONIUS

As well as being a prime source for Chrysippus' theory of the passions, Books 4–5 of *PHP* also constitute the main evidence for Posidonius' (alleged) critique of this theory. Galen presents Posidonius as having rejected Chrysippus' psychological ideas fundamentally, despite being himself a leading Stoic thinker. He also claims that Posidonius took over, broadly speaking, the

[276] See text to nn. 270–1 above.

[277] See text to nn. 185, 253, 263 above.

[278] See Tieleman (2003), 188–90, referring to Pl. *Ti.* 86b–88d, linking especially the combination of physical and social causes of corruption (Pl. *Ti.* 86e–87b) with Stoic accounts of the two causes of corruption, 'the persuasiveness of impressions and the conversation of the majority' (text to nn. 233–6 above). On this passage of Pl. *Ti* as a possible source of influence on Stoic thought, see also 3.5 above, text to nn. 324–34.

same tripartite Platonic model that Galen himself adopted.[279] The issue of the nature of Posidonius' position is a crucial one for the history of Stoic thinking on the passions and, indeed, of the relationship between part-based and holistic conceptions of personality in the later Hellenistic period. The question is also important for understanding the relationship between Platonic thinking and Stoicism, a question broached here and pursued in Chapter 5.

How credible is Galen's account of Posidonius? As regards Chrysippus, scholars have mostly accepted that Galen offers a partisan and incomplete picture and have seen his theory as more coherent and credible than Galen maintains.[280] Although scholars allow that there may be some bias in Galen's account of Posidonian psychology, it has been more normal to accept as accurate Galen's claim that Posidonius rejected Chrysippus' unified model and adopted the Platonic tripartite picture.[281] However, John Cooper, developing a view advanced by Janine Fillion-Lahille, has argued that Galen's account of Posidonius is as unreliable as that of Chrysippus and for similar reasons. Although Cooper accepts that Posidonius saw some weaknesses in Chrysippus' theory and made some significant modifications, notably regarding the idea of emotional movements, he argues that Posidonius retained the core principles of Stoic psychology.[282] Teun Tieleman (2003: ch. 5), goes further still, arguing that Posidonius made *no* significant changes to Chrysippean theory and that Galen's picture is thus even more misleading than Cooper maintains. Tieleman argues that Galen's presentation of Posidonius as adopting Platonic ideas is based on cases where Posidonius reinterprets Platonic psychology on Stoic lines. The views of Cooper and, still more, Tieleman, are, at first sight, surprising in the extent to which they challenge Galen's analysis, while accepting that he is an invaluable source of evidence. However, I think that both discussions are highly cogent in their rereading of Galen's evidence and their reconstruction of Posidonius' real objectives. I will review key features of the alternative pictures offered by these scholars, together with some of the evidence on which their claims are based. I believe that their interpretations open the way to a substantially more plausible reading of Posidonius' contribution than Galen provides and that even Tieleman's more radical view is highly tenable.

[279] Galen acknowledges in *PHP* 5.4.2–3 that Posidonius did not allocate the different functions of the psyche to different bodily parts, as Galen did (4.4 above), but saw them as different 'capacities' (*dunameis*), presumably of the unified control-centre situated in the heart.

[280] See references in n. 147 above; an exception is Sorabji (2000), part 1, who largely accepts Galen's view of Chrysippus.

[281] See e.g. Kidd (1971*a*),(1988), 553–625; also LS i. 421–3.

[282] See Cooper (1998*a*); also Fillion-Lahille (1984), part 3, chs. 1–3.

On Cooper's view, which I take first, Posidonius does not reject the central Stoic thesis that a passion, which is a function only of adult humans, involves rationality.[283] To this extent, Posidonius does not reject Chrysippean unified psychology; and the evidence that he adopts the Platonic tripartite model is much weaker than Galen claims.[284] The only significant Posidonian innovation in this area, as Cooper maintains, is the idea that adult humans, as well as non-human animals and human children, are subject to 'affective [or passionate or emotional] movements' (*pathētikai kinēseis*), that is, affective responses to impressions (*phantasiai*). Galen presents the idea of affective movements, in Posidonian psychology, as replacing that of passions in Chrysippean psychology. Galen characterizes *pathētikai kinēseis* as 'movements ... of non-rational capacities' (or 'faculties') (*dunameōn alogōn*), which Galen identifies with those 'which Plato called appetitive and spirited'.[285] But Galen also provides evidence that Posidonius retains Chrysippus' view that passions are 'impulses' (*hormai*) which, in adult humans, require 'assent' to rational impressions to produce their full psychological effect, and that the idea of 'affective movements' is introduced by Posidonius alongside that of passions.[286]

It is Galen who presents this innovation as part of a radical critique of Chrysippus' monistic psychology and a reversion to the Platonic tripartite model. But, Cooper maintains (1998*a*: 81–90), the evidence provided by Galen allows us to discern a more limited ground of dispute, which emerges from within Chrysippean psychology, which Posidonius largely accepts. Posidonius' criticism seems to be that Chrysippus did not explain adequately the 'cause' (*aitia*) of a passion, which is conceived by Posidonius, in Chrysippean terms, as 'impulse in excess' (*hormē pleonazousa*).[287] Chrysippus' explanation, outlined earlier (257–8 above), centres on the defective development of beliefs. Most human beings fail to evolve fully from pursuing primary natural goods ('preferables') to seeking virtue, understood as the only good. The fresh application to specific cases of the resulting false beliefs causes excessive value

[283] The following five paragraphs are based on Gill (1998*a*), 124–7.

[284] For the claim that Posidonius adopted tripartition, see Gal. *PHP* 4.3.3, 5.6.38, 8.1.14. In no case is Galen able to cite Posidonius *explicitly saying* that he is adopting the tripartite psyche; on *PHP* 5.1.5, see below. See Cooper (1998*a*), 106 n. 32; Tieleman (2003), 202–6.

[285] *PHP* 5.1.5, p. 293, 24–5; the identification with Plato's tripartite model is here explicitly presented as *Galen's* own, not that of Posidonius. On affective movements, see also *PHP* 4.7.37, p. 288, 28, and 5.5.26.

[286] See e.g. *PHP* 5.5.21, discussed below; also 4.7.28 (referring to Posidonius' view, cf. 4.7.24–9, in which Posidonius is presented as criticizing Chrysippus), and 4.7.33. See further Cooper (1998*a*), 85, 103–4 n. 24.

[287] *PHP* 4.3.4, p. 248, 7–8; also 4.5.30, p. 266, 5–7; 4.5.41, p. 268, 22; 4. 4.44; 5.5.9. See also, on the importance of the question about causes, Cooper (1998*a*), 81–2; also Kidd (1971*a*), 206–7, 210–11.

to be attached to preferables, generating an excessive impulse to obtain these, together with the correlated psychophysical reactions. Posidonius thought that Chrysippus' explanation raised a further question: what provides the motivational force that makes humans form the beliefs that generate passions, and that makes those beliefs activate impulses (*hormai*) and the correlated psychophysical responses? For Chrysippus, the answer is provided simply by the interlinked operations of impression, assent, and impulse, regarded as functions of the rational *hēgemonikon* or 'control-centre'. Posidonius argues that we also need to invoke the existence of affective movements, which occur in both rational and non-rational animals, but which contribute crucially to the way in which rational animals (adult humans) experience passions.

'Affective movements' seem to be conceived as natural—instinctive or automatic—reactions to the impression that such-and-such is good or desirable and worth pursuing or the reverse. As Cooper reconstructs Posidonius' theory, affective movements play a number of roles in explaining the motivational basis of passions in adult human beings. The occurrence of these affective reactions to primary natural goods helps to explain why people tend to develop false action-guiding beliefs, such as that pleasure is not simply preferable but also a good in its own right. The 'affective pull' (*pathētikē holkē*) exerted by these movements helps to explain why the passionate impulse is excessive both in the overvaluation of preferables and in the type of psychophysical response produced.[288] The motivational force of these affective movements helps also to explain why passions, once formed, can (like 'running legs'), overwhelm the person's recognition of the irrationality of the passionate impulse. They also provide an alternative form of explanation, considered shortly, for the inner conflicts which Chrysippus analysed as being between competing sets of beliefs.[289] But, in Cooper's view, the explanation provided in this way is designed to supplement Chrysippus' framework of explanation, not to replace it, as Galen argues.

Crucial support for scholars who see Posidonius as maintaining orthodox (Chrysippean) Stoic psychology is provided by one important passage in Galen, translated by Cooper (1998*a*: 88) as follows:

In fact, Posidonius criticizes Chrysippus on these points and tries to show that the causes of all the false suppositions [in question] (*hupolēpseis*) lie indeed in their theoretical views (*to theorētikon*), due to the force of affect (*pathētikē holkē*), but this force is preceded by the false beliefs of a rational power that is weak in judgement. For

[288] See *PHP* 5.5.19–21, discussed below.

[289] See *PHP* 4.7.28, p. 286, 23–4; 4.7.37, p. 288, 28–30; also Cooper (1998*a*), 89. On the relevant features of Chrysippus' analysis of emotional conflict, see Gill (1998*a*), 120–2, and text to nn. 321–6 below.

impulse (*hormē*) in animals is generated sometimes on the basis of the judgement (*krisis*) of the rational power (*to logistikon*), but often on the basis of the affective power (*to pathētikon*). (*PHP* 5.5.21)

According to Cooper and Fillion-Lahille,[290] the content of the passage is as follows. Posidonius shows that the causes of false suppositions (such as that pleasure is the good, 5.5.16–20) lie in the rational part (*to theorētikon*, taken to be a synonym for *to logistikon*, used twice later in the passage). This part operates under the influence of ('through') the affective pull, presumably, that of affective responses to impressions which 'pull' the adult human to draw a certain inference, such as that 'this is pleasurable and therefore choiceworthy'. What precedes the affective pull and the impulse that follows are false beliefs which arise from a *logistikon* that is weak as regards judgment (*krisis*). The passage ends by distinguishing, it would seem, between impulses (*hormai*) in adult humans and other creatures. In adult humans (affective) impulse involves the judgement of the rational part (assent to rational impressions), but in other creatures it involves only affective movement.[291] On this view, Posidonius' psychological model gives two principal roles to rationality in the occurrence of passions. (1) The affective movement motivates the passionate impulse by activating the rational application of a false belief, for instance, that pleasure is the good. (2) It is the past development of such false beliefs, a process promoted by affective movements, which makes a psyche 'weak' as regards the judgements made and thus makes it liable to apply false ethical beliefs in specific situations.

This passage, as so interpreted, illustrates with great clarity the way in which the idea of affective movements is inserted into a basically Chrysippean framework, rather than forming part of a fundamentally different model, as Galen suggests. It is true that the passage has been seen as raising textual difficulties. Some scholars think that certain words have dropped out of our manuscripts, and the words suggested by editors to fill this gap would remove the direct link between the rational operations of *to theorētikon* and 'the affective pull'.[292] However, even if some words have dropped out,[293] the

[290] See Cooper (1998*a*), 88–9; Fillion-Lahille (1984), 156–7.

[291] *PHP* 5.5.21, p. 321, 27–8; see further below.

[292] De Lacy (1978–84), translates 'the causes of all false suppositions [arise] in the theoretical sphere [through ignorance, and in the practical] through the pull of the affections' (p. 320, 24–5, words supplied in square brackets). Edelstein and Kidd (1972/1989), fr. 169, p. 161, adopt a similar emendation. Kidd (1988), 620–1, suggests adding 'in the affective part (*to pathētikon*)' before 'through the affective pull'. These editors also think it unlikely that *to theorētikon* functions purely as a synonym for *to logistikon*.

[293] Editors who posit a lacuna argue that the *men* ('on the one hand') on p. 320, 24, requires us to supply a *de* ('on the other'). But Cooper and Fillion-Lahille take this to be the *d'* in p. 320, 25, and think that the contrast is a purely temporal one. See Cooper (1998*a*), 107–8 n. 37.

passage still presents the passionate impulse as involving 'the judgement of the rational part' and as having been 'preceded' by 'false beliefs' (such that 'pleasure is the good'). Hence, the 'affective pull' occurs *because* of this weakness of belief and takes effect *through* the formation of a passionate judgement.[294] The last sentence states that, in living creatures (human beings and animals), impulses 'often' involve affective movements, but 'sometimes' involve a judgement of the rational part. I take it that what is implied is that, in adult humans, passionate impulses (as just described) *always* involve a combination of affective movement and rational judgement, but that these only form a small subdivision of the impulses experienced by living creatures, including human children, as a whole.[295]

Tieleman (2003) supports this type of interpretation of the passage with further important points. The contrast between 'theoretical' and 'practical', familiar in Platonic–Aristotelian thought and sometimes used by editors filling the supposed gap in the text, is not a standard feature of Stoic thought.[296] On the contrary, we regularly find the claim that the wise person is equally capable of reflective and of practical activity.[297] Also, and probably for similar reasons, we are told that, in Stoicism, the virtues are seen as inter-entailing because they have their *theōrēmata* (concepts or ideas) in common. We also hear that the virtues consist in 'theorems', and that other qualities 'supervene' on these theorem-based virtues to make up the overall 'symmetry' or 'beauty' or 'health' of the personality as a whole.[298] This suggests that *theōrēmata*, in Stoicism, are not conceived as being, in a Platonic–Aristotelian sense, purely 'theoretical', but as shaping practical actions and qualities of character. In other words, terms such as 'theorems' and 'theoretical' need to be located in the unitary or holistic psychological framework characteristic of Stoicism. Hence, Tieleman suggests, the phrase 'in *to theōrētikon*' means 'in the sphere of knowledge', without any need to supply a contrast with 'in the practical sphere'. What Posidonius is stressing is the way that passions are produced in adult humans by an intricate combination of

[294] See De Lacy p. 320, 25–8, taken with discussion above.

[295] I take this to be the basis of the 'often–sometimes' distinction; see also Fillion-Lahille (1984), 157. The alternative reading (Kidd 1988: 622–3), is that in *all* living creatures (including adult humans), impulses are 'often' activated solely by affective movements (without rational judgements).

[296] For famous passages employing this contrast, see e.g. Pl. *R* 519b–521c; Arist. *NE* 10.7–8.

[297] See e.g. D.L. 7.126; Stob. 2.63.8–10 (also LS 61 G–H, 67 W–X); see further Tieleman (2003), 322–3.

[298] See D.L. 7.125; Stob. 2.63.6–8 (LS 61 D, esp. (1)) (also LS 61 C, F). See also D.L. 7.90; Stob. 2.62.15–63.5. See further Tieleman (2003), 233–7, 240, emphasizing that these ideas are ascribed to a wide range of Stoic thinkers including Panaetius' pupil Hecaton, contemporary with Posidonius. On ideas of this type, see also 3.3 above, text to nn. 114–25.

rational ('theoretical') judgement and—causally linked with judgement—the 'affective pull' and 'movement'. Tieleman also highlights the similarity between this passage and those illustrating Chrysippus' thinking, which also present passions as caused by a combination of wrong judgements and psychic 'weakness' (*astheneia*) or 'lack of tension' (*atonia*).[299] Tieleman thus helps us to see that the connection between this passage and the Chrysippean (holistic) analysis of passion is even closer than had been recognized.

Tieleman finds further support for the claim that Posidonius retained a holistic view of emotion in evidence from two sources other than Galen. Lactantius, in a passage based on Seneca, ascribes this definition of anger to Posidonius: 'the desire to punish him by whom you consider yourself to be unjustly harmed'. This definition, a variant of the standard Stoic one cited by Lactantius ('the desire to avenge an injustice') focuses on the cognitive content of the emotion rather than introducing reference to an irrational psychic part.[300] Second, an essay attributed to Plutarch records a schematic analysis of types of affection (*pathos*) ascribed to Posidonius. These include affections of the psyche, consisting of 'judgements (*kriseis*) and assumptions (*hupolēpseis*), e.g. desires, fears, fits of anger'. They also include affections of the body which also involve the psyche, for instance, 'pangs (*dēgmoi*), appearances (*phantasiai*) and feelings of relaxation (*diachuseis*)'. A further relevant type is affections of the psyche which involve the body: 'tremors, pallors and other changes of appearances related to fear and distress'.[301] The schematic distinctions between mental and bodily aspects of affection recall Platonic–Aristotelian thinking rather than Stoic.[302] But the various aspects of affections included here can be paralleled in other sources for Stoic thinking, including Plutarch's discussion in *On Ethical Virtue*.[303] The key point is that the passage ascribes to Posidonius the standard Stoic combination of cognitive or rational beliefs ('judgements' and so on) and psychophysical reactions

[299] See Tieleman (2003), 237–9, referring to *PHP* 4.6.2–3, on Chrysippus' theory. On Tieleman's account of the terminology used in the passage, see further text to nn. 307–13 below.

[300] Lactantius, *On God's Anger* 17.13 (Posid. fr. 155 in Edelstein and Kidd 1972/1989), trans. Tieleman (2003), 278, slightly modified. The passage is taken to supply words lost from Sen. *Ira* 1.2.3; for this type of Stoic definition, see Cic. *Tusc.* 3.11, 19, 4.44. The cognitive type of definition goes back to Aristotle (*de An.* 1.1, 403^a29–$^b1$, *Rh.* 2.2, 1378^a30–2).

[301] [Plu.], *Whether Appetite and Distress Belong to the Soul or Body*, ch. 6 (Posid. fr. 154 in Edelstein and Kidd 1972/1989), trans. based on Tieleman (2003), 278–9.

[302] See e.g. the subdivision of psychic and bodily aspects of anger in Arist. *de An.* 1.1, 403^a3–$^b19$, noted by Tieleman (2003), 279.

[303] See e.g. Plu. *Mor.* 449 D A–B , including 'tremors' and 'pangs' or 'bites' (*dēgmoi*). In Stoic theory, more technically described, these might be classed as 'pre-emotional' reactions or as psychophysical components of a passion. See further Graver (1999), 316–17; Tieleman (2003), 280–3; and text to nn. 336–45 below on pre-emotions.

('pangs', 'feelings of relaxation'), including visible ones ('tremors', 'pallors').[304] There is, again, no indication that Posidonius' thinking on emotions was associated with the idea of (Platonic) irrational parts such as spirit or appetite. In both these passages, Posidonius' name is attached to what seem to be quite typical Stoic (holistic) ideas. This is consistent with the fact that—apart from Galen—ancient sources typically present Posidonius as maintaining standard Stoic theses, for instance on ethics, rather than abandoning these in favour of Platonic–Aristotelian ones.[305]

Evidence of this type lends support to Tieleman's view that Posidonius made *no* significant modification to Chrysippean theory, rather than Cooper's belief that Posidonius modified Chrysippus' theory without rejecting it. For Cooper, although Posidonius' modifications were relatively localized, they had potentially large ethical implications, in allowing that adult humans *might* act on a purely non-rational motive (an affective movement), even if they do not normally act on this basis.[306] But Tieleman seems to face a difficulty in that Galen's evidence indicates that Posidonius made *some* terminological innovations with substantial conceptual implications. These include the contrast between *to logistikon* (or *to theorētikon*) and *to pathētikon* in the Galenic passage discussed earlier (*PHP* 5.5.21) which he, like Cooper, sees as reflecting genuine Posidonian thinking. Tieleman argues, convincingly, that, in Galen's verbatim quotations of Posidonius (by contrast with Galen's own summary), terms such as *pathētikon* are not presented as constituting distinct 'parts' (*merē*) or 'powers' (*dunameis*), that is, psychophysical organs or independent sources of motivation.[307] Tieleman is also sceptical about whether Posidonius regularly uses *to logistikon*, either on its own or in contrast to *to pathētikon*.[308] He does allow that Posidonius seems to have made regular use of the notions of 'affective motions' and of *to pathētikon*.[309] However, he suggests that Posidonius, like earlier Stoics, used *to pathētikon*, sometimes in combination with *alogon*, not to denote a separate psychic 'part',

[304] Cf. LS 65 B–D; see further 4.5 above, text to nn. 184–7. Sorabji (2000), 104–5, accepts that these passages present emotions as based on judgements, but suggests that, for Posidonius, emotions sometimes do and sometimes do not involve judgements.

[305] See e.g. D.L. 7.39, 40–1, 54, 60; Cic. *Tusc.* 2.61; *Fin.* 1.6. See further Tieleman (2003), 199–200; and Cooper (1998*a*), 100 nn. 4–5, who discusses one exceptional ethical idea ascribed to Posidonius in D.L. 7.103.

[306] Cooper (1998*a*), 72, 94–9; also Tieleman (2003), 199–200.

[307] Tieleman (2003), 202–6, noting, among other passages, *Galen*'s claim that affective movements 'are those of other, irrational powers (*dunameis*) which Plato called desiderative and spirited' (*PHP* 5.1.5, cited in text to n. 285 above).

[308] Tieleman (2003), 223, suggests that the contrast between these terms in *PHP* 5.5.33, may reflect Posidonius' way of summarizing Plato's theory (or Galen's report of this summary). On *PHP* 5.5.21, see below.

[309] Tieleman (2003), 203–4.

but in a broader sense, suggesting the complex of factors that lead to the occurrence of passions.[310] For instance, in one well-known passage on the cause of the passions, he takes 'what is irrational (*alogon*) and unhappy and godless in the psyche' to denote the complex of factors (not, significantly, characterized as 'parts' or 'powers') that produce *pathē*.[311] The same principle is seen at work in the passage discussed earlier (*PHP* 5.5.21), in the use of the terms 'affective pull' (*pathētikē holkē*) and 'movement of *to pathētikon*'. Tieleman also sees here an allusion to the active–passive contrast which is fundamental to Stoic thinking on causation as well as being a pervasive Greek concept. 'The term [*pathētikē/on*] indicates the soul's susceptibility to external influences, its passive side, whereas the active side is represented by the act of giving or withholding assent to mental appearances', the latter idea being here linked with *to logistikon* or *to theōrētikon*.[312] 'The passive moment in the genesis of emotion occurs when a mental appearance is formed... its impact causes a physical process. When the soul's physical tension is weak, the "first movement" thus caused may slip into the excessive motion that is technically a mental affection or emotion.'[313] In other words, *to pathētikon* represents an aspect of (adult human) experience, out of which belief-based passions emerge, rather than an independent 'part' or locus of motivation.

To put the point differently, one might see the terms *pathē* and *to pathētikon* as connotating, in part at least, a type of psychophysical inertia,[314] one which derives from a failure in development. This idea applies to Chrysippus as much as Posidonius. Chrysippus' image of a passion as like 'running (out of control) legs' suggests this kind of psychophysical inertia; one fails to exercise the kind of rationality of which one is essentially capable.[315] This image may have been one of the factors that prompted Posidonius to evolve the idea of 'affective *movements*', which manifest themselves in reactions which fail to

[310] For this usage in earlier Stoics, see e.g. Stob. 2.39.5–9 (*SVF* 1.206, first text), Plu. *Mor.* 441 C; Tieleman (2003), 206, n. 29.

[311] *PHP* 5.6.4–5 (Posid. fr. 187 in Edelstein and Kidd 1972/1989), final phrase; see Tieleman (2003), 228–30 (also text to nn. 389–92 below).

[312] Tieleman (2003), 237, slightly modified. On *to pathētikon* and the active–passive contrast, see Tieleman, 211–12 (on the Stoic contrast, see 1.3 above, text to nn. 53–4). That is, neither *to pathētikon* nor *to logistikon* signify 'parts' (independent sources of motivation) but rather coordinate aspects of psychological (psychophysical) experience that work together to produce passion.

[313] Tieleman (2003), 284; on 'first movements', see text to n. 338 below.

[314] This is my suggestion, though based on Tieleman's readings of the relevant evidence. Cf. 'psychological inertia', as used by Inwood (1993), 182, in connection with Chrysippus' and Seneca's analysis of passion.

[315] See e.g. Gal. *PHP* 4.2.14–18, taken with text to nn. 205, 216–18, 238–42 above. The physical dimension seems to be recognized in the rather bizarre suggestion that the 'excessive' impulse in a passion is caused by a non-rational factor, namely the 'weight of the body'. Though often treated as Posidonian, the comment may be Galen's own; see Tieleman (2003), 250–2.

express our common latent rationality.[316] Chrysippus' view that passions result from a combination of wrong judgements and 'lack of tension' (*atonia*) or slackness can also be seen as identifying a form of psychophysical inertia.[317] We may also link with this point Posidonius' interest in the way that innate or environmental factors influence psychophysical character and thus encourage the development of certain types of 'affective movements'.[318] As noted earlier (265 above), although Galen ignores this fact in *PHP*, Chrysippus *shares* with Galen as well as Posidonius this interest in the physical shaping of character. For both Stoic thinkers, it would seem, the occurrence of passions is an index of the type of psychophysical inertia (manifested in 'running legs', 'affective movements', or 'lack of tension') that is the outcome of a failure to achieve the recognition that virtue is the only good, which both thinkers regard as the proper outcome of human development.[319] If Posidonius, as it would seem, made extensive use of the terms 'affective movements' and *to pathētikon*, it may have been to underline the importance of an idea that was important for Stoic thinking on the passions, both in Chrysippean and Posidonian versions.

The idea of psychophysical inertia may have a significant role to play in helping us to make sense of Posidonius' criticisms of Chrysippus' theory. Galen gives a prominent place to these criticisms in *PHP* Book 4, suggesting that, in Posidonius' eyes, Chrysippus' failure to recognize an irrational part of the psyche made him incapable of giving a credible account of the cause of the passions.[320] As elsewhere, the material which is recorded by Galen allows us to form a very different picture. Posidonius' comments seem to be made in response to the series of problems (*aporiai*) which Chrysippus set out in *On Passions* Book 2. Many of these problems centre on cases in which Chrysippus acknowledges types of internal conflict, in spite of the psychological holism characteristic of the theory. Posidonius is, thus, contributing to a line of enquiry initiated by Chrysippus himself, and not, as Galen suggests, taking the initiative in finding weaknesses in Chrysippus' approach.[321] Many of the comments recorded by Galen show Posidonius remaining very much within the framework for analysing passions deployed by Chrysippus himself.

316 Chrysippus also describes the activation of passions in terms of 'movement' (*kinein/kineisthai*), e.g. Gal. *PHP* 4.5.26, 4.7.17.

317 Gal. *PHP* 4.6.2–3 (LS 65 T); Tieleman (2003), 238–9.

318 Gal. *PHP* 5.5.22–3, 26, cited by Tieleman (2003), 240–1.

319 On Posidonius' retention of orthodox Stoic ideas in ethics. see n. 305 above.

320 *PHP* 4.5.24–46 (Posid. fr. 164 in Edelstein and Kidd 1972/1989), 4.7.1–44. For Galen's comments on what he thinks is shown by the exchange, see e.g. 4.7.34–5, 38, 45–6.

321 For other such cases, see *PHP* 4.6.7–48, cited in Galen's report of the exchange between Chrysippus and Posidonius (but, apparently, drawn from Book 4 of Chrysippus' *On Passions*). See Tieleman (2003), 250–64, also 122–32, taken with his reconstruction of Chrysippus' treatise in 325–6.

Posidonius' aim seems to be to probe Chrysippus' explanations of mixed or complex cases and to suggest possible incompleteness or contradiction. For instance, one of Chrysippus' examples is of a Homeric figure (Agamemnon) who asks for sound advice *in spite of* being in a state of passion and thus calls into question the idea that passion involves a 'rejection of reason'. The example is taken by Posidonius to show that 'those in passions do *not* think it in line with their assessment of the situation that they should accept *no* reasoning'; they *do* accept reasoning, in some cases, despite their passionate state (4.5.40 p. 268, 17–18, my trans.). This example also illustrates that, 'when the same supposition and the same weakness underlie (their acts) some persons reject reasoning whereas others accept it', a further point on which Posidonius asked for further explanation.[322] It is not easy to gauge from Galen's report how important Posidonius saw these problems as being or how far he saw them as soluble. What does seem clear is that the questions are being raised from within a conceptual framework set by Chrysippus, in which passions are explained by a combination of wrong judgements and psychic 'weakness', rather than within the part-based conceptual framework that Galen holds and which he attributes to Posidonius.[323]

One topic on which we can discern some difference of approach between the two Stoic thinkers—though it may not turn out to be a large one—is on the explanation of two related kinds of phenomenon. These are the fading of grief in time despite the fact that one retains belief in the badness of death, and the occurrence of tears although one does not actively want to grieve. Chrysippus' explanation, cited by Galen, raises a number of interpretative difficulties. But the main relevant point is that Chrysippus frames the explanation purely in terms of belief. More precisely, his explanation involves two kinds of belief: (1) the judgement that, for instance, someone's death is bad and (2) the judgement that it is therefore appropriate to 'contract' with grief. As I read the passage, his line of explanation centres on the idea that the first belief remains present but the second one changes over time as circumstances alter. It may be, for instance, that the passage of time no longer makes it seem socially appropriate to grieve for someone's death. Hence, the impulse to grieve abates in time; but the belief in the badness of death remains and so tears may still arise, even though the person does not now think it appropriate to grieve. On another possible reading of the passage, the problem is that the psychophysical reactions (weeping or ceasing to weep) fail to match the second belief about what is appropriate. Thus, in one type of case, although grief still seems appropriate, changing circumstances have created new

[322] See 4.5.41 p. 268, 20–1, De Lacy trans.; see also *PHP* 4.5.33.
[323] See e.g. *PHP* 4.5.29–34. See also Tieleman (2003), 252–8.

preoccupations, leading to an abatement of grief. In the second type, tears arise although this is not seen as appropriate, perhaps because (as in the alternative type of case) the belief in the badness of death remains. In Chrysippus' own words:

On the lessening of distress, the question might be asked how it occurs, whether because a particular opinion is altered, or with them all persisting, and for what reason this will be so... I think that this kind of opinion does persist—that what is actually present is something bad—but as it grows older the contraction and, as I take it, the impulse towards the contraction, lessen. It might happen that, even though *this* [belief type 1 or 2] persists, the consequences will not correspond because a differently qualified condition (*diathesis*)[324] supervenes, which does not reason from those events. So it is that people cease weeping and people weep who do not want to, when different impressions are created by different external objects (*ta hupokeimena*), and something or nothing stands in the way.[325]

The italicized '*this*' (*tautēs*, p. 284, 10) may signify either the belief (1) that, for instance, someone's death is bad or the belief (2) that it is appropriate to grieve. But on either reading, the explanatory framework is couched wholly in terms of beliefs, of various kinds, as these are affected by the circumstances at the relevant time.[326]

What is Posidonius' response to this explanation? Galen, waxing eloquently on the inadequacies of Chrysippus' analysis, suggests that Posidonius shares his own rejection of any treatment which is not based on Platonic–Aristotelian part-based psychology and that Posidonius' explanation reflected this view.[327] But the one section of Galen's discussion that seems to cite Posidonius' actual comments suggests a more nuanced response. Posidonius is said to be sceptical about Chrysippus' explanation for the disparity between belief (taken to be belief type 2) and reaction.[328] His own response is then reported:

Posidonius again asks the reason why ordinary people often weep when they do not wish to and are unable to check their tears, while others who still want to weep find their tears stopping—obviously because the affective movements press so hard they cannot be mastered by the wish (*boulēsis*), or are brought to so complete a halt that it [the wish] can no longer arouse them.[329]

324 For this translation of *diathesis* (normally a permanent disposition), see Tieleman (2003), 128 n. 150.

325 Gal. *PHP* 4.7.12–17, excerpted (LS 65 O, trans. modified).

326 For detailed discussion of the meaning of the passage, see Inwood (1985), 149–52; Gill (1998*a*), 121–3; Sorabji (2000), 109–10; Tieleman (2003), 123–30, 259–60.

327 Gal. *PHP* 4.7.18–35, 38–44, also 5.6.30–2; Sorabji (2000), 112–14, follows this account.

328 Gal. *PHP* 4.7.36–7, p. 289, 19–24, citing two sentences from Chrysippus' comments. Posidonius takes 'this' to mean 'the impulse' (i.e. belief type 2).

329 *PHP* 4.7.37, p. 288, 25–30, De Lacy trans. modified.

The main point of difference seems to be that Chrysippus' explanation was couched solely in terms of beliefs, which change under different circumstances, whereas Posidonius introduces also reference to the idea of affective movements. These are presented as providing a further dimension of explanation why, in such cases, reactions fail to match beliefs (or 'wish'), at least the belief (type 1 or 2) with which they are in conflict. One might redescribe this response as being that Chrysippus' explanation does not bring out fully the element of psychophysical inertia in such situations, which Posidonius conveys, here as elsewhere, by reference to the idea of affective movements. More precisely, the criticism may be that Chrysippus does not *here*, in the analysis cited earlier (*PHP* 4.7.12–17), whose wording Posidonius examines, bring out this element. The qualification is needed because in other passages cited by Galen (which Posidonius himself notes), Chrysippus does bring out this idea by saying that emotions subside in time because the desire for grief is 'sated' (*emplēsthentes*) or because the 'inflammation' (*phlegmonē*) abates.[330] Also, as noted earlier, Chrysippus often explains passions by reference to a combination of a wrong judgement and 'weakness' or 'absence of tension', which is another way of expressing what I am calling 'psychophysical inertia'.[331] Indeed, even in the relevant passage, Chrysippus refers to the idea that 'in the beginning' passions such as grief 'cause greater motion' (*kinein*), a phrase which anticipates Posidonius' term 'affective movements' and thus Posidonius' way of bringing out the dimension of psychophysical inertia in passions.[332]

But, when these points are taken into account, how great is the difference between Chrysippus and Posidonius? As is clear from one important passage in Galen (*PHP* 5.5.21), discussed earlier, as well as other sources, both thinkers see passions as involving beliefs, even if Posidonius at least also sees them as activated by affective movements. It is also evident from this passage that Posidonius, like Chrysippus, recognizes the importance of two kinds of factor, the occurrent (mistaken) judgement or judgements and the longer-term state of psychological weakness.[333] Other passages indicate that Posidonius, like Chrysippus, regarded the dispositional states of the non-wise as only *relatively* stable in their proneness to specific forms of passion or 'disease'.[334] Against this background of largely shared ideas, Posidonius' criticism in this context seems to be directed simply at the narrowness of focus (on occurrent beliefs) in the Chrysippean passage he comments on. Galen himself fully acknowledges—and

[330] Gal. *PHP* 4.7.26 (ascribed to *On Passions* Book 2), 27. See also Tieleman (2003), 259–61.

[331] See e.g. Gal. *PHP* 4.6.2–3; this type of combination is noted by Posidonius (*PHP* 4.5.29).

[332] 4.7.17 p. 284, 15–16; see also text to n. 325 above.

[333] Cf. Gal. *PHP* 5.2.21 and 4.6.2–3; see also text to nn. 177, 291–5 above.

[334] Posidonius' only modification to Chrysippus' comparison of the condition of the non-wise to a body which is liable to fall into fevers from a slight or random cause is that the

is a prime source for—Chrysippus' thinking about (longer-term) psychological weakness or 'absence of tension', and about the other states of internal conflict that can be seen as expressing psychophysical inertia. But Galen presents this aspect of Chrysippus' thought, like Posidonius' ideas on affective movements, as an acknowledgement of the existence of irrational parts, and one which is flagrantly inconsistent with Chrysippus' overall theory.[335] This in turn reflects the fact that Galen interprets Chrysippus' approach to emotions as narrowly cognitive or rationalistic. He does not see Chrysippus as offering an inclusive or holistic account, as I am doing here. Hence, any reference by Chrysippus to a longer term state of character, particularly one described in psychophysical terms, is seen by Galen as a recognition of the essential truth of Platonic–Aristotelian part-based psychology. This point underlies Galen's (overstated) picture of the differences between the two Stoic thinkers. It is more plausible, I think, to see both Chrysippus and Posidonius as highlighting—at most—minor points of difference within a shared framework that reflects psychological and psychophysical holism.

This way of interpreting what—Galen presents as—Posidonius' critique of Chrysippus regarding hard or marginal cases has implications for a subject that has recently attracted scholarly interest. This is how to make sense of evidence for Stoic thinking about *pre-* or quasi- emotions.[336] These are affective experiences, which may be characterized in either physical or mental terms, but which fall short of being passions or emotions (*pathē*) in the full sense, as understood in Stoicism. That is, they do not involve the assent to impressions and the consequent impulse (believing that it is appropriate to react in a certain way) which normally trigger the psychophysical reactions characteristic of a passion. The fullest discussion of this phenomenon is in Seneca, *On Anger* (*Ira*) 2.1–4; but there is also evidence in authors from the first century BC onwards, including Cicero, Philo of Alexandria, and Epictetus. It seems clear that one important function of this idea was to show how even perfectly wise people might experience *some kinds of* affective reactions—apart from 'good emotions' (*eupatheiai*)—which, none the less, do not count as complete, and completely defective, passions.[337]

condition is like 'either physical health with a proneness to (*euemptōton*) disease ... or the disease itself' (*PHP* 5.2.2–7, quotation from p. 296, 14–15). Even Galen allows this is a minor difference: see *PHP* 5.2.6, 10; also 4.5 above, text to nn. 252–66.

[335] Gal. *PHP* 4.6.1–48, esp. 4.6.1–9, 28, 37, 47–8.

[336] Terms used for this phenomenon include *propatheiai*, 'pre-emotions' (first occurrence in this sense in Philo, *Q. Gen* 1.79), 'first motions' (*primi motus*), and 'preliminaries to emotion' (*principia proludentia adfectibus*) (Sen. *Ira* 2.2.5, 2.4.1).

[337] For an appraisal of the full range of ancient evidence, especially that of Philo, see Graver (1999), including an analysis of recurrent themes in 319–20. See also Inwood (1985), 175–81, (1993), 164–83; Sorabji (2000), 66–75, who both focus on Seneca's evidence.

Among the questions recently raised by scholars is how the treatment of this theme in later writers such as Seneca relates to earlier Stoic thinking. Sorabji, for instance, sees Seneca's discussion (*Ira* 2.1–4) as designed to defend Chrysippus' theory of passions against Posidonius' criticisms. By distinguishing explicitly between 'first movements' or 'pre-emotions' and passions proper, which involve 'third movements', Seneca reinstates Chrysippean theory in a way that defends it against Posidonius' claims (as interpreted by Sorabji) that emotions can occur without judgements.[338] One difficulty with this view is that Seneca makes no explicit reference to Posidonius in this context nor does he signal that his discussion forms part of a debate within Stoicism.[339] A further problem with Sorabji's view, if one accepts the interpretation offered here, is that Posidonius' critique of Chrysippus is much less radical than Sorabji (following Galen) assumes. In essence, Posidonius' objection is only that Chrysippus does not make sufficient reference—at least in one important discussion—to the idea of psychophysical inertia, in particular that of affective movements. But, as I see it, Posidonius does not challenge the Chrysippean idea that passions involve assent to impressions and so Seneca's reformulation is not needed as a defence of this idea against Posidonius.[340]

But the question then arises: how *do we* explain Seneca's—very striking and emphatic—analysis? A related question is this: how far back can we trace the introduction of the idea of pre-emotions in Stoic theory? Does it derive from Posidonius' innovative emphasis on 'affective movements'[341] or does it go back even to Zeno?[342] Or does Seneca's discussion, in effect at least, mark a new recognition of the importance of this idea for Stoic theory?[343] Margaret Graver's appraisal of the evidence (1999: 318–23) leads her to suggest that the idea was known already as a Stoic theme by Cicero and Philo of Alexandria (before Seneca's discussion in *On Anger*), even though it is not easy to pinpoint an earlier statement of the idea. Tieleman suggests that the idea is

[338] Sorabji (2000), 61–3, 66–75 (esp. 72–3), with special reference to Sen. *Ira* 2.4.1. For his interpretation of Posidonius' critique of Chrysippus on emotional hard cases, which closely follows Galen's analysis, see Sorabji (2000), chs. 7–8, also (1998).

[339] For related criticisms of Sorabji on this point, see Gill (2005*a*), 457–8; also Graver (2002*b*).

[340] See text to nn. 361–9 below. For the view that Posidonius does not think that affective movements can cause passions, in the full sense, without assent to impressions, see (in spite of other differences of interpretation) Cooper (1998*a*), 72–3, 87–9; Tieleman (2003), 284.

[341] As suggested by Cooper (1998*a*), 99. A problem with this idea is highlighted by Graver (1999: 322): 'pre-emotions', though they sometimes precede passions, 'never function as causes of them', as Posidonius' affective movements do.

[342] As suggested by Sen. *Ira* 1.16.7 (*SVF* 1.215); see further Abel (1983), 89.

[343] For this view, see Sorabji (2000), 70–3. Inwood (1993), 164–83 sees a more modest degree of innovation: a new stress on the conscious or voluntary dimension of emotions (and on the limits of this dimension).

already present in Chrysippus' thinking, though not formulated in those terms. Chrysippus' explanation for the occurrence of tears unwilled presupposes that certain kinds of affective reactions (though not full-scale passions) can take place without the normal type of assent to impressions.[344] This seems a reasonable suggestion and one which can be put in more general terms. The intellectual context in which the idea of pre-emotions may well have arisen is the attempt by Chrysippus to explore marginal and complex cases in which his belief-based analysis does not apply obviously or straightforwardly, though it can be shown to provide effective explanation. Chrysippus' examination of problem cases (*aporiai*) in Book 2 of *On Passions,* continued by Posidonius, like his study of instances of internal conflict, such as Medea, in Book 4, form part of this programme. Chrysippus' discussions may have contained some more explicit formulation of the idea of pre-emotions than is apparent in extant material. Alternatively, the discussions we do have, including that on cases such as tears unwilled, may have helped to generate subsequent treatments which formulate this idea more explicitly. This suggestion helps to explain why—as is widely agreed—the later versions of the idea, including Seneca's, are in line with Chrysippus' cognitive theory of the passions, rather than any (supposedly) non-cognitive version of the theory.[345] If this line of thought is accepted, it brings out in another way that Chrysippus' central concern was not only with stressing the cognitive or rationalistic basis for emotions. This concern forms part of the larger Stoic project of offering a unified or holistic explanation for human (and animal) psychology, including complex, marginal, and non-standard manifestations of psychology. The recognition that some affective reactions by rational animals (adult humans) do not fully express the rationality of which they are capable—including the formulation of the idea of pre-emotions—forms an intelligible part of this project.

So far, I have been arguing that Tieleman's view that Posidonius retains, and at most refines, the Chrysippean framework of thought about passions is highly plausible. But can this view really be maintained? Is there *nothing* in Galen's claim that Posidonius adopts the Platonic tripartite psyche in favour of Stoic psychological monism?[346] It is not credible that there is nothing

[344] Tieleman (2003), 127–8, who does not claim Chrysippus used the term 'first movements'. The sense in which Chrysippus postulated pre- or quasi- emotions depends on the precise interpretation taken of Gal. *PHP* 4.7.12–17 (see text to nn. 324–6 above).

[345] See Graver (1999), 318–23; Sorabji (2000), 66–73; Inwood (1993),164–83. Inwood (1993), 154–6, also challenges the claim of Fillion-Lahille (1984) that the discussion of Sen. *Ira* 2.1–4 is based on Posidonius rather than Seneca.

[346] Or, at least, the claim that Posidonius, *in effect,* does so. Galen himself sometimes makes the claim in this weaker form; see nn. 285–6 above.

behind the claim; but it seems likely that what underlies this is much less than, and very different from, what Galen maintains. As several scholars have recently argued, the period of Panaetius and Posidonius seems to mark a major shift in approaches to earlier thinkers, and one that is not confined to the Stoic school. Whereas earlier Hellenistic thinkers adopted or rejected previous ideas, without seeing it as necessary to comment explicitly on this process of selection,[347] later Hellenistic thinkers seem to have discussed what they took or rejected from earlier thought. An associated move was that of presenting one's own philosophy as part of an unfolding intellectual tradition which went back well beyond the start of one's own school or movement.[348] In the case of Stoicism, there is the further point that Platonic, or Academic, thought constituted a key influence on its thought from its inception.[349] The change, associated especially with Panaetius and Posidonius, seems to lie in the explicitness with which the linkage with Platonic, and other earlier, thought is acknowledged.[350] As I have also argued, Stoicism took from Plato ideas which promoted a combination of a holistic philosophical outlook and Socratic ethical ideals; and it is material of this kind, rather than (for instance) the part-based psychology shared by Plato and Aristotle that Stoics, both early and late, would be likely to be most interested in discussing.

Tieleman underlines evidence which supports this understanding of Posidonius' attitude to Plato. Galen himself at one point says that Posidonius 'attempts to bring over not only himself but also Zeno... to the side of the Platonists'. This comment implies that Posidonius tried to identify common ground between the Platonic and Stoic positions, acknowledged as being distinct approaches. It does not suggest that Posidonius silently merged the two positions, let alone (as Galen maintains elsewhere) that he abandoned the Stoic—or, at least, Chrysippean—position in favour of the Platonic one.[351] Galen also reports that Posidonius wrote, in *On Passions* Book 1, 'a kind of epitome' (*hoion epitomēn*) of what Plato said in *Laws* 8 about the shaping of children before and after birth. This again suggests that Posidonius distinguished Plato's ideas (in his 'epitome') from his own.[352] Some of the other reports suggest that there has been—what one might call—creative assimilation of one position to the other. But, in at least some cases, what seems to have occurred is the assimilation of Platonic to Stoic approaches, rather than

[347] One of Galen's complaints about Chrysippus is that he rejected Platonic ideas about the tripartite psyche without explicitly arguing against them; see text to nn. 22, 25–9 above.

[348] See n. 30 above.

[349] See 1.3 above, text to nn. 41–68, 2.2, text to nn. 22–34.

[350] See text to nn. 30–4 above.

[351] Gal. *PHP* 4.4.38; Tieleman (2003), 207.

[352] Gal. *PHP* 5.5.32, referring to Pl. *Lg*. 789a–792e.

the reverse process. This move was not peculiar to Posidonius. We are told that Antipater, head of the Stoic school *c.*159–*c.*129 BC, wrote three books arguing that Plato maintained the Stoic thesis of the self-sufficiency of virtue and 'presented more doctrines [of Plato] as consonant with the Stoic ones'.[353]

This is the process that seems to be at work in Posidonius' reading of Plato's *Timaeus*. As already indicated, this was a work which had a special significance for the evolution of the Stoic world-view. It can be read as expressing Plato's most 'one-world' vision, and it seems to have made an important contribution to Zeno's formulation of a holistic view of the principles of reality.[354] Posidonius appears to interpret the work in the light of earlier Stoic reception of its ideas. For instance, he looked for support for the (Stoic) idea that psychic *pneuma* is scattered throughout the bones in Homeric phraseology and in the claim of Plato, *Timaeus* 73b, that the chains of the psyche lie 'in the roots of the bone'.[355] In other words, Posidonius projected Stoic psychophysical holism, on this point at least, on to the *Timaeus*. A similar move is suggested in a comment made by Plutarch in an essay on the world psyche in the *Timaeus*: '[Posidonius and his followers] did not withdraw far from matter... they declared the psyche to be the form (*idea*) of what is everywhere extended, constituted according to number that comprises harmony'.[356] The interpretation of this passage, together with a related comment that the psyche is intermediate between the intelligibles and perceptibles, is quite difficult and has generated extensive scholarly discussion.[357] But I think that some relevant points emerge clearly enough for the present purpose. In Plato's *Timaeus*, on a straightforward reading, the universe is a combination of an extended but non-material world psyche and a material world body. Earlier Stoicism translated this into the idea that the universe is a fusion of active and passive principles, both of which are physical.[358] Posidonius, it would seem, presupposes that view. Plutarch, writing from the standpoint of dualist Platonism, complains that Posidonius' account of the psyche 'did not withdraw far from matter'; that is, Posidonius (and his followers) presented the psyche as material. Also, the world psyche is presented, in the second sentence cited earlier, as, like the Stoic active principle or god, the immanent

[353] Clement, *Stromateis* 5.97.6 (*SVF* 3.56); trans. Tieleman (2003), 225.

[354] See 1.3 above, text to nn. 41–61; also 5.1 below.

[355] See Posid. fr. 28a (cf. 28b), in Edelstein and Kidd (1972/1989), a scholion (ancient commentary) on Homer's *Iliad*; Tieleman (2003), 209–10.

[356] Plu. *Mor.* 1023 B, from *On the Generation of the Psyche in the Timaeus*, trans. Cherniss (1976), slightly modified.

[357] See e.g. Cherniss (1976), 217–21; Kidd (1988), 530–55; Reydams-Schils (1999), 96–100; Tieleman (2003), 210–13.

[358] See LS 44 and 1.3 above, text to nn. 53–5.

structure or 'form' of the extended, material universe.[359] The mathematical relations and proportions ascribed by Plato's *Timaeus* to the nature and movements of the world psyche are taken by Posidonius as a way of analysing the structure or 'harmony' of the material universe.[360] Although Posidonius may have in some way modified earlier Stoic ideas, the main impression is that he has continued the typical Stoic reading of Plato's universe, as being in line with Stoic psychophysical holism, though in a way that is more explicitly presented as exegesis of Plato's text.

It is worth noting that Plutarch himself advances an ultra-dualist view of the generation of the world psyche, non-standard even among ancient Platonists. He argues that the world psyche was created by the imposition of order and mind on a pre-existing disordered psyche. That is to say, in addition to the dualism of body and psyche, evident in Plato's account, we have a further dualism, between rational and irrational psyche.[361] A striking, and perhaps surprising, feature of Plutarch's essay *On Ethical Virtue*, noted earlier in this chapter, is that he introduces reference there to the world psyche and the human psyche of Plato's *Timaeus* (441 E–442 B). Both of these are characterized in terms that are taken to support the dualism that is Plutarch's explicit position (441 D–E). In the cosmic psyche, as characterized by Plutarch, the contrast is between a part marked by uniform and regular motions and one marked by variable and disorderly motion, giving rise to change and variety in the universe (441 F).[362] In Plutarch's account of Plato's human psyche, the contrast is between a part which is 'endowed with mind and reason, whose natural role is to control and rule the human being', and another which is 'emotional and irrational, wandering and disorderly and in need of a supervisor'.[363] In both essays, a similar conception of rationality or order is assumed, that based on the imposition of order by rational element

[359] Plu. *Mor.* 1023 C understands 'form' (*idea*) as the Platonic Form; but this is inconsistent with his claim that Posidonius conceives the world psyche in material terms (or as intermediate between intelligible and perceptibles) and cannot represent Posidonius' own view.

[360] Pl. *Ti.* 35b–36d; see further on this linkage between Pl. *Ti.* and the Stoic world-view, 5.1 below, text to nn. 10–20.

[361] Plutarch appeals to indications of duality in the world psyche in *Plt.* 273b–e, *Lg.* 896e–898c, as well as the contrast between 'indivisible' and 'divisible' being in *Ti.* 35a. As Cherniss (1976: 148) explains (his wording modified slightly): 'the demiurge ... compounded the soul of the universe by blending *nous* [mind] with irrational soul, the vestigial irrationality of which is the cause of evil in the universe as the rationality imposed on it by god is the cause of the good'; see also Cherniss, 136–49. See further on Plutarch's reading Opsomer (2004).

[362] Plutarch combines the contrast between indivisible (and changeless) being and divisible (and physical) being in *Ti.* 35a with that between the motion of the same and different in 36c–d, 37a–c.

[363] Plutarch builds on the contrast between embodied reason (in the brain) and emotions and appetites based in the heart and liver area in *Ti.* 69c–71e, also 90a–d.

on an essentially irrational one. The Stoic interpretations of the relevant Platonic passages, in so far as these can be reconstructed, stress, rather, the idea of the cosmos or human being as unified psychophysical wholes or structures.[364]

Plutarch's reference in the essay *On Ethical Virtue* to these aspects of Plato's *Timaeus* indicates his awareness that the dualism to which he is committed (of which he sees Plato as an authoritative exponent) applies in analogous ways at the human and cosmic level.[365] In *On Ethical Virtue*, emphatically, and, to a lesser extent, in the essay on the *Timaeus*, Plutarch pits his dualist outlook against the unified or holistic standpoint of Stoicism and, in the latter case, against the Posidonian view of the world psyche. In doing so, Plutarch, like Galen, shows how the debate between part-based or dualist and holistic approaches to human psychology and reality as a whole became in this period an increasingly important and well-defined feature of intellectual life. Plutarch also indicates how competing interpretations of Plato became an integral part of this debate. Posidonius' Stoicizing reading of Plato, both as regards the *Timaeus* and (I shall suggest) human and animal psychology, probably figured as a significant factor in this emerging debate about the significance of Plato's thought. Certainly, we can see how Posidonius' interpretations of Plato are drawn into this debate by both Plutarch and, more fully, by Galen. This is so although, as suggested earlier (4.1 above), full-scale debate and polemic between the two approaches probably only emerges in the era of Plutarch and Galen, rather than that of Posidonius.

I turn now to the evidence for Posidonius' discussions of Plato in connection with ethical psychology. I think we can see how Posidonius' responses to Plato are linked with a set of topics in which Posidonius had a special interest, centring on the question which he is said to have raised repeatedly (*PHP* 4.3.4): what is the cause (*aitia*) of the 'excessive impulse' that constitutes a passion? These topics include the relationship between the motivation of humans and non-human animals, and the early development of human children and the growth of rationality, understood in psychophysical terms. Posidonius' special focus on affective movements, which form part of the experience of animals as well as human children and animals, can be linked with this set of topics. Galen presents these special interests of Posidonius as reflecting an acknowledgement of the existence and motivational power of irrational parts of the psyche. But they can, more plausibly, be seen as

[364] For Zenonian and Posidonian interpretations of Plato's world psyche, see text to nn. 355–7 above; for a reconstructed Stoic reading of Plato's human psyche, see 5.1 below, text to nn. 35–62.

[365] See further Opsomer (1994), 36–41; also Babut (1969*b*), 298–317; Dillon (1977), 199–208.

supplementing Chrysippus' own exploration of these areas, and as expressing the unified or holistic picture of natural kinds and motivational patterns that Posidonius shares with other Stoics.[366]

As noted earlier, the Stoics conceive the universe as an integrated system of more or less complex entities, ranging from material objects to rational animals, unified by differing degrees of 'tension'. They also map natural kinds in complexity of types of animation or motivation. Whereas the activities of plants (nutrition and growth) are shaped by 'nature' (*phusis*) alone, non-rational animals possess in addition perception and 'impulse' (*hormē*), which, in adult humans, is informed by rationality (*logos*).[367] Galen attributes to Posidonius a variant of this scheme, in which immobile and plant-like animals are activated only by appetite (*epithumia*), whereas mobile animals are governed by both appetite and spirit (*thumos*), and humans also by reason (*PHP* 5.6.37–8). This corresponds precisely neither with Stoic or Platonic patterns: for instance, in Stoicism, plants differ from animals in being activated by nature not psyche, whereas the Stoic scheme, rather than any Platonic treatment, gives a determinate place for the capacity for motion.[368] But the closest parallels are with Plato's *Timaeus*, which attributes non-rational appetite to plants (77b) and which, at its close, presents various types of animals (including shellfish) as devolved human beings in a way that reflects the dominance of non-rational motives in their make-up.[369] The last section of the *Timaeus*, including the presentation of psychic illness as body-based and of intellectual activity as assimilation of oneself to the patterns of the cosmos, is one that seems to have held special interest for Stoic thinkers.[370] It is difficult to gauge precisely what kind of Posidonian material underlies Galen's report. But a plausible suggestion is that Posidonius (as suggested by Galen elsewhere)[371] is trying to find common ground between Stoic and Platonic patterns, in particular, by correlating the Stoic schema of types of motivation (as in D.L. 7.86) and Plato's mapping of natural kinds in terms of motives.[372] This need not imply that Posidonius

[366] On these topics as constituting an interconnected complex, see also Cooper (1998*a*), 89–93; on the linkage with Posidonius' readings of Plato, see Tieleman (2003), 214–30.

[367] See e.g. D.L. 7.86 (linked in 87 with a conception of the goal of life shared by leading Stoics including Posidonius). See also 1.4 above, text to nn. 113–17 and Inwood (1985), 18–41.

[368] Galen's phrasing (*PHP* 5.6.38), 'plant-like animals' cuts across the Stoic distinction. For the Stoic linkage between impulse and motion, see e.g. D.L. 7.86.

[369] *Ti.* 77b–c also links non-rational appetite with immobility. See *Ti.* 91d–92c, including 92b6–c1 on shellfish and other fish.

[370] On body-based psychic illness, see *Ti.* 86b–87b, on assimilation to the cosmos, see 90a–d. On links with Stoicism, see 3.5 above, text to nn. 324–34, 4.5, text to n. 278, and text to nn. 377, 389–92 below; also Gill (2000*b*), 70–7.

[371] See text to n. 351–2 above.

[372] See further Tieleman (2003), 214–20.

himself adopted the threefold Platonic subdivision of motives (reason, spirit, and appetite) or regarded them as independent sources of motivation.[373]

PHP 5.5.1–29 is an extended discussion of childhood development, including reference to Posidonius' (alleged) criticisms of Chrysippus and to his interest in Plato's *Laws*. This discussion includes the idea that 'appropriation' (*oikeiōsis*) has three aspects, namely to pleasure, victory, and the ethically fine (correlated with the three Platonic psychic parts), and that children develop from the first two to the third as they grow up (5.5.6–8). This idea is often attributed to Posidonius;[374] but, in this case, Galen does not even claim to be summarizing Posidonius. The passage seems better taken as an attempt by Galen—parallel to earlier attempts by Antiochus and Arius Didymus—to rework the Stoic idea of development as 'appropriation', in this case by assimilation to Platonic part-based psychology.[375] However, more suggestive is Galen's report that Posidonius 'admires what Plato said about the shaping of unborn children in the womb and about their rearing and training after birth' and that Posidonius wrote 'a kind of epitome' of Plato's ideas in his treatise *On Passions*.[376] The passage to which Galen refers (*Lg.* 789a–792e) is striking and unusual, in Plato's writings, in tracing the start of character development in the embryo and infancy and in the focus on the influence of certain types of movement. The close linkage implied between physical and psychological character is parallel in part to the presentation of psychic illness as body-based in the *Timaeus*.[377] It is not difficult to see what may have attracted Posidonius' interest. The treatment of the developing human being as, to a degree at least, a psychophysical unit might interest any Stoic thinker. Galen notes in the same context Posidonius' ideas about the physiological basis for character (which were shared by Chrysippus).[378] In particular, Plato's stress on the potential long-term ethical effect of the handling of infants by nurses recalls Calcidius' reports of early Stoic thinking about the impact of the midwife's bath on newborn infants in shaping their ideas about the goodness of pleasure.[379] Plato's stress on the influence of different kinds of motion

[373] On Galen's claims about Posidonius in this respect, see nn. 284–5 above.

[374] *PHP* 5.5.8 is excerpted as Posid. fr. 160 by Edelstein and Kidd (1972/1989), also as *SVF* 3.54.

[375] See further Cooper (1998*a*), 107 n. 35; Tieleman (2003), 221–2. For appropriation in Antiochus and Arius, see 3.4 above. See also Tieleman (2003), 132–9, who, comparing Gal. *PHP* 5.5.1–26 with Calcidius, *in Timaeum* 165–7 (*SVF* 3.228), sees Galen's discussion as largely commentary (from Galen's standpoint) on *Chrysippus'* theory.

[376] Gal. *PHP* 5.5.32, p. 324, 3–7.

[377] See esp. *Lg.* 789d–e, 790c–792e; cf. *Ti.* 86b–87b (3.5 above, text to nn. 324–34).

[378] Gal. *PHP* 5.5.22–4; on Chrysippus' parallel ideas, see 3.5 above, text to nn. 226–9 (also 4.4, text to nn. 160–1).

[379] See Calcidius, *in Timaeum* 165–7 (*SVF* 3.228); also 4.5 above, text to n. 274. See further Tieleman (2003), 132–9, esp. 134–5, which forms part of his reconstruction of Chrysippus' *On Passions* Book 2.

would have a particular resonance for Posidonius, given his innovative focus on 'affective movements'.[380] Taking all these points together, it seems plausible to think that Posidonius' interest in this discussion of Plato was based on the extent to which it prefigured *Stoic* thinking on childhood development and the physical basis of character.

A further response to Plato is highlighted by Galen in the same context:

At first (he [Posidonius] says) this (rational part) is small and weak, but it acquires size and strength at about the fourteenth year, which is the proper time for it to take control and rule, as a kind of charioteer, the team of horses conjoined with it, namely desire and anger, so long as they are not excessively strong or weak, sluggish or restive, or in general disobedient or disorderly or lawless, but ready to follow and obey reason in everything.[381]

One point in this report is clearly Stoic: the idea that human beings become rational at 14 and that rationality then informs, to some degree, at least, all their psychological functions.[382] But what about the apparent Posidonian interest in the image of the charioteer and horses of *Phaedrus*, 253d–256d, one of Plato's versions of the idea of the tripartite psyche? One might see this as purely Galenic elaboration, based, perhaps, on a more plausibly Posidonian image, that of the charioteer and runaway horses, cited by Galen elsewhere.[383] But perhaps Posidonius was actually interested in the image of the *Phaedrus*. I have suggested in another context that Chrysippus' own usage of the term 'throwing off the reins' (*aphēniazein*) to convey the idea of the 'rejection of reason' may indicate an allusion to Plato's image, which Chrysippus could have read as supporting his conception.[384] If so, that makes it more likely that Posidonius too might have drawn on the charioteer–horse image. It does not follow, of course, that Posidonius used it to express the idea that Galen attributes to him, that being virtuous is a matter of reason exercising authority over separate psychic 'parts' or independent sources of motivation.[385] But Posidonius could have used the image, perhaps even in the words cited earlier, to convey the orthodox Stoic idea that, at 14, the human being, in becoming rational, becomes capable of *passions* (*pathē*), in a full sense, as distinct from

[380] On this Posidonian interest, see text to nn. 285–7 above; on the possible Chrysippean basis for this idea, see text to n. 316 above.

[381] Gal. *PHP* 5.5.34, p. 324, 11–18.

[382] See 3.2 above, text to nn. 55–61.

[383] Gal. *PHP* 5.6.31, used by Galen in connection with the idea of emotions as abating in time. For this suggestion, see Tieleman (2003), 223–4.

[384] For this usage, see Gal. *PHP* 4.2.27, 4.5.18. See Gill (1998*a*), 136–7, which also suggests that Chrysippus might have read the dialogue between charioteer and horses, like Medea's monologue, as expressing the conscious rejection of reason by a figure (the composite of charioteer and horses) essentially capable of accepting reason. See also Price (1995), 150.

[385] For this as being Galen's conception of virtue, see Hankinson (1993), 204–12.

the passionate or affective movements shared by human children and non-human animals.[386] At this age, the 'control-centre' or *hēgemonikon*, like a charioteer, takes charge of the psychic functions in a new (rational) way.[387] From now on, the (rational) impulses are either in accordance with (normative) reason or they are passions, such as desire and anger, which are, in Galen's words, 'disobedient or disorderly'; that is, in Chrysippean terms, they 'reject' reason.[388] As so interpreted, Galen's report, which may be accurate in its phrasing (though not its analysis), shows a further case in which Posidonius interpreted a Platonic image as prefiguring Stoic theory.

I conclude this discussion of Posidonius by considering a quotation by Galen which is often, and plausibly, seen as based on Plato's *Timaeus*:

> The cause of the passions, that is, of inconsistency and the unhappy life, is not to follow in everything the divinity (*daimōn*) within oneself who is of the same stock and has a similar nature to the one who governs the whole cosmos but *at times* to allow oneself to be distracted and carried along by what is worse and beast-like. But *those who overlook this* have neither got the cause of the passions right in these matters nor the correct view with respect to happiness and consistency; for they do not see that this consists first of all in not being led *in anything* by what is irrational and unhappy and godless in the psyche.[389]

As has been recognized, this passage alludes both to an orthodox Stoic definition of the goal of life[390] and to a passage in Plato, *Timaeus* 90a–d, which advocates assimilating the divinity (*daimōn*) in us to that in the cosmos by giving priority to rational understanding rather than other desires. But the passage is also usually seen as supporting Galen's account of Posidonius, by including reference to non-rational motives in the definition of the overall goal, albeit in the form of advocating the rejection of those motives.[391]

However, Tieleman has now offered an intriguing, and credible, rereading of the passage. The key point is to see that those criticized in the passage (as 'those who overlook this') are not Chrysippus and his followers, as Galen claims (*PHP* 5.5.6), but Plato, in the *Timaeus* passage alluded to, and those who follow him in adopting a part-based psychology. The criticism is that these thinkers define happiness in terms of reason's rule over (distinct)

[386] See the interpretation of Gal. *PHP* 5.5.21 offered earlier (text to nn. 290–9 above).

[387] In Posidonius' own phrasing, this, rather than *to logistikon*, may well have been the subject of this sentence (if Galen is here drawing directly on Posidonius).

[388] On 'normative' reason and the 'rejection' of reason in Stoic thought, see 4.5 above, text to nn. 197–205.

[389] Gal. *PHP* 5.6.4–5, trans. Tieleman (2003), 228, slightly modified and with added italics.

[390] D.L. 7.87–8, ascribed to Chrysippus.

[391] See e.g. Reydams-Schils (1999), 111–13; also, despite his general misgivings about Galen's presentation of Posidonius, Cooper (1998*a*), 94–5.

non-rational parts; but they do not see that this is an inadequate conception of happiness. Happiness is a state in which the wise person is *completely* rational (in a normative sense). Put differently, the wise person is not '*at times*... distracted and carried along by what is worse and beast-like' nor is he 'led *in anything* by what is irrational and unhappy and godless'. The reason that such thinkers fail to grasp the *complete* consistency of which human beings are capable is that they posit irrational parts which are independent sources of motivation. Inevitably, once this move is made, their conception of happiness will be, at best, that of the (unstable and uneasy) rule of the rational part over the irrational.[392] On this interpretation, Posidonius is implicitly criticizing Plato, even in his most 'one-world' and pre-Stoic dialogue, for not going far enough in counteracting psychological and ethical dualism. On this reading too, Posidonius' interest in, and responses to, Plato do not constitute the vehicle of a compromise with dualism but, rather, a means of reasserting orthodox Stoic psychological holism.

[392] Tieleman (2003), 228–30; for a contrasting interpretation, see e.g. Edelstein and Kidd (1972/1989); Kidd (1988), 676–7. A possible problem with Tieleman's suggestion is that the passage cited seems to refer to ethical *experience* rather than to *analysis* of this experience, as Tieleman assumes.

5

Competing Readings of Platonic Psychology

5.1 GALEN AND CHRYSIPPUS ON THE *TIMAEUS*

This, relatively short, chapter develops in a concentrated way one of the themes of the previous chapter, the reception of Platonic psychology in Hellenistic and Roman thought. This provides a further way of locating the idea of the structured self (in its Stoic version) within its ancient intellectual context. In particular, it shows how debate about the nature and significance of Platonic psychology became intertwined in this period with the conflict between holistic and part-based conceptions of psychology.

Specifically, I contrast Galenic and Stoic readings of Plato's tripartite psyche as presented in the *Timaeus* and *Republic*. More precisely, I contrast Galen's *actual* comments on this topic with those which Chrysippus *might have* made. Because of the difference between attitudes to earlier thought in the early and later Hellenistic (and Imperial Roman) periods, it is unlikely that, in fact, Chrysippus explicitly discussed this topic or others in quite the way that Posidonius, or still more, Plutarch and Galen did (212–14 above). Also, a reconstruction of Chrysippus' reading of Plato, without supporting ancient evidence, is, inevitably, speculative. None the less, a contrast between a Galenic and a (reconstructed) 'Chrysippean' interpretation of Platonic thought can be illuminating, for several reasons. We have already seen ways in which, it seems very likely, Platonic thought influenced the formation of Stoic philosophy from its origins. This applies not just to the Socratic ethical claims, presented by Plato, which form one side of the set of ideas I am associating with the structured self (Chapter 2 above). There is also good reason to think that Platonic thought, especially that of the *Timaeus*, helped to shape the Stoic version of the holistic world-view. As well as giving an influential picture of a providential universe, the *Timaeus* also, it would seem, helped to shape Stoic thinking on the core principles (active and passive) that give structure and coherence to this universe (17–19 above). Reconstructing an early Stoic (Chrysippean) view of the embodied tripartite psyche can help us to see how far this aspect of Platonic thought might also have influenced Stoic psychology.

As suggested below, *Timaeus* 69–72 offers a picture of the psyche as, first, integrally linked with the body and, second, a coordinated system or structure. It thus anticipates key elements of Stoic thinking, namely psychophysical and psychological holism. On the other hand, Plato's account also contains a feature which is, fundamentally, at odds with the Stoic holistic view of personality, namely the idea of the psyche as consisting of separate parts in the sense of independent sources of motivation.[1] Hence, Plato's picture of the tripartite psyche in the *Timaeus* contains the potentiality for internal conflict (between autonomous parts) in a way that is not true of the Stoic model. Galen's reading of the *Timaeus* passage shares with Stoicism an interest in the idea that psychic functions are fully integrated with the body. However, he also stresses—and perhaps overstates—the internal conflict which is latent in the idea that the psyche consists of independent sources of motivation. Thus, taken together, the Galenic and 'Chrysippean' readings of Plato's account bring out both sides of the Platonic conception. This helps us to see how Plato's account may have contributed to the formation of Stoic psychology. But it also brings out how Platonic ideas were used to support the non-Stoic side of the debate, favouring part-based psychology. This seems to have occurred especially in the first and second centuries AD, as the issues in the debate between holistic and part-based approaches were defined with increasing explicitness and polemical vigour, as suggested earlier (4.1 above).[2]

I focus on the comments on *Timaeus* 69–72 made by Galen in *PHP*, and on the contrasting points that Chrysippus might have made. But I begin by placing this detailed comparison in the wider context of the relationship between Galenic and Stoic psychology, a relationship outlined earlier (4.4 above).What Galen has in common with the Stoics, broadly speaking, is a physicalist conception of the psyche. What he does not share with them is the idea that the embodied psyche forms a unified or whole *structure*. These points of similarity and difference come out in a number of ways, including their respective views of Plato's embodied tripartite psyche. The physicalism of Galen's approach, and the point of contact with Stoic thinking, is most obvious in *The Soul's Dependence on the Body* (*QAM*), rather than *PHP*. Here, Galen develops the thesis that the body is '"proximately composed" of the four humours (blood, black bile, yellow bile and phlegm) whose proper blend is different in different parts of the body, so that the brain, the heart, and the liver, for example, each has its own proper blend'.[3] Galen refers to ideas from a

[1] This theme is even more prominent in Pl. *R.* 4, discussed in 5.2 below.

[2] On indications in Plutarch that the interpretation of Plato's *Timaeus* became involved with this debate, see 4.6 above, text to nn. 361–5.

[3] Von Staden (2000), 106, cited more fully in 4.4 above, text to n. 157.

wide range of earlier thinkers, who are presented as holding one or other aspect of the kind of physicalism that Galen is affirming. These examples include the Stoics in general (not just Posidonius), who are described as maintaining that 'the substance (*ousia*) of the psyche comes to be according to a particular mixture (*krasis*) of air and fire.'[4] Galen also cites certain passages from Plato's *Timaeus* as expressing a similar view. He refers to the description of the effect of the (gradually diminishing) 'stream of growth and nourishment' in the composition and development of the human being in support of his own claim that 'wetness brings about mindlessness and dryness understanding.' He also presents the account of psychic illness (as body-based) in *Ti.* 86b–87b as showing that 'Plato is... aware of the negative effect of bad bodily humour (*kakochumia*) on the psyche'.[5] There is, of course, scope for debate about the plausibility of Galen's reading of these and other such passages, and also about how to locate this strand of Galen's thinking within his—rather diverse—range of ideas about the body–psyche relationship.[6] The only points I want to underline here are that Galen has in common with the Stoics—as he sometimes acknowledges—a physicalist approach to the psyche and that the *Timaeus* is a context in which this physicalism is exemplified in a way that seems to have influenced both Galen and the Stoics.[7]

Where Galen diverges from the Stoics, in a way that bears on the interpretation of Plato's *Timaeus*, is on the question of the extent to which the embodied psyche constitutes a unified whole or structure. Galen's critical attitude towards the Stoic, and especially Chrysippean, conception of the psyche as a unified whole has been illustrated fully here (4.5 above). Galen's criticism of this Stoic idea reflects his general belief, which he sees as supported by a combination of medical experiment and philosophical tradition, that the embodied psyche consists of three independent sources of motivation, housed in different parts of the body. This overall view is reflected in Galen's comments on the tripartite psyche in *Timaeus* 69–72 as well in *Republic* Book 4. In both cases, Galen focuses on passages which he takes to show internal conflict which derives from the independence of the psychic parts. As regards the *Republic*, Galen's response registers an explicit and fundamental feature of the argument—though he de-emphasizes, I think,

[4] Gal. *QAM*, ch. 4, trans. Tieleman (2003), 150, slightly modified; see also 4.4 above, text to nn. 158–60. Contrast *PHP* 5.5.23, 26, where this idea is ascribed to Posidonius (and *not* Chrysippus); Tieleman (2003), 240–1.

[5] Gal. *QAM*, chs. 4 and 6, trans. Singer (1997*a*), 156, 160, referring to Pl. *Ti.* 43a–b, 44a–b, and 86e–87a, respectively.

[6] On the second question, see Singer (1997*a*), pp. xxx–xxxix (also Singer 1997*b*), and von Staden (2000), 105–16.

[7] See further, on the body-based approach to Plato's *Timaeus*, as presented in Gal. *QAM*, Gill (2000*b*), 65–70 (on *Ti.* 86b–87b and psychic illness).

the indications of internal cohesion there.[8] But Galen, arguably, fails to bring out a salient difference between the accounts of *Republic* 4 and *Timaeus* 69–72. In the *Timaeus*, the focus is less on the idea of the psyche as a composite of independent, and potentially conflicting, sources of motivation, and more on the psyche as an integrated set of cooperative functions. This contrast has been brought out clearly by Thomas Johansen. He highlights the emphasis in *Ti.* 69–72 on the way that the physiological system is designed to enable the various psychic parts to achieve rational objectives, by contrast with the focus in *Republic* 4 on the capacity for conflict between reason and appetite. The idea that humans, and other animals, function as cohesive psychological wholes, and that this integration is reflected at the physiological level is fundamental to Stoicism. It is reflected in their view, often supposed to have been influenced by the *Timaeus*, that the configuration of the human body is providentially designed to enable human beings to exercise the rationality of which they are constitutively capable.[9] Hence, Stoics such as Chrysippus are likely to have been better placed than Galen to recognize this feature of Plato's picture of the embodied tripartite psyche in the *Timaeus*, a point brought out shortly in my 'Chrysippean' reading of Plato's account.

There is a further way in which the Stoics might have seen the embodied psychology of the *Timaeus* as expressing the idea of wholeness or structure. Several recent accounts have emphasized that mathematical ideas permeate the *Timaeus*, in a way that informs the presentation of psyche and body, at the level of both the universe and the human being.[10] Psyche and body do not only constitute a structure in the sense that they combine or interact, as separate types of entity—though this is a well-marked dimension of the dialogue.[11] Also, psyche and body equally form part of a larger structure or system, in which their separate identities are merged, a structure which can be analysed in terms of number, ratio, or analogy. For instance, the idea of proportion is introduced in the dialogue as a means of creating the best kind of bond, namely one 'which makes a unity of itself together with the things bonded by it'.[12] This idea is then applied to the relationship between the four elements making up the universe as a solid object and to the relationship between the components and movements of the world psyche,

[8] On the latter point, see 5.2 below, text to nn. 83–91.

[9] See Johansen (2000), 104–11, (2004), 153–9; on the providential approach to the body in *Ti.*, see also Steel (2001), 14–20.

[10] On mathematical ideas in *Ti.*, see Burnyeat (2000), 57–67; also references in nn. 11–13 below.

[11] See e.g. *Ti.* 86b–87b, also 87c–90d; see further Gill (2000*b*), 68–9; Johansen (2000), 108–9, (2004), 156–7.

[12] *Ti.* 31c2–3, trans. Zeyl in Cooper (1997). For the points made in the remainder of this paragraph, see also Gill (2000*b*), 70.

analysed in terms of ratio.[13] A similar set of ideas is applied to the human being. The human body is characterized, like the cosmos, as a unified structure, informed by a psyche which, like the world psyche, is constructed according to a determinate set of ratios. The initial impact of the conjunction of psyche and body disrupts this set of ratios; but they can be restored by a proper process of development and education.[14] The correspondence between the human being and the cosmos is reinforced by the idea that humans should use their senses and mind to restore in themselves the ratio-governed movements which are also found in the universe.[15] Recent accounts have shown how fully Plato works out the idea of the human being as a psychophysical unit structured on mathematical principles. Sedley argues that the idea that philosophical activity consists in circular movements which mirror those of the universe is meant to be taken quite literally and is supported by the roundness of the human head that houses the brain.[16] Johansen shows how the marrow serves as a physical vehicle for a psyche that combines circular and rectilinear movements in a way that informs the relatively rational (circular and rectilinear) movements of the psyche–body complex.[17]

This type of conception of structure, which embraces the relationship between psyche and body, universe and human, is one that is more congenial to Stoic thought, with its systematically holistic outlook, than to Galenic thought. It is possible, at least, that Posidonius had this kind of structure in mind in characterizing Plato's world psyche (which he conceived in physical terms) as 'the form of what is everywhere extended, constituted according to number that comprises harmony'.[18] It is true that the Stoics do not, in general, conceive the universe as structured on mathematical principles, in the way suggested in the *Timaeus*.[19] But they do see the universe as a unified structure. For instance, they see the universe as constituting varying degrees of 'tension' of *pneuma* (or the active cause) operating on matter. Bodily entities, psyche, and 'reason' (*logos*) are all conceived as grades on a single scale of 'tension'. It follows that psyche and body are not the basic building blocks of the universe; they are manifestations of a more inclusive or fundamental type of structure

[13] *Ti.* 31b–32c, 35a–36d. For systematic study of ratio in the *Timaeus*, especially in the world psyche, see Zedda (2000, 2003).

[14] *Ti.* 43a–44c; see also, for analogous features in the world psyche, 36e–37a.

[15] *Ti.* 47b–d, 90c–d.

[16] Sedley (1997*a*), 329–30, referring esp. to *Ti.* 44d, 76a, and 91e–92a.

[17] Johansen (2000), 102–4, (2004), 150–2, referring esp. to *Ti.* 73c–d. On the body in Pl. *Ti.* as an integrated structure, see also Burgess (2000, 2004), and Joubaud (1991), 281–8.

[18] Plu. *Mor.* 1023 B; for interpretations of what Posidonius meant, see 4.6 above, text to nn. 356–60.

[19] However, a related Stoic line of thought, with Platonic antecedents, that virtue constitutes a type of (quasi-mathematical) harmony, is explored by Long (1996), ch. 9.

or system. This point, I suggested earlier, forms a crucial part of the holism of the Stoic world-view, which underlies their understanding of humans and other animals as psychophysical wholes.[20] There is, at least, an analogy between the way that psyche and body are seen as part of a larger mathematical structure in Plato's *Timaeus* and the way they are conceived as expressions of 'tension' of *pneuma* in Stoicism. Against the background of the larger influence of Plato's *Timaeus* on the Stoic holistic world-view (16–20 above), it is entirely possible that this feature was also influential on Stoic thought, even though it was not adopted in precisely the same form. This is a further suggestive point of contact, which underlies the analogies between Platonic and Stoic thought about embodied psychology discussed shortly.

I now highlight salient features of Galen's actual and Chrysippus' reconstructed reading of the embodied tripartite psyche of Plato's *Timaeus*.[21] Galen uses *Ti.* 69–72 as part of his overall project of showing that the tripartite psyche, which was adopted, as he claims, by Hippocrates as well as Plato, is compatible with the experimental findings of medical science.[22] On the face of it, Galen's interpretation of Plato is highly plausible, since this is the only passage in Plato's dialogues where the three parts of the tripartite psyche are located in specific parts of the body. However, if closely examined, it is less clear that the account in the *Timaeus* does provide support for the kind of conception that Galen advocates. There are related reasons, outlined earlier (243–4 above) for doubting whether Galen's model, taken on its own terms, is internally consistent. A key aspect of Galen's theory is that the three major organs of the body (brain, heart, and liver) are the sources or principles (*archai*) of three types of faculty or capacity (*dunamis*) both of psyche and body. Galen also adopts what he sees as Plato's view that the three psychological capacities (reasoning, emotions such as anger, and appetite) should not be seen as functions of a unified organic system but as fundamentally different 'forms' or 'parts' (*eidē* or *merē*), which differ in 'essence' (*ousia*). They are also seen as distinct, and potentially conflicting, sources of motivation.[23] Galen finds support for this view in Plato's *Republic*, especially in the argument in Book 4, in which conflict between parts, especially reason and appetite, is taken as proof that they are distinct sources of motivation.[24] In

[20] See 1.4 above, text to nn. 110–17.

[21] For an earlier version of this exercise, see Gill (1997*a*).

[22] See 4.4 above, text to nn. 155–6, 162–4. Galen's main comments on *Ti.* 69–72 are in *PHP* 3.1.26–33, 6.2.9–10, 6.8.39–40, 48–52, 69–72, 74.

[23] For this terminology, see *PHP* 6.2.5, which contrasts Plato with other thinkers (Aristotle, Posidonius, and Chrysippus). See further Tieleman (1996), pp. xxiii–xxvi, (2003), 34–9; also Hankinson (1991), 205 n. 32; Mansfeld (1991), 138–45.

[24] See *PHP* 5.7.1–82, which discusses at length the argument of *R.* 435e–441c, used as support against Chrysippean unified psychology; see further 5.2 below, text to nn. 81–6.

referring to Plato, Galen tends to assimilate the psychological models of the *Republic* and the *Timaeus* to each other.[25] For instance, in describing the relations between the parts in the *Timaeus*, Galen uses terms such as 'dog' or 'savage many-headed beast' that are based on the description of conflict between parts in the *Republic*.[26] In discussing *Ti.* 69–72, Galen gives particular emphasis (regarding the heart) to Plato's phrase, 'fountain-head of blood that moves violently (*sphodrōs*) through all the limbs', and (regarding the liver) to Plato's phrase, 'appetitive (*epithumētikon*) of food and drink'. In Book 6, his argument is centred on physiological, rather than psychological, questions.[27] But the effect is to reinforce his general picture of the psyche as a collection of independent sources of motivation with their own, sometimes irrational, mode of operation.

Galen's interpretation of Platonic texts in support of his theory is problematic in certain ways. For one thing, as Tieleman points out, Galen links psychological parts or functions with anatomical organs in a way that is more definite and precise than Plato's *Timaeus* allows. In Plato's account, 'spirited' and appetitive parts are allocated a general location, rather than a specific organ.[28] Also, Galen's procedure glosses over significant differences between the psychology of the *Republic* and the *Timaeus*. For one thing, the scope of the appetitive part is different in the two dialogues. In the *Timaeus*, the focus is on the stomach and liver as means of digestion and divination, and there is no explicit mention of sexual functions.[29] In the *Republic*, by contrast, sexual desire is included in the appetitive functions; and sexual desire plays a prominent role in the extreme case of the psyche ruled by appetite, the tyrannical (or tyrannized) character.[30] It is partly the inclusion of sexual desire that makes it plausible to describe the appetitive part as 'most

[25] See e.g. *PHP* 6.2.1–12, which follows reference (in 6.1.25–7) to the argument in *R.* 4 (that conflict between psychic parts shows they are independent sources of motivation).

[26] See *PHP* 6.2.14, using the language of *R.* 440c–d and 588c–589b to characterize the relation between parts in *Ti.* 70a–b.

[27] See e.g. (on the heart) *PHP* 6.8.40, 49 (also, with fuller quotation, 6.8.72, 3.1.31), and 6.8.74 ('when the strength of anger boils'); (on the liver) 6.8.51–2, 69–70). See esp. *Ti.* 70b1–3, d7–8. Galen also refers to *Ti.* 70c1–5 in *PHP* 3.32–3, challenging Chrysippus' claim that the presence of anger in the heart demonstrates that this is the seat of the ruling part of the psyche (*PHP* 3.1.24–33); see also Tieleman (1996), 156–7.

[28] The gods placed 'the part of the psyche that shares in courage and spirit ... nearer the head between the midriff and the navel', and 'the part of the psyche that has appetites for food and drink ... in the area between the midriff and the boundary towards the navel' (*Ti.* 70a3–4, d7–e2), second passage, trans. Zeyl in Cooper (1997), slightly modified. See further Tieleman (1996), pp. xxx–xxxi; Steel (2001), 120–3.

[29] See *Ti.* 70e–72d. The location seems to rule out the genital organs: see 77b4; 'between the midriff and the navel', 77b4, trans. Zeyl in Cooper (1997); also 70e1–2, cited in n. 28 above.

[30] See *R.* 439d6, 580e4, 439e–440a (Leontius example): on sexual desire in the tyrannized psyche, 572e, 573d–e, 574b–c, 574e.

insatiable' and liable to conflict with reason and spirit.[31] When sexual desire figures in the *Timaeus*, in connection with the idea of body-based psychic illness, it is linked with bone-marrow, which is, in turn, associated with the brain rather than the liver.[32] Also, although the appetitive part is characterized as 'irrational' in both dialogues, this is so in different senses. In the *Republic*, the appetitive part seems to be conceived as rational (or cognitive) in the sense that it can, in principle, collaborate with, or be 'persuaded by', reason. But it is described as 'irrational', and characterized in bestial language, because (in many people) it is in conflict with reason as a source of authority.[33] In the *Timaeus*, the appetitive functions of the stomach and liver are 'beast-like' because they are more limited in their rational or cognitive capacities; hence, communication must be through physiological processes and images. But the operations of these parts are 'rational' in the sense that they form a coherent part of an overall organic system.[34] In other words, whereas the *Republic* presents the psychological interplay between competing sources of motivation, the *Timaeus* depicts the coordination of different types of psychophysical function. Galen's tendency to assimilate the two Platonic accounts obscures this important difference.

How, by contrast, might Chrysippus have read *Timaeus*. 69–72? Thanks to Galen, we know that Chrysippus *did* read this passage, but we do not know very much about *how* he read it. In an extended quotation from Chrysippus' *On the Psyche*, Galen includes this comment: 'Plato, who said that the psyche has three parts, placed the rational part in the head, the spirited in the region of the chest, and the desiderative in the region of the navel'.[35] The passage from which this comment is taken comes at the start of the second half of Book 1 of Chrysippus' treatise (*PHP* 3.1.16). Mansfeld, in particular, has attempted to explain Chrysippus' line of thought, which he sees as reflecting the conceptual pattern of early examples of the doxographical or *placita* tradition. Chrysippus refers to questions central to this emerging tradition, derived from earlier philosophical debate: the nature or 'essence' (*ousia*) of the psyche, its parts, and the character of the ruling part.[36] The topic on which

[31] See *R.* 442a6–b3, 588e–589b.

[32] *Ti.* 86c–d, and (on marrow and brain), 73b–d. The linkage between 'control-centre' and genitals prefigures that in Stoic theory (LS 53 H(4)).

[33] On the 'rationality' of this part, see e.g. *R.* 442d10–d1, 548b4–c2, 554d2–3; on its 'irrationality' (rejecting reason) see e.g. 439d6–8, 442a5–b3, 588e–589a. The contrast can be characterized as that between 'functional' and 'normative' rationality. See further Gill (1996*b*), 245–60, 4.5 above, text to nn. 197–212 also text to nn. 42–3 below.

[34] *Ti.* 71a (also 71b–72d), 77b. On this contrast, see also Johansen (2000), 105–7, (2004), 153–5.

[35] Gal. *PHP* 3.1.14, p. 170, 20–2, trans. De Lacy, slightly modified.

[36] These topics are taken to derive from Aristotle (and Plato), mediated by Theophrastus, and to have found their way at some date before Chrysippus into early doxographical accounts.

Chrysippus focuses here is that of the location of the ruling part; he notes the division of opinion about whether this is the head or the chest. Plato's position is cited, Mansfeld suggests, as a compromise between these two dominant views; but Chrysippus goes on to claim that the issue still remains unresolved. The reference to unresolved contradictions in philosophical debate evokes the approach of Academic scepticism. But it is clear that Chrysippus went on to try to resolve the contradictions by arguing that the unitary control-centre was located in the heart.[37] Galen criticizes Chrysippus, here and subsequently, for citing Plato's view and then failing to argue against Plato, despite putting forward a radically different position.[38] Tieleman claims that Galen's charge is, at best, a half-truth. In his arguments for the location of the control-centre (which Tieleman seeks to reconstruct), it seems clear that Chrysippus, in effect, aimed to answer Plato.[39] For instance, Chrysippus seems to have taken up Plato's idea that anger and other emotions are located in the chest, and argued that this is because the heart is the centre of rational activity. Rational activity includes, for Chrysippus, emotions such as anger, which are also physical processes of whose presence, and indeed location within us, we are to some degree aware.[40] However, Tieleman does not suggest that Chrysippus argues explicitly against Plato, in the way that, for instance, Galen argues against Chrysippus. His lack of explicit commentary reflects what seems to be the normal, if not invariable, practice of Stoics in the early Hellenistic period.[41]

My aim here is not to pursue the question of how Chrysippus actually did, in his essay, contradict the *Timaeus* on this point. My project—an explicitly speculative one—is to ask how Chrysippus might have interpreted the embodied tripartite psyche if he had seen it as prefiguring Stoic thought, given that, as it seems, other aspects of the *Timaeus* anticipated, and helped to

See Mansfeld (1990), 3062–4, 3172–3, 3212–16; also Tieleman (2003), 34–5. Alternatively, Chrysippus' line of thought could be seen as an independent response to the way that previous philosophers had formulated psychological questions.

[37] See further Mansfeld (1989), 311–14, 334–42, (1990), 3167–77; also Tieleman (1996), 158–60.

[38] Gal. *PHP* 3.1.14, 19–27, also 5.7.43, 51. See also 4.1 above, text to nn. 22–4.

[39] See Tieleman (1996), 140–6, criticizing the explanation for Chrysippus' silence offered by Gould (1970), 133–7. For Tieleman's reconstruction of the start of Chrysippus' response to Plato, see his 158–88.

[40] See Gal. *PHP* 3.1.25; this response is taken by Galen to show Chrysippus' failure to recognize that he has been contradicted by Plato, e.g. in *Ti.* 70a–c, cited earlier (text to n. 27 above). See further Tieleman (1996), 168–76, 185–8; and for a different reading of *PHP* 3.1.25, Sorabji (2000), 39–40.

[41] See further 4.1 above, text to nn. 25–8. Chrysippus' treatise *On Justice* (*SVF* 3.195), apparently directed against Plato (noted by Tieleman (1996: 140–1), may be an exception. See also n. 68 below.

shape, Stoic thought.[42] I think that we can offer in this way what is both a plausible reading of salient features of Plato's account and one which brings out real points of resemblance to the Stoic conception of the embodied human personality. The main points bear on the way in which, in the *Timaeus*, spirit and appetite function rationally, in certain senses, and also on the way in which their operation forms part of a coherent psychophysical system. There are two principal senses of rationality relevant to the passage. One is that of responding, directly or indirectly, to reason, understood as a locus of beliefs, judgements, and so on. The other is that of forming part of an organic system, whose rationality (in the sense of order or structure) is intelligible to a human observer.

Both senses of rationality are relevant to the description of the spirited element, located in the region of the heart. Chrysippus might well have seen this description as prefiguring his thinking about the way that a passion expresses the rationality of the adult human being, as well as about the human body as a rationally intelligible organic system. Stress is laid in Plato's account on the idea that the spirited part responds to the rational part. Put differently, it responds to grounds for anger, 'when reason gives the message that some unjust action is occurring... either outside or from any of the appetites inside.'[43] The ideas that spirit is the natural assistant of reason and that reactions such as anger depend on judgements about injustice recall the *Republic*.[44] What is distinctive in the *Timaeus* is the coupling of this belief-based view of emotion with a conception of the human body as a psychophysical system. The intensity of the reaction is presented as a direct result of the reason given. It is when 'reason gives the message' that 'the excitement (*menos*) of spirit boils'. This, in turn, stimulates the movement of 'the blood that moves violently through all the limbs' (one of the phrases highlighted by Galen) that communicates this message to the body as a whole.[45] This description combines two aspects that Aristotle sees as belonging to two different types of analysis of anger: the dialectician's definition of anger as a desire for retaliation and the natural scientist's definition of it as the boiling of blood around the heart.[46] However, it is precisely this combination that is characteristic of the Stoic analysis of passions. Passions depend on beliefs, specifically, the belief 'that it is appropriate to react' in a given way. Passions

[42] See 1.3 above, text to nn. 41–68.

[43] *Ti.* 70b4–5, also a4–7, b7–c1.

[44] Cf. *Ti.* 70a5 and *R.* 441a2–3, *Ti.* 70b4–5 and *R.* 440c. Galen's conflation of the two Platonic accounts (*PHP* 6.2.9–10, 14) brings out this point of resemblance from a different standpoint.

[45] *Ti.* 70a6–c1, quotations from b3–4, b1–2. On Galen's interest in the latter phrase, see text to n. 27 above.

[46] See Arist. *de An.* 403^{a}29–^{b}1; the linkage with Pl. *Ti* 70a–b is noted by Cornford (1937), 283.

also constitute the intense psychophysical reactions (such as 'swelling' or 'shrinking') that are triggered by these beliefs. More precisely, the reactions depend on assent to the rational impression that, for instance, 'this act is wrong and justifies anger'.[47] Chrysippus, reading *Timaeus* 70a–b, might well have seen in the description of anger 'obeying' reason's message and reacting accordingly a striking anticipation of this conception of a passion.[48] In *On the Psyche*, it seems that Chrysippus cited our awareness of emotions such as anger in the heart as evidence that the (rational) control-centre is also present there. That is, he drew out in another way the linkage between rational beliefs and psychophysical reactions that Plato's picture also highlights—though Plato, of course, separates the locations of reason and spirit.[49]

Chrysippus might also have seen the account of the spirited part in the *Timaeus* as prefiguring his view of the body as a psychophysical system. In Stoicism, the animal body is seen as a unified system of communication, in which 'impressions' are sent as messages to the control-centre (*hēgemonikon*) in the heart. The veins and arteries form a key part of this system, though the messages are transmitted through vital *pneuma* (warm breath) rather than blood.[50] As noted earlier, the Stoics, like Hellenistic medical science, adopted the picture of animal physiology as an integrated system. However, unlike the Hellenistic doctors (but like some earlier thinkers, including Aristotle), they saw this system as centred on the heart rather than the brain.[51] Similarly, in the *Timaeus*, sensation is depicted as taking place in a communication system in which messages are sent (*exangeilē*(*i*)) to the rational part (*to phronimon*, 64b5–6). The rational part is located in the brain; but, in advance of the Hellenistic discovery of the brain-centred nervous system, Plato makes no attempt to define a chain of communication from the brain. It is not clear how communication is seen as occurring; but blood is sometimes involved and this plays an important role in communicating anger throughout the body.[52] The heart is described as the 'knot' and 'source' of violently moving blood that responds to reason's 'message' of the grounds for anger. This

[47] See 4.5 above, text to nn. 184–7.

[48] For another way in which Plato's *Timaeus* can be seen as anticipating Stoic thinking on the passions, namely in Plato's 'first creation moment', in which the newly created (rational) human being reacts irrationally (42b–44b), linked by implication with the account of the passions of 69c–d in the 'second creation moment', see Reydams-Schils (1999), 62–4.

[49] Gal. *PHP* 3.1.23–5; see also text to n. 43 above.

[50] See LS 53 E–N, esp. G–H. See also Solmsen (1961), 180–1; Gould (1970), 50–6; Sedley (1993), 326–31.

[51] See 1.4 above, text to nn. 118–22, 4.4, text to nn. 162, 167–9; also Mansfeld (1991), 138–41.

[52] For the role of blood in communication, see *Ti.* 65c7–d1, 66d4–8, 67b3. See also Solmsen (1961), 160–7; also 181, noting the similarity between Platonic and Stoic theories; Brisson (1997), 311–16.

ensures that all the blood vessels of the body become aware of the orders given and allow 'the best part to be the leader' (*hēgemonein*, 70a7–c1). The last term, in particular, could have been taken by Chrysippus as prefiguring the Stoic communication system, centred on the heart as the seat of the control-centre (*hēgemonikon*).[53]

As well as being rational in the sense that it responds to reason's messages, the heart as described in the *Timaeus* is also rational in the sense of forming a coherent part of an intelligible system. The idea, more precisely, is that the parts of the human body, like other features of the universe, can be understood as functionally adapted to work for the good of the creature concerned and thus to form part of a providentially designed universe. This is a theme which is common to Plato's *Timaeus* and to Stoicism; and, in this general idea at least, it is plausible to see Plato as influencing, and not simply prefiguring, Stoic thought.[54] To see the scope for rationality in this sense in *Timaeus* 69–72, we need to see that the two lower parts form a system consisting of two, functionally related, pairs: (1) spirit centred on heart and lungs and (2) appetite centred on stomach and liver. Just as the lungs have the function of cooling the heart when this is inflamed by spirit, so the liver has the function of 'frightening' the stomach and causing contraction, presumably when the stomach's natural desire for food leads to excessive consumption.[55]

However, different parts of this system differ in the degree of rationality (in the previous sense considered) that is involved in this process. Spirit–heart, as just noted, acts in response to reason's messages, and communicates these throughout the body. The lungs, however, merely provide a physiological means by which spirit can play this role without 'being troubled' by the heat and agitation incurred in fulfilling its function (70c1–d5). Appetite–stomach seems to occupy an intermediate status. It is made explicit that it is incapable of responding to reason, though it is adapted to be guided (*psuchagōgein*) by images. These images are, in part, simply physiological reactions, such as the bilious contractions produced in the liver (71b7–c3). However, it is also suggested that both positive and negative reactions (images) are, in some sense, the product of 'thoughts sent down from the mind' (71b3–4, c4). The ambiguous status of these images is taken further by exploring the traditional idea that the liver is the seat of prophecy or divination. The liver is said to enable divination in dreams; in this way, a part of us that 'has no share in reason and understanding' has 'some grasp of truth'.[56] In explanation, it is

[53] See also *Ti.* 41c6–d1 (*hēgemonoun*); and Reydams-Schils (1999), 60–1.

[54] See 1.3 above, text to nn. 41–68.

[55] *Ti.* 71a–c, esp. b5, c3; the spleen is attached to the second set of organs to keep the liver clean (72c–d).

[56] *Ti.* 71d–e, esp. d4 and e1, trans. Zeyl in Cooper (1997).

said that people only prophesy when their state of mind is altered by sleep or mental disturbance, but that their prophecies need to be interpreted by those in sound mind (*Ti.* 71e–72b). This is one of the more puzzling details in the *Timaeus*' picture of embodied psychology.[57] But the main point, made explicitly, is that the use of the 'base' (*phaulon*) organ of the liver for divination serves the larger, providential objectives of the cosmos because it enables a non-rational part to 'have some grasp of truth'.[58] To put the point differently, the rationality of the cosmos is not realized only by the fact that the organs fulfil their function within an organic system whose internal organization and structure we can recognize. They also do so by sharing, partly or indirectly, in the more complex (cognitive or belief-based) functions of reason. Spirit–heart does so by acting directly on reason's judgements and the liver does so by communicating an image of truth, which is grasped non-rationally but is open to rational interpretation.[59]

Taken as a whole, Plato's account of the embodied human psyche can be seen as anticipating Stoic thought in several ways. The presentation of the organs, and correlated psychic parts, functioning as a cohesive system anticipates the Stoic conception of animals (including humans) as psychophysical wholes. In particular, the description of the heart responding to reason's messages prefigures the Stoic conception of passions as functions of the rational (adult human) psyche. The rationality, in the sense of intelligible order, of this psychophysical model evokes the Stoic providential world-view, which was probably modelled on that of the *Timaeus*. The ambiguous kind of rationality displayed by the liver is less easy to correlate with Stoic theory. The function of nutrition associated with the stomach and liver is allocated to 'nature' (*phusis*) rather than psyche in Stoicism. It is seen as a biological or physiological process rather than a psychological one, even in the qualified sense envisaged by Timaeus.[60] The closest parallel to the process of 'picturing' attributed to the Platonic liver may be Posidonius' idea that passions are produced more effectively by pictures than words, perhaps because this activates affective movements, even in adult humans.[61] One point of

[57] See further Pender (1997), 286–8; Rotondaro (1997); Steel (2001), 117–19. There are partial parallels in Platonic ideas about prophetic madness and related types of madness (*Phdr.* 244b–245b, also *Ion* 533d–535a).

[58] *Ti.* 71d5–e2, referring back to 41b–d (and 30a–c).

[59] For some analogous comments on the 'devolved rationality' in Plato's account of the function of the two lower parts, see Johansen (2000), 106–7, (2004), 154–5.

[60] See LS i. 319–20; also von Staden (2000), 102–4. The comparable section of the account of Stoic thinking in Cic. *N.D.* 2 (156–7, on the stomach) only illustrates the sense of 'rationality' according to which the organ is well adapted to perform its function.

[61] See Gal. *PHP* 5.6.24–6; both accounts use a similar term for the 'picturing' involved (*apozōgraphoi*), *Ti.* 71c4; *anazōgraphēsis*, Gal. *PHP* 5.6.25, p. 330, 28.

difference is that Posidonius seems to have in mind cases where picturing supplements, and gives added force to, rational impressions in words, rather than the process of communicating with a non-rational organ or part, as in the *Timaeus*.[62] In general, however, a 'Chrysippean' reading of Plato's account of the embodied tripartite psyche brings out strong points of resemblance with the Stoic approach based on psychophysical holism, in spite of the initial appeal of the Galenic interpretation.

5.2 GALEN AND CHRYSIPPUS ON THE *REPUBLIC*

To suggest that Chrysippus might have seen the account of the embodied tripartite psyche in *Timaeus* 69–72 as prefiguring the Stoic theory—that it might even have influenced the theory—is not so surprising, given the general acceptance that some aspects of the *Timaeus* may have helped to shape the Stoic world-view. To propose a similar idea about the tripartite psyche of the *Republic* is much more controversial. It is much more common to suppose that Stoic ethics and psychology were influenced by *Socratic* thought, as represented especially in the early Platonic dialogues. The Stoics are often seen as offering a more fully theorized version of the psychology implied in Socratic arguments such as the denial of *akrasia* ('weakness of will') in *Protagoras* 353–60. The Socratic paradox that virtue is knowledge reappears as the Stoic claim that all psychological functions of adult humans, including passions, are acts of a unitary, and fundamentally rational, control-centre.[63] The tripartite psyche of the *Republic*, like that of the *Phaedrus*, by contrast, is naturally taken as shaping the competing part-based psychological framework that we find in thinkers such as Plutarch and Galen.[64] The previous discussion in this book has tended to support this way of conceiving the contrasting influence of 'Socratic' and 'Platonic' (or Platonic–Aristotelian) psychology.

Whether the Stoics themselves saw the situation in this way is rather less clear. For one thing, as Sedley points out, 'it would be misleading to imply

[62] Posidonius, for instance, refers to the way in which mental picturing can supplement a 'verbal account' (*diēgēsis*), Gal. *PHP* 5.6.26. I am assuming that Posidonius' thinking reflects orthodox (Chrysippean) psychology (4.6 above). For a discussion of picturing based on the idea that Posidonius revises Stoic thinking, see Sorabji (2000), 114–15.

[63] See e.g. M. Frede (1986), 96, 98; Gosling (1990), 48–9; Sedley (1993), 313–14. See also 2.2 above, text to nn. 23–6.

[64] See further, on Plutarch, 4.3 above, on Galen, 4.4 above. For a contrasting suggestion about the influence of the psychology of the *Phaedrus* on Stoic thought, see 4.6 above, text to nn. 383–8.

that any ancient reader of Plato operated with an entirely clearcut distinction between historically Socratic texts on the one hand and Platonic texts on the other'.[65] So we cannot simply assume that the Stoics drew a sharp contrast between 'Socratic' and 'Platonic' psychology. On some topics, it seems clear, the Stoics found congenial material in what are, for modern scholars, 'Platonic' dialogues such as the *Timaeus* or *Laws*.[66] When Antipater argued that Plato anticipated Stoic thought on the self-sufficiency of virtue for happiness, it is likely that he drew on the core claims of the *Republic* as well as on 'Socratic' dialogues such as the *Euthydemus*.[67] Political theory seems to be one topic on which the early Stoics, both Zeno and Chrysippus, explicitly took issue with Plato's *Republic*.[68] But it is less obvious that this also happened with psychology. As noted earlier, Galen complains repeatedly that Chrysippus, though citing Plato's theory of the tripartite psyche in *On the Psyche*, fails to argue explictly against Plato's view.[69] Galen makes similar criticisms of Chrysippus' practice in *On Passions*, though in that case it is not clear that Chrysippus specifically mentioned Plato's theory at all.[70] In connection with *On the Psyche*, Tieleman has argued (299 above) that Chrysippus, in effect, if not explicitly, aimed to counter Plato's theory with his arguments for a unified psyche in one location (the heart). There is, I think, no evidence to suggest that Chrysippus deliberately set out to contest the tripartite psychology of Plato's *Republic* in *On Passions*. At all events, it is far from obvious that Chrysippus or other Stoics distinguished systematically between a 'Socratic' view of the psyche, which they favoured, and a 'Platonic' one, which they did not.

But, even if Chrysippus dissented, explicitly or implicitly, from the tripartite theory of the *Republic*, taken as a whole, it does not follow that Plato's theory *in no way* prefigures the Stoic one. In fact, I think that, in spite of appearances to the contrary, there are important ways in which the *Republic* anticipates Stoic psychology.[71] In the first instance, the *Republic* is the first

[65] Sedley (1993), 314, discussing the possible influence on Chrysippus of the *Phaedo*, often seen as 'Platonic' in approach. On the issues raised by the Socrates–Plato distinction in both ancient thought and modern scholarship, see 2.2 above, text to nn. 29–31.

[66] On Posidonius' interest in *Laws*, see 4.6 above, text to nn. 352, 374–80.

[67] On Antipater, see 4.6 above, text to n. 353; on Stoic readings of *Euthydemus*, 2.2 above, text to n. 22; for relevant material in *Republic*, see e.g. 358b–367e, 444c–445b, 588b–592a.

[68] See Schofield (1991), ch. 2, esp. 22–6, (2000), 443–6; Vander Waerdt (1994*a*), 294–308.

[69] See *PHP* 3.1.14 (and subsequent comments in *PHP* 3, e.g. 3.19–27). These seem to refer, primarily at least, to Chrysippus' response to *Ti.* 69–72, since they refer to the *embodied* tripartite psyche, as does 4.1.6 (on which, see Sedley 1993: 313 n. 1). For the suggestion that Chrysippus was referring to a pre-existing, doxographical merger of the psychological position of *R.* and *Ti.*, see Mansfeld (1989), 336. See also 4.1 above, text to nn. 22–3, 5.1, text to nn. 35–41.

[70] See Gal. *PHP* 4.1.14–15, also 4.3.6, 5.7.43, 52.

[71] For a previous, less detailed, version of the argument of this section, see Gill (1998*a*), 130–5.

ancient work which gives an absolutely central role to the concept of reason in ethical psychology,[72] even though this role is implied in what modern scholars regard as the 'Socratic' psychology of *Protagoras* 353–60. In this respect, the *Republic* prefigures the dominant role played by reason in Stoic psychology. More precisely, the *Republic*, especially in Books 8–9, presents reason as interlocked with other psychological functions in a way that anticipates Stoic ideas about the way that (adult) human psychology is pervaded by rationality. To this extent, Plato's discussion anticipates what I am characterizing as psychological holism; and it does so in a way that prefigures—and might have helped to shape—Stoic ideas and even terminology.[73] In this respect, I think, Plato's theory might have contributed to one aspect of the set of the ideas that make up the Stoic version of the structured self (psychological holism). But the *Republic* also offers its own version of one of the 'Socratic' claims seen here as combined with holism in Stoic thought. Parts of Books 8–9 represent one of the clearest expressions of an idea taken over by both Stoicism and Epicureanism. This is that psychological stability and cohesion are confined to those who are fully rational or 'wise', whereas the non-wise are more or less conflicted and unstable.[74] I cannot claim that we *know* that the Stoics derived these two themes from the *Republic*; as just noted, the evidence for Chrysippus' reaction to the Platonic theory in *On Passions* (the most relevant treatise for this subject) gives us little to go on. But, given their evident familiarity with Plato's dialogue, and the fact—as I shall suggest—that the *Republic* strikingly prefigures these key motifs of Stoic thought, it is plausible to suppose that the Stoics may have been directly influenced by this work. Hence, a 'Chrysippean' reading of the tripartite psyche of the *Republic*, as well as the *Timaeus*, can be a revealing exercise.

However, an obvious problem for the hypothesis that Stoic holistic psychology was in any way inspired by the theory of the *Republic* is posed by the argument in Book 4 (435–441) for the existence of separate and independent parts in the human psyche. Galen discusses this argument at length at the end of *PHP* 5 (5.7.1–82) and assumes that it presents a radically different theory from the Stoic one. Although Platonic psychology is not in itself a primary topic for this book, this argument in *Republic* 4 is worth examining here for several reasons. This seems to have been the first explicit claim in Greek philosophy that the psyche contains separate parts. Unusually, among ancient treatments of psychology, it is formulated as a logical argument, and one

[72] Reason, or the reasoning part, is formally introduced in the argument of *R.* 435–41, and the ideal of the psyche harmonized by reason's rule is presented in 441d–444e and 589c–592b.

[73] See further text to nn. 71–118 below.

[74] See further text to nn. 121–35 below.

which also lays bare the substantive conceptual issues raised by this topic. The argument was, evidently, regarded by later ancient thinkers such as Galen as a classic statement of the case for part-based psychology. Plato's treatment thus provides a point of access to a question which is central for Part III of this book and in a sense for the book as a whole. Why did the conflict between part-based and unified conceptions of the psyche become such an important and keenly contested issue in Hellenistic–Roman philosophy?[75] In considering Plato's argument, I draw on both ancient and modern responses; as will become clear, there are illuminating points of contact between recent scholarly discussions and those in Hellenistic and Roman thought.

Plato's argument, in outline, takes this form. After raising the question whether the psyche has parts comparable with those of the state, Socrates states a general principle by which this question can be determined. The principle is that 'the same thing will not be willing to do or undergo opposites in the same part of itself, in relation to the same thing, at the same time'.[76] This principle, that of non-contrariety or conflict, is then applied to the psyche.[77] Socrates distinguishes as opposites such processes as assent and dissent, desiring to take and refusing, drawing to and thrusting away. He locates appetites (*epithumiai*) within the first of these two types of process. He gives thirst as an instance of appetite, directed at drinking. He considers a case in which someone is thirsty (wants to drink) but also does not want to drink. He argues that this must be understood as the simultaneous presence of 'something in their psyche ordering them to drink and something different, forbidding them to drink'. The forbidding element is said, in such cases, to derive from reasoning; and this argument is said to establish the difference between the reasoning (*logistikon*) and appetitive (*epithumētikon*) parts of the psyche (*R.* 437b–d, 439b–d). Similarly, instances of conflict between anger or indignation (characterized as 'spirit', *thumos*) and appetite are presented as enabling us to distinguish these two parts from each other. Spirit is said never to conflict with reason, although it can occur separately from it (as it does in animals and children); and on this basis it is distinguished as a third part of the psyche (439e–441c).

What, exactly, is this argument designed to show? Its objectives are stated in rather general terms, as that of determining whether the psyche is 'one or

75 This is a different question from that raised in 4.1 above: that is, how and when did the contrast between part-based and unified conceptions of the psyche become an explicit and central issue of philosophical debate? However, as Galen's use of Plato's argument indicates, these two questions are interconnected.

76 *R.* 436b8–9, trans. Grube, rev. Reeve in Cooper (1997).

77 For these ways of characterizing the principle involved, see, respectively, Price (1995), 40–1, and Annas (1981), 137.

many', and whether it has the same 'forms' (*eidē*) or 'kinds' (*genē*) as the state.[78] This vagueness of formulation goes some way towards explaining the different ways that the argument has been understood in modern scholarship. But it is possible to claim, as some recent accounts have, that the general form of the argument implies a more precise objective. The aim is not simply to show that the three parts of the psyche are *in some way* different and distinct, or that the psyche is *in some sense* many rather than one. It is, more precisely, to show that these parts or forms constitute independent sources of motivation. Otherwise, it can be argued, the emphasis on psychological *conflict* would have no point. The (alleged) fact of psychic conflict is presented as evidence for the existence of distinct parts; and their distinctness, as parts, consists in their being independent sources of motivation.[79] This, more precise, understanding of the aim of the argument gives rise to another question: what are the preconditions of the kind of conflict which establishes independent sources of motivation? What capacities or qualities must parts have in order to be able to *conflict*, as distinct from simply being different? There is room for argument, of course, about the correct answer to that question. But we can claim that, in order to compete, as independent sources of motivation, psychological parts need to have *some* similar capacities even though they differ in other ways. We might argue, for instance, that competing parts must be alike in being goal-directed; and that being goal-directed implies having beliefs about what goals are worth pursuing.[80] If we explore these implications of Plato's argument, we will, I think, be better able to make sense of its influence in antiquity as well as the differing responses it aroused. We will also become clearer about what was at issue in the ancient debates about psychological models.

I turn first to Galen's reading of the argument in *PHP* 5.7.1–82. To call this discussion a 'reading' may seem an overstatement, since all Galen does is to summarize *Republic* 435–441 and to present it as undermining the Stoic model by posing a challenge which Chrysippus fails to confront.[81] However, this account needs to be placed in the larger context of Galen's dispute with Stoic psychology and his use of Plato in that connection. As explained earlier

[78] See e.g. *R.* 435b9–c6, 441c5–7. For 'one (literally, "the same thing") or many', see 436b10–c1.

[79] This point applies with full force to the distinction between reason and appetite (see e.g. *R.* 437b–d, 439b–d). Spirit, while independent of appetite, is presented as deriving its responses from reason, at least in adult humans; but it is independent (or at least separate) in animals and children, in whom reason has not developed (440b–d, 441a–b). On the key role of conflict in the argument, see e.g. Annas (1981), 137–9; Price (1995), 40–8, also 1–2.

[80] Put differently, we might claim that conflict between psychological parts requires that the parts have comparable cognitive or evaluative capacities. For one way of pursuing this line of thought, see Penner (1990), 49–61, discussed in text to nn. 92–7 below.

[81] On the last point, see nn. 69–70 above.

(4.4 above), Galen combines the idea that the control-centre is located in the brain with the idea that there are three separate sources of motivation, in the brain, heart, and liver. The point at issue, then, is whether or not there are independent (and separate) sources of psychological, and psychophysical, motivation or only one such source. Mansfeld, in particular, brings out the centrality of this question for Galen, and the way that it arises out of his response to Stoicism. Mansfeld also, as noted earlier (244 above), highlights the serious problem raised by Galen's attempt to combine a brain-centred physiological model with the idea that three separate parts of the body contain independent sources of motivation.[82] Galen's larger theoretical objective helps to explain the prominence that he gives to the argument in *Republic* 4. He takes the argument as offering a logical proof for the claim that the three parts of the psyche constitute independent sources of motivation.

For Galen, the three sources of motivation are located in separate locations and are in that sense 'parts' (*moria*) as well as distinct 'powers' (*dunameis*). Galen acknowledges that this is not also true for Plato in *Republic* 4, by contrast with the *Timaeus* (*PHP* 5.7.1–7).[83] How, then, does he suppose that Plato, in that context, understands the distinctness and independence of the psychic parts? To judge from his summary, Galen sees the parts as differentiated, and conflicting, simply because of the difference in their function or mode of operation. He underlines those passages in Plato's argument in which the mode of operation is specified as appetite, reasoning, or anger.[84] It is clear that he takes this differentiation of psychological mode as sufficient to generate the conflict identified in Plato's argument, and thus to establish the three parts as independent sources of motivation. In this respect, Galen's summary does, of course, follow the main explicit thrust of Plato's argument, in which the divergent psychic parts are defined by reference to function or mode.[85] But, read in this way, Plato's argument runs into two major difficulties, which have been underlined in recent discussions. It is open to question whether the argument, interpreted as Galen does, succeeds in defining psychological parts which are capable of generating *conflict*, in a strong sense. If these parts have sharply different functions and do not share, for instance, some cognitive or evaluative capacities, it can be argued that we

[82] See Mansfeld (1991), 126–45, stressing the connection between Galen's experiments on the psychophysical source (*archē*) of movement and his emphasis on the questions of the basis for 'impulse' (*hormē*) or 'choice' (*prohairesis*) and the respective strength of different psychophysical parts. See also Hankinson (1991), esp. 205, 212–15, 225; Tielemann (1996), pp. xxix–xxxi.

[83] Gal. *PHP* 5.7.1–4, by contrast with 6.2.5; but Galen thinks the theory of the embodied tripartite psyche is also assumed in *R.* 4 (*PHP* 5.7.5–9).

[84] See e.g. *PHP* 5.7.16, 26, 40, 45, 57, 67–8.

[85] See esp. *R.* 436a, 439c–d, 440a–d.

do not have the requisite basis for motivational conflict. This difficulty has led some scholars to reformulate the significance of Plato's argument. This reformulation has the special interest, in the present context, that it brings us closer to the way that the Stoics may have read this argument.

This issue arises especially in connection with the differentiation between reason and appetite or desire (*epithumia*) in *Republic* 437d–439d. Socrates stresses there that thirst should be understood as appetite for drink as such, not drink qualified in any specific way, for instance, as good; and he seems to present this feature as typical of appetite in general (437d–e, 439a). On the face of it, the point seems to be that appetite is a 'brute', instinctive motive, whose mode is sharply contrasted to that of rational consideration. This is how Galen seems to understand the point of the argument.[86] One difficulty with this reading is that the argument of the *Republic* as a whole requires a quite different conception of appetite or desire, not as a merely brute instinct but as a part with more complex cognitive or rational capacities. Even in Book 4, appetite is presented as capable of 'agreeing' to be harmonized by reason's rule. In Books 8–9, appetite has a complex range of capacities, including those of being 'persuaded' by education, of means-end reasoning (of using money as a means of satisfaction), and of 'ruling' the psyche in three different ways. In Book 10, the non-rational part of the psyche is characterized as the one which forms opinions 'contrary to measurement'.[87] This range of capacities goes well beyond those that can plausibly be attributed to a merely 'brute', unreasoning instinct or drive.

One way of responding to this problem is to say that the argument in Book 4 (435–441) understates the conception of desire and the nature of the distinction between reason and desire, and that the more complex psychic parts presented later are what is required by the argument of the *Republic* as a whole. So, if the argument in Book 4 is to be consistent with the rest of the *Republic*, it must in some way imply a more cognitive conception of appetite.[88] Another response is to suggest that the argument in Book 4 does not aim simply to differentiate the parts by reference to their function or mode but also by their object, as is done elsewhere in the *Republic* (580d–581c). It has been claimed that the purpose of *R.* 437d–439d is to differentiate reason from appetite by the fact that reason is directed at the good. The point is not

[86] Gal. *PHP.* 5.7.21–5, 34–42, highlighting in 5.7.37 (p. 344, 24) Plato's phrase in *R.* 439b4, 'like a brute'.

[87] See *R.* 443c, 554c10–d3, d9–10, 553d1–7 (taken with 580d11–581a7), 602e4–603a2. In *R.* 8–9, the oligarchic, democratic, and tyrannical types are all characterized as 'ruled by appetite'. See further text to nn. 109–11 below.

[88] For versions of this view, see e.g. Annas (1981), 139–46; Price (1995), 40–57; Gill (1996*b*), 245–60.

that appetite is 'brute' instinct (that it lacks any cognitive or rational capacities), but, rather, that it is directed at achieving its own satisfaction, and not at the good. In this interpretation, the rest of the *Republic* explores further the cognitive capacities of appetite and the way in which reason is constitutively directed at the good. But, it is claimed, the rest of the *Republic* does not introduce a radically different conception of the parts from that presupposed in the argument in Book 4.[89] This reading can itself be questioned, on various grounds. It is not obvious that the function of *R.* 437d–439d is to introduce a substantive claim about reason, namely that it is constitutively directed at the good. Later in the *Republic*, it is difficult to exclude the possibility that the education of desire includes modifying the understanding of what is good and therefore worthy of desire.[90] There is the further problem of determining whether the natural goal of reason is presented as the good or knowledge of the truth (or both).[91] However, this reading of Plato's argument also brings out a possible dimension in the differentiation of psychic parts that is not reflected in Galen's interpretation, which is narrowly focused on differentiation by function or mode.

Both these limitations in Galen's reading bear on the question of how the Stoics might have responded to this argument and to the psychology of the *Republic* more generally. In trying to reconstruct their response, I turn first to another recent discussion of Plato's argument, that of Terry Penner.[92] Penner argues for a version of the 'Socratic' psychological position—that of Plato, *Protagoras* 353–60—which is, in crucial respects, virtually identical with the Stoic position. In the course of maintaining this position, Penner denies that Plato's argument in *Republic* 4 is successful in establishing the existence of independent sources of motivation. The key relevant point in Penner's discussion is his account of the preconditions of psychological conflict of a type that would prove the existence of independent sources of motivation. What he takes to be required is the simultaneous presence of two 'executive desires', both directed at particular objects or courses of action. In psychological conflict, as so understood, someone must both desire and not desire to do something. In the terms used in *R.* 437b–c, 439b–c, the person concerned would need to be drawn both to and from a given action in a given situation. Plato's argument, Penner maintains, fails to meets these conditions, because it

[89] For versions of this view, see Irwin (1977), 191–5, 226–33, (1995), 203–22, 245–8; Cooper (1984), 4–8; Kahn (1987), 82–91.

[90] That is, concern for the good is not necessarily confined to reason but can be shared by appetite or the psyche more broadly. On this point, see Price (1995), 50–1, 63–5.

[91] Kahn (1987), 84–9, outlines a response to that question.

[92] Penner (1990). See also Penner (1971), (1997), (1991, on related ideas in *Grg.*), and (2005), encapsulating his analysis of Socratic philosophy.

presents a conflict between merely generalized desires, such as for drink in general (which Penner calls 'drives') and 'executive desires', including reason's judgement that it is best not to drink in this situation.[93]

The relevance of Penner's view to reconstructing the Stoic reading of Plato's argument is this. I think that the Stoics would have specified similar preconditions for psychological conflict—if they were to allow that there could be such conflict between independent sources of motivation. They would have required a demonstration that someone could simultaneously believe 'that it is appropriate to do (or feel) this in this situation' and 'that it is not appropriate'.[94] If they had interpreted Plato's argument as Penner does, as describing a conflict between a reasoned wish and a 'blind' or 'brute' desire ('drive'), they too would have regarded the argument as unsuccessful as well as based on a false pychological picture. However, it is possible that they interpreted the argument rather differently. They may have thought that the argument is effective, and that it implies the kind of psychological conflict that they *did* acknowledge. This is conflict between different states of the person as a whole, namely between the person *as* rational and *as* passionate. This kind of conflict would be like that between Penner's 'executive desires',[95] but on the understanding that such conflict consists in *alternation* between differing 'executive desires'. An alternative Stoic analysis, exemplified in Medea, is that the person (as a whole) acts or feels 'passionately' but also has a (more or less explicit) awareness of what it would mean to act or feel 'rationally'.[96]

I noted earlier the views of modern scholars for whom Plato's argument in Book 4, if it is to be consistent with the *Republic* as a whole, must imply a rather different psychological model from that presumed in Galen's reading. The argument must imply that appetite has some cognitive or rational capacities and is not simply brute instinct. Alternatively, the argument must represent a conflict between motivation directed at the good and motivation directed at some other aim, such as gratification.[97] The Stoics too might have thought that Plato's argument implied that appetite has richer cognitive or

[93] Penner (1990), esp. 49–61. Penner himself does not discuss the Stoic psychological position or the way that the Stoics might have read Plato's argument.

[94] For this way of characterizing motivation in Stoicism, see 2.2 above, text to nn. 10–13, 3.2, text to nn. 47–54, 4.5, text to nn. 185–7.

[95] See also Price (1995), 43, who reformulates Plato's argument as being about two different ways of 'being set on' doing something. We may compare Cooper's suggestion that a Stoic impulse (including a passionate one) expresses the belief that 'this is the thing to do' (1998*a*: 75).

[96] For Stoic models of psychological conflict, see 4.2 above, text to nn. 76–9, 4.5, text to nn. 214–45. For the idea that Plato's example of Leontius prefigures the latter (Medea-type) model of conflict, see discussion below.

[97] See, respectively, text to nn. 88 and 89 above.

evaluative capacities than are explicit in the text. They may have understood the conflict as being between states of the whole person which are more or less rational in the sense that they are closer to, or more remote from, ideal wisdom. The Stoics do, indeed, recognize conflict of this sort, and may have read the argument in the light of this model of conflict.

Are there specific features of Plato's argument that might have encouraged the Stoics to read it in this way? There are, certainly, some suggestive phrases. For instance, the idea that desire is the result of 'assent' (*epineuein*) to a question put by the psyche to itself anticipates the Stoic view that, in human adults, impulses are the outcome of assent to verbal impressions.[98] Also suggestive is the description of the appetitive part as one that 'flutters' (*eptoētai*) in its desire for satisfaction, and as moved by 'feelings and sicknesses' (*pathēmata* and *nosēmata*) in its conflict with reason. Both phrases are linked for Stoics with the idea of 'passion' and might have been interpreted by then as indicating that the conflict was between the (whole) person as, alternately, both rational and passionate.[99] Also, the characterization of 'spirit', in the *Republic* as well as the *Timaeus*, could have been seen as prefiguring Stoic thinking about passion. This is not only because spirit, as the 'natural auxiliary' of the rational part (441a2–3), normally acts in line with its commands. Also, the idea that an emotional response such as anger or indignation depends on the (rational) judgement that 'it is appropriate to react with anger' is one that the Stoics could easily have read into the description of the workings of spirit.[100] Socrates uses the example of Leontius, angry at his own desire to gaze at corpses, to show that spirit, though naturally disposed to reason, can come into conflict with desire (*R.* 440a–b). Chrysippus might well have seen in Leontius' conscious surrender to desire, expressed in his bitterly ironic words to his own eyes, 'Wretches, take your fill of the lovely sight', a phenomenon comparable to Medea's conscious surrender to passionate anger in Euripides' *Medea* 1079–81. In Leontius' words, as in Medea's final words in her great monologue (1020–81), Chrysippus could have seen a similarly partial (and ineffective) awareness of the 'irrationality' of the passion to which the person was surrendering himself.[101]

If we move from the argument in Book 4 to the psychology of the *Republic* as a whole, we find much that Stoics could have taken as prefiguring their

[98] *R.* 437c4–5; on the Stoic analysis, see 3.2 above, text to nn. 47–54.

[99] See *R.* 439d7; for passions as a type of *ptoia*, 'fluttering', see *PHP* 4.5.6 and LS 65 A(2). See also *R.* 439d2; for passions as 'sicknesses', which alternate 'feverishly' with each other and with more rational responses, see 4.2 above, text to nn. 79–82, 4.5, text to nn. 261–6.

[100] See *R.* 440c1–d2, esp. c7–d2; see also *Ti.* 70b (5.1 above, text to nn. 43–9).

[101] See *R.* 439e–440b, esp. 439e9–440a3, b1–4; for analysis of Leontius' surrender, see Price (1995), 52–3, 97–8. On Chrysippus' reading of Medea, see 4.5 above, text to nn. 216–44.

thought. This applies, for instance, to the idea, central to the *Republic*, that virtue (in the person) consists in a psyche harmonized by reason's rule.[102] Psychic harmony is analysed in terms that presuppose a high degree of cooperation and cohesion between the functions of reason and those of appetite as well as spirit. The just psyche is characterized by 'the friendship and harmony of these parts, when the ruling and the two ruled parts agree about who should rule' (442c10–d1). The just psyche, by contrast with the oligarchic one, is 'unanimous' and 'harmonized' because its desires can been 'persuaded' (or 'tamed') by reason (554c12–d4, d9–10, e4). A related idea is that the philosopher's love of truth brings with it a fundamental redirection of desire from sensual to intellectual goals (485d–e). Another is that the unification of the psychic parts under the direction of reason enables each of them to satisfy its desires and pleasures in the best possible way (586d–587a). Implied in such passages are ideas which are absent from, or not explicit in, the argument in Book 4. These include the idea that desire or appetite, as well as spirit, has cognitive or rational capacities, such as means-end reasoning or beliefs. The last two passages cited, in particular, imply that desire is open to modification in the light of changes in belief about what is good.[103] The idea that the wise person is someone whose character is exceptionally unified, coherent, and harmonized is also prominent in Stoicism. Earlier, in connection with the idea of 'ethical holism', I discussed the Stoic idea that the presence of the virtues as a unified set produces further types of symmetry and cohesion, which inform all aspects of the person's personality and life. The Stoic version of the ideal of the harmonized psyche is also, as in the *Republic* (and, of course, in a fuller and more systematic way), combined with the idea that cognitive or rational functions inform emotions and desires.[104]

However, Plutarch, in his essay *On Ethical Virtue*, also sees the ideal of the psyche harmonized by reason's rule, as presented by Plato and Aristotle, as one that prefigures his—Middle Platonic—ideas. Indeed, he seems to assume that the Platonic and Aristotelian thought supports, unequivocally, the part-based psychological framework he adopts, by contrast to the Stoic unified psychological approach.[105] Galen argues, explicitly, for the same

[102] See e.g. *R.* 441e–442a, 443d–e, 591a–e.

[103] See further Gill (1996*b*), 245–60, 295–7; also (1998*b*), esp. 211–25, on Platonic and Stoic ethical education. See also 3.2 on the psychology of ethical development in Stoicism (esp. text to nn. 5–14, 42–6, 72–8 above).

[104] On the Stoic ideal of the unified and harmonized character, see 150–7 above, also Long (1996), 202–23, on the language of 'harmony' in Stoic ethics. On parallels between Platonic and Stoic thought about the cognitive or rational basis for emotions and desires, see 3.3 above, esp. text to nn. 113–25.

[105] This is implied in Plutarch's references to Plato and Aristotle (4.3, text to nn. 111–14). However, as illustrated in 4.3 above, Plutarch's approach represents a creative synthesis of Platonic–Aristotelian themes, and not a textually based interpretation of their thought.

view.[106] Of course, this does not rule out the possibility that the Stoics also found such Platonic ideas a source of inspiration. Plutarch's approach reflects the intensification in this period of debate between part-based and unified psychology and also the increasing tendency to cite the authority of earlier thinkers to support one's position.[107] But Plutarch's move does raise the question whether there is anything in the *Republic* which prefigures specifically Stoic (holistic) psychology, as distinct from anticipating a range of Hellenistic ideas, some of which are holistic and some part-based. In fact, I think that certain features of Books 8–9, in particular, strikingly prefigure Stoic psychology. These features are not found, for the most part, in Aristotle or in the Middle Platonic synthesis of Plato and Aristotle. In some cases, the resemblance is so striking that it seems plausible to think that the Stoics drew the ideas from Plato rather than simply recognizing in his philosophy anticipations of their theory. The ideas involved partly express holistic psychology and partly the 'Socratic' theme according to which all non-wise people are, to some degree, psychologically incoherent. Indeed, as in Stoic thinking, these two themes are combined in Books 8–9 of Plato's *Republic*.

I take first the Platonic ideas which prefigure features of Stoic psychological holism. In Stoicism, emotions (or passions) involve rational beliefs in two ways. On a given occasion, the person in a state of passion forms the (false) belief 'that it is appropriate to react' in a given way, for instance, angrily. This occurrent reaction depends, in turn, on the formation of (false) long-term, dispositional beliefs about what is good, which shape beliefs about how it is right to react on any given occasion.[108] The formation of false dispositional beliefs is explained by Chrysippus by reference to two factors, the 'persuasiveness of impressions' and the 'conversation' of the majority of people (or 'those around one'). These two factors, taken together, lead people to form false beliefs, notably that 'indifferents' such as health and wealth are good, and thus lead people to react passionately (257–8 above). This set of Stoic ideas is anticipated by certain features of the presentation of the emergence of the defective types of personality in Books 8–9 of the *Republic*. Although the different types are characterized by reference to the psychic part which rules each person,[109] the account of the formation of these character-types is also

[106] This is an emphatic theme in Gal. *PHP*; see 5.1 above, text to nn. 21–7, text to nn. 81–2; also 4.1, text to nn. 22–4, 5.1, text to nn. 35–8, on Chrysippus' failure to disprove the alleged Platonic view.

[107] On the first point, see 4.1 above, and, on the second, Ch. 4 n. 30 above.

[108] See references in n. 94 above; also, on passionate dispositions, 4.5, text to nn. 253–66. Brennan (1998), 39–44, stresses that it is dispositional beliefs underlying passions (rather than occurrent ones) which are false.

[109] Since three of the types are ruled by the same part (the oligarchic, democratic, and tyrannical types are all ruled by appetite), this form of characterization is, obviously, incomplete.

framed in terms of the rejection and adoption of sets of beliefs. For instance, in the development of the 'democratic' type, the disposition to refuse to give priority to necessary over non-necessary desires is brought about by replacing one set of ideas and beliefs (*logoi* and *doxai*) about what should count as virtues and vices by another set. Similarly, the emergence of the 'tyrannical' (or 'tyrannized') psychic type occurs through the replacement of the beliefs (*doxai*) implanted in childhood about what is fine and disgraceful by those which were formerly suppressed and which manifested themselves only in dreams.[110] In the development of these and other psychic types, the relevant disposition emerges out of a conflict between two competing sets of beliefs about what counts as good.[111] The outcome of this conflict determines the way that the person subsequently experiences emotions and desires on any given occasion.

The link between the Platonic and Stoic pattern lies, in the first instance, in the idea that a person's emotions and desires reflect her beliefs about what is good. As suggested earlier, Stoics would probably have seen Plato's description of psychic conflict in Book 4 as being, like that in Books 8–9, an account of conflict between better and worse sets of beliefs.[112] A further link is that Plato stresses what Chrysippus calls the 'conversation of the majority' (or 'those around one') in analysing the formation of defective sets of beliefs.[113] *Republic* 8–9 shows how the discourse of one's family and community plays a crucial role in shaping the emergence of a given belief-set and structure of character. For instance, the timocratic psychic type is shown as emerging in response to the competing claims about life-goals by his father (a just person in an unjust community) and his mother and family slaves, who point out what they see as the disadvantages of the father's goals and way of life.[114]

As in the argument in Book 4, or, indeed, even more so, there are specific phrases that Stoics might have read as prefiguring their own psychological theory. For Chrysippus, every instance of passion is understood as the 'rejection' or 'disobedience' of reason, a rejection of which the person is at some level aware, thus producing the psychic conflict associated with a passion (257–60 above). In *R.* 8–9, the emergence of a specific character-type is presented as deriving from the rejection of a better belief-set in

[110] See *R.* 560c2–d6, taken in the context of 559d–561e; 573b1–4, 574d5–e2; also 571b–572b.

[111] *R.* 549e–550b, 553a–d.

[112] See 312–13 above; on such accounts of conflict in *R.* 8–9, see n. 111 above. A relevant difference, of course, is that Book 4 describes occurrent conflict, whereas the conflicts described in Books 8–9 form part of the explanation of dispositional belief-sets.

[113] On this Stoic theme, see Gal. *PHP* 5.5.14, D.L. 7.89.

[114] *R.* 549c–550b; also 553a–e, 559c–561c, 572c–573c. On the interplay between social and psychological factors in these descriptions, see Lear (1992), esp. 202–4; Gill (1996*b*), 256–9; Ferrari (2003).

preference for a worse. For instance, the democratic person is presented as 'refusing to accept' (*ou prosdechomenos*), and as someone who 'denies' (*ananeuei*), the true belief that some pleasures are better than others. In this sense, he rejects reason. In a related form of description, this process is described as 'handing over' rule in oneself to a part other than reason (its natural ruler).[115] We do not need to suppose that what is involved is a consciously akratic process, in which someone knowingly adopts a worse kind of psychic structure and set of goals in preference to a better one. Rather, Plato is presenting in this way the emergence of a character-structure that is, by objective standards, less (normatively) rational than the preceding character-type.[116] But this form of description carries two implications which would have been congenial to the Stoics. One is that the emergence of a character-type involves reason in the form of rational functions such as belief-formation and practical inference.[117] The other is that the surrender of rule to a part other than reason constitutes the abandonment of a psychic structure of which all human beings are, at some level, capable. The latter idea is more explicit in Stoicism, which presupposes that 'all human beings have the starting-points of virtue.'[118] But the idea is implied in the sequence described in *R.* 8–9, in which each psychic type is presented as evolving out of its predecessor and as 'rejecting' or 'handing over' the previous structure and belief-set. In effect, this cycle of decline is the story of a single person, a human being who progressively abandons the rule of reason that is fundamental to his nature.

Some of the points highlighted in *Republic* 8–9 also have analogues in Aristotle. Aristotle sees in human psychology a close interconnection between beliefs or reasoning and emotions or desire, sometimes expressed through his use of the 'practical syllogism' to express motivation.[119] This feature of Aristotelian thought is sometimes seen as prefiguring, and perhaps influencing, Stoic psychology.[120] Aristotle also recognizes social discourse as a factor which can shape action-guiding beliefs and promote or impede ethical development.[121] But there are certain features shared by *R.* 8–9 and Stoicism

[115] See *R.* 550b, esp. b6, 553b–d, esp. b8, c5–6, 561b4.

[116] See further Gill (1996*b*), 257–8; on the combination of (functional) rationality and (normative) rationality involved, see Irwin (1977), 226–332, (1995), 283–8, taken with the commentary on Irwin's approach in Gill (1996*b*), 260–6. On the contrast between functional and normative senses of rationality, see 4.5 above, text to nn. 197–205.

[117] See text to nn. 108–14 above.

[118] LS 61 L, LS trans. modified; see further 3.2 above, text to nn. 11–14.

[119] See e.g. Arist. *NE* 7.3, esp. $1147^a24–^b17$. For a powerful analysis of Aristotle's thinking on the linkage between belief and desire, see Charles (1984); on the cognitive basis for emotions in Aristotle's theory of virtue, see Sherman (1997), chs. 2, 6.

[120] See further Inwood (1985), ch. 1; Gill (1991), esp. 188–92.

[121] Social discourse is seen as a key contributor of 'habituation'; see e.g. *NE* 2.1, 10.9. See further Burnyeat (1980); Sherman (1989), ch. 4, (1997), ch. 6, esp. 241–3, 259–62.

which diverge from Aristotle's characteristic line of thought. An important one, highlighted earlier (95–6, 232 above), centres on the question whether defective people can have stable and coherent characters. Aristotle's ethical psychology seems to presuppose that this is so. This is clearest in the distinction he draws between 'self-indulgence' (*akolasia*) and 'weakness of will' (*akrasia*). The self-indulgent person is stably and consistently disposed towards excessive sensual gratification. The akratic person is marked by psychic conflict and inconsistency in this respect, being drawn, periodically, towards sensual pleasures in contradiction to her ethical beliefs.[122] In one striking discussion (*NE* 9.4), Aristotle does suggest that this kind of inner conflict is characteristic of defective people in general, and that this explains why they are incapable of self-love.[123] But this view is unusual for Aristotle. Elsewhere, he seems to assume that defective, as well as good, people develop stable dispositions to think, act, and feel in largely consistent ways.[124]

The Stoics, by contrast, believe that only the ideal wise person is fully stable and coherent, and that all other psychic states are marked by incoherence and instability. Although both Chrysippus and Posidonius recognize quasi-dispositional states, these are seen as essentially unstable and 'feverish'. Hence, Aristotle's distinction between self-indulgence (or vice generally) and *akrasia* does not hold good in Stoicism, in which all instances of passion are, in a sense, akratic.[125] Where should Plato be placed on this question? As noted earlier, in *On Ethical Virtue*, Plutarch presents as a shared Platonic and Aristotelian theme the idea that ethical character (*ēthos*), in good and bad alike, constitutes a stable pattern, implanted in the non-rational part by reason. He sees Plato's picture of the tripartite psyche in the *Phaedrus* as expressing essentially the same model as Aristotle's, in which the distinction between self-indulgence and *akrasia* marks different degrees of the harmonization of the non-rational by reason.[126]

It is possible to read *Republic* 8–9 as expressing the idea that defective psychic types, as well as the ideal type, achieve consistency and stability of character. This seems plausible especially if we focus on the point that three of the types, in some sense, 'choose' their goal and psychic structure and achieve

[122] See e.g. Arist. *NE* 7.8, also 1.13, 1102^{b}13–28, on the related contrast between (complete) temperance and (less complete) self-control as regards sensual pleasure.

[123] See *NE* 1166^{b}6–29, also, less emphatically, *EE* 1240^{b}12–13; on this feature as exceptional, see Price (1989), 127–9; Gill (1996*b*), 358–60.

[124] This comes out clearly in *NE* 3.5, which refers to the case of someone who has developed a stable disposition to self-indulgence which he may now regret (but which cannot now be changed); see esp. 1114^{a}3–21.

[125] See text to n. 122 and Ch. 4, n. 227 above.

[126] See Plu. *Mor.* 443 C–D, 445 B–E, contrasted with the Stoic (monistic) account of psychic conflict in 446F–447A. See further 4.3 above, text to nn. 110–20.

a relatively determinate character and way of life.[127] However, this reading fails to bring out indications of a contrasting line of thought in Plato's account, and one which strongly prefigures Stoic thinking. This is that the progressive ethical deterioration in the character of the psychic types is expressed, in part, in an increasing degree of psychological conflict and incoherence. This derives from the progressive weakening of the psychic stability and 'harmony' produced by reason's rule. This theme is signalled first in the account of the timocratic state, in whose rulers the covert desire for money arises, in addition to the predominant desire for honour, because they have been educated 'not by persuasion [which depends on proper education] but by force'.[128] This motif is developed by the presentation of the oligarchic type as dominated by an uneasy combination of necessary and non-necessary—and sometimes bad—desires. Although such a person seems to be just in his business dealings, in fact, 'by a certain decent self-enforcement, he restrains other, bad desires present in himself, not persuading them that this is the better way, nor taming them by reason but by compulsion or fear'. For this reason, he is said to be never 'free of internal strife' and to be a 'double person', by comparison with the genuinely 'single-minded and harmonious psyche' of the truly just person.[129] In the next stage, the outcome of conflict between two sets of beliefs and correlated desires (both necessary and non-necessary ones) is that the democratic person 'hands over rule of himself to whatever pleasure happens to come along'. If anyone tells him that good pleasures must be valued and bad ones restrained, he 'rejects' this 'true statement', and treats them all equally. His life is then characterized as a random mix of activities in which there is no 'order or necessity'.[130]

The final outcome of this sequence is the tyrannical type. This character emerges out of the conflict between two types of non-necessary desires, the lawful and the lawless. This type is marked by his subjection to the power of intense erotic desire and a mass of uncontrolled and unlimited appetites: 'Erotic love (*erōs*) lives tyrannically in him, in total anarchy and lawlessness as his monarch, and drives him . . . to dare anything to feed itself and the chaotic mob (*thorubos*) around it . . .'.[131] As indicated in this passage, the theme of psychic disorder and instability is combined with that of lack of real freedom;

[127] See *R.* 550a–b, 553b–d, 561a–d. The ideas of choice and stable pattern are less clear in the emergence of the tyrannical psyche (572c–573b). The motifs of choice and stable pattern of character are stressed by Irwin (1995), 284–7.

[128] *R.* 548b–c, esp. b7–8. The same phenomenon in the timocratic psychic type is attributed to the lack of 'reason' (or 'argument', *logos*), combined with artistic education (*mousikē*), 549b6–7.

[129] *R.* 554c–e, esp. c11–d2, e4–5.

[130] *R.* 561a–c, esp. b3–4, 7–8, d5.

[131] *R.* 575a1–4; see also 571b–d, 572d–573b, 574d–e.

the 'tyrannical' type is also presented as *tyrannized* by its worst desires. Hence, 'the tyrannized psyche will least of all do what it wants... always forcibly driven by the gadfly's sting [*erōs*], it will be full of confusion and regret' (577e2–3). This psychic state is also characterized as a form of 'madness' (*mania*), which is defined by the absence of temperance (*sōphrosunē*) and by association with drunkenness and uncontrolled, intense erotic desire.[132]

The key relevant point in this powerful and lurid sequence of characterizations is this. The further one moves from the ideal, reason-ruled personality, the more the psychic state is marked by inner conflict, instability, and confusion.[133] Although, on the surface, we have a series of distinct types, deeper analysis suggests that what is described is the progressive decline of a single personality from reason-ruled harmony to psychic chaos. Taken as a whole, the sequence strongly prefigures the Stoic view, by contrast with the Aristotelian one, that defective psychic states necessarily lack coherence and permanence. As noted earlier, the phraseology of the sequence evokes the language of Stoic passions, such as the idea of the 'rejection of reason'. However, what Plato's description suggests is not so much that the person concerned is, at the moment of passion, like Medea, aware of rejecting the rationality of which she is constitutively capable. Rather, the sequence suggests that, from an objective standpoint, the further one moves from normative rationality, the further one advances into psychic incoherence.[134] One of the clearest ways in which Plato's account prefigures Stoic thought is in the idea that this decline carries with it loss of real 'freedom' and entry into a kind of 'madness'. This evokes two of the most famous of Stoic paradoxes: that only the wise person is free and that everyone except the wise person is mad.[135] Indeed, the presence of these themes, combined with the ideas about psychic conflict and confusion, make it plausible to see this whole account not simply as anticipating but also as influencing Stoic thought. The presence of a whole complex of pre-Stoic ideas, forcefully presented in a text that the Stoics knew well, makes it reasonable to see in the *Republic*, as well as the *Timaeus*, a source

[132] *R.* 573a–c, esp. a8, b4, c3, c9.

[133] This point is also stressed by Annas (1981), 294–305.

[134] This point explains the apparent paradox that Pl. *R.* 8–9, despite exploring thoroughly the interconnection and possible 'harmony' between psychic functions, concludes with an image of the human psyche (588b–592a) that stresses its internal plurality. The image emphasizes the potentiality for psychic conflict, a potentiality that is realized by ethical decline from reason-ruled harmony. See Gill (1996*b*), 245 n. 7, 259 n. 66.

[135] For these paradoxes, see *SVF* 3.589–603, 657–70. The theme that the tyrant does not do what he wants, and hence lacks real freedom, is also prominent in *Grg.* 467b–468b. See further Long (2002), 70–4, on the influence of this type of thinking (in Pl. *Grg.*) on Epictetus, and Bobzien (1998*a*), 338–44, on 'freedom' as an ethical ideal in Stoicism.

of inspiration for some of the most distinctive Stoic ideas about ethical psychology.

How far does this discussion, taken with preceding ones, help us to answer the question raised earlier (307 above): why does the conflict between unified and part-based conceptions of psychology become so important and intense in later Hellenistic and Roman philosophy? This conflict becomes important partly because it is linked with other major issues, which bear on the whole nature and basis of ethical character. This conflict is linked with the question whether character is a product of the shaping of the non-rational part or parts by reason or the achievement of complete consistency in a personality conceived as unified whole.[136] This point is linked, in turn, with the question whether stability and consistency of character is a property available, to some extent at least, to good and defective alike, or whether it is restricted (as Stoics and Epicureans maintain) to the fully wise and virtuous.[137] These questions are intertwined with other issues which emerge in the Hellenistic period, such as whether 'moderation of passion' (*metriopatheia*) or 'absence of passion' (*apatheia*) is the ideal emotional state.[138] As emerges very clearly in 5.1 above, the conflict between part-based and holistic models of the psyche is closely linked, for Galen, with the question how far the human body functions as an integrated system or as a combination of quasi-independent agencies. These issues may also reflect the larger world-view of the thinker or theory involved. Thus, for instance, for Plutarch, a part-based psychology reflects a dualistic outlook that is, fundamentally, at odds with the Stoic holistic world-view.[139] It is, in part, these links with other important conceptual issues that make the question whether the psyche is unified or part-based such an urgent one in this period.

There is a broader and more revealing way of putting this point, which goes to the heart of my project in this book. As argued in earlier chapters, what is innovative about Stoicism (and Epicureanism) is not simply psychological monism, but, rather, a conception of humans and other animals as integrated psychophysical and psychological wholes or structures. Human beings are conceived as structures, in the first instance, because, like other animals, they constitute cohesive organic and psychological units. They are also seen as

[136] See further 3.2–3 and 4.2–3 above. This issue manifest itself, in part, through the deliberate use of different terminology; e.g. Plutarch takes over the Aristotelian terms 'disposition' (*hexis*) and 'character' (*ēthos*), *Mor.* 443 C–D, whereas, in Stoicism, *hexis* has a different meaning ('tenor'), and (stable) 'character' (*diathesis*), in the full sense, is reserved for the wise; see LS 47 S, and i. 289, 376–7.

[137] See e.g. 2.2 above, text to nn. 76–92, 2.3, text to nn. 209–17, 4.3, text to nn. 115–19, 4.5, text to nn. 245–66.

[138] See e.g. 3.4 above, text to nn. 207–224, 4.3, text to nn. 121–45.

[139] See 4.2 above, text to nn. 100–1, 4.6, text to nn. 362–5.

naturally adapted to develop towards an ideal condition (perfect wisdom or happiness) which is itself conceived as a structured state of the whole personality, defined by reference to a set of 'Socratic' ideals. In both Hellenistic theories, though in different ways, both kinds of human structure (the organic and the ideal) are also correlated with a conception of the physical universe as a unified and intelligible whole (1.3 above). This conception of human personality as structure is also linked with an innovative understanding of value and of rationality. Value is not attached to one part of the personality, for instance, psyche rather than body, or mind rather than emotion or desire. Rather, it is attached to the whole personality, in so far as this realizes the kinds of organic and psychological structure of which it is capable. Similarly, 'reason' or 'rationality' is not conceived as a distinct psychological part or independent source of motivation. Rather, it is conceived as a condition of the whole person both as an organic and as a psychological whole.[140]

In reacting against Stoic psychological monism, thinkers such as Plutarch and Galen are also, and more fundamentally, reacting against this conception of human personality as structure. In doing so, they appeal to the idea, well established in earlier Greek philosophy, that human beings constitute a combination of body and psyche, and that the psyche is itself a combination of reason or mind, emotion, and desire (1.2). Plutarch, in particular, embraces the correlated belief that value attaches not so much to the personality as a whole, but to one, especially valuable part (mind or reason), and to the personality as a whole only as it is ruled or shaped by reason.[141] In maintaining this view against the innovations of Stoicism, these thinkers see themselves as perpetuating the—traditional and well-grounded—thinking of Plato and Aristotle (4.3–4 above). In fact, as I have argued, the truth is more complex; and the Stoics could reasonably have seen their psychological and psychophysical holism, together with the Socratic ideals with which they are combined, as a development of earlier thought, including that found in the Platonic dialogues. To this extent, the idea of the structured self, at least in its Stoic version, can be understood—and may have been regarded by the Stoics—not as marking the rejection of Platonic thought but as a logical extension of it.

[140] See e.g. 1.2, text to nn. 18–23, 1.4, text to nn. 111–17, 1.5, text to nn. 202–9, 2.3, text to nn. 199–206, 3.2, text to nn. 47–61, 4.5, text to nn. 209–12.

[141] See 4.3 above; on Galen's, more nuanced or elusive thinking on this subject, see Hankinson (1993), esp. 198–212.

PART III

Theoretical Issues and Literary Reception

6

Issues in Selfhood: Subjectivity and Objectivity

6.1 PRELIMINARIES

In Part I of this book I have explored a set of converging ideas in Stoicism and Epicureanism which I have characterized as the conception of the structured self. In Part II I have examined in detail a single theory (the Stoic analysis of passion) which exemplifies the salient characteristics of this conception and of the debates (especially about the reception of Plato) to which this theory gave rise in later Hellenistic and Roman Imperial thought. Part III of this book explores two kinds of issue which are raised by the Hellenistic–Roman ideas discussed in Parts I and II. One relates to conceptions of selfhood and personality and to the history of such conceptions. The other is that of the possible impact on literature of the early Roman Imperial period of the understanding of character and emotion expressed in the philosophical ideas and debates considered in Parts I and II.

The aim of the present chapter is twofold. First, I discuss the relationship between the thesis presented in this book, about what is new in Hellenistic–Roman thinking about personality, and other scholarly accounts of what is innovative in this respect. Second, I relate the claims made here to those made in an earlier general study of Greek thinking about personality, centred on Greek epic and tragedy, and Plato and Aristotle (Gill 1996*b*). These two objectives are, in fact, closely connected. There are some recent scholarly discussions which suggest that what is new or distinctive about Hellenistic or Graeco-Roman thought in the first and second centuries AD is the emergence of an idea of selfhood centred on self-consciousness, unique individuality, or the first-personal perspective. In my earlier book, I associated ideas of this type with (what I called) a 'subjective-individualist' conception of personality, by contrast with an 'objective-participant' one. I argued that Greek thinking, at least in the period from Homer to Aristotle, consistently expressed an objective-participant conception of person. What is the position, in this respect, in Hellenistic–Roman thought? Should we suppose that there is a major shift, from an objective-participant to a subjective-individualist conception? Or are scholars mistaken in seeing a move towards a more subjective and individualist way of understanding personality? This question is connected to a second one. What is the relationship between the contrast drawn in this book, between holistic and core-centred or part-based conceptions of personality, and the distinction drawn in my earlier book, between subjective-individualist and objective-participant conceptions? Are these distinctions in competition with each other or are they different in kind but compatible?

In the course of this chapter, I suggest answers to these questions, which are outlined here. As regards the second question, my view is that the contrasts are of different types but compatible with each other. To bring this out it is helpful to refer to a distinction sometimes drawn in anthropological discussion between categories framed in 'observer's' and in 'participant's' language.[1] The contrast central to this book, between holistic and part-based conceptions of personality, belongs to participant's, rather than observer's, language. By the latter part of this period, at least, the time of Plutarch and Galen, this contrast had become an important explicit theme of psychological debate. This reflects the fact, explored in detail in the preceding chapters, that one of the main innovative moves made in Stoicism (and also Epicureanism) was to introduce a systematically unified idea of personality, as part of a larger holistic world-view, by contrast with some leading tendencies in Platonic and Aristotelian thought. On the other hand, the contrast between subjective-individualist and objective-participant conceptions of person, at least as applied to Classical antiquity, is an observer's one. Although my claim in 1996*b* was that the objective-participant conception can appropriately be used to characterize the type of thinking about the person found in Greek philosophical—and in a different way—poetic thinking, I did not maintain that the distinction itself was articulated, or even implied, in ancient Greek categories or debates. My thesis was that the idea of an objective-participant conception was an effective way *for us* to define salient features of Greek thinking and to recognize points of resemblance with some aspects of modern thinking.[2]

I turn now to the question whether there is a shift, in Hellenistic–Roman thought, from an objective-participant to a subjective-individualist conception of personality. I am highly sceptical about this idea. It seems to me much

[1] This is sometimes presented as a contrast between 'emic' and 'etic' language. On the methodological issues, see further Pike (1954), Bourdieu (2003), and, on questions relating to the study of concepts of person and self in other periods and cultures, Carrithers, Collins, and Lukes (1985), esp. Collins (1985) and Lukes (1985).

[2] See Gill (1996*b*), introduction and ch. 6, esp. 10–18, 455–69.

more plausible that Hellenistic–Roman thought represents a continuation of earlier Greek thinking in this respect. But, if so, why do scholars of the period sometimes suggest that there is such a shift? The answer to this question is quite complex. But part of the explanation, I think, is that these scholarly accounts are informed by certain prevalent (subjective-individualist) modern ways of thinking about selfhood and personality. More precisely, the assumption is that *if*, as is sometimes supposed, there is a new or heightened awareness of the concept of self in this period, this will take a subjective-individualist form.[3] In questioning the idea that there is a shift of this type in Hellenistic–Roman thought, I am not supposing that there are *no* new features in thinking about human personality in this period. I have argued at length that there *are* innovative features in Hellenistic–Roman thought, centring on the combination, in Stoicism and Epicureanism, of certain kinds of holism and naturalism and 'Socratic' ethical ideas, adding up to the idea I have called 'the structured self'. Indeed, I think aspects of this new type of thinking, particularly those which relate to development, *might* be taken as involving a move towards a more subjective-individualist pattern of thought. But my view is that these aspects, and the larger Stoic–Epicurean pattern of thinking described here, are better interpreted in objective-participant terms. The same is true, I think, of the contrasting, part-based, strand of Hellenistic–Roman thinking about psychology, exemplified here by Plutarch and Galen.

In this chapter, I pursue this set of questions in the following way. First (6.2), I consider some examples in recent scholarship of the idea that Hellenistic–Roman thought evolved what is, in my terms, a more subjective-individualist conception of selfhood or personality than we find in Classical thought. I then discuss, in general terms, what is involved in the contrast between subjective-individualist and objective-participant concepts of self. I suggest that the *appearance* of a shift towards a more subjective-individualist conception is to be explained, partly, by some of the innovations I associate with the idea of a structured self. In subsequent sections, I explore the relationship between the two contrasts deployed here, that is, between holistic or part-based ideas of psychology and subjective-individualist or objective-participant conceptions of personality. The main focus is on the contrast between subjectivity and objectivity rather than on individuality

[3] This may be because scholars assume that 'self' is, inherently, a subjective-individualist concept or because they are concerned to study 'self' (understood in subjective-individual terms), by contrast with 'personality' (on this point, see Introd. above, text to n. 6). Or it may be because *development* in ancient thinking about selfhood is assumed to have taken the same form that it did in modern times (until quite recently), that is, towards a subjective-individualist conception; see further 6.2 below, esp. text to nn. 10–21.

and participation.[4] Next, I examine the kind of terminology and type of thinking linked with the idea of self-knowledge in Plato's *Alcibiades 1* (6.3). This is taken here as a pre-Hellenistic, fourth-century example of core-centred or part-based thinking. I consider how far the dialogue contains, as is sometimes supposed, an equivalent for the modern coinage '*the* self' and I also examine the conceptual implications of the dialogue's characterization of reflexive relationships. I suggest that these features are best analysed in objective-participant terms, and that the dialogue provides a Classical formulation of this type of thinking, against which to locate Hellenistic–Roman ideas.

In the following two sections (6.4–5), I consider two aspects of Stoic thought which have sometimes been taken as displaying a shift towards a more subjective or individualist notion of self. These are the theory of personal development as 'appropriation', as interpreted by Troels Engberg-Pedersen, and Epictetus' thinking about 'choice' or rational agency (*prohairesis*) and about examination of impressions, as characterized in discussions by Charles Kahn and A. A. Long. In both cases, I point to ways in which the features presented in this book as expressing the idea of the structured self might *seem* to reflect a more subjective or individualist approach to personality, while arguing that they are better interpreted in the light of the objective-participant conception. Finally (6.6), I consider more broadly whether and in what sense the notion of subjectivity is relevant to ancient thought in the Hellenistic–Roman period. I do so by examining an argument by Gail Fine that this notion *is* appropriately applied in the case of certain theories, notably those of the Cyrenaics and the Sceptic Sextus, although this has been denied by some scholars, particularly Myles Burnyeat. Again, I am doubtful about the relevance of subjectivity (at least in a strong sense) to the ancient context; but examining Fine's arguments provides a useful way of considering what is involved in correlating this modern concept with ancient material.

6.2 SUBJECTIVE AND OBJECTIVE SELVES

I begin by noting examples of the scholarly view that what is new or distinctive about Hellenistic–Roman thought about personality or selfhood in the first and second centuries AD is the emergence of an idea of selfhood centred on self-consciousness, unique individuality, or the first-personal perspective.

[4] As highlighted in Introd. n. 27, fuller study of the question of individuality would require a more thorough examination of Hellenistic–Roman social ethics than I can undertake here.

I then suggest that this view is informed by a rather prevalent (subjective-individualist) modern way of understanding selfhood, and outline an alternative, objective-participant conception of the person. This alternative pattern also draws on modern ideas, but it is designed to provide a framework which helps us (modern thinkers) to engage more closely with ancient ideas, including Hellenistic-Roman ones. The contrast offered here between alternative conceptions of the person forms a framework for the examination of specific ancient ideas in the remainder of the chapter.

Charles Kahn, in a step-by-step history of the 'discovery' of the 'will' from Aristotle to Augustine, places special importance on the significance of Epictetus' use of the notion of *prohairesis* (usually translated 'choice' or 'decision'). One comment is particularly revealing and worth citing at some length (Kahn 1988: 53):

> [*Prohairesis*] is presented not only as the decisive factor in practical existence but as the true self, the inner man, the 'I' of personal identity. By contrast, for Plato and Aristotle, the 'I' or true self was *nous*, the principle of reason most fully expressed in theoretical knowledge. This shift is a momentous one for the evolution of the idea of person and selfhood. For theoretical reason is essentially impersonal, and the Platonic–Aristotelian identification of the person with his intellect offers no basis for a metaphysics of the self in any individual sense. Epictetus, on the other hand, identifies himself with something essentially personal and individualized: not with reason as such but with the practical application of reason in selecting his commitments, in keeping his emotional balance, his serenity, by not extending himself to goals and values that lie beyond his control.

A. A. Long develops this idea in a discussion of 'representation and the self' in Stoicism (1996: ch. 12). Long begins by locating certain key features of Stoic psychology, notably the role given to 'impressions' and 'assent', within the larger perspective of the history of ideas about the self. This stress on *phantasia* ('representation' or 'impression') 'is best interpreted . . . as a new focus on consciousness, on the individuality of the perceiving subject, as the fundamental feature of the mental' (1996: 266). Long elaborates this view of the significance of the Stoic concept of *phantasia* in these terms: '[in so far as *phantasiai* are] appearances to *this* individual, they have an irreducible particularity—they are mental affections of this and only this person . . . what it is for [a given] person to assent to [a given *phantasia*] will remain something unique . . . how to deal with the representations one has is a matter for each person's individual decision'.[5] Long, analysing Epictetus' use of the idea of 'examining' impressions or representations, notes that this account 'might

[5] Long (1996), 276, referring also to Kahn (1988), 253.

suggest that Epictetus is feeling his way towards' the post-Cartesian[6] idea of a 'free-floating ego', 'subject', or 'the "I" of reflective consciousness' of (some) modern theories of personal identity. He also suggests that Stoic thought, in forming part of the 'prehistory', at least, of this development, deploys the idea that we have 'a persisting view of ourselves, a bottom-line representation or narrative, which is called into play whenever an "I" is called upon to register and evaluate new experience'.[7]

The third example is that of Michel Foucault, whose study, *The Care of the Self* (1988*b*) has been particularly influential on scholarship on Graeco-Roman ideas on selfhood in the early Roman Empire. Foucault cites as a special feature of this period 'the insistence on the attention that should be brought to bear on oneself', and, more precisely, 'an intensification of the relationship to oneself by which one constituted oneself as a subject of one's acts' (1988*b*: 41). What exactly does this mean, and what view does it imply about historical changes in conceptions of selfhood? Foucault notes the rather common belief that the Hellenistic and Roman Imperial periods saw the introduction of individualism, in comparison with earlier Greek culture. He expresses scepticism about this idea, but argues that, to make sense of the process involved, we need to distinguish three different senses of 'individualism'. One is 'the individualistic attitude, characterized by the absolute value attributed to the individual in his singularity'. A second is 'the positive valuation of private life', as distinct from public life. The third is 'the intensity of the relations to self', as expressed in 'taking oneself as an object of knowledge and field of action, so as to transform, correct, and purify oneself'. Foucault is not convinced that Hellenistic–Roman culture, though different in some ways from earlier Greek life, saw the introduction of 'individualism' in the first two senses. However, he does see a development, or at least 'intensification' in the third form of individualism, namely in 'the cultivation of the self' (1988*b*: 41–50). Foucault sees this as a matter of degree, 'a difference in emphasis', rather than a sharp break with the past. It involves, for instance, more elaborate techniques of self-scrutiny and self-examination to ensure that desire matches 'the aesthetic and ethical criteria of existence' (1988*b*: 67).

Although these three scholarly views reflect rather different perspectives and raise distinct issues, a shared theme is that Hellenistic–Roman thought is marked by a heightened focus on self-consciousness or unique individuality,

[6] In this discussion, the terms 'post-Cartesian' and 'post-Kantian' signify 'following and influenced by Descartes/Kant', and not 'following and reacting against Descartes/Kant'; contrast the way the terms 'post-modernist' or 'post-structuralist' are generally used.

[7] Long (1996), 282; Long's phraseology refers especially to Rorty (1976), 11, on the history of modern ideas of the self.

associated by Long, in particular, with the first-personal view. What underlies this response, which is, to some degree at least, also shared by other scholars?[8] Of course, the response is partly based on readings of the relevant ancient material, which I examine more fully later.[9] But it also reflects certain dominant ways of thinking about selfhood in modern Western culture. In addition, it reflects the assumption that we can reasonably expect to find *development* in the idea of selfhood within a culture, and particularly development towards a subjective-individualist conception.[10] I first explore this suggestion, with reference to some significant features of modern thinking about selfhood, and then outline some alternative ways of thinking about selfhood and personality. A striking encapsulation of some of the shaping influences on the conception of the person as self-conscious 'I' is given by Amélie Rorty, in comments noted by Long.[11] Her remarks also sum up certain salient features of the development of this kind of conception in modern Western thought.

> First, let us sketch the historical conditions that gave rise to the view of the person as the 'I' of reflective consciousness, owner and disowner of its experiences, memories, attributes, attitudes. The philosophical conditions: the movement from Descartes's reflective 'I' to Locke's substantial center of conscious experience, to Hume's theater of the sequence of impressions and ideas, to Kant's transcendental unity of apperception and the metaphysical postulate of a simple soul, to Sartre's and Heidegger's analyses of consciousness as the quest for its own definition in the face of its own non-Being. The social conditions: the movement from the Reformation to radical individualism. The cultural conditions: Romanticism and the novel of first person sensibility.

I explore first one aspect of these influences, which associates selfhood closely with 'I' centred self-consciousness, and bring out the relevance of these ideas to the scholarly views about Hellenistic–Roman thought outlined earlier.

In historical analyses of the development of modern Western ideas about self, particularly those involving subjectivity, it is common to give a special role to Descartes and his famous claim, *cogito ergo sum* ('I think therefore I am'). In the sceptical enquiry presented in the Second Book of his *Meditations*, Descartes assumes that the one thing beyond doubt was, first, that he

[8] See further Edwards (1997), 25–9, who also refers to Misch (1950), ii. 420–2; see also Rudd (1976), ch. 6, discussed in Gill (1994), 4599–4600, 4638.

[9] On the interpretation of Epictetus by Kahn and Long, see 6.5 below. On Foucault's reading of Pl. *Alc.* see also 6.3 below, text to nn. 67–72.

[10] On issues raised by positing development in the conceptualization of personality within ancient culture (in particular, development *towards* a specific modern idea), see further Gill (1996*b*), 3, 29–41, 65–7, referring also to Williams (1993), esp. chs. 2, 4. Both Gill and Williams are critical of the type of developmental accounts offered by Bruno Snell and A. W. H. Adkins. On methodological questions raised by the study of ideas of self and person in other cultures, see Carrithers, Collins, and Lukes (1985).

[11] Rorty (1976), introd., 11, referred to by Long (n. 7 above).

exists: '*I am, I exist*, is necessarily true whenever it is put forward by me or conceived in my mind'. He then infers that what exists is a 'thinking thing' (*res cogitans*).'But what then am I? A thing that thinks. What is that? A thing that doubts, understands, affirms, denies, is willing, is unwilling, and also imagines and has sensory perceptions.'[12] This supposed absolute certainty was used by him as the basis for reconstituting his knowledge of the world. Descartes also assumed that 'thought', meaning any psychological process, was necessarily accompanied by consciousness.[13] By this crucial move, the idea of the person as, essentially, a conscious mind and an 'I' was formulated in a way that, when developed by subsequent philosophers, became central to much modern thought about selfhood and personhood. The implications of this move were drawn out in certain influential formulations of key concepts by Locke. One is that of 'self': '*Self* is that conscious thinking thing ... which is sensible, or conscious of Pleasure and Pain, capable of Happiness and Misery, and so concern'd for it *self*, as far as that consciousness extends'.[14] The influence both of Descartes and Locke is apparent in the 'philosophical' sense of 'self' included in the *Oxford English Dictionary* (*OED*) (Ce3): 'That which in a person is really and intrinsically *he*... the ego (often identified with the soul or mind as opposed to the body); a permanent subject of successive and varying states of consciousness'. Another influential definition by Locke is that of 'person', namely as 'a thinking, intelligent Being, that has reason and reflection, and can consider it self as it self, the same thinking thing, in different times and places; which it does only by that consciousness which is inseparable from thinking and, as it seems to me essential to it'.[15]

These formulations reflect the early history of a long series of discussions about the mind and personal identity that have helped to shape modern Western assumptions and concepts.[16] These concepts include the idea of the

[12] Descartes, *Second Meditation*, cited from Cottingham, Stoothoff, and Murdoch (1984–91), ii. 17, 19.

[13] 'Thought is a word that covers everything that exists in us in such a way that we are immediately conscious of it... Thus all the operations of will, intellect, imagination and the senses are thoughts.' Descartes, *Arguments Demonstrating the Existence of God*, cited from Haldane and Ross (1967), ii. 52. See also: 'nothing can be in me, that is to say, in my mind, of which I am not aware', Descartes, Letter to Mersenne 31 December 1640, cited from Cottingham, Stoothoff, and Murdoch (1984–91), iii. 165. See further Wilkes (1988), 216–17; on the overall form of Descartes's argument, see Smith and Jones (1986), ch. 3.

[14] Locke, *Essay Concerning Human Understanding*, 2.27.17, his italics, cited from Nidditch (1975), 341.

[15] Locke, *Essay*, 2.27.9, cited from Nidditch (1975), 335.

[16] For surveys of the modern concept of self or person which highlight (sometimes from a critical standpoint) the significance of the Cartesian model of mind and Locke's conception of the conscious self, see e.g. Perry (1975), 12–30; Wilkes (1988), 214–21; C. Taylor (1989), esp. chs. 8–9; Kenny (1988–9).

person as 'subject'. The 'subject' signifies, minimally, the (more or less) unified and continuing locus of psychological experience, that is, that which 'underlies', or is the 'subject' of, such experiences.[17] But the term 'subject', in this sense, has been closely associated with consciousness or self-consciousness in post-Cartesian thought, as is noted in the relevant *OED* entry.[18] In recent thought, the ideas of 'subject' and 'subjectivity' are often also linked with that of the 'first-personal' view. The first-personal view idea can be defined in relatively narrow terms, for instance those of 'indexicality', meaning the awareness that 'I' am 'this person here now'.[19] But the scope and importance of the first-personal viewpoint can also be conceived much more broadly. Thomas Nagel and Richard Wollheim, for instance, see the first-personal viewpoint as one which shapes, for instance, not only memory but also ethical judgement and one's whole understanding of oneself and the world. For Nagel, it is a fundamental fact about human beings that we have, ineluctably, both a subjective (first-personal) and an objective (impersonal) view of ourselves and the world.[20] A further relevant strand of modern thought is the association between being a person or self and reflexivity. The relevant kind of reflexivity may be simply self-consciousness. But it can also be conceived in more complex terms, as in Harry Frankfurt's famous theory that the mark of a 'person' is having desires *about* one's desires or having 'second-order' desires. A key component in Frankfurt's theory is the association between being a person and being capable of (self-conscious) reflexivity, specifically the reflexivity that consists in having desires about *one's own* desires.[21]

This strand of modern thinking helps to explain the conceptual language used by modern scholars to analyse Hellenistic–Roman thought about the self. It may also contribute to the view that there is a development in ancient thought of this period, and one that leads towards this conception, as there has been in modern Western thought (though there has recently been a reaction against this development). It explains why scholars such as Kahn

17 *OED*, 'subject' II notes the link, via the Latin *subiectum*, with Aristotle's *to hupokeimenon* 'in the three-fold sense of (1) material out of which things are made, (2) subject of attributes, (3) subject of predicates'.

18 *OED*, 'subject' IIb9: '*Modern Philos.* More fully *conscious* or *thinking subject*. The mind, as the "subject" in which ideas inhere; that to which all mental representations or operations are attributed; the thinking or cognizing agent; the self or ego'. The entry also notes the 'tendency in modern philosophy since Descartes to make the mind's consciousness of itself the starting-point of enquiry'.

19 On indexicality as fundamental for personhood, see Morton (1990). On the first-personal perspective, see e.g. Shoemaker (1996), 50–73.

20 See Nagel (1986), chs. 8–11; Wollheim (1984), chs. 1, 3–4, 6–7.

21 Frankfurt (1971), often reprinted. For discussion, see Dennett (1976), 192–3; Morton (1990), 41–3; Gill (1996*b*), 413–14, 418–21.

and Long stress the importance of reflexivity, in the form of self-awareness, and, in particular, the kind of self-awareness that involves a uniquely individual or first-personal viewpoint. Thus, Kahn characterizes as a 'momentous shift for the development of the idea of person and selfhood' the emergence in Epictetus of the use of *prohairesis* to signify 'the "I" of personal identity', an 'I' which is 'essentially personal and individualized'. This idea is explicitly identified as 'the late Stoic parallel to a Cartesian *cogito* or focus on consciousness'.[22] Long elaborates this theme in equally significant language: 'If my representations are up to me to interpret, accept or reject, there must be a "me" to which they appear and an "I" which reacts to them—a subject that is identifiable precisely by the representations that it receives and by what it does with them' (1996: 276). In specifying the way in which Epictetus' idea of *prohairesis* anticipates the modern post-Cartesian self, he speaks of 'a persisting view of ourselves, a bottom-line representation or narrative which is called into play whenever an "I" is called upon to register and evaluate new experience' (1996: 282). These interpretations select as the crucial innovation in Epictetus the combination of the idea of self-consciousness with that of a uniquely first-personal, 'I'-centred viewpoint. In other discussions, Long draws on Nagel's distinction between the objective and subjective perspectives, assumed to be a fundamental feature of human capacities, to interpret some key themes in Heraclitus and Lucretius.[23]

What conception of self underlies Foucault's view of the kind of 'care of the self' found in this period? In general, Foucault is critical of the modern Western conception of self or subject with its roots in Cartesian ideas about self-consciousness and Kantian thinking on autonomy. Much of his work (1973, 1977) has explored the way that political, legal, and religious constraints have controlled how people think about their mental states and selfhood. He has used the term 'assujettissement' to link the idea of 'subjection' and 'subjectivity', implying that people are 'subjected' to certain norms of what it means to be a (post-Cartesian) 'subject'. The idea of 'objectivity' is also presented as the (false) 'objectification' of the self that results from the imposition of external norms. Some readers have been puzzled, therefore, by the absence of these themes in his work on 'the care of the self' in Greco-Roman culture. He has sometimes been supposed to have relapsed into a more conventionally 'humanist' stance towards his material. He has also been taken to have idealized ancient culture and presented it as permitting a more authentic kind of self-cultivation than has been possible in most periods of modern Western history, in which sexual behaviour has been subjected to

[22] Kahn (1988), 253, word-order of first phrase slightly rearranged.
[23] Long (1992) and (1997). See further on Nagel and ancient thought 369–70 below.

powerful legal, religious, and social restraints. Foucault has rejected these claims about his approach to Hellenistic and Roman thought and has argued that his concern has always been with three dimensions of power, that exercised in the household, in society, and over oneself. In *The Care of the Self*, the focus is mainly on the last theme, reflecting the rich body of resources in Hellenistic–Roman thought relating to self-management. But Foucault recognizes that this is only one aspect of the larger set of factors, both external and internal, by which selfhood is shaped.[24]

It has also been argued that Foucault's account of Hellenistic–Roman self-scrutiny leaves out the elements that provide an absolute or, in my terms, 'objectivist', normative framework. These include ideas such as reason (*logos*) in Stoicism, conceived as a normative idea and linked with belief in a providential universe and a moral world-community. This criticism has been made by Pierre Hadot, whose work on Hellenistic–Roman practical ethics first stimulated Foucault's study of this area.[25] As a result, Hadot maintains, the 'care for the self' attributed by Foucault to ancient culture gives a greater weight to individual preference and to eclecticism than is appropriate, at least for Stoic or Epicurean thought. Foucault's presentation of Hellenistic–Roman self-cultivation as centred on 'the aesthetics of existence' suggests 'a culture of the self which is *too* aesthetic' for the material described, and seems to reflect 'a new form of Dandyism, later twentieth-century style'.[26] To rephrase this criticism, Foucault's account of the care of the self in Hellenistic–Roman philosophy *seems*, at least, to reflect a subjective-individualist approach to personality. This is so even though Foucault himself is far from endorsing the ideas of the post-Cartesian and post-Kantian tradition from which this approach typically derives.

What other modern ideas about selfhood or personality can we draw on to frame an appropriate way of analysing ancient ideas, including Hellenistic–Roman ones? In fact, the conception of person as self-conscious 'I' is not universally accepted in modern thinking. There are, for instance, several theories in psychology and the philosophy of mind which are critical of Cartesian assumptions, including the view of the person as an 'I'-centred

[24] This paragraph is indebted to Pradeau (2002*a*, 2003). See also Foucault (1988*a*), 16–19. On the interplay between self-government and politics in the Hellenistic–Roman period, see Foucault (1998*b*), 81–95, esp. 94–5, and on Hellenistic–Roman 'care of self', viewed in a larger historical perspective, 235–40. On Foucault on morals, knowledge, and power, see further Detel (2005*a*) ch. 1, centred on Foucault (1984).

[25] P. Hadot (1995), 206–13. On Foucault's interest in Hadot's application of the idea of 'spiritual exercise' to Hellenistic–Roman thought, see P. Hadot (1995), 1, 206.

[26] P. Hadot (1995), 210–11, quotations from 211. See also P. Hadot (1995), 24–5 (introduction by Davidson), recording Foucault's dismissal of Hellenistic logic and physics as 'enormous excrescences', in conversation with Paul Veyne.

locus of self-consciousness. It has been argued, for instance, that consciousness is a more internally complex and conflicted phenomenon than is presupposed in Cartesian-style theory. The idea that we have direct and incorrigible access to all our mental states is vulnerable to common-sense objections and scientific research. Correspondingly, there are problems with the idea that 'I' should be identified as a unitary locus of consciousness, or that the first-personal viewpoint, in so far as this is conceived as centred on self-consciousness, should be taken as fundamental in our accounts of personhood and personal identity. If there is a good deal in our mental processes of which we are not directly aware, the third-personal perspective—for instance, the standpoint of scientific enquiry—may offer greater insight into our motivation and state of mind.[27] Several important theories in the modern philosophy of mind have developed approaches which are *not* based on giving authoritative status to the 'I', taken as the centre of subjectivity, self-consciousness, and agency. These include functionalism, of the type developed by Daniel Dennett, Donald Davidson's action-theory, and the theory of cognitive content offered by Christopher Peacocke. For instance, Davidson's theory assumes that a person's actions are properly explained by her beliefs and desires. But Davidson does not presuppose that the beliefs and desires which represent the reasons for a given action are necessarily conscious to the person concerned, either before or after the action. Hence, beliefs and desires, as understood by Davidson, differ from the conscious volitions taken to motivate action in post-Cartesian thought.[28]

It has been argued that these features of the contemporary philosophy of mind represent not just a move away from post-Cartesian ideas but also one that brings us closer to earlier ways of understanding psychology, including those in Greek thought. This has been maintained, for instance, by some scholars working in the modern philosophy of mind, such as Elizabeth Anscombe, O. R. Jones and Peter Smith, and Kathleen Wilkes.[29] The related view, that these features of contemporary thought form the best starting-point for our study of ancient thought, has been argued for, or deployed as a basis of interpretation, by a number of scholars, including David Charles and Martha Nussbaum. One ancient idea often noted in this connection is

[27] See Smith and Jones (1986), ch. 15; Wilkes (1988), ch. 6. The contemporary critique of Cartesian-style ideas about consciousness was anticipated, of course, by Freud (on his theory of mind see e.g. Wollheim and Hopkins 1982). However, Freud's theory continues to give the idea of 'I' (Ego) a more central place than the contemporary theories noted below, although Freud's 'I' is a very different concept from that presupposed in Cartesian-style thinking.

[28] See e.g. Dennett (1979), ch. 9, (1993); Davidson (1980), chs. 1–3; LePore and McLaughlin (1985), 3–13; Peacocke (1983).

[29] See Anscombe (1957), 79; Smith and Jones (1986), ch. 6; Wilkes (1988), ch. 7, esp. 209–14.

Aristotle's use of the practical syllogism to spell out both human and non-human motivation. The practical syllogism has been seen as significant partly because it serves as a way of analysing motivation in terms of a connected set of reasons (or motives or content) without making reference to *conscious* intentions.[30] More broadly, Aristotelian thought has been commended for analysing psychology by reference to a set of functions, such as movement, perception, and thought, all of which count as expressions of 'psyche', rather than in terms of conscious mental states. The distinctive feature of human psychology is defined as the presence of advanced or complex functions, for instance, in Aristotle's analysis of *prohairesis*, 'choice', and not as that of 'I'-centred self-consciousness or subjectivity.[31]

Elsewhere, I have also suggested that reference to contemporary non-Cartesian, or anti-Cartesian, theories can help us to form a better understanding of ancient thought about what distinguishes human from non-human animals or about what constitutes a normative or ideal type of human being. For instance, I have presented as a point of contact between Aristotle and Dennett the fact that they see distinctively human functions, such as acting on the basis of belief or reflection, as more complex versions of functions also found in non-human animals, and not as radically different in kind, namely, conscious or self-conscious rather than unconscious, as in the Cartesian model. I have also argued that the Stoic characterization of humans as distinctively rational, rather than distinctively self-conscious, can be usefully compared to Davidson's account of rational animals. Both Davidson and the Stoics identify as the crucial marker of rationality the presence of a structured set of capacities, notably those for holding reasoned beliefs expressed in language and for logical inference.[32] The question of how to approach ancient criteria for normative status, or for what makes someone fully 'human' or 'divine'—in the way that a human being can be—is more complex, and involves ethical as well as psychological considerations. But, on this topic too, I have suggested that we should begin from modern non-Cartesian discussions of personhood or rationality, rather than from the 'I'- centred or subjective definitions of personhood or personal identity that have played an important role in much modern thought.[33]

[30] See e.g. Arist. *de Motu Animalium* (*M.A.*), ch. 7, *NE* 7.3, esp. 1146^{b}35–1147^{a}10, 1147^{a}24–^{b}5. See further Nussbaum (1978), 165–220; Charles (1984), pp. ix–x, chs. 3–4.

[31] See Arist. *NE* 3.3, 6.2, on *prohairesis*. See esp. *NE* 1139^{b}4–5: 'choice is either desiderative reason or ratiocinative desire, and *such a source of action is a man*', cited by Wilkes (1988), 213, her translation and italics.

[32] See Gill (1991), referring esp. to Dennett (1976), Davidson (1985); see also Davidson (2001), essays 1–9, on the concepts of 'subjective' and 'intersubjective'. On the (distinct) question how far Aristotle's theory can be compared with modern functionalism in its assumptions about the mind–body relationship, see Nussbaum and Rorty (1992), chs. 1–3.

[33] See further Gill (1996*b*), ch. 6, esp. 430–43.

In my earlier book on Greek concepts of selfhood and personality (1996*b*), I suggested that debate in the current philosophy of mind provides us with two sets of contrasts which we can deploy in our analysis of ancient ideas. The first contrast is between subjective and objective psychological concepts. The second is between correlated types of methodology, in the theory of mind and ethics; this contrast can be characterized as that between subjectiv*ist* and objectiv*ist* types of methodology.[34] I summarize these contrasts, based on the kind of modern ideas just discussed, before considering their implications for the present enquiry.

The use of *subjectivity* as a criterion of selfhood or personhood reflects the influence of Descartes's move of taking the 'I', conceived as a self-conscious, unitary subject, as fundamental to our understanding of reality. In post-Cartesian thought, the 'I' can be understood simply as the more or less unified centre of psychological experience, such as perception and memory, and of self-consciousness. But the 'I' can also be conceived as the centre of a uniquely 'first-personal' viewpoint. The first-personal viewpoint can be defined narrowly, for instance, in terms of 'indexicality', the awareness that 'I' am *this* person *here now*. But this viewpoint can also be defined more broadly, as one that shapes not only perception and memory but also one's whole psychological and ethical world-view.[35] The contrasting criterion of *objectivity* can be been linked with the reaction in many contemporary theories of mind against the post-Cartesian emphasis on subjectivity. It has been stressed that the human mind and personality can be understood just as well, or better, from a third-personal as from a first-personal viewpoint. From a third-personal standpoint, human psychology can be analysed as the complex of psychological functions or the set of beliefs and desires that best explains human behaviour to an observer. The objective approach rejects the idea that there is a peculiarly private, first-personal sphere of experience to which the person as subject has privileged access. The idea of 'self' (and sometimes that of 'person') has sometimes been seen as inseparably linked with the subjective conception of personality. In consequence, alternative concepts have sometimes been adopted by modern thinkers working from an objective standpoint, such as 'rational animal' or 'human being' (the latter idea being taken as having normative and not simply biological connotations).[36]

As an example of *subjectivist* methodology, we can take the use of arguments about personal identity based on intuitions about who 'I' am. Typical examples of such arguments in modern philosophy include thought-experiments centring on the question whether 'I' am identical with my mind

[34] See also Gill (1996*b*), 7 n. 21, 10–11.
[35] See text to nn. 12–20 above.
[36] See references in nn. 27–33 above.

or my body. Such arguments are often subjective in the criteria used to determine who 'I' am, for instance, as a locus of first-personal perceptions and memories, and are subjectivist in the means used to apply these criteria, such as personal intuitions about who 'I' am. Objectivist methodology gives no such status to the first-personal standpoint and focuses on procedures which can be applied from a third-personal standpoint. Modern scientific experiments, for instance, into states of the brain would count as a classic example of the objectivist approach. There are also purely philosophical methods, such as those of functionalism or action-theory, which deliberately adopt a third-personal, though not specifically scientific, approach to the analysis of human psychology.[37] An analogous distinction can be drawn between subjectivist and objectivist approaches to ethical questions. The contrast, broadly, is between those who assume that ethical questions depend, ultimately, on subjective criteria and perspectives and those who think that they are amenable to independent or absolute (objective) determination.[38]

In my earlier book (1996*b*), I combined this set of contrasts with a second one, centred on divergent approaches to ethics, namely between 'individualist' and 'participant' conceptions of the person. This contrast is not so fully elaborated in this discussion as in my previous book,[39] but I outline it here because it contributes to the composite conceptions of person (subjective-individualist, contrasted with objective-participant) which I do deploy here.

An idea which has had great influence in modern Western ethics, analogous to the role played by the Cartesian conception of the self-conscious 'I' in the philosophy of mind, is that the individual agent has a crucial, even foundational, role in setting moral standards. This idea has its roots in Kant's thinking about the moral agent as capable of 'autonomy' or self-legislation.[40] But the full implications of line of thought are brought out more clearly in the radical moral individualism of more recent thinkers such as Nietzsche and Sartre.[41] There has also been a reaction against the kind of post-Kantian moral theory that gives a crucial or foundational role to the individual agent as a locus of autonomy. Alasdair MacIntyre and Bernard Williams, in famous

[37] See further Gill (1996*b*), 41–5, 423–4, referring especially to the critique by Wilkes (1988) of subjectivist methodology as deployed in the theory of personal identity e.g. by Parfit (1984), chs. 10–13. See further on the methodology of personal identity, including responses to Wilkes (1988), in Cockburn (1991), 117–22, 138–41, 147–51, 153–4, 213–14; also McGinn (1997), ch. 9.

[38] On ancient and modern approaches to this issue, see Gill (2005*d*).

[39] This is simply for reasons of space and focus in the present study. I think the contrast could be used effectively to analyse Hellenistic–Roman thinking on social ethics and hope to do so in another context.

[40] On Kantian 'autonomy', see Kant, *Groundwork*, Prussian Academy edition, iv. 402–3 (Kant 1948: 67–8); also T. E. Hill (1989).

[41] See further Gill (1996*b*), 110–11, 126–7, 445–7. On Nietzsche and Sartre, see also text to n. 46 below.

books published in the 1980s, re-asserted the importance of the communal and interpersonal basis of ethical life. Both thinkers stressed, from differing standpoints, the idea that social participation plays a key part in shaping the dispositions and attitudes that are fundamental for ethical life. Both thinkers were also sceptical of the idea that, without this kind of social basis, moral philosophy could play what Williams calls an 'Archimedean' role in providing a foundation for moral life. I have suggested that ethical approaches of this kind could be described as 'participant' in approach, by contrast with the various kinds of 'individualism' that are crucial for the post-Kantian tradition.[42]

This area of debate provides us with a second contrast, between individualist and participant approaches to the person. The idea of *individuality* can be used in a relatively neutral way; the aim may simply be to distinguish the person considered on her own rather than as a member of a group. However, the idea of individuality becomes more significant when it is coupled with a stronger claim, such as that the individual, rather than the group, plays the key role in grounding morality, and that, in this respect, she expresses most fully her selfhood or personhood.[43] Individuality is sometimes contrasted with membership of a community or group; but I focus here, rather, on the idea of *participation* in interpersonal or communal relationships and in the modes of discourse by which these are constituted. The term 'participation' is designed to avoid the rather common modern idea that there is a radical dichotomy between 'individual' and 'society', which may be taken to imply that social involvement requires the individual to surrender her identity. Rather, participation in interpersonal or social relations can be seen as absolutely central to one's selfhood or personality.[44] The kind of participation involved may be reflective and philosophical as well as involving social interaction. Shared reflection or debate can be seen as the appropriate context for grounding morality, and the capacity to take part in such debate can be taken as a mark of personhood in the full sense.[45]

These four ideas (subjective and objective, individual and participant) can be combined with each other to identify different types of psychological and ethical approaches to the person. Two combinations of special importance here are 'subjective-individualist' and 'objective-participant'. The idea of

[42] See MacIntyre (1985), esp. chs. 1–6; Williams (1985), esp. 28–9 (on the Archimedean point) and chs. 4, 9, 10. See further Gill (1996*b*), 7–8, 62–8, referring also to Strawson (1974) and C. Taylor (1985).

[43] For some example of the latter move, see n. 46 below. On 'individualism' as a (multi-faceted) modern normative concept, see Lukes (1973).

[44] See e.g. C. Taylor (1985) on the concept of person as 'interlocutor' (see also other references in n. 42 above).

[45] See further Gill (1996*b*), 11–12, also 279–87, 370–83, 430–43.

individuality is sometimes combined with that of subjectivity and the first-personal viewpoint. The resulting idea is that to realize one's individuality is to express oneself as a locus of first-personal subjectivity (as 'I' or 'me' in that sense). Self-expression is sometimes presented as a more important or profound moral claim or need than the obligations of group-membership. In modern Western culture, this combination has been especially important, and has been informed by the combination of post-Cartesian influence in the philosophy of mind and post-Kantian thought in ethics. One striking example is that of Nietzsche, whose ideal of 'self-creation' (sometimes linked with that of the 'Superman' or *Übermensch*) is envisaged as going 'beyond good and evil' in a conventional sense. A second example is that of Sartre, in whose earlier thought 'existentialist' self-realization is presented as an overriding goal, while reliance on standard moral norms is seen as a surrender to 'bad faith'.[46] As indicated in a comment by Amélie Rorty (1976: 11, quoted on 331 above), in the development of this kind of modern idea, philosophical shifts were reinforced by literary or cultural movements such as Romanticism and the emergence of 'the novel of first person sensibility'. These intellectual movements took place against a background of substantive political and socio-economic change through which individuals in fact acquired much greater autonomy in relation to family and communal groups than in any previous culture or period. To this degree, it is unsurprising that the ethic of radical self-realization is still a recognizable presence in our culture, even if it currently lacks any powerful philosophical exponent.

I have argued that the contrasting objective-participant conception of person, which combines an objective psychological standpoint with a participant (and, typically, objectiv*ist*) ethical one, was characteristic of Archaic and Classical Greek thought. I think this kind of conception is implied in central works of Classical Greek theory such as Plato's *Republic* and Aristotle's *Nicomachean Ethics*, and that aspects of this idea are also embodied in the presentation of heroic figures in Homer's *Iliad* and Greek tragedy. I have offered the image of 'the self in dialogue' as a symbol for this conception of the person. The image is that of the person as a locus of three interlinked types of dialogue: internal dialogue between the parts of the psyche, discourse between people as engaged social participants, and shared debate or dialectic about the fundamental norms of human life.[47] However, I have also suggested that this conception is not peculiar to ancient Greek culture. As noted earlier,

[46] See Gill (1996*b*), 109–11, 115–116, 125–9, referring to the accounts of Trilling (1972), chs. 4–5; MacIntyre (1985), esp. ch. 9, 18; Solomon (1988), 111–26, 173–93; C. Taylor (1989), 440–55. See esp. Gill (1996*b*), 110–11, citing Nietzsche (1974), 290; also, on Sartre, Kerner (1990), part 3, and Dilman (1991).

[47] See Gill (1996*b*), 14–16, 255–6, 387–9, 453–4, 458–9.

in contemporary thought, there has been both a strong ('objective') reaction in the philosophy of mind against the post-Cartesian conception of person and an equally powerful ('participant') reaction against the kind of individualism expressed in the post-Kantian ethical tradition. In principle at least, these two strands of reaction can be combined to make a modern version of an objective-participant conception of person, and this can in turn be combined with (psychological or ethical) objectivism.[48] Hence, it is possible to argue that the study of objective-participant conceptions of person in ancient culture is not simply of historical importance but is of special significance *to us*, in our specific intellectual and cultural situation.[49]

The last point is worth developing in order to clarify the assumptions of this discussion. A theme of recent scholarship has been that interpretation, including that of past cultures, is also a matter of reception, and that the way we receive ideas from other cultures is shaped by our own pre-existing assumptions and ideas. I take the force of this point, which explains, in part, why I have drawn on modern Western ideas in defining categories such as subjective or objective by which to analyse ancient Greek thinking. However, the interpretative framework just outlined shows that we can take a more active and discriminatory role in reception than is sometimes acknowledged. For instance, we can select, from within modern ideas, those which seem to correspond most closely with the ancient ideas we are seeking to understand. This process can go hand in hand with using our study of antiquity to think critically about the ideas that are prevalent in our own culture. In this way, our response to the ideas of the past can be conceived as an attempt to engage in responsive dialogue with them, rather than simply superimposing our own assumptions and categories on the ancient material. Thus, the objective-participant conception, defined by contrast with the subjective-individualist, is designed to act as—what Steven Lukes calls—a 'bridgehead' in the project of taking forward our dialogue with the conception of person or self in another age and culture.[50]

[48] I have not argued that any one modern theory combines *all* these aspects, though that of David Wiggins is a possible candidate. See further Gill (1996*b*), 6–16, 423–43, 455–69. See also Detel (2005*b*) on types of objectivism in some modern theories of psychological and ethical normativity compared with ancient (especially Platonic) thought.

[49] However, other combinations of these ideas are conceptually possible. 'Objective-individualism', combining a focus on the individual agent with the assumption of ethical objectivism, has been especially prominent in modern post-Kantian moral thought; see further Gill (1996*b*), 278–9, 366–9.

[50] For this type of approach, see also Gill (1996*b*), 17–18. On reception-theory, see Holub (1984); on reception and antiquity, Martindale (1992). For the idea of using 'bridgeheads' towards the conceptions of person and self in other cultures, see Lukes (1985), esp. 297–9.

The framework just outlined, centred on the contrast between subjective and objective, individualist and participant, was formulated to carry forward dialogue with the conceptions of selfhood and personality in ancient Greek culture from Homer to Aristotle (Gill 1996*b*). However, it seems to me equally valid as an interpretative framework for analysing the ideas about the person embodied in Hellenistic–Roman thought. What is, of course, more open to debate is whether the application of this framework should yield the same result as my analysis of Homer and Classical Greek thought. It would be possible to argue that a new, or at least modified, notion of self emerges in the Hellenistic and Graeco–Roman eras, and that this version is closer to the subjective-individualist conception than are the ideas embodied in preceding Greek culture. The implication of the comments of Kahn and Long cited earlier is that a new focus on subjectivity and individuality emerges in Hellenistic–Roman thought, especially as exemplified in Epictetus (329–30, 334 above). Also, Foucault alludes to the longstanding scholarly idea that socio-political changes in Hellenistic–Roman society led to the emergence of certain kinds of individualism, by contrast with the more communal approach that is characteristic of earlier Greek culture. Foucault, along with some other recent discussions, is sceptical of that idea. But he presents as a more credible view that the Hellenistic and Graeco–Roman periods saw the rise of a body of reflective writing and discussion that promoted a culture which gave a prominent role to *le souci de soi*, that is, 'care of oneself' in the form of (individual) self-examination and self-fashioning.[51] Foucault's view might be seen as implying that Hellenistic–Roman thought introduces what is, in this respect, a more subjective-individualist conception of selfhood. Thus, on these grounds and others, the claim can be made that, although the same interpretative framework for analysing personality is applicable to Hellenistic–Roman thought, the outcome of the analysis will differ from that of earlier Greek thought. I will argue for an opposing view, namely that an objective-participant approach underlies Hellenistic–Roman thought as it does Classical thought. This claim is supported by readings of Plato, *Alcibiades 1*, representing fourth-century BC thinking, and aspects of Stoic thought, including features of Epictetus' teaching taken by Kahn and Long to indicate a shift towards a more subjective or individualistic conception. But I also suggest, particularly in connection with Epictetus, that some of the innovative features of Stoicism (and Epicureanism) that I am associating with the idea of a structured self go some way to explaining the *apparent* shift towards

[51] See text to nn. 7–8 and 24–6 above.

a more subjective-individualistic conception of the person.[52] However, my view remains that these features are best explained in terms of objective-participant concepts and objectivist methodology.

6.3 CONCEPTS OF SELF IN PLATO'S *ALCIBIADES*

The first topic considered here is the presentation of the idea of self-knowledge in Plato, *Alcibiades 1*.[53] I focus first on the language used and its conceptual implications, in particular, the question whether we find here, as is sometimes supposed, the—surprisingly modern—phrase 'the self itself'. I also examine the mode of argument, especially its implications as regards the relationship between the core or essence of personality and reflexivity. My overall aim is to locate the conception of self expressed in the dialogue in the context of the contrast between subjective-individualist and objective-participant approaches in the preceding section. The kind of core-centred thinking found here and in other Platonic dialogues resembles Descartes's thinking in its dualism.[54] But this does not mean that we should interpret the argument in terms of the subjective concepts or subjectivist methodology explored by Descartes and developed in the post-Cartesian tradition. On the contrary, I think that the conception of self-knowledge presented in the dialogue is best understood in terms of the objective-participant approach that is prevalent in Classical Greek thought, which is also expressed in certain well-known features of Aristotelian thought.

As explained earlier, this dialogue is also deployed here as an example of Classical thought (of a core-centred type) to serve as a reference-point by which to define what is innovative in Hellenistic–Roman thought. Plato's *Alcibiades* might seem a questionable text to use for this purpose, since, in modern times, its authenticity has often been questioned. However, as Annas points out (1983: 114–15), the grounds for doubting that it is Platonic are far from decisive. It was widely taken to be authentic in antiquity; and several recent treatments accept it as a—probably early—Platonic dialogue. Even scholars who dispute its authenticity tend to regard it as originating from

[52] See 6.5 below, text to nn. 184–93 on some implications of Stoic (and Epicurean) thinking about development. On another change from earlier Greek thought, which renders less relevant the idea of internal dialogue *between psychic parts*, see 6.5 below, text to nn. 243–5.

[53] Hereafter, simply *Alcibiades* (*Alcib.*).

[54] On Descartes's dualism, contrasted both with Aristotelian ideas and with contemporary functionalism, see (from a critical standpoint), Smith and Jones (1986), parts 1–2; Wilkes (1988), ch. 7.

the fourth century BC.[55] So it seems reasonable to take the *Alcibiades* as an expression of Classical, and specifically fourth-century, thinking. The dialogue as a whole represents Socrates showing Alcibiades that he wants to take charge of the politics of Athens before he has learnt to take care of himself.[56] It is from this topic that there arises, in the last third of the dialogue, the question of what it means to know and take care of yourself. Other Platonic dialogues also show Socrates giving a prominent role to the importance of 'knowing yourself' and 'taking care of' or 'cultivating' (*epimeleian poieisthai*) yourself.[57] However, more explicitly than any other such dialogue, this one proceeds to analyse what the 'self' is that is known. Beginning from the question what it means to 'take care of oneself' (128a), the question focuses on knowing 'what we ourselves are' (128e11), meaning, as I show shortly, what we are essentially.

What is identified as essential is the mind, soul, or personality (psyche) rather than the body, on the grounds that the user is distinct from what is used and the ruler distinct from what is ruled (129c–130c). The discussion explicitly rejects the idea that 'the combination of the two' (*sunamphoteron*, 130a9), that is, body and psyche, could be assigned this status (130b–c). Towards the end of the dialogue our essence is specified more precisely as an aspect of the psyche. Socrates elucidates the idea of self-knowledge by that of mutual knowledge, and he elucidates the latter idea by the image of two eyes looking at each other and seeing their reflection in the other eye (132c–133b). More precisely, the mutual seeing occurs through the pupil, 'that region of the eye in which good activity (or virtue, *aretē*) is present' (133b3–4). By analogy, the psyche recognizes itself when it looks at that region of the psyche in which its good activity or virtue is present, namely wisdom (*sophia*), or 'knowing and thinking' (*eidenai* and *phronein*, 133b9–10, c2). This region is said to be that which resembles god (or 'the divine'), and whoever understands 'god and wisdom (*phronēsis*)' is said also to understand himself and to have the virtue of moderation or self-control, *sōphronein* (133c).

In considering the significance of this argument for this enquiry, I focus on two questions. One concerns a point of language: is it the case, as may at first

[55] See the outline of modern scholarly views in Marboeuf and Pradeau (1999), 219–20. Marboeuf and Pradeau, 24–9, and Annas (1985), 112–15, take it to be an early Platonic dialogue. D. S. Hutchinson, in Cooper (1997), 557–8, suggests it was written shortly after Plato's death, that is, contemporary with similar ideas in Aristotle (on which see text to nn. 87–93, 98–100 below).

[56] See esp. *Alc.* 116d–118c, 124a–c, 127d–e, 133c–135e. For this type of dialogue between Socrates and Alcibiades, see e.g. Pl. *Smp.* 216a, (in Giannantoni 1991) Aeschines VI A 46, 49–50, summarized in Kahn (1996), 20–1.

[57] See e.g. *Alc.* 119a, 124a–b, 128a; also Pl. *Ap.* 29e–30b, 36c; *Chrm.* 164e–174e.

appear, that the argument introduces an exact equivalent for the modern English usage 'the self'? Second, in the form of argument, what is the relationship between reflexivity and essence? In particular, is our essence presented as a certain type of reflexivity, namely that expressed in knowing ourselves? Both these questions can also be raised in connection with Aristotle's accounts of friendship. Discussion of these questions can help us to distinguish the conception of selfhood implied in the ancient texts from subjective, post-Cartesian, conceptions that may seem initially similar.

In the *Alcibiades*, there are two passages (129b and 130d) in which we find the puzzling phrase, *auto to auto*, which is sometimes translated 'the self itself'. In the second passage, the phrase is contrasted with *auto* (or *auton*) *hekaston*, sometimes translated as 'a particular self'.[58] The phraseology has been found striking and puzzling since antiquity, and has been interpreted in several different ways. Some have seen a reference to the Platonic Forms and have taken *auto to auto* to mean 'the same itself', on the analogy of Forms such as 'the beautiful itself' *auto to kalon*.[59] In antiquity, Neoplatonic interpreters found these terms of special interest and interpreted them in the light of their own concern with higher and lower levels of the psyche. Damascius saw *auto to auto* as an elaboration of *auto* (129a8). He understood *auto* as the rational psyche which uses the body as its instrument, and *auto to auto* as the 'purified' (*kathartikē*) and 'contemplative' (*theōrētikē*) rational psyche, disembodied and directed at truth. Despite regarding the latter sense as the higher one, Damascius saw the argument of *Alcibiades* as a whole as focused on the first ('political') sense, the embodied psyche which engages, as Alcibiades does, in political action. Proclus identifies three key terms: *auto* and *auto to auto*, understood much as they are by Damascius, and *auto to auto hekaston* (*Alc.* 130d4), understood as the essential but also individual psyche. Olympiodorus takes the same view of *auto* and *auto to auto*, while seeing the third idea (in 130d4) as being *auto hekaston*, meaning each embodied psyche as an individual.[60]

Modern interpretations tend to analyse the discussion, instead, in terms of 'self'.[61] Julia Annas sees the discussion as, progressively, identifying, one's true

[58] 129b1, contracted to *auto tauto* in one ms. (d), followed by Burnet (1901); 130d4. The translations given are those by D. S. Hutchinson in Cooper (1997).

[59] See e.g. Pl. *Phd.* 78d3, *Smp.* 211d3. Hence, Lamb (1927) translates as 'the same-in-itself', seeing a reference to Forms. Jowett (1892), gives 'the self-existent' at 129b1 and 'absolute existence' at 130d4. Croiset (1946) translates as 'ce que c'est au juste que soi-mēme' (explained in 129 n. 1, as literally 'ce qu'est au juste "un ētre lui-mēme", le fond de l'être').

[60] The text of *Alc.* 130d4 is uncertain, allowing different readings (and interpretations); see Burnet (1901) and Denyer (2001), ad loc., and Segonds (1985), p. lx n. 2. On Neoplatonic interpretations, see Segonds (1985), pp. lv–lxi, and, more briefly, Annas (1985), 131; Marboeuf and Pradeau (1999), 22–4.

[61] See e.g. Hutchinson's translation in Cooper (1997): 'the self itself' (129b and 130d).

self as the 'self-itself' (*auto to auto*), which is 'impersonal' and, 'like a Form, is the same in all its instances' (1983: 131). Jean-François Pradeau also reads the argument as concerned with the concept of *soi* (understood as the equivalent of the English 'self') or *sujet* ('subject'). In the relevant passages (129b, 130d), he sees a deliberate move, on Plato's part, to convert a reflexive pronoun (*soi*) into a noun or substantive (*le soi*); hence, the unusual phrase *auto to auto*.[62] Like Annas, and also Jacques Brunschwig (and, in a different way, the Neoplatonists), Pradeau sees the argument as designed to define an 'objectivized' or impersonal self as our real self.[63] Annas and Pradeau, while interpreting the argument in terms of 'self' or 'subject', do not claim that this marks a substantive innovation or a shift towards (what can be called) a more subjective conception of self. But a version of this claim is made by Foucault in an important discussion considered shortly.

The interpretation of these passages (129b and 130d) raises two kinds of issue. One concerns the relationship between the language of the *Alcibiades* and the terms used to interpret it. The other concerns the conception of selfhood or personality that is implied in the argument of the *Alcibiades*. Although these two issues are distinct, they can easily become intertwined. There is, for instance, a potential danger in analysing the argument in terms of 'self'. The English term, 'self' (even more, '*the self*') is a rather peculiar usage, representing the conversion of a reflexive suffix (as in 'himself') into a noun. In French, the same process has occurred with a reflexive prefix (*soi* or *le soi*, as in *soi-mēme*).[64] One factor that has surely promoted this usage is the tendency, in post-Cartesian European thought, to give a privileged status to a certain kind of reflexivity, namely that involved in 'I'-centred self-consciousness.[65] In general, this linguistic phenomenon did not take place in Greek or Latin, where the key terms are, in Greek, *psuchē* ('personality'), *nous* ('mind'), *logos* ('reason') or *anima* ('spirit' or psyche), *animus* ('mind'), *ratio* ('reason'), rather than *heauton* or *se* ('himself'). Similarly, at least on the view taken here, we do not find in ancient thought the post-Cartesian shift towards a notion of personality centred on subjective reflexivity (self-consciousness).

62 Marboeuf and Pradeau (1999) (introd. by Pradeau), 47–53, esp. 71. Their translation renders the phrase as 'ce/le soi-mēme lui-mēme' (129b and 130b), i.e. (presumably) 'this/the oneself itself'; see also 210 n. 121.

63 Marboeuf and Pradeau (1999), 210 n. 121, 212 n. 129; also introd., 70–80; Brunschwig (1996), 68.

64 However, in French, we also find the same process occurring with 'I' or 'me' (*le je* or *le moi*), as also in German (*das Ich*). See further on these linguistic variations and their conceptual implications, Toulmin (1977), 295–300; Carrithers, Collins, and Lukes (1985), 20–2, 282–3.

65 See the 'philosophical' sense of 'self' cited from the *OED* (text to n. 15 above); the influence of the post-Cartesian tradition in shaping this linguistic usage is stressed by Kenny (1988–9), 4–6.

However, Plato's *Alcibiades* gives a prominent place to the unusual phrase *auto to auto* (129b, 130d), and this *might* seem to mark innovation both at the linguistic and the conceptual level. It *might* seem to introduce an ancient equivalent for the modern term 'the self' and do so as a means of signalling conceptual innovation, perhaps prefiguring the modern post-Cartesian conception of self. As just noted, among modern scholars, Annas and Pradeau have analysed the topic of the dialogue in terms of 'self', and Pradeau sees the usage as innovative, at the linguistic level at least. However, neither Annas nor Pradeau sees any indication of a move towards a more subjective or post-Cartesian sense of 'self'; rather, they see the argument as identifying our real self (or what is essential to us) as something objective and impersonal, in line with core-centred Platonic thought elsewhere.[66]

By contrast, as Inwood brings out in a recent discussion, Foucault sees the usage as innovative at the conceptual as well as linguistic level.[67] This is clearer in the lectures published as *L'Herméneutique du sujet* (2001) than in Foucault's other treatments of the dialogue.[68] Foucault suggests there that Plato is not simply, as elsewhere, asking about what is essential to human nature but raising a different kind of question: not, what is a human being but '"What is the subject?" That is, "What is the *auto*?"'.[69] Subsequently, Foucault develops the idea that Plato's question here does not only have methodological but also substantive importance. The question is: '[What is] this relationship which is denoted by this reflexive pronoun *heauton*; what is this element which is the same from the standpoint of subject and object?'[70] At the conceptual level, Foucault finds here a move towards an idea of the self which is fundamentally reflexive, in which the person is both subject and object. What he has in view here is not so much the Cartesian or Lockean conception of self, in which the form of reflexivity is that of ('I'-centred) self-consciousness. What he seems to have in mind is, rather, the kind of reflexive self-attention and self-fashioning (in line with 'the aesthetic and ethical criteria of existence') that he explores in his study of Hellenistic–Roman thought.[71] As Inwood underlines, Foucault

[66] See text to nn. 62–3 above, and 1.2 above, esp. text to nn. 5–6, 14–22.

[67] Inwood (2005), ch. 12, centred on the question whether a new concept of self emerges in Seneca. I am grateful to Brad Inwood both for drawing my attention to Foucault's comments and for showing me his chapter before publication.

[68] See also Foucault (1988*a*), 24–6, (1988*b*), 44–5.

[69] Foucault (2001: 39), 6 Jan., second lecture, trans. Inwood (2005: 333).

[70] Foucault (2001: 52), 13 Jan., first lecture: 'c'est en quelque sorte une question méthodologue et formelle mais, je crois, tout à fait capitale dans tout ce mouvement... [Quel est] ce rapport, qu'est-ce qui est désigné par ce pronom réfléchi *heauton*, qu'est-ce que c'est que cet élément qui est le mēme du coté du sujet et du coté de l'objet?'

[71] On Cartesian and Lockean ideas, see 6.2 above, text to nn. 12–15 On Foucault's philosophical position and approach to Hellenistic–Roman thought, see 6.2 above, text to nn. 23–6; the phrase cited is from Foucault (1998*b*: 67).

finds in this passage of Plato's *Alcibiades* a crucial innovative move towards that idea of self-fashioning. Foucault is not wholly explicit about how he interprets the relevant texts. But he seems to read *auto to auto* in 129b1 as 'the very same thing' which is both subject and object of the kind of reflexive relationships (taking care of and knowing oneself, *heauton*) discussed in 128a–129a. Foucault finds here a fundamentally reflexive relationship, in which both partners are 'the same', as distinct from the relationship between user and used discussed in 129e–130c, in which the partners are presented as different (psyche and body).[72]

I now offer my own account of the meaning of *auto to auto*, as a basis for considering the conception of selfhood expressed in Plato's dialogue. My interpretation of this phrase follows that adopted in Nicholas Denyer's commentary.[73] In 128a, Socrates raises the question, what it means 'to take care of yourself', a question elucidated by drawing a distinction between taking care of yourself and of the things that belong to you. He suggests that we will be better able to take care of ourselves if we know 'what we ourselves are' (*ti pot' esmen autoi*, 128e10–11). The word 'ourselves' (*autoi*) is used in what is sometimes called the 'intensive' sense; and this, I think, rather than the reflexive sense, is the crucial one here.[74] The expression 'what we ourselves are' is repeated later, in the immediate context of the phrase (*auto to auto*); and this may give us the key to the meaning. I think the passage should be translated in this way: 'Come now, how might the itself itself be discovered? In this way we could perhaps discover what we ourselves are, but if we don't know this [what the itself itself is] we never could' (129b1–3). Socrates, having raised the question of what 'we ourselves' are, suggests that they examine what it means to consider something 'itself'. The phrase resembles the type used in connection with Forms, for instance, 'the beautiful itself', *auto to kalon*. But the aim does not seem to be to create a Form of 'the itself', but, rather, to ask what is the core or essential features of 'the itself'. Though

[72] Foucault (2001: 54–7); my interpretation here follows Inwood's (2005: 331–4).

[73] Denyer (2001). I am grateful to Christopher Rowe for first suggesting this reading to me, and to Nicholas Denyer for sending me relevant extracts of his commentary prior to publication. A similar reading is adopted in Inwood (2005), 335–8.

[74] For the distinction between intensive and reflexive senses, see Goodwin (1951), sections 989–90 (pp. 213–15). See also the usages listed as '*the very*' in LSJ, *autos*, sense II, of which the philosophical sense 4, 'itself', seems to be an extension. The term *autos is* used in the reflexive sense in this context, e.g. 128d11, e2, 129a9, cf. *heauton* in 129a2. Allen (1962), 188–9, thinks that *auto tauto* in 129b1 refers to both senses. But the logic of the argument requires that we focus on the intensive sense in 129b1. We need to find out what we *ourselves* (intensive sense) are (129b2, picking up 128e11), so that we can give a proper account of what it means to care for and know ourselves (reflexive sense).

striking and exceptional, the phrase is intelligible and is reinforced by another intensive usage, 'ourselves' (*autoi*, 129 b2).[75]

The phrasing of the sentence ('...how might the itself itself be discovered?') in 129b1–2 seems to lead us to expect some general analysis of what is meant by speaking of something 'itself'. Instead, the argument takes the more restricted form of considering, in effect, 'what we ourselves are';[76] the question is then rephrased as asking what a human being is (*anthrōpos*, 130b–c). The fact that the discussion has become restricted in this way may be the main point of the second passage in which the phrase *auto to auto* occurs, which I would translate in this way:

> 'What was said just now was that we should first of all examine what the itself itself was. In fact, instead of the itself itself (*anti autou tou autou*), we've examined what each himself is (*auton hekaston*).[77] But perhaps this will be enough. Surely we would not say that there is anything of us ourselves (*hēmōn autōn*)[78] that is more authoritative than the psyche.' (130d3–6)

The gist of the passage, as so translated, is this. The fact that, in the preceding discussion (129b–130c), they have focused on what each person is in himself, instead of examining the concept of 'itself' in broader terms,[79] has not prevented them from reaching a conclusion which is adequate for their present purpose. They have established that the 'authoritative' or ruling element in a human being is the psyche;[80] and this is enough to answer the question what 'we ourselves' are, which was the starting-point of the enquiry. Commentators, from the Neoplatonists on, have tended to overinterpret this passage (130d3–6), assuming that it distinguishes between more or less essential parts or functions of the psyche, for instance, disembodied mind and embodied practical reason.[81] But, in so far as the argument contains a

[75] See also Denyer (2001), note on 129b1–3, esp. (p. 212, Greek term transliterated): 'Thus "to discover the itself itself" would be to find a formula which spells out the common feature of those cases in which the expression *autos* can rightly be applied'. For a different (but detailed and helpful) reading, see Allen (1962).

[76] In 129b, Socrates asks who 'you' and 'I' (who are speaking) are. As the continuation shows, he means to ask who they are 'themselves' or essentially.

[77] This translation assumes the reading *autou tou autou* (the same meaning would be given by *tou autou autou*) and the *auton* of mss. B and T; see Denyer's (2001) text. See also Denyer's notes on 130d5–6; Allen (1962), 188 n. 4, and contrast Burnet's (1901) text.

[78] On this phraseology, see n. 108 below. An alternative translation would be 'As regards us ourselves, surely we would not say anything is more authoritative than the psyche'.

[79] They have considered what each person is *himself* (see 129b–130c, summarized above); hence, the translation 'each himself', meaning 'each person in himself'.

[80] 'More authoritative' (*kuriōteron*) picks up the question, 'which rules, body or psyche or both?', in 130a–b.

[81] See e.g. Croiset (1946), 105 n. 1, whose translation of 130d3–6 distinguishes between '"soi-mēme" consideré absolument' and '"soi-mēme" en particulier' (i.e. 'the self itself' and each

distinction between more or less essential functions of the psyche, this comes later (133b–c), following the introduction of a new phase of the argument in 132c. At this stage, both before and after this passage (130d3–6), the argument is focused on the question whether the psyche or body is what we are 'ourselves'.[82]

An advantage of the reading offered here is that it offers a translation of *auto to auto* ('the itself itself') which shows how the phrase, while unusual, is intelligible as Greek and makes sense within the immediate context. The alternative sometimes adopted ('the self itself') is more familiar as English. But the familiarity is deceptive because 'the self' is not a normal way of translating *to auto*.[83] If *auto to auto* is translated as 'the self itself', there is a danger that modern readers will think that the Greek carries the complex psychological connotations—and the same *kind of* connotations—that 'the self' or 'le soi' has acquired. These include the sense of 'self' noted earlier, which reflects the post-Cartesian tradition of thinking about personality: 'That which in a person is really and intrinsically *he*...the ego (often identified with the soul or mind as opposed to the body): a permanent subject of successive and varying states of consciousness'.[84] Foucault, although not translating this phrase as 'the self itself', interprets it as expressing an innovative idea (the fundamentally reflexive self, the agent of self-fashioning), which prefigures both Hellenistic–Roman ideas and also, more indirectly, Foucault's own conception of the self.[85] But, as underlined earlier, *auto to auto* in *Alc.* 129b and 130d does not have a specifically psychological sense but simply conveys the general idea of 'the itself itself', though this notion is introduced in connection with the idea that the psyche is 'what we ourselves are'.[86]

The importance of not translating key terms in a way that imports inappropriate modern connotations is also relevant to the language of some

individual thing, reading *auto hekaston*); cf. Olympiodorus' reading (text to n. 60 above). See also Marboeuf and Pradeau (1999), 212 n. 129. For this type of reading to be credible, *auto to auto* must mean, in effect, 'the psyche itself' (i.e. what is essential in the psyche), and *auto(n) hekaston* must convey 'the psyche as found in the embodied particular person'.

82 The continuity of argument is marked, for instance, by the reference back from 130d–e to 129a–b ('we' are those in dialogue with each other), and by the re-use of the distinction between 'what belongs to yourself' and 'yourself' (128a–e) in connection with the distinction between psyche and body (131a–c). The body–psyche contrast is the main theme up until the new phase of argument, which is marked by the re-introduction of the Delphic oracle at 132c (cf. 129a).

83 Normally, one would take *to auto* to mean 'the same thing'.

84 *OED*, sense Ce3; see text to n. 15 above. For this point, see also Denyer (2001), p. 212. LSJ is, surely, misleading in identifying as sense I1 of *autos* 'one's true self', from Homer onwards; the meaning is simply the intensive 'itself' or 'oneself', as LSJ translates some of the usages listed in I1.

85 See text to nn. 69–72 above; also 6.2 above, text to nn. 23–6.

86 For a similar view, responding especially to Foucault's interpretation, see Inwood (2005), 333–8.

well-known chapters of Aristotle's *Nicomachean Ethics* (9.4, 9.8), which also illustrate 'core-centred' thinking about personality.[87] These chapters contain three ideas which are often translated into English by phrases involving the term 'self'. One idea is that of loving oneself or being a 'self-lover'. Another is that of what is essential to us, often rendered as 'our real' (or 'essential') 'self'. The third is the idea that a friend is 'a second self' or 'another self'.[88] However, in Greek, these three ideas are expressed either in different terms or in different senses of the same term. The first idea is expressed through reflexive forms: 'loving himself', *philein heauton*, or being a 'self-lover', *philautos*.[89] The second idea is expressed in a quite different form, as 'what each one is' (or 'seems to be') (*ti hekastos esti*), implying what each human being is in his essence.[90] The third is *allos autos*, meaning 'another oneself', that is, another equivalent to oneself.[91] These three ideas are linked in the arguments of these chapters; they are also linked with a related idea, that true friendship is directed at what someone is 'in himself' (*kath' hauton*).[92] But the key terms expressing these ideas are not verbally linked in the same way as they are in English, in which all three ideas can readily be translated by 'self'. The terminological linkage between the English terms might lead us to read the argument as unpacking different senses of a single well-established notion, 'the self'. In particular, the linkage in English might seem to lend support to one particular type of recent interpretation of Aristotle's theory of friendship. In this interpretation, Aristotle's theory is taken as implying that a proper understanding of one's selfhood as a rational agent leads one to see altruism as the deepest kind of self-realization. I have argued elsewhere that this interpretation is conceptually inappropriate to Aristotle's argument, in part because it gives a pivotal (or 'Archimedean') role to the notion of self.[93] It is important that we should not be drawn towards this type of interpretation

[87] See further on 'core-centred' thinking in these passages, 1.2 above, text to nn. 7–11, 15–21. *NE* 9.9 is closely related in thought and is also cited below.

[88] See e.g. Thomson (1976) (Penguin trans.), 294, which renders the latter two ideas as 'the self of the individual' (or 'the individual self') and 'another self'.

[89] On relationship to oneself, including friendship/love (*philia*), see 9.4, esp. 1166^{a}1–34; 9.8 is focused on whether someone should 'love himself' and be a 'self-lover'.

[90] See *NE* 9.4, esp. 1166^{a}14–23; 9.8, esp. 1168^{b}28–1169^{a}6.

[91] *NE* 9.4, 1166^{a}32; 9.9, 1170^{b}6. (For related examples, see Price 1989, 110.) The sense is, presumably, the (intensive) 'oneself/himself' of LSJ, sense I1, rather than the reflexive sense.

[92] *NE* 8.3, 1156^{b}8–12, an idea presupposed in the passages listed in n. 90 above.

[93] See further Gill (1996*b*), ch. 5, esp. 323, 328–31, 334–46, discussing Irwin (1988), chs. 16–18. Irwin's argument, like Engberg-Pedersen's treatment of the Stoic theory of development (on which see 6.4 below) is characterized as subjective-individualist in giving 'Archimedean' weight to the individual's conception of himself but as objectivist in its assumptions about ethical knowledge (Gill 1996*b*: 345). For a contrasting (objective-participant) reading of the language and methodology of Aristotle's arguments, see Gill (1996*b*), 346–70.

by a false impression about the meaning of the key terms of Aristotle's discussion.

I turn now from the question of phraseology to the form of argument and its conceptual implications. In the terms offered earlier, my concern is especially with the *criteria* of personhood or selfhood, though pursuing this question also involves consideration of the *methodology* of argument.[94] First, although the *Alcibiades* and *NE* 9.4, 8 give a role both to reflexivity and to essence, reflexivity is not used as a criterion of what is essential to us. In this respect, there is a contrast with the post-Cartesian subjective approach, in which the essence of personality is defined by reference to *a certain kind of* reflexivity, namely the subject's relation to herself. I noted earlier Locke's famous definition of 'person' as 'a thinking intelligent Being, that has reason and reflection, and can consider it self as it self, the same thinking thing, in different times and places; which it does only by that consciousness which is inseparable from thinking, and, as it seems to me, essential to it'.[95] Here, the subject's relation to herself, defined as self-consciousness, is presented as the criterion of being a 'person' and hence, as Locke also puts it, of being 'capable of a Law, and Happiness, and Misery'. The underlying thought is that, unless you are conscious of yourself as a continuing subject, you are not capable of acting as a moral and legal agent, who is responsible for herself.[96] Similarly, in a celebrated modern theory of personhood, that of Harry Frankfurt, persons are defined by a certain kind of reflexivity. This is that of having desires and motives *about* one's own desires and motives, or what Frankfurt calls having 'second-order' desires. In this theory, the reflexivity consists in the fact that the second-order desires must be about *one's own* (first-order) desires. It is this kind of 'capacity for reflective self-evaluation' that, for Frankfurt, marks off humans—at least if they develop into full 'persons'—from animals. Frankfurt's definition is less obviously subjective in conception than Locke's, and is capable of being developed in either subjective or objective versions. However, I have argued elsewhere that it derives much of its significance from the modern subjective-individualist tradition of thinking about personhood. Thus, it can serve as another example of how reflexivity can be used in a subjective approach to provide a definition of personhood.[97]

[94] See 6.2 above, text to nn. 34–8. Methodology is especially important in text to nn. 97–100, 104–14 below.

[95] Locke, *Essay*, 2.27.9, cited from Nidditch (1975), 335; see also text to n. 15 above.

[96] See Locke, *Essay*, 2.27.26, cited from Nidditch (1975), 346. See further Perry (1975), 12–15; Wilkes (1988), 218; C. Taylor (1989), 159–76.

[97] See Frankfurt (1971), esp. 6–7; also Gill (1996*b*), 413–22. Frankfurt's theory is criticized for (what I am calling) its subjectivist-individualist character by C. Taylor (1976), 281–8, (1977),

In the *Alcibiades* and Aristotle *NE* 9.4, 8, by contrast, the essence of personality is not defined by reference to either of these two types of reflexivity, or, indeed, by reflexivity at all. In fact, these Greek discussions exhibit a different, and, in this context, highly suggestive, pattern. Reflexive relations (relations to oneself), rather than being treated as fundamental to the essence of personality, are taken to require explanation or justification by reference to a concept of one's core or essence which is independently conceived. In the *Alcibiades*, the ideas of 'care for oneself' and 'knowledge of oneself' are explained by the idea that the psyche is the authoritative part of the human being, or 'what we *ourselves* are'. Later in the argument, self-knowledge is explained further by the idea that the highest, most divine, region of the psyche is that in which wisdom is found (that is, mind or reason).[98] Similarly, in *NE* 9.4, the claim that friendly relations towards others are derived from relations towards oneself is justified by the idea that 'what each one is' is the thinking and reasoning part of the psyche.[99] In 9.8, the claim that the good person should love himself most is supported by the argument that the good person loves 'what each one is', that is, his mind and practical reason.[100] Reflexivity is taken to be an idea that requires explanation or justification by reference to the core of the personality. This core is not defined by reflexivity, including reflexivity of the kind used by Locke and Frankfurt to define personhood.

So far, my case has been negative. I have maintained that the form of argument in the *Alcibiades* and *NE* 9.4, 8 is not well understood in terms of the methodology associated with a subjective or subjective-individualist conception of personality. I now claim, more positively, that the argument and concepts of these discussions can be rendered more intelligible by interpreting them in objective or objective-participant terms. A key feature of what I have presented as the objective-participant conception is that human personality is conceived as being formed and expressed through a combination of interactive and reflective dialogue or discourse. More broadly, human beings are seen as interlocutors in three related types of dialogue: the interplay

103–10; G. Taylor (1985), 111–20. Frankfurt's theory is developed in a non-subjectivist (functionalist) way by Dennett (1976), 191–3, and in a subjectivist way (by reference to the first-personal viewpoint), by Morton (1990).

98 For these two phases of argument, see *Alc.* 128a–132b (discussed above) and 132c–133d (discussed below).

99 More precisely, the claim is that, in the case of a good person, at least, wishing another well for the other's sake is derived from wishing himself (his essence) well for its own sake; *NE* 1166^{a}1–4, 14–23; also *NE* 8.3, on the related point that perfect friendship includes wishing the other well for the sake of what he is 'in himself' or essentially (1156^{b}6–12).

100 1168^{b}1–6, 1168^{b}28–1169^{a}11; on these passages see further 1.2 above, text to nn. 7–11, 15–21.

between parts or functions of the psyche, interactive discourse within the family or community, and reflective debate or dialectic.[101] A further relevant feature of this conception is that objective truth is taken to be determined through some combination of interactive discourse and reflective dialectic. This point applies to the determination of, for instance, normative ideas about what is essential to us as human beings.[102]

This conception can help to place in perspective aspects of the *Alcibiades* and Aristotle's *Nicomachean Ethics* that might otherwise seem puzzling. One small but striking point in Plato's dialogue is that, when Socrates takes up the question of 'who we ourselves are', his initial suggestion is that 'we' (Socrates and Alcibiades) are to be understood as interlocutors, engaged in dialogue with each other. This idea is not pursued as an independent claim. Instead, Socrates assumes the availability of this idea as the basis for establishing the more controversial idea, that our essential aspect is our psyche, and that we use discourse as the medium to communicate with each other's psyche.[103] However, the fact that he assumes the availability of the idea of the person as interlocutor, rather than one which suggests a more private or subjective conception of selfhood, is itself significant.

Reference to the objective-participant conception of personality can also help us to make sense of a much more famous and problematic passage near the end of the dialogue (*Alc.* 133a–c). After defining 'what we ourselves are' as the psyche, Socrates pursues the question of how 'we', as so understood, can gain knowledge of ourselves, and draws an analogy with sight. Just as an eye can see itself by looking into another eye, so a psyche can know itself by looking at another psyche. More precisely, it does so by looking 'at that region (*topos*) of the psyche in which the virtue of the psyche is present, namely wisdom (*sophia*), and at anything else which is similar to this' (133a9–10). This region of the psyche is presented as the most divine part of it; and looking at this region—or perhaps at god, identified here with wisdom—is said to be the best way of gaining knowledge of oneself (133c). This knowledge is then presented as the basis of moderation or self-control (*sōphronein*), since it provides knowledge of what does and does not belong to us (133d–e). It is offered as

[101] On this image and its significance, see Gill (1996*b*), 14–16, 252–8, 387–90, 453–4. For modern versions of this idea, see Strawson (1974) and C. Taylor (1985), discussed in Gill (1996*b*), 64–5.

[102] The precise form that such a combination should take represents a key issue of debate among those sharing this framework of thought; for varying ancient approaches to this question, see Gill (1996*b*), 289–301. On objectivist-participant thinking (both ancient and modern) about norms of human nature, see Gill (1996*b*), 423–43.

[103] *Alc.* 129a–c, 130d–e. The idea that 'we' are different from the words we use is taken to support the claim that 'we' (as psyches) are different from the bodies which we use (and rule); therefore, 'we' are using words as psyches, not as bodies or as combinations of psyche and body.

the basis for the political power which Alcibiades wants to exercise, the source of which he has been shown not to understand (134b–135e).

This passage (*Alc.* 133a–c) suggests that self-knowledge is best achieved by looking at someone else rather than by introspection. This idea is sometimes compared with the claim in the *Magna Moralia* (ascribed to Aristotle, but often thought to be post-Aristotelian) that we can know ourselves better by observing, as though in a mirror, a close friend who is 'another oneself' than by observing ourselves. Also, in Aristotle's *Nicomachean* and *Eudemian Ethics*, the friend is said to provide a means by which the good person can extend his own pleasurable perception of his goodness of character.[104] The way of thinking about self-knowledge expressed in these Aristotelian passages is in sharp contrast to the idea, central to the Cartesian tradition in modern thought, that consciousness or knowledge of oneself is primary and fundamental to other kinds of awareness. For Descartes, the belief that he was a 'thinking thing' (that 'I think, therefore I am') was the one belief that was beyond doubt, and which could therefore ground his reconstitution of reality as a whole. In post-Cartesian thought, we find various versions of this type of idea. These include the belief that the person as subject has immediate, incorrigible access to her own mental experience and that the first-personal perspective has a unique authority in all aspects of psychological and ethical life.[105] The contrast between these subjective-individualist ideas and Aristotle's thinking on self-knowledge indicates the presence of a quite different conception of personality in the Greek texts.

However, although it may be right to say that these Aristotelian passages and *Alcibiades* 133a–c express a shared objective-participant conception of personality, this does not mean they do so in exactly the same way. In the Aristotelian passages, the point is that interpersonal relationships create a context in which friends can communicate to each other knowledge or awareness of the character they share, in particular, their shared virtue.[106] In the *Alcibiades*, as Pradeau underlines, following Brunschwig, the idea of knowing oneself through another is not the central point.[107] Despite the image of two people recognizing themselves in each other (as psyches) (133b7–10), the interpersonal theme is less strong. The focus is on knowing

104 Self-knowledge through others, Arist. *MM* 2.15, 1213^{a}10–26, also *NE* 9.9, 1169^{b}28–1170^{a}4; self-perception (of one's own virtue) through another, *NE* 9.9, 1170^{a}13–^{b}13, *EE* 7.12, 1244^{b}23–1245^{b}19. Annas (1985), 117 n. 23, takes the use of the mirror-image in the *MM* passage to be based on that in *Alc.* 133a–c.

105 See 6.2 above, text to nn. 12–21.

106 See refs. in n. 104 above. See further Cooper (1980), 318–24; Price (1989), 120–4; Sherman (1989), 140–4; Gill (1996*b*), 353–4.

107 See Marboeuf and Pradeau (1999), Pradeau's introd., 74–81; also Brunschwig (1996), 72–8.

yourself in the sense of knowing 'what you *yourself* are'. The stress is also on the idea that knowing yourself consists in knowing *the best thing* about you, which is later identified with god.

> SOCRATES: So if an eye is to see itself, it must look at an eye, and at that region of the eye in which the virtue of an eye is to be found; and that virtue is surely sight (*opsis*)?
>
> ALCIBIADES: That's right.
>
> SOCRATES: Well then, my dear Alcibiades, if a psyche is to know itself, it must look at a psyche, and especially at that region in which the virtue of the psyche is to be found, namely wisdom or at anything else that this [aspect of the psyche] is similar to.[108]
>
> ALCIBIDES: That is how it seems to me, Socrates.
>
> SOCRATES: Can we say that there is a feature of the psyche that is more divine than that which is involved in both knowing and thinking?
>
> ALCIBIADES: We cannot.
>
> SOCRATES: So this feature of the psyche is like god, and anyone who looked at this and knew everything that was divine, god and wisdom, would also know himself most. (133b2–c6)

As this quotation brings out, the stress is not so much on mutual recognition of shared goodness of character as on recognizing your essential character, identified with wisdom or god. As Pradeau emphasizes (Marboeuf and Pradeau 1999: 76–8), self-recognition is conceived in aspirational terms: to see 'yourself' is to see what you could become, namely the god-like wisdom that is able genuinely to make you a better person. The image, then, is not so much that of a mirror, reflecting what is already there to be seen, as that of recognizing (through another) what you are, essentially, and what you could become. The image is that of the pupil, recognizing itself (through another) as an active and potentially developing capacity. The significance of this image, rather than that of the ordinary mirror, is that both what sees and what is seen are *active* capacities—for sight, which signifies wisdom. As so interpreted, this text resembles two passages in Plato's *Republic* which also convey an essence-centred conception of personality. One is the image of education as turning round the mind, the 'eye' of the psyche, towards truth, understood as the Form of the Good. The other passage is one which suggests that, if we want to

[108] This translation of 133b10 follows Marboeuf and Pradeau (1999), ad loc (see also 215, n 151). An alternative translation, that of Hutchinson in Cooper (1997), is 'at anything else which is similar to it [i.e. wisdom]'. The language used, i.e. 'region', b9, 'that of [the psyche]', c1–2, seems designed to avoid the awkwardness of saying that the essence of the psyche is just a *part* of a larger whole; see also Marboeuf and Pradeau (1999), 214–15 n. 149; Denyer (2001), note on 133c1–2.

understand the true nature of the psyche, we have to look at its 'love of wisdom' (*philosophia*), as expressed in its attempt to grasp what is permanent and divine.[109] *Alcibiades* 133a–c is couched in terms of the idea that mutual recognition serves as a means of self-recognition. But what is expressed in that way is a similar set of ideas to those found in the *Republic* about the 'eye' of the psyche or about what constitutes its true, essential nature.

On this interpretation, it may perhaps seem unclear why we should regard this passage as expressing an objective-*participant* conception of personality. If the focus is on recognizing what we essentially are rather than on mutual recognition of a shared nature, it is not clear what constitutes the 'participant' dimension of this idea. Perhaps the whole process of self-recognition could be conducted within ourselves. However, although the image of mutual reflection does not have to be taken literally, as signifying that self-understanding comes through mutual recognition, it surely allows this interpretation. Also, the idea of self-recognition through mutual reflection is linked with a whole series of other themes in the *Alcibiades* which suggest the idea of learning through interpersonal dialogue. One motif, noted earlier, is that of Socrates and Alcibiades as interlocutors, an idea introduced into the dialogue in connection with the question of defining 'who we ourselves are'.[110] Also, the stretch of dialogue following 133a–c spells out a recurrent theme of the dialogue as a whole. This is that, if Alcibiades is to acquire the kind of ethical knowledge that would justify his exercising political rule, he needs to 'know himself' first. His dialogue with Socrates serves both as the means of teaching him this lesson and of providing the starting-point for acquiring this knowledge.[111] Against this background, it is plausible to see the image of mutual 'seeing' in 133a–c as representing the ideal outcome of Socrates' dialectical encounter with Alcibiades. The idea that Socratic dialectic is needed to enable interlocutors to 'know themselves', in part by seeing the inadequacy of the ethical 'knowledge' they have acquired through their families and larger communities is, of course, a recurrent one in the early Platonic dialogues.[112] Another is that standard types of interactive discourse need to be examined and reshaped through reflective discourse (dialectic), if such discourse is to

[109] *R.* 518c and 611c–612a (on the second passage, see also 1.2 above, text to n. 6).

[110] *Alc.* 129a–c, 130d–e.

[111] See *Alc.* 134c–135e, taken with 109d–e, 112e–113b, 118a–119a, 124a–b, 127d–128a, 131d–132c, 133c–d. See further on the structure of the argument, Annas (1985), 115–33; Marboeuf and Pradeau (1999), 13–14 (summary), also 34–81.

[112] On self-knowledge in the early Platonic dialogues, see references in n. 57 above, also Schmid (1998), chs. 3–4. The inadequacy of conventional social discourse as a means of achieving knowledge is underlined in *Alc.* 110d–112d.

serve as a medium for achieving objective truth.[113] These ideas can be linked, in turn, with Plato's standard representation of dialectic between two properly prepared interlocutors as the primary context in which the mind is best able to achieve knowledge of the most profound, 'divine', truths.[114]

In this discussion of Plato's *Alcibiades*, I have aimed, first, to argue against the idea that it contains a linguistic equivalent of 'the self'. Second, I have tried to clarify that the form of argument, found also in Aristotle *NE* 9.4, 8, is one in which reflexivity—for instance, self-knowing—is explained by essence; also, essence does not consist in a type of reflexivity. The underlying aim of these two points has been to bring out the larger conception of personality involved, which I see as objective-participant rather than subjective (or subjective-individualist). The fact that the dialogue centres on self-knowledge, and on exploring the nature of the self which is known, does not mean that its project is subjective in a post-Cartesian sense. This provides a reference-point, in a text of the Classical period, against which to correlate the contrasting and innovative features of Hellenistic–Roman thought. Do we find here, as has sometimes been suggested, a heightened focus on subjectivity and individuality alongside the emergence of the features I am associating with the structured self?

6.4 SUBJECTIVE AND OBJECTIVE READINGS OF STOIC DEVELOPMENT

In considering the relevance of the idea of subjectivity to ancient thought, I turn now to the Stoic theory of development as 'appropriation' (*oikeiōsis*), more specifically the interpretation of this theory offered by Troels Engberg-Pedersen.[115] His reading is especially relevant because he discusses explicitly the relationship of the theory to the modern subjective–objective distinction. He also argues that one ancient version of the theory, that of Cicero, offers a deliberately subjective presentation. In responding to his claims, I adopt a type of approach which will be deployed more fully in 6.5 below. I acknowledge that his account fastens on what are, indeed, distinctive and important features of the theory or of its presentation, but I maintain that these features are better analysed in objective (or objective-participant) terms. In offering an

[113] On this pattern, and for alternative, but equally objective-participant, patterns of thinking about discourse, see Gill (1996*b*), 288–300.

[114] See e.g. Pl. *R.* 534b–c (also 534d–540a); *Ep.* 340c–d, 341c, 343c–344b; also Gill (1992), (1996*a*), esp. 285, (1996*b*), 281–3.

[115] Engberg-Pedersen (1986) (1990*a* and *b*).

alternative reading of the theory, I draw on aspects of the account already given of the Stoic theory, in terms of a combination of types of holism and 'Socratic' ethical ideals. In doing so, I bring out how this account lends itself to analysis in objective, rather than, subjective, terms.[116]

There are several respects in which, according to Engberg-Pedersen, Cicero, in *On Ends* 3, offers a specifically subjective version of the Stoic theory of *oikeiōsis*. One relates to the overall presentation of the theory in the two key relevant passages (*Fin.* 3.16–17, 20–22, and 62–8). The other relates to the central concepts within the theory, at least as characterized by Cicero. I consider each of the stages of Engberg-Pedersen's interpretation, offering a competing account at each stage.[117] As regards the overall presentation, he suggests that Cicero's version is 'subjective', by contrast with what is, on the face of it at least, the more 'objective' account offered in other sources, notably, that of Diogenes Laertius 7.85–9.[118] Why does he regard Cicero's version as more subjective? Partly this is because Cicero's version is couched in terms of human action and motives, with which we can engage subjectively, rather than in the universal or cosmic and teleological framework offered by Diogenes. Also, for related reasons, we can also engage, as moral agents—in a subjective or 'internal' way—with the narrative of ethical progress of which Cicero offers an especially full account. Our engagement enables Cicero's version to serve as an effective practical demonstration of the conception of good which underlies both these ancient versions of the theory.[119]

The contrast to which Engberg-Pedersen draws attention is, I think, a real one. It is similar to the distinction drawn by Julia Annas between different ancient versions of the Stoic theory, framed in terms of human virtue and happiness or of cosmic order. As Annas brings out, these different forms of presentation also carry different implications about the nature of the more advanced stages of human ethical development, and about how far this depends on the idea of patterning yourself on the order of the cosmos.[120]

[116] See also 6.1 above, text to n. 1, on the distinction between analysis framed in participant's and observer's language. This discussion builds on the comments on Engberg-Pedersen's approach to the Stoic theory in Gill (1996*b*), 332–3, 338–40, 364–70, 408.

[117] I comment only briefly on his account of *social* development, in line with the main focus of this book (Introd. above, n. 27).

[118] See D.L. 7.85–9, also LS 57A, 63 C. However, Engberg-Pedersen (1990*b*), 24–5, 32–5, 36–63, argues that D.L. 7.85–9 also implies the more 'subjective' or 'internalist' view that is explicit in Cicero's presentation.

[119] Instead of simply arguing in abstract terms for a certain conception of the goal of life, Cicero's version shows how the recognition of the validity of this goal grows out of each person's deepening understanding of herself; see Engberg-Pedersen (1990*b*), 65–6, 72–9.

[120] See 3.3 above, esp. text to nn. 85–91, 148–60; also n. 90 for other scholars who recognize differing versions of the Stoic theory. See also Long (1996), 154–5, discussing the challenges of Engberg-Pedersen and Annas to the 'cosmic' reading of Stoic ethics.

What is less clear to me, however, is that this contrast is appropriately-characterized by reference to the subjective–objective distinction. On the face of it, the contrast is between a focus on human good and on cosmic order, as Annas suggests. The human focus is not, obviously, subjective, in any of the senses so far considered, nor is Cicero's presentation framed in a way that is clearly designed to appeal to the reader's subjectivity, for instance, in the sense of a (uniquely individual) first-personal view. However, what gives force to Engberg-Pedersen's interpretation of Cicero's account is his analysis of the substantive content of the theory set out in that account, in which (according to Engberg-Pedersen) subjectivity, in a recognizably modern sense, *does* have a significant role. What is this role?

The Stoic theory subdivides development into personal and social aspects, and the personal side of development is subdivided into two stages.[121] As regards the first stage of development, that of primitive self-love and self-awareness, Engberg-Pedersen recognizes that this is attributed to animals in general and not just humans. However, he sees this as providing the basis, in human beings, for self-awareness of a complex type, namely consciousness of oneself as an individual 'I' or subject and for attachment to the 'self' as so understood. In the second stage, this self-conscious attachment is directed at oneself understood as rational. The shift from selecting natural advantages to choosing virtue for its own sake is taken to be the outcome of understanding oneself as rational. The person concerned moves from recognizing, and loving, herself as an 'I', an individual subject, to seeing herself as a rational agent who transcends her own individuality by understanding the objectivity of reason and its universal application. In the social side of development, understanding oneself as rational is seen as bringing with it an attitude of care for all human beings as such, as rational beings who share one's essential identity.[122]

Engberg-Pedersen's analysis is conceptually sophisticated and coherently maintained. How credible is it? His view that the Stoic theory introduces a new focus on subjectivity and individuality depends to a large extent on his interpretation of the role of self-awareness and self-love in the first stage of development. He takes this as indicating, first, that the subjective (agent-centred) perspective is fundamental to the theory, and, second, that a certain kind of reflexivity, namely 'I'-centred self-consciousness, is central to the conception of human nature expressed throughout the theory. The crucial passage is this one:

121 See Cic. *Fin.* 3.16–17, 20–2, and 62–8; key extracts are given in LS 59 D and 57 F. (On the first stage of personal development see also LS 57A–E.)

122 On these three aspects of the Stoic theory, see Engberg-Pedersen (1986), 150–3, 156–62, 175–7; (1990*b*), 66–71, 84–7, 100–15, 123–5; also the summary in (1990*a*), 119–23, 126–7.

[The Stoics] hold that as soon as an animal is born—for this must be the starting-point—it is appropriated to itself (*ipsum sibi conciliari*) and led to preserve itself and to love its own constitution (*suum statum*) and those things which preserve its constitution, and to be alienated from its death and from those things that seem to lead to death. They prove that this is so from the fact that, before either pleasure or pain has affected them, infants seek what preserves them and rejects the opposite, something which would not happen unless they loved their constitution and feared death. But it cannot be the case that they desire anything unless they have a sense of themselves (*sensum sui*) and therefore love themselves. Hence it must be realized that the principle (*principium*) has been drawn from self-love.[123]

Engberg-Pedersen presents this process as one in which the human being, or other animal, becomes conscious of herself as a unified subject and attached to herself as subject. He lays special stress on Cicero's comment that infants 'have a sense of themselves and *therefore* love themselves (*sensum haberent sui eoque se diligerent*)'.[124] Engberg-Pedersen anticipates the criticism that he is over-interpreting Cicero's account in the light of modern (post-Cartesian) thinking: '... is [my interpretation] not just blatantly anachronistic in the use it makes of the notions of self-consciousness, of a bearer of consciousness and of a resulting "full" self or I?'.[125] He also explains that he has in mind a process that could reasonably have been attributed to infants by the Stoics. However, I think that there are, indeed, real difficulties in matching the conceptual language of the ancient theory with that deployed by Engberg-Pedersen. By contrast, I think there are good reasons for us to characterize the argument as 'objectivist' in its methodology and 'objective' in its conceptual language.[126]

I take the question of methodology first. As Jacques Brunschwig has brought out, the Stoic account of the first stage falls into a general type of argument found in Hellenistic, but not earlier Classical, thought, namely the 'cradle-argument'.[127] The salient feature of such arguments is that the

[123] Cic. *Fin.* 3.16, trans. Brunschwig (1986), 128, slightly modified. This passage is also quoted in 1.4 above, text to n. 134.

[124] Cic. *Fin.* 3.16. See Engberg-Pedersen (1986), 150–3, (1990*b*), 66–71.

[125] See Engberg-Pedersen (1990*b*), 71; also (1990*a*), 120–1. He finds support for the relevance of the concept of 'I' by reference to the theory of indexicality, as in some modern theories of personhood (see e.g. Morton 1990: 43–9). But the Stoic text cited in 1990*b*: 89 (S.E. *M.* 8.98, 100, extracts in *SVF* 2.205, LS 34 H) does not refer to *first-personal* indexicality.

[126] For the suggestion that these categories are useful ones *for us* to deploy in analysing ancient thought, even if the distinctions are not themselves recognized in this form in antiquity, see 6.1 above, text to n. 2.

[127] The use of the cradle argument goes along with the importance given in Stoic–Epicurean thought about development to *natural* capacities of human beings (or animals) as such, by contrast with those which are (in the Platonic–Aristotelian pattern) the product of the combination of inborn natural character and habituation. See 3.2 above, esp. text to nn. 43–6, 3.5, esp. text to nn. 236–44.

naturalness of certain types of motivation in animals, including humans, from 'the cradle' onwards, is used to support a certain conception of the goal of life. Although this motivation is presented—at least partly—in reflexive form in most versions of this argument, including the Stoic one, it is not so presented in the Epicurean version, which is likely to be among the earliest examples of this type of argument.[128] If we take this Hellenistic pattern of argument as a whole, considering both the conception of human nature and the methodology of argument, it is hard to see any reason for describing the pattern as 'subjective' or 'subjectivist'.[129] The forms of motivation described, such as desire for pleasure or instinctive appropriation of what suits one's constitution, make no explicit reference to the ideas of 'I' or 'individual subject'. Also, no special status is given to 'first-personal' intuitions, for instance, about who 'I' am or where 'I' belong.[130] On the contrary, it is assumed that the motives concerned—which belong, it should be remembered, to animals and human infants—can be effectively characterized, as 'self-love' or the desire for pleasure, from a third-personal perspective. The claims are presented as either self-evident or empirically based.[131] In the case of the Epicurean version, there has been dispute about whether the argument is based on a thesis about animal motivation in infancy or about *our* (adult rational human) inferences from infant animal behaviour.[132] However, on either view, what is claimed is *consistency* between the animal's perspective and that of reflective human observers. There is no attempt to contrast the (first-personal, subjective) standpoint of the animal and the (third-personal, objective) perspective of the human observers. The assumption is, rather, that reference to both kinds of viewpoint can provide evidence for a single, shared, objective truth—the nature of the human good. In other words, the form of argument seems clearly objectivist, in a number of ways.

However, Engberg-Pedersen's view is not based on the Hellenistic pattern in general but on the Stoic theory, especially as presented by Cicero in *Fin.* 3.16, cited earlier. What reasons are there for regarding the account of self-appropriation, including self-awareness and self-love, as objective or

128 See Brunschwig (1986), esp. 115–28 on the Epicurean version, referring to Cic. *Fin.* 1.30, 2.31–2. On the later Hellenistic versions of the argument (those of Antiochus and Arius Didymus), and on the role of reflexivity in those versions, see 3.4 above.

129 On the application of the terms 'subjective'/subjectivist' and 'objective'/'objectivist' in connection with the criteria and methodology of normative concepts, see 6.2 above, text to nn. 34–8.

130 For this as a mark of modern subjective-individualist thinking about personal identity, see 6.2 above, text to nn. 34–5.

131 Brunschwig (1986) gives special attention to the question whether those claims are fully justified in either case: see 117–19, 122, 125–7, 133–4, 137–9.

132 See Sedley (1998*b*), 136–7, responding to Brunschwig (1986), 115–22.

objectivist in its approach? In 1.4 above, I considered this passage in some detail, along with related treatments of self-perception in Hierocles and self-awareness in Seneca. My overall claim is that these discussions presuppose a conception of human beings and other animals as organic psychophysical wholes. The reflexive terminology is used to express the idea that we (animals) have an instinctive attachment to ourselves as organic units. In the course of exploring this idea in the Stoic texts, I highlighted the contrast between Hierocles' notion of consciousness or self-perception and Cartesian 'I'-centred self-consciousness, and also between Seneca's thinking on appropriation to oneself at any stage of life and modern, post-Cartesian thinking about diachronic personal identity, conceived as that of the 'I' or unique individual. I suggested that Stoic thinking on this subject was comparable with modern, non-Cartesian concepts such as Sherrington's idea of 'proprioception' or Dennett's view of animals as 'intentional systems', whose beliefs are displayed by the 'an order that is there' in their behaviour rather than by conscious volitions. I also highlighted the significance of the fact that Stoics seem to treat as synonymous and interchangeable the idea of 'appropriation' to oneself and to one's 'constitution' as a psychophysical and psychological whole.[133] In terms of the contrast drawn earlier, the implication of my account is that the Stoic theory is conceived in terms of 'objective' concepts and 'objectivist' methodology. The passage cited earlier (*Fin.* 3.16), which Engberg-Pedersen takes as lending crucial support for his interpretation,[134] seems to me to fall squarely within this line of thought. Among other indications of this approach is the alternation between loving oneself and loving one's constitution, suggesting that these ideas are regarded as synonymous. This runs counter to the assumption, typical of post-Cartesian thought, that certain types of reflexive or self-related experiences, notably self-consciousness, have a special status as an expression of personhood. If this way of reading Cicero's passage is accepted, this casts doubt on Engberg-Pedersen's claim that 'I'-centred subjectivity is presented in Cic. *Fin.* 3.16 as fundamental to the Stoic conception of development.

Engberg-Pedersen interprets the second stage in personal development (Cic. *Fin.* 3.20–1), as grounded on the emergence of individual subjectivity in the first stage. After coming to see herself, and becoming attached to herself, as a unified subject or 'I', the person gradually reaches an understanding that this self is essentially rational. This brings the recognition that rational self-expression consists in acting virtuously rather than in pursuing the natural advantages that are the outcome of the previous attachment to

[133] See 1.4 above, text to nn. 143–58, 165–73.

[134] See text to n. 123 above.

oneself.[135] Engberg-Pedersen emphasizes two aspects of this process. One is that this recognition is based especially on observation of *one's own* past behaviour and of the rationality expressed in the deliberate selection of 'preferable' natural advantages.[136] The other is that this recognition constitutes a substantive change in self-understanding, which he describes in terms such as 'transcending the individual' and 'self-objectification'. The process is also characterized as movement from a subjective to an objective viewpoint. The key idea is that one comes to grasp 'the objectivity of reason', as applying universally; this understanding is also taken to be identical with understanding 'the good'.[137] The outcome of the process is to negate the importance of individuality. But this presupposes that 'individuality' plays a significant role in the theory and that it represented something that had previously been important to the agent. The agent is also taken as retaining her status as an individual subject throughout the whole process.[138] A further step in the same process is taken to explain the process of social development that leads from attachment to those close to one, above all one's children, to human beings in general. This stage is analysed as the growing recognition that one's own virtuous rationality brings with it 'an other-regarding attitude of care' not only for the people who are specifically 'one's own' but for all rational agents as such, who share the core (rational) element of one's identity.[139]

Engberg-Pedersen's account raises two related issues. One relates to the general conceptual form of his analysis, and its appropriateness to Stoic theory; the other concerns the textual support for his interpretation. As regards the conceptual form, I have argued elsewhere that Engberg-Pedersen's analysis of the Stoic theory, like Terence Irwin's reading of related themes in Plato and Aristotle,[140] is informed by certain leading ideas in modern Western moral theory. One salient influence is Kant's idea that, as individual rational agents, we (human beings) are constitutively capable of 'autonomy' (self-legislation), in the form of recognizing that moral laws apply universally, to ourselves as much as others.[141] A second theme, found in various forms in post-Kantian moral theory, is that development in self-understanding, leading us to recognize our nature or identity as rational agents, can transform

[135] Engberg-Pedersen (1986), 156–62, (1990*b*), 84–7, 100–15.

[136] Engberg-Pedersen (1986), 160–2, (1990*b*), 84–7.

[137] Engberg-Pedersen (1986), 168–72, (1990*b*), 88, 91–7, 98–100.

[138] Engberg-Pedersen (1986), 164–5, (1990*b*), 88–91.

[139] See Cic. *Fin.* 3.62–8 (LS 57 F); also Engberg-Pedersen (1986), 175–7, (1990*b*), 123–5, quoted words from 125.

[140] See especially Irwin (1977), 232–45, (1988), chs. 16–18. See further Gill (1996*b*), 326–32, also 260–6.

[141] See Kant, *Groundwork*, Prussian Academy edition iv. 420–1, 446–8 (Kant 1948: 83–4, 107–8). See further Gill (1996*b*), 336, 338, also 37–8.

our moral attitudes and behaviour and promote reason-based altruism in our treatment of other people.[142] I have suggested that this conceptual pattern has helped to shape Engberg-Pedersen's account of the second and third (social) stages in the Stoic picture of development. In particular, it underlies his stress on the idea that growing awareness of one's own rationality, as expressed in increasingly rational selection of indifferents, plays a key role in enabling us to understand the absolute (universal) value of (moral) goodness.[143] This pattern also serves to explain why Engberg-Pedersen stresses, in the social side of development, that recognition of the idea that one's identity (as a rational moral agent) is shared with all human beings as such leads to the view that moral norms apply universally, and not just to those with whom we have conventional bonds.[144] Engberg-Pedersen combines this pattern with a two-fold use of the subjective–objective distinction. In the Stoic theory, as he interprets this, the person is conceived, in psychological terms, as an 'I' or individual subject and locus of perception throughout the process of development. However, in epistemological terms, there is a development from a 'subjective'—that is, immature and partial—understanding of moral truth to an 'objective'—that is, mature and complete—one.[145] This helps to explain why Engberg-Pedersen characterizes growth in moral understanding in terms such as 'transcending the individual' and 'self-objectification'.[146] His conceptual language represents a combination of the Kantian and post-Kantian pattern outlined earlier with the (post-Cartesian) subjective–objective contrast used in both psychological and ethical senses.

To underline (what seem to me to be) the modern conceptual influences on Engberg-Pedersen's interpretation of the theory is not, by itself, to say anything about the appropriateness of his approach to the Stoic theory. It is, in principle, entirely possible that an interpretation could both draw on modern conceptual models and use these motifs to identify core distinctive features of an ancient theory.[147] However, I think that one strand, in particular, in Engberg-Pedersen's analysis is not really appropriate to Cicero's account. This is the emphasis on the idea that growth in moral understanding depends, in a quite fundamental way, on *one's own* observation of *one's own* identity as an emerging rational agent, and on the idea that such change in self-

[142] See Gill (1996*b*), 337–40, referring, for instance, to Rawls (1971), Gewirth (1977), and (despite his critical stance towards some Kantian ideas), Parfit (1984).

[143] See Gill (1996*b*), 332–3, 338–40, 364–7. See also references in nn. 135–7 above.

[144] See Gill (1996*b*), 333, 367–8.

[145] This combination of ideas is especially clear in his (1990*a*), 121–7.

[146] See references in n. 137 above.

[147] This feature is common to Engberg-Pedersen's approach and the one adopted here, that of attempting to engage in 'dialogue' with ancient ideas from (what is acknowledged to be) a specific modern standpoint (6.2 above), text to nn. 49–50.

understanding has the power to transform one's pattern of moral motivation and attitude towards others.[148] This emphasis represents, in part, a reaction against the 'cosmic' reading of Stoic development, illustrated earlier by reference to Gisela Striker, according to which the crucial shift in motivation, affecting one's attitude to oneself and others, is brought about by recognizing the order and rationality in the cosmos as paradigmatic for one's ethical character and interpersonal attitudes. Engberg-Pedersen maintains that this pattern does not correspond to the explicit content or emphases of Cicero's account in *Fin.* 3.20–2, and that even apparently 'cosmic' treatments such as that in D.L. 7.85–9 allow a more 'subjective' or 'internalist' reading.[149] In my earlier discussion, following certain aspects of Annas's view, I also expressed reservations about the cosmic reading of Cicero's account, which, like some other Stoic treatments, seems to be couched wholly in terms of human ethical agency and development. However, I also underlined the relevance of certain other aspects of human ethical life that do not figure in Engberg-Pedersen's interpretation. One is the role of observation of the qualities of other people in helping us form a conception of virtue as order and harmony. The other is (what I called) 'ethical holism', particularly in the form of the idea that virtue and the good constitute the expression of types of unified or complete wholeness. My overall claim is that these elements help us to see how Cicero's account can offer a credible account of ethical development without our needing to invoke the cosmic pattern stressed by Striker and others—though that pattern may be relevant for other Stoic discussions.[150]

What features of Cicero's account in *Fin.* 3.16–22 lend support to Engberg-Pedersen's reading or to my (partly) competing view? As noted earlier, Engberg-Pedersen thinks that the first stage of personal development, presented in 3.16, identifies the person as an individual (self-aware and self-loving) subject or 'I' in a way that underpins the whole account.[151] But I have just argued, by contrast, that this stage is presented in objectivist terms; so we cannot presume that the idea of the self-conscious subject is carried into the next stage. In 3.20–1, the passage which might seem to give most support to Engberg-Pedersen's focus on individual self-observation is the account of increasingly rational selection. He takes this account as providing a paradigm of rationality, which underlies the final recognition of virtue (understood as 'rationality') as the only real good.

[148] See references in n. 136 above.

[149] See Engberg-Pedersen (1990*b*), 65–6, 72–5, 78–9, 82–4 (on Striker), 95–7; see also n. 118 above; and on Striker's view, 3.3 above, text to nn. 80–3.

[150] See 3.3 above, esp. text to nn. 91–125, 162–71.

[151] See references in nn. 123–5 above.

the first 'proper function'... is to preserve oneself in one's natural constitution ... Once this procedure of selection and rejection has been discovered, the next consequence is selection exercised with proper functioning; then such selection performed continuously; finally selection which is absolutely consistent and in full accordance with nature.[152]

It is certainly the case that this account, like that of the culminating recognition of virtue as the only genuinely good thing, is presented as a description of the developing capacities of a single agent,[153] without explicit reference either to involvement in social action and relationships or to shared philosophical activity. But there is no question that the Stoics *did* see the latter features as integral elements in a complete human life and also as contributing crucially to full ethical development.[154] Hence, the fact that this part of the account is couched in terms of the experience of a single agent does not mean that any special weight is being given to the role of individual reflexivity or, more broadly, that changes in self-understanding are pivotal in ethical development. However, one might ask what reason there is to prefer my interpretation of the ethical ideal—in terms of unified or structured wholeness—rather than of rationality, which is taken, by Engberg-Pedersen, as implying the capacity to recognize the universal force of moral principles. The reason for thinking that phrases such as 'the regularity and ... harmony' of conduct (3.21) imply an ideal of wholeness is, partly, the prevalence of this ideal in Stoic thinking about virtue and the good, and partly the larger philosophical or substantial holism that I see as typical of the theory.[155] But also, although Cicero's account gives a role to developing rationality, the main thrust of the account is on the thought that the entire personality is affected by the focusing of motivation on the good.[156] Cicero's account thus encapsulates two features presented here as fundamental to Stoic thinking about personality: psychological holism and the 'Socratic' claim that only the wise person (the implied paradigm for the final stage of development) is psychologically cohesive and whole.[157] In short, my suggestion is that Cicero's description of the second stage of ethical development is best understood in terms of the themes that I have presented as fundamental to the Stoic version of the ideal of the structured self. It is also that the account is best understood in objective

[152] Cic. *Fin.* 3.20 (= LS 59 D(3)), also 3.21 (LS 59 D(4)).

[153] Striker, for instance, despite her different interpretative standpoint, describes the process in terms of individual self-observation, in part at least (1996: 230, cited in 3.3 above, text to n. 82).

[154] See, on these two elements, 3.3 above, text to nn. 161–79.

[155] See 1.4 and 3.3 above.

[156] For this view (and the contrast with the Platonic–Aristotelian, part-based) view of development, see 3.2 above.

[157] See 2.2 above, esp. text to nn. 76–92.

terms (those of wholeness, for instance) and as involving, by implication, a participant dimension, in the form of social and philosophical cooperation.

Although I have reservations about certain aspects of Engberg-Pedersen's reading of the Stoic theory, I strongly endorse one point he makes about different versions of the subjective–objective distinction, in a way which bears directly on the project attempted by both of us, that of correlating ancient and modern thinking about selfhood.[158] Engberg-Pedersen, as noted earlier, sees the Stoic theory as involving a progression from a subjective (immature and partial) grasp of moral truth to an objective (mature and complete) one. To this degree, he too presents the Stoic theory as an objectivist one, as regards ethical epistemology, even though his account assumes that, psychologically, agents are to be understood as individual subjects.[159] Although I would be more cautious then he is about attributing to the Stoics an awareness of the significance of the subjective–objective distinction, I share his view that the Stoic account describes progress in knowledge or understanding and not simply a change in perspective or attitude.

The contrast between a subjective and an objective viewpoint is also central to a famous modern moral theory, that of Thomas Nagel's *The View from Nowhere* (1986). However, Engberg-Pedersen highlights a crucial difference between the Stoic conceptual framework and Nagel's. For the Stoics, this development consists in the acquisition of objective ethical knowledge and the associated reshaping of character and desires. For Nagel, the subjective and objective viewpoints are unavoidable features of everyone's experience. They are also fundamentally distinct and incompatible, so that the subjective viewpoint can never be replaced by the objective one. Nagel sees the difference between the viewpoints as one of perspective or attitude, not of knowledge or truth-status; the objective viewpoint is 'impersonal' or 'detached' or 'centreless', but it does not therefore confer a greater understanding of truth. In this respect, although Nagel contrasts subjective and objective viewpoints, *both* his viewpoints are (in epistemological terms) subjective, because neither of them allows the notion of (objective) knowledge and truth that is fundamental for Stoic and other Greek theories.[160]

Engberg-Pedersen's clarification of the difference between Nagel and Stoicism on this point represents an original and substantive contribution to debate on these questions. I would draw the distinction even more sharply,

[158] See Engberg-Pedersen (1990*a*), a chapter in Gill (1990*d*), a volume centred on the question of the relationship between ancient and modern conceptions of person.

[159] On this combination, in Engberg-Pedersen's approach, of characterization of the agent in subjective terms and of ethical objectivism, see also Gill (1996*b*), 406–8.

[160] See Engberg-Pedersen (1990*a*), 117–118, 124–6, 132–3, referring to Nagel (1986), 149, 151, 155; also Nagel (1974).

since I do not think the first stage of Stoic development is usefully described as 'subjective' at all. However, Engberg-Pedersen's point is important and also has implications for understanding the relationship between Nagel's views and other ancient theories. In some recent work, A. A. Long has compared Nagel's two viewpoints to certain standpoints marked as contrasted in ancient thought. For instance, he sees in Heraclitus' distinctive world-view a Presocratic equivalent of Nagel's objective viewpoint (including a version of the attempt at 'self-transcendence'), which is deliberately contrasted with the subjective viewpoint to which the experience of most people is limited. In Lucretius' version of Epicureanism, Long sees both a systematic aspiration towards an objective view of oneself and the world and a recognition that this needs to be squared with human subjectivity, a recognition he sees as shared with Nagel.[161] Long, to be sure, is not claiming an exact parallel between Nagel's twofold viewpoints and those identified by any ancient thinker. Also, the ancient contrasts which Long highlights are themselves real ones, though they could be described in different terms. None the less, I think Engberg-Pedersen has performed an important service in underlining the precise conceptual character of Nagel's distinction and the difficulty in correlating this with ancient analogues. The key point of difference from ancient thought is Nagel's belief that human subjectivity is an ineliminable aspect of human existence. Hence, his so-called 'objective' viewpoint is, in effect, a variant of the subjective one; although it is external instead of internal; it is not objective in terms of epistemology and truth-status.[162] Among ancient theories, including Scepticism, as I argue later (6.6), this belief in a pervasive, ineliminable subjectivity is absent. For Engberg-Pedersen, this is a reason for seeing a distinction between ancient and modern ways of conceiving the subjective–objective distinction. I am not convinced that the idea of the subjective is relevant to ancient thought at all, except in a very weak sense.[163] Engberg-Pedersen's clarification of the difference between Stoic thinking and that of one of the most famous modern theories of subjectivity helps us to see one of the reasons for doubting the relevance to ancient thought, of any period, of the idea of subjectivity, at least in the philosophically strong senses this has acquired in post-Cartesian modern thought.

[161] See Long (1992), 262–3, 270–3, on Heraclitus; 275–7, on Marcus Aurelius; (1997), 138–9, on Lucretius; also, briefly (1996), 259, on Hierocles.

[162] For analogous reservations about Long's comparison between Heraclitus and Nagel, and for an alternative, objective-participant, interpretation of Presocratic psychology, see Gill (2001*a*), esp. 172–6.

[163] For a weak sense of 'subject' (as psychological seat or centre) that could serve as the basis for such as weak sense of 'subjectivity', see 6.6 below, text to nn. 283–4.

6.5 EPICTETUS: A NEW SUBJECTIVE-INDIVIDUALIST SELF?

In my second discussion of Stoic ideas in this connection, I return to the comments of Charles Kahn and A. A. Long cited earlier (6.2 above). Both scholars suggest that in Stoicism, especially as formulated by Epictetus, we can find a substantively new concept of self, characterized especially by individuality, self-awareness and, in Long's account, a first-personal view. I focus on their comments here because they offer clear articulation of a view about what is innovative in Stoic and, to some extent, Hellenistic–Roman thought more generally, which is rather widely held (329–31 above). I have already suggested ways in which I think these comments are informed by subjective and individualistic strands in modern Western thought about selfhood since Descartes. Their views also seem to reflect the assumption that we can reasonably expect to find a gradual development towards the post-Cartesian notion of self, both within the history of Graeco–Roman antiquity and in subsequent Western thought.[164] As already stated, I do not think that the modern subjective-individualist conception of person forms the best starting-point for understanding Hellenistic–Roman thought or that we should expect to find in this period a gradual movement towards this conception. I have suggested that (what I am calling) the objective-participant approach provides a better interpretative framework for Hellenistic–Roman, as well as earlier Greek, understanding of human personality (6.2 above).

However, this does not mean that I think the comments of Kahn and Long about what is new in Stoic thought about the self, particularly as presented by Epictetus, have no basis. On the contrary, I examine their views more closely precisely because they highlight features which, I accept, *are* innovative within the history of ancient thought about selfhood. I maintain, however, that these features are best explained by the combination of types of holism and naturalism and of Socratic ideals that I have presented as characteristic of Stoic, and in a different way, Epicurean thinking about the person. Also, I claim that these features are best analysed in terms of an objective-participant, rather than subjective-individualist, conception of person. First, I consider more closely the views of Kahn and Long, calling into question aspects of the conceptual language they use to characterize Stoic thinking on selfhood, especially as expressed by Epictetus. Second, I re-examine a contrast drawn earlier between Platonic–Aristotelian and the Stoic–Epicurean accounts of ethical development (3.2 above); I focus on the question of the conception of

[164] See 6.2 above, esp. text to n. 10.

selfhood (whether objective-participant or subjective-individualist) that is implied in those accounts. Against the background of these two issues, I discuss what is widely recognized as an important and (partly) innovative dimension of Epictetus' thought, a three-point programme of practical ethics. I consider what this programme implies as regards Epictetus' understanding of the nature and contributory factors—social, individual, and philosophical—of ethical development. In this way, I draw out the implications of the programme for the conception of self which Epictetus presupposes.

Kahn and Long, in the comments noted earlier, give special attention to certain distinctive features of Epictetus' terminology and intellectual idiom, viewed in relation to Stoic conceptual language generally. One is his recurrent use of the term *prohairesis*, the standard Aristotelian word for 'choice' or 'decision', where we might have expected to find 'reason' (*logos*) or 'control-centre' (*hēgemonikon*). A related theme is the emphatic contrast between what is or is not 'up to us' (*eph' hēmin*), sometimes expressed as what is or is not 'within the scope of *prohairesis*' (*prohairetika* or *aprohaireta*). Another theme is that we should exercise our *prohairesis* in 'using' or 'examining' impressions (*phantasiai*). This extract from *Handbook* 1 illustrates some of these features:

> Practise, then, from the start to say to every harsh impression, 'You are an impression, and not at all the thing you appear to be'. Then examine it and test it by the rules which you have, and firstly and chiefly, by this: whether the impression has to do with the things which are up to us, or those which are not; and, if it has to do with the things that are not up to us, be ready to reply, 'It is nothing to me'.[165]

The question how far we should suppose that distinctive motifs or vocabulary denote substantive conceptual innovations in Epictetus, or in works of practical ethics by other Stoic thinkers of the first and second centuries AD, is a complex one and is the subject of continuing debate among scholars.[166] In Epictetus, a further factor is that the *Discourses* (and shorter *Handbook*) are not authored books but reports of Epictetus' oral teachings by Arrian, an independent writer and, for some years, a student of Epictetus.[167] What he records are not the technical lessons in the school, which seem to have been based on exposition of classic Stoic texts, especially by Chrysippus, but less formal discussions centred on putting Stoic ethics into practice. These discussions, presented either in dialogue or monologue form, seem to have been

[165] Trans. Hard in Gill (1995). On innovations of terminology in Epictetus, see Inwood (1985), 115–26, also appendix 2 (224–42); for comments on Inwood, Long (2002), 126–7.

[166] See further Gill (2003*d*), 36–50. 'Practical ethics' is not an ancient term, but it does seem to capture the character of much practically oriented ethical writing and teaching in Hellenistic–Roman philosophy, especially between the 1st c. BC and the 2nd c. AD.

[167] See Stadter (1980), 26–8.

conducted mainly with Epictetus' students, though also sometimes with other people, in a semi-public, rather than private, setting.[168] These features of the form of the writings, obviously, have a bearing on how far we can reasonably look for theoretical innovation in Epictetus' distinctive ideas and expressions. Although various positions have been taken on this question, I find most persuasive the view of Long's book on Epictetus (2002), that Epictetus' discourses assume and reflect a largely orthodox Stoic theoretical framework, but that his formulations and approach are often strikingly original, in ways that partly reflect the essentially practical nature of his objectives in this context.[169] This does not rule out the possibility that Epictetus' teachings imply an innovative conception of the self; but I think they are more credibly seen as representing a personal expression of Stoic thought.

Kahn (1988) finds in Epictetus a crucial stage in the 'discovery of the will', a process that he traces from Aristotle to Augustine and, finally, Thomas Aquinas. What is the salient mark of 'the will' for Kahn, by contrast with other psychological concepts? The main point is the idea of a highly unified locus of motivation and action. In medieval thought, the will (*uoluntas*) is seen as a single psychological agency that takes over functions played in Aristotelian thought by four different rational and desiderative elements.[170] A related factor is the religious and ethical demand for total, unified commitment towards God, reflecting, though imperfectly, the unity of divine will.[171] Kahn finds in Stoicism, especially as expressed by Epictetus, the closest ancient analogue or forerunner of this idea. The Stoic view of motivation, analysed in terms of an interlocking set of factors (impression, assent, and impulse), all of which are rational in adult humans, is more tightly integrated than the Aristotelian picture, in which action results from a combination of desire and practical reason. In Stoic psychology, in its original Hellenistic form, this motivational process is standardly seen as based on the unified control-centre (*hēgemonikon*). In Stoicism in the late Roman Republic and early Empire, Kahn finds the emergence of a new vocabulary for expressing this integrated conception of motivation, in the use of *uoluntas* ('wish' or 'will') in Seneca and *prohairesis* ('choice', 'decision', 'rational agency') in

[168] See Long (2002), 43–5.

[169] See Long (2002), chs. 1–2; also (briefly) Gill (2003*d*), 47–8; for a similar view (on determinism and freedom), Bobzien (1998*a*), ch. 7. Bonhöffer (1890, 1894 (1996)), author of the most substantial earlier studies of Epictetus, argued for a more systematic degree of orthodoxy. See also Dobbin (1998), pp. xiv–xxiii.

[170] Kahn (1988), 239–45. The four features in Aristotle are (1) the idea of action being 'up to us' (*eph' hēmin*), i.e. attributable to us, (2) *to hekousion*, the 'voluntary', (3) *prohairesis* ('choice'), (4) *boulēsis* ('wishing') as the rational aspect of desire (Kahn: 240).

[171] Kahn (1988), 245. Kahn's account of the relationship between ancient and medieval ideas of the will draws on Dihle's book-length treatment (1982).

Epictetus. A further analogue to the medieval view of will is the Stoic belief, vividly conveyed by Epictetus, that the proper function of *prohairesis* lies in responding whole-heartedly to the 'will' of Zeus as embodied in the natural cosmos (Kahn 1988: 245–54).

Kahn couples these ideas with the claim that Epictetus' Stoicism also introduces a 'metaphysics of the self in [an] individual sense' not found in the Platonic and Aristotelian identification of the 'I' with 'mind', as the locus of theoretical wisdom. 'Epictetus . . . identifies himself with something essentially personal and individualized: not with reason as such but with the practical application of reason in selecting his commitments, in keeping his emotional balance, his serenity, by not extending himself to goals and values that lie beyond his control'. Kahn also characterizes Epictetus' standpoint as that of 'intense preoccupation with inner life, the late Stoic parallel to a Cartesian *cogito* or focus on consciousness' (1988: 253).

In this account of Stoic innovations, Kahn identifies several features that I also regard as distinctively Stoic but which I explain by a different framework of analysis. One is the integration or 'holism' of the Stoic psychological model, by (partial) contrast with earlier Greek theories. As argued in Chapters 1–3 above, this forms part of a holistic world-view which includes the idea of humans, and other animals, as unified psychophysical and psychological organic entities. There is at least a partial contrast with types of core-centred and part-based thinking about human nature found in Plato, Aristotle, and their Middle Platonic successors. To this degree, at least, I think Kahn is right to claim that Stoicism offers a 'metaphysics of the self' which is substantively different from that of Plato and Aristotle. In so far as this 'metaphysics' is centred on the notion of human beings, and other animals, as *particular* psychophysical wholes, it does, in a way, include what Kahn calls an 'individual' dimension, a feature reflected in the Stoic puzzle about identity considered earlier.[172] The motivational unity that Kahn sees as expressed both in Stoic psychology and medieval conceptions of will can be seen as reflecting a Socratic view of motivation.[173] Also, other features highlighted by Kahn can be linked with the 'Socratic' ethical ideas that I see as characteristic of Stoic (and, in a different way, Epicurean) thought. For instance, Epictetus' focus on what is 'up to us' evokes the Socratic idea that we are all capable of developing towards ethical perfection. Also, the Stoic ideal of unified, total commitment evokes the idea of the wise person as the (sole) exemplar of motivational

[172] Kahn (1988), 253. See 1.6 above, esp. text to nn. 277–83. On the question of Epictetus and individuality, see also text to nn. 216–18, 237–45 below.

[173] On Socratic thinking as prefiguring Stoic in this respect, see 2.2 above, text to nn. 23–6, 3.2, text to nn. 47–75.

unity, in whom desire is focused on the good.[174] Where I dissent from Kahn's account is in the conceptual language he uses to characterize these—typically Stoic—features. The comparison with the medieval concept of will goes beyond my concerns here. But the linkage with the Cartesian *cogito* and the allusions to 'I'-centred subjectivity and self-consciousness seem to me to be simply importations from modern European thinking, with no clear echo in the Stoic material. Revealingly, Kahn offers little detailed textual support for this suggestion.

However, Long, who cites approvingly Kahn's view that Stoicism introduces a new metaphysics of the individual self (1996: 275–6) provides more supporting evidence. In the first place, he suggests that the Stoic model, in using the combination of impression and assent to explain both perception or thought and motivation, anticipates modern (post-Cartesian) thinking about the self. Just as in this kind of modern thinking, the person, as 'I' or subject, sees the world as mediated through 'representations', so the Stoic control-centre, which is also an individual 'I' or subject, does so through the mediation of *phantasiai*, which can be translated as 'impressions' or, to use a modern post-Cartesian term, 'representations' (265–75). How does Long support the claim that the Stoic notions of 'control-centre' and 'impressions' carry connotations similar to those of modern, post-Cartesian concepts of self? He does so partly by reference to the Stoic idea, which we find in Hierocles, of self-perception as a primary feature of animal psychology (268–9). Also, Long sees in Epictetus' emphasis on the use of impressions a move that prefigures modern thinking about the nature of individual self-consciousness or self-examination. The fact that, for Epictetus, and Stoicism more generally, different individuals form different 'representations' of themselves and the world is taken to provide a point of comparison with, for instance, Richard Wollheim's understanding of self-examination.[175] As in modern theories of this type, if 'my representations are up to me to interpret, accept or reject, there must be a "me" to which they appear and an "I" which reacts to them—a subject that is identifiable precisely by the representations that it receives and by what it does with them' (276).

The discussion in which Long makes these points (an essay on 'Representation and the Self in Stoicism')[176] is thoughtful and suggestive, and underlines several major features of Stoicism, including the highly unified character

[174] For these ideas, see Kahn (1988), 253, cited above (Epictetus' self-identification with what is in one's control), and, on Stoic and medieval thought about unified motivation/will, 245–54. On these 'Socratic' ideas, in their Stoic version, see 2.2 above, text to nn. 37–45, 76–88, 3.2 above, text to nn. 10–18; also text to nn. 197–202 below.

[175] See Long (1996), 275–82, esp. 281, referring to Wollheim (1984), 163.

[176] Originally published as Long (1991), it appears as ch. 12 of Long (1996).

of the psychological model, that I also stress here.[177] But some at least of his phraseology is open to similar kinds of objection to those made here regarding Engberg-Pedersen's reading of the Stoic theory of *oikeiōsis* as the development of the person as 'I'-centred subject (6.4 above). In fact, I think that some of Long's other discussions can help us to qualify the reading of the Stoic theory suggested in his essay. Long's reference to Hierocles' account of self-perception does not emphasize, what he himself brings out elsewhere, the difference between the Stoic idea of instinctive self-perception, as a function of animals as psychophysical organisms, and the post-Cartesian conception of (uniquely human) self-consciousness.[178] Long's reference to the idea that, in Stoicism, impressions are not necessarily truth-bearing is not sufficient to establish that they are seen as fundamentally subjective or first-personal. They can simply be understood as wrong or false (in some cases), from a realist or objectivist standpoint.[179] A similar, though more complex, point applies to Long's comparison between the understanding of self-examination by Epictetus and by Wollheim. For Wollheim, it is not just a post-Cartesian conception of subjectivity, but also a post-Freudian view of the role of unconscious belief that makes our view of ourselves ineluctably first-personal. For Wollheim, this makes moral judgement a fundamentally private matter: only 'I' can, in any serious or profound way, understand and judge myself.[180] The contrast with Stoicism, especially as expressed by Epictetus, is stark. Epictetus' discourses sometimes represent a searching, quasi-Socratic examination of his interlocutors (real and imagined) in which their 'impressions' are dragged into the open and subjected to public scrutiny and correction. Long himself, in his book on Epictetus (2002), has brought out very clearly the quasi-Socratic character of Epictetus' discourses. As he stresses, a key aim of Epictetus' method, whether conducted through actual dialogue, reported dialogue, or monologue, is to induce his audience to examine their own impressions with a view to making them consistent with objective norms.[181] Indeed, in the essay on 'Representation and the Self', Long also highlights the connection between this procedure and the Stoic view that such consistency can only be obtained through achieving complete wisdom, and that failure to achieve this state necessarily leads to internal (including emotional)

[177] Long (1996), 270, 272–3, 277; see also refs. in n. 173 above.

[178] See Long (1996), ch. 11, esp. 257–9, also 1.4 above, text to nn. 143, 153.

[179] Long (1996), 272–3. For a brief 'objectivist' account of Stoic 'impressions' (and Epicurean 'feelings', *pathē*), as well as Cyrenaic 'appearances', see Everson (1991*a*), esp. 132–5.

[180] See Wollheim (1984), chs. 1, 3–7, esp. pp. 276–8; on the contrast with ancient ideas (e.g. in Plutarch), see Gill (1994), 4637.

[181] Long (2002), ch. 3, esp. 79–86. On this point, see further text to nn. 224–7, 236–7 below.

conflict.[182] Long's cogent analysis of the function of Epictetus' emphasis on examining impressions is, essentially, objectivist in conception, both in psychological and ethical terms. To this degree, it is at least potentially at odds with the more subjective-individualist terminology which he sometimes uses to characterize Stoic thinking about selfhood.

Subsequently, I develop these comments about Epictetus' method by reference to his three-stage programme of practical ethics. Before doing so, I re-examine a broader contrast between divergent ancient ways of understanding ethical development, which has implications for the study of ancient conceptions of selfhood. Earlier, I identified two main differences between Platonic–Aristotelian and Stoic–Epicurean ways of conceiving ethical development. In the Platonic–Aristotelian pattern, this is envisaged as constituting two inter-related stages. The first stage is habituation in the norms, roles, and practices of one's community; the second is that of reasoned reflection on ethics, based on the beliefs developed in the first stage. These stages are correlated with the development of different parts of the personality. The first stage is seen, primarily, as a process of shaping appropriate dispositions of emotion and desire, while the second is more purely rational or cognitive, though it also takes further the development of emotion and desire. The contrasting Stoic–Epicurean pattern is informed by the Socratic idea that all human beings are constitutively capable of developing towards ethical perfection, regardless of their inborn nature or social context. Humans are seen as having the rational or cognitive resources to acquire an understanding of goodness even if they are brought up in societies whose belief-structures are largely misguided or corrupt. Also, since these Hellenistic theories presuppose a unified or holistic psychological model, the process of development is not seen as directed at different parts of the personality at different stages. Development affects the personality as a whole, and can do so, in principle, at any stage of life once rational capacities have been formed. To put the point differently, the Platonic–Aristotelian pattern assumes that ethical development depends on the right combination of (inborn) nature (*phusis*), habituation (*ethos*), and reason (*logos*). The Epicurean–Stoic pattern, by contrast, eliminates or radically reconceives the role of habituation. Human nature is seen as constitutively rational, and rationality is seen as capable of shaping or reshaping the personality as a whole at any stage of adult life.[183]

[182] Long (1996), 279–80; for this Stoic idea, see 2.2 above, text to nn. 76–80, 4.5, text to nn. 251–66.

[183] See 3.2 above, esp. text to nn. 10–77, 3.5, esp. text to nn. 225–43; on Plutarch's version of the Platonic–Aristotelian pattern, see 4.3 above, text to nn. 113–14.

In my earlier book on Greek conceptions of personality (1996*b*), I suggested that the Platonic–Aristotelian pattern expressed an objective-participant approach to personality.[184] I also claimed that this pattern reflects certain longstanding ways of thinking in Greek culture, manifested, for instance, in Homer's *Iliad* and Attic tragedy. The pattern is objective in characterizing the agent as a bearer of psychological capacities or functions rather than as a locus of self-consciousness or unique individuality. It is also objectiv*ist* in its thinking about knowledge; development is conceived not as the realization of a subjective or uniquely individual vision but of objective knowledge and correlated character and action. The pattern is participant because of the role given to involvement in communal practices and internalization of communal norms in the first, habituative, stage, which also forms a necessary basis for the second stage. It is also participant in that ethical reflection, in the second stage, is also, typically, conceived in cooperative terms, as shared enquiry or dialectic based on agreed presuppositions and directed at establishing common standards. I suggested that this pattern could be seen as underlying the two-stage education of the guardians in Plato's *Republic* and analogous features of Aristotle's ethical writings.[185] I also maintained that a similar pattern of thinking underlies the presentation of heroic figures in Homer and tragedy. Homer's Achilles and Euripides' Medea, for instance, are often seen as self-assertive individuals, radically questioning or rejecting communal or shared human standards. I argued, however, that their non-standard actions should be seen as 'exemplary gestures', designed to dramatize, and protest at, exceptional breaches in communal or common human norms.[186]

If the Platonic–Aristotelian pattern, together with its Greek poetic precursors, is taken as reflecting an objective-participant approach to personality, does it follow that the Stoic–Epicurean one, with its salient differences, reflects a contrasting subjective-individualist one? There are certain features of the Hellenistic pattern which *might* seem to point in that direction. One distinctive feature is that ethical development is *not* seen as depending on an upbringing in a family or community which instils soundly based ethical standards. The claim is that human nature is constitutively capable of forming preconceptions of good, for instance, even if people are brought up in societies which are not permeated by true ethical beliefs. This might seem to amount to the claim that ethical development is a purely individual process, conducted without reference to the surrounding community.[187]

[184] See, in outline, Gill (1996*b*), 11–12, esp. point 2 in the 'objective-participant' conception.
[185] See Gill (1996*b*), ch. 4, esp. 266–87, ch. 5, esp. 356–83.
[186] See Gill (1996*b*), ch. 2, esp. 148–74.
[187] See 3.2 above, text to nn. 10–19, 3.5, text to nn. 230–44.

This feature also goes some way towards explaining the importance of self-scrutiny and self-examination that is emphasized by scholars such as Kahn, Long, and Foucault (329–31 above). I accept that, to some degree at least, self-scrutiny *does* have a more integral place in the Stoic–Epicurean than in the Platonic–Aristotelian pattern. Since ethical development is not conceived as dependent on the foundation of a soundly based set of communal beliefs,[188] the developing agent must continually examine her current belief-set to see how far they match her preconceptions.[189] Hence, we find Epictetus' stress on the importance of 'examining your impressions' before giving assent and Seneca's focus on 'self-scrutiny' as regards actions and beliefs.[190] This is a process which continues, in principle, throughout adult life, and is one which *may* have to be conducted by the person on her own—in the absence of any suitable teachers or collaborators.[191] Also, there is no point at which ethical progress is conceived as being blocked by emotional dispositions ingrained by nature or habituation.[192] Hence, self-examination and self-modification can bring about changes in a way that does not depend on the social context of one's upbringing or adult development. One can see a contrast with the Platonic–Aristotelian pattern, especially as presented in the two-stage educational programme of Plato's *Republic*. Here, as outlined earlier, ethical development is seen as closely integrated with the social and dialectical practices of the ideal community, and the stages of the programme are correlated with the development of distinct psychic parts.[193] But I do not think that these differences mean that the Stoic (or Epicurean) pattern expresses a shift towards an individualist or subjective (or subjectiv*ist*) conception of the person. The second and third stages of Epictetus' ethical programme especially bring out its participant and objectivist dimensions. Also significant, and exemplified in Epictetus' methods, is the role of (philosophically informed) interpersonal discourse in ethical development. Epictetus' stress on examining impressions, like Sereca's emphasis on self-scrutiny, can thus be understood as expressing an objective-participant conception of personality.

[188] This is postulated as a feature of the ideal pattern of development by Plato and Aristotle (e.g. Pl. *R.* 401a–402c; Arist. *NE* 1.4, 1095^{b}2–8, 10.9, 1179^{b}20–31), though both thinkers recognize that this is often not available (e.g. Pl. *R.* 491e–497c; Arist. *NE* 1179^{b}4–19).

[189] On preconceptions in Stoicism and Epicurearism, see refs. in n. 187 above.

[190] See further Long (2002), 79–86, referring to Epict. *Diss.* 2.11.1–8, 1.22.1–2, 4.1.42–3; and Edwards (1997), 28–34, referring esp. to *Ira* 3.36.1–3, *Ep.* 6.1–3.

[191] On the question of the *form* of such scrutiny (whether internal or interpersonal), see text to nn. 237–45 below.

[192] Contrast the situation envisaged in Arist. *NE* 3.5, 1114^{a}15–21; see also 2.3 above, text to nn. 131–43.

[193] See Pl. *R.* 441d–442c, 518d–519b. See further Gill (1985), (1996*b*), 266–71, 275–87, 292–5; also (1998*b*), (2004*d*).

Against this larger background, I turn specifically to Epictetus' programme, as presented in his most complete statement of the method.

(1) There are three topics, in which the would-be honourable and good person needs to have been trained. (2) That of desires and aversions, to ensure that he succeeds in getting what he desires and does not encounter what he seeks to avoid. (3) That of impulses and repulsions, or the appropriate (*kathēkon*) as a whole, to ensure that he acts in ways that are orderly, well reasoned and not thoughtless. (4) The third has to do with infallibility and uncarelessness, or assents in general. (5) Of these [three] the most important and urgent is the one concerned with the passions [i.e. the first]. A passion only occurs if a desire is unsuccessful or an aversion encounters [what it seeks to avoid]. This is the topic which brings up disturbances, confusions, misfortunes, disasters, sorrows, lamentations, envies . . . through which we are unable even to listen to reason.(6) The second has to do with the appropriate; I should not be impassive like a statue, but maintain my natural and acquired relationships, as a religious person, as a son, a brother, a father, and a citizen. (7) The third topic applies to those who are already making progress, and concerns security in just those matters mentioned, to ensure that even in dreams or intoxication or depression an impression (*phantasia*) should not slip by which has not been tested.[194]

Epictetus' schema is one of a number of ways of subdividing the project of practical ethics in this period. A similar pattern can be found in Seneca, which consists in (1) assessing the value of each thing, (2) adopting an appropriate and controlled impulse towards the objects pursued, (3) achieving consistency between impulse and action.[195] In drawing out the significance of Epictetus' version, I focus first on the ethical programme taken as a whole, and then on the interplay between individual and social factors and the model of personality implied in the programme. In broad terms, I take it that Epictetus sets out in plain language a pathway in ethical progress based on the central Stoic idea of development as 'appropriation', as illustrated in Cicero's account in *Fin.* 3.16–22.[196] In examining Cicero's treatment earlier (3.2–3 above), I stressed that the Stoic view of development implies psychological holism, by contrast with the part-based Platonic–Aristotelian pattern, and also—what I called—ethical holism, as regards the ideal outcome of development. These features are also implied here. The background presence of these motifs helps to explain two of the features of Epictetus' conception of

[194] Epict. *Diss.* 3.2–15, with omissions (= LS 56 C, trans. modified, numbers as in LS). On one or more of these three topics, see *Diss.* 1.4.11, 2.17.14–18, 3.12.13–15, 4.10.13. For discussion, see LS ii. 342; Bonhöffer (1890), 19–28; Inwood (1985), 116–19; P. Hadot (1995), 12–13, 193–5; Dobbin (1998), 91–4; Long (2002), 112–18; Sellars (2003), 134–42.

[195] *Ep.* 89.14 (LS 56 B). On programmes of this type, see further n. 234 below.

[196] That is, Cicero's account of personal appropriation (LS 59 D); his account of social appropriation (Cic. *Fin.* 3.62–8, LS 57 F) is also relevant, especially to the second of Epictetus' stages.

selfhood stressed by Kahn and Long, noted earlier, namely the highly integrated view of motivation and the unified 'metaphysics of the self' linked with that view.[197]

The linkage between Epictetus' programme and these features of Stoic theory is most obvious in the characterization of the first of the three stages. It is plausible to connect the first stage of Epictetus' programme with his recurrent advice to direct desire towards what is 'up to us', 'ours', and 'within *prohairesis*', rather than what is not 'up to us', what is not 'external', and what 'falls outside *prohairesis*'. Another reiterated theme in Epictetus is that focusing desire on the first type of object leads to peace of mind, whereas pursuing the second leads to passions.[198] We can also link these themes with the central Stoic ethical claim that humans are naturally adapted to develop from seeking to obtain primary natural things (preferable indifferents) to recognizing that only the good (expressed in particular as virtue) is inherently valuable.[199] It is this crucial shift in motivation that yields freedom from passion, whereas failure to develop in this way generates passion.[200] Epictetus' programme implies the psychological holism characteristic of the theory, according to which cognitive or rational progress affects one's emotional state directly without any need for *separate* training of an irrational part, of the kind found in the Platonic–Aristotelian model adopted by Plutarch, for instance.[201] Similarly, Epictetus' characterization of the third, final, stage implies the ideal I linked earlier with the notion of ethical holism. This is the ideal of a *completely* consistent and unified character, in which rational coherence (wisdom) confers emotional unity and the absence of the kinds of inner conflicts associated with the passions. This stage aims at 'infallibility and uncarelessness' and 'security', qualities which are elsewhere in Stoic theory associated with the consistency of understanding and correlated character-state of the wise person.[202]

To connect this passage with the Stoic theory of development as appropriation might seem implausible, since Epictetus here avoids distinctions central to this theory, such as between pursuing indifferents and seeking virtue as the

[197] Kahn (1988), 253; Long (1996), 270, 272–3, 277. See also text to nn. 172–4 above.

[198] *Diss.* 3.2.1, 3 (LS 56 C(2, 5)). See also e.g. *Handbook* 1, 2, 5; *Diss.* 1.1.7–12, 1.4.1–3, 1.12.

[199] In Stoic thought, the good, characterized by structure and wholeness, is a broader concept than virtue; but virtue is the manifestation of goodness that is most relevant to human ethical development; See 3.3 above, esp. text to nn. 93–103, 174–9.

[200] See 4.5 above, esp. text to nn. 225–44. Note the characterization of passion in Epict 3.2.3 (LS 56 C(5)), cited above, especially 'through which we are unable even to listen to reason'.

[201] On this point in Stoic theory, see 2.2 above, text to nn. 36–46, 3.2, text to nn. 10–20, 42–77; contrast Plutarch's version of the part-based account, 4.3 above.

[202] Cf. Epict. *Diss.* 3.2.2, 5, with D.L. 7.46–8 (LS 31 B); see further on this linkage text to nn. 228–9 below. On the ideal linked with 'ethical holism', see 3.3 above, text to nn. 92–127.

good. As elsewhere in the *Discourses*, Epictetus, strikingly, avoids the technical terms and neologisms that figure in most ancient accounts of Stoic ethics.[203] However, there are clear indications that Epictetus uses his distinctive, though non-technical, vocabulary to convey an orthodox Stoic picture of ethical development. In *Diss.* 1.4, for instance, the first stage of the programme of practical ethics (the focusing of desire on what is 'up to us') is explicitly presented as learning to take virtue as one's goal, rather than what Epictetus calls 'externals', which are characterized elsewhere in Stoicism as 'preferable indifferents'. Peace of mind (understood as freedom from passion), happiness, and harmony with nature are described as the outcome of the 'perfection' of virtue, and not as goals to be pursued independently.[204] A similar line of thought is implied by the recurrent theme that desire (*orexis*) should be deferred until there is complete understanding of the good.[205] This recommendation not to have desire seems rather startling, especially when expressed in Epictetus' common-sense, non-technical vocabulary. But it is consistent with the standard Stoic view that the only unqualified desire should be for the good, a desire which, in the strict sense, can only be experienced by the wise, who know fully what the good is.[206] At the same time, again consistently with Stoic theory, the achievement of this state is presented as the appropriate target for anyone, regardless of their current state of character or background.[207]

In examining the implications of the three-point programme for understanding human personality, I begin with two questions which have not, I think, been much raised, at least in this form.[208] Is the programme—like the Stoic theory of appropriation on which it is based—a universal account of ethical development or a specific teaching method, which requires expert

[203] On Epictetus' avoidance of the standard distinctions between, for instance, 'choice' (*hairesis*) and 'selection' (*eklogē*), and between 'perfect acts' (*katorthōmata*) and 'appropriate acts' (*kathēkonta*), see Inwood (1985), 115–119.

[204] See esp. *Diss.* 1.4.3–4: 'If virtue holds out this promise, of creating happiness, freedom from passion (*apatheia*) and a smooth flow [of life] (*eurhoia*), certainly, progress towards virtue is progress towards each of these. Wherever the perfection (*teleiotēs*) of something tends, progress is always an approach to that.' See also 1.4.11–12, 18, 23–8. For a discussion of 'indifferents', characterized in those terms, see *Diss.* 2.6.

[205] See Epict. *Handbook* 2, 'For the present, totally remove desire', *Handbook* 48.3, and *Diss.* 3.13.21: 'Abstain from desire altogether for the present, to do so later with good reason (*eulogōs*). If you do so with good reason, whenever you have some good in you, you will direct your desire well.'

[206] On this point, see Long (2002), 126, clarifying the features of Epictetus' vocabulary highlighted by Inwood (1985), 119 (also 116); see also Bonhöffer (1890), 240–2; and Dobbin (1998), 91–3.

[207] This is implied in the three-stage programme (see text to n. 194 above). See also e.g. *Diss.* 1.1, and 1.2, esp. 35–7, 1.4, taken with Gill (1988), 187–9, (1998*b*), 220–2.

[208] For scholarship on the three-topic programme, see n. 194 above.

philosophical training, of the type offered in Epictetus' school? There are certain ways, explored shortly, in which Epictetus' characteristic teaching techniques are designed to play a special role in this developmental programme. But the programme is presented in quite general terms; it also presupposes that human beings as such have certain constitutional capacities.[209] So it seems plausible to think that this is a process that *anyone* can carry out, in quite different social and intellectual contexts. Second, are the three topics (*topoi*) of the programme to be understood as temporal stages or as coordinated aspects? The third topic is presented as designed for 'those who are already making progress' (*Diss.* 3.2,5, LS 56(7)) suggesting that the division corresponds to temporal stages. On the other hand, there are also reasons, explained shortly, for seeing the three topics as marking out non-temporal, coordinated aspects of ethical life.[210] So, although the programme, overall, has a progressive dimension, it also depends crucially on simultaneous development of the personality in various aspects. These are, broadly, those of ethical attitudes and motivation, social relationships, and cognitive understanding.

I now explore the programme in more detail, holding in mind the questions just raised, with a view to bringing out the relationship between social or interactive and individual dimensions of the process and the model of personality implied. The account of the first topic is in one respect rather puzzling, when set against a more typical Stoic account of personal ethical development, by Cicero, for instance. Although presented as coming first in the sequence, it deals with what is, in Cicero's version, the climactic recognition that what matters is not securing preferable indifferents through selection but valuing the good in itself.[211] The explanation for Epictetus' mode of presentation may be this. The first move in ethical development is to realize that, unlike obtaining preferable indifferents, or 'externals', as Epictetus calls them, this process is wholly 'up to us'.[212] But this topic also comes first because it is *primary*. The reorientation of motivation is fundamental to the Stoic conception of development, and needs also to be reflected in the conduct of social relationships and the shaping of the belief-structure in the second and third topics. The completion of the first topic thus depends on development in

209 See text to nn. 213–14 below.

210 Analogous issues arise in connection with the three branches of philosophy in Stoicism, on which see LS 26 A–D, and 3.3 above, text to nn. 148–60. On the question of the relationship between these two tripartite schemas, see text to nn. 230–4 below.

211 Contrast Epict. *Diss.* 3.2. 1, 3 (LS 56 C(2, 5)) with Cic. *Fin.* 3.21–2 (LS 59 D(4–6)) in this respect; see also 129–31 above.

212 On this claim, see Bobzien (1997), 79–82, (1998*a*), 331–8, stressing the essentially practical ethical implications of the claim and arguing against the idea that Epictetus advances a new theory about human agency and determinism, distinct from that of Chrysippus.

social behaviour and cognitive understanding, that is, the subjects of the second and third topics. Hence, although the three topics form what is sometimes presented as a progressive sequence, they also map out an integrated process involving three related aspects of human experience, and this integration carries implications for the conception of personality implied.[213]

What does the programme suggest about the interrelationship of individual and social or interactive dimensions, including collaborative philosophical activity? Epictetus emphasizes that human beings have certain natural capacities which are relevant for carrying out this programme. One is the natural capacity to form preconceptions (*prolēpseis*), for instance, that of good, which play a crucial role in the 'examination of impressions' through which people can take forward their ethical development.[214] He also stresses that human beings have a natural capacity for forming a coherent and rational set of beliefs; more precisely, they are naturally orientated towards forming the stable and consistent structure of understanding that is the basis of wisdom.[215] These natural capacities are, clearly, relevant to the three-topic programme of ethical development, especially the first and the third topics.

Does the fact that human beings have these natural capacities imply that they are developed and expressed in a specifically individual, and self-related, way? In fact, there are clear indications in the opposite direction, both as regards the social relationships that are the focus of the second topic and the construction of a framework of beliefs that is central for the third. The second topic is focused on motivation (defined as 'impulse') towards the appropriate, notably the kind of 'appropriate acts' (*kathēkonta*) that derive from one's social relationships (for instance, 'as a son, a brother, a father, and a citizen').[216] This topic explicitly centres on social participation, but what is the proper form of such participation? Crucial for the programme is correlating the orientation of motivation that is central for the first topic (towards what is 'up to us', that is, progress towards virtue and not preferable indifferents) with the conduct of social relationships, specifically conventional family and communal ones.[217] Another way of putting this point is to say that Epictetus urges

[213] For the three topics, see text to. n. 194 above. See esp. LS 56 C(5): 'Of these [three] the most important and urgent [is the first]', i.e. it is primary or fundamental; and (7) 'The third topic applies to those who are already making progress', for the idea of progressive sequence.

[214] See Long (2002), 79–85, referring to *Diss.* 1.22.1–2, 2.11.1–8, 13–25, 3.12.15, 4.1.41–6. On Stoic 'preconceptions', see also 3.2 above, text to nn. 10–19, 3.5, text to nn. 230–44.

[215] See Long (2002), ch. 4, esp. 97–104, referring to Epict. *Diss.* 1.2.1–4, 1.28.1–5, 2.26.3, 3.3.2–4; also 112–18, linking this point with Epictetus' three-topic programme.

[216] Epict. *Diss.* 3.2.1, 4 (= LS 56 C(3, 6)), also 1.4.11, 3.12.13, 4.10.13. On 'appropriate actions' and social behaviour, see further LS 59, esp. E(2), (Q); also Inwood (1999), 100–26.

[217] See further Gill (1988), 187–92; also on Epictetus' concern with both conventional and cosmopolitan social relations, Gill (2000*d*), 609–11.

his listeners to correlate with each other the two types of ethical development—personal and social appropriation—that are both seen as expressing fundamental parts of human motivation.[218]

One aspect of this process seems especially to underlie Epictetus' thinking in the *Discourses* about social relationships, viewed as part of the three-stage programme. On the one hand, involvement in familial and communal relationships helps someone to learn what 'the appropriate' means. It also helps someone to understand the nature of the virtues and so, gradually, to move towards an understanding of the good.[219] On the other hand, the 'influence' or 'conversation' (*katēchēsis*) of the many can also pervert development, above all, by encouraging someone to regard indifferents as good (or bad) and so promoting the 'passions' and misguided behaviour that derive from this (256–8 above). Recurrent features of the *Discourses* express this twofold point. On the one hand, Epictetus stresses that social 'roles' (*prosōpa*) and relationships (*scheseis*) constitute a guide for reasonable direction of our impulses towards what is appropriate.[220] On the other, he underlines that conflict can arise in such relationships if they involve us in overvaluing indifferents, or in cooperating with others who do overvalue then. For instance, in *Diss.* 3.3, Epictetus says that, if relationships are consistent with right judgement, then 'the very preservation of relationships becomes a good' (3.3.8). But this is coupled with the assertion that, if the demands of meeting family obligations come into conflict with the good, 'off go father and brother and fatherland and everything else of that kind' (3.3.6). A related point is conveyed in Epictetus' famous, and seemingly shocking, advice that, when you kiss your child, friend or wife, you should remind yourself that 'tomorrow, you or I may die'.[221] The underlying point is that relationships should be conducted in a way that develops the recognition that what matters, ultimately, is not indifferents, including the preferable indifferent of continued life, but the good, as this is progressively understood.[222] As so understood, the second stage fits coherently both into Epictetus' three-point programme and the Stoic pattern of ethical development outlined earlier (377 above). Although this stage involves

218 See further Inwood (1996); also, on the larger question of the relationship between the two types of appropriation, see esp. Reydams-Schils (2002), (2005), ch. 2.

219 This line of thought is very clear in Cic. *Off.* 1 (e.g. 1.15–23, 107–25). This is based on Panaetius' *On Appropriate Actions*, but seems also to reflect Chrysippean thinking about social engagement (e.g. in Cic. *Fin.* 3.62–8 (LS 57 F, esp. 2–3, 7–8)). See further (on Cic. *Off.* and Stoic theory), Annas (1993*b*), 302–11, esp. 310–11; Inwood (1999), 112–26; Atkins (2000), 505–14, esp. 506–7.

220 See especially *Diss* 4.12.16–17 (= LS 66 F(2)), also 2.10.21.

221 See *Diss.* 3.24.84–8, *Handbook* 3; see also *Diss.* 1.2.1–11.

222 See further Inwood (1985), 123–4, (1996); Gill (1988), 187–92, (1998*b*), 214–25 (2000*d*), 608–11; Long (2002), 232–44, 247–9.

social 'participation', this does not take the form of habituation in the belief-set and practices of one's community, on the assumption that these are well grounded. Rather, it takes the form of a critical engagement with those beliefs, a 'dialogue', in a sense, between conventional beliefs and the emerging belief-set that reflects one's own progress in personal ethical development. To this extent, the process involves both an individual and a participant dimension, though the former one is not 'individualistic' in the sense of giving positive value to individuality or to one's own individual views as such.[223]

What contribution is played by philosophical teaching in promoting this critical engagement and also in developing the stable and coherent structure of beliefs described in the third topic? Long, in his book on Epictetus (2002), has brought out very clearly how Epictetus' teaching methods, as displayed in the *Discourses*, reflect his thinking on natural human capacities and on the three-point programme. He stresses that Epictetus deploys a distinctive blend of the modes of discourse explored in Hellenistic–Roman practical ethics, including elenctic (Socratic), doctrinal (Stoic), and reproving (Cynic) modes.[224] He emphasizes especially that several of Epictetus' discourses constitute quasi-Socratic dialogues, in which the interlocutor is led to recognize the incoherence of his opinions and to move towards a more coherent and, it is claimed, true or 'natural' belief-set. As in Plato's 'Socratic' dialogues, as sometimes interpreted, the dialectic proceeds on the assumption that the only fully coherent set of beliefs are true ones, which can also be understood as constituting objective knowledge.[225] In Epictetus' version, this process is grounded on the assumption that all human beings, as such, have the capacity to form preconceptions, for instance, of what is good, which form the basis at least for acquiring this knowledge.[226] Several points follow from Long's analysis which bear on my concerns here. First, he brings out that Epictetus' philosophical methods are conceived very much as modes of *discourse*, which complement—partly by counteracting—the communication of beliefs which forms part of conventional interactive discourse. To this extent, he shows that

[223] See Foucault on different senses of Hellenistic–Roman 'individualism', 6.2 above, text to nn. 7–8. Philosophical critical engagement with social and political discourse could also lead to an antagonistic relationship between philosophers and the dominant forces or trends in society. On aspects of this (very complex) subject, see e.g. Griffin (1976), 363–6; Vegetti (1986) and Cambiano (1988), ch. 5 (both of whom criticize Foucault (1988*b*) for neglecting this point).

[224] Long (2002), 52–66; for these three modes, see Epict. *Diss.* 3.21.19; on genres of practical ethics in Hellenistic–Roman philosophy, see n. 234 below.

[225] Long (2002), ch. 3, esp. 74–96, referring e.g. to Epict. *Diss.* 1.11.5–15, 2.11.1–8. On Socratic elenctic method, see Vlastos (1994), ch. 1; Benson (2000); on the relationship between the methods of Socrates and Epictetus, see Gill (2000*a*), 137–9. On the linkage between truth and consistency in Stoic epistemology, see Annas (1990), especially 185–8.

[226] See references in nn. 214–15 above.

philosophical teaching and learning is also a mode of social participation. Second, his account shows how this form of participation, and the critical engagement with conventional discourse, are conceived in objectivist terms, rather than as the expression of individual views or perspectives.[227]

However, this raises one of the questions underlined earlier: do Epictetus' teaching methods imply that the three-topic programme of ethical development can *only* be carried through with the help of practical philosophical discourse of the type deployed by Epictetus and other Stoic teachers? This issue emerges with special force in connection with the third topic. This stage 'has to do with infallibility (*anexapatēsia*) and uncarelessness (*aneikaiotēs*) or assents in general' and concerns the kind of 'security' (*asphaleia*) involved in ensuring that an 'impression should not slip by that has not been tested'.[228] As noted earlier, Epictetus' language evokes features which are elsewhere presented as typical of the state of mind of the wise person who has mastered fully the 'virtue' of dialectic or logic.[229] Does this imply that completion of the ethical programme depends on formal philosophical training, for instance, in Stoic logic? A much-discussed idea in recent scholarship is also worth noting here. It has been suggested, in particular by Pierre Hadot, that the three topics in Epictetus' programme correspond to the three main branches of Stoic philosophy: the first to physics, the second to ethics, and the third to logic or dialectic. The two schemas are not, of course, identical: Epictetus' topics consist in drawing out *the ethical implications* of the three branches of knowledge, or, as Hadot sometimes puts it, they represent these three branches as 'lived philosophy'.[230] Although sometimes criticized, Hadot's view has been influential.[231] It seems to carry the clear implication that the completion of Epictetus' ethical programme depends on following through the Stoic philosophical curriculum, conducted in a way that draws out its significance for leading a good life.

I think that Hadot's idea that Stoic practical ethics was informed by a synthesis of the three branches of philosophy is a suggestive one, with important implications for the interpretation of Hellenistic–Roman practical

[227] See also text to nn. 181–2 above, presented as qualifying the view offered in Long (1996), ch. 12.

[228] *Diss.* 3.2.1, 5 (LS 56 C(4, 7)); also 1.4.11, 1.17.22, 3.12.14–15, 4.10.13.

[229] See D.L. 7.46–8 (LS 31 B), esp. 'uncarelessness' (*aneikaiotēs*) (LS 31 B(3)), 'secure (*asphalē*)... in the reception of impressions' (LS 31 B(6)). See further Long (1996), ch. 4, esp. 92–5. See also text to n. 202 above.

[230] See P. Hadot (1995), 11–12, 191–5; also (1991), 218, (1998), 89–98. For this idea, see also Bonhöffer (1890), 22–8, (1894) 46–9, 58–60 (= 1996: 78–85).

[231] For criticism, see e.g. Dobbin (1998), 94, 164; Barnes (1997*a*), 34. For support, see, briefly, Gourinat (1996), 14–15; Long (2002), 117–18, 126; more fully, Sellars (2003), 134–6, who develops this approach in 136–43.

philosophy. It can be linked with the theme of 'rich naturalism' which I have argued is important in both Stoicism and Epicureanism (186–94 above). However, I have reservations about the specific connection Hadot makes between this idea and Epictetus' three-topic programme. For one thing, the match between the three branches of philosophy and the first two topics seems rather strained. 'Ethics', in Stoicism, and ancient thought generally, is much broader than the conduct of social relations that forms the second topic. In fact, the orientation of desire in the first topic (to the progress towards the good that is 'up to us') highlights what are, arguably, the key claims in Stoic ethics. Although Stoic 'physics' can include the understanding of human psychology or human agency as a form of causation that is implied in the first topic, I see little reason to supply that connection here.[232] The linkage between the third topic and logic is more plausible; and this can be connected with Epictetus' recurrent concern in the *Discourses* with using logic to advance ethical progress and not treating it as an end in itself.[233] But recognizing this connection does not require us to correlate each of the three topics with the three standard branches of Stoic knowledge. Like most other such schemas in Hellenistic–Roman philosophy, Epictetus' three-topic pattern is, essentially, a programme in *ethics*,[234] and allusions to other branches of knowledge are, I think, less integral to their conception than Hadot maintains.

Also, I am not sure we should conclude that the description of the third stage implies that study of formal Stoic logic is a prerequisite for the completion of this stage. What is suggested here is the coherence and stability of belief-structure (or knowledge) that, together with a similar character-state and affective pattern, is typical of the normative wise person.[235] For committed Stoic students and teachers, of course, the projected route to wisdom must lie in the combination of philosophical understanding, based on the integration of the three branches of knowledge, and ethical progress, as embodied both in character-development and in practical action. But the tendency in Stoicism to present as candidates for wisdom pre-Stoic thinkers such as Socrates and Diogenes the Cynic, and also non-philosophers such as Odysseus

[232] On the scope of Stoic physics and related subjects cited in the text, see LS 43, 53, 55. See further Long (2002), 118; Sellars (2003), 136–9. On the practical (ethical) focus in Epictetus' use of ideas such as what is 'up to us', see Bobzien (1998*a*), 331–8.

[233] See Epict. *Diss.* 3.2.6–12, 1.7.1–2, 1.8.6–10, 2.17.34, 2.23.41. See further Bonhöffer (1894) 122–4 (= 1996: 158–61); Nussbaum (1994), 348–9; Long (1996), 104–6, (2002), 117, 120–1; Dobbin (1998), 113–18.

[234] See e.g. Sen. *Ep.* 89.14 (LS 56 B), cited in text to n. 195 above; Stob. 2.39.20–45.6 (Philo of Larissa and Eudorus); on Philo see Brittain (2001), ch. 6; on Eudorus, Dillon (1977) 122–6. M.A. *Med.* 3.11, 8.7 (on which see P. Hadot 1995: 195–202) raises further complex issues. On these schemas, see, in outline, Gill (2003*d*), 42–3.

[235] For this ideal in Epictetus and Stoic thought generally, see refs in n. 202 above.

and Hercules, points towards a broader view.[236] This is that, as stressed elsewhere, *all* human beings as such have the natural capacity to make progress towards perfect wisdom, a belief which also implies a confidence that this progress is possible despite wide varieties in social, cultural, and intellectual contexts of development.

I now sum up the implications of Epictetus' three-topic programme for my enquiry. What I have suggested is that, although it assumes a different pattern of thinking about development from the Platonic–Aristotelian one outlined earlier (377–8 above), Epictetus' programme is no less objective-participant and objectivist in its assumptions about human nature and personality. His programme envisages the person developing through engagement in a critical dialogue with the belief-set of her social context, in a way that may be supplemented by the modes of (practically directed) philosophical discourse deployed by Epictetus and other Stoic teachers. Although this programme presupposes a greater measure of critical detachment from one's social context than is assumed in the accounts of (at least) ideal ethical development in Plato and Aristotle, there is no evidence of a positive evaluation of individual perspectives or opinions as such. On the contrary, the programme is thoroughly objectivist in its conception of ethical knowledge. Although Epictetus' description of ethical progress assumes a Stoic theoretical and educational framework, his aspiration, shared by Stoicism more generally, is to characterize ethical development and its ideal outcome in a form that applies to human nature universally and that is realizable in a wide variety of contexts.

I conclude by offering a description in objective-participant terms of a feature of Epictetus' discourses that is sometimes taken to mark a shift towards a more subjective and individualist conception of selfhood. Epictetus' theme of the examination of impressions, like Marcus Aurelius' composition of meditations ('to himself'), is sometimes seen as significant in the history of ideas of selfhood because it implies that introspective, self-related activities have a special significance which does not attach to interpersonal discourse. An instance often cited in this connection is Seneca's report of his own nightly self-examination (*On Anger* 3.36.1–3).[237] In similar vein, Long, in the essay cited earlier, characterizes Epictetus' examination of impressions as a process involving a (first-personal) 'I' and 'me' and describes Epictetus' invented conversations as 'the way of exhibiting the self to itself'.[238] The

[236] See further on the implications of Stoic use of such figures, Kerferd (1978), esp. 124; Schofield (2003), 233–5. Sedley (1999*c*), 150–1, esp. n. 86, suggests that this feature only emerges in later Stoicism.

[237] See e.g. Rudd (1976), 163–4; Edwards (1997), 25–31; Sellars (2003), 147–8; on self-addressed 'meditation' as an ancient practice, Newman (1989).

[238] Long (1996), 276, 282, and 281 n. 28; see also 6.2 above, text to nn. 174–5.

post-Cartesian thinking outlined earlier (331–4 above) indicates why this should be so: such reflexive, introspective activities seem to express—or, at least, prefigure—the idea of the person as a self-conscious 'I', with privileged access to her own mental states. Epictetus' own practice, however, indicates no such priority of inner, reflexive states over interpersonal discourse. Epictetus seems to regard it as equally appropriate to examine his interlocutor's impressions through dialogue as to urge his interlocutor to do so for himself.[239] Indeed, one might suggest that, for Epictetus and other thinkers of this period, private thought or meditation is conceived as the internalization of the kind of practical ethical teaching that is standardly conducted through oral interchange (or sometimes its written equivalent).[240] This view finds support, for instance, in the fact that Epictetus sometimes presents the examination of impressions in the form of internal dialogue (between the person and his impressions) as though such examination represented a continuation of the dialogue between teacher and pupil.[241] To this degree, interpersonal discourse, the more participant mode, retains the kind of primacy over internal discourse which (I have suggested elsewhere)[242] it had in earlier Greek culture.

Comparison with earlier Greek practice can help to sharpen this point. In my earlier book (1996*b*), I discussed especially two forms of internal dialogue, the deliberative monologues in Homer's *Iliad* and the presentation of relationships between psychic parts in Plato's dialogues. The use of interior monologue in Homer, I suggested, does not imply that deliberation standardly or necessarily takes this form; indeed, much deliberation in Homer is collaborative and takes the form of public debate. The use of internal dialogue reflects, rather, special situations of crisis or isolation when the figure is presented as speaking to himself because he has no one else with whom to share the deliberative process.[243] In Plato, in partial contrast, the idea of inner dialogue has a different, and more positive, significance. It expresses the idea of the personality as a complex of different parts which are also conceived as

[239] See e.g. the quasi-Socratic dialogue *Diss.* 1.11, which is, in effect, an examination of the interlocutor's impressions or judgements (and which concludes by urging such examination, 1.11.39); for convincing analysis of this dialogue, see Long (2002), 77–9. See 3.9.12–13, dialogue as mutual examination of judgements; 2.19.29–34, in which the dialogue is presented as the means by which Epictetus 'crafts' the other person's rational agency until it becomes 'free' (i.e. perfect).

[240] Seneca's *Letters* to Lucilius constitute an extended representation of practical ethical teaching.

[241] *Diss.* 2.18.24, 3.8.1–3, 3.12.15, *Handbook* 1, cited in text to n. 165 above.

[242] Gill (1996*b*), see references in general index to 'internal dialogue', esp. 15–16, 58–60, 182–3, 186–7, 252–3.

[243] See Gill (1996*b*), 46–7, 58–60; for public deliberation, see e.g. Hom. *Il.* 14.37–134 (analysed by Schofield 1986: 22–4), 18.510–12, 22.174–6 (and contexts).

independent, and sometimes conflicted, sources of motivation.[244] In Stoic and Epicurean thought, at least as presented in this study, the holistic conception of personality renders inappropriate Plato's reason for using internal dialogue to portray a part-based conception of personality. Although inner dialogue does, occasionally, figure in Stoic texts, it is for special reasons; and it also carries the implication that each of the partners in dialogue represent the whole personality (in its 'rational' or 'passionate' modes) and not long-term 'parts' or quasi-independent agents.[245] Hence, contrary to the impression often given by modern scholars, the idea that internal dialogue expresses the nature of selfhood or personality in some fundamental way is more appropriate to fourth-century, Classical, thought than to Hellenistic–Roman thought, at least in its Stoic–Epicurean version. The use of internal discourse in Epictetus to convey self-scrutiny or the examination of impressions seems to be more like the use of internal monologue in Homer. It reflects the internalization of aspects of ethical development that are typically expressed in the discourse of practically directed philosophical discourse, as suggested earlier. Although a full-scale demonstration of this point is not appropriate here, it is worth indicating in this way my view that the combination of an innovative holistic model of personality in Stoicism with a continuing objective-participant conception of the person militates against the idea that inner dialogue has a special status as an expression of selfhood.

6.6 A SUBJECTIVIST STRAND IN ANCIENT THOUGHT?

I have argued that Classical (fourth-century) accounts of self-knowledge and related notions, as exemplified in Plato's *Alcibiades*, are not best understood in subjectivist, or subjective-individualist, terms. I have also made a similar claim about the Stoic theory of development as appropriation and about Epictetus' method of practical ethics, which I see as based on this theory. In doing so, I am following the lead of scholars of ancient thought such as Burnyeat and Everson who doubt the relevance of the idea of subjectivity to ancient thought, seeing it as a notion which derives from modern philosophical innovations starting with Descartes.[246] In a more general way, I am influenced by those working on the philosophy of mind

244 See further Gill (1996*b*), 252–9, on this aspect of Pl. *R.*, and 386–8, on Pl. *Phdr.*

245 On this point, regarding Chrysippus' (probable) reading of the monologue in Euripides' *Medea*, esp. 1078–80, see Gill (1983*a*), 138, 141 (also 4.5 above, text to nn. 216–45), and, on Cleanthes' dialogue between reasoning and anger, Tieleman (2003), 264–77.

246 On Burnyeat and Everson, see further below.

and personhood such as Peter Smith and O. R. Jones or Kathleen Wilkes. These scholars (together with some other modern thinkers)[247] are sceptical about the philosophical validity of ideas which are often linked with subjectivity in modern thought. These include the ideas that we are unified centres of consciousness (and have incorrigible access to our mental states) and that we have a uniquely first-personal viewpoint.[248] This scepticism about subjectivity is coupled with a commendation of the kind of philosophy of mind found in ancient thinkers such as Aristotle, in which (they maintain) psychological states are analysed in terms which do not involve the notion of the self-conscious, 'I'-centred subject.[249] But is this view credible? Is it not more plausible to assume that the idea of subjectivity is a universally available human concept? More specifically, can we not find in at least some ancient theories what can reasonably be characterized as a subjectivist strand, implying that the idea of subjectivity was, indeed, an available one in Graeco-Roman thought? This, in effect, is the claim made by Gail Fine, in several recent, powerfully argued, discussions. Her claims are based mainly on evidence for the thinking about the theory of knowledge of a fourth-century post-Socratic group, the Cyrenaics, and of the Pyrrhonian Sceptics, for which our main source is Sextus Empiricus (second century AD). These theories, while falling broadly within the period of thought covered in this book, have not been central to my enquiry so far; and a full response to her arguments is not appropriate here. But her claims pose a serious challenge for the kind of approach being taken in this book. So I discuss some of the issues she raises for the historical study of the idea of subjectivity, after locating her challenge in its scholarly context.[250]

I begin by noting some relevant features of these ancient theories, taken together with a line of thought in the first part of Plato's *Theaetetus* that seems partly to anticipate their approach. The shared idea—in broad terms—is that we do not have knowledge of the truth about the world; all we have access to is how things appear to us; more precisely, in some formulations, how things appear to *me*, or to *me at any one time*. The version found in the *Theaetetus* is, in some ways, the most extreme. It is suggested that there are no independently existing objects or qualities but only products of a particular perceptual encounter between a perceiver and an object of perception. Hence, 'what we

[247] See e.g. Davidson (2001), ch. 3 on 'the myth of the subjective', esp. 51–2 (also chs. 1–6).

[248] See Smith and Jones (1986), ch. 15, esp. 216–19; Wilkes (1988), chs. 6–7, esp. 224–7, both directed especially against the conception of subjectivity advanced by Nagel (1974).

[249] See Smith and Jones (1986), ch. 6; Wilkes (1988), 209–14. See the survey of scholars holding this type of view in 6.2 above, text to nn. 28–9; also Gill (1991), 168–71, (1996*b*), 41–5.

[250] I am most grateful to Gail Fine for helpful comments on an earlier version of this section. Of course, this does not mean that she is responsible for the account of her views I offer here.

naturally call a particular colour is neither that which impinges nor that which is impinged upon, but something that has come into being between the two, and which is private to the individual percipient (*hekastō(i) idion*)' (153e7–154a3, trans. Levett in Cooper 1997). Socrates reiterates the point that perceptions are private to individual observers, or, as it is sometimes put, to 'me' or what is 'mine'.[251] However, as the full implications are drawn from the position being examined, it is stressed that we cannot properly even speak of 'me' or 'mine' or of an individual perceiver, if this is taken to signify that there is a stable entity on either side of the encounter. There are no permanent or unchanging factors in perception but only a series of localized encounters between perpetually changing partners (182d–183b).

The Cyrenaics, active in the later fourth century BC, are best known for a version of hedonism; but they also adopted an epistemological position according to which '*pathē* ("experiences") alone are apprehensible'. Put more precisely, '*pathē* alone are apprehended and they are infallible; of the items that have produced the *pathē*, none is either apprehensible or infallible'.[252] As in the *Theaetetus*, this involves the claim of the privacy of our own experiences.

> Everyone grasps his own *pathē*. Whether a particular *pathos* comes to him and his neighbour from something white neither he nor his neighbour can say, since neither receives the other's *pathos*. Since there are no *pathē* common to us all, it is rash to say that what appears thus-and-so to me also appears thus-and-so to my neighbour.

This is coupled with a conception of language according to which the names which we assign to things are common (*koina*) but the *pathē* corresponding to those names are private (*idia*).[253]

There are similarities between these positions and that of the Pyrrhonian Sceptics, as presented by Sextus Empiricus. Sceptics are presented as searching for truth about the world, but prevented from determining what is true by the conflicting appearances that the world presents, including the conflicting appearances that different people have concerning the same object. The Sceptics hold, in contrast to most other Hellenistic–Roman schools, that there is no convincing criterion for establishing the truth when appearances

[251] See *Tht.* 160c4–5 ('for me and no one else'), c7–8 ('my reality'), 'perceptions that are private to each of us' (166c3–4).

[252] D.L. 2.92; Sextus Empiricus (S.E.), *Against the Mathematicians* (*M.*), 7.191; for translations and discussion see Brunschwig (1999), 256. Brunschwig translates *pathē* as 'feelings' but the Greek terms is broader or more open in meaning, referring to anything experienced or undergone. The translation 'feelings' might seem to beg the question at issue, how far the Cyrenaics are concerned with (what we call) 'subjective' responses.

[253] S.E. *M.* 7.197, trans. Brunschwig (1999), 254, but replacing his 'feeling(s)' with *pathos*/*pathē*; also S.E. *M.* 7.198, on which see Tsouna (1998*b*), 246–7.

conflict. So Sceptics are forced to suspend judgement, at least about what is true in reality. However, they accept the validity of their own appearances—indeed, they regard this acceptance as inevitable—while denying that this gives them a basis for beliefs or knowledge about what is really the case. Hence:

we do not overthrow the things which lead us, without our willing it, to assent in accordance with passive impressions—and these are the things which are apparent...For example, it appears to us that honey sweetens...but whether...it is actually sweet is something we investigate: and this is not what is apparent but something said about what is apparent.[254]

Clearly, there are similarities between these three positions; and all of them might be characterized as involving 'subjectivity' in some sense. Recurrent themes are the privacy of perceptions, feelings, or appearances and the idea that these experiences are 'incorrigible' in their content, that is, not open to correction by reference to a norm external to the perceiver.[255] How far can these positions be seen as influencing each other and forming part of a larger intellectual tradition? One relevant point is that the theory examined in the *Theaetetus* is not one that Plato's Socrates positively adopts but is explicitly constructed for dialectical purposes, as a fusion of Protagorean relativism and Heraclitean flux-doctrine, and is eventually shown to be self-contradictory.[256] However, if this section of Plato's dialogue *does* embody a type of subjectivism, that is in itself significant; also Plato's presentation of this theory may have been influential on these later ideas. The *Theaetetus* was a widely studied text in the Hellenistic–Roman period, especially in the ('Academic') version of scepticism dominant in Plato's school between the third and first centuries BC, which in turn influenced Sextus' type of scepticism.[257] This line of argument in the *Theaetetus* was known to Sextus Empiricus,[258] who is our main source for Pyrrhonian Scepticism, and could also have been known by the Cyrenaics, a school tracing their origins from Socrates.[259] The links between the Cyrenaics and Pyrrhonian Scepticism are much closer. Sextus is the principal source on the Cyrenaics and explicitly discusses their relation-

[254] S.E. *Outlines of Pyrrhonism* (*PH*), 1.19–20, trans. Everson (1991*a*), 126–7.

[255] On the possible senses of 'subjectivity' see text to nn. 280–6 below.

[256] See Burnyeat (1982), 4–14 (page references to original journal article), (1990), 7–31, 39–42.

[257] On the influence of *Tht.*, see Sedley (1996), referring especially to the partly extant commentary on *Tht.* which he dates in the 1st c. BC (83–4). On the Pyrrhonian Sceptics and their links with Academic Sceptics, see, in outline, LS 71–2.

[258] See *PH* 1.216, *M.* 7.389.

[259] The theory outlined here is generally ascribed to Aristippus the Younger, active in the later 4th c. BC, and grandson of Aristippus the follower of Socrates.

ship.[260] So these two approaches form a 'tradition', in this limited sense, with the *Theaetetus* as a well-known forerunner.

I noted earlier that these theories seem, on the face of it, to express—or perhaps to introduce—ideas that strike modern readers as subjectivist in approach. But does this impression stand up to examination? Can we really find here an anticipation of the focus on subjectivity in modern, post-Cartesian thought? This question has, in fact, been actively pursued in scholarship of the last twenty years. The terms of debate have largely been set by a wide-ranging and suggestive article by Myles Burnyeat (1982). Burnyeat's central thesis was that Descartes's sceptical strategy was more radical than any ancient version of scepticism, in that he questioned the very existence of the external world as well as our ability to gain knowledge of, or determine the truth about, this world. Also, Descartes's response to his own sceptical doubt, the claim that the only secure basis for knowledge is the conviction that 'I am', elaborated as the claim that 'I' am a thinking thing, has no parallel in ancient thought. More broadly, Burnyeat argued that the modern contrast, developed in philosophy since Descartes, between an inner world of subjective experience, to which we have privileged access, and an objective, external world has no real equivalent in ancient philosophy. Even theories such as those outlined earlier (in Plato's *Theaetetus*, and that of the Cyrenaics and Pyrrhonian Sceptics) are, actually, realist or objectivist in assuming that what is at issue is our knowledge of the real world, and not our access to a distinct sphere of subjective experience.[261]

In maintaining this thesis, Burnyeat (1982: 32, his italics) poses three salient questions bearing on the relationship between ancient and modern philosophy:

(1) How did it come about that philosophy accepted the idea that *truth* can be obtained without going outside subjective experience?
(2) When and why did philosophers first lay claim to *knowledge* of their own subjective states?
(3) When and why did one's own *body* become for philosophy a part of the external world?

The answer to all these questions, for Burnyeat, centred on Descartes's innovations, and he defined in this way the key contrast between ancient and modern thought. In a thorough re-examination of the same material, Stephen Everson queries and refines, but then reasserts, Burnyeat's claim that

[260] See e.g. S.E. *PH* 1.215.

[261] Burnyeat (1982), esp. 11–14, 23–9, 32–40. For this summary, cf. Gill (1996*b*), 409; on Descartes's argument, see 6.2 above, text to nn. 12–13, also Everson (1991*a*), 122–3.

there is a radical difference between the ancient and the Cartesian standpoint. Everson questions whether Burnyeat's first two questions succeed in pinpointing the essential contrast. The Cyrenaics and Sceptics *do* claim that they have knowledge—or at least apprehension—of their feelings or appearances. They also regard themselves as having inner or privileged access to these feelings or appearances and to that degree their views seem at least close to that of thinkers in the post-Cartesian approach.[262] But this apparent similarity is illusory. Even more explicitly than Burnyeat, Everson stresses that the subjective–objective distinction is not drawn in the ancient framework and that Cyrenaic feelings and Pyrrhonian appearances are not 'subjective' states in the modern, post-Cartesian sense but reflect the fundamentally realist or objectivist outlook of ancient thought[263]

He supports this view especially by arguing that the mental–physical contrast does not operate for the Cyrenaics and Sceptics in the way it does in Cartesian thought. Also, these theories share the standard ancient view that perceptions reflect facts about the world—although they refrain from claiming knowledge about *what* these facts are. Thus, for the Cyrenaics, for instance, 'it is possible to say infallibly and incontrovertibly that we are whitened or sweetened—but that the thing which brings about the affection [or feeling, *pathos*] is white or sweet, it is not possible to show'.[264] Whatever model of perception the Cyrenaics presuppose, to say 'we are whitened' seems to imply a physical process and one that is, in principle, produced by a physical external object ('that which brings about the affection') even if they deny that we can securely say whether that object is white.[265] Analogously, for the Sceptics, differences in 'appearances' may be seen as the result of physiological differences between different people or parts of the body or types of animal, thus presupposing that appearances reflect the impact of an external object, even though the appearances do not confer knowledge of the nature of that object (136–40). Hence, the radical gulf presupposed in post-Cartesian thought between an inner, mental, subjective realm and an outer, physical, objective one fails to fit the categories of these ancient theories. The contrast

[262] Everson (1991*a*), 127–8, 133–4, 136–7, 139–40. Hence, his comment (130) on S.E. *M.* 7.196 (cited above): 'At first sight, it would be difficult to read this as anything other than an argument for the privacy, and hence subjectivity, of experience'.

[263] Everson (1991*a*), 141–2. Everson presents his view as a revision of Burnyeat (1982: 32–3), on the assumption that Burnyeat ascribes to the ancient theories the idea of subjective states (though not that these states constitute a source of knowledge of truth). I think Burnyeat also denies a role to subjectivity in ancient thought, and that Everson is thus restating his view. See also on Burnyeat's position text to nn. 277–9 below.

[264] Everson (1991*a*), 129, including his translation of S.E. *M.* 7.192.

[265] Everson (1991*a*), 130–2. To this extent, the Cyrenaics share a widely held view in the 4th and 3rd BC, that perception is produced by an external object (Everson, 132–4).

with modern ideas is not limited to subjectivity as defined by Descartes's mental–physical dualism. Everson also argues that we can find no ancient equivalent for, for instance, Nagel's characterization of subjectivity in terms of a distinctive and irreducibly first-personal 'point of view', which makes it impossible for us to imagine 'what it is like to be a bat' even if we have a complete knowledge of the bat's psychophysical nature. This is, again, because the ancient theories do not posit an epistemological or ontological gap between subjective experience and physical, external states which needs to be bridged. To this degree, the idea of subjectivity does not figure in these ancient theories at all.[266]

Everson's line of argument is supported by a discussion by Voula Tsouna, which also considers the same three theories as those outlined here.[267] Tsouna takes up the question why these ancient theories, despite positing in some sense privacy of experience, do not give rise to the problem of the existence of other minds. This problem arises in Cartesian thought because the individual subject has incorrigible (first-personal) access to her own mental states but not to those of other people. Hence, the existence of other minds, as well as that of the external world as a whole, can be called into question in Cartesian thought. In the case of the Cyrenaic and Sceptic theories, Tsouna's response, like Everson's, is to say that the Cartesian problem does not arise because the categories of those theories cut across the Cartesian mind–body distinction; hence, for instance, the privacy of Cyrenaic 'feelings' is not that of private *minds*, in a Cartesian sense.[268] Other scholars too have accepted the main thrust of Burnyeat's view,[269] so that, until recently, there has seemed to be rather general agreement on the topic.

This consensus has now been challenged by Gail Fine.[270] Her discussions constitute both a searching critique of those holding this view, especially Burnyeat, and a detailed re-examination of the relevant theories as they bear on this issue. The nub of her position, I think, is this. In the Cyrenaics, and, arguably, Sextus, we find the claim that the only basis for belief, knowledge, and

[266] Everson (1991*a*), 140–5, referring to Nagel (1974).

[267] Tsouna (1998*b*); her account of Cyrenaic thought is based on Tsouna (1998*a*). She refers to Burnyeat (1982) in her (1998*b*), 260 n. 19, and to Everson (1991*a*) in her (1998*a*).

[268] Tsouna (1998*b*), esp. 250–3, 258–9. In the first part of the *Theaetetus*, the unbridged gap is between the world as it seems to a perceiver (at any one time) and as it is in reality; there is no special problem of the existence of other minds, as distinct from that of the knowability of states of affairs in general (253–7).

[269] See e.g. McDowell (1986); Forster (1989); Hankinson (1995); Mates (1996).

[270] Fine (2003*b*) tackles the question of the relationship between ancient and modern thought on subjectivity, with reference to both the Cyrenaics and Sceptics. Fine (2003*a*) focuses on the question whether we find scepticism about the external world in Sextus; Fine (2004) overlaps in scope with (2003*b*), but is limited to the Cyrenaics.

truth is constituted by our own appearances. Fine suggests that (using various criteria for 'subjectivity'), this amounts to the thesis, first, that we have subjective states and, second, that these subjective states constitute the only secure basis for knowledge of truth.[271] Therefore, Burnyeat's view that Descartes was the first person to maintain this thesis is wrong; more generally, he is wrong in denying the relevance to ancient thought of the contrast between the private world of subjective experience and the external, objective world.

In the case of the Cyrenaics, Fine presents her case as a relatively straightforward one, in that their conception of 'appearances' is, in a clear sense, 'subjective'. Their statements imply that we have incorrigible access to mental states, and they also clearly regard appearances as the only basis of knowledge of truth.[272] The main obstacle she confronts is Everson's argument that Cyrenaic perceptions, because they are conceived in physical terms, are not subjective.[273] In the case of the Sceptic Sextus, Fine acknowledges that her case is a harder one. It is less clear in what sense his conception of appearances is subjective.[274] However, as Fine points out, the Sceptics 'say what is apparent to themselves and report their own affections without holding opinions, affirming nothing about external objects' (S. *PH* 1.15, trans. Fine 2003*a*: 369). Fine argues that this procedure (described in a number of passages) amounts to the claim that we have a radically first-personal stance, involving privileged access to our own subjective states (2003*a*: 369–75). It might be argued that the Sceptics cannot be said to accept the validity of *subjective* beliefs or knowledge because they do not accept the validity of beliefs or knowledge *at all*. But, Fine argues, Sextus accepts the validity of *some* types of belief, namely 'assent to the affections (*pathē*) forced upon them by appearances'.[275] She also maintains, more speculatively, that Sextus does not disown—and so, by implication, accepts—the Cyrenaic thesis that 'only

[271] On her criteria for subjectivity, see (2003*b*), 193–4 and text to nn. 280–2 below; on the application of these marks of subjectivity to specific ancient theories, see below.

[272] See Fine (2003*b*), 201–6, esp. 206, referring to S.E. *M.* 7.191–2. This includes the statement (in the reading she follows) that: 'it is possible to assert infallibly (*adiapseustōs*) *and truly* (*alēthōs*) and certainly (*bebaiōs*) and incorrigibly (*anexelenktōs*) that we are whitened' (her translation, 202, italics added).

[273] Fine (2003*b*), 201–6, also (2004), 390–4; on Everson (1991*a*), see text to nn. 263–6 above. Fine (2003*b*: 204) points out that some modern theories see materialism as compatible with subjectivity; so, even if Cyrenaic *pathē* are physical, this does not rule out the idea of subjectivity.

[274] We do not find, for instance, an explicit equivalent to the Cyrenaic view that feelings are private, not common (see S.E. *M.* 196–7, cited at text to n. 253 above), though this is implied in the Sceptics' stress on the point that differences between people entail different appearances (S.E. *PH* 1.87).

[275] S.E. *PH* 1.13, trans. Fine (2003*a*: 372); the beliefs presented as invalid are based on 'assent to some unclear object of investigation in the sciences' (*PH* 1.13). As Fine recognizes, interpretation of this passage is difficult and some scholars take it as ruling out the validity of beliefs as such. See Fine (2003*a*), 370–5, also Everson (1991*a*), 125.

affections are known'[276] On this basis, Fine maintains that we can find in Sextus, as well as the Cyrenaics, at the least what she calls the 'core conception of External World Scepticism'. According to this conception, the mind is treated as 'the locus of subjective states' to which we have 'privileged access', while judgement is suspended 'about whether any inferences from claims about one's subjective states to anything else are justified' (2003*a*: 380). Thus, the contrast between an inner realm of subjective states (which may be seen as providing knowledge) and an outer world about which we suspend judgement is not an innovation of Descartes, as Burnyeat argues, but is already present in the Cyrenaics and Sextus.

Fine's claims are likely to attract responses which discuss in detail the ancient theories on which she bases her thesis. My response focuses on the implications of her procedure for the general question of whether or not we can find the idea of subjectivity in the ancient material. First, however, I make a more localized point. She maintains that Burnyeat (1982) is self-contradictory in suggesting, on the one hand, that Sextus sees appearances as subjective experiences and, on the other, that the subjective–objective distinction was an innovation of Descartes.[277] I find this criticism of Burnyeat unpersuasive. Her view that Burnyeat attributes subjectivity to Sextus' appearances is based especially on a (rather compressed) footnote in which he says that, for Sextus, statements about appearances have 'incorrigibility' (1982, 39 n. 53). Burnyeat refers back to a previous comment (p. 26): '[Statements about appearances] are immune from enquiry (*azētētos*)... because they make no claim as to objective fact. They simply record the sceptic's present experience... leaving it open whether external things really are as they appear to him to be'. Fine takes Burnyeat to be suggesting in these passages that Sextus holds the view that we have first-personal authority and are incorrigible about our experiences, which is a standard mark of subjectivity. She finds a contradiction with Burnyeat's main claim that views of the latter type form part of Descartes's innovative strategy. Perhaps Burnyeat's wording was rather unguarded, at least in the footnote.[278] But I see little doubt what his overall thesis is.

[276] Fine (2003*a*), 380 (see also 379–81), and (2003*b*), 207–8, referring esp. to S.E. *PH* 1.215, and acknowledging that her view is highly conjectural.

[277] See esp. Fine (2003*b*), 194–9, where she offers seven possible ways of interpreting Burnyeat's view (though it seems rather clear to me that his position is her (*C*), combined with (*F*), but without the assumption that the ancients operate with the concept of the subjective at all). See also Fine (2003*a*), 374–8, and (2004), 387–90.

[278] Burnyeat (1982), 39 n. 53, might appear to say that Sextus anticipated Descartes in 'the idea that we have incorrigible knowledge of our own subjective states'; but Burnyeat's point, I think, is, rather, that Sextus anticipates Descartes in the idea of 'incorrigibility' (of statements about appearances), whereas Descartes innovates in seeing appearances (conceived as subjective) as the basis of knowledge of truth.

Knowledge and truth are seen as matters of (what we call) objective fact, which belong to a public arena, about which there can be shared enquiry and dispute. Sextus—who, in Burnyeat's opinion, denies the possibility of knowledge—regards statements about appearances as 'immune from enquiry' because they make no claim to objective truth, not because appearances have a privileged status as the bearers of subjective truth.[279]

My own response to this debate is twofold. First, I re-examine the question of the sense in which these ancient theories presuppose or introduce—what we call—subjectivity. Given the larger aims of this study, I am especially interested in senses of 'subjectivity' which are rich or complex enough to constitute what one might call a subjective sense of selfhood or personhood. Second, I reconsider the question of the larger conceptual framework, or context of debate, within which these theories seem to be framing their contribution, in particular, whether this framework or context seems to be conceived in objective or subjective terms.

How, in the case of such material, should we set about trying to establish the relevance of the idea of subjectivity? In (2003*b*), 193–4, where this question is tackled explicitly, Fine begins by offering what she calls 'a working account of subjectivity'. She lists psychological phenomena about whose status (as 'subjective states') there is 'rough agreement': these are: 'being in pain, having a sensation, experiencing something, and being appeared to'. She also lists criteria for defining the subjective character of such phenomena: these include 'characteristic phenomological feel' (Nagel), 'availability to introspection' (McDowell), and the idea that the subject has privileged access to her mental states and that this access is 'incorrigible'.[280] She then suggests that, 'if someone discusses appropriate examples . . . and describes them along the lines just mentioned', this is sufficient to establish belief in the subjective status. Subsequently, she takes the combination of (*a*) one of the relevant types of phenomena and (*b*) one or more of the criteria to establish the presence of the idea of subjectivity either in the ancient theories or in a modern scholarly discussion. This procedure raises several methodological questions.[281] But, initially, I focus

[279] Burnyeat (1982), 26. Fine (2003*a*), 375–6, notes the kind of view outlined here, and lays less stress on Burnyeat's alleged inconsistency than in (2003*b*). But her argument assumes (I think, wrongly) that Burnyeat holds that Sextus sees appearances as subjective; see Fine (2003*a*), nn. 20, 68, 78.

[280] Fine's references include Nagel (1974); McDowell (1986); and Shoemaker (1991). See also Fine (2004), 384–5.

[281] Her use of examples seems to imply that some phenomena *must* be explained in subjective terms; but at least some (objectivist) modern theories would deny this, e.g. those of Smith and Jones (1986); Wilkes (1988), cited in text to nn. 248–9 above; also Davidson (n. 248). Fine (2003*b*), 216 n. 18, notes this issue indirectly, in connection with the question whether subjectivity is compatible with functionalism or materialism.

on two points. Fine here assembles a number of criteria, some quite complex in formulation, without indicating how this list might be structured into more basic or complex senses of 'subjectivity'. Also, she draws on ideas about subjectivity from the whole range of post-Cartesian theorizing up to the present, although the main thrust of her argument is centred on arguing that the ancient theories anticipated Descartes's theory, specifically.[282]

My first move is to present criteria for subjectivity in a way that attempts to distinguish simpler from more complex senses and to indicate their interrelationship. I begin by outlining basic or 'thin' senses of 'subject', which could, perhaps, be seen as relevant to any psychological framework, not just specifically 'subjective' ones.[283] This term may mean no more than the seat or locus of a specific psychological process or experience, for instance, perceiving.[284] But, more typically, I think, it is taken to signify the (at least relatively) unified centre of a set of coordinated psychological processes or experiences. The question of the nature and degree of this unity or coordination is a recurrent question in psychology, both in ancient and modern thought. This question can be raised in synchronic or diachronic terms (that is, at any one time or over time); the question of unity thus converges with that of identity or sameness. The general points just made could apply to psychological theories of various types and periods. I now turn to senses of 'subject' that are more specifically linked with the notion of 'subjectivity'. The two main characteristics of the 'subject', from Descartes onwards, are self-consciousness and 'I'-centredness or the first-personal viewpoint.[285] The question of the unity or identity of the subject is, typically, linked with one or other or both of these features of subjectivist thought. For instance, Locke's definitions of 'self' and 'person', cited earlier (332 above) presuppose the diachronic extension of the subject as a locus of unified self-consciousness. The first-personal viewpoint can be tied, simply to 'indexicality' ('I' am *this* person *here now*') or to more complex features, including (first-personal) memory, imagination, attitudes, and judgements. The first-personal viewpoint can be seen as closely linked with consciousness or self-consciousness, as, for instance, by McDowell

[282] See (2003*b*), 209–14, where her concern is with distinguishing Descartes's theory from McDowell's account, not with McDowell's theory as such. See also (2003*a*), 341–2, 376–83; in this focus on Descartes, she is, of course, responding to Burnyeat's view.

[283] It could be argued that the term 'subject' is so closely linked with the 'subjectivist' strand in modern thought that there are no such neutral senses. In that case, these basic senses should be seen as characterizations of 'mind' or 'psychological centre'.

[284] That is, that which 'underlies' the process; on the etymology of the English term, see n. 17 above.

[285] To say this is not to treat as settled the point at issue, whether these kinds of subjectivity are *also* relevant to other (for instance, ancient) psychological frameworks. On Descartes's contribution, see 6.2 above, text to nn. 12–13.

or Nagel (thinkers cited by Fine).[286] Alternatively, the first-personal viewpoint, broadly understood, can be seen as expressed in subconscious forms of life, such as dreams and fantasies, as in Wollheim (1984). The features of incorrigibility and privileged access are also, typically, associated with self-consciousness and the first-personal view.

If we turn back to the ancient material from this set of criteria, set out in this way, what is striking is the limited nature of the conceptualization of subjectivity. The clearest feature in the ancient material, as already underlined, is that of incorrigibility and privileged access. This kind of feature can be seen in all three theories discussed here, especially that of the Cyrenaics.[287] But what can we say about the content of the idea of 'subject' implied by the theories? It is not clear there is anything more than a basic or 'thin' sense involved. Is self-consciousness present? We can, of course, *supply* this as an implied idea: how else can the Cyrenaics, for instance, say, 'Everyone grasps his own *pathē*'.[288] (One has to grasp first that they are *his own* experiences.) But the focus of these theories is not on coordinated functions or capacities such as self-consciousness, which implies at least an 'I' or mind which is conscious of some other mental state, or at least conscious of itself. Rather, the focus is on perception, understood in a more or less complex way, as a sensation, 'feeling', or 'being appeared to', but taken largely in isolation from other psychological functions or capacities.[289] What about the first-personal viewpoint? The *Theaetetus* sometimes refers to perceptions as 'mine' or 'for me'; the Cyrenaics stress that feelings are 'private', not shared with other individuals; for the Sceptics, what matters are the specific observer's (often conflicting) appearances, not an allegedly external standard.[290] But what does this terminology imply? Again, we can say very little, beyond noting the idea of privacy or differentiation between one person's perceptions, feelings, or appearances and another's. The kind of theorizing about the first-personal viewpoint (by McDowell or Nagel, for instance) used by Fine (2003b: 193) to illustrate the idea of subjectivity finds little echo here. Even Descartes's 'I', as a locus of self-consciousness, cannot be securely linked with any determinate feature of the theories. Relevant too is the absence of stress on

[286] Fine (2003*b*), 193; on the linkage between the first-personal viewpoint and self-consciousness in Frankfurt's theory of personhood, see 6.2 above, text to n. 21.

[287] See text to nn. 252–3 above.

[288] S.E. *M.* 7.196, cited at text to n. 253 above.

[289] On the nature and scope of these functions, see further (on the Cyrenaics), Brunschwig (1999), 254–6; (on the Sceptics), Fine (2004), 347–56; on both, Everson (1991*a*), 129–32, 135–40. The use of the term 'function' is not meant to signify an implicit acceptance of the modern theory of 'functionalism'; 'function' or 'capacity' stands simply for some such ancient term as *dunamis*.

[290] See e.g. Pl. *Tht.* 160c4–5, 7–8, 166c3–4; S.E. *M.* 7.196–8, *PH* 1.87.

the diachronic unity of the subject. In the *Theaetetus*, indeed, the 'subject' (in the sense of individual perceiver) is shown, under investigation, to break down into a series of isolated encounters between different partners (perceiver-perceived, 182a–183b). This extreme negation of diachronic unity is not found in the later theories. None the less, the focus is on specific occurrences of feelings or appearances taken in isolation; and, in the Cyrenaic theory, in particular, as I suggest shortly, this episodic character may be especially significant. In all these respects, anyone searching in these ancient theories for a rich or complex exploration of the notion of 'subject', as we now understand this term, will find rather limited and unrewarding material.

If we accept this account of the ancient material, how should we explain it? One response, in line with Fine's approach, would be to say that these ancient theories concentrate on the bare fact of subjectivity or the minimum needed to establish this fact, namely the epistemic preconditions of privileged access or incorrigibility. The further elaboration of subjectivity in post-Cartesian philosophy can be seen as a response to a different conceptual situation. But, one might say, this does not mean that ancient thought did not, in its own way, define the essential core of subjectivity, namely, the definition of a realm of 'private' perceptions or appearances, not open to correction by external standards. This response would not be unreasonable; but it could be criticized for assuming—unnecessarily—that the idea of subjectivity is part of the standard furniture of any conceptual framework.[291] Another response is possible, and one which would more plausibly explain several features just noted of the ancient theories.

The starting-point of this response is the hypothesis that the ancient theory of knowledge is conceived, uniformly, in objective-participant terms.[292] The characteristic move, from at least Socrates onwards, is to seek to define common standards or criteria for knowledge of truth, conceived as objective. To say that the framework is objective-*participant* does not mean that knowledge of truth is understood as intersubjective. Rather, the normal approach (displayed in the Platonic dialogues, for instance) is that of seeking through shared enquiry and debate to establish what should be universally recognized as common standards of knowledge of truth.[293] A related feature of standard ancient approaches to the theory of knowledge is this. The achievement of knowledge, to put the point very broadly, is conceived as dependent on the

[291] As pointed out in n. 281 above, some contemporary theories do without the idea of subjectivity altogether.

[292] This response is, obviously, more in line with the approaches of Burnyeat (1982), as interpreted here, and Everson (1991*a*).

[293] See further Gill (1996*a*), 284–6, (1996b), 279–87; on the question of the relevance of intersubjectivism to Platonic thought, see also Rowe (2005).

effective coordination of interconnected psychological (or psychophysical) functions. In the empirical approach, in Aristotle, for instance, the achievement of knowledge depends on the coordination of a series of functions, including perception, memory, 'appearance' (*phantasia*), and belief.[294] In Plato's idealist theory, in the *Republic*, for example, knowledge also depends on the transition from perception and belief to knowledge, but with crucial intermediate or intervening roles played by the kind of understanding conferred by mathematics and dialectic.[295]

This characterization of standard approaches in the ancient theory of knowledge is, obviously, very generalized. But it is sufficient for my immediate aim, which is to identity a determinate role for the ancient theories discussed in this section. These theories, together with Academic Scepticism, play a dissident or challenging role within a body of theory which is, typically, positive or constructive.[296] They exercise their dissident or challenging role by denying or questioning key features of the process by which other theories construct their positive accounts. But they do so—I suggest—within the objective-participant conceptual framework which they share with the theories they challenge, rather than by adopting or introducing a different—subjective, or subjective-individualist—approach. This point bears on both aspects of the standard ancient approach to the theory of knowledge. There is a rejection of, or challenge to, the idea of common or shared standards of knowledge of truth and the idea that knowledge can be based on the effective coordination of psychological or psychophysical functions. But this challenge is a fundamentally negative or questioning one, and does not give rise to a radically new line of approach (a subjective one). There is a sharp contrast to the way in which Descartes's style of sceptical enquiry gave rise, under quite different conceptual and cultural conditions, to the idea of subjectivity and the body of modern theory associated with that idea.[297] The very limited content or significance that we can give to the notion of 'subject' or 'subjectivity' in these ancient theories, by contrast with the post-Cartesian approach, is an indication that the essential move made in these ancient theories is a negative one, and not the exploration of a new outlook.

[294] See e.g. (on relevant aspects of the coordination of functions), Arist. *A. Po.* 1.18, *Metaph.* 1.1, $980^{b}25$–$^{a}1$, *NE* 6.6, 7.3, $1147^{b}4$–5, *de An.* 3.3, $428^{a}19$–24. See further C. C. W. Taylor (1990).

[295] See e.g. Pl. *R.* 508d–513e, 531c–534c. See further Fine (1990), and, on the role of mathematics, Burnyeat (2000).

[296] This body of theory is positive in asserting that knowledge of truth, defined according to common norms or criteria, can—in principle at least—be achieved by the appropriate coordination of functions.

[297] On those conditions and the progressive emergence of subjective conceptions of self, see, in outline, 6.2 above, text to nn. 11–21.

This view can be illustrated by reference to some of the passages cited earlier to introduce these theories. In the *Theaetetus*, for instance, it is claimed at one stage that 'what we naturally call a particular colour is neither that which impinges nor that which is impinged upon, but something that has come into being between the two, and which is private to the individual percipient (*hekastō(i) idion*)' (153e7–154a3, trans. Levett in Cooper 1997). This is an idea which could have been developed in the direction of a subjective theory of perception; but, instead, the theory is presented as undermining any common or shared account of knowledge of truth, including any that Protagoras might have wanted to offer.[298] The same point might be made about the passage cited earlier as illustrating the Cyrenaic theory:

> Everyone grasps his own *pathē*. Whether a particular *pathos* comes to him and his neighbour from something white neither he nor his neighbour can say, since neither receives the other's *pathē*. Since there are no *pathē* common to us all, it is rash to say that what appears thus-and-so to me also appears thus-and-so to my neighbour.[299]

This positive claim, expanded elsewhere, could have been used as the basis of a full-scale account of individual subjectivity, for instance, by exploring the idea of the first-personal viewpoint. But, instead, it is used to draw the negative conclusion, that we have no 'common' or shared feelings, and therefore, as it is put earlier in the same passage, no 'common criterion' (of knowledge). Analogously, some at least of the 'conflicting appearances' which Sextus cites are conflicts between what appears to different people, or different animals.[300] Again, this point could have served as the basis for a theory of subjective individuation. But, instead, the idea is combined with that of conflict within the appearances of a single person to support the negative claim that knowledge (at least as standardly conceived)[301] is unavailable.

A related emphasis in these theories is that perceptions, feelings, or appearances *cannot* be used as building-blocks in a coordinated set of functions taken, as a whole, to provide knowledge. The theory in the *Theaetetus* differs from the others in that it is, at least in the section combining Protagoreanism and Heracliteanism, a Platonic construction designed to make a negative point: that perception does not constitute knowledge.[302] But, at the same

[298] Pl. *Tht.* 154a–162a, 163a–171c; in other words, the theory of Protagoras, in so far as it claims to present a shared account of knowledge of truth, is shown to be 'self-refuting'.

[299] S.E. *M.* 7.196–7, trans. Brunschwig (1999), 254, 'feeling(s)' replaced by *pathos*/*ē*.

[300] See e.g. S.E. *PH* 1.87; also Everson (1991*a*), 135–40.

[301] For Fine's suggestion that a special kind of (subjective) knowledge, limited to appearances, is conceived as available in Scepticism, see text to n. 276 above.

[302] On this combination, see further Burnyeat (1990), 7–31, 39–42; Fine (1996). For the idea that the epistemological position of the historical Protagoras, which we can reconstruct (in part) from Pl. *Tht.*, is best understood as 'intersubjectivist', see Zilioli (2002).

time, perception, as characterized in the theory, is disabled from providing an element or component in a structure of processes or states accounting for knowledge. A comparable claim is made, in a less dialectical mode, by the Cyrenaics and Sextus. For the Cyrenaics, 'feelings (*pathē*) alone are apprehended and they are infallible'. This point, taken on its own, seems positive, but it is then coupled with the negative claim: 'of the items which have produced the *pathē*, none is either apprehensible or infallible'.[303] Analogously, for the Sceptics: 'it appears to us that honey sweetens . . . but whether . . . it is actually sweet is something we investigate: and this is not what is apparent but something said about what is apparent'.[304] Put positively, the thesis is that feelings or appearances are the only basis for knowledge (or, at least, 'apprehension'). But, put negatively—and the emphasis is often negative, especially for the Sceptics—these functions *cannot* be used as components in a positive account of how a structured set of psychological functions provides knowledge of truth.[305] The outcome is a critique of positive (objective-participant) models of knowledge, empirical or idealist, which are premised on the possibility of such a structured set of functions. It is a critique rather than a constructive exploration of subjective knowledge.

A related feature of the theories, linked with the last point, is the failure to develop an integrated picture of the person as a locus of coordinated functions. We may contrast with this absence the positive development in Cartesian and post-Cartesian theory of models of the subject as locus of self-consciousness, and in some cases of agency or will, or of a (sometimes multi-faceted) first-personal viewpoint.[306] This failure appears in its most extreme form when the combination of Protagorean and Heraclitean elements in Plato's *Theaetetus* is shown to lead to what is—in modern parlance—the dissolution of the subject. The perceiving person has neither synchronic cohesion nor diachronic identity; there are only localized encounters between mutable perceiver and perceived.[307] The Cyrenaic theory seems, in effect, to give a comparable picture of life as a series of episodic feelings, with no obvious structure among feelings at any one time or over time. It is plausible to connect this picture with the main features of the Cyrenaic ethical theory. Unlike virtually all other ethical theories, the Cyrenaics offered no general account of happiness, as the organizing goal of a human life; in effect, they simply advocated accumulating episodes of pleasure (conceived as 'smooth

[303] S.E. *M.* 7.191, trans. Brunschwig in Algra *et al.* (eds.) (1999), 256.

[304] S.E. *PH* 1.20, trans. Everson (1991*a*), 126.

[305] See, again, for possible qualifications to this view, text to n. 276 above.

[306] See 6.2 above, text to nn. 16–21.

[307] See e.g. Pl. *Tht.* 158e–160c, on discontinuities between 'Socrates ill' and 'Socrates well' or between versions of 'me' at different times and in different states.

movements'). In both aspects of the theory, we seem to lack any coherent picture of the person as a psychological subject or agent.[308] The Sceptical theory is different to some extent; its goal (of freedom from distress) depends for its achievement on drawing reasoned conclusions over time about the implications of conflicting appearances and on deliberately suspending judgement. But, although this goal is elaborated in certain ways, this is not done in a way that involves giving an extended account of the person as subject and locus of (subjective) appearances. The focus, again, is rather on the negation of other accounts of knowledge that imply, or are linked with, a model of the person as a coordinated set of functions.[309] There are, of course, modern accounts of the self or person which also stress the idea that we lack any coherent centre (Hume) or that we consist only of person-states and have no deep metaphysical personal identity (Parfit);[310] and it would be possible to argue that these ancient theories are comparable to these accounts.[311] However, an obvious difference is that these modern theories are conceived in a context of developed accounts of the person as subject or self, against which they react. Also, it is doubtful that the theories of Hume and Parfit count as *constructive* accounts of subjectivity, so this does not quite meet the present purpose.

There is, of course, much more that could be said, about these ancient theories and about their relationship to modern thought, including modern thought about selfhood and personal identity.[312] All I have tried to do is to indicate my reasons for being disinclined to adopt Fine's view that these ancient theories embody a subjectivist pattern of thought which is broadly comparable with that of Cartesian theory. Although her contributions to debate on this point are important and challenging, my view remains that an objective-participant approach offers the best framework for understanding these theories as well as other Classical and Hellenistic ones.

[308] See further Irwin (1991*a*); Annas (1993*b*), 37–9, 227–36, 329–30; Brunschwig (1999), 252–6; key relevant sources include D.L. 2.87–96; Eus. *PE* 14.18.31–2. For a challenge to the view that the Cyrenaic position derives from assumptions about personal identity, see Warren (2001*a*), 167–74, outlined in ch. 2 n. 221 above.

[309] See further Bett (forthcoming).

[310] Hume, *Treatise of Human Nature*, 1.4.6, repr. in Perry (1975), 161–72; Parfit (1971) and (1984), part 3, chs. 10–12.

[311] See Fine's (2003*a*: 367–8) comparison between Hume's thinking (on whether he is or has a self) and that of Sextus (on whether he is or has a soul), in connection with the question whether Sextus is an External World Sceptic or not.

[312] See also, on the relationship between ancient theory and modern theory of personal identity, 1.6 above, esp. text to nn. 298–307.

7

Literary Reception: Structured and Unstructured Selves

7.1 PRELIMINARIES

In this final chapter, I take up another type of issue raised by the preceding analysis of ideas about selfhood and personality in Hellenistic–Roman thought. The issue pursued here represents one aspect of a much larger topic. The larger topic is the question how far philosophical theories and issues about human personality relate to thought-forms and practices in other aspects of ancient culture of the time. One dimension of this question is the direct influence of philosophical ideas on other aspects of the culture, in a way that helps to shape, for instance, practical decision-making or the presentation of figures in works of literature. A related question is whether analogous perspectives and issues on this topic arise in both literature and philosophy in a given period, regardless of whether this involves direct influence in either direction. A further line of enquiry centres on the possible shaping influences, which might include socio-political or economic factors, on patterns of thinking about selfhood in both philosophy and literature.

There are several ways in which questions of this general type could be raised in connection with the main themes of this book. One would be to pursue in broader cultural terms the issues raised by the distinction drawn, in Chapter 6, between 'subjective-individualist' and 'objective-participant' conceptions of personality. In a previous book (1996*b*), I examined in some depth the relationship between—what I presented as—the objective-participant approach to personality in Homer and Greek tragedy, on the one hand, and Plato and Aristotle, on the other. There, my concern was with analogous thought-patterns, in poetry and in philosophy, rather than with direct influence in either direction. In the Hellenistic–Roman period, there is scope for a study centred wholly on this topic. This could embrace questions about direct influence, for instance, from philosophy to literature and vice versa, and also about analogous thought-patterns in philosophy, literature, and other forms of socio-cultural life. There has been, in fact, some scholarly discussion of this distinction or a related one (between 'character' and 'personality'), particularly in connection with Plutarch's biographies.[1] But this line of enquiry could be developed much further. As indicated here (especially in 6.2 and 6.5 above), there are important questions to be raised about the significance of these conceptions of selfhood for understanding the aims and methods of philosophical practical ethics and their role within the culture. Also, the ideas examined here provide the basis for exploring further the question sometimes posed of how far and in what sense 'individuality' and 'individualism' figure as salient ideals in Hellenistic and Roman social ethics, and whether what are sometimes taken as expressions of those ideals are better interpreted in objective-participant terms.[2] There has also been important recent work on social ethics in Epicureanism and Stoicism,[3] and also on the possible influence of this on practical decision-making and patterns of thought in Hellenistic–Roman culture.[4] The discussion of psycho-ethical ideals here, especially in Chapters 2, 4, and 6, could form the basis for further study of the relationship between philosophical norms of personality and Hellenistic–Roman social ethics more generally.

However, the question which I actually pursue in this chapter is more narrowly focused than those just outlined and more closely related to the main lines of argument in this book. My principal theme (the topic of Part I) has been the idea of the structured self in Stoicism and Epicureanism, centred on the combination of various types of holism or naturalism and 'Socratic' ethical claims. A related theme, important in both Parts I and II, has been the relationship between this conception of selfhood and other, part-based approaches, in earlier, contemporary, or later philosophy, especially in Plato and Middle Platonism. The issue broached in this chapter is this. Should we see these ideas and debates as restricted to philosophy or as ones which influence, or have analogues in, Hellenistic–Roman literature? In particular, can we discriminate in literature as well as philosophy between the features linked here with the idea of the structured self and those which reflect contrasting ways of thinking about human personality?

Even to pursue this, relatively limited, question as a whole would be a large undertaking, given the possible range of Hellenistic and Roman literature potentially relevant to the topic. So I focus on three examples or case-studies:

[1] See 7.2 below, esp. references in n. 12; also Levene (1997), esp. 132–6, applying a related distinction between 'analytic' and 'audience-based' reactions to the presentation of emotions in Roman historiography.

[2] For some relevant points, see 6.2 above, esp. text to nn. 7–8, 50–1, and 6.5, esp. text to nn. 172–81, 184–93.

[3] See, most recently, Warren (2004), ch. 5; Reydams-Schils (2005).

[4] See e.g. Sedley (1997*c*); Griffin (1986), (1995).

selected aspects of Plutarch's biographies or *Lives*, Senecan tragedy, and Virgil's *Aeneid*. I choose these examples because relevant aspects of these works have been studied in recent years in a way that enables us to specify with some precision possible links between philosophical ideas and literary characterization. There are two kinds of link I am concerned with. One is that in which we have grounds for seeing the direct influence of philosophy on literature. The other is that in which, regardless of influence, a determinate type of approach to personality is evident in literature, which resembles one or other of the philosophical patterns studied here.

I also choose these examples because they display differing approaches to a shared theme, and one which is of special relevance to this book. This is that of stability and disintegration of character, especially the disintegration of a relatively stable adult character. This theme raises a series of related questions. How is structure of character and the collapse of this structure understood in these literary works? What picture of human psychology and of ethical development is implied? What is the relationship between literary patterns of thought on this topic and the idea characterized here as the (Stoic–Epicurean) structured self, in its ideal and imperfect versions, or contrasting Platonic or Aristotelian ways of conceiving structure and collapse? As the material in this chapter indicates, the question of what constitutes stability of character, and what promotes or disrupts stability, are recurrent themes in Hellenistic–Roman literature as well as philosophy, and are related in various ways to the prevalent ideal of 'invulnerability' from internal or external collapse.[5] The present discussion represents a selective exploration of this terrain, centred on points of possible linkage between philosophical ideas and literary expression.

These examples are discussed, perhaps surprisingly, in reverse chronological order. There are two reasons for doing so. One is that the material involved presents what are, for this enquiry at least, interpretative issues of increasing complexity. The other is that the discussions of Plutarch and Seneca are intended to provide exemplification of two contrasting ways of understanding collapse of character, both of which are potentially relevant for understanding this theme in Virgil's *Aeneid*. Plutarch's *Lives* embody, I take it, in a relatively straightforward way a Platonic–Aristotelian (or Middle Platonic) pattern of thinking about ethical development and psychological stability and collapse. In Senecan tragedy, there is more room for debate about how far philosophical patterns are relevant. But, at least in the material discussed here, I think we can see a distinctively Stoic pattern of thought

[5] The role of this ideal in Hellenistic–Roman thought and culture still awaits systematic investigation; the present book offers material for doing so, especially in 2.2–3, 3.3, 4.3, and 4.5.

about psychological and ethical disintegration. There is yet more scope for argument about the nature and extent of philosophical influence on the portrayal of structure and collapse of character in Virgil's *Aeneid.* Indeed, the whole question of philosophical influence on Virgil's presentation of human psychology has been much debated recently, especially as regards the presentation of anger. I suggest that, underlying certain key aspects of the poem, we can see a considered blend or 'layering' of Platonic–Aristotelian and Stoic–Epicurean approaches. There is also, I think, a rather persistent tendency to give greater weight or emphasis to the Stoic–Epicurean mode than the Platonic–Aristotelian. Taken together, these literary examples provide an illuminating point of access to the question how far the philosophical ideas considered here (in particular, the contrast between holistic and part-based approaches to psychology) influence, or intersect with, thinking on human personality in other aspects of Hellenistic–Roman culture.

There are two features of my analysis that require special explanation. After discussing Plutarch's (Middle Platonic) understanding of stability and disintegration of character, I refer to the 'Plutarchean' approach in gauging the pattern of thinking found in Senecan tragedy and Virgil's *Aeneid.* Also, I sometimes discuss the sense in which these two types of literature present the 'biography' of their figures. In doing so, I am not ignoring the fact that Plutarch is the last, chronologically, of the three writers and that his work could not have influenced the earlier writers.[6] I am also fully aware of the difference in genre between the three types of literature discussed and the difference this may make to the presentation of character. The Plutarchean approach is taken, in discussion of the other works, as exemplary of a certain *type* of thinking about personality. The salient marks of this approach include a part-based psychological model and the assumption that ethical development depends on a combination of inborn nature, habituation, and reason. A further feature is that a person's character (and happiness or misery) is viewed in relation to the unfolding narrative of a human life. These marks can be contrasted with features of Stoic–Epicurean thinking already examined fully here: a holistic approach to psychology and a view of ethical development in which progress to perfect happiness—or slippage from this progress—is possible at any stage of life. This is linked with a conception of happiness as based on 'time-independent' perfection of character and not bound up so closely with the unfolding narrative of a human life.[7] Although the first set of

[6] The relative dates of their lives are: Virgil 70–19 BC, Seneca *c.*4 BC–AD 65, Plutarch *c.*AD 50–*c.*120.

[7] On relevant features of Hellenistic–Roman thought, see 2.2 above, esp. text to nn. 35–51, 2.3, esp. text to nn. 124–50, 207–9, 223–31, 3.2, esp. text to nn. 10–46, 75–7; also 7.2 below, text to nn. 14–18 on contrasting attitudes to the significance of the unfolding narrative of a life.

features noted are clearly displayed in Plutarchean biography, they are not, of course, peculiar to that genre.[8] They reflect, on the one hand, longstanding features of philosophical thought going back to Plato and Aristotle and, on the other, familiar dimensions of conventional thought in Hellenistic–Roman culture.[9] The 'Plutarchean' approach is thus used here to highlight, by contrast, the Stoic or Epicurean standpoint, and so to provide determinate reference-points against which to locate the thinking about character displayed in Seneca and Virgil.

A second aspect of my discussion which needs clarification is this. In considering these works of literature, I focus on the question whether their presentation of stability and disintegration of character seems to be informed by (roughly) Platonic–Aristotelian or Stoic–Epicurean patterns of thinking about selfhood. I do not take up the issue whether they are also shaped by other factors including genre, intertextual influences, or socio-political connotations. This is not because I do not think those other factors are important. Indeed, elsewhere (2004*a*), I have explored the interplay between possible philosophical models and intertextual or political influences on the presentation of character and passion in Virgil's *Aeneid.* My exclusion of these other aspects here is simply a by-product of the aims of this discussion. I want to explore the hypothesis that the presentation of structure and collapse of character in these literary works is informed by one or other (or both) of the main patterns of philosophical thinking examined here. This requires me to focus on this specific question; but it does not mean that I think this is the only significant factor, or that I fail to recognize that this factor is intertwined with others in the literary work and its reception.

7.2 PLUTARCH'S *LIVES*

Some years ago, I wrote an article (1983*b*) challenging the rather common assumption, at that time, that character, in the ancient world, was seen as inborn and unchanging, by contrast with the modern view that character develops. This assumption was taken to explain certain striking features of Greek or Roman historiography and biography, especially Tacitus' presentation of Tiberius as a person whose (unchanging) character was gradually

[8] The articles on 'Biography, Greek' and 'Biography, Roman' by Pelling in *OCD* bring out clearly the way in which ancient biography overlaps with other genres and is informed by well-marked Greek and Roman socio-cultural thought-patterns and practices.

[9] For instance, on 'vernacular' (conventional, non-philosophical) analogues for the Aristotelian approach to emotions, see further Braund and Gill (1997), introd., 7–8, 12–14.

revealed, rather than as someone who deteriorated in the course of his life.[10] One of the points I highlighted was the disparity between this scholarly assumption and the manifest interest, in Classical Greek and Hellenistic–Roman philosophy, in the development of character, both during childhood and adult life. I also suggested that the most important point of contrast, between ancient and modern approaches, did not centre on the question whether character did or did not develop in the course of one's life. It hinged, rather, on the contrast between a focus on making (broadly) moral judgements about a person's character, as shown in his life, taken as a whole, and on exploring, from the inside, as it were, the narrative of an individual's life, with a view to understanding the special, perhaps unique, character of this life. I described these two approaches as focused on 'character' and 'personality', respectively, and suggested that the first approach was typical of Greek and Roman biography and historiography, by contrast with at least some modern biography, including that written from a psychoanalytic standpoint.[11] The contrast drawn in (1983*b*) between 'character' and 'personality' represents an earlier version of the distinction between objective-participant and subjective-individualist conceptions of personality outlined in Chapter 6.[12]

There is, obviously, scope for debate about how far the contrast between character and personality, or between objective-participant and subjective-individualist conceptions of person, pinpoints the distinctive approach to character in Plutarch's *Lives*. Much depends, as Christopher Pelling brings out, in his discussions of the distinctions, on the precise significance attached to these ideas.[13] But I focus here on the first issue noted, that relating to character-development, and the significance of this question for understanding Plutarch's thinking about psychological stability and collapse. In the light of the treatment of ethical development in this book (especially Chapter 3), I would now draw a much sharper distinction than I did earlier (in 1983*b*) between two alternative ancient philosophical patterns. In one (Platonic–Aristotelian or Middle Platonic) pattern, character is analysed in terms of the interrelated effects of inborn nature, habituation, and reasoned choice on a personality conceived as a combination of rational and non-rational parts. In this pattern, it is generally assumed that character, both good and bad, once formed in this way, is relatively determinate and stable—though this does not mean that it has achieved complete stability. In an alternative (Stoic–Epicurean) pattern, the formation of character is conceived as the realization of the

[10] Tac. *Ann.* 6.51; for this scholarly assumption, see references in Gill (1983*b*), 469, 471.

[11] Gill (1983*b*), 469–78, referring to modern biographies by Lytton Strachey and Erikson (1958).

[12] See Gill (1983*b*), 470–2, also (1990*b*), 1–9, and 6.2 above, text to nn. 34–49.

[13] See Pelling (1990*a*), 228–35, (2002), 321–9. See also Duff (1999), 13 n. 3, 69–70, 228 n. 70.

(universal) natural capacity for perfection of character ('wisdom'). This involves the progressive development of the personality as a whole and not the shaping of independent (rational and non-rational) parts. For this pattern, as underlined earlier, all character-states which fall short of perfect wisdom are relatively incoherent and unstable, by comparison with the complete coherence and stability (and 'invulnerability') that is the mark of wisdom.[14]

In his essay *On Ethical Virtue*, discussed earlier (4.2–3), and to a large extent in his philosophical writings generally, Plutarch emerges as a committed exponent of the Platonic–Aristotelian pattern of thinking about psychology and character-development.[15] This way of thinking also, and explicitly, underlies his writing of the parallel lives of Greek and Roman statesmen, which can be seen as an extension of his concern with ethical education. Indeed, it is not difficult to see how adoption of the Platonic–Aristotelian pattern, with its focus on the way that interrelated factors shape a character, expressed in a relatively stable set of actions over a life-time, might lead someone towards the project of biography, understood as the narrative of an unfolding life, with its stages, achievements, and vicissitudes.[16] By the same token, a biography, written in the alternative, Stoic–Epicurean, style, would need to be differently conceived. To take one such example, Seneca's *Letters* to Lucilius depict a developmental sequence, in which Seneca helps Lucilius (a middle-aged man, like himself), to move progressively towards a more coherent and stable way of thinking and path of life. In so far as the *Letters* embody a—partly fictional—biography, it is one whose framework is set by the Stoic theory of ethical development as 'appropriation' (*oikeiōsis*), rather than the unfolding narrative and specific events of Lucilius' life.[17] Alternatively, one could imagine a Stoic–Epicurean biography as being one in which the main figure makes a series of salient decisions which show how near he or she comes at any one

[14] See 3.2 above, 4.3, esp. text to nn. 113–20, and 4.5 above.

[15] Plutarch's relationship to Stoicism and Epicureanism is not uncomplicated. Although some works criticize both theories systematically, following the approach of Carneades and the New Academy, Plutarch also sometimes writes less technical essays which are more sympathetic to Stoic attitudes (e.g. *On Control of Anger*, see Babut (1969*b*), ch. 2, esp. 94–7) or which synthesize Stoic, Epicurean, and Platonic–Aristotelian themes (e.g. *On Peace of Mind*, see Gill (1994: 4624–31)). On the complexity of his response to Epicureanism, see Boulogne (2003), esp. 32–9. But, overall, Plutarch's stance is, clearly, Platonic (sometimes couched in Platonic–Aristotelian mode); see Dillon (1988).

[16] By contrast, the biographical approach of Plutarch's Roman contemporary Suetonius (born *c.*AD 70) is thematic rather than presenting an unfolding narrative; his approach is not explicitly shaped by a Platonic–Aristotelian (or other) philosophical pattern.

[17] On the *Letters* (and other Senecan prose works) as partly fictional presentation of ethical progress, see Griffin (1976), 346–55; on Seneca's conception of ethical development and education, I. Hadot (1969), part 2; on Stoic development, see 3.2–3 above.

time to the stability and coherence of perfect wisdom. As I bring out subsequently, one can interpret Senecan tragedy and perhaps Virgilian epic as embodying, to some extent, biography in this latter sense. In focusing on significant moments which display degrees of ethical understanding (or the opposite), rather than the overall shape of a life and the expression of a relatively stable character, the latter type of biography prefigures later religious life-narratives, above all that of Augustine's *Confessions*, centred on conversion.[18]

In his study of Plutarch as a writer of (broadly) ethical biography, Tim Duff shows very clearly how the *Lives* reflect the Platonic–Aristotelian way of thinking about character-development.[19] Plutarch's biographies express both the idea that goodness of character depends on a combination of inborn nature, habituation, and reasoned choice, and also that it consists in the rational control of emotions and desires. Although the subjects of the *Lives* tend to be relatively good men, who can provide paradigms for self-patterning, Plutarch, increasingly, includes figures who are at least partly defective.[20] As Duff stresses, these are often presented as instances of a pattern of 'great natures gone wrong'. They are depicted as people whose exceptional natural capacity is not supported by good education or social environment, and who, as a result, never realize the goodness of character which lies within their potential. This mode of presentation is explicitly based on Plato's account in *Republic* 6 of great ('philosophical') natures developing badly in the absence of a proper ethical environment.[21] In a broader way, it reflects the two-stage, psychologically part-based, model of ethical development, which I highlighted in both Plato's *Republic* and Aristotle's ethical writings (134–7 above). As Duff also shows, the idea of the 'great nature' who goes wrong is one of the ways in which Plutarch qualifies the judgemental or moralizing tendency in his biography by an attempt to understand the person's development in a relatively sympathetic way.[22] It is also a feature which promotes the educational objectives of his biography, by unpicking the combination of factors that make for the development of goodness of character or its opposite, and by highlighting the importance of education (broadly understood) among those factors.[23]

[18] The classic study of Classical prefiguring of Christian 'conversion' is Nock (1933). For some related points, see P. Hadot (1995), 51–2, 126–44; Edwards (1997), 25–8; on ancient biography and the Christian gospels, Burridge (1992).

[19] Duff (1999), chs. 1–3, esp. 31–45, 72–82; also Russell (1973), chs. 5–6. See also Whitmarsh (2001), 208–10, on a similar pattern in Dio Chrysostom, Plutarch's contemporary.

[20] Duff (1999), 63–5.

[21] Duff (1999), 48–9, 60–1, 101, 156, 224–5; Pl. *R.* 491b–495b.

[22] Duff (1999), 58–65; see also 66–71, 252–67, 283–6. See also Pelling (1995).

[23] Duff (1999), 76–8, 109–10, 224–7.

It is within this framework that we need to locate Plutarch's thinking about stability and disintegration of adult character. Three suggestive comments, in different *Lives*, provide a basis for analysing his approach.[24]

Philip (V) seems to have undergone the greatest and most problematic (*paralogōtaton*) type of change: from being a gentle king and self-controlled young man, he became a licentious man and an utterly corrupt tyrant. But in fact this was not a change in nature (*phusis*), but a revelation—at a time when he had nothing to fear—of a wickedness that went unrecognized for a long time while he acted out of fear (*Aratus* 51.4).

Marius was harsh from the start and this just became more intense; he did not change his nature (*phusis*) when he gained power. Sulla, on the other hand, responded at first to good fortune in a moderate and statesmanlike way and gave the impression of being an aristocratic leader who also helped the people... [but his subsequent behaviour] made it reasonable to make against great power the accusation that it does not allow people's characters (*ēthē*) to maintain their original pattern (*tropoi*) but makes them unstable (*emplēkta*), arrogant, and inhumane. Whether this was a movement and change of nature (*phusis*) as a result of good fortune or rather a revelation of underlying wickedness when he gained power would need to be settled by another kind of discussion. (*Sulla* 30.4–5)

Towards the end of [Sertorius'] life, the savagery and bitterness of his behaviour towards the hostages seems to show that his nature (*phusis*) was not gentle but was covered up in a calculating way in response to necessity. My view is that, when virtue is complete and rationally established, it is impossible that good fortune would change it (*ekstēsai*) to the opposite state. But it is not impossible that good principles [literally, 'decisions', *prohaireseis*] and natures (*phuseis*), damaged by great and undeserved disasters, should change their character (*ēthos*), along with their fate (*daimōn*). But I think this is what happened to Sertorius, when his good fortune abandoned him, and he was made harsh by bad circumstances in his treatment of those who had done wrong. (*Sertorius*, 10.3–4).

It is clear from these passages that Plutarch finds especially puzzling, and needing explanation, actions which suggest that someone's character has changed markedly for the worse at some point in adult life. But where, exactly, does the puzzle lie? In part, it seems to derive from the belief, which certainly does form part of Plutarch's (Middle Platonic) approach, that, in general, once adult character is formed, it tends to remain unchanged throughout life.[25] This belief seems to underlie some of the comments made in these passages, notably the suggestion at two points that what is involved may be, not a change of character but, rather, the revelation of qualities that were

[24] The following three paragraphs are based on Gill (1983*b*), 478–87.

[25] See Swain (1989); on the Middle Platonic assumptions, see Duff (1999), 72–8, referring to *On Ethical Virtue*, esp. 443 C–D, 451 B–452 D.

previously unrecognized or covered up. A similar belief, and analysis, seems also to underlie Tacitus' famous final judgement on Tiberius, whose later years were seen as marred by cruelty and licentiousness.[26] Consistent with this idea is Plutarch's use of the term *phusis* in these passages, sometimes coupled with other terms, including 'character' (*ēthos*) and 'decisions' (*prohaireseis*, implying 'principles' or perhaps 'disposition'), to denote the—relatively stable—adult character. (A similar point could be made about Tacitus' use of the term 'nature' (*ingenium*) in his judgement on Tiberius.) It is much less plausible to think that Plutarch's comments imply a belief in the persistence of *inborn* nature, given his emphasis on the interplay of nature, education, and choice in shaping adult character. Also, although it is sometimes thought that Plutarch regularly uses *phusis* to denote inborn nature and *ēthos* for developed adult character, this terminology is not consistently maintained. In so far as Plutarch finds apparent change late in life puzzling, this reflects thinking about the durability of adult, and not specifically innate, character.[27]

But this is only part of what makes these cases puzzling, as comes out particularly in the comments cited on Sulla and Sertorius. Also crucial is the thought that *complete* virtue is marked by the kind of stability that can surmount *any* contingency or the internal pressures (emotions or desires) that circumstances may produce. The point is made explicitly elsewhere in the *Lives*: 'A body that can bear only heat or cold is less powerful than one which is naturally capable of bearing both changes. Similarly, a psyche is *completely* (or purely, *akratos*) vigorous and strong if prosperity does not spoil it with arrogance (or lawless violence, *hubris*) or poverty and misfortune degrade it.'[28] The comments on Sulla and Sertorius allude to the longstanding idea that both good and bad fortune can challenge and undermine a generally good character.[29] In Sulla's case, the emphasis is on the idea that external success can disrupt previous patterns of character (*tropoi*) and produce 'unstable' or 'capricious' (*emplēkta*) arrogance and loss of humanity. A similar explanation for Tiberius' later behaviour is entertained by the historian Dio Cassius: 'although he had a naturally good character (*pepheukōs eu*), he ran aground (*exokeilas*) when he was deprived of a rival' (after the death of Germanicus). Tacitus also reports a similar view, ascribed to the Roman Lucius Arruntius: 'Tiberius after such great experience of affairs was undermined (or collapsed, *conuulsus*) and changed (*mutatus*) by the force exerted

[26] See Plu. *Arat.* 51–3, *Sulla* 30.5, cited above; also *Arat.* 49.1 (Philip V); Tac. *Ann.* 65.1 (Tiberius).

[27] See further Gill (1983*b*), 478–80, 481, 484–7; also Swain (1989), 63; on *prohairesis* in Plutarch, see Duff (1999), 39–40.

[28] *Comparison of Timoleon and Aemilius* (2.5).

[29] A few examples: Aesch. *Agam.* 750–6; Hdt. 3.80.3; Thuc. 3.45.4; Pl. *Prt.* 339, *Lg.* 875a–c.

by absolute power'.[30] In Sertorius' case, Plutarch makes the point that, for much of his life, he seemed able to maintain his character in both favourable and unfavourable circumstances. 'He was not easily caught either by pleasure or by fear; being naturally undisturbed (*phusei anekplēktos*), he was moderate in bearing both terrible things and good fortune.' But, eventually, he proved unable to withstand adversity and 'was made harsh by bad circumstances'. Here, Plutarch rejects the explanation considered in the case of Sulla of a revelation of underlying badness; his explanation is that Sertorius lacked the *complete* virtue (*aretēn* ... *eilikrinēn*), 'rationally established' (*kata logon sunestōsan*), that *no* circumstances can reverse.[31]

Two other *Lives*, though also introducing other motifs, seem to reflect the same (Platonic–Aristotelian) pattern. Alcibiades is presented as another instance of unstable character; indeed, his entire life is marked by 'inconsistency' (*anōmalia*). As Duff brings out, Plutarch's own interpretation is itself rather complex and elusive, in this respect reflecting contemporary and later estimates of this figure.[32] On the one hand, Alcibiades serves as a classic instance of the Platonic pattern of a 'great nature gone wrong', a pattern which the historical Alcibides may have helped to suggest. The influence of Socrates is presented as ineffective in correcting certain bad features of an otherwise gifted nature.[33] Plutarch also twice suggests that what produced Alcibiades' apparent inconsistency was a powerful 'natural ambition and desire to come first', which led him to adopt a different 'facade and fiction' in different situations, rather than a real change in character (*ēthos* and *tropos*).[34] The *Life* also suggests a persistent and rather wilful effeminacy of attitude and life-style, a trait seen as consistent with heterosexual promiscuity, and one traced back into his youth.[35] However, these seemingly divergent indications may be underpinned by a single line of explanation, which is similar in basic type to those applied in other cases, including that of Sertorius. This is that a potentially good nature which is not 'harmonized' by education and reason never acquires complete stability of character. In this instance, this leads to capricious variety in satisfying desires that would otherwise

[30] D.C. 57.13.6 (Dio also considers the possibility of revelation of previously concealed nature); Tac. *Ann.* 6.48.2. On the connotations of *exokellō*, 'be shipwrecked', see Gill (1983*b*), 481–2 n. 79; Duff (1999), 110. On elements in Tacitus' account of Tiberius that *could have* been used to present the idea that Tiberius detoriarated in character, Gill (1983*b*), 483.

[31] Plu. *Sertorius* 10.3–4, cited above.

[32] Duff (1999), 230–2; also Gribble (1999).

[33] *Alc.* 2.1, 4.1–4; also Duff (1999), 224–8.

[34] *Alc.* 2.1, 23.5–6.

[35] Duff (1999), 236–7, referring esp. to *Alc.* 23.6. On the foreshadowing of adult character in anecdotes about Alcibiades' childhood and youth, see Duff (2003).

have been moderated or removed.[36] In other words, Alcibiades' inconsistency, like the lapses which occur late in life in Sulla and Sertorius, represent the expression of a failure to develop—or to develop fully—the stability and coherence of character that depend on virtue.[37]

Alexander is also presented in Plutarch as having a volatile and unstable character in adult life. Although there are some distinctive elements in this *Life* (brought out clearly by Tim Whitmarsh 2002), the basic pattern seems to me to be the same. One distinctive aspect is a quasi-medical description of his natural qualities. His unusually sweet body odour is explained by reference to the 'mixture' (*krasis*) of his body, which was exceptionally hot (and moist). Plutarch also comments that his unusual heat made him 'bibulous and spirited' (*potikon kai thumoeidē*).[38] The presentation of the influence of education (*paideia*) is also unusual. Although open to philosophical types of advice throughout his life, Alexander's response to advice is unpredictable. In one case, he reacts to ethical criticism from a friend (Clitus) with passionate anger and barbaric, as well as tyrannical, violence.[39] His extraordinary conquest of the East represents both a further source of (largely negative) social influence, promoting an autocratic and luxurious style, and a challenge, in the form of extreme success, to stability of character.[40] Plutarch's analysis of his downfall is thus complex; as Whitmarsh puts it, 'Nature and nurture are fused . . . it is both his innate barbarism and the influence of the East that undermine his paradigmatically Hellenic *paideia*'.[41] Despite this complexity, the analysis reflects, I think, the same underlying pattern found in the other *Lives* discussed here. Stability of character is a product of the interplay of inborn nature, education, and environmental influences; the failure to develop a *fully* coherent and reason-based type of virtue leaves Alexander liable to respond to pressures with passionate lack of emotional control or tyrannical violence.[42]

I now return to the question of the intellectual framework within which Plutarch approaches this subject, especially the question of consistency

36 See Plu. *Alc.* 16.1–6, also 2.1; also Gill (1983*b*), 475.

37 For a similar analysis, see also Plu. *Them.* 2.7: he was 'uneven and unstable, since his nature (*phusis*) was unadulterated. This nature, without reason or education, produced great changes of habit to both good and bad, and often degenerated for the worse' (trans. Duff 1999: 62).

38 Plu. *Alex.* 4.5, 7. Plutarch cites Theophrastus as his source for this idea. Gal. *QAM* argues that this type of physiological explanation for character (in terms of 'mixtures') can be traced back to Hippocrates. See Whitmarsh (2002), 188–90.

39 Plu. *Alex.* 51; see Whitmarsh (2002), 182–3 (also 180–6).

40 See further Whitmarsh (2002), 186–92. On the idea that good fortune as well as bad threatens stability of (virtuous) character, see text to n. 28 above.

41 Whitmarsh (2002), 190, also 187: 'Alexander's death in the East from wine is thus presented as the final victory of the Dionysiac stratum over . . . philosophical *paideia*.'

42 See also, in line with this interpretation, Duff (1999), 76, 85–6.

between ethical theory and the *Lives*. As underlined earlier (232–3 above), Plutarch, in *On Ethical Virtue* adopts the (broadly) Aristotelian view that there can be stable though defective characters, by contrast with the Stoic position that only the wise person is coherent and stable. On the face of it, the Plutarchean examples considered here, and the analysis applied to Sertorius (which seems to underlie the other cases) might suggest that Plutarch too assumes that only someone of perfect virtue is really stable.[43] This analysis seems to presuppose an ideal of invulnerable virtue, capable of surmounting any internal and external pressures, which again might seem to imply a Stoic ideal rather than a Platonic–Aristotelian one. It is, indeed, possible, that Stoic thinking is exercising some influence on Plutarch's thought, despite his explicit critique of Stoic psychology in *On Ethical Virtue* and elsewhere.[44] However, the way in which Plutarch formulates this ideal of completely stable and invulnerable character, both in *On Ethical Virtue* and the *Lives*, seems to be consistent with the Platonic–Aristotelian approach he adopts in both genres. In both cases, stability is conceived in terms of the outcome of the interplay between inborn nature, upbringing, education, or social influence, and reason, and also as the control or 'harmonization' of emotions by reason.[45] There is nothing to indicate, in the *Lives*, for instance, that *all* his subjects are constitutively capable of achieving complete virtue at *any* point in their lives.[46] Nor is there any evident attempt to depict emotional states in a way that implies that people (in passionate as well as rational states) respond in a unified or holistic way. On the contrary, emotional outbursts such as Alexander's are presented as lapses in the control of reason over (distinct) anger or spirit.[47] (By contrast, I shall suggest, a key strand in Seneca and Virgil's *Aeneid does* reflect Stoic holistic psychology: the depiction of 'akratic' surrender to passion as triggering collapse into self-division, irrationality, and

[43] For this analysis, see text to nn. 28–31 above.

[44] On Plutarch's relationship to Stoicism, see n. 15 above. Stoicism often set the intellectual agenda of debate for ethics in the Hellenistic–Roman period, e.g. in the concept of development as appropriation, adopted also by Middle Platonic thought (3.4 above), or in their ideal of *apatheia*, which Plutarch both criticizes and tries to rival in his own (Platonic) terms (4.3 above, text to nn. 123–5, 144–5).

[45] See 4.3 and discussion above; also Duff (1999), ch. 3, which correlates analogous features of *On Ethical Virtue* and *Lives*. The ideal for the *Lives* is more plausibly taken as being 'moderation of passion' than the quasi-Socratic 'absence of passion' also outlined in *On Ethical Virtue* (references in n. 44 above).

[46] Contrast the Stoic pattern implied in Seneca's 'biography' of Lucilius' development (text to n. 17 above).

[47] See Plu. *Alex.* 51.1, 5: Alexander is 'incensed' (*paroxuntheis*), and cannot bear (*pherein*) his anger (*orgē*) (text to n. 39 above). See further Duff (1999), 78–89, on reason and passion in conflict in the *Lives*.

a kind of madness.)[48] Also, although I have focused on cases in the *Lives* where there is instability and variation in adult behaviour, it is more typical of Plutarch to show his subjects as relatively consistent in their character, even when they are not people of exceptional virtue.[49]

One might want to question whether Plutarch's ethical and psychological assumptions entitle him to hold an ideal of fully stable or 'invulnerable' virtue. This type of question is raised, for instance, as regards Antiochus' account of happiness, in the Stoic-based critique of Cicero, *On Ends* 5.[50] But Plutarch himself does not, as far as I am aware, explicitly address this possible criticism of his Middle Platonic ethical stance, and seems to assume that he too, like the Stoics, is entitled to maintain this as an ideal and assume it in his characterization in the *Lives.* If we set aside the reservations that a Stoic critic might have of Plutarch's use of this ideal, I think we can accept that it is consistently maintained and that Plutarch's thinking on stability and collapse of character in the *Lives* coherently reflects his Platonic–Aristotelian theoretical standpoint.

7.3 SENECAN TRAGEDY

Plutarch's *Lives*, I have suggested, express a Middle Platonic (Platonic–-Aristotelian) pattern of thinking about stability and collapse of character. I now examine a strand in Senecan tragedy which I see as displaying a contrasting, Stoic, line of thought. In Seneca's *Phaedra*, taken as a whole, and in the monologue towards the end of his *Medea*, surrender to passion generates self-division and a kind of madness, which constitutes in both cases a collapse of character.[51] This feature of Senecan drama seems to me to reflect certain distinctively Stoic ways of thinking about passion and self-division, and about structure and incoherence of character, which can be contrasted with the Plutarchean, Middle Platonic pattern.

[48] See 7.3 below, esp. text to nn. 77, 87–112, 7.4, text to nn. 133–8, 145–60, 185–8, 223–4, 233–43. The pattern is holistic in assuming that passion involves the person as a whole abandoning, perhaps consciously, the virtuous rationality (or at least progress towards this state) of which all human beings are fundamentally capable.

[49] Hence, change and variation in adult character presents a *problem* for Plutarch, needing explanation, as illustrated in text to nn. 25–6 above.

[50] See Cic. *Fin.* 5.77–86. See further 3.4 above, esp. text to nn. 27–8, 44. The debate in Cic. *Fin.* 5 centres on the question of invulnerable happiness but also refers to invulnerable virtue (e.g. Cic. *Fin.* 5.32); see further Annas (1993*b*), 415–25, esp. 417, 420–3.

[51] This section builds on previous treatments of these texts in Gill (1997*c*), 215–18, 225–8, and (forthcoming).

I do not tackle here the larger question whether Seneca's tragedies, taken as a whole, embody a Stoic conception of human psychology or world-view. Scholars have taken sharply different positions on this question. Senecan tragedy is sometimes interpreted as designed to promote Stoic ethical objectives by presenting figures which serve as negative or cautionary exemplars of passion, seen as a destructive and self-destructive force.[52] Other scholars are cautious about, or critical of, this view.[53] For instance, Alessandro Schiesaro has argued, on the basis of a detailed reading of *Thyestes*, that there are profound difficulties in a Stoic, moralizing interpretation of Seneca's drama. On the contrary, he maintains, there are well-marked features of Senecan dramaturgy, including 'meta-dramatic' elements, which promote audience identification and emotional engagement with figures, such as Thyestes and Medea, who are morally repellent by Stoic, or conventional, standards.[54] Schiesaro also questions the claim sometimes made, that Stoic aesthetic theory or psychology offers a credible explanation of how the representation of morally objectionable figures is compatible with ethical education. In particular, he calls into question Martha Nussbaum's view that Stoic theory defines a kind of 'critical spectatorship', which enables us to observe without emotional involvement the depiction of ethically problematic figures.[55]

A full response to Schiesaro's claims would require a more systematic examination of Senecan drama, including *Thyestes*, than I can attempt here, and also further scrutiny of the (rather limited) evidence we have for Stoic thinking about audience responses to poetry. What I offer is a more limited exercise, centred on the implications of points of resemblance between Seneca's *Medea* and *Phaedra*. However, if my reading of these features is accepted, it carries implications that bear on the larger debate about Senecan tragedy and Stoicism. This discussion shows, I think, the shaping influence on Senecan tragedy of a determinately Stoic—by contrast with a Platonic–Aristotelian—way of conceiving collapse or disintegration of character. It also indicates how such representation might influence audience responses, for instance, by bringing out the naturalness and unnaturalness of certain attitudes, or by showing how states of passion involve internal conflict and disintegration. This point bears on the issues about emotional engagement

[52] See e.g. Marti (1945); Pratt (1948), (1983); Herington (1966); D. and E. Henry (1985); Rosenmeyer (1989). See the résumé of scholarship which adopts this approach in Nussbaum (1994), 448–9 n. 13; also Nussbaum's reading of Seneca's *Medea* in (1994), 439–83, esp. 448–53.

[53] See e.g. Coffey and Mayer (1990), 26, 29, and Hine (2000), 27–30, in commentaries on the two Senecan dramas discussed here.

[54] Schiesaro (2003), esp. 6–7, 20–5, 133–8, 147–51, 214–20, 252–5.

[55] Schiesaro (2003), 221–51, esp. 229–35, 244; also Nussbaum (1993), esp. 136–45. See also Schiesaro (1997).

raised by Schiesaro. Although the powerful representation of evil and destructiveness by Seneca can, perhaps, be seen as inviting identification by the audience, it is less plausible to think that the depiction of psychological disintegration and irrationality or madness does so. These are not obviously appealing or desirable states of mind. Indeed, as I suggest later, this form of representation is better taken as one which supports the Stoic view that passion is a form of psychic sickness or mental disorder.[56]

Also, in considering how far Seneca's tragic characterization reflects a Stoic approach, it is important to have in view the most credible picture of the nature and history of Stoic thinking about emotions and psychology. Norman Pratt, for instance, supposes that Senecan tragedy reflects Posidonian thinking about emotions (which he calls 'Neo-Stoic'), assumed to be sharply different from earlier Stoic theory. Nussbaum's reconstruction of Stoic thinking on poetry also involves a distinction between 'cognitive' and 'non-cognitive' views of emotion, the latter taken to be Posidonian.[57] I have argued here (4.6 above) that there is no substantive difference between Posidonian and early Stoic thinking about emotions, especially that of Chrysippus. If this view is accepted, it is inappropriate to look in Senecan drama for the influence of a distinctively Posidonian (by contrast with mainstream Stoic) line of thinking. In fact, as I suggest shortly, the features of Senecan tragedy examined here seem to be strongly informed by Chrysippean thinking about passion as internal conflict. This vein of Stoic thought is already linked with tragic characterization through Chrysippus' use of Euripides' Medea as an exemplar of passion. So there is a special appropriateness in this set of ideas being reapplied by Seneca to tragic portrayal, including his version of Medea.[58]

I begin by highlighting a common element in Seneca's presentation of Medea and Phaedra, in spite of other important differences: namely the way that surrender to passion generates internal conflict, madness, and psychological disintegration.[59] I bring out the distinctive character of this pattern by contrast with Euripidean versions of similar material, and also with Plutarch's (Middle Platonic) conception of collapse of character. I then identify what seems to me to be the distinctively Stoic line of thought underlying Seneca's dramatic presentation of these figures.

[56] Schiesaro (2003) does not bring out these aspects of the dramas. He stresses in Medea (as in Atreus), the linkage between passion and destructive power (16–19, 208–14); also 158 on Phaedra. See also text to nn. 115–16 below.

[57] Pratt (1983), esp. 59–61, 64–5, 76, 89–93, including discussion of Sen. *Med.* and *Phaed.*; Nussbaum (1993), esp. 109–14.

[58] On Sen. *Med.*, see discussion below; for a possible echo of E. *Med.* 1078–80 in Sen. *Phaed.*, see text to n. 100 below.

[59] The following five paragraphs are based on one section of Gill (forthcoming).

Seneca's Medea, on the face of it, like his Atreus, is a highly integrated and consistent character, single-mindedly focused on hatred, revenge, and violence, and revelling in her own evil motivation.[60] Yet, in the course of the monologue in which she decides to satisfy her destructive hatred by killing her own children (893–977), her personality disintegrates. Medea urges herself to an 'innovative' (*haut usitatum*) form of punishment, which will enable her to express her conception of herself as an evil and destructive person and thus become truly *Medea*.[61] The idea of killing her children presents itself to her as the 'ultimate crime' (*ultimum scelus*). It is chosen as a means of revenge by the rather tortuous reasoning that *her own* children will serve as a substitute for those whom Jason's new bride (already killed by Medea) had no time to generate (921–5). Finding the ultimate crime and thus fulfilling her self-image brings about internal conflict—which is not the result you would expect. The thought of infanticide produces intense revulsion in Medea and an upsurge of maternal feeling,[62] in spite of the fact that motherly love has figured very little in the play up to this point.[63] The emergence of maternal feelings threatens her decision to take revenge through a supremely evil act and leads to psychological disintegration, expressed first as inner division and then as a kind of madness.

Her internal conflict is shown in two main ways. One is that of debate between alternating voices, expressing the maternal or the angry, avenging self.[64] The other is a quasi-narrative commentary, mostly couched in third-personal form, in which she describes her inner conflict and emphasizes its intensity.[65] Although there are analogues for this mode elsewhere in Seneca and in earlier Latin poetry,[66] it has a jarring impact in a monologue which, at first, is marked by single-minded commitment to the course of action chosen (895–925). The effect is, partly, to accentuate the internal conflict by describing it and by identifying the various psychological agents in Medea's conflicted state.[67] But also, since the narrator is the person concerned, the

[60] Cf. her opening speech (1–55, esp. 45–52) and 129–36, with 893–925, esp. 905–19; and cf. 171 ([Medea] 'is what I shall become', [*Medea*] *fiam*) with 910 ('Now I am Medea', *Medea nunc sum*). For this view, see e.g. Schiesaro (2003), 208–14, and, on analogous features in Atreus, 117–38.

[61] 910–15, esp. 899 and 910 (n. 60 above).

[62] 'Horror has struck my heart, my limbs have gone numb with chill and my heart has trembled. Anger has left its post and the mother has completely returned (*materque tota... redit*), with the wife thrown out' (926–8).

[63] Instead, Jason's fatherly love has been stressed, which Medea sees as allowing scope for revenge (437–41, 544–50); see also 1002–5.

[64] For the phases, see (motherly voice) 929–32, 944–7; (wifely anger) 933–6, 948–51, 953–7.

[65] 926–8, 937–44 (including a full-scale simile in 940–3), 951–3.

[66] Cf. Sen. *Ag.* 131–44, esp. 138–40, *Phaed.* 177–94; Virg. *A.* 4.15–23; Ov. *Met.* 7.18–21, 8.506–11.

[67] That is, the mother (*mater*) and the wife (*coniunx*), 928, anger (*ira*), 927, 938, 943–4, bitter grief (*dolor*), 944, 951, hatred (*odium*), 952, love (*amor*), 938, duty or piety (*pietas*), 943–4; on the significance of the plurality of psychological agents, see n. 99 below.

impression is given that she is separate from *both* the selves she describes and that she depicts her state of mind from a distinct, self-conscious standpoint. In the final phase of her self-division, she embraces her children—for the first time in the play—and considers sparing them (945–8). But the thought that the children will be left only for the father and not the exiled mother leads to the re-emergence of her grief, hatred, and anger, which are again described in quasi-narrative style (948–53). This produces two more, rather bizarre, responses: the wish that she had produced a whole 'crowd' (*turba*) of children to maximize her vengeance, and the thought that the two produced are sufficient to pay for the harm she has done to the father she betrayed and the brother she killed (954–7). The introduction of the second theme, in a sense, resolves the conflict between motherly love and anger: Medea is enabled to reconceive her revenge as a mode of justified self-punishment.[68] But this quasi-resolution is achieved at the cost of a further form of self-division. Medea goes mad, in some sense; she sees herself as the target and intended victim of a crowd of avenging Furies and of the ghost of her dismembered brother. In this way too, she is separated from her sane, but now hopelessly conflicted, self.[69]

In Seneca's *Phaedra*, by contrast, self-division is a recurrent theme throughout the play, and is, arguably, the key to the characterization of the central figure. Scholars have asked whether Phaedra should be seen as a depraved, manipulative figure or as a sincere victim of her own destructive passion.[70] However, as Tim Hill suggests, she is best understood as radically conflicted throughout the play, divided between passionate love (*amor*/*furor*) and a sense of shame (*pudor*). Indeed, the basic pattern is the same as in the monologue in Seneca's *Medea.* A person who gives herself up to passion finds that she is—in Phaedra's case, repeatedly—affected by shame in a way that creates internal conflict and ambivalence. This point of similarity coexists with other differences between the two Senecan figures. Whereas Seneca's Medea positively urges herself into a passionate state (of anger, hatred, and violence), Phaedra's initial entry into passion is more indirect, though it also involves some agency on her part. In her first speech, she seems to be constructing a set of beliefs that make it 'appropriate' for her to react with passionate love for her stepson. (She alludes to her husband's absence on a morally dubious mission, as well as his infidelity to her sister Ariadne; she also refers to her family's tendency to love in a criminal or perverted way, like

68 'brother, use this hand [hers], which has drawn the sword—with that victim, we appease your ghost' (969–71), also *poenas* ('punishment'), 956.

69 958–71. On this point, see further Gill (1987), 35–6, (1997*c*), 218.

70 See e.g. Croisille (1964); Davis (1983), esp. 122; Coffey and Mayer (1990), 27–8; Roismann (2000). The following treatment of *Phaedra* is indebted to T. D. Hill (2003), 193–214. Hill is preparing a book based on (2003).

Pasiphaë or Ariadne.)[71] Subsequently, she presents herself to the nurse as completely possessed by her passion, in spite of recognizing its wrongness.[72] However, when the nurse strongly criticizes her self-abandonment to love (129–249), Phaedra threatens suicide to preserve her shame, and then seems to change her mind again when the nurse modifies her attitude (250–73). What underlies these divergent responses is that Phaedra *both* recognizes what is wrong in her passionate love *and* is powerfully affected by it, so that both motives are at work in her at the same time.

A similar ambivalence is implied in her reply to Hippolytus' threat to kill her in his horror at the revelation of her love: 'You cure my madness. This is more than I could have prayed for—that I should die at your hands with my shame intact' (... *sanas furentem. maius hoc uoto meo est | saluo ut pudóre manibus immoriar tuis*) (711–12). Although these lines express relief at the thought of dying with her shame intact, they also indicate a quasi-erotic pleasure at the thought of dying with Hippolytus' sword inside her—an implication that Hippolytus seems to recognize, prompting him to discard his 'polluted sword' (*contactus ensis*, 714) and run away. The same pattern can be seen later, when Phaedra responds obliquely to Theseus' questions about her motive for suicide and thus allows Hippolytus to be incriminated. The scene has been interpreted in various ways;[73] but it seems to make most sense as an expression of Phaedra's ambivalent motives. On Theseus' arrival, her intention seems to be to kill herself to preserve (what remains of) her sense of shame and her reputation, but to do so with Hippolytus' sword inside her, a wish coloured by her passion.[74] But this is not a motive she can disclose to Theseus without discrediting herself—hence her cryptic replies (868–81). When Theseus threatens to torture the nurse to force Phaedra to give a direct reply (882–5), Phaedra responds with a series of ambiguous comments, which reflect the true facts while allowing Theseus to place the blame on Hippolytus (891–3).[75]

> Though assailed by prayers, I resisted; before weapon and threats
> My mind did not give way, but my body endured violence.
> My blood will wash out this stain on my honour.

[71] See 91–8, 113–18, 127–9. For Medea's self-urging, see n. 61 above. For the idea that a passion involves the belief that it is 'appropriate' to react in a given way, see 3.2 above, text to nn. 72–4, 4.5, text to nn. 184–7.

[72] See nn. 100–1 below.

[73] See n. 70 above. The main competing view to that offered here is that Phaedra's suicide plan is a fiction and that her only objective is to incriminate Hippolytus and save her reputation and life.

[74] See 854–68 (the sword is in her right hand, 866). Note also Phaedra's earlier wish to die to save her shame (250–4) and to die with Hippolytus' sword inside her (710–12).

[75] See also Davis (1983), 122–4; Boyle (1987), 31–2; and T. D. Hill (2003), 207.

temptata precibus restiti; ferro ac minis
non cessit animus; uim tamen corpus tulit.
labem hanc pudoris eluet noster cruor.

In these words and those which follow (894–7), her language allows Theseus to think that she has been the victim of sexual assault by an adulterer (*stuprator*), described 'as the one whom you least suppose' (*quem rere minime*) and identified by the sword she holds. But the words also convey a private significance, which reflects her judgements on her own actions. She resisted the nurse's appeals to her to control herself (125–249). Although her body did suffer some violence at Hippolytus' hands (704–9), her mind did not give way to this violence, but, rather, to her own passionate love. It is this passion which has stained her honour in a way that only her death will wash out. Again, the one who 'defiled our honour' was, indeed, 'the one whom you least suppose' (894–5), namely herself, while the identifying sword (earlier described by Hippolytus as 'polluted', 714) is linked with adultery by her desire rather than by any act of Hippolytus (896–7). If her intention was simply to incriminate Hippolytus, such many-layered language would be pointless. While protecting her own reputation, the lines form a guilt-laden commentary on the actions that have brought close to death both herself and the man she loves. It is only Hippolytus' death, hideously achieved, that prompts her to make fully explicit her inner ambivalence before she brings about her own death. She tells herself: 'Die for your husband, if you are pure, for your love if you are impure' (*morere, si casta es, uiro; | si incesta, amori*, 1184–5). She invokes 'Death, the only remedy for a wicked love, death, greatest glory of blighted shame' (*o mors amoris una sedamen mali | o mors pudoris maximum laesi decus*, 1188–9). She sees death as a fitting punishment (*poenas*) for the wrong she has done to Hippolytus and also declares that she will, even so, pursue him 'madly' (*amens*) through the underworld.[76] Thus, her conflicted state is presented as one which will persist beyond the grave.

What line of thought underlies this shared pattern? The common thread, I think, is that self-surrender to passion—or, in Medea's case, to a more intense level of passion—generates internal conflict and mental instability or madness. This distinctive feature comes out, in the first instance, if we compare these plays to the Euripidean plays which form a key part of the intertextual background for these Senecan dramas. Although Euripides' (surviving) *Hippolytus* and *Medea* have been noted since antiquity for their powerful expression of internal conflict,[77] there are, none the less, salient points of contrast in the Senecan version of self-division.

[76] 1176–8, also 1192–8, 1179–80; for the motif of wanting to pursue Hippolytus, see also 235, 700.

[77] See further Snell (1964), ch. 3; Irwin (1983); Gill (1983*a*), (1996*b*), 216–39, (2005*c*).

The sustained internal conflict in Seneca's Phaedra, between shame and passionate love (*pudor* and *amor*), might seem, at first glance, to recall that of Phaedra in the extant *Hippolytus* of Euripides; Phaedra's revelation of this conflict to the nurse (373–430), like the monologue of Euripides' *Medea*, is one of the most powerful presentations of psychological division in fifth-century tragedy. But there is an important difference from Seneca's *Phaedra*. Whereas Euripides' Phaedra, in this version, consistently identifies herself as a would-be virtuous person trying to control or conceal the alien force of her passionate love (*erōs* or *Kupris*), Seneca's Phaedra engages herself more fully with her passion and acts on it, while still being conscious of its wrongfulness. As a result, ambivalence enters more deeply into Phaedra's motivation and agency in Seneca's play than in Euripides'.[78] The Phaedra of Euripides' first *Hippolytus*, of which we have only fragments, has sometimes been seen, notably by Bruno Snell, as anticipating Seneca's Phaedra in both actively pursuing her lover and dissociating herself from her love. I think it is likely that Euripides' first version of Phaedra, like Seneca's, was active in trying to satisfy her passion. But the evidence is much weaker for thinking that Euripides' figure also repudiated her love, and was thus internally conflicted in the same way as in Seneca's version.[79] So Seneca's depiction of Phaedra, as caught in a prolonged internal conflict which informs all her ethical and emotional responses, reflects a substantively new conception.

The monologue near the close of Seneca's *Medea* (893–977) represents a response to the famous monologue in Euripides' play (1021–80) and shows some of the same features. Both versions express a conflict which arises between the plan of taking vengeance on Jason by killing their joint children and an upsurge of maternal feelings. Both monologues also exhibit some common formal features, notably the use of alternating voices to express competing (avenging or maternal) aspects of the self, including an appeal by one self to another.[80] But there are also major differences. For one thing, the motivation of Seneca's Medea is more radically internalized. For related reasons, the conflict generated is more intense and irrational; notably it gives rise to a kind of madness, though one that is partly self-induced. The so-called monologue in Euripides' *Medea* is, in fact, for much of the time,

[78] See e.g. E. *Hipp.* 392–402, 413–14, 426–7, 725–31. Euripides' Phaedra shows ambivalence in her change of mind (revealing her love to the nurse and allowing her to approach Hippolytus), but not the explicit and systematic conflict of motivation found in Seneca's play. See further Gill (1990*a*), esp. 86–9.

[79] For the fragments, see Barrett (1964), 18–22; also Coffey and Mayer (1990), 5–6. See Snell (1964), ch. 2; and Gill (2005*c*), 166–71, for the view outlined here.

[80] In Sen. *Med.*, see references in n. 64 above. In E. *Med.*, see (motherly voice) 1021–48, 1056–8, 1067–77, (wifely anger) 1049–55, 1059–66.

couched in *dialogue* form, with the chorus or the children.[81] This, in turn, reflects a strongly interpersonal conception of her vengeance-plan and of the countervailing motive. As I have argued elsewhere, the play as a whole suggests that taking revenge by infanticide is conceived as an exemplary gesture (of an appalling kind) designed to dramatize to Jason the intolerable breach in interpersonal bonding (*philia*) created by his one-sided repudiation of their marriage. It is also stressed that the conflict between this exemplary gesture and her love for her children is deeply felt by Medea and is conceived as one between two justified ethical claims.[82]

In the Senecan monologue, by contrast, both the conflict and its resolution are expressed in more internalized, or self-related, forms. As illustrated earlier, Medea arrives at the plan of infanticide through a search for the 'ultimate crime', which will consummate her career of wrongdoing and fulfil her self-image as supremely evil.[83] The plan is finalized, and reinforced, by strained, barely intelligible, reasoning, with only vestigial contact with interpersonal ethics, as normally understood.[84] The upsurge of motherly feeling, in reaction to her own plan, and the conflict that this creates are depicted as real and intense.[85] But her response to the conflict is, again, bizarrely motivated and self-related. The children are represented to herself as sacrificial victims to enable her to bring about her self-punishment for the abandonment of her father and the murder and dismemberment of her brother. It is this line of thought that produces the peculiar 'madness' in which she sees her dead brother and the furies and offers her right hand as the vehicle by which her brother can take vengeance on her.[86] The radical internalization of the conflict, the unnatural reasoning, and the irrationality or madness involved are all features which mark a sharp difference from the Euripidean version.

[81] E. *Med.* 1021–41 are addressed to the children, as are 1069–77; 1042–8 (and perhaps 1049–55) are addressed to the chorus. Thus, only 1056–69 and 1078–80 are formally monologue, and even these lines can be regarded as a continuation of the confidential address to the chorus in 1042–8. See further Gill (1996*b*), 217.

[82] See further Gill (1996*b*), 217–26, and, for a detailed comparison between the two monologues, Gill (1987).

[83] See text to n. 61 above.

[84] See Sen. *Phaed* 919–25 (her children are to take the place of those who cannot be born from Jason's new bride, whom Medea has killed); 933–5 (the children must die for the guilt of their father—and mother), 948–51 (if the children are lost to the mother, they must be killed to deprive their father too).

[85] Sen. *Med.* 926–52, esp. 926–32, 945–7; on the significance of this motif, see text to nn. 107–9 below.

[86] Sen. *Med.* 952–71. The only (partial) parallel for this type of strained reasoning is in E. *Med.* 1059–64, whose authenticity has been questioned (the authenticity of lines 1056–80 has also been questioned, although the last three lines were certainly treated as authentic in the Hellenistic–Roman period). See further Gill (1987), esp. 25–6, 29, and 35–6, (1997*c*), 217–21.

What conceptual framework, among those current at that time, best explains the distinctive type of breakdown of character we find displayed in these examples? I consider first the Platonic–Aristotelian framework found in Plutarch's *Lives.* The main potentially relevant features are the part-based psychology and the idea that the development of character depends on a combination of inborn nature, habit or social environment, and rational decision. In this framework, it is assumed that adult character, both virtuous and defective, is relatively stable. Marked change in behaviour is interpreted either as the disclosure of a previously concealed type of disposition or as collapse or disintegration, which shows that the character was not completely 'harmonized' and stable.[87] There are aspects of the Senecan tragic pattern that *might* seem to support this type of analysis. For instance, Phaedra's sustained ambivalence between shame and passionate love and the internal conflict that arises in Medea's monologue (involving a plurality of distinct forces) could be taken as reflecting the idea of division between independent psychic parts, such as reason and anger or desire.[88] In both plays, there are references to the main figure's nature or character (including some by the figure herself) treated as a causal factor that determines her current behaviour.[89] The emotional trajectory of Phaedra could be interpreted as the collapse of—a previously good—character under the impact of overwhelming passion. Alternatively, the drama could be taken, in terms that Phaedra herself supplies, as the revelation of a previously unrecognized tendency to criminality, including polluted love, of a type to which her family is subject.[90] Seneca's Medea, in one way, lends herself more easily to a Plutarchean type of approach in that her (long-term) character is more clearly defined within her drama than Phaedra is in hers. Hence, the occurrence of internal conflict in the monologue can be seen as the—temporary—collapse of a determinate character, like that of Sertorius, for instance.[91] In another way, however, Medea's collapse is quite different from anything in Plutarch's *Lives.* Hers is the disintegration of a thoroughly and determinedly evil character under the impact of moral revulsion at her own brutal plans. Although Plutarch's biographical project does accommodate the idea of representing people of bad character, there is no instance, as far as I am

[87] See 7.2 above, esp. text to nn. 28–31.

[88] See e.g. Sen. *Phaed.* 177–9, 184 (discussed further below), *Med.* 926–30, 937–44.

[89] See e.g. Sen. *Phaed.* 112–28, 169–77, 687–93, *Med.* 902–10, cf. 45–52.

[90] See *Phaed.* references in n. 89 above.

[91] Medea's collapse lasts from lines 926 to 970 (including the 'madness' in which she kills the first child), before she reassumes in 976–7 the confident tone of 893–925 (with a further short lapse in 989–90). On Plutarch's Sertorius, see 7.2 above, text to nn. 25–31.

aware, of inner conflict generated in a bad Plutarchean person by competing virtuous motives.[92]

Although we could (apart from the last point) construct in this way a Plutarchean interpretation of Seneca's presentation of these two figures, I do not think that this would take us to the heart of these dramas. This is not only, or primarily, because of the generic contrast between Plutarch's biography and Senecan tragedy; more important is the question of the underlying ethical and psychological assumptions.[93] As already indicated, I think that Stoic ideas take us much further in interpreting what is distinctive in the Senecan depiction, outlined earlier. Indeed, these distinctive features in the plays can be seen as reflecting central and characteristic dimensions of Stoic thinking. A crucial part of Chrysippus' theory is that passionate states of mind are inherently unstable, fluctuating or 'feverish', and internally conflicted. What underlies this idea is the Stoic version of the 'Socratic' claims that only the wise person is psychologically coherent whereas all non-wise people are relatively incoherent and that all human beings are constitutively capable of developing towards (perfect) wisdom, whatever their current state of mind. This is combined with a holistic psychological model in which emotions, though (normatively) 'irrational', are seen as states of the whole person which embody rational judgements, including those expressing the person's latent or imperfect understanding of goodness. It is the presence of judgements reflecting this partial understanding that generates the conflict with the primary ('irrational') passionate judgement that it is 'appropriate' to feel anger or grieve or love in this situation. This explains Chrysippus' interest in Euripides' Medea as an exemplar of passion, since she is able to say, even as she surrenders to her own anger, that she knows what is 'bad' (*kakon*) in acting as she does now.[94]

Seneca's philosophical prose writings show familiarity with this type of thinking.[95] Although the chronological and conceptual relationship between Seneca's philosophical and dramatic writings remains a matter of conjecture

[92] On Plutarch's attitude to the inclusion of bad subjects, see Duff (1999), 45–71. In practice, Duff points out, Plutarch's 'bad' figures are often represented as 'great natures' gone wrong (47–8, 60–2, 64), and criticism is nuanced by recognition of better aspects; this framework is not congenial to the type of psycho-ethical state depicted in the monologue in Sen. *Med.*

[93] As highlighted in 7.1 above (text to nn. 6–9), this chapter compares and contrasts literary works in different genres with a view to gauging the influence of competing intellectual frameworks in this period. See also 7.2 above (text to nn. 13–18) for the idea that different frameworks promote different conceptions of 'biography'.

[94] See 4.5 above, esp. text to nn. 212–18, 226–51.

[95] For the idea that only the wise person is unified and the non-wise incoherent, see e.g. *Ep.* 120, esp. 11–12, 19, 20–2. Seneca's best-known analysis of emotion, in *Ira* 2.4.1, is taken by e.g. Inwood (1993), esp. 180–3, and Sorabji (2000), chs. 3–4, as expressing a basically Chrysippean (unified) psychological model.

and debate,[96] both these Senecan dramas, in the aspects described earlier, can be seen as expressing this way of thinking about passion. Both figures decide, in different ways, that it is 'appropriate' to feel and act in a certain (passionate) way; in both cases, this generates a countervailing ethical judgement or set of judgements in a way that gives rise to internal conflict. In Phaedra's case, the outcome is a sustained tension between passionate love and her own sense of shame at this love. In Medea's case, we have a more localized phase of conflict between a passionate (though deliberate) desire for the ultimate crime and the morally informed reactions, including outrage, maternal love, and guilt, generated in response to this desire. But both portrayals seem to reflect the same, Chrysippean, conception of passion.[97] In Plutarch's analysis of problematic variation in behaviour, the focus is on the contrast (real or apparent) between the behaviour in question at any one time and the long-term (adult) character.[98] In these Senecan cases, as in the relevant aspects of Chrysippus' theory, the emphasis falls on internal contradictions or the simultaneous presence of competing (normatively) rational or irrational judgements and correlated psychophysical reactions and actions.[99]

In Phaedra's case, one clear link with Chrysippus' analysis comes in the famous lines, echoing the conclusion of the monologue in Euripides' Medea, in which she tells the nurse that her reason can no longer control a passion whose badness she herself recognizes: 'I know that what you say is true, nurse, but frenzy (*furor*) compels me to follow the worse course of action ... What could reason (*ratio*) do? Frenzy has won and rules ...'[100] The 'reason–frenzy' contrast in these lines might seem to express psychological dualism; what makes plausible a Stoic, rather than Middle Platonic, framework? Phaedra's phrasing needs to be taken in context. She is defending herself against the nurse's critical tirade (129–77) by presenting herself as subject to an overwhelming force, that of the divine power of love—a claim abruptly dismissed by the nurse (195–217). But, even so, the overall emphasis in her speech, as in the conclusion of Euripides' monologue, is that she (the person as a whole) is aware of what is wrong in what she wants to do but is still powerless to correct

[96] The dating of tragedies and most prose works is uncertain, but Seneca's commitment to Stoicism seems to be longstanding (Griffin 1976: 37–43). For scholarly debate, see text to nn. 52–5 above.

[97] See text to nn. 59–76 above, on the relevant features of the plays, taken with the preceding paragraph on the Stoic analysis of passion.

[98] See 7.2 above, text to nn. 25–7.

[99] On Chrysippus' theory, see 4.5 above, esp. text to nn. 180–7, 201–51. For the view that the psychology of Seneca's monologue, including the language identifying different psychic parts (n. 67 above) is consistent with Stoic thinking on passion and inner conflict, see Nussbaum (1994), 448–53; also Pigeaud (1981), 398–405, esp. 402.

[100] Sen. *Phaed.* 177–9, 184. Cf. E. *Med.* 1078–80, also Ov. *Met.* 7.19–21.

this. Chrysippus, as argued earlier, showed that this phenomenon, perhaps surprisingly, could be effectively explained in holistic psychological terms.[101] This speech by Seneca's Phaedra can be taken as expressing the same set of assumptions, particularly when located in the larger emotional sequence depicted in the play as a whole. Once Phaedra has, in the opening scene, justified or rationalized her passionate love—in part by reference to her own, inherited nature (91–8, 112–28)—she exhibits the conflicted, 'feverish' state of mind that Chrysippus presents as typical of passion. In the lines just cited (177–9, 184), Phaedra herself articulates the contradiction between her moral awareness and the passionate judgements that are activating her feelings and actions. Subsequently, her words imply the simultaneous presence of judgements expressing a sense of shame and those reflecting intense erotic desire. At the close of the play, she renders this ambivalence explicit; but the conflict implicitly informs her responses throughout the action, thus producing the enigmatic or ambiguous quality often noted in her characterization.[102]

In Seneca's Medea-monologue, the Chrysippean framework comes out especially in the conflict between her deliberate but passionate desire to commit the 'ultimate crime' and the complex of moral responses that this provokes within her. Euripides' Medea, it would seem, was taken by Chrysippus as a paradigm, because her judgement on the 'badness' of her own passionate actions show that, as Cleanthes had put it, 'all human beings'—even Medea—'have the starting-points of virtue'.[103] In Seneca's monologue, there is a special significance in the fact that what produces this conflict is an (uncharacteristic) upsurge of maternal love.[104] The Stoics present parental love as a paradigm of the motivation towards sociability and benefiting others that is fundamental to one side of human (and animal) development as 'appropriation' (*oikeiōsis*), a point underlined in a key Cicero text.[105] The idea that (proper forms of) parental love constitute an exemplary way of realizing other-directed ethical motivation is brought out strongly in early Imperial Roman practical ethics.[106] This point, we may suppose, explains the specific way that Medea's internal conflict is dramatized here. Medea's view of

[101] See text to n. 94 above. In Sen. *Phaed.* 177–94, note especially 'I know...' (cf. E. *Med.* 1078) and the combination of analysis (178–80, 184) and imagery (181–3, 186–94) expressing her consciousness of her akratic state (or her 'psychophysical inertia', 4.6 above, text to nn. 314–19).

[102] See text to nn. 70–6 above; also Gill (1997*c*), 215–16.

[103] See E. *Med.* 1078, Stob. 2.65.8 (LS 61 L) my trans., and 3.2 above, text to nn. 11–13.

[104] See text to nn. 62–3 above.

[105] See Cic. *Fin.* 3.62–8, esp. 62 (LS 57 F, esp. (1)); also Plu. *Mor.* 1038 E (LS 57 E). See also Blundell (1990).

[106] See e.g. Musonius Rufus, *Discourses* 13A–B; also Reydams-Schils (2002), 247–8 and (2005), ch. 4. See Epict. *Diss.* 1.11, esp. 5–15, taken with Long (2002), 77–9.

herself, strongly conveyed in the opening lines of the monologue, is as a person who is equal to carrying out the 'ultimate crime' of infanticide to satisfy her anger and thus fulfilling her image of herself as 'Medea'. But the underlying fact of her mother-love, the expression of the natural motive to benefit others, *forces itself on her*, and brings about the violent internal conflict that she herself describes so vividly.[107] A similar line of thought helps to explain the strained, implausible reasoning by which Medea determines on infanticide, first, as the appropriate form of vengeance and then as the best way of punishing herself for her brother's dismemberment and murder.[108] The effect of such tortuous reasoning is to suggest that Medea is persuading herself, *against nature*, of the appropriateness of killing her children in these circumstances.[109] Also significant in this connection is the temporary phase of delusive madness in which she carries out the killing of the first child (*Med.* 958–70). This is a peculiar type of madness, sharply contrasted to the 'raving' madness we sometimes find in Greek tragedy: for instance, the state in which Euripides' Heracles kills his children.[110] In one way, the madness of Seneca's Medea can be taken as a further extension of the internally conflicted state of mind produced by the tension between her deliberated plan of infanticide and her horror at this plan. In another way, the madness presents itself as a kind of internal ruse, by which she deceives herself into accepting the appropriateness of infanticide on the spurious or unnatural ground that it is justified morally, as a means of self-punishment.[111]

Despite their complexity, these features of Medea's monologue, like those of Phaedra's extended state of inner ambivalence, are, credibly, taken as expressions of Chrysippus' conception of passion as a form of 'rejection' of reason (by an essentially rational animal), marked by 'feverish' instability and internal conflict.[112] This feature of Senecan drama, considered in the light of the analysis of Chrysippus' thinking about passion offered earlier, lends support to the idea that Senecan drama is, as is sometimes claimed, strongly informed by Stoic ethical psychology.[113] If this line of interpretation is accepted, it has implications for Schiesaro's criticism of the Stoic reading of Senecan tragedy, noted earlier. Schiesaro underlines in Seneca's portrayal of Medea, as of Atreus, the triumphant realization of her self-image as evil that

[107] See Sen. *Med.* 893–925, especially 910 and 923; 925–51.

[108] See Sen. *Med.* 919–25, 933–6, 950–7, and text to nn. 62–9, 83–6 above.

[109] On the (unnatural) reversal of time and of natural process (reproduction and growth) in her description of her infanticide, esp. in *Med.* 984, 1012–13, see Schiesaro (2003), 210, 212.

[110] Contrast E. *HF* 822–1015; see further Padel (1994). On this contrast in types of madness see Gill (1997*c*), 219–23.

[111] See also Gill (1987), 35–6.

[112] See 4.5 above, esp. text to nn. 197–205, 213–18, 225–44.

[113] See n. 52 above.

forms a powerful strand in the drama and one aspect of the monologue. Schiesaro find here grounds for scepticism that Senecan dramaturgy can really be squared with the objectives of Stoic ethical education.[114] However, the preceding discussion brings out a dimension of Seneca's *Medea*, and *Phaedra*, which can, plausibly, be seen as promoting those aims. As suggested earlier, although audiences, ancient and modern, can be envisaged as identifying with powerful representations of evil,[115] it is less easy to see why one should engage with internal conflict, 'feverish' instability, tortuous reasoning, and the kind of 'madness' which Medea induces in herself. In Stoic thought, it seems that these dimensions of human experience were taken as—in modern terms—'objective' indicators of the idea that passion was, as the Stoics claimed, a kind of sickness or madness.[116] Seneca's dramatization of these dimensions may then, be taken as conveying the same message. If even his Medea or Phaedra can, in these ways, recognize or express the badness of their passionate state or of its consequences, that carries implications for the type of message which is also conveyed to the audience.

7.4 VIRGIL'S *AENEID*

The examples considered so far in this chapter, as illustrations of differing approaches to structure and disintegration of character, have been relatively straightforward. Plutarch's *Lives* are largely explicit in their overall objectives and in the Platonic–Aristotelian ethical and psychological framework applied to the question of stability and breakdown. Although there is more room for argument about the standpoint of Senecan tragedy, I have maintained that the presentation of psychological collapse in *Phaedra* and *Medea* reflects central features of Stoic thinking about passion and internal conflict. Virgil's *Aeneid*, the final example considered here, raises more complex issues. There is scope for debate, first, about how far we should suppose that *any* philosophical framework underpins the characterization of the epic. Second, if we allow the likelihood of some philosophical influence, there is room for argument about

114 See Schiesaro (2003), 16–18 (referring especially to *Med.* 13–17, 45–52), 208–14 (referring to passages including 166, 171, 910); see also *Med.* 900–25, 982–8. See also text to nn. 54–5 above.

115 For some 19th- and 20th-c. formulations of this idea, see Gill (1996*b*), 107–12.

116 A similar point could be made about Plato's analysis of psychic disintegration in the tyrannical type; see 5.2 above, text to nn. 125–35; also Annas (1981), 303–4. On Stoic passion as psychic sickness and madness, see e.g. Cic. *Tusc.* 3.7–11, 4.52–4, 77; Sen. *Ira* 1.1.2–4, 2.36.4–6; also Gill 1997*c*: 231–2.

which theory is most relevant. We also need to consider the possibility that several (more or less) theorized approaches to emotions are combined in the poem, integrated with other informing influences on characterization. A third issue is suggested by the present context. There are a number of cases in the *Aeneid* where the main figures seem to be presented as lapsing from standards of (normatively) rational and virtuous behaviour and attitude. Are these cases better seen in quasi-Plutarchean terms as breakdown under pressure of a normally stable—and broadly virtuous—character? Or are these instances better interpreted in the light of Stoic or Epicurean psychology and ethics? In particular, do we find in the *Aeneid* signs of the influence of Stoic or Epicurean versions of the 'Socratic' claim that deflection from the highest standards of virtuous rationality generates psychological instability, internal conflict, or 'madness', in some sense? Obviously, these are very large questions; and my response here, as elsewhere in this chapter, can only be selective. But it is worth considering at least some of the relevant evidence against the background of the philosophical ideas examined in this book, in particular the contrast between Stoic–Epicurean and Platonic–Aristotelian conceptions of personality.

Why, in broad terms, is it plausible to think that philosophical theories of any sort might be a significant influence on characterization in the *Aeneid*? The most explicitly philosophical section of the poem is Anchises' visionary picture of the universe in Book 6. This account does not seem to reflect the world-view of any single theory, and its interpretation is still debated. But its presence at a crucial moment in the poem indicates a readiness to deploy philosophically informed ideas in a way that is integral to the poetic project.[117] More external or general considerations are also germane to this question. The period of the late Roman Republic, immediately prior to Virgil's composition of the poem, was one of intense philosophical activity, as regards the Roman reception of Greek theories and debate among Romans about the rival merits and implications of these theories. Works of this period that have a direct bearing on the topics of character and emotion include Cicero's *Tusculan Disputations*, Philodemus' *On Anger*, and Lucretius' *On the Nature of the Universe* (which includes a large-scale critique of erotic passion).[118] As some recent discussions have brought out, our evidence suggests that at least some members of the Roman ruling elite in the late Republic were not only familiar with philosophical ideas but also tried seriously to apply them in determining difficult ethical or political

[117] Virg. *A.* 6.724–51, which combines (at least) a Stoic world-view and Platonic eschatology. See further Austin (1977), 220–1; Hardie (1986), 66–84; Braund (1997), 217–18.

[118] Lucr. 4.1037–1207; see further text to nn. 167–71 below.

questions.[119] Virgil's friend and contemporary, Horace, explicitly deploys philosophical ideas and themes in a series of poetic genres.[120] External evidence, including some recently discovered, suggests that Virgil, like Horace, was associated with the Epicurean circle centred on the school of Philodemus at Herculaneum.[121] These are just the most obvious of the points that make it plausible, in principle, to think that Virgilian presentation of character—including breakdown of character—might be significantly shaped by philosophical ideas.

The question, in this area, that has so far attracted most scholarly attention is that of possible philosophical influences on Virgil's presentation of anger. This is partly because relevant evidence is relatively full. Philodemus' *On Anger*, of which a number of extracts survive, provides access to Epicurean views and debate within the school.[122] Cicero's *Tusculans* give a prominent role to contrasting approaches to anger and other emotions from a Stoic and 'Aristotelian' standpoint (as these are understood in this period), and Seneca's *On Anger* confirms the main lines of argument.[123] Anger has also figured prominently in scholarly discussion because it is a major subject in the poem and the source of a longstanding particular critical problem. This is the question of how we should interpret the uncharacteristic outburst of anger in which Aeneas kills Turnus at the end of the *Aeneid* (12.930–52). Should this be taken as a response which is justified as motivation for a legitimate punishment for exceptional wrongdoing? Or is Aeneas' upsurge of anger, following initial restraint, an indication that he too—like other figures—is subject to lapses into irrational frenzy? Reference has been made to Stoic, Epicurean, and (in some sense) 'Aristotelian' or Platonic–Aristotelian approaches, to define Virgil's presentation of anger in general and at the end of the poem in particular.[124] Some discussions have also stressed that philosophical influences need to be considered in conjunction with other possible shaping factors, in particular intertextual factors as well as Virgil's response to Roman political and ethical events and attitudes.[125] A further relevant

119 See Sedley (1997*c*), referring esp. to Plu. *Brut.* 2.3–4; Griffin (1995), 343–6, referring to Cic. *Fam.* 15.17.3 and 15.19.2. Another important text for this question is Cic. *Off.* 3; see Long (1995). See also Clark and Rajak (2002).

120 See references in n. 129 below.

121 See further Gigante and Capasso (1989); Armstrong *et al.* (2004), introd. 1–3.

122 See Indelli (1988); also Annas (1989); Procopé (1998); Fowler (1997).

123 See e.g. Cic. *Tusc.* 4.39–46, esp. 43; Sen. *Ira* 1.7, 8–14. On conceptions of 'Aristotelian' ideas in this period, see Braund and Gill (1997), 6–7.

124 See text to nn. 190–207 below.

125 See e.g. (on interplay between philosophical and political factors), Harris (2001), 217–18, 244–7, discussed in R. J. Tarrant (2004), 118–23; (on interplay between all three factors), Gill (2004*a*).

question, raised especially by the last scene of the *Aeneid*, is whether the poem aims at offering a unified ideological, moral, and emotional vision or is fractured into two or more modes or 'voices'.[126]

I have contributed in previous discussions to the question of the possible philosophical background to Virgil's presentation of emotions in the *Aeneid*.[127] The main points I want to emphasize here are these. I am sceptical of the idea that we should assume that Virgil necessarily deploys a single philosophical approach to emotions in the *Aeneid*. Perhaps, like some other Romans in his day, he aimed at consistency in adopting a specific philosophical theory or in applying this to practical decision-making. But it does not follow that he pursued uniformity of this sort in writing an epic poem.[128] Horace, his friend and (arguably) fellow-Epicurean, does not aim at this kind of consistency in his *Odes*, let alone his poetic corpus as a whole.[129] I think that there are aspects of the presentation of character and emotions in the *Aeneid* which lend themselves to analysis in Stoic, Epicurean, and (in various senses) 'Aristotelian' terms[130]—hence *all* the competing scholarly views noted earlier have material to draw on. However, I am not suggesting that Virgil just applies a promiscuous 'pick-and-mix' approach to philosophical connotations. It is more plausible to think that the poem, typically, deploys a 'layered' mode or presentation. Virgil combines, in different parts of the poem or even the same part, Aristotelian and Stoic or Epicurean ideas or attitudes. But the Stoic or Epicurean approach is, typically, given greater prominence or weight; also Stoic and Epicurean themes are sometimes used in such a way that they reinforce each other and mark a distinction from the Aristotelian approach.[131] Also, specific philosophical themes—and the overall effect or 'layering' of philosophical colours—are integrated with intertextual and political or ideological factors. To this extent, the presentation of emotions, while certainly complex—more so than is often acknowledged in discussions of this type—can be seen as contributing to a poem that has a unified overall vision or 'voice'.[132]

[126] The 'two-voices' view, especially associated with the 'Harvard school', tends to see Aeneas' final outburst of anger as problematic. For a survey of views, see Harrison (1990); also Fowler (1997), 30–5; for recent examples of the 'Harvard school' approach, see Thomas (2000), (2001), esp. 25–54. For a more unified reading (stressing intertextuality), Galinsky (2003).

[127] See Gill (1997*c*), (2003*c*), and (2004*a*); these discussions form the basis for some parts of this section.

[128] For this point, see Gill (2003*c*), 217; for a similar view, see Harris (2001), 216–17.

[129] Horace, for instance, satirizes Stoic ideas in *Satires* 3.3, 7, but adopts a Stoic–Roman idiom in *Odes* 3.2–3, 5. On Horace and Stoicism, see Colish (1985), 160–8; on Horace and Epicureanism, see Armstrong *et al.* (2004), 1–3; Armstrong (2004).

[130] On these various senses of 'Aristotelian', see text to n. 191–4 below.

[131] For this view, see also Gill (2003*c*), 218–21; Stoic and Epicurean readings diverge on Aeneas' killing of Turnus (text to nn. 230–41 below).

[132] On the latter two points, see further Gill (2004*a*).

This is the line of interpretation I pursue here, directed especially towards the following question, which reflects the overall theme of this chapter. A well-marked feature of the *Aeneid* is the way in which the key figures experience what seem to be (on virtually any type of interpretation) ethical and emotional lapses from the standards which the figures themselves, or the poem as a whole, set for them.[133] The two preceding sections of this chapter have presented competing ways of understanding such lapses. In the Plutarchean framework, shaped by Middle Platonic (or Platonic–Aristotelian) thinking, such lapses tend to be understood either as the revelation of longstanding, but previously undisclosed, dispositions or as the breakdown of a (previously stable) character under exceptional pressure. In Stoic—and also Epicurean—thinking, they are explained as symptoms of the instability and incoherence to which all non-wise people are subject, a form of explanation which I see as relevant to Senecan tragedy (7.3 above). I raise here the question of which framework of interpretation seems better to explain Virgilian characterization. I consider this question in connection with both Dido and Aeneas, with specific reference to some salient episodes.[134] In comparing Virgil's modes of presenting figures with those of Plutarchean biography and Senecan tragedy, I am well aware of the differences in genre and chronology between the three types of literature being considered. As explained earlier (411–12 above), my aim is to chart different ways of representing human personality and, as far as possible, the philosophical approaches which inform them. These are topics which cut across different genres and periods of Hellenistic and Roman literature.

In general terms, my answer to the question raised is this. In the case of both Dido and Aeneas, there are grounds for applying a quasi-Plutarchean framework and for seeing their lapses as indicating a more or less temporary deflection from a generally stable and virtuous character. One of the considerations supporting this kind of reading is the use of (broadly) Aristotelian ethical and emotional language in relevant stretches of dialogue. However, there are also indications that these lapses are conceived in Stoic or Epicurean terms or some combination of the two. These indications point to a rather different interpretative model: namely that the figures, in failing to match the highest normative standards, have plunged into the instability and incoherence that characterizes the absence of wisdom. In this model, the question of

[133] However, some incidents are, arguably, only lapses from a Stoic standpoint (and not an Aristotelian or Epicurean viewpoint), e.g. Aeneas' killing of Turnus: see text to nn. 223–43 below.

[134] I consider the presentation of Dido and Aeneas separately, without taking up the further (and very complex) question of the rights and wrongs of their relationship and its breakdown.

stability or variation of character is less important than that of the relative success or failure of the figure in matching—or at least aspiring and making progress towards—ideal standards at any one time. I think that the second (Stoic–Epicurean) framework provides a deeper understanding of these lapses and also takes us further in making sense of the kind of literary project undertaken there. The *Aeneid*, like Seneca's tragedies, as interpreted here, embodies—predominantly at least—the kind of biography that shows how near or how far its figures come at any one time to matching the ideal norms associated in this book with the idea of the structured self. Their lapses tend to be marked as deflections into the *un*-structured state that is characteristic of Stoic or Epicurean passions or errors, rather than the stable but defective vices of the Platonic–Aristotelian framework deployed by Plutarch.[135] One indication of the importance of this second framework is the well-recognized prevalence of the opposition in the ethical language of the *Aeneid* between *uirtus* ('virtue') or *pietas* ('piety') and *furor* ('frenzy') rather than between virtue and vice, or reason and emotion or desire, as one might expect in a more consistently Platonic–Aristotelian framework.[136] Another is the recurrence at key moments in the imagery of the poem of descriptions of *exceptional* firmness and cohesion on the one hand and of *chaotic* violence on the other.[137] Both these features imply the strong contrast in a Stoic–Epicurean pattern between (stable, unified) wisdom and (unstable, incoherent) folly, rather than the more graded Platonic–Aristotelian contrasts between degrees of largely stable virtue and vice.[138]

I begin with Dido, considering the rival merits of a quasi-Plutarchean and a Stoic–Epicurean reading. A key feature of her presentation is the contrast between the composed and virtuous figure shown in Book 1 and the progressive movement in Book 4 towards emotional violence, culminating in a destructive curse and self-destruction (4.584–665). One factor promoting a Platonic–Aristotelian reading is the presence of a strongly Aristotelian idiom in Dido's exchanges with Aeneas, for instance after his announcement that he plans to leave her. In 4.305–8, 320–6, her expression of anger and her appeal for pity are presented as appropriate (in modern terms) 'reactive attitudes',

[135] I have in view here mainly the three Plutarchean cases discussed in 7.2 above, text to nn. 24–31 especially Sertorius. Plutarch does also present some people as unstable *in character* (e.g. Alcibiades and Alexander), but I see this type as less relevant to Virgil's Dido and Aeneas.

[136] Virgil's antithesis cuts across the Platonic–Aristotelian dichotomies; it implies, at least, the Stoic–Epicurean view that virtue/reason and vice/passion are states of the whole personality. For a striking example, see Virg. *A.* 1.292–6; the antithesis pervades the interpretation of Otis (1964), chs. 6–7, e.g. 215–46.

[137] For an early and characteristic example, see Virg. *A.* 1.81–156; on such imagery and its implications, see Hardie (1986), e.g. 90–119.

[138] On this contrast in philosophical ideas, see e.g. 4.3 above, text to nn. 115–20.

given the actions of the people concerned and standard expectations about interpersonal conduct.[139] There are also certain features which might be taken as pointing towards a Plutarchean, character-based interpretation. Dido is introduced as someone who not only has a (relatively) stable political role but also—what seems to be—a developed and settled character. She is depicted, in her dealings with her own people and the Trojan refugees, displaying in a 'kingly' way virtues such as justice, piety, and humanity.[140] As emerges in Book 4, her ethical, and perhaps political, conception of herself is closely linked with the maintenance of loyalty (*fides*) to her dead husband Sychaeus, whose murder led her to take up her monarchic role in founding Carthage.[141] Dido's famous final speech, just before her suicide (especially 6.654–8), might also be taken as supporting this type of reading. This quasi-obituary outlines her achievements and, by inference, her virtues, and places the blame for her disaster on the accident of the arrival of the Trojan ships on her shores. Her comments, though first-personal in form, might be compared with Plutarch's overall judgements on the character and lives of his subjects, or with those of pre-Virgilian writers such as Sallust.[142]

So, overall, we might, in this reading, form a view of Dido not unlike that offered by Plutarch on Sertorius, cited earlier:

> But it is not impossible that good principles [literally, 'decisions', *prohaireseis*] and natures (*phuseis*), damaged by great and undeserved disasters, should change their character (*ēthos*), along with their fate (*daimōn*). But I think this is what happened to Sertorius, when his good fortune abandoned him, and he was made harsh by bad circumstances in his treatment of those who had done wrong. (*Sertorius*, 10.4).

We might see Dido as someone whose adult life, for the most part, shows that she has developed a strongly virtuous character, but who, none the less, changes for the worse at the end of her life. Under the impact of her abortive love affair and her abandonment by Aeneas, she is 'made harsh' and ends by cursing the man she sees as having done her wrong, and his descendants.[143] For Plutarch, the implication of such an analysis is that the person concerned

[139] On Aristotle and 'reactive attitudes', see text to nn. 189–94 below. On Dido's language in 4.305–8, 320–4 as more 'layered' than it initially seems, see text to nn. 172–5 below.

[140] Virg. *A.* 1.507–8, 522–3 (justice), 603–6 (and Dido's response in 615–30) (piety), 461–3, 565–78 (humanity). On Dido and the virtues of 'kingliness', see Cairns (1989), 40–2.

[141] Virg. *A.* 1.340–68, 4.15–29 (also 4. 457–9). See also Monti (1981), 21–2, 32, 69; T. D. Hill (2003), 129.

[142] For such judgements in Plutarch, see 7.2 above, text to nn. 24–5; also Duff (1999), 243–86 on summarizing 'comparisons' of character. For judgements of this kind in Sallust, based on behaviour in various stages of life, see e.g. *Cat.* 23.1–2 (Quintus Curius), 54 (Caesar and Cato), *Jug.* 6.1, 7.3–7 (Jugurtha).

[143] See Virg. *A.* 4.607–29, also 305–30, 365–87.

has not acquired the 'complete virtue' that would enable her to surmount either great success or great misfortune without loss of ethical stability.[144]

I think this type of interpretation is tenable. But another understanding of Dido's breakdown is, I think, more credible. This is a version of the pattern displayed in Senecan tragedy (6.3 above), in which surrender to passion generates a prolonged state of emotional instability, involving irrational reasoning, internal conflict and self-blame, and a kind of 'madness'. Several of the most striking features of Book 4 support this reading.[145] For instance, once Dido has surrendered herself to her love (a surrender she herself presents as against her better judgement),[146] her behaviour is described as 'frenzied' or 'mad', in the sense that it is intensely emotional and uncontrolled.[147] This 'madness' is intensified after she receives news of Aeneas' departure (300–1); her subsequent speeches are marked, increasingly, by conflicting emotions, including passionate love, intense anger, and self-blame at breaking her vow to Sychaeus. Though she is compared at one point to Greek tragic figures who experience raving madness, her 'madness', like that of Seneca's Medea, is not of that type.[148] The fact that she is conflicted in this way, and that she herself characterizes her behaviour as 'mad',[149] implies an idea also suggested by the Senecan pattern. This is that, in spite of being in the grip of intense passion, she is still able to exercise her fundamental human rationality, a point also displayed in the—almost cosmic—detachment of her quasi-obituary speech before her death.[150]

What is the conceptual basis for this type of pattern? In considering this strand in Senecan tragedy, I have highlighted the likely influence of Stoic thought, notably Chrysippus' thinking on passion as self-division (431 above). Although there is no reason to suppose that Virgil was a committed Stoic, in the way Seneca was, Stoic thought was probably a key influence on this mode of representing Dido and other figures in the *Aeneid*. For both Virgil and Seneca, works such as Cicero's *Tusculans* are likely to have been an important

[144] See 7.2 above, text to nn. 28–31.

[145] The rest of this paragraph is based closely on Gill (1997*c*), 229.

[146] Virg. *A.* 4.15–19, 24–9, 55, also 548–9; see further below. Dido's passionate love is also presented as the outcome of Venus' intervention (1.657–722, 4.1–5). I take it that Virgil, like Homer, employs the kind of 'double-motivation', in which divine intervention, signifying, for instance, the world-historical significance of events, is compatible with human agency. On the idea of Virgil's gods 'working with' human emotions, see Lyne (1987), 66–71; Feeney (1991), 164–80.

[147] Virg. *A.* 4.68–9 ('frenzied', *furens*), 78–9 ('mad', *demens*), 91, 101 ('frenzy', *furorem*).

[148] She is compared to Pentheus and Orestes (4. 465–73). For the contrast between this type of 'madness' and 'raving' madness in Greek tragedy, see Gill (1997*c*), 218–22, and text to n. 110 above on Sen. *Med.* On madness in Virg. *A.* in general, see Hershkowitz (1998), ch. 2.

[149] Virg. *A.* 4.376, 433, 548, 595–6.

[150] Virg. *A.* 4.653–8. For this reading of this passage, see text to nn. 177–81 below; for a competing ('Plutarchean') reading, text to n. 142 above.

source for Stoic ethical psychology.[151] The *Tusculans* contain a series of ideas relevant to this poetic pattern, including the contrast between the self-consistent and emotionally invulnerable wise person and the sickness, madness, and feverish incoherence of the passions to which the non-wise are subject.[152] One point of special relevance is Cicero's claim—made in criticism of the Aristotelian ideal of 'moderation' of passion—that to give way to passion at all is to throw oneself 'headlong' (*praeceps*), as though from a precipice, into a passionate state that one can no longer control.[153] However, the fact that Stoicism is the most likely source for this poetic pattern does not mean that it is the only source. As I have suggested elsewhere (1997*c*: 230–4), Stoic ideas may converge with certain, characteristically Roman, themes in suggesting this mode of presentation. These themes include a tendency in late Republican political rhetoric to deploy a sharp virtue–madness contrast.[154] Also relevant is ideological pressure on the Roman ruling elite to set the standards of virtue and rationality very high, thereby widening the scope for falling short of these standards. We can see a similar convergence of Stoic and Roman ideals in the 'Roman' *Odes* of Horace, another non-Stoic.[155] Virgil's presentation of Dido's plunge from kingly rationality and virtue to inner conflict, instability, and 'madness', which is, at least partly, counterpointed by Aeneas' aspiration to gain or recover stability and virtue,[156] implies this fusion of Stoic and Roman motifs.

Another influence on this pattern, and one which may reinforce its main features, is Epicurean thinking on ethical psychology. Some ancient thinkers in this period, especially those writing from (some version of) the Platonic standpoint, such as Cicero and Plutarch, tend to take a negative view of Epicurean ethics and to discourage comparisons between Stoic and Epicurean thought.[157]

[151] On the likely influence of Cic. *Tusc.* on Virgil, see Putnam (1990), 13–18. For similarities between Cic. *Tusc.* and Sen. *Ira* in thinking about passions, see 4.3 above, text to nn. 126–8; also I. Hadot (1969), 81–4; Fillion-Lahille (1984), 112–18

[152] See e.g. Cic. *Tusc.* 3.18–21, 4.37–8 (wise person), 4.23–30 (passions as psychic sicknesses, which are unstable and inconsistent, 4.24, 29–30, even though there are dispositional tendencies to certain passions), anger as 'madness', and the link with Stoic ideas of (non-wise) 'madness' (4.52–4). See further on Cic. *Tusc.* as a vehicle of Chrysippean theory, Tieleman (2003), 288–320; on *Tusc.* 3–4 more generally, Graver (2002*a*).

[153] Cic. *Tusc.* 4.41–2, cf. Sen. *Ira.* 1.74. These passages echo Chrysippean ideas about passions (as 'running legs') and 'psychophysical inertia' (4.6 above, text to nn. 314–19); see also Gill (1997*c*: 321–2).

[154] See e.g. Cic. *Parad.* 4.1.27, *Sest.* 97, 99, *Cael.* 15, *Pis.* 46–7; [Sal.] *Cic.* 7.

[155] See e.g. Hor. *Carm.* 3.5, esp. 41–56, 3.3.1–8; also Cic. *Off.* 3.99–111, taken with 1.66–7, 69, 80. See further Gill (1997*c*), 233–4, also (1994), 4609–10, on Cic. *Off.* 1. On Horace and philosophy, see n. 129 above.

[156] See esp. Virg. *A.* 4.279–95, 331–61, 437–49.

[157] See e.g. Ch. 2 above, text to n. 235. See also, on Cicero's philosophical stance, Glucker (1988); Powell (1995), introd. and on Cicero's criticisms of Epicurean ethics, Stokes (1995). On Plutarch's position, see 4.3 above, text to nn. 101–4 and on his relationship to Epicureanism, Boulogne (2003), esp. 32–9.

But I have argued here that these two innovative Hellenistic theories converge, even if they do not explicitly agree, in their views on key aspects of psychology and ethics. Notably, they converge in combining versions of—what I am calling—'Socratic' ethical claims with certain kinds of holism and naturalism. These shared Stoic–Epicurean ethical claims include the idea that only the wise person is fully coherent in psychological make-up and behaviour and that all non-wise people are more or less incoherent. Related ideas in Epicurean ethics include the contrast between 'empty' and 'natural' desire and emotions, together with a critique of (many) conventional emotions and desires as based on a false conception of what is naturally good and bad, pleasant and painful, for human beings.[158] To some degree, at least, Epicureanism thus shares the Stoic rejection of the conventional, and also Aristotelian, view of emotions as reactive attitudes, or justified responses to deliberate actions in interpersonal exchange.[159] Epicureans are, I think, less inclined than Stoics to characterize non-wise responses in terms of 'madness'.[160] But, in other respects, Epicurean thinking provides connotations which reinforce the main lines of the second, Stoic-inspired, pattern of interpretation of Dido's emotional trajectory, in which surrender to passion generates a plunge into irrationality and inner conflict.

I now illustrate this Stoic–Epicurean convergence with reference to certain passages in Book 4.

> 'If my mind were not fixed and immovably settled against wanting to unite with another in the marriage-bond after my first love cheated me and deceived me with death; if my attitude were not wholly negative about the bridal bedroom and wedding-torch—this is perhaps the one failing to which I could have given way (*huic uni forsan potui succumbere culpae*).' (Virg. *A.* 4.15–19.)

Dido's revelatory words to her sister Anna imply that her surrender to passionate love is against her better judgement or 'akratic'. The narrator's subsequent comment on the effect of Anna's encouraging reply reinforces that impression: 'with these words, she inflamed a heart already charged with love and gave hope to a wavering mind and broke down her shame (*spemque dedit dubiae menti soluitque pudorem*)' (Virg. *A.* 4.54–5). These passages illustrate a feature which is recurrent in Book 4: Dido herself sees her passionate love for Aeneas as a fault or source of blame (here, *culpa*, 19), especially because it runs counter to her longstanding commitment (*fides*) to her first husband Sychaeus.[161] This presentation of passion as involving inner conflict, because of the person's continuing rational awareness of going wrong, is one of the

[158] See Ch. 2 above, esp. 2.2, text to nn. 76–80, 2.3, text to nn. 179–93, 210–22.

[159] See Gill (2003*c*), 213–16; also 450–3 below.

[160] But see e.g. Phld. *On Anger* 44.5–35, trans D. Armstrong, cited by Fish (2004), 114–15, in which 'madness' (*mania*) is twice used as a synonym for (non-wise) folly.

[161] Dido reaffirms this commitment in 4.20–9; see also n. 141 above.

features of Virgil's description of Dido that most strongly evokes the kind of Stoic thinking that seems to underlie Seneca's presentation of Phaedra and Medea. Line 19, with its unexpected idea of giving way to—what the person concerned sees as—a fault (*succumbere culpae*) might be an echo of the paradoxical declararation by Euripides' Medea (1078) that she knows that what she is doing is 'bad' (*kaka*), an assertion which had such resonance for the Stoic Chrysippus.[162] The echo is less evident than in the case of Seneca's *Phaedra*, and it is also more open to question whether Virgil would have been aware of Chrysippus' interest in Euripides' lines.[163] But this passage as a whole, taken in the context of the larger pattern charted in Book 4, has a strongly Stoic colour.

This connotation coexists with others, including intertextual responses to other poetic representations of hesitation and conflict. For instance, in Apollonius, *Argonautica* 3, the dialogue between Chalciope and her sister plays a similar role in inducing Medea to act on her intense (though concealed) love rather than on her sense of shame.[164] There may also be echoes of Catullus' Lesbia-poems, which accentuate inner conflict and include telling use of the term *culpa*, though not applied by the speaker to himself.[165] However, my focus here is philosophical influences; the possible echo of Medea's lines is cited primarily because of the resonance these lines had acquired in Stoic writings, especially Chrysippus' *On Passions*.[166]

Epicurean themes may also reinforce this aspect of Virgil's presentation of Dido's love. Epicureans regarded passionate or romantic love as a clear case of an 'empty' or ungrounded desire. Lucretius, a poet seen as widely influential on Virgil,[167] wrote an extended critique of passionate love, presenting it as a species of illusion or deception (and self-deception).[168] His analysis in Book 4

[162] *Culpa* is a term we might expect another person to use of one's actions (see e.g. 4.171–2). Another possible echo of Medea-type expressions is Turnus' line (12.680): 'Let me do this one mad act (*furere... furorem*) before I die'. See further Gill (1997*c*), 238–9, noting the paradox that this line signals the moment at which Turnus *throws off* his passionate folly.

[163] On Sen. *Ph.* 177–9, 184, see 7.3 above, text to nn. 100–2. It is not certain that Seneca was aware of Chrysippus' interest in Medea's line but Galen's evidence suggests this was a well-known feature of Chrysippean thought.

[164] A.R. *Arg.* 3, esp. dialogue between the sisters (673–743), Medea's hesitations (645–63, 771–801), conflict between desire and shame (649, 652–3, 681, 687), Medea's indirectness about her love (687–92), Chalciope's ready response (697–704).

[165] Catul. 75, esp. line 1, also poems 85, 72; see further Lyne (1980), 26–41, on the interplay between erotic and ethical language in Catullus.

[166] On this focus, see 7.1, first para; on Chrysippus and Medea, 4.5 above. On the combination of intertextual and philosophical connotations, see Gill (2004*a*), esp. 114–15, on this passage.

[167] See e.g. Hardie (1986), ch. 5; Armstrong *et al.* (2004), 91–6.

[168] On 'empty' desires, see 2.3 above, text to nn. 179–87. On Epicurean thinking about sexual desire, see LS 21 G(3) (= *VS* 51), and Lucr. 4. 1037–1207. See also Graver (1990), 108–12; Nussbaum (1994), ch. 5, esp. 166–72, who both stress the significance of the linkage between erotic and sensory illusions, for instance, in Lucr. 4.1024–36.

of the way in which romantic love involves delusions about sexual desire is parallel to his study in Book 3 of the way that most people misunderstand their emotions and desires and the real motives underlying these.[169] In the opening dialogue between Dido and Anna, from which the lines cited are taken (4.15–19, 54–5), there are possible echoes of both of Lucretius' critiques. Dido's opening speech exemplifies the persuasive description of a loved one that Lucretius sees as promoting the error of romantic love.[170] Anna's response, offering an ethical and political justification for Dido's feelings, provides a justification for a passion already aroused.[171] Anna promotes Dido's self-deception about her real motives, thus encouraging her to *succumbere culpae*, to 'give way' to what Dido herself at some level recognizes as wrong. So we can see how the connotations of Epicurean thinking about romantic love may reinforce those of Stoic thinking about surrender to passion.

In this passage, as so interpreted, the relevant philosophical connotations are Stoic–Epicurean. Elsewhere, we find what can be termed a 'layered' presentation, which, on the surface, invites an Aristotelian interpretation, but, on closer reading, contains a Stoic–Epicurean sub-text.

> 'Traitor (*perfide*), did you even hope that you could cover up so great a crime and silently leave this land? Aren't you held here by our love or [our] right hands once given as a pledge (*data dextra quondam*) or by Dido, soon to die with a cruel end ... It is because of you that the Libyan peoples and the Numidian lords hate me and that the Tyrians are my enemies. It is because of you also that my sense of shame has been lost (*extinctus pudor*) as well as my earlier fame, my only means of immortality. To whom do you abandon me to meet my death, guest (this name alone is left in place of "husband").' (4.305–8, 320–4)

On the face of it, the language reflects the Aristotelian—and conventional—view that emotions such as anger or pity are reactive attitudes, which are presented as justified by the interpersonal behaviour of the agents involved.[172] But fuller reflection suggests that Dido's claims may not be wholly justified; and this, in turn, prompts a different way of interpreting her speech. The appeal to the right hand pledged in marriage and to Aeneas' role of husband is thrown into question by the ambiguous status of their liaison.[173] The claim

[169] See Lucr. 3.31–93, 1053–94; also 2.3 above, text to nn. 188–93.

[170] Cf. Virg. *A.* 4.10–14 (also 3–4 and 54–5) and Lucr. 4.1153–70.

[171] Virg. *A.* 4.31–53 (also 1–2). The importance of Anna's persuasion is stressed by Dido in 4.548–52.

[172] See text to nn. 189–94 below.

[173] See 4.165–72, esp. 172: 'She calls it a marriage (*conubium*); with this name she screens wrongdoing (*culpam*)'. Aeneas' denial that they were married (4.338–9) is not challenged by Dido in her following speech (4.365–87).

that Aeneas—by implication, alone—is responsible for the hostility of the surrounding Africans and the Tyrians, and also for Dido's abandonment of her commitment to Sychaeus, is also not borne out by the situation presented earlier in Book 4.[174] The assertion that Dido is now condemned to death at the hand of her enemies (*moritura*, 308, *moribundam*, 323) goes beyond what can credibly be attributed to Aeneas' agency and taken to justify anger or pity. My aim, in making these points, is not to assert that Dido is, clearly, in the wrong, in this exchange or in the relationship generally. My suggestion is that we may not, on reflection, interpret her remarks in the way she intends (as providing grounds for anger or pity), but rather, in a more Stoic or Epicurean way, as the expression of irrational passion or as self-delusion. The allusion in the latter part of the passage to the breach in her fidelity to Sychaeus (4.322–3) recalls the start of Book 4 (1–55). Here, I argued earlier, Stoic and Epicurean connotations converge to convey the impression that Dido is surrendering herself to passion or 'empty' emotion. The speech cited here is preceded by a description of how Dido 'raged out of her mind (*saeuit inops animi*) like an inflamed Bacchant' (*incensa... bacchatur*, 300–1). This alerts us to the indications of irrational passion in Dido's words. The signs of strained reasoning and the conflict between passionate love and self-blame indicated in these lines become more pronounced in the course of Book 4.[175]

I return now to Dido's famous pre-death speech.

> 'I have lived my life and completed the course which fortune has given me, and now my shade, in its greatness, will go under the earth. I have established a famous city, I have seen my own city-walls, I took revenge for my husband, punishing a brother who had become our enemy. I was happy—all too happy—if only the Trojan ships had never touched our shores.' (4.654–8).

As noted earlier, these lines serve as a quasi-obituary. They could also be compared to a biographer's final judgement on a life or a character, and might seem to support a quasi-Plutarchean interpretation of Dido's story. In this view, the events of Book 4, including the abandonment of her kingly role and decline into emotional violence and hatred, might be seen as marking a lapse in a life otherwise marked by great achievements and the expression of the virtues.[176] On the other hand, the tone of exceptional, rational detachment in an extreme situation has powerful Epicurean and Stoic resonance.

[174] Virg. *A.* 4.36–41 suggests that the African leaders are already angry at their rejection as Dido's suitors. Neither the enmity of Dido's brother (cited in 4.325) nor the weakening of Dido's commitment to Sychaeus (which is portrayed in 4.1–55) can credibly be attributed to Aeneas as a responsible agent.

[175] See further Gill (2004*a*), 116–17, referring to 4.534–6, 543–52, taken as illustrating irrationality (as understood in Stoic or Epicurean terms). See also nn. 146–8 below.

[176] See text to nn. 142–4 above.

An Epicurean parallel is Epicurus' famous death-bed letter.[177] For Stoics, Socrates' speeches before his death in Plato's *Phaedo* might come to mind, which served as a paradigm for subsequent Stoic modes of preparation for death.[178] However, there are important qualifications to this apparent adoption of the accent of Stoic or Epicurean wisdom and emotional invulnerability. Dido's summary of her life wholly elides her own agency (as depicted in the course of Book 4) in cutting short this life of virtuous achievement. Her rational tone is also in sharp contrast to her situation and intended actions: she is sitting on top of a funeral pyre on her quasi-marital bed and about to die by plunging Aeneas' sword into her breast (642–50, 663–5). The speech is also in striking contrast to the terrible curse she has just uttered against her former lover and his descendants (607–29). The philosophical tone of this speech is at odds with the expressions of anger, vengeance, and wounded love just before and after these lines.[179] This juxtaposition of tones brings out in another way the Stoic theme that all human beings are fundamentally capable of exercising rationality even at moments, such as this, when their emotions and actions seem in some ways deeply irrational. Elsewhere in Dido's speeches, this theme appears in the form of self-blame alongside bitter anger and continuing passionate love.[180] Here, the contrast, and conflict, is between the detached rational tone and the passions (unacceptable by Epicurean as well as Stoic standards)[181] that are still at work in her. Thus, overall, I think Dido's biography in the *Aeneid* is told in a predominantly Stoic–Epicurean mode, even though there are features that might seem to suggest a Platonic–Aristotelian, and quasi-Plutarchean, pattern.

I now raise a similar question as regards Aeneas. Obviously, the potential material here is more extensive, and my treatment will need to be yet more selective. The question whether the poem embodies a quasi-Plutarchean or Stoic–Epicurean 'biography' of Aeneas overlaps with the much-discussed issue of whether Aeneas develops as a character, and what form of

177 See LS 24 D, and 2.3 above, text to nn. 234–9.

178 See Pl. *Phd.* 115c–118a. The self-killings of the Stoics Cato and Seneca were explicitly modelled on Socrates' death; see Griffin (1986); T. D. Hill (2003), 218–21, referring esp. to Tac. *Ann.* 15.62–4.

179 Contrast 653–8 with 643–50, esp. 642–6, and also the implied passionate love in 651–2 and the anger in 659–62; also the confused riot of emotions in 590–606. See also 2.2 above, text to nn. 67–9.

180 See e.g. 4.534–52 (taken with the narrative comment in 531–2), 590–606. A similar point is implied in the combination of (confused) emotions (including grief, love, and madness) and virtuous attitudes (*uirtus* and *pudor*) ascribed to Turnus and Mezentius as they go to meet their deaths (10.870–1, 12. 667–8). For a similar combination, signifying the same idea, in Seneca's *Phaedra*, see 7.3 above, text to nn. 70–6.

181 On Epicurean criticism of revenge, taken as a source of pleasure, see 452 below; contrast Dido's intensely passionate desire for revenge in her curse (607–29).

character-development can be expected in this type of epic poem and in this intellectual and cultural context.[182] For a Plutarchean framework, based on Platonic–Aristotelian assumptions, the normal expectation is that a developed adult character is unlikely to change during adult life; apparent change of character thus requires special explanation. (This is not, of course, to rule out extension of ethical understanding through further education and experience; Plutarch's *Lives*, like his essays in practical ethics, are designed to produce this result.)[183] For a Stoic–Epicurean framework, by contrast, the possibility of life-long development is a key assumption. This derives in both theories, as shown in Chapter 3, from the combination of the 'Socratic' claim that virtue and happiness are 'up to us' with psychological holism, in which there are no non-rational 'parts' incapable of modification. The central role given in Stoic–Epicurean thinking to philosophical therapy, directed primarily at adults (at any stage of their life) reflects this pattern of thinking about development.[184] This view of the possibility of life-long development is combined with the belief that failure to develop in this way brings with it psychological and ethical instability, incoherence, and inner conflict.

Against this background, I see two possible ways of viewing Aeneas' biography in the poem, with some partly overlapping features. From a broadly Plutarchean standpoint, Aeneas can be viewed as someone with a relatively stable character, and a settled disposition to exercise virtues such as courage, piety, and humanity, in a kingly or leaderly way. This character is indicated in Aeneas' presentation of his past life (in Books 2–3), in the 'present' of the poem's narrative, and in prophetic glimpses of his future.[185] However, the narrative also highlights certain episodes, in Books 2 and 4, and—possibly—Books 10 and 12, where he falls short of the highest standards of conduct and character.[186] These might be taken as instances, like that of Plutarch's Sertorius, where the exceptional pressures of circumstances produce an episodic lapse in stability, thus implying that Aeneas falls short of 'complete' virtue, though less markedly so than other figures such as Dido.[187] For the contrasting,

[182] On this issue, see e.g. Otis (1964), 308; Fish (2004), 125, 135 n. 56; more generally, on Virgilian characterization, Laird (1997).

[183] See Duff (1999), 37, 39, 42–3, 73–4, also 103–11; Gill (1994), 4624–31.

[184] See 3.2 above, esp. text to nn. 11–20, 42–7, 3.5, text to nn. 225–43; on therapy, 6.5 above, text to nn. 182–93.

[185] For such prophetic glimpses, see e.g. Virg. *A.* 1.257–66, 6.756–886 (Aeneas' character indicated by his descendants, e.g. 6.769–70), 8.729–31, taken with 8.626–728.

[186] See e.g. 2.567–633 (the Helen-episode, discussed below), 4.160–278 (the liaison with Dido); on 10.510–42 (violent anger after Pallas' death), see Gill (2003*c*), 223, and on 12.919–52 (the killing of Turnus), text to nn. 223–41 below. Whether or not the incidents in Books 10 and 12 count as lapses depends on the ethical (and philosophical) framework being applied, as indicated in discussion of the anger of Aeneas below.

[187] See 7.2 above, text to nn. 24–31, text to nn. 139–44.

Stoic–Epicurean, framework, it is not assumed that adult human beings—apart from the normative wise person—are stable in ethical character. Also, the criteria for what counts as an ethical or emotional lapse are different from, and in some ways more rigorous than, those in a Plutarchean (Platonic–Aristotelian) approach.[188] From a Stoic–Epicurean standpoint, what is important is whether Aeneas, at any one point, is at least aspiring towards the complete consistency and stability of perfect wisdom or is falling back into the instability, irrationality, inner conflict, or 'madness' to which the non-wise are subject.

How can we adjudicate between these two possible readings, both of which are tenable in terms of the thought-world of Virgil's time? As a point of access to this question, I focus on Virgil's presentation of anger. This topic has been much debated by scholars wanting to correlate Virgilian characterization with ancient philosophical approaches. But there are still important points to be made, notably regarding Virgil's layered mode of representation, combining the connotations of different philosophical perspectives. As in the case of Dido, I think that greater emphasis is given to the indications of a Stoic or Epicurean (or Stoic–Epicurean) approach to anger than of an Aristotelian approach in Virgil's portrayal of Aeneas. This point does not, by itself, settle the question whether we should see the *Aeneid* as embodying a quasi-Plutarchean or Stoic–Epicurean conception of biography; but it is an important indicator.

What, in essence, is the difference between these philosophical approaches to anger? One way of defining these differences which I have deployed elsewhere, is in terms of P. F. Strawson's contrast between 'reactive' and 'objective' attitudes. In the case of reactive attitudes, the other person is treated as an equal partner in relationships and as fully responsible, by her actions, for praise and blame and other such reactions, including anger and resentment. In the contrasting objective attitude, the relationship is asymmetrical: the leading partner refrains from reactive responses such as blame or anger. The leading partner's attitude is 'objective' in the sense of being dispassionate, rather than subjectively engaged, and also in that she takes account of objective factors not necessarily grasped by the other person. Strawson presents reactive attitudes as the normal mode of interpersonal exchange, while objective attitudes are appropriate in special cases, such as the relationship of parent to child or psychiatrist to patient.[189]

[188] The norm is 'absence of passion/disturbance', not 'moderation of passion'; see e.g. 4.3 above, text to nn. 121–8; also text to nn. 195–207 below (Epicurean and Stoic readings of anger in the *Aeneid*).

[189] Strawson (1974); see further Gill (2003*c*), 208–9. Strawson's objective-reactive contrast has some points of resemblance with the objective–subjective contrast drawn in 6.2 above, but the two distinctions are not identical in conception or reference. Strawson's distinction is focused on types of interpersonal relation; the contrast drawn in 6.2 is broader, relating also to psychology and epistemology.

This contrast can help us to differentiate key features of Aristotelian and Stoic or Epicurean thinking on anger.[190] Aristotle's definition of anger in *Rhetoric* 2 illustrates the main features of his view:

> Let anger be defined as a desire, accompanied by pain, for revenge at what is taken to be an insult to oneself or those close to one, in a situation where insult is not appropriate... Every case of anger must be accompanied by a certain type of pleasure, namely that which derives from the hope of taking revenge.[191]

Aristotle presents anger as an emotional response derived from judgements about the other person treated as a responsible agent in interpersonal relations, based on (conventional) expectations about appropriate standards of conduct.[192] This characterization of anger as a 'reactive attitude' does not only hold good in Aristotle's school-texts (of which Virgil may not have had detailed knowledge)[193] but also applies to contemporary accounts of Aristotelian or Peripatetic thought. It also applies to what one might call 'vernacular' Aristotelianism, that is, conventional Greek or Roman attitudes which share the reactive approach illustrated by Aristotle's definition.[194] The Stoic concept of anger differs in several ways: in the psychological model, the conception of value, and the norm of interpersonal relationship. Anger is seen as a (normatively) irrational passion, based on a mistaken belief about what is really good and involving intense psychophysical reactions.[195] These features of Stoic thinking are well known and have been fully examined here (251–2 above). What is less often recognized is that Stoic thinking on anger and other passions is linked with a revisionary view of interpersonal relations. This is brought out especially in Stoic practical ethics, as presented by Epictetus and Marcus Aurelius. Anger and other passions are repudiated in part because they imply (mistakenly) that another person can harm or benefit you. In reality, Stoics maintain, you are the only person who can harm or benefit yourself, by advancing or preventing your own progress towards

190 For a similar contrast between Aristotelian and Stoic–Epicurean social attitudes (centred on rivalry) to that drawn here, see Gill (2004*a*).

191 Arist. *Rh.* 2.2, 1378^{a}30–2, ^{b}1–2; see also Arist. *de An.* 1.1, 403^{a}29–^{b}3, and *NE* 4.5.

192 See further Fortenbaugh (1975), 12–18, 80–1; Sherman (1989), 169–71; Gill (1996*b*), 198–9; M. R. Wright (1997), 170–3, who sees the pattern as Platonic–Aristotelian. Konstan (2001), esp. 128–36, highlights parallels between Aristotle's thinking on anger and on pity.

193 See further Barnes (1997*b*), 44–59, attempting to reconstruct Cicero's knowledge of Aristotle's school-texts.

194 On these senses of 'Aristotelian', see Braund and Gill (1997), introd. 6–9. For the second sense, see e.g. Cic. *Tusc.* 3.22, 74, 4.39–46; Sen. *Ira* 1.7, 8.4–5, 9, 10.4, 11.1, 12.1–3, 14.1, 17.1. For 'vernacular Aristotelianism' in the thinking about emotions in Roman historiography, see Levene (1997), esp. 128–36.

195 These points only emerge by implication in standard Stoic definitions of anger, e.g. 'a desire for revenge on one who seems to have done one an injustice inappropriately', D.L. 7.113, cf. Stob. 2.91.10–15 (10c), trans. Inwood and Gerson (1997), pp. 198, 218.

goodness or wisdom. In Strawson's terms, the Stoics advocate an 'objective' rather than 'reactive attitude'. This attitude is dispassionate, though this is compatible with a real desire to benefit the other person. It is also based on an understanding of 'objective' features of human and cosmic life that hold good for people even if they do not generally recognize them.[196]

The Epicurean position is less easy to define, in part because there are no teachings on anger surviving from Epicurus. Our fullest source, extracts of Philodemus' *On Anger*, represents only one position in a debate in which other Epicureans adopted sharply different views.[197] Philodemus' own position seems to contain features that might be taken as either 'reactive' or 'objective'. On the one hand, he draws a distinction between 'natural' and 'empty' anger; 'natural' anger is defined by matching response correctly to the situation.[198] The distinction is also drawn in terms of the contrast between the Greek terms *orgē* (natural anger) and *thumos*.[199] Also, we hear that what causes gratitude, anger, or resentment is the 'voluntary' (intentional) nature of the actions involved, a point which seems to bring Philodemus' account close to Strawson's notion of 'reactive attitudes'.[200] On the other hand, there is explicit rejection of the kind of 'reactive' response embodied in Aristotle's definition, cited earlier. It is not reasonable to feel the kind of anger ('empty' anger or *thumos*) that is based on the belief that punishment of others is pleasurable or is a good in itself. Hence, the wise person 'neither falls into such intense emotions as these... nor is impelled to punishment as something enjoyable... but approaches it as something most unpleasurable, as he would the drinking of apsinthion [bitter medicine] or the doctor's knife'.[201]

One way of interpreting these apparently contrasting emphases is this.[202] Anger may be understood as a natural defence mechanism, in response to—and as a means of pre-empting—aggression. However, the expression of this natural reaction varies sharply according to the person's overall belief-set

[196] See Gill (2003*c*), 210–13, referring to M.A. *Med* 2.1, 12.24, 26; Epict. *Diss.* 1.28; also Bobzien (1998*a*), 336–7; Long (2002), 250–4.

[197] For instance, Nicasicrates sees no role for anger in an Epicurean life and holds a position very close to Stoicism on this point; see Fowler (1997), 24–30; Procopé (1998), 186–9.

[198] 'it arises from insight into the state of the nature of things and from avoiding false opinion in calculating the disadvantages and in punishing those who do harm', Phld. *On Anger* (*Ira*) 37.52, trans. Procopé (1998), 181. See also Procopé, 178–82; Annas (1989), 147.

[199] See Indelli (2004), who also applies this distinction to Virgil's presentation of anger in the *Aeneid*.

[200] *Ira* 46.28–35; Procopé (1998), 177, referring to Strawson (1974), 5.

[201] *Ira* 44.5–35 (in part), trans. D. Armstrong, cited by Fish (2004), 114–15. The wise person also responds to aggression 'gritting his teeth' (*dakōn*), i.e. without battle-lust, Phld. *Ira*. 41.8, trans. Procopé (1998), 180; see also Annas (1989), 155–9. Contrast the Aristotelian linkage between anger and the desire for the pleasure of revenge (text to n. 191 above).

[202] This paragraph is based on Gill (2003*c*), 214–16.

(about what is valuable, especially) in a way that also shapes her interpersonal relationships. For instance, most people (mistakenly) see wealth and honour as inherently valuable, instead of seeing them as valuable only in so far as they produce freedom from physical pain and mental disturbance.[203] The mistaken desire to punish, as though such punishment were good or pleasurable, derives from this kind of mistake. This line of thought may also explain the seemingly contradictory statements about whether or not the normative wise person is susceptible to anger. Philodemus tells us that the wise person is 'susceptible to anger of a kind' (presumably, 'natural' anger). But we are also told that he will not be much harmed by anyone else because 'he is not even susceptible to great troubles in the presence of great pains, and much more is this so with anger.'[204] We also hear that Epicurus as a teacher used anger—or perhaps the appearance of anger—in the therapeutic discourse that figured prominently in his interpersonal relationships. Epicurus is described as 'reproaching out of friendship all his acquaintances or most of them, frequently and intensely, and often abusively'.[205] Hence, 'even such a wise person as Epicurus gave some people the impression [of being angry]'. In fact, however, he was 'unangered' (*aorgētos*) and of a 'completely opposite disposition' to the angry person.[206] In terms of conventional reactive attitudes, it would seem, Epicurus was not angry. But he used the reactive attitude, or its appearance, in an 'objective' way, in Strawson's sense, as a therapeutic strategy, to help people ('out of friendship') to work towards leading better, more Epicurean, lives.[207]

This outline of ancient approaches to anger (with which Virgil is likely to have been familiar) provides a basis for considering relevant episodes in the *Aeneid*, and thus for gauging the kind of biography of Aeneas embodied in the poem. A clear instance of the layering of different approaches, and also of a lapse in virtue, comes in Book 2, where Aeneas considers killing Helen in vengeance after the fall of Troy but is restrained by his divine mother Venus (567–633).[208] This passage offers vivid illustration of the contrast between (ancient versions of) reactive and objective attitudes. Aeneas narrates his own thoughts at the time: 'yet I shall be praised for having put an end to a source of crime and taking justified retaliation, and there will be pleasure in satisfying

203 For relevant Epicurean thinking about what is valuable, see 2.3 above, text to nn. 161–83.

204 Phld. *Ira* 41.28–42.14, trans. Annas (1989), 158–9.

205 Phld. *Ira* 35.18–40, trans. Procopé (1989), 177. On the role of 'frank speaking' (*parrhēsia*) in Epicureanism, see Konstan *et al.* (1998), esp. introd. See also Nussbaum (1994), 117–27; Armstrong *et al.* (2004), index under *parrhēsia*.

206 Phld. *Ira* 34.31–35.5, trans. Annas (1989), 163.

207 On the role of 'vituperation' in Epicurean and Stoic therapeutic strategies, see Procopé (1998), 184–6; Fish (2004), 117–18.

208 The remainder of this paragraph is based on Gill (2003*c*), 219.

my feelings and the shades of my ancestors with avenging flames' (2.585–7). Aeneas' reference to a desire for 'justified retaliation' (*merentis poenas*) and the 'pleasure' he anticipates (*iuuabit*) strongly evokes the Aristotelian definition of anger, cited earlier. However, Aeneas' subsequent description of his response, and, still more, Venus' reported words express a contrasting, objective approach. Aeneas says that his plan was formed 'with a frenzied mind' (*furiata mente*), and that his divine mother criticized his 'uncontrolled rage' (*indomitas iras*), asking him 'why are you frenzied?' (*quid furis?*, 2.588, 594–5). Venus goes on to say that neither Helen nor Paris are 'to be blamed' (*culpatus*); in explanation she strips away Aeneas' human blindness and shows him that Troy is now being destroyed by the combined work of the gods.[209] Venus thus counteracts Aeneas' impulse to reactive anger and blame, and also the desire for revenge, advocating a dispassionate attitude that recognizes (to an exceptional degree) objective factors which provide a deeper than normal understanding of events.[210]

As Michael Putnam has brought out, Venus' reaction can be seen as having a strongly Stoic character, underlined by contrast with Aeneas' initial, Aristotelian, response.[211] Her language, like Aeneas' own later comment, suggests that his reaction was an irrational passion, motivated by misguided beliefs, such as that anger and the desire for revenge are appropriate in this situation.[212] Venus' unveiling of the divine world-view may also evoke the 'cosmic' perspective that is, at least sometimes, part of Stoic ethical understanding.[213] Marcus Aurelius, in particular, illustrates how the adoption of this perspective, and the correlated move to view fellow human beings as brothers or part of the same body, can counteract normal reactive attitudes.[214] Approaching the scene from another standpoint, Jeffrey Fish has also highlighted the Epicurean connotations of this exchange. Aeneas presents himself as making the mistake that Philodemus especially stigmatizes, of regarding revenge as a source of pleasure. Venus' response also brings home to Aeneas that his anger and desire for revenge are leading him to neglect things that are really in his best interest, a further motif in Philodemus' critique of anger. Fish also compares the blunt, sarcastic tone of Venus' reprimand (combined with the vivid picture of the damaging consequences of anger) with the technique of 'blunt speaking' (*parrhēsia*) that forms part of Epicurean therapeutic

[209] Virg. *A.* 2.589–623, esp. 595–8, 601–3.

[210] Cf. text to nn. 189, 196 above, outlining Strawson's (1974) distinction and relevant Stoic ideas.

[211] Putnam (1990), 24–5, 35–9.

[212] On Stoic thinking on anger as a passion, see text to n. 195 above.

[213] On the role (which is more limited than is sometimes supposed) of the cosmic perspective in Stoic ethics, see 3.3 above, text to nn. 79–84, 145–8, 3.5, text to nn. 320–3.

[214] See M.A. *Med.* 2.1. taken with Gill (2003*c*), 211–12 and 219.

discourse.[215] In the context of philosophical debate, there is, of course, scope for argument about how far the Stoic and Epicurean conceptions of anger are compatible. But, in the Virgilian context, it seems to me quite conceivable that evocations of Stoic and Epicurean approaches to anger—both of which advocate in different ways objective attitudes—could be combined to mark a contrast to the reactive, Aristotelian tone of Aeneas' initial response.

To what extent is this layering of reactive and objective attitudes regarding anger typical of Virgil's presentation of Aeneas? The relevant material is quite complex, and often less clear-cut than in the Helen-episode. But I think there are grounds for seeing this as a recurrent pattern, and one that may explain the problematic final scene of the poem.[216] In Book 8—by contrast with the surrounding books[217]—the dominant motif appears to be that of reactive anger, presented in a way that is not undercut or qualified, at least on the face of it. This point applies to three types of reactive anger: that of the people of Argylla against Mezentius, of Hercules against Cacus, and that associated with the Evander–Pallas theme.[218] This mode of presentation appears to prepare us for a strongly reactive approach in Aeneas' campaign against Turnus in Italy. However, closer inspection brings out a more subtle picture. There is an implicit contrast between the reactive attitudes expressed by Evander and the Argyllans and those of Aeneas himself. Evander, after describing the 'unspeakable slaughter... the savage acts of the tyrant' presents the Argyllans' response as one of 'justified bitterness' (*iustus... dolor*) and 'well-deserved anger' (*merita... ira*).[219] Aeneas' tone is rather different. After receiving a divine signal to prepare for war, he responds with these words:

> Ah, how great is the slaughter that stands in wait for the poor Laurentine people! What a penalty you will pay to me, Turnus! How many are the shields, helmets, and brave bodies of fine men that you will turn over with your flow, father Tiber! So let them demand the clash of battle and break their treaties. (8.536–40)

215 Fish (2004), 120–5, referring esp. to Phld. *Ira* 14.17–29, 29.20–9. On 'blunt speaking' in Epicureanism, see n. 205 above. Fish, 125–9, defends the authenticity of the Helen-episode (which has been questioned since antiquity).

216 The following two paragraphs are based on Gill (2003*c*), 218, 220–3.

217 In Book 7 the outbreak of war in Italy is presented as a collective plunge into irrational madness (see e.g. 7.341–407, 435–76, 481–2, 519–30, 550, 580–5). Book 9 is dominated by Turnus' irrational frenzy in battle, which is defective by both Stoic and Epicurean standards. See further on Turnus, Putnam (1990), 29–30; Gill (1997*c*), 236–8; Indelli (2004), 109–10.

218 See (anger against Mezentius) 8.494, 501; (Hercules' anger) 219–20, 228–30; for Evander–Pallas, 508–19, 560–83. Related themes include Augustus' retributive attack on Antony and Cleopatra at Actium (675–728) and Aeneas taking the whole burden (of retributive action) on his shoulders (729–31).

219 8.482–3, 500–1. The related phrase 'with just fury' (more precisely, 'furies', *furiis... iustis*, 8.494) is more negatively coloured, given the problematic associations of fury (and furies) in the poem. See further Putnam (1990), 23–34.

Although Aeneas registers the thought that Turnus and the Laurentines must pay the penalty for breaking the treaty and so provoking war, there is a notable absence of reactive anger in his words. Instead, we find a rather generalized pity, at least in his attitude towards the 'poor' (*miseris*) Laurentine people, whose bodies will fill the Tiber. As in the Helen-episode, Aeneas' response evokes both Stoic and Epicurean norms. Here too, we can see indications of a cosmic perspective on events (produced in this case by the divine portent), combined with the detached, non-reactive pity that is commended by Stoics such as Epictetus and Marcus.[220] The response also meets Epicurean norms in confronting the prospect of justified retribution as something to be approached without pleasure, like medicine or the doctor's knife.[221]

In subsequent books, other incidents fit the same pattern. In Book 11, following Pallas' funeral, Aeneas' words show a marked absence of anger, when this might be expected: 'the same dreadful fates of war call from here to other tears' (*alias*... *ad lacrimas*, 11.96–7). This response can also be taken as expressing quasi-Stoic cosmic detachment and pathos or, in Epicurean style, as facing the prospect of retribution without pleasure. It is, again, Evander, rather than Aeneas, who acts as the mouthpiece of reactive anger, as he places on Aeneas the obligation of revenging his dead son:

> your right hand... owes [the death of] Turnus to the son and his father. This is the only scope that is left open for you to combine doing what is right and achieving success. I seek no joy (*gaudia*) in life—that would be wrong—but only to bring some joy to my son among the shades. (11.178–81).

Evander's message implies the Aristotelian view that anger is desire for justified retaliation and that such retaliation brings pleasure, which in this case is reserved for the dead Pallas. In Book 10 Aeneas too might seem to exhibit a more reactive mode, in his rapid, brutal, and 'blazing' (*ardens*) responses to Pallas' killing by Turnus, including taking prisoners alive for sacrifice and rejecting suppliants.[222] Even here, however, it is not wholly clear that he is presented as acting out of anger; the picture may be of someone responding in a quasi-instinctive way or making an exemplary military gesture. Although the obligations to Evander and Pallas are said to be 'before his very eyes'(515–17), it is not also said that this image stimulates anger.

[220] See references in n. 196 above. In Aristotelian terms, pity, like anger is a reactive attitude, that of emotional response to a belief in the merits of an agent's case and situation. See Arist. *Rh.* 2.9; also Konstan (2001), esp. 128–36.

[221] For this reading of the lines, see Fish (2004), 121; also text to n. 201 above.

[222] 10.510–42, including 'blazing (*ardens*)... he drives on with the sword... seeking you, Turnus' (513–14); also 'frenzied' (*furens*) in 604; see also Gill (2003*c*), 223.

Against this background—if one accepts this way of reading these incidents—it is the more surprising that the poem ends with an outburst of what seems to be violently reactive anger. Aeneas is at first inclined to respond positively to Turnus' moderately phrased appeal for his life, coupled with a full admission of defeat (12.931–40). But his mind is changed by the sight of the breast-plate wrenched from the dying Pallas by Turnus.[223]

> inflamed by fury [or the furies] and terrible in his anger (*furiis accensus et ira terribilis*) [he said]: 'are you to be snatched away (*eripiare*) from me, dressed in the spoils of my own people (*meorum*)? It is Pallas, Pallas, who sacrifices you (*immolat*) and exacts the penalty from your criminal blood (*poenam scelerato ex sanguine sumit*).' Saying this, boiling (*feruidus*), he buried his sword full in Turnus' breast. (12.946–51)

I outline the main competing readings of this much-debated scene before considering the implications of my preferred view for the larger issue being considered here. Different interpretations appeal to the implications of divergent ancient philosophical approaches to anger.[224]

For an 'Aristotelian' reading,[225] emotions such as anger are taken to be (in principle) justified reactive attitudes to appropriate or inappropriate interpersonal behaviour. Here, Aeneas is first of all swayed by pity, understood as a reactive attitude,[226] at Turnus' appeal, which is replaced by a surge of anger at the sight of Pallas' breast-plate. The breast-plate stimulates anger because it evokes Pallas' death at Turnus' hands, which was, in this interpretation, a source of intense (reactive) anger and grief in Aeneas.[227] It also evokes Evander's grief-inspired injunction on Aeneas to avenge his son's death by killing his murderer; more broadly, it evokes the theme of justified anger or merited grief which is a significant strand in Books 8 and 11.[228] Aeneas' final response, his being 'inflamed' (*accensus, feruidus*) with anger, his intense bitter words and violent action, express the emotional response of someone who feels himself wholly justified in his anger and in acting as the agent of Pallas' revenge (*poenas*).[229]

The Epicurean reading, like the Aristotelian, finds Aeneas' final attitude acceptable, though on rather different grounds. As indicated earlier, 'natural' anger may be shown by someone with a good character (*diathesis*) and not

223 Virg. *A.* 12.941–6, cf. 10.495–505.

224 The following four paragraphs are based on Gill (2004*a*), 118–20.

225 On the various possible relevant senses of 'Aristotelian', see text to n. 191–4 above.

226 That is, an Aristotelian interpersonal response rather than generalized Stoic-style pity; see nn. 192 and 220 above.

227 10.510–42, 552, 602–4, 11.26–9, 11.39–44.

228 11.177–81, cf. 10.515–17; see references in nn. 217–19, 222 above.

229 For the emotional dimension in Aristotelian anger (conceived in terms of part-based psychology), see n. 191 above. For readings of this type, see Galinsky (1988), esp. 321–7, 330–5; Cairns (1989), 78–84; M. R. Wright (1997), 183–4.

typically prone to anger, if a correct examination of the situation shows that anger is appropriate. A crucial point of distinction from the Aristotelian view is that anger is not seen as pleasurable, but painful. Pursuing revenge as a source of pleasure is seen a mark of 'empty', misguided, anger or *thumos*.[230] Here, Aeneas' willingness to suppress the desire for revenge and to show pity is a mark of the reasonable character or attitude shown in earlier cases such as his killing of Lausus.[231] The shift from restraint to (natural) anger is brought about by recognition that this response is merited by Turnus' brutal killing of Pallas. But, it is claimed, Aeneas is not presented at aiming at pleasure through retaliation. He seeks revenge on Pallas' behalf (*Pallas... Pallas... poenam... sumit*, 948–9, translated above), while aware of the grim, painful nature of the task ('memorials of savage grief', *saeui monimenta doloris*, 945).[232]

The Stoic reading of the passage differs from the other two in that Aeneas' final reactive anger is *not* seen as acceptable, but as a lapse, like that envisaged in the Helen-episode. This interpretation gives weight to the fact that Aeneas, as indicated earlier, refrains elsewhere from violent anger when it might have been expected. By contrast with the reactive anger shown by figures such as Evander, Aeneas responds on other occasions with (what seems to be) an expression of generalized or 'cosmic' pity.[233] Aeneas' initial readiness to respond to Turnus' appeal for mercy may also derive from this kind of response.[234] The sudden change of plan triggered by the sight of Pallas' breast-plate appears, by contrast, as a virtually 'akratic' impulse.[235] It is marked as a 'passion' (non-rational, excessive, uncontrolled) by the narrative language (*furiis accensus et ira | terribilis... feruidus*, 946–7, 951), and by Aeneas' use of the language of human sacrifice (*immolat*). Although the reiteration and alliteration (*Pallas... Pallas... scelerato ex sanguine sumit*, 948–9) of Aeneas' words express passionate intensity, the use of the third-personal form may suggest that Aeneas is implicitly distancing himself from acts and attitudes that he would elsewhere repudiate. Hence, this final scene resembles Dido's surrender to passion; the contrast between Aeneas' initial

[230] See text to nn. 198–203 above.

[231] See 10.808–32, esp. 823, 825; also Fish (2004), 119.

[232] See Erler (1992); Galinsky (1994), esp. 197–200; Indelli (2004), 108–9.

[233] See text to nn. 219–22 above. Aeneas' response to Lausus (10.808–32, esp. 823, 825), might seem to express a more reactive pity, responding (with emotion) to special grounds for pity (see n. 220 above on Aristotelian pity).

[234] There are no explicit indications about how to interpret Aeneas' forbearance in 12.938–41. However, as suggested in Gill (2003*c*), 227, the Homeric parallel (Achilles' response of generalized humanity to Priam's supplication, *Il.* 24.486–551), might suggest that Aeneas is considering a similar type of response.

[235] For a passion as activated by assent to a 'fresh' impression, especially one presented in visual form, see Gal. *PHP* 4.7.3–5, 5.6.24–6 (Posidonius); also Gill (1997*c*), 240 n. 99.

and final reactions enacts the inner conflict between passionate and rational responses implied in her case too.[236]

What can be said for or against these readings, in the light of the previous discussion here? The main problem with the Aristotelian reading is that the presentation of Aeneas as expressing full-hearted engagement with vengeful anger runs counter to most, though not all, his previous attitudes.[237] The Epicurean view seems more credible, particularly since it accommodates the idea of an atypical outburst of (justified) anger in a characteristically mild-tempered person.[238] However, Aeneas' state of mind in the final lines does not match the Epicurean norm of someone going towards punishment as something 'most unpleasant' and 'gritting his teeth' (*dakōn*).[239] Aeneas is described as carried away by intense, burning emotion (*furiis accensus et ira | terribilis... feruidus*), expressed also in his bitter, reiterative words, which is not the state of mind associated with the Epicurean good person. So, overall, I think, the Stoic reading seems most plausible, on the assumption that, under the extreme pressure of this situation, Aeneas fails to live up to the norms which are elsewhere set for him, by implication, and which he often matches.[240] This reading perhaps best explains the puzzling fact that the passage shows Aeneas *nearly* reacting in a different way—with restraint and humanity. It may also explain why Aeneas' final words and narrative comments suggest an uncharacteristic brutal intensity and are marked by other connotations (frenzy or Furies, *furiis*, and human sacrifice, *immolat*) which are particularly disturbing at the very close of the poem.[241]

On this reading, the final scene falls into the pattern found often elsewhere in the poem. We find a layered presentation of emotions, in which the connotations of different approaches to emotions can be found. But the Stoic connotations (elsewhere combined with Epicurean ones) are given greater weight and significance than the Aristotelian ones. This discussion of the anger of Aeneas provides the basis for, at least, a partial response to the question broached earlier, whether we should see the *Aeneid* as taking a quasi-Plutarchean (and Platonic–Aristotelian) view of its figures or a Stoic–

[236] See text to nn. 161–6, 176–80 above. For this type of reading, see Gill (1997*c*), 239–40; also Lyne (1983),199–202; Putnam (1990), 14–18, (1995), 157–60; and (with more qualifications) R. J. Tarrant (2004), 119–20. See also n. 241 below.

[237] For earlier outbursts of anger, see text to nn. 208–9, 222; for contrasting attitudes, see text to nn. 210–11, 220–1 above. For previous outbursts of anger by Aeneas in Book 12, see 12.494, 499, also 569–73, 580–2.

[238] See e.g. Phld. *Ira* 34.31–35.5, taken with Galinsky (1994), 196.

[239] See text to n. 201 above.

[240] See text to nn. 233–6 above.

[241] Cf. *furiis accensus* (12.946) with Dido's self-description as *furiis incensa* (4.376). See also Thomas (1991), arguing against the view of Cairns (1989), 83–4, that *furiis* differs substantively in ethical colour from *furore*; see also Putnam (1990), 23–32.

Epicurean one.[242] In the case of Aeneas, even more than Dido, a Plutarchean reading is possible, in which a figure with a generally good and relatively stable character experiences periodic lapses.[243] However, I think that the layered presentation of Aeneas' emotions, in the passages discussed here, leads us to give greater weight to a Stoic–Epicurean view. Thus, in so far as the poem embodies a biography of Aeneas, the dominant concern is with seeing how near or how far he comes, at any one time, to meeting—or at least aspiring and making progress towards—very demanding normative standards of rationality and virtue, those of Stoic–Epicurean wisdom.

To a remarkable degree, given the vicissitudes of Aeneas' life and his complex political role (with its gradually emerging world-historical significance), Aeneas often *does* come close to meeting Stoic or Epicurean norms. However, in this conceptual framework, it is far from surprising if any human being fails to meet these standards. The Stoics, in particular, acknowledge the extreme difficulty and rarity of achieving complete wisdom, although they also insist it is the proper target for all of us.[244] So we should not be dismayed if Aeneas from time to time fails to achieve wisdom, even if he is also presented as having aspirations towards this state. Failure to meet this standard, at key decisive moments, is also depicted as constituting a plunge towards irrational passion and frenzy or, in some sense 'madness', in the case of Aeneas as of Dido and other figures.[245] For this reason, among others, it seems to me that the *Aeneid* is written predominantly from a Stoic or an Epicurean standpoint (perspectives which often, if not always, converge with each other) rather than the kind of Platonic–Aristotelian approach presupposed by Plutarch in his day and by earlier Middle Platonists in the late Roman Republic.[246] Whether my interpretation of the *Aeneid* is correct is, of course, open to debate. But I hope, at least, to have brought out some of the criteria by which one could confirm or deny such a view. In doing so, I have also wanted to show how the issues seen as fundamental for philosophical debate in the Hellenistic and early Roman Imperial periods—notably the contrast between Platonic–Aristotelian and Stoic–Epicurean conceptions of personality—are also relevant to literature at this time. The distinction drawn in this book between the Stoic–Epicurean ('structured') conception of the self and the

[242] A fuller response would, among other points, locate the depiction of Aeneas' emotions within the larger narrative shape and organization of the poem, and consider in what sense the poem presents a 'life' or 'biography' of Aeneas or other figures.

[243] Cf. the analogy considered earlier between Dido and Plutarch's Sertorius (text to nn. 139–44 above).

[244] See LS 54 D(2), 61 N(2), LS i. 383.

[245] In Aeneas' case, this is most marked in the killing of Turnus; see also nn. 146–50, 217, 222, 241 above.

[246] Such as Antiochus; see 3.4 above.

Platonic–Aristotelian ('part-based') one, together with related ideas about social ethics, are not only central features of philosophical controversy, with urgent practical and political implications.[247] They also take us to the heart of key themes and issues of great literature in this period.

[247] Sedley (1997*c*), in particular, brings out the political implications of adopting a Stoic or Platonic standpoint in the late Republic; see also other references in n. 119 above.

REFERENCES

Abel, K. (1983). 'Das Propatheia-Theorem: Ein Beitrag zur stoischen Affektenlehre'. *Hermes*, 111: 78–97.

Alberti, A. (1990*a*). 'Paura della morte e identità personale nell'epicureismo', in Alberti (1990*b*: 151–206).

—— (1990*b*) (ed.). *Logica, mente, persona: Studi sulla filosofia antica*. Florence: Olschki.

Alesse, F. (2000). *La stoa e la tradizione socratica*. Naples: Bibliopolis.

Algra. K. A., van der Horst, P. W., and Runia, D. T. (1996) (eds.). *Polyhistor: Studies in the History and Historiography of Ancient Philosophy*. Leiden: Brill.

Algra, K. A., Koenen, M. H., and Schrijvers, P. H. (1997) (eds.). *Lucretius and his Intellectual Background*. Amsterdam: Dutch Academy of Sciences, Arts, and Letters.

Algra, K. A., Barnes, J., Mansfeld, J., and Schofield, M. (1999) (eds.). *The Cambridge History of Hellenistic Philosophy*. Cambridge: Cambridge University Press.

Allen, R. E. (1962). 'Note on *Alcibiades I*'. *American Journal of Philology*, 83: 187–90.

Annas, J. (1981). *An Introduction to Plato's Republic*. Oxford: Oxford University Press.

—— (1985). 'Self-Knowledge in Early Plato', in D. O'Meara (ed.). *Platonic Investigations*. Studies in Philosophy and the History of Philosophy, 13. Washington, D.C.: Catholic University of America Press, 111–38.

—— (1989). 'Epicurean Emotions'. *Greek, Roman, and Byzantine Studies*, 30: 145–64.

—— (1990). 'Stoic Epistemology', in Everson, 184–203.

—— (1991). 'Epicurus' Philosophy of Mind', in Everson (1991*b*), 84–101.

—— (1992). *Hellenistic Philosophy of Mind*. Berkeley: California University Press.

—— (1993*a*). 'Epicurus on Agency', in Brunschwig and Nussbaum, 53–71.

—— (1993*b*). *The Morality of Happiness*. Oxford: Oxford University Press.

—— (1994). 'Virtue as the Use of Other Goods', in Irwin and Nussbaum, 53–66.

—— (1995). 'Reply to Cooper'. *Philosophy and Phenomenological Research*, 55: 599–610.

—— (1999). *Platonic Ethics, Old and New*. Ithaca, NY: Cornell University Press.

—— (2002). 'Democritus and Eudaimonism', in V. Caston and D. Graham (eds.), *Presocratic Philosophy: Essays in Honour of Alexander Mourelatos*. Aldershot: Ashgate, 169–81.

—— (2004). 'Marcus Awelius: Ethics and its Background'. *Rhizai*, 2: 103–19.

—— and Rowe, C. J. (2002) (eds.). *Perspectives on Plato: Modern and Ancient*. Cambridge, Mass.: Harvard University Press.

Anscombe, E. (1957). *Intention*. Oxford: Oxford University Press.

Armstrong, D. (2004). 'Horace's *Epistles* 1 and Philodemus,' in Armstrong *et al.* (2004: 267–98).

—— , Fish, J., Johnston, P. A., and Skinner, M. (2004) (eds.). *Vergil, Philodemus, and the Augustans*. Austin: Texas University Press.

Arnim, H. von (1903–5) (ed.). *Stoicorum Veterum Fragmenta*, 4 vols. Leipzig: Teubner (= *SVF*).

—— (1906). *Hierokles: Ethische Elementarlehre.* Berliner Klassikertexte, 4. Berlin: Weidmann.

Arrighetti, G. (1973, 2nd edn.). *Epicuro: Opere.* Turin: Biblioteca di cultura filosofia, 41.

Asmis, E. (1990). 'Free Action and the Swerve'. Review of W. Englert, *Epicurus on the Swerve and Voluntary Action. Oxford Studies in Ancient Philosophy,* 7: 275–91.

—— (1999). 'Epicurean Epistemology', in Algra *et al.*, 260–94.

Atkins, E. M. (2000). 'Cicero', in Rowe and Schofield, 477–514.

Austin, R. G. (1977) (ed.). *P. Vergili Maronis: Aeneidos Liber Sextus.* Oxford: Oxford University Press.

Babut, D. (1969*a*) (ed.). *Plutarque de la vertu éthique.* Bibliothèque de la Faculté des Lettres de Lyon, 15. Paris: Les Belles Lettres.

—— (1969*b*). *Plutarque et le Stoicisme.* Paris: Presses Universitaires de France.

Barnes, J.(1989). 'Antiochus of Ascalon', in Griffin and Barnes, 51–96.

—— (1997*a*). *Logic and the Imperial Stoa.* Philosophia Antiqua, 75. Leiden: Brill.

—— (1997*b*). 'Roman Aristotle', in Barnes and Griffin (1997), 1–69.

—— and Griffin, M. (1997) (eds.). *Philosophia Togata II: Plato and Aristotle at Rome.* Oxford: Oxford University Press.

—— and Mignucci, M. (1988) (eds.). *Matter and Metaphysics.* Fourth Symposium Hellenisticum. Elenchos, 14. Naples: Bibliopolis.

Barney, R. (2003). 'A Puzzle in Stoic Ethics'. *Oxford Studies in Ancient Philosophy,* 24: 303–40.

Barrett, W. S. (1964) (ed.). *Euripides: Hippolytos.* Oxford: Oxford University Press.

Bastianini, G., and Long, A. A. (1992). 'Hierocles', in *Corpus dei papiri filosofici greci e latini, 1.1* **. Florence: Olschki, 268–451.

Beauchamp, T. (1999) (ed.). *David Hume: An Enquiry Concerning Human Understanding.* Oxford: Oxford University Press.

Becchi, F. (1975). 'Aristotelismo ed antistoicismo nel "De virtute morali" di Plutarco'. *Prometheus,* 1: 160–80.

—— (1978). 'Aristotelismo funzionale nel "De virtute morali" di Plutarco'. *Prometheus,* 4: 261–75.

—— (1981). 'Platonismo medio ed etica plutarchea'. *Prometheus,* 7: 125–45, 263–84.

—— (1990*a*). 'La nozione di *orgē* e di *aorgēsia* in Aristotele e in Plutarco'. *Prometheus,* 16: 65–87.

—— (1990*b*) (ed.). *La virtù etica.* Corpus Plutarchi Moralium, 5. Naples: M. d'Auria.

Benson, H. H. (2000). *Socratic Wisdom: The Model of Knowledge in Plato's Early Dialogues.* Oxford: Oxford University Press.

Betegh, G. (2003). 'Cosmological Ethics in the *Timaeus* and Early Stoicism'. *Oxford Studies in Ancient Philosophy,* 24: 273–302.

Bett, R. (forthcoming). 'What Kind of Self is a Greek Sceptic Entitled To?', in P. Remes and J. Sihvola (eds.), *Ancient Philosophy of the Self.*

Beversluis, J. (2000). *Cross-examining Socrates: A Defense of the Interlocutor in Plato's Early Dialogues.* Cambridge: Cambridge University Press.

Bignone, E. (1936, 2nd edn. 1973). *L'Aristotele perduto e la formazione filosofica di Epicuro,* 2 vols. Florence: La nuova Italia.

Bloch, E. (2002). 'Hemlock Poisoning and the Death of Socrates: Did Plato Tell the Truth?', in Brickhouse and Smith, 255–78.

Blundell, M. W. (1990). 'Parental Nature and Stoic *Oikeiōsis*.' *Ancient Philosophy*, 10: 221–42.

Bobonich, C. (1996). 'Reading the Laws', in Gill and McCabe, 249–82.

—— (2002). *Plato's Utopia Recast: His Later Ethics and Politics*. Oxford: Oxford University Press.

Bobzien, S. (1997). 'Stoic Conceptions of Freedom and their Relation to Ethics', in R. Sorabji (ed.), *Aristotle and After. Bulletin of the Institute of Classical Studies*, supplement 68, 71–89.

—— (1998*a*). *Determinism and Freedom in Stoic Philosophy*. Oxford: Oxford University Press.

—— (1998*b*). 'The Inadvertent Conception and Late Birth of the Free-Will Problem'. *Phronesis*, 43: 133–75.

—— (1999). 'Chrysippus' Theory of Causes', in Ieradiakonou, 196–242.

—— (2000). 'Did Epicurus Discover the Free Will Problem?' *Oxford Studies in Ancient Philosophy*, 19: 287–337.

Bonhöffer, D. (1890, repr. 1968). *Epictet und die Stoa: Untersuchungen zur Stoischen Philosophie*. Stuttgart: Frommann.

—— (1894, repr. 1968). *Die Ethik der Stoikers Epictet*. Stuttgart: Frommann. Trans. by W. O. Stephens (1996). *The Ethics of the Stoic Epictetus*. New York: Peter Lang.

Boulogne, J. (2003). *Plutarque dans le miroir d'Épicure: Analyse d'une critique systématique de l'épicurisme*. Villeneuve d'Ascq Cédex: Presses Universitaires du Septentrion.

Bourdieu, P. (2003). 'Participant Objectivation'. *Journal of the Royal Anthropological Institute*, 9: 281–94.

Bowin, J. (2003). 'Chrysippus' Puzzle about Identity'. *Oxford Studies in Ancient Philosophy*, 24: 239–51.

Boyle, A. J. (1987) (ed.). *Seneca's Phaedra*. Leeds: Francis Cairns.

Boys-Stones, G. R. (2001). *Post-Hellenistic Philosophy: A Study of its Development from the Stoics to Origen*. Oxford: Oxford University Press.

Braund, S. M. (1997). 'Virgil and the Cosmos: Religion and Philosophical Ideas', in Martindale, 204–21.

—— and Gill, C. (1997) (eds.). *The Passions in Roman Thought and Literature*. Cambridge: Cambridge University Press.

Bremmer, J. (1983). *The Early Greek Concept of the Soul*. Princeton: Princeton University Press.

Brennan, T. (1998). 'The Old Stoic Analysis of the Emotions', in Sihvola and Engberg-Pedersen, 21–70.

—— (2001). 'Fate and Free Will in Stoicism: A Discussion of Susanne Bobzien, *Determinism and Freedom in Stoic Philosophy*'. *Oxford Studies in Ancient Philosophy*, 21: 259–86.

—— (2003). 'Stoic Moral Psychology', in Inwood, 257–94.

Brickhouse, T. C., and Smith, N. D. (2002) (eds.). *The Trial and Execution of Socrates: Sources and Controversies*. Oxford: Oxford University Press.

Brisson, L. (1992). *Platon: Timée-Critias*, trans. with introduction and notes. Paris: Flammarion.

—— (1997). 'Perception sensible et raison dans la Timée', in Calvo and Brisson, 307–16.

Brittain, C. (2001). *Philo of Larissa: The Last of the Academic Sceptics*. Oxford: Oxford University Press.

Brunschwig, J. (1986). 'The Cradle Argument in Epicureanism and Stoicism', in Schofield and Striker, 113–44.

—— (1988). 'La Théorie stoïcienne du genre suprēme et l'ontologie platonicienne', in Barnes and Mignucci, 19–127.

—— (1991). 'On a Book-title by Chrysippus: *On the Fact that the Ancients admitted Dialectic along with Demonstrations*'. *Oxford Studies in Ancient Philosophy*, supplementary volume, 81–95.

—— (1996). 'La Déconstruction du "connais-toi toi-mēme" dans l'Alcibiade Majeur'. *Recherches sur la Philosophie et la Langage*, 18: 61–84.

—— (1999). 'Introduction: the Beginnings of Hellenistic Epistemology', in Algra *et al.*, 229–59.

—— and Nussbaum, M. C. (1993) (eds.). *Passions and Perceptions: Studies in Hellenistic Philosophy of Mind*. Cambridge: Cambridge University Press.

Burgess, S. A. (2000). 'How to Build a Human Body: An Idealist's Guide', in Wright, 43–58.

—— (2004). 'The Human Body in Plato's *Timaeus*'. University of Wales Ph.D. thesis.

Burnet, J. (1901) (ed.). *Platonis Opera*, ii. Oxford: Oxford University Press.

Burnyeat, M. F. (1978). 'The Upside-down Back-to-front Sceptic of Lucretius IV 472'. *Philologus*, 122: 197–206.

—— (1980). 'Aristotle on Learning to be Good', in Rorty (1980*a*), 69–92.

—— (1982). 'Idealism and Greek Philosophy: What Descartes Saw and Berkeley Missed'. *Philosophical Review*, 91: 3–40. Reprinted in G. Vesey (1982) (ed.), *Idealism Past and Present*. Royal Institute of Philosophy Lecture Series, 13. Cambridge: Cambridge University Press, 19–50.

—— (1990) (ed.). *The Theaetetus of Plato*, trans. M. J. Levett, revised with introduction by Burnyeat. Indianapolis: Hackett.

—— (1992). 'Is an Aristotelian Philosophy of Mind Still Credible? A Draft', in Nussbaum and Rorty, 15–26.

—— (2000). 'Plato on Why Mathematics is Good for the Soul', in T. Smiley (ed.), *Mathematics and Necessity*. Oxford University Press for the British Academy. *Proceedings of the British Academy*, 103: 1–81.

Burridge, R. A. (1992). *What Are the Gospels? A Comparison with Graeco-Roman Biography*. Cambridge: Cambridge University Press.

Cairns, F. (1989). *Virgil's Augustan Epic*. Cambridge: Cambridge University Press.

Caizzi, F. D. (1993). 'Early Hellenistic Images of Philosophical Life', in A. W. Bulloch, E. S. Gruen, A. A. Long and A. Stewart (1993) (eds.), *Images and Ideologies: Self-Definition in the Hellenistic World*. Berkeley: University of California Press, 303–29.

Calvo, T., and Brisson, L. (1997) (eds.). *Interpreting the Timaeus and the Critias*. St. Augustin: Academia Verlag.

Cambiano, G. (1988). *Il ritorno degli antichi.* Roma: Laterza.

Carratelli, G. P. (1983) (ed.). *SUZĒTĒSIS: studi sull' epicureismo greco et romano offerti a Marcello Gigante*, 2 vols. Naples: Bibliopolis.

Carrithers, M., Collins, S., and Lukes, S. (1985) (eds.). *The Category of the Person: Anthropology, Philosophy, History.* Cambridge: Cambridge University Press.

Charles, D. (1984). *Aristotle's Philosophy of Action.* London: Duckworth.

Cherniss, H. (1976) (ed. and trans.). *Plutarch's Moralia*, 13.2. Loeb Classical Library. Cambridge, Mass.: Harvard University Press.

Chilton, C. W. (1971). *Diogenes of Oenoanda: The Fragments, A Translation and Commentary.* Oxford: Oxford University Press for University of Hull.

Clark, G., and Rajak, T. (2002) (eds.). *Philosophy and Power in the Graeco-Roman World: Essays in Honour of Miriam Griffin.* Oxford: Oxford University Press.

Claus, D. B. (1981). *Toward the Soul: An Inquiry into the Meaning of Psyche before Plato.* New Haven: Yale University Press.

Cockburn, D. (1991) (ed.). *Human Beings.* Cambridge: Cambridge University Press.

Coffey, M., and Mayer, R. (1990) (eds.). *Seneca: Phaedra.* Cambridge: Cambridge University Press.

Cohen, S. M. (1992). 'Hylomorphism and Functionalism', in Nussbaum and Rorty, 57–73.

Colish, M. (1985). *The Stoic Tradition from Antiquity to the Early Middle Ages*, i: *Stoicism in Classical Latin Literature.* Leiden: Brill.

Collins, S. (1985). 'Categories, Concepts or Predicaments? Remarks on Mauss's Use of Philosophical Terminology', in Carrithers, Collins, and Lukes, 46–82.

Cooper, J. M. (1980). 'Aristotle on Friendship', in Rorty (1980*a*), 301–40.

—— (1984). 'Plato's Theory of Human Motivation'. *History of Philosophy Quarterly*, 1: 3–21. Reprinted in (1999: 118–37).

—— (1995). 'Eudaimonism and the Appeal to Nature in the Morality of Happiness: Comments on Julia Annas, *The Morality of Happiness*'. *Philosophy and Phenomenological Research*, 55: 587–98.

—— (1996). 'Eudaimonism, the Appeal to Nature, and "Moral Duty" in Stoicism', in Engstrom and Whiting, 261–84. Reprinted in (1999), 427–48.

—— (1997) (ed.). *Plato: Complete Works.* Indianapolis: Hackett.

—— (1998*a*). 'Posidonius on Emotions', in Sihvola and Engberg-Pedersen (1998: 71–111). Reprinted in (1999), 449–84.

—— (1998*b*). 'The Unity of Virtue'. *Social Philosophy and Policy*, 15.1: 233–74. Reprinted in (1999), 76–117.

—— (1999). *Reason and Emotion: Essays on Ancient Moral Psychology and Ethical Theory.* Princeton: Princeton University Press.

—— (2004*a*). 'Moral Theory and Moral Improvement: Marcus Aurelius', in (2004*b*), 335–368.

—— (2004*b*). *Knowledge, Nature and the Good: Essays on Ancient Philosophy.* Princeton: Princeton University Press.

Cornford, F. M. (1937). *Plato's Cosmology: The Timaeus of Plato.* Translation with running commentary. London: Kegan Paul.

Cottingham, J., Stoothoff, R., Murdoch, D., and (for vol. iii) Kenny, A. (1984–1991) (eds. and trans.). *The Philosophical Works of Descartes*, 3 vols. Cambridge: Cambridge University Press.

Croiset, M. (1946). *Platon: Oeuvres complètes*, i Paris: Les Belles Lettres.

Croisille, J.-M. (1964). 'Lieux communs, *sententiae*, et intentions philosophique dans la *Phèdre* de Sénèque'. *Revue des Études Latines*, 42: 276–301.

Damasio, A. R. (1994). *Descartes' Error: Emotion, Reason, and the Human Brain*. New York: Putnam.

Davidson, D. (1980). *Essays on Actions and Events*. Oxford: Oxford University Press.

—— (1985). 'Rational Animals', in LePore and McLaughlin, 473–80.

—— (2001). *Subjective, Intersubjective, Objective*. Oxford: Oxford University Press.

Davis, P. J. (1983). '*Vindicat Omnes Natura Sibi*: A Reading of Seneca's *Phaedra*', in A. J. Boyle (ed.), *Seneca Tragicus: Ramus Essays on Seneca's Drama*. Berwick, Victoria: Aureal Publications, 114–27.

Defilippo, J. G., and Mitsis, P. T. (1994). 'Socrates and Stoic Natural Law', in Vander Waerdt (1994*b*), 272–308.

Dennett, D. C. (1976). 'Conditions of Personhood', in Rorty, 175–96.

—— (1979). *Brainstorms*. Hassocks, Sussex: Harvester.

—— (1984). *Elbow Room: The Varieties of Free Will Worth Wanting*. Oxford: Oxford University Press.

—— (1993). *Consciousness Explained*. London: Penguin.

Denyer, N. (2001) (ed.). *Plato: Alcibiades 1*. Cambridge: Cambridge University Press.

De Lacy, P. (1978–84) (ed. and trans.). *Galen: De Placitis Hippocratis et Platonis*, 3 vols. Corpus Medicorum Graecorum. Berlin: Akademic Verlag.

Detel, W. (2005*a*). *Foucault and Classical Antiquity: Power, Ethics and Knowledge*, trans. D. Wigg-Wolf. Cambridge: Cambridge University Press.

—— (2005*b*). 'Hybrid Theories of Normativity', in Gill (2005*d*), 113–44.

Diano, C. (1935). 'Note epicuree'. *Studi Italiani di Filologia Classica*, 12: 61–86, 237–89.

—— (1974). *Scritti epicurei*. Florence: Olschki.

Diels, H. (1879). *Doxographi Graeci*. Berlin: De Gruyter.

—— and Kranz, W. (1961, 10th edn.) (eds.). *Die Fragmente der Vorsokratiker*, 2 vols. Berlin: Weidmann. (= *DK*)

Dihle, A. (1982). *The Theory of Will in Classical Antiquity*. Berkeley: University of California Press.

Dillon, J. (1977, 2nd edn. 1995). *The Middle Platonists: A Study of Platonism 80 B.C. to A.D. 220*. London: Duckworth.

—— (1983). '*Metriopatheia* and *Apatheia*: Some Reflections on a Controversy in Later Greek Ethics', in J. P. Anton and A. Preus (eds.), *Essays in Ancient Greek Philosophy*, ii. Albany, NY: State University of Albany Press, 508–17.

—— (1988). 'Orthodoxy' and "Eclecticism": Middle Platonists and Neo-Pythagoreans', in Dillon and Long, 103–25.

—— (1993) (trans. with introduction and commentary). *Alcinous: The Handbook of Platonism*. Oxford: Oxford University Press.

—— (2003*a*). *The Heirs of Plato: A Study of the Old Academy (347–274 BC)*. Oxford: Oxford University Press.

Dillon, J. (2003*b*). 'The *Timaeus* in the Old Academy', in Reydams-Schils, 80–94.
—— and Long, A. A. (1988) (eds.). *The Question of 'Eclecticism': Studies in Later Greek Philosophy.* Berkeley: University of California Press.
Dilman, I. (1991). 'Sartre and Our Identity as Individuals', in Cockburn, 245–64.
—— (1998). *Epictetus: Discourses Book I.* Translation with introduction and commentary. Oxford: Oxford University Press.
Donini, P. L. (1974). *Tre studi sull'aristotelismo nel II secolo d. C.* Torino: G. B. Paravia.
—— (1986). 'Lo scetticismo academico, Aristotele e l'unità della tradizione platonica secondo Plutarco', in G. Cambiano (ed.), Storiografia e dossografia nella filosofia antica. Turin: Tirrenia Stampatori, 203–26.
—— (1988). 'The History of the Concept of Eclecticism', in Dillon and Long, 15–33.
Dover, K. J. (1974). *Greek Popular Morality in the Time of Plato and Aristotle.* Oxford: Oxford University Press.
Duff, T. E. (1999). *Plutarch's Lives: Exploring Virtue and Vice.* Oxford: Oxford University Press.
—— (2003). 'Plutarch on the Childhood of Alkibiades (*Alk.* 2–3)'. *Proceedings of the Cambridge Philological Society,* 49: 89–117.
Dumortier, J., and Defradas, J. (1975) (eds.). *Plutarque: Oeuvres morales,* 7.1. Translation with introduction and notes. Collections des Universités de France. Paris: Les Belles Lettres.
Edelstein, L., and Kidd, I. G. (1972, 2nd. edn. 1989) (eds.). *Posidonius I: The Fragments,* Classical Texts and Commentaries 13.1. Cambridge: Cambridge University Press.
Edwards, C. (1997). 'Self-Scrutiny and Self-Transformation in Seneca's Letters'. *Greece and Rome,* 44: 23–38.
Engberg-Pedersen, T. (1986). 'Discovering the Good: *oikeiosis* and *kathekonta* in Stoic Ethics', in Schofield and Striker, 145–83.
—— (1990*a*). 'Stoic Philosophy and the Concept of a Person', in Gill (1990*c*), 109–35.
—— (1990*b*). *The Stoic Theory of Oikeiosis: Moral Development and Social Interaction in Early Stoic Philosophy.* Aarhus: Aarhus University Press.
Engstrom, S., and Whiting, J. (1996) (eds.). *Aristotle, Kant, and the Stoics: Rethinking Happiness and Duty.* Cambridge: Cambridge University Press.
Erikson, E. (1958). *Young Man Luther.* London: Faber.
Erler, M. (1992). 'Der Zorn des Helden, Philodems "De Ira" und Vergils Konzept des Zorns in der "Aeneis"'. *Gräzer Beiträge,* 18: 103–26.
—— and Schofield, M. (1999). 'Epicurean Ethics', in Algra *et al.,* 642–74.
Everson, S. (1990) (ed.). *Epistemology: Companions to Ancient Thought, 1.* Cambridge: Cambridge University Press.
—— (1991*a*). 'The Objective Appearance of Pyrrhonism', in Everson (1991*b*), 121–47.
—— (1991*b*) (ed.). *Psychology: Companions to Ancient Thought, 2.* Cambridge: Cambridge University Press.
—— (1999). 'Epicurean Psychology', in Algra *et al.,* 542–59.
Feeney, D. C. (1991). *The Gods in Epic.* Oxford: Oxford University Press.
Ferrari, G. R. F. (2003). *City and Soul in Plato's Republic.* St Augustin: Academia Verlag.

Fillion-Lahille, J. (1984). *Le 'De ira' de Sénèque et la philosophie stoïcienne des passions.* Paris: Klincksieck.

Fine, G. (1990). 'Knowledge and Belief in *Republic* V–VII', in Everson, 85–115.

—— (1996). 'Conflicting Appearances: *Theaetetus* 153d–154b', in Gill and McCabe, 105–33.

—— (2003*a*). 'Sextus and External World Scepticism'. *Oxford Studies in Ancient Philosophy,* 24: 341–85.

—— (2003*b*). 'Subjectivity, Ancient and Modern: The Cyrenaics, Sextus, and Descartes', in Miller and Inwood, 192–231.

—— (2004). 'The Subjective Appearance of Cyrenaic *Pathē*', in V. Karasmanis (ed.), *Socrates: 2400 Years from his Death.* Athens and Delphi: European Cultural Centre of Delphi, 383–94

Fish, J. (2004). 'Anger, Philodemus' Good King, and the Helen Episode of *Aeneid* 2.567–589: A New Proof of Authenticity from Herculaneum', in Armstrong *et al.*, 111–38.

Forster, M. (1989). *Hegel and Ancient Skepticism.* Cambridge, Mass.: Harvard University Press.

Fortenbaugh, W. W. (1970). 'On the Antecedents of Aristotle's Bipartite Psychology'. *Greek, Roman, and Byzantine Studies,* 11: 233–50.

—— (1975). *Aristotle on Emotion.* London: Duckworth.

—— (1983) (ed.). *On Stoic and Peripatetic Ethics: The Work of Arius Didymus.* Rutgers University Studies in Classical Humanities, 1. New Brunswick: Transaction Books.

—— Huby, P. M., Sharples, R. W., and Gutas, D. (1992) (eds.). *Theophrastus of Eresus: Sources for his Life, Writings, Thought, and Influence,* 2 vols. Leiden: Brill.

Foucault, M. (1973). *Madness and Civilization: A History of Insanity in the Age of Reason,* trans. R. Howard. New York: Vintage/Random House.

—— (1977). *Discipline and Punish: The Birth of the Prison,* trans. A. Sheridan. London: Allen Lane.

—— (1984). *The Use of Pleasure: History of Sexuality,* ii, trans. R. Hurley. London: Allen Lane.

—— (1988*a*). 'Technologies of the Self', in L. H. Martin, H. Gutman, and P. H. Hutton (eds.), *Technologies of the Self: A Seminar with Michel Foucault.* Amherst: University of Massachusetts Press, 16–49.

—— (1988*b*). *The Care of the Self: The History of Sexuality,* iii, trans. R. Hurley. London: Penguin.

—— (2001). *L'Hermeneutique du sujet: Cours au Collège de France (1981–2),* ed. F. Ewald, A. Fontana, and F. Gros. Paris: Gallimard.

Fowler, D. P. (1997). 'Epicurean Anger', in Braund and Gill, 16–35.

Frankfurt, H. (1971). 'Freedom of the Will and the Concept of a Person'. *Journal of Philosophy,* 68: 5–20.

Frede, D. (1996). 'The Philosophical Economy of Plato's Psychology: Rationality and Common Concepts in the *Timaeus*', in Frede and Striker, 29–58.

—— (2003). 'Stoic Determinism', in Inwood, 179–205.

—— and Laks, A. (2002) (eds.). *Traditions of Theology: Studies in Hellenistic Theology, its Background and Aftermath.* Philosophia Antiqua, 89. Leiden: Brill.

Frede, M. (1986). 'The Stoic Doctrines of the Affections of the Soul', in Schofield and Striker, 93–110.

—— (1996). 'Introduction', in Frede and Striker, 1–28.

—— (1999*a*). 'Epilogue', in Algra *et al.* (1999: 771–97).

—— (1999*b*). 'On the Stoic Conception of the Good', in Ieradiakonou, 71–94.

—— (1999*c*). 'Stoic Epistemology', in Algra *et al.* (1999), 295–322.

—— and Striker, G. (1996) (eds.). *Rationality in Greek Thought.* Oxford: Oxford University Press.

Frischer, B. (1982). *The Sculpted Word: Epicureanism and Philosophical Recruitment in Ancient Greece.* Berkeley: University of California Press.

Furley, D. (1967). *Two Studies in the Greek Atomists.* Princeton: Princeton University Press.

—— (1999). 'Cosmology', in Algra *et al.*, 412–51.

Galinsky, K. (1988). 'The Anger of Aeneas'. *American Journal of Philology*, 109: 1–11.

—— (1994). 'How to be Philosophical about the End of the *Aeneid*'. *Illinois Classical Studies*, 19: 191–201.

—— (2003). 'Greek and Roman Drama and the *Aeneid*', in D. Braund and C. Gill (eds.), *Myth, History and Culture in Republican Rome: Studies in Honour of T. P. Wiseman.* Exeter: University of Exeter Press, 275–94.

Gaskin, J. (1995) (ed.). *The Epicurean Philosophers.* Translations with introduction and notes. Everyman edition. London: Dent.

Gerson, L. P. (2002). *Knowing Persons in Plato.* Oxford: Oxford University Press.

—— (2004). 'The Unity of Intellect in Aristotle's *De Anima*'. *Phronesis*, 49: 348–73.

Gewirth, A. (1977). *Reason and Morality.* Chicago: Chicago University Press.

Giannantoni, G. (1991) (ed.). *Socratis et Socraticorum Reliquiae*, 4 vols. Naples: Bibliopolis.

Gigante, M., and Capasso, M. (1989). 'Il ritorno di Virgilio a Ercolano'. *Studi Italiani di Filologia Classica*, 3rd series, 7: 3–6.

Gill, C. (1973). 'The Death of Socrates'. *Classical Quarterly*, 23: 25–8. Reprinted in Brickhouse and Smith (2002), 251–5.

—— (1983*a*). 'Did Chrysippus Understand Medea?' *Phronesis*, 28: 136–49.

—— (1983*b*). 'The Question of Character-Development: Plutarch and Tacitus'. *Classical Quarterly*, 33: 469–87.

—— (1985). 'Plato and the Education of Character'. *Archiv für Geschichte der Philosophie*, 67: 1–26.

—— (1987). 'Two Monologues of Self-Division: Euripides *Medea* 1021–80 and Seneca *Medea* 893–977', in M. Whitby, P. Hardie, and M. Whitby (eds.), *Homo Viator: Classical Essays for John Bramble.* Bristol: Bristol Classical Press, 25–37.

—— (1988). 'Personhood and Personality: The Four-*Personae* Theory in Cicero, *De Officiis* 1'. *Oxford Studies in Ancient Philosophy*, 6: 169–99.

—— (1990*a*). 'The Articulation of the Self in Euripides' *Hippolytus*', in A. Powell (ed.), *Euripides, Women, and Sexuality.* London: Routledge, 76–107.

—— (1990*b*). 'The Character-Personality Distinction', in Pelling (1990*b*: 1–31).

—— (1990*c*). 'The Human Being as an Ethical Norm', in Gill (1990*d*: 137–61).

—— (1990*d*) (ed.). *The Person and the Human Mind: Issues in Ancient and Modern Philosophy.* Oxford: Oxford University Press.

—— (1991). 'Is There a Concept of Person in Greek Philosophy?', in Everson (1991*b*), 166–93.

—— (1992). 'Dogmatic Dialogue in *Phaedrus* 276–7?', in Rossetti, 156–72.

—— (1993). 'Platonic Dialectic and the Truth-Status of the Unwritten Doctrines'. *Methexis*, 6: 55–72.

—— (1994). 'Peace of Mind and Being Yourself: Panaetius to Plutarch', in Haase and Temporini, 2.36.7: 4599–4640.

—— (1995) (ed.). *Epictetus: The Discourses, Handbook, Fragments*. Translation by R. Hard with introduction and notes by C. Gill. Everyman edition. London: Dent.

—— (1996*a*). 'Afterword: Dialectic and the Dialogue Form in Late Plato', in Gill and McCabe, 283–311.

—— (1996*b*). *Personality in Greek Epic, Tragedy, and Philosophy: The Self in Dialogue*. Oxford: Oxford University Press.

—— (1997*a*). 'Galen versus Chrysippus on the Tripartite Psyche in *Timaeus* 69–72', in Calvo and Brisson, 267–73.

—— (1997*b*) (ed.). *Marcus Aurelius: Meditations*. Translation by R. Hard with introduction and notes by C. Gill. Ware: Wordsworth Classics.

—— (1997*c*). 'Passion as Madness in Roman Poetry', in Braund and Gill, 213–41.

—— (1998*a*). 'Did Galen Understand Platonic and Stoic Thinking on Emotions?', in Sihvola and Engberg-Pedersen, 113–48.

—— (1998*b*). 'Ethical Reflection and the Shaping of Character'. *Proceedings of the Boston Area Colloquium in Ancient Philosophy* (1996 Colloquia), 12, eds. J. J. Cleary and W. Wians. Lanham, Md.: University Press of America, 193–225.

—— (2000*a*). 'Protreptic and Dialectic in Plato's *Euthydemus*', in T. M. Robinson and L. Brisson (eds.), *Plato: Euthydemus, Lysis, Charmides*. St Augustin: Academia Verlag, 133–43.

—— (2000*b*). 'The Body's Fault? Plato's *Timaeus* on Psychic Illness', in Wright, 59–84.

—— (2000*c*). Review of S. Bobzien, *Determinism and Freedom in Stoic Philosophy*, *Times Literary Supplement*, 15 Sept., 28.

—— (2000*d*). 'Stoic Writers of the Imperial Era', in Rowe and Schofield, 597–615.

—— (2001*a*). 'La "Psychologie" présocratique: Quelques questions interprétatives', in Morel and Pradeau (2001), 169–89.

—— (2001*b*). 'Speaking up for Plato's Interlocutors': Discussion of J. Beversluis, *Cross-examining Socrates: A Defense of the Interlocutors in Plato's Early Dialogues*. Oxford Studies in Ancient Philosophy, 20: 297–321.

—— (2003*a*). 'Is Rivalry a Virtue or a Vice?', in D. Konstan and K. Rutter (eds.), *Envy, Spite and Jealousy: The Rivalrous Emotions in Ancient Greece*. Edinburgh: Edinburgh University Press, 29–51.

—— (2003*b*). 'Plato's *Laws*—is it a Real Dialogue?', in L. Brisson and S. Scolnicov (eds.), *The Laws: From Theory into Practice*. St Augustin: Academia Verlag, 42–7.

—— (2003*c*). 'Reactive and Objective Attitudes: Anger in Virgil's *Aeneid* and Hellenistic Philosophy', in *Yale Classical Studies*, 32: *Ancient Anger: Perspectives from Homer to Galen*, eds. S. M. Braund and G. Most. Cambridge University Press, 208–28.

—— (2003*d*). 'The School in the Roman Imperial Period', in Inwood, (2003), 33–58.

Gill, C. (2004*a*). 'Character and Passion in Virgil's *Aeneid*'. *Proceedings of the Virgil Society*, 25: 111–24.

—— (2004*b*). 'Plato and the Scope of Ethical Knowledge'. *Plato* (<http://nd.edu~plato>) 4.

—— (2004*c*). 'Plato, Ethics and Mathematics', in M. Migliori, L. M. Napolitano Valditara, D. Del Forno (eds.), *Plato Ethicus: Philosophy is Life*. St Augustin: Academia Verlag., 165–76.

—— (2004*d*). 'Plato's *Republic*: An Ideal Culture of Knowledge', in A. Becker, W. Detel, and P. Scholtz (eds.), *Ideal and Culture of Knowledge in Plato*. Stuttgart: Steiner, 37–55.

—— (2004*e*). 'The Impact of Greek Philosophy on Contemporary Ethical Philosophy', in L. Rossetti (ed.), *Greek Philosophy in the New Millenium: Essays in Honour of Thomas M. Robinson*. St Augustin: Academia Verlag, 209–26.

—— (2004*f*). 'The Stoic Theory of Ethical Development; in What Sense is Nature a Norm?', in J. Szaif and M. Lutz-Bachmann (eds.), *Was ist das für den Menschen Gute? Menschliche Nature und Güterlehre. What is Good for a Human Being? Human Nature and Values*. Berlin: De Gruyter, 101–25.

—— (2005*a*). 'Competing Readings of Stoic Emotions', in Salles, 445–70.

—— (2005*b*). 'In What Sense are Ancient Ethical Norms Universal?', in Gill (2005c: 15–40).

—— (2005*c*). 'Tragic Fragments, Greek Philosophers, and the Fragmented Self', in F. McHardy, F. D. Harvey, and J. Robson (eds.), *Lost Dramas from Ancient Athens: Greek Tragic Fragments*. Exeter: University of Exeter Press, 151–72.

—— (2005*d*) (ed.). *Virtue, Norms, and Objectivity: Issues in Ancient and Modern Ethics*. Oxford: Oxford University Press.

—— (forthcoming). 'Seneca and Selfhood: Integration and Distintegration', in S. Bartsch and D. Wray (eds.), *Seneca and the Self*.

—— and McCabe, M. M. (1996) (eds.). *Form and Argument in Late Plato*. Oxford: Oxford University Press.

Glucker, J. (1978). *Antiochus and the Late Academy*. Hypomnemata, 56. Göttingen: Vandenhoeck and Ruprecht.

—— (1988). 'Cicero's Philosophical Affiliations', in Dillon and Long, 34–69.

Goodwin, W. W. (1951, 2nd edn. reprint). *A Greek Grammar*. London: MacMillan.

Görannson, T. (1995). *Albinus, Alcinous, Arius Didymus*. Studia Graeca et Latina Gothoburgensis, 61. Göteborg: Acta Universitatis Gothoburgensis.

Görgemanns, H. (1983). '*Oikeiōsis* in Arius Didymus', in Fortenbaugh (1983), 165–89.

Gosling, J. C. B. (1990). *Weakness of the Will*. London: Routledge.

—— and Taylor, C. C. W. (1982). *The Greeks on Pleasure*. Oxford: Oxford University Press.

Gould, J. (1970). *The Philosophy of Chrysippus*. Leiden: Brill.

Gourinat, J.-P. (1996). *Les stoïciens et l'âme*. Paris: Presses Universitaires de France.

Graver, M. (1990). 'The Eye of the Beholder: Perceptual Relativity in Lucretius', in Nussbaum, 91–116.

—— (1999). 'Philo of Alexandria and the Origins of the Stoic *propatheia*'. *Phronesis*, 44: 300–25.

—— (2002*a*). *Cicero on the Emotions: Tusculan Disputations 3 and 4*. Translation with introduction and commentary. Chicago: Chicago University Press.

—— (2002*b*). Review of R. Sorabji, *Emotion and Peace of Mind*. *Ancient Philosophy*, 22: 225–34.

Gribble, D. (1999). *Alcibiades and Athens: A Study in Literary Presentation*. Oxford: Oxford University Press.

Griffin, M. T. (1976). *Seneca: A Philosopher in Politics*. Oxford: Oxford University Press.

—— (1986). 'Philosophy, Cato and Roman Suicide: I and II'. *Greece and Rome*, 33: 64–77, 192–202.

—— (1995). 'Philosophical Badinage in Cicero's Letters to his Friends', in Powell, 325–48.

—— and Barnes, J. (1989) (eds.). *Philosophia Togata I: Essays on Philosophy and Roman Society*. Oxford: Oxford University Press.

Gros, F. *et al.* (2002). *Foucault: Le Courage et la vérité*. Paris: Presses Universitaires de France.

Gundert, B. (2000). 'Soma and Psyche in Hippocratic Medicine', in J. P. Wright and Potter, 13–35.

Guthrie, W. K. C. (1969). *A History of Greek Philosophy*, iii. Cambridge: Cambridge University Press.

Haase, W., and Temporini, H. (1972–) (eds.). *Aufstieg und Niedergang der römischen Welt / Rise and Decline of the Roman World* (multi-volume series). Berlin and New York: De Gruyter.

Hadot, I. (1969). *Seneca und die griechisch-römische Tradition der Seelenleitung*. Berlin: De Gruyter.

Hadot, P. (1979). 'Les Divisions des parties de la philosophie dans l'Antiquité'. *Museum Helveticum*, 36: 210–23.

—— (1991). 'Philosophie, discours philosophique, et divisions de la philosophie chez les stoiciens'. *Revue internationale de la philosophie*, 178: 205–19.

—— (1995). *Philosophy as a Way of Life: Spiritual Exercises from Socrates to Foucault*. Trans. M. Chase with introduction by A. Davidson. Oxford: Blackwell.

—— (1998). *The Inner Citadel: The Meditations of Marcus Aurelius*. Trans. M. Chase. Cambridge, Mass.: Harvard University Press.

Hahm, D. E. (1977). *The Origins of Stoic Cosmology*. Columbus: Ohio State University Press.

—— (1983). 'The Diairetic Method and the Purpose of Arius' Doxography', in Fortenbaugh, 15–38.

—— (1991). 'A Neglected Stoic Argument for Human Responsibility'. *Illinois Classical Studies*, 17: 23–48.

Haldane, E. S., and Ross, G. R. T. (1967) (eds. and trans.). *The Philosophical Works of Descartes*, 2 vols. Cambridge: Cambridge University Press.

Hankinson, R. J. (1991). 'Galen's Anatomy of the Soul'. *Phronesis*, 36: 197–233.

—— (1993). 'Actions and Passions: Affection, Emotion and Moral Self-Management in Galen's Philosophical Psychology', in Brunschwig and Nussbaum, 184–222.

Hankinson, R. J. (1995). *The Sceptics.* London: Routledge.
—— (1998). *Cause and Explanation in Ancient Greek Thought.* Oxford: Oxford University Press.
—— (1999). 'Explanation and Causation', in Algra *et al.*, 479–512.
—— (2003). 'Stoic Epistemology', in Inwood, 59–84.
Hardie, P. R. (1986). *Virgil's Aeneid: Cosmos and Imperium.* Oxford: Oxford University Press.
Harkins, P. W., and Riese, W. (1963). *Galen on the Passions and Errors of the Soul,* trans. with introduction and interpretation Columbus: Ohio State University Press.
Harris, W. V. (2001). *Restraining Rage: The Ideology of Anger Control in Classical Antiquity.* Cambridge, Mass.: Harvard University Press.
Harrison, S. (1990). 'Some Views of the *Aeneid* in the Twentieth Century', in Harrison (ed.), *Oxford Readings in Vergil's Aeneid.* Oxford: Oxford University Press, 1–20.
Helmbold, W. C. (1970) (ed.). *Plutarch: Moralia,* 6. Loeb Classical Library. Cambridge, Mass.: Harvard University Press.
Henry, D. and E. (1985). *The Mask of Power: Seneca's Tragedies and Imperial Rome.* Warminster: Aris and Phillips.
Herington, C. J. (1966). 'Senecan Tragedy'. *Arion,* 5: 422–71.
Hershkowitz, D. (1998). *The Madness of Epic: Reading Insanity from Homer to Statius.* Oxford: Oxford University Press.
Hill, T. D. (2003). '*Ambitiosa Mors*; Suicide and the Self in Roman Thought and Literature'. University of London Ph.D. thesis.
Hill, T. E. (1989). 'The Kantian Concept of Autonomy', in J. Christman (ed.), *The Inner Citadel: Essays on Individual Autonomy.* Oxford: Oxford University Press, 91–105.
Hine, H. M. (2000) (ed.). *Seneca: Medea.* Warminster: Aris and Phillips.
Holub, R. C. (1984). *Reception Theory: A Critical Introduction.* London: Methuen.
Hursthouse, R. (1980–1). 'A False Doctrine of the Mean'. *Proceedings of the Aristotelian Society,* 81: 57–72.
Ieradiakonou, K. (1999) (ed.). *Topics in Stoic Philosophy.* Oxford: Oxford University Press.
Indelli, G. (1988) (ed.). *Filodemo: L'ira.* Text and translation, with introduction and commentary. Naples: Bibliopolis.
—— (2004). 'The Vocabulary of Anger in Philodemus' *De Ira* and Vergil's *Aeneid*', in Armstrong *et al.*, 103–10.
Inwood, B. (1983). 'Comments on Professor Görgemann's Paper: The Two Forms of *Oikeiōsis* in Arius and the Stoa', in Fortenbaugh, 190–201.
—— (1984). 'Hierocles: Theory and Argument in the Second Century AD'. *Oxford Studies in Ancient Philosophy,* 2: 151–84.
—— (1985). *Ethics and Human Action in Early Stoicism.* Oxford: Oxford University Press.
—— (1993). 'Seneca and Psychological Dualism', in Brunschwig and Nussbaum, 150–83.

—— (1995). Review of J. Annas, *The Morality of Happiness*. Ancient Philosophy, 15: 647–66.

—— (1996). 'L'*Oikeiōsis* chez Epictète', in Algra *et al.*, 243–64.

—— (1999). 'Rules and Reasoning in Stoic Ethics', in Ieradiakonou, 95–27.

—— (2003) (ed.). *The Cambridge Companion to the Stoics*. Cambridge: Cambridge University Press.

—— (2005). *Reading Seneca: Stoic Philosophy at Rome*. Oxford: Oxford University Press.

—— and Donini, P. (1999). 'Stoic Ethics', in Algra *et al.*, 675–738.

—— and Gerson, L. (1997, 2nd edn.). *Hellenistic Philosophy: Introductory Readings*. Indianapolis: Hackett.

Ioppolo, A. M. (1984). *Aristone di Chio e lo stoicismo antico*. Naples: Bibliopolis.

Irwin, T. (1977). *Plato's Moral Theory*. Oxford: Oxford University Press.

—— (1980). 'Reason and Responsibility in Aristotle' in Rorty (1980*a*), 117–55.

—— (1983). 'Euripides and Socrates'. *Classical Philology*, 78: 183–97.

—— (1985). *Aristotle: Nicomachean Ethics*, trans. with notes. Indianapolis: Hackett.

—— (1986). 'Stoic and Aristotelian Conceptions of Happiness', in Schofield and Striker, 205–44.

—— (1988). *Aristotle's First Principles*. Oxford: Oxford University Press.

—— (1991*a*). 'Aristippus against Happiness'. *The Monist*, 74: 55–82.

—— (1991*b*). 'Aristotle's Philosophy of Mind', in Everson, 56–83.

—— (1995). *Plato's Ethics*. Oxford: Oxford University Press.

—— (1996). 'Stoic Individuals'. Philosophical Perspectives, 10 (Metaphysics): 459–80.

—— and Nussbaum, M. (1994) (eds.). *Virtue, Love, and Form: Essays in Memory of Gregory Vlastos*. Edmonton, Alberta: Academic Printing and Publishing (= *Apeiron* 26.3–4).

Jackson-McCabe, M. (2004). 'The Stoic Theory of Implanted Preconceptions'. *Phronesis*, 49: 323–47.

Jeffrey, R. (1985). 'Animal Interpretation', in LePore and McLaughlin, 481–7.

Johansen, T. (2000). 'Body, Soul, and Tripartition in Plato's *Timaeus*'. *Oxford Studies in Ancient Philosophy*, 19: 87–111.

—— (2004). *Plato's Natural Philosophy*. Cambridge: Cambridge University Press.

Joubaud, C. (1991). *Le Corps humain dans la philosophie platonicienne*. Paris: Vrin.

Jowett, B. (1892, 3rd edn.). *The Dialogues of Plato*, ii. Translation with introduction and analyses. Oxford: Oxford University Press.

Kahn, C. H. (1985). 'Democritus and the Origins of Moral Psychology'. *American Journal of Philology*, 106: 1–31.

—— (1987). 'Plato's Theory of Desire'. *Review of Metaphysics*, 41: 77–103.

—— (1988). 'Discovering the Will: From Homer to Augustine', in Dillon and Long, 234–59.

—— (1992). 'Aristotle on Thinking', in Nussbaum and Rorty, 359–79.

—— (1983). 'Drama and Dialectic in Plato's *Gorgias*'. *Oxford Studies in Ancient Philosophy*, 1: 75–121.

Kahn, C. H. (1996). *Plato and the Socratic Dialogue: The Philosophical Use of a Literary Form.* Cambridge: Cambridge University Press.

—— (2001). *Pythagoras and the Pythagoreans: A Brief History.* Indianopolis: Hackett.

—— (2002). 'On Platonic Chronology', in Annas and Rowe, 93–127.

Kant, I. (1948, repr. 1951–86). *Groundwork of the Metaphysic of Morals.* Translation and analysis (as *The Moral Law*), H. J. Paton. London: Hutchinson.

Kenny, A. (1988–9). 'The Self', *The Aquinas Lecture.* Maquette University, Wisconsin.

—— (1992). *Aristotle on the Perfect Life.* Oxford: Oxford University Press.

Kerferd, G. B. (1971). 'Epicurus' Doctrine of the Soul'. *Phronesis,* 116: 80–96.

—— (1972). 'The Search for Personal Identity in Stoic Thought'. *Bulletin of the John Rylands University Library of Manchester,* 60: 482–94.

—— (1978). 'What Does the Wise Man Know?', in Rist, 125–36.

—— (1983). 'Two Problems concerning Impulses', in Fortenbaugh, 87–98.

Kerner, G. C. (1990). *Three Philosophical Moralists: Mill, Kant, and Sartre: An Introduction to Ethics.* Oxford: Oxford University Press.

Kidd, I. G. (1971*a*). 'Posidonius on Emotions', in Long, 200–15.

—— (1971*b*). 'Stoic Intermediates and the End for Man', in Long, 150–72.

—— (1983). '*Euemptōsia*-Proneness to Disease', in Fortenbaugh, 107–13.

—— (1988). *Posidonius II: The Commentary,* 2 vols. Classical Texts and Commentaries 14 A–B. Cambridge: Cambridge University Press.

—— (1992) (ed.). *Plutarch: Essays,* trans. R. Waterfield with introduction and notes by I. G. Kidd. Penguin Classics. London: Penguin.

Kleve, K. (1983). 'Scurra Atticus: The Epicurean View of Socrates', in Carratelli, i. 227–53.

Konstan, D. (2001). *Pity Transformed.* London: Duckworth.

—— Clay, D., Glad, C. E., Thom, J. C., and Ware, J. (1998). *Philodemus: On Frank Criticism.* Translation with introduction and notes. Atlanta, Georgia: Society of Biblical Literature, Texts and Translations, 43, Graeco-Roman, 13.

Kuiper, T. (1925) (ed.). *Philodemos over den Dood.* Amsterdam: H. J. Paris.

Laird, A. (1997). 'Approaching Characterisation in Virgil', in Martindale, 282–93.

Lamb, W. R. M. (1927) (ed. and trans.). *Plato,* 7. Loeb Classical Library. Cambridge, Mass.: Harvard University Press.

Laursen, S. (1987). 'Epicurus, *On Nature* Book XXV'. *Cronache Ercolanesi,* 17: 77–8.

—— (1988). 'Epicurus *On Nature* XXV (Long–Sedley 20, B, C and J)'. *Cronache Ercolanesi,* 18: 7–18.

—— (1995). 'The Early Parts of Epicurus, *On Nature,* 25th Book'. *Cronache Ercolanesi,* 25: 5–109.

—— (1998). 'The Later Parts of Epicurus, *On Nature,* 25th Book'. *Cronache Ercolanesi,* 28: 5–82.

Lear, J. (1988). *Aristotle: The Desire to Understand.* Cambridge: Cambridge University Press.

—— (1992). 'Inside and Outside the *Republic*'. *Phronesis,* 38: 184–215.

LePore, E., and McLaughlin, B. P. (1985) (eds.). *Actions and Events: Perspectives on the Philosophy of Donald Davidson.* Oxford: Oxford University Press.

Levene, D. (1997). 'Pity, Fear and the Historical Audience', in Braund and Gill, 128–49.

Lévy, C. (1992). *Récherches sur 'Les Académiques' et sur la philosophie cicéronienne.* Rome: École Française de Rome.

—— (2003). 'L'âme et le moi dans les *Tusculanes*'. *Revue des Études Latines*, 80: 78–94.

Lewis, E. (1995). 'The Stoics on Identity and Individuation'. *Phronesis*, 49: 89–108.

Liddell, H. G., Scott, R., and Jones, H. S. (1940, 9th edn.). *Greek–English Lexicon.* Oxford University Press (= LSJ).

Lloyd, A. C. (1978). 'Emotion and Decision in Stoic Psychology', in Rist, 233–46.

Lloyd, G. E. R. (1991). *Methods and Problems in Greek Science: Selected Papers.* Cambridge: Cambridge University Press.

—— (1996). 'Theories and Practices of Demonstration in Galen', in M. Frede and Striker, 255–77.

Long, A. A. (1971, repr. 1996) (ed.). *Problems in Stoicism.* London: Athlone Press.

—— (1986). 'The Stoic Concept of Evil'. *Philosophical Quarterly*, 18: 329–43.

—— (1988). 'Socrates in Hellenistic Philosophy'. *Classical Quarterly*, 38: 150–71 Reprinted in Long (1996), 1–34.

—— (1991). 'Representation and the Self in Stoicism', in Everson (1991*b*), 102–220. Reprinted in Long (1996), 264–85.

—— (1992). 'Finding Oneself in Greek Philosophy'. *Uit Tijdschrift voor Filosofie*, 54.2: 257–76.

—— (1995). 'Cicero's Politics in *De Officiis*', in A. Laks and M. Schofield (1995) (eds.), *Justice and Generosity: Studies in Hellenistic Social and Political Philosophy.* Cambridge: Cambridge University Press, 213–40.

—— (1996). *Stoic Studies.* Cambridge: Cambridge University Press.

—— (1997). 'Lucretius on Nature and the Epicurean Self', in Algra *et al.*, 125–40.

—— (1998). 'Theophrastus and the Stoa', in Ophuisen and Raalte, 355–83.

—— (1999*a*). 'Stoic Psychology', in Algra *et al.*, 560–84.

—— (1999*b*). 'The Socratic Legacy', in Algra *et al.*, 617–41.

—— and Sedley, D. N. (1987). *The Hellenistic Philosophers*, 2 vols. Cambridge: Cambridge University Press (= LS).

—— (2002). *Epictetus: A Stoic and Socratic Guide to Life.* Oxford: Oxford University Press.

Lukes, S. (1973). *Individualism.* Oxford: Blackwell.

—— (1985). 'Conclusion', in Carrithers, Collins, and Lukes, 282–301.

Lynch, J. P. (1972). *Aristotle's School: A Study of a Greek Educational Institution.* Berkeley: University of California Press.

Lyne, R. O. A. M. (1980). *The Latin Love Poets: From Catullus to Horace.* Oxford: Oxford University Press.

—— (1983). 'Vergil and the Politics of War'. *Classical Quarterly*, 33: 188–203.

—— (1987). *Further Voices in Vergil's Aeneid.* Oxford: Oxford University Press.

McCabe, M. M. (2002). 'Indifference Readings: Plato and the Stoa on Socratic Ethics', in T. P. Wiseman (ed.), *Classics in Progress: Essays on Ancient Greece and Rome.* Oxford: Oxford University Press for the British Academy, 363–98.

McDowell, J. (1986). 'Singular Thought and the Extent of Inner Space', in P. Pettit and J. McDowell (eds.), *Subject, Thought and Context*. Oxford: Oxford University Press, 137–68.

McGinn, C. (1982, 2nd edn. 1997). *The Character of Mind: An Introduction to the Philosophy of Mind*. Oxford: Oxford University Press.

MacIntyre, A. (1985, 2nd edn.). *After Virtue: A Study in Moral Theory*. London: Duckworth.

Mackenzie, M. M. (now McCabe) (1981). *Plato on Punishment*. Berkeley: University of California Press.

McKirahan, V. T. (1994). 'The Socratic Origins of the Cynics and Cyrenaics', in Vander Waerdt (1994*b*), 367–91.

Mansfeld, J. (1989). 'Chrysippus and the Placita'. *Phronesis*, 34: 311–42.

—— (1990). 'Doxography and Dialectic: The *Sitz im Leben* of the *Placita*', in Haase and Temporini, 2.36.4: 3056–3229.

—— (1991). 'The Idea of the Will in Chrysippus, Posidonius, and Galen'. *Boston Area Colloquium in Ancient Philosophy*, 7: 107–45.

—— and Runia, D. T. (1997). *Aëtiana: The Method and Intellectual Context of a Doxographer*, i: *The Sources*. Philosophia Antiqua, 73. Leiden: Brill.

Marboeuf, C., and Pradeau, J. F. (1999), *Platon: Alcibiade*, translation, with introduction and notes by J.-F. Pradeau. Paris: Flammarion.

Marquardt, I., Müller, I., and Helmreich, G. (1967) (eds.). *Claudii Galeni Pergameni: Scripta Minora*, 3 vols. Amsterdam: Hakkert.

Marti, B. (1945). 'Seneca's Tragedies: A New Interpretation'. *Transactions of the American Philological Association*, 76: 216–45.

Martindale, C. (1992). *Redeeming the Text: Latin Poetry and the Hermeneutics of Reception*. Cambridge: Cambridge University Press.

—— (1997) (ed.). *The Cambridge Companion to Virgil*. Cambridge: Cambridge University Press.

Mates, B. (1996). *The Skeptic Way*. New York: Oxford University Press.

Miller, J., and Inwood, B. (2003) (eds.). *Hellenistic and Early Modern Philosophy*. Cambridge: Cambridge University Press.

Misch, G. (1950). *A History of Autobiography in Antiquity*, 2 vols. Cambridge, Mass.: Harvard University Press.

Mischel, T. (1977) (ed.). *The Self: Psychological and Philosophical Issues*. Oxford: Blackwell.

Mitsis, P. (1988). *Epicurus' Ethical Theory: The Pleasures of Invulnerability*. Ithaca, NY: Cornell University Press.

Monti, R. C. (1981). *The Dido Episode and the Aeneid*. Leiden: Brill.

Morel, P.-M. (1996). *Démocrite et la recherche des causes*. Paris: Klincksieck.

—— and Pradeau, J.-F. (2001) (eds.). *Les Anciens Savants: Études sur les philosophies préplatoniciennes*. Strasbourg: Les Cahiers Philosophiques de Strasbourg.

Morton, A. D. (1990). 'Why There is No Concept of a Person', in Gill (1990*d*), 39–59.

Nagel, T. (1974). 'What it is Like to be a Bat?' *Philosophical Review*, 83: 435–50.

—— (1986). *The View from Nowhere*. Oxford: Oxford University Press.

Newman, R. J. (1989). '*Cotidie meditare*: Theory and Practice of the *meditatio* in Imperial Stoicism', in Haase and Temporini, 2.36.3: 1473–1517.

Nidditch, P. H. (1975) (ed.). *John Locke: An Essay Concerning Human Understanding*. Oxford: Oxford University Press.

Nietzsche, F. (1974). *The Gay Science*, trans. W. Kaufmann. New York: Vantage Books.

Nock, A. D. (1933). *Conversion*. Oxford: Oxford University Press.

Norton, D. F., and Norton, M. J. (2001) (eds.). *David Hume: A Treatise of Human Nature*. Oxford: Oxford University Press.

Nussbaum, M. C. (1986). *The Fragility of Goodness: Luck and Ethics in Greek Tragedy and Philosophy*. Cambridge: Cambridge University Press.

—— (1990) (ed.). *The Poetics of Therapy: Hellenistic Ethics and its Rhetorical and Literary Context*. Edmonton, Alberta: Academic Printing and Publishing (= *Apeiron* 23.4).

—— (1993). 'Poetry and the Passions: Two Stoic Views', in Brunschwig and Nussbaum, 97–149.

—— (1994). *The Therapy of Desire: Theory and Practice in Hellenistic Ethics*. Princeton: Princeton University Press.

—— (2001). *Upheavals of Thought: The Intelligence of Emotions*. Cambridge: Cambridge University Press.

—— and Putnam, H. (1992). 'Changing Aristotle's Mind', in Nussbaum and Rorty, 27–56.

—— and Rorty, A. O. (1992) (eds.). *Essays on Aristotle's De Anima*. Oxford: Oxford University Press.

O'Keefe, T. (2002). 'The Reductionist and Compatibilist Argument of Epicurus' *On Nature*, Book 25'. *Phronesis*, 47: 153–86.

Ophuisen, J. M. van, Raalte, M. van (1998) (eds.). *Theophrastus: Reappraising the Sources*. Rutgers University Studies in Classical Humanities, 4. New Brunswick: Rutgers University Press.

Opsomer, J. (1994). 'L'Âme du monde et l'âme de l'homme chez Plutarque', in G. M. Valdés (1994) (ed.), *Estudios sobre Plutarco: Ideas Reliogosas*. Actas del III Simposio Internacional sobre Plutarco, Oviedo 1992. Madrid: Ediciones Clásicas, 33–49.

—— (2004). 'Plutarch's *De Animae procreatione in Timaeo*: Manipulation or Search for Consistency?', in P. Adamson, H. Baltussen and M. W. F. Stone (eds.), *Philosophy, Science and Exegesis in Greek, Arabic and Latin Commentaries*, 2 vols. *Bulletin of the Institute of Classical Studies*, Supplement 83: 1, 137–62.

Osborne, C. (1996). 'Space, Time, Shape and Direction: Creative Discourse in the *Timaeus*', in Gill and McCabe, 179–211.

Otis, B. (1964). *Virgil: A Study in Civilized Poetry*. Oxford: Oxford University Press.

Oxford Classical Dictionary (1996, 2nd. edn.). (eds.) S. Hornblower and A. Spawforth. Oxford: Oxford University Press (=*OCD*).

Padel, R. (1994). *Whom Gods Destroy: Greek Images of the Tragic Self*. Princeton: Princeton University Press.

Parfit, D. (1971). 'Personal Identity'. *Philosophical Review* 80: 3–27, reprinted in Perry (1975), 199–220.

Parfit, D. (1984). *Reasons and Persons*. Oxford: Oxford University Press.

Peacocke, C. (1983). *Sense and Content: Experience, Thought, and Their Relations*. Oxford: Oxford University Press.

Pelling, C. (1990*a*). 'Childhood and Personality in Greek Biography', in Pelling (1990*b*), 213–44.

—— (1990*b*) (ed.). *Characterization and Individuality in Greek Literature*. Oxford: Oxford University Press.

—— (1995). 'The Moralism of Plutarch's *Lives*', in D. Innes, H. Hine, and C. B. R. Pelling (eds.), *Ethics and Rhetoric: Classical Essays for Donald Russell on his Seventy-fifth Birthday*. Oxford: Oxford University Press, 205–20.

—— (2002). *Plutarch and History: Eighteen Studies*. London: Classical Press of Wales and Duckworth.

Pembroke, S. (1971). '*Oikeiōsis*', in Long (1971*b*), 114–49.

Pender, E. (1997). 'The Language of Soul in Plato's *Timaeus*', in Calvo and Brisson, 281–8.

Penner, T. (1971). 'Thought and Desire in Plato', in Vlastos, 96–118.

—— (1973). 'The Unity of Virtue'. *Philosophical Review*, 82: 35–68.

—— (1990). 'Plato and Davidson: Parts of the Soul and Weakness of the Will'. *Canadian Journal of Philosophy*, 16: 35–74.

—— (1991). 'Desire and Power in Socrates: The Argument of *Gorgias* 466a–468e that Orators and Tyrants Have No Power in the City'. *Apeiron*, 24: 147–202.

—— (1997). 'Socrates on the Strength of Knowledge: *Protagoras* 351b–357e'. *Archiv für Geschichte der Philosophie*, 79: 117–49.

—— (2005). 'Socratic Ethics: Ultra-Realism, Determinism and Ethical Truth', in Gill (2005*d*), 157–88.

—— and Rowe, C. J. (2005). *Plato's Lysis*. Cambridge: Cambridge University Press.

Perry, J. (1975) (ed.). *Personal Identity*. Berkeley: California University Press.

Pigeaud, J. (1981). *La Maladie de l'âme: Étude sur la relation de l'âme et du corps dans la tradition médico-philosophique antique*. Paris: Les Belles Lettres.

Pike, K. L. (1954). 'Emic and Etic Standpoints for the Description of Behaviour', in Pike (ed.), *Language in Relation to a Unified Theory of the Structure of Human Behaviour*, Part 1. Glendale: Summer Institute of Linguistics, 8–28.

Pohlenz, M. (1940). *Grundfragen der Stoischen Philosophie*. Göttingen: Vandenhoeck and Ruprecht.

—— (1959, 2nd edn.). *Die Stoa: Geschichte einer geistigen Bewegung*. Göttingen: Vandenhoeck and Ruprecht.

Powell, J. G. F. (1995) (ed.). *Cicero: The Philosopher: Twelve Papers*. Oxford: Oxford University Press.

Pradeau, J.-F. (1995). *Le Monde de la politique*. St Augustin: Academia Verlag.

—— (2002*a*). 'Le Sujet ancien d'une politique moderne: à propos des exercises spirituels anciens dans *L'Histoire de la sexualité* de Michel Foucault', in Gros (2002), 131–54.

—— (2002*b*). *Plato and the City: A New Introduction to Plato's Political Thought*, trans. J. Lloyd. Exeter: University of Exeter Press.

—— (2003). 'Le Sujet ancien d'une politique moderne: sur la subjectivation et l'éthiques anciennes dans les *dits et écrits* de Michel Foucault', in P.- F. Moreau (2003) (ed.), *Lectures de Michel Foucault*, iii: *Sur les dits et écrits*. Lyons: École normale supérieure, Lettres et sciences humaines, 35–51.

Pratt, N. T. (1948). 'The Stoic Base of Seneca Drama'. *Transaction of the American Philological Association*, 79: 1–11.

—— (1983). *Seneca's Drama*. Chapel Hill: University of North Carolina Press.

Price, A. W. (1989). *Love and Friendship in Plato and Aristotle*. Oxford: Oxford University Press.

—— (1995). *Mental Conflict*. London: Routledge.

—— (2005). 'Were Zeno and Chrysippus at Odds in Analysing Emotion?', in Salles, 471–88.

Procopé, J. (1998). 'Epicureans on Anger', in Sihvola and Engberg-Pedersen, 171–96. Originally published in G. W. Most, H. Petersmann, and A. M. Ritter (1993) (eds.), *Philanthropia kai Eusebeia: Festschrift für Albrecht Dihle zum 70. Geburtstag*. Göttingen: Vandenhoeck and Ruprecht, 363–86.

Purinton, J. (1999). 'Epicurus on "Free Volition" and the Atomic Swerve', *Phronesis*, 44: 253–99.

Putnam, M. (1990). 'Anger, Blindness and Insight in Virgil's *Aeneid*', in Nussbaum, 7–40.

—— (1995). *Virgil's Aeneid: Interpretation and Influence*. Chapel Hill: University of North Carolina Press.

Rawls, J. (1971). *A Theory of Justice*. Cambridge, Mass.: Harvard University Press.

Reydams-Schils, G. (1999). *Demiurge and Providence: Stoic and Platonist Readings of Plato's Timaeus*. Turnhout: Brepols.

—— (2002). 'Human Bonding and *Oikeiōsis*'. *Oxford Studies in Ancient Philosophy*, 22: 221–51.

—— (2003) (ed.). *Plato's Timaeus as Cultural Icon*. Notre Dame: University of Notre Dame Press.

—— (2005). *The Roman Stoics: Self, Responsibility, and Affection*. Chicago: Chicago University Press.

Riley, M. T. (1980). 'The Epicurean Criticism of Socrates'. *Phoenix*, 34: 55–68.

Rist, J. M. (1969). *Stoic Philosophy*. Cambridge: Cambridge University Press.

—— (1972). *Epicurus: An Introduction*. Cambridge: Cambridge University Press.

—— (1978) (ed.). *The Stoics*. Berkeley: California University Press.

Roisman, H. (2000). 'A New Look at Seneca's *Phaedra*', in G. W. M. Harrison (ed.), *Seneca in Performance*. London: Duckworth, 73–86.

Rorty, A. O. (1976) (ed.). *The Identities of Persons*. Berkeley: California University Press.

—— (1980*a*) (ed.). *Essays on Aristotle's Ethics*. Berkeley: California University Press.

—— (1980*b*) (ed.). *Explaining Emotions*. Berkeley: University of California Press.

Rosenbaum, S. (1990). 'Epicurus on Pleasure and the Complete Life'. *The Monist*, 73: 21–41.

Rosenmeyer, T. G. (1989). *Senecan Drama and Stoic Cosmology*. Berkeley: University of California Press.

Rossetti, L. (1992) (ed.). *Understanding the Phaedrus.* St Augustin: Academia Verlag.

Rotondaro, S. (1997). 'Il *pathos* della ragione e i sogni: *Timeo* 70D7–72B5', in Calvo and Brisson, 275–80.

Rowe, C. (2005). 'What Difference Do Forms Make for Platonic Epistemology?' in Gill (2005d), 215–32.

—— and Schofield, M. (2000) (eds.). *The Cambridge History of Greek and Roman Political Thought.* Cambridge: Cambridge University Press.

Rudd, N. (1976). *Lines of Enquiry: Studies in Latin Poetry.* Cambridge: Cambridge University Press.

Russell, D. A. (1973). *Plutarch.* London: Duckworth.

Rutherford, R. B. (1989). *The Meditations of Marcus Aurelius: A Study.* Oxford: Oxford University Press.

Sacks, O. (1987). *The Man who Mistook his Wife for a Hat.* London: Duckworth.

Salles, R. (2005) (ed.). *Metaphysics, Soul, and Ethics: Studies in Honour of Richard Sorabji.* Oxford: Oxford University Press.

Sandbach, F. H. (1971). '*Ennoia* and *Prolēpsis*', in Long (1971*b*), 22–37.

—— (1985). *Aristotle and the Stoics.* Cambridge Philological Society, supplementary volume 10. Cambridge: Cambridge University Press.

Schiesaro, A. (1997). 'Passion, Reason and Knowledge in Seneca's Tragedies', in Braund and Gill, 89–111.

—— (2003). *The Passions in Play: Thyestes and the Dynamics of Senecan Drama.* Cambridge: Cambridge University Press.

Schmid, W. T. (1998). *Plato's Charmides and the Socratic Ideal of Rationality.* Albany: State University of New York Press.

Schofield, M. (1984). 'Ariston of Chios and the Unity of Virtue'. *Ancient Philosophy,* 4: 83–96.

—— (1986). '*Euboulia* in the *Iliad*'. *Classical Quarterly* NS, 36: 6–31.

—— (1991). *The Stoic Idea of the City.* Cambridge: Cambridge University Press.

—— (1996). 'Epilogismos: An Appraisal', in M. Frede and Striker, 221–37.

—— (2000). 'Epicurean and Stoic Political Thought', in Rowe and Schofield, 435–56.

—— (2003). 'Stoic Ethics', in Inwood, 233–56.

—— and Striker, G. (1986) (eds.). *Norms of Nature: Studies in Hellenistic Ethics.* Cambridge: Cambridge University Press.

Scott, D. (1995). *Recollection and Experience: Plato's Theory of Learning and its Successors.* Cambridge: Cambridge University Press.

Sedley, D. N. (1973). 'Epicurus, On Nature Book XXVIII'. *Cronache Erciolanesi,* 3: 5–83.

—— (1982). 'The Stoic Criterion of Identity'. *Phronesis,* 27: 255–75.

—— (1983). 'Epicurus' Refutation of Determinism', in Carratelli, i. 11–51.

—— (1988). 'Epicurean Anti-Reductionism', in Barnes and Mignucci, 295–327.

—— (1993). 'Chrysippus on Psychophysical Causality', in Brunschwig and Nussbaum, 313–31.

—— (1996). 'Three Platonist Interpretations of the *Theaetetus*', in Gill and McCabe, 79–103.

—— (1997*a*). '"Becoming like God" in the *Timaeus* and Aristotle', in Calvo and Brisson 327–39.

—— (1997*b*). 'Plato's *Auctoritas* and the Rebirth of the Commentary Tradition', in Barnes and Griffin, 110–29.

—— (1997*c*). 'The Ethics of Brutus and Cassius'. *Journal of Roman Studies*, 87: 41–53.

—— (1998*a*). *Lucretius and the Transformation of Greek Wisdom*. Cambridge: Cambridge University Press.

—— (1998*b*). 'The Inferential Foundations of Epicurean Ethics', in S. Everson (ed.), *Ethics: Companions to Ancient Thought, 4*, Cambridge: Cambridge University Press, 129–50.

—— (1999a). 'Hellenistic Physics and Metaphysics', in Algra *et al.*, 355–411.

—— (1999b). 'The Ideal of Godlikeness', in G. Fine (ed.), *Plato*, ii: *Ethics, Politics, Religion, and the Soul*. Oxford Readings in Philosophy. Oxford: Oxford University Press, 309–328.

—— (1999*c*). 'The Stoic–Platonist Debate on *kathēkonta*', in Ierodiakonou, 128–52.

—— (2002). 'The Origins of Stoic God', in D. Frede and Laks, 41–83.

—— (2003). 'The School, from Zeno to Arius Didymus', in Inwood, 7–32.

—— (2004). *The Midwife of Platonism: Text and Subtext in Plato's Theaetetus*. Oxford: Oxford University Press.

Segal, C. P. (1990). *Lucretius on Death and Anxiety*. Princeton: Princeton University Press.

Segonds, A. P. (1985–6) (ed.). *Proclus: Sur le premier Alcibiade de Platon*. Translation with introduction and notes, 2 vols. Paris: Les Belles Lettres.

Sellars, J. (2003). *The Art of Living: The Stoics on the Nature and Function of Philosophy*. Aldershot: Ashgate.

Sharples, R. W. (1991–3). 'Carneades and Epicurus on the Atomic Swerve'. *Bulletin of the Institute of Classical Studies*, 38: 174–90.

—— and Sheppard, A. (2003) (eds.). *Ancient Approaches to Plato's Timaeus. Bulletin of the Institute of Classical Studies*, Supplement 78.

—— and Sorabji, R. (forthcoming) (eds.). *Greek and Roman Philosophy, 100 BC to AD 200. Bulletin of the Institute of Classical Studies* Supplement.

Sherman, N. (1989). *The Fabric of Character: Aristotle's Theory of Virtue*. Oxford: Oxford University Press.

—— (1997). *Making a Necessity of Virtue: Aristotle and Kant on Virtue*. Cambridge: Cambridge University Press.

Sherrington, C. (1906). *The Integrative Action of the Nervous System*. Cambridge: Cambridge University Press.

Shoemaker, S. (1991). 'Qualia and Consciousness'. *Mind*, 100: 507–24, repr. in Shoemaker (1996), 50–73.

—— (1996). *The First Person Perspective and Other Essays*. Cambridge: Cambridge University Press.

Sihvola, J., and Engberg-Pedersen, T. (1998) (eds.). *The Emotions in Hellenistic Philosophy*. Dordrecht: Kluwer.

Singer, P. N. (1997*a*). *Galen: Selected Works*. Translation with introduction and notes. The World's Classics. Oxford: Oxford University Press.

Singer, P. N. (1997*b*). 'Levels of Explanation in Galen'. *Classical Quarterly*, 47: 525–42.

Smith. P., and Jones, O. R. (1986). *The Philosophy of Mind: An Introduction*. Cambridge: Cambridge University Press.

Snell, B. (1964). *Scenes from Attic Drama*. Berkeley: University of California Press.

Solmsen, F. (1961). 'Greek Philosophy and the Discovery of the Nerves'. *Museum Helveticum*, 18: 150–67, 169–97.

Solomon, R. C. (1988). *Continental Philosophy since 1750: The Rise and Fall of the Self*. Oxford: Oxford University Press.

Sorabji, R. (1980). *Necessity, Cause and Blame: Perspectives on Aristotle's Theory*. London: Duckworth.

—— (1993). *Animal Minds and Human Morals: The Orgins of the Western Debate*. London: Duckworth.

—— (1998). 'Chrysippus–Posidonius–Seneca: A High-level Debate on Emotion', in Sihvola and Engberg-Pedersen, 149–69.

—— (1999). 'Soul and Self in Ancient Philosophy', in J. Crabbe (ed.), *From Soul to Self*, Wolfson Lectures, London: Routledge, 8–32.

—— (2000). *Emotion and Peace of Mind: From Stoic Agitation to Christian Temptation*. Oxford: Oxford University Press.

Staden, H. von (2000). 'Body, Soul, and the Nerves: Epicurus, Herophilus, Erasistratus, the Stoics, and Galen', in J. P. Wright and Potter, 79–116.

Stadter, P. (1980). *Arrian of Nicomedia*. Chapel Hill: University of North Carolina Press.

Steel, C. (2001). 'The Moral Purpose of the Human Body: A Reading of *Timaeus* 69–72, *Phronesis*, 46: 105–28.

Stokes, M. C. (1995). 'Cicero on Epicurean Pleasures', in Powell, 145–70.

Straaten, M. van (1962, 3rd. edn.). *Panaetii Rhodii Fragmenta*. Leiden: Brill.

Strawson, P. F. (1974). 'Freedom and Resentment', in *Freedom and Resentment and Other Essays*. London: Methuen, 1–25.

Striker, G. (1989). 'Comments on Mitsis'. *Proceedings of the Boston Area Colloquium in Ancient Philosophy*, 4: 315–20.

—— (1994). 'Plato's Socrates and the Stoics', in Vander Waerdt (1994*b*), 241–51.

—— (1996). *Essays on Hellenistic Epistemology and Ethics*. Cambridge: Cambridge University Press.

Swain, S. (1989). 'Character Change in Plutarch'. *Phoenix*, 43: 62–8.

Tarrant, R. J. (2004). 'The Last Book of the *Aeneid*'. *Syllecta Classica*, 15: 103–29.

Tarrant, T. H. (1985). *Scepticism or Platonism?* Cambridge: Cambridge University Press.

Taylor, C. (1976). 'Responsibility for Self', in Rorty, 281–99.

—— (1985). 'The Person', in Carrithers, Collins, and Lukes, 257–81.

—— (1989). *Sources of the Self: The Making of the Modern Identity*. Cambridge: Cambridge University Press.

Taylor, C. C. W. (1990). 'Aristotle's Epistemology', in Everson, 116–42.

Taylor, G. (1985). *Pride, Shame and Guilt: Emotions of Self-Assessment*. Oxford: Oxford University Press.

Thomas, R. F. (1991). '*Furor* and *Furiae* in Virgil'. *American Journal of Philology*, 112: 261–2

—— (2000). 'A Trope by Any Other Name: "Polysemy", Ambiguity and *Significatio* in Virgil'. *Harvard Studies in Classical Philology*, 100: 381–407.

—— (2001). *Virgil and the Augustan Reception*. Cambridge: Cambridge University Press.

Thomson, J. A. K. (1976). *Aristotle: Ethics*. Translation with introduction, revised by H. Tredennick. Penguin Classics. Harmondsworth: Penguin.

Tieleman, T. L. (1996). *Galen and Chrysippus on the Soul: Argument and Refutation in the De Placitis Books II-III*. Philosophia Antiqua, 68. Leiden: Brill.

—— (2003). *Chrysippus' On Affections: Reconstruction and Interpretation*. Philosophia Antiqua, 94. Leiden: Brill.

Toulmin, S. E. (1977). 'Self-Knowledge and Knowledge of the "Self"', in Mischel, 291–317.

Trilling, L. (1972). *Sincerity and Authenticity*. Oxford: Oxford University Press.

Tsouna, V. (1998*a*). *The Epistemology of the Cyrenaic School*. Cambridge: Cambridge University Press.

—— (1998*b*). 'Remarks about Other Minds in Greek Philosophy'. *Phronesis*, 43: 245–63.

Tye, M. (1995). *Ten Modes of Consciousness*. Cambridge, Mass.: Massachusetts Institute of Technology Press.

Usener, H. (1887). *Epicurea*. Leipzig: Teubner.

van der Eijk, P. J. (2000). 'Aristotle on the Soul–Body Relationship', in J. P. Wright and Potter, 57–77.

Vander Waerdt, P. A. (1985). 'Peripatetic Soul–Division, Posidonius, and Middle Platonic Moral Psychology'. *Greek, Roman and Byzantine Studies*, 26: 373–94.

—— (1994*a*). 'Socrates and Stoic Natural Law', in Vander Waerdt (1994*b*), 272–308.

—— (1994*b*) (ed.). *The Socratic Movement*. Ithaca, NY: Cornell University Press.

Vegetti, M. (1986). 'Foucault et les anciens'. *Critique*, 43: 325–32.

Vlastos, G. (1945–6). 'Ethics and Physics in Democritus'. *Philosophical Review*, 54: 578–92 and 55: 53–64.

—— (1971). *Plato. A Collection of Critical Essays*, ii: *Ethics, Politics and Philosophy of Art and Religion*. Notre Dame: University of Notre Dame Press.

—— (1973, 2nd edn. 1981). *Platonic Studies*. Princeton: Princeton University Press.

—— (1991). *Socrates: Ironist and Moral Philosopher*. Cambridge: Cambridge University Press.

—— (1994). *Socratic Studies*, ed. M. F. Burnyeat. Cambridge: Cambridge University Press.

von Staden: see Staden, H. von.

Wachsmuth, C., and Hense, O. (1884–1912, repr. 1958) (eds.). *Ioannis Stobaei: Anthologium*, 5 vols. Berlin: Weidmann.

Warren, J. (2000). 'Epicurean Immortality'. *Oxford Studies in Ancient Philosophy*, 18: 231–61.

—— (2001*a*). 'Epicurus and the Pleasures of the Future'. *Oxford Studies in Ancient Philosophy*, 21: 135–79.

Warren, J. (2001*b*). 'Epicurus' Dying Wishes'. *Proceedings of the Cambridge Philological Society*, 47: 23–46.

—— (2001*c*). 'Lucretian *Palingenesis* Recycled'. *Classical Quarterly*, 51: 499–508.

—— (2001*d*). 'Lucretius, Symmetry Arguments, and Fearing Death'. *Phronesis*, 46: 466–91.

—— (2002). *Epicurus and Democritean Ethics: An Archaeology of Ataraxia*. Cambridge: Cambridge University Press.

—— (2004). *Facing Death: Epicurus and his Critics*. Oxford: Oxford University Press.

White, N. P. (1979). 'The Basis of Stoic Ethics'. *Harvard Studies in Classical Philology*, 83: 143–78.

—— (1985). 'The Role of Physics in Stoic Ethics'. *The Southern Journal of Philosophy*, 23 (Supplement, Proceedings of the Spindel Conference): 57–74.

—— (2002). *Individual and Conflict in Greek Ethics*. Oxford: Oxford University Press.

Whitmarsh, T. (2001). *Greek Literature and the Roman Empire: The Politics of Imitation*. Oxford: Oxford University Press.

—— (2002). 'Alexander's Hellenism and Plutarch's Textualism'. *Classical Quarterly*, 52: 174–92.

Wilkes, K. V. (1988). *Real People: Personal Identity without Thought Experiments*. Oxford: Oxford University Press.

Williams, B. (1981). *Moral Luck: Philosophical Papers, 1973–1980*. Cambridge: Cambridge University Press.

—— (1985). *Ethics and the Limits of Philosophy*. London: Fontana.

—— (1993). *Shame and Necessity*. Berkeley: California University Press.

Wollheim, R. (1984). *The Thread of Life*. Cambridge: Cambridge University Press.

—— and Hopkins, J. (1982) (eds.). *Philosophical Essays on Freud*. Cambridge: Cambridge University Press.

Wright, J. P., and Potter, P. (2000) (eds.). *Psyche and Soma: Physicians and Metaphysicians on the Mind-Body Problem from Antiquity to Enlightenment*. Oxford: Oxford University Press.

Wright, M. R. (1991) (ed.). *Cicero: On Stoic Good and Evil. De Finibus 3 and Paradoxa Stoicorum*, with introduction, translation, and commentary. Warminster: Aris and Phillips.

—— (1997). '*Ferox uirtus*: Anger in Virgil's *Aeneid*', in Braund and Gill, 169–84.

—— (2000) (ed.). *Reason and Necessity: Essays on Plato's Timaeus*. London: Duckworth and the Classical Press of Wales.

Zanker, P. (1995). *The Mask of Socrates: The Image of the Intellectual in Antiquity*, trans. A. Shapiro. Berkeley: University of California Press.

Zedda, S. (2000). 'How to Build a World Soul: A Practical Guide', in M. R. Wright, 23–41.

—— (2003). 'The World Soul and the Universe as Structure in Plato's *Timaeus*'. University of Exeter Ph.D. thesis.

Zilioli, U. (2002). 'The Epistemology of the Sophists: Protagoras'. University of Durham Ph.D. thesis.

Index of Ancient Passages

Entries for each author are arranged by alphabetic order of Greek or Latin titles even if English titles are also given. For the full details of the editions cited here by editor's name alone, see References or Note on Conventions. Passages listed under *Hellenistic Philosophers* or *Stoicorum Veterum Fragmenta* are only those so identified in the book; passages also identified by author and work are so cited here.

General Index

Modern scholars are included only when their works are discussed in the text or are especially relevant to the argument of the book; all secondary works cited in the book are listed in the References or the Note on Conventions.